The American REPUBLIC

for Christian Schools®

Rachel C. Larson with Pamela B. Creason

Bob Jones University Press, Greenville, SC 29614

Advisory Committee

John A. Matzko, Ph.D.
Professor, Department of History, Bob Jones University

Daniel P. Olinger, Ph.D.
Project Director, Secondary Level

Mark Sidwell, Ph.D.
Editor, Bob Jones University Press

David Fisher, M.A.
Instructor, Bob Jones Academy

Elizabeth Olsen, M.Ed.
Instructor, Bob Jones Junior High School

Alvin E. Iten, B.S.
Supplementary Author

NOTE:
The fact that materials produced by other publishers are referred to in this volume does not constitute an endorsement by Bob Jones University Press of the content or theological position of materials produced by such publishers. The position of the Bob Jones University Press, and the University itself, is well known. Any references and ancillary materials are listed as an aid to the student or the teacher and in an attempt to maintain the accepted academic standards of the publishing industry.

THE AMERICAN REPUBLIC for Christian Schools®
Rachel C. Larson, M.A., with Pamela B. Creason, M.Ed.

Produced in cooperation with the Bob Jones University Departments of History and Social Studies of the College of Arts and Science, the School of Education, and Bob Jones Academy and Junior High School.

ISBN 0-89084-446-1

20 19 18 17 16 15 14 13 12 11

Contents

List of Maps

Special Features

To the Student

Pronunciation Guide   The pronunciation key used in this text is designed to give the reader a self-evident, acceptable pronunciation for the word as he reads it from the page. For more nearly accurate pronunciations, the reader should consult a good dictionary.

Stress   Syllables with primary stress appear in LARGE CAPITAL letters. One-syllable words and syllables with secondary stress appear in SMALL CAPITAL letters. Unstressed syllables appear in lower-case letters. Where two or more words appear together, hyphens separate the syllables within each word. For example, the pronunciation of *Sante Fe* appears as (SAN-tuh FAY).

Consonant Sounds   Most consonants and consonantal combinations in the key have only their one visual sound. There are a few exceptions:

Symbol	Example	Symbol	Example
c	voice = VOYCE	th	thin = THIN
g	get = GET	*th*	then = *THE*N
j	gentle = JEN tul	zh	fusion = FYOO zhun

Vowel Sounds

Symbol	Example	Symbol	Example
a	cat = KAT	ar	car = KAR
a-e	cape = KAPE	aw	all = AWL
ay	paint = PAYNT	o	bone = BOHN
e	jet = JET	oa	don't = DOANT
eh	spend = SPEHND	o-e	groan = GRONE
ee	fiend = FEEND	oh	own = OHN
i	swim = SWIM	u	some = SUM
ih	pity = PIH tee	uh	ăbet = uh BET
eye	icy = EYE see	oo	crew = CROO
i-e	might = MITE	*oo*	push = P*OO*SH
y	pint = PYNT	ou	loud = LOUD
ye	Levi = LEE vye	oy	toil = TOYL
ah	cot = KAHT		

Introduction

A Baptist minister asked a midwestern audience in the 1930s, "Who, knowing the facts of our history, can doubt that the United States of America has been a thought in the mind of God from all eternity?" Indeed, Christians must realize that nothing in history is accidental; our sovereign God directs the affairs of men and nations to accomplish His will. As you begin your study of the history of the United States, keep in mind that God has likewise directed—and is still directing—America's history. The story of the United States is but one part of God's overall design for the ages. You will read about human failure and weakness, but remember that God superintends all things for His glory and purpose. "For of him, and through him, and to him, are all things: to whom be glory for ever. Amen" (Rom. 11:36).

x

Canada

Washington
Olympia •

River

Columbia

Salem •

Helena •   Montana   North Dakota
                                             Bismarck •

Oregon

Boise •   Idaho   South Dakota
                                             Pierre •   *Missouri Riv*

                    Wyoming

                              Rocky Mountains

                         Salt Lake City •   Cheyenne •   *Platte River*   Nebras

Sacramento •   Carson City •   Nevada   Linc

Sierra Nevada   *Great*   Utah   Denver •   *Great Plains*
                        Basin   Kansas
                                                  Colorado
California   *Arkansas*   *Ri*

                              Colorado *River*

                         Arizona   Sante Fe •   Oklaho
PACIFIC   Oklahoma •
                         Phoenix •   New Mexico
OCEAN

                                                                                  Texas

                                                                     Rio Grande   Austin •
Honolulu •

Hawaii   *Yukon River*   *Mexico*

same scale as large map   Alaska

                                             Juneau •

                    0 100 200 300 400 500

                         scale in miles

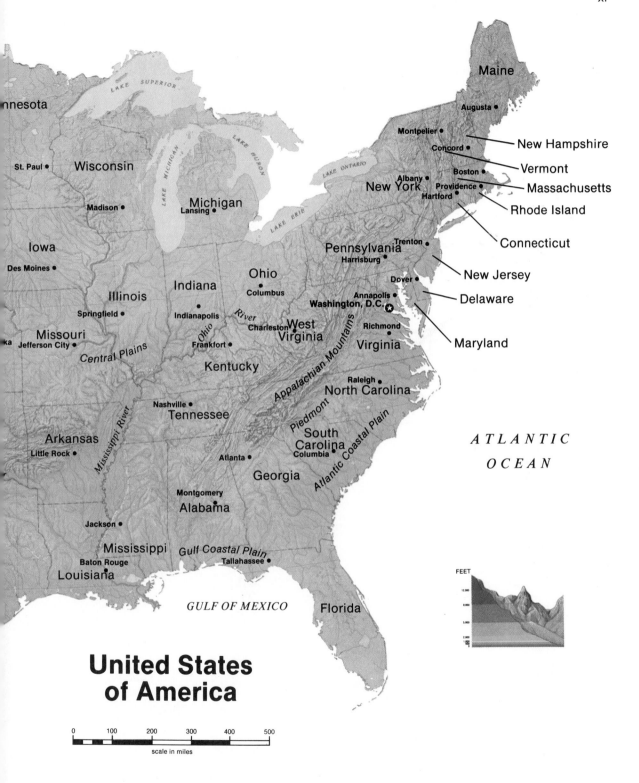

United States
of America

LAKE SUPERIOR

nnesota

St. Paul ●

Wisconsin

LAKE MICHIGAN

Madison ●

Michigan

Lansing ●

LAKE HURON

LAKE ERIE

LAKE ONTARIO

Maine

Augusta ●

Montpelier ●

Concord ● —— New Hampshire

—— Vermont

Albany ●   Boston ●

New York   Providence ● —— Massachusetts

Hartford ● —— Rhode Island

Iowa

Des Moines ●

Illinois

Springfield ●

Missouri

ka

Jefferson City ●

Central Plains

Indiana

Columbus ●

Indianapolis ●

River

Ohio

Frankfort ●

Kentucky

Ohio

Charleston ●

West
Virginia

Pennsylvania

Harrisburg ●

Trenton ●

—— Connecticut

—— New Jersey

Dover ●

Annapolis ●

Washington, D.C. ✪

Richmond ●

Virginia

—— Delaware

—— Maryland

Appalachian Mountains

Raleigh ●

North Carolina

Nashville ●

Tennessee

Piedmont

Mississippi River

Arkansas

Little Rock ●

Atlanta ●

South
Carolina

Columbia ●

Atlantic Coastal Plain

ATLANTIC

OCEAN

Georgia

Montgomery ●

Alabama

Jackson ●

Mississippi

Gulf Coastal Plain

Baton Rouge ●

Tallahassee ●

Louisiana

GULF OF MEXICO

Florida

FEET

12,000

8,000

5,000

2,000
1,000
0

0   100   200   300   400   500

scale in miles

165° 180° 165° 150° 135° 120° 105° 90° 75° 60° 45° 30°

GREENLAND

(DENMARK)

Longitude

Arctic Ocean

75°

Arctic Circle

Latitude

60°

CANADA

45°

Atlantic

UNITED STATES

Pacific

Ocean

30°

Tropic of Cancer

Gulf of
Mexico

MEXICO

CUBA HAITI
DOMINICAN REPUBLIC

Ocean

BELIZE

JAMAICA

15°

GUATEMALA
EL SALVADOR
HONDURAS
NICARAGUA
COSTA RICA
PANAMA

Caribbean Sea

GUYANA
SURINAM

VENEZUELA

COLOMBIA

Equator

0°

ECUADOR

BRAZIL

PERU

15°

BOLIVIA

Tropic of Capricorn

PARAGUAY

CHILE

30°

ARGENTINA

URUGUAY

NEW

ZEALAND

45°

60°

Antarctic Circle

165° 180° 165° 150° 135° 120° 105° 90° 75° 60° 30°

15° 0° 15° 30° 45° 60° 75° 90° 105° 120° 135° 150°

Prime Meridian

Longitude

Arctic Circle

U. S. S. R.
S.
U.
(Soviet Union)
Latitude

75°

ICELAND

NETHERLANDS
UNITED KINGDOM
DENMARK
EAST GERMANY
POLAND
IRELAND
CZECHOSLOVAKIA
BELGIUM
AUSTRIA
WEST GERMANY
HUNGARY
FRANCE
ROMANIA
SWITZERLAND
YUGO-
BULGARIA
SLAVIA
ALBANIA
PORTUGAL
SPAIN
ITALY
GREECE
TURKEY

MONGOLIA

NORTH
KOREA

PEOPLE'S REPUBLIC OF
CHINA

SOUTH
KOREA

JAPAN

45°

Mediterranean Sea
LEBANON
SYRIA
TUNISIA
ISRAEL
IRAQ
IRAN

MOROCCO
ALGERIA
LIBYA
EGYPT
JORDAN
KUWAIT
QATAR

AFGHANISTAN
PAKISTAN
NEPAL
BHUTAN

REPUBLIC OF CHINA
(TAIWAN)

Tropic of Cancer

30°

SAUDI
OMAN
INDIA
ARABIA

BURMA
LAOS

SENEGAL
MAURITANIA
MALI
NIGER
CHAD
SUDAN

UNITED ARAB
EMIRATES
SOUTH YEMEN
NORTH YEMEN
DJIBOUTI

BANGLADESH
THAILAND
KAMPUCHEA
(CAMBODIA)
SRI LANKA

VIETNAM

PHILIPPINES

15°

GAMBIA
GUINEA-
BISSAU
GUINEA
SIERRA LEONE
LIBERIA
NIGERIA

ETHIOPIA
SOMALIA

MALAYSIA

PAPUA
NEW GUINEA

UPPER VOLTA
(NOW BURKINA FASO)
IVORY COAST
GHANA
BENIN
KENYA

Equator

Indian

INDONESIA

0°

TOGO
CAMEROON
EQUATORIAL GUINEA
CENTRAL AFRICAN REPUBLIC
GABON

CONGO
ZAIRE
UGANDA
RWANDA
BURUNDI
TANZANIA
MALAWI
ZIMBABWE

Ocean

ANGOLA
ZAMBIA

15°

NAMIBIA
MADAGASCAR
Tropic of Capricorn

AUSTRALIA

BOTSWANA
MOZAMBIQUE
SWAZILAND
SOUTH
AFRICA
LESOTHO

30°

45°

Prime Meridian

60°

Antarctic Circle

15° 0° 15° 30° 45° 60° 75° 90° 105° 120° 135° 150°
ANTARCTICA

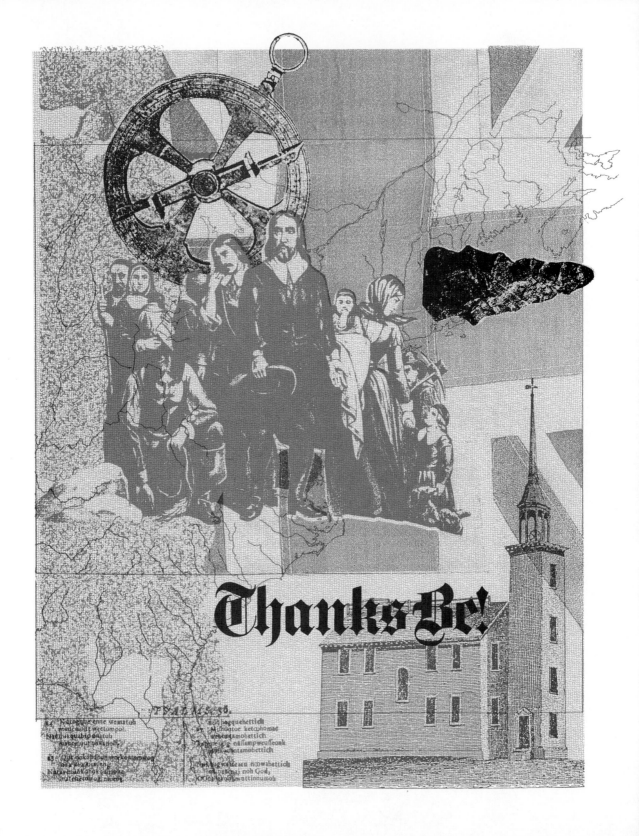

Thanks Be!

1

Finding a New World

After sailing for thirty-three days and nearly three thousand miles, ninety men and boys in three small ships searched the horizon for signs of land. The sailors were reluctant to sail on into the unknown waters far to the west of Europe, but their leader, Christopher Columbus, was determined to find the riches of the Orient. He was sure that he could reach the lands of spices and gold in the East by sailing west.

At ten o'clock that night, Columbus saw a dim light on the horizon. It may have been the moonlight reflecting on an island beach or cliff, or it may have been a fire used by natives on an island. Columbus pressed toward the light, and four hours later, in the early morning of October 12, 1492, Columbus, his men, and his three ships, the *Niña,* the *Pinta,* and the *Santa Maria,* reached sight of land. Later that day Columbus went ashore on the island he named San Salvador (Holy Saviour).

Recent evidence indicates that the island Columbus saw first was Samana Cay in the Bahamas, but Columbus believed it was an island in the Orient, perhaps in the East Indies. Therefore, he called the natives "Indians." Even after four voyages to the

"New World" he had found, Columbus continued to believe he had reached the Far East. He failed, however, to find the spices and riches he sought, and he died in 1506, poor and powerless. Nevertheless, Columbus's discovery of America opened the door to the exploration and development of two continents and gave the United States of America an important piece of its early heritage.

A. The New World Until Columbus

Columbus introduced Europe to the Americas, but those lands were not empty and unknown before his discovery.

The First Americans

Almost everywhere Europeans explored in the New World, they came into contact with the people whom Columbus mistakenly called "Indians." It is still uncertain how and when these first Americans came to North and South America. They probably came to the land shortly after the scattering of the nations at the Tower of Babel in Genesis 11. Perhaps they crossed a land bridge that may have linked Asia to Alaska. However they came to America, it is clear they lived in the New World centuries before the Europeans came.

Spread out across North and South America, the Indians were not a unified people. They were divided into hundreds of clans or tribes, each with its own language, lifestyle, and leader or chief. Some Indians were **nomadic,** constantly on the move in search of game animals, fish, and wild plants. Other groups settled in one area and farmed the land, raising crops such as maize (corn), potatoes, squash, and beans. The various groups lived in different kinds of shelters. The nomadic Indians often lived in portable shelters such as the cone-shaped tepees covered with the hides of animals. But more often Indians lived in more permanent housing such as dome-shaped wigwams covered with leaves and bark, or adobe houses built of sun-dried bricks.

Although most Indians throughout the Americas lived in small villages, there were three groups that built large civilizations before the white man came. In Central and South America, the **Mayas,** the **Aztecs,** and the **Incas** lived in large cities and developed many skills. The Mayan (MAH yuhn) civilization, located on the Yucatan (YOO kuh TAN) Peninsula of Mexico and in Guatemala, flourished from A.D. 300 to 900. The Mayas were amazing builders; they built their temples, for example, on top of large stone pyramids. Unlike most Indian groups, they developed a system of writing and of mathematics. They also studied the stars and the planets. Their calendar was more nearly accurate than the one used in Europe at the time of Columbus.

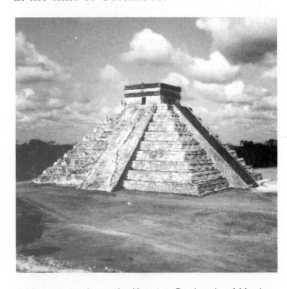

A Mayan temple on the Yucatan Peninsula of Mexico

Although the Mayan civilization had fallen five hundred years before Columbus's arrival, the Aztecs and the Incas were strong when he came. The Aztecs (AZ TEKS) were fierce warriors who conquered other Indian tribes in what is now Mexico. They built their capital city, Tenochtitlán (teh NOCH tee TLAN), on an island in the middle of Lake Texcoco (tay SKOH KOH) in Central Mexico. It was a beautiful city with large plazas, pyramid temples, and adobe houses. A network of canals flowed through the city. Connecting the capital to the mainland were massive earthen bridges. An estimated 100,000 people lived in the city at the time of the arrival of the first Europeans. Today, Mexico City, the present-day capital of Mexico, is located in the same area.

The Incas built an empire in the mountainous region of present-day Peru. They looked on their ruler, "the Inca," as a god. Like the Mayas and Aztecs, the Incas were excellent builders. Ruins of their well-planned cities and roads still exist. Inca craftsmen produced fine metal work, textiles, and pottery.

White Men Before Columbus

Although the Indians lived in America long before the arrival of the first Euro-peans, it is not known when they saw the first white men. Columbus is generally regarded as the "discoverer" of America, but almost certainly he was not the first European to see the Americas.

Many theories have arisen about who did arrive first. Stories are told of Phoenician (fih NISH un) sailors who came to the New World centuries before the birth of Christ. There is a legend of Madoc, a Welshman who founded a settlement among the Indians during the Middle Ages. Legends of Welsh-speaking, blue-eyed Indians persisted from the 1600s to the 1800s. Many explorers, such as Lewis and Clark, looked for these Welsh-speaking Indians. Other tales tell of Irish monks who visited America over a thousand years ago.

Evidence indicates that the **Vikings** visited America around A.D. 1000. The Vikings, or Norsemen, were courageous seamen from northern Europe. They planted colonies in Iceland and Greenland. From Greenland, the Vikings sailed their brightly painted ships westward to America. The best known of the Viking adventurers is **Leif Ericson,** the son of Eric the Red who colonized Greenland. Leif found "the strange land to the west" and called it "Vinland." Archaeologists have uncovered some evidence of the Viking visits in eastern Canada.

Other Vikings journeyed to America after Leif. But the rest of Europe was unaware of their voyages. Their discoveries went unnoticed and had no lasting effect on Europe or the New World. It was not until the "discovery" by Columbus that a new era dawned for both Europe and the Americas. This was the age of exploration and discovery.

An artist's view of the Aztec capital, Tenochtitlán

Columbus's Contribution

Europe had entered a new era of exploration in the late 1400s. The Europeans had new ship designs and new instruments to help them sail the seas. Much of the early exploration centered on finding new routes to the Orient (the Far East), where spices and wealth were readily available. Europeans greatly desired the spices of the East, which would help them improve the taste of their food. They also wanted the fine products of the East—silk, porcelain, gems, and precious metals. Because great profits could be made by obtaining these goods for Europe, merchants and rulers were willing to search for new trade routes. While some, like the Portuguese, tried to find a way eastward around Africa, others wondered whether the Orient could be reached by sailing west. It was this belief that led to the discovery of the New World.

The Italian sailor **Christopher Columbus** was convinced that by sailing west he could reach the rich lands of the Indies. For many years he tried to persuade the Portuguese king to finance his voyage. Having no success, he turned to Portugal's rival, Spain, for help. There he secured the support of **King Ferdinand** and **Queen Isabella.**

In August of 1492, Columbus set sail on his historic voyage with his three ships. Each day his men grew more anxious and impatient. Some of the sailors, who believed the earth was flat, feared that they would sail off the edge. Others, who believed the earth was round, feared that the ships would sail "downhill" so far that they would not be able to sail back "uphill" to Spain. There was also the fear of "sea monsters." Who could know what great beasts lived in unexplored seas? Despite the fears, Columbus was able to keep his concerned crew on course until land was in sight.

Columbus made his discovery that October and then returned to Spain with news of what he thought was the Far East. Soon swarms of other explorers came to investigate the lands across the Atlantic. Before long they realized that what Columbus had found was really a roadblock in their path to the Orient. One of the first to suggest that these lands were not the East

Christopher Columbus at the court of Ferdinand and Isabella

was an Italian merchant and explorer named **Amerigo Vespucci.** Having made several voyages westward, Vespucci offered proof that the lands were not the Orient, but instead a "new world." A German mapmaker included the new land on his map and named it after Amerigo. The map became popular and with it the name "America." Thus Columbus was denied the honor of having the two continents of the Western Hemisphere named for him.

Nonetheless, Columbus had pointed the way for European countries to explore the lands to the west. His voyages encouraged Spain and other countries to seek out the extent and the riches of these lands. Without a courageous adventurer like Columbus to lead the way, discovery, further exploration, and settlement of the Americas would have been postponed.

Section Review

1. Identify the two general types of Indian lifestyles and list important characteristics of each.
2. What three groups of American Indians had built impressive civilizations before the Europeans arrived?
3. What Viking adventurer set out to find the strange land west of Greenland? What did he call this area?
4. What prompted early explorers to risk their lives exploring uncharted seas?
5. What nation financed Columbus's voyage to prove his theory that by sailing west he could reach the Orient in the east?
6. Name the Italian explorer who offered proof that Columbus had in fact discovered a new world and not a new route to the Orient. How was he honored?

B. Claiming a New World

With Columbus's discovery Spain got off to a fast start in the exploration of the Americas. Other countries, however, soon saw that there was much to be gained by making claims in the New World. The resulting struggle for the lands of the New World helped shape the heritage of the United States.

Spanish Conquests

Spain's original goal had been to find the wealth of the Orient. Because Columbus had not found great treasures in the New World, a desire for Oriental trade remained; so Spain continued to search for a route around the Americas to the Far East. Such desire led to further exploration such as **Vasco de Balboa**'s crossing of the Isthmus of Panama (1513) and **Ferdinand Magellan**'s circumnavigation of the earth (1519-22). (*Circumnavigation* means "sailing around.") Even so, Spain continued to explore the Americas in hopes of finding treasure there.

Conquistadors—Spain's early expeditions to the New World remained primarily along the coastal region of Central and South America. However, they did eventually push inland. The inland explorations were led by **conquistadors** (conquerors). The colonies established by these conquerors became the backbone of the Spanish Empire in the New World. The land they claimed extended over most of South and Central America and into what is today Florida, Texas, and the Southwestern United States. The two most famous conquistadors were **Hernando Cortés** and **Francisco Pizarro.**

Cortés landed in Mexico the same year that Magellan began his famous voyage.

With a small army he marched to Tenochtitlán, the capital of the mighty Aztec empire. Montezuma, the Aztec king, welcomed Cortés, thinking that he was a god. Cortés, however, took Montezuma captive. He then defeated the Aztec warriors, destroyed their capital, and built on its site Mexico City.

Pizarro had accompanied Balboa on his journey across Panama and had later settled there. But on hearing of the wealth of the Incas in the Andes Mountains of South America, he organized an expedition and traveled south. With only 180 men he conquered the entire Inca Empire.

Both the Aztecs and the Incas were intelligent and brave, but they could not stand against the Spanish guns, armor, and horses. By conquering these two civilizations, the Spanish finally found what they wanted from the New World—treasures. The Spanish confiscated gold, silver, and gems from the Indians, and then the Spanish forced the Indians to work mining more of the precious metals and stones. This wealth

Aztec ruins in Mexico

kept the Spanish interest primarily in Central and South America instead of North America, which lacked large deposits of these treasures.

As we look at Latin America today, we can still see the strong influence of the Spanish culture that grew there. The Spaniards implanted their language, customs, and the Roman Catholic religion in the New World. But to gain such a strong hold on those New World lands, the conquistadors were often cruel and ruthless. They killed or mistreated the Indians and plundered their wealth, often under the guise of converting them to Roman Catholicism. The Spanish also set up governments in the Americas controlled by officials called viceroys, and these men were often corrupt and self-seeking. The Spanish came to take what they could from the New World; they rarely sought to improve it and make it their home.

Portuguese Agreement—Portugal had begun its voyages in search of the Orient before Spain had. With Vasco da Gama's trip around Africa to India in 1497-99, the Portuguese were actually successful first. But Spain's discovery and exploration of the New World made the two countries realize that if they both continued their exploration, they would have territorial conflicts. Since these two nations were Roman Catholic, they called in the pope to "settle" their growing disputes. In 1493 he drew an imaginary line, called the **Line of Demarcation** (DEE mahr KAY shun), dividing the world in half.

According to the pope's decree, Portugal was free to claim all the lands east of the line, and Spain was free to claim those to the west. The following year, the line was slightly altered when the two countries signed a treaty moving the line farther west.

This alteration eventually allowed Portugal to claim the South American land of Brazil.

The pope's Line of Demarcation offered only a temporary solution, however. In his decree he had recognized only Spain and Portugal. It was only a matter of time before other European countries would rise up to challenge this Portuguese and Spanish supremacy in the New World.

English Rivalry

Throughout the 1500s tension between Spain and England mounted. The Spanish objected to English intrusion into the New World, which they had claimed as their own. They were especially angered by the plundering activities of the English **"Sea Dogs."**

The "Sea Dogs" were a group of bold and daring English sea captains who struck at the heart of Spanish power. Acting as pirates, they disrupted the flow of gold and silver from the New World to Spain. They raided coastal towns, destroying Spanish harbors and ships. They also seized Spanish ships full of treasure and took their booty back to England.

The most courageous of the "Sea Dogs" was **Sir Francis Drake,** a favorite of **Queen Elizabeth I.** In 1577 he sailed down the coast of South America, plundering Spanish ports and capturing treasure ships. His ship was soon weighted with gold and silver. To escape the Spanish patrols, Drake sailed around South America, across the Pacific, and returned to England by sailing around the Cape of Good Hope. He duplicated the feat of Magellan, becoming the first Englishman to circumnavigate the earth.

Drake became the hated enemy of the Spanish. They called him "the master thief" and "the dragon." But in England he became a popular hero. Queen Elizabeth I, who had secretly encouraged his pirating

raids, now openly knighted him on board his ship, the *Golden Hind.*

Perhaps the most significant difference between Spain and England was their difference in religion. The Reformation started by Martin Luther had spread to England, and the nation had shifted toward Protestantism and had renounced the authority of the pope. Spain, on the other hand, was the bitter enemy of the Protestant Reformation. The king of Spain, Philip II, was the strongest champion of Roman Catholicism in Europe. He wished to restore England to the Catholic fold.

To conquer his political and religious rival, Philip II organized a large invasion force known as the "Invincible Armada." In 1588 his proud fleet of 130 ships sailed toward England. The English navy, ably commanded by "Sea Dogs" such as Francis

The "Rediscovery" of God's Word

At the same time that the explorers were discovering the New World, Europeans were also "rediscovering" God's Word. The invention of movable-type printing made copies of the Scripture readily available, and the revival of learning spawned by the Renaissance helped more people learn to read and write. As a result, people began to explore God's Word for themselves. This "exploration" revealed the errors taught by the Roman Catholic church and encouraged a spiritual revival.

Almost twenty-five years after Columbus stood before Ferdinand and Isabella to proclaim that the earth was round, Martin Luther stood before their grandson Charles V to proclaim his faith in God's Word. Luther's actions turned men's attention back to the Bible as the source of authority and exposed the accepted, but false, teachings of Rome. Other preachers also began to proclaim the truth of God's Word. As is often the case, however, revival was followed by persecution for many European Christians. But God had provided a "way of escape" through the New World. It seemed as though He had preserved America through the centuries for the time when His people would need to flee the religious persecution in Europe.

Drake, met the Spanish Armada in the English Channel. The lighter and faster English ships inflicted heavy damages on the Spanish galleons. The battered armada fled back to Spain, but fierce storms wrecked even more ships along the way. Only about half of the Spanish ships returned to Spain.

The English leaders praised God for destroying the powerful Spanish navy. Spain never recovered, and England eventually took her place as "the Mistress of the Seas." The weakening of Spanish sea power opened the door for English colonization in the New World. Spain could no longer threaten English activity in most of North America. Thus a Protestant land gained the opportunity to settle what would become the United States. Had it not been for the defeat of the Spanish Armada, Spain might have kept control of the New World, and North America might have become Spanish-speaking and Roman Catholic just as Central and South America are today.

French Activity

The French were also interested in the Americas. Because the Spanish had a strong hold on the Caribbean area, however, France concentrated on exploring parts of North America. Like Spain and other coun-

Because the Bible had become available to Europeans, they were able to bring it with them to America and even share it with the Indians. This 1663 Algonquin Bible was the first Bible printed in the New World.

tries, France hoped to find a water passageway through America to the Far East. **Jacques Cartier** (KAHR tee AY) sailed for France in search of such a waterway, and in the process he found the St. Lawrence River. His exploration of this important river of eastern Canada helped to give France a claim to a large section of North America. Other French explorers added to that claim. Most significant was **Robert de La Salle's** claim to the Mississippi River and the land that it drained.

France was slow to develop its claims in the New World. The French were preoccupied by European affairs and did not find gold and silver as did their Spanish counterparts to the south. It was almost a century after the first French explorers laid claim to North America that the French began to explore the land in earnest.

Throughout the seventeenth century the French settled up and down the major rivers, especially the St. Lawrence and the Mississippi, and around the Great Lakes. The lakes and rivers served as "roads," opening up the interior to French traders. Trading tools, trinkets, clothing, axes, and pots for the skins of fox, moose, otter, wolverine, and beaver became a lucrative business for the French in the land that they called "New France."

The French did not establish well-organized towns as did the English. The most permanent signs of French civilization were the military forts, missions, and trading posts built at key places to protect the traders and trappers. These outposts—such as Quebec, Montreal, Detroit, and New Orleans—became the centers of French culture and religion in the New World.

Because of the lack of opportunity for quick riches or prosperous farms, French colonies did not attract as many settlers as did the English. The French colonies were under the strict control of the French king. There was no local government or self-rule. In addition, the early traders cornered the fur market, discouraging others who might have come to seek their fortune. Furthermore, only French Roman Catholics were allowed to settle in the French colonies. They even excluded their own highly skilled, industrious group of Protestants called **Huguenots** (HYOO guh NOTS). These French Protestants were eventually forced to flee France because of religious persecution. When they did flee, many of them settled in English territory.

A few other countries, most notably the Netherlands, sent explorers to the New World in hopes of gaining land and treasures. Yet the Spanish, French, and English ended up with most of the claims. While the Spanish concentrated on mining the New World's riches and the French cornered the fur trade market, the British would take another approach to developing their land in the Americas.

Section Review

1. Name two men who conquered outstanding Indian civilizations, thereby bringing much wealth to Spain.
2. How did Spain and Portugal settle their disputes about territories in the New World?
3. What famous English sailor circumnavigated the globe?
4. What effect did the defeat of the Spanish Armada have on England and the future United States?
5. How did France profit from its New World claims?

C. The English Come to Stay

The English had begun to explore the eastern coast of what is now the United States long before they defeated the Spanish Armada. In fact, the explorer **John Cabot** had laid claim to the Atlantic coast of North America for England in 1497 and 1498. In less than a century, interest was growing in the possible founding of an English colony in this new land.

The Lost Colony

Although he did not go to the New World himself, **Sir Walter Raleigh,** an English nobleman, organized several colonizing expeditions to Roanoke Island off the coast of North Carolina. The first attempt, in 1585, failed because of poor leadership, Indian attacks, and famine. After one year the settlers returned home.

In 1587 Raleigh tried again. John White was placed in charge of the new group sent to found a colony. Shortly after they landed, White returned to England for supplies, but his return to America was delayed for three years by war with Spain. When he finally did return, the colony had disappeared. Along with the other colonists, White's daughter and baby granddaughter were missing. The baby, Virginia Dare, had been the first English baby born in the New World. The only clue to the disappearance of the colonists was the word *Croatoan* carved in a tree. It was thought that the nearby Croatan Indians had taken the people captive, but to this day no one knows what happened to the "Lost Colony" of Roanoke Island.

Jamestown

Nearly twenty years later the English established their first permanent colony. In

New World Colonies

Dutch
English
French
Spanish

CARTIER
1534

CABOT
1497

Early Explorers
and Colonies

0   100   300   500
Scale of Equitorial Miles

Mississippi RIVER

LASALLE
1681-82

COLUMBUS 1492

May 1607 three small ships containing just over one hundred men and boys sailed into Chesapeake Bay. These colonists had been sent by a group of London merchants to establish a money-making colony. Full of hope, they sailed up the James River and selected a site near the Virginia coast to build a settlement. They named it **Jamestown** in honor of their king, James I.

The settlers had trouble right from the start. Many were noblemen who considered themselves too good to work; they preferred to spend their time searching for gold. Those who did labor to plant crops were discouraged when all their harvest was placed into a common storehouse. As a

When Smith was injured in a gunpowder explosion and had to return to England, problems mounted once again. There were Indian attacks, fires, and disease. But most devastating was a terrible famine that plagued the settlement during the winter of 1609-1610. It was called the "starving time" because so many men died. The colonists ate anything they could find—horses, dogs, snakes, and even mice. In the first year and a half, six hundred men had come to Jamestown; by the end of the "starving-time," only sixty were left.

result these men stopped working, and soon there was a shortage of food. Disease also took its toll among the settlers. Their drinking water was impure, and malaria-carrying mosquitoes bred in the swamps that surrounded Jamestown.

One man who helped Jamestown survive was **John Smith,** a rough, hard-talking soldier who demanded obedience. In keeping with the teaching of II Thessalonians 3:10, he ruled that any man who did not work could not eat. Soon everyone was busy planting, hunting, or building.

In the spring of 1610, the few remaining settlers decided to abandon the settlement and return to England. Just after they had made this decision, however, ships arrived from England with more men and supplies. Encouraged, they decided to stay. Soon

Views of the reconstructed settlement at Jamestown, Virginia

they learned to plow and plant the crops that could support the colony. Although it proved to be an unhealthful product, the tobacco plant, introduced by colonist John Rolfe, became a profitable money crop for the early colonists.

Their troubles were not over, of course; there were more sickness, more hunger, and more Indian attacks. But the colony continued to grow. In 1619, twelve years after the settlers had arrived, the first women arrived from England. Many of these women married settlers and began to raise families. They were an important influence on the colony, for with the families came stability and morality that the colony had lacked before. Few women had come to the New World colonies of Spain and France, but the English quickly settled in to make this new land their home. Jamestown was the first success, but the English soon planted many successful colonies.

Also in Jamestown in 1619, the Virginia **House of Burgesses,** the first representative government in America, began meeting. The burgesses, representatives of the people, gathered to pass laws for the good of the colony. In this way Jamestown provided the beginning of the American republic.

Section Review

1. Name the Englishman who sponsored two colonizing attempts on Roanoke Island, and describe their outcome.
2. What group sponsored the settlement at Jamestown?
3. List the hardships faced at Jamestown.
4. What two important events took place in Jamestown in 1619? Why was each important?

Summary

Columbus's discovery of America in 1492 was not the beginning of American history. Indians had lived in the Americas for centuries; and the Mayas, Aztecs, and Incas had built great civilizations. Vikings had come to North America about five hundred years earlier, but Columbus opened the way for European exploration and colonization of the New World.

The Spanish took great interest in the gold, silver, and gems that they found in Central and South America. They concentrated their colonizing efforts in those regions, spreading their culture and Roman Catholicism. The French, also Roman Catholics, made their claims in North America where their chief activity became the fur trade. The English grew as a sea power in the late 1500s and were free to explore and settle along the east coast of North America. In contrast to the Spanish and the French, the English were mostly Protestant. Thus, while Roman Catholicism claimed much of the New World, the English preserved a part of North America for more religious freedom and the influence of the Bible. Jamestown, Virginia, founded in 1607, was the first successful English settlement.

Chapter Review

Do You Remember?

■ Answer the following questions.
1. On what day did Columbus discover America?
2. What were the names of Columbus's three ships?
3. What did Columbus name the island on which he first landed?
4. Which Indians built a large capital in central Mexico?
5. Which Indian civilization grew in the Andes Mountains of South America?

■ Name the persons described below.
6. He came to America five hundred years before Columbus.
7. They helped Columbus finance his voyage.
8. The new lands were named for him instead of Columbus.
9. He crossed the Isthmus of Panama.
10. He was the first to circumnavigate the earth.

■ Fill in the blank.
11. _____ was a conquistador who conquered the Aztecs.
12. The Line of Demarcation temporarily settled claim disputes between _____ and _____.
13. _____ explored the St. Lawrence River for France.
14. The _____ were French Protestants who were not allowed to settle in New France.
15. _____ gave the English claim to the eastern coast of North America.
16. In 1607 the first permanent English settlement, _____, was founded.

Why Is It So?

1. Why were the sailors who accompanied Columbus fearful about the voyage?
2. Why did Columbus name the natives of the New World *Indians?*
3. Why did the religious difference between Spain and England have a major effect on the Americas?
4. Why was the House of Burgesses in Jamestown significant?

What Do You Think?

1. What do you think might have happened if Columbus had failed to find land?
2. How might the colonization of the Americas have been different if the Spanish Armada had defeated England?
3. What do you think might have happened if women settlers had not come to Jamestown?

How to Study

"Whether therefore ye eat, or drink, or **whatsoever ye do,** *do all to the glory of God."* (I Cor. 10:31)

Preparing for Study

Success in doing an assignment begins in class. Listen carefully to the instructions, and write them down accurately in an assignment book. Before you leave school at the end of the day, check your assignment book, and make sure you have all the books, notebooks, and supplies necessary to do the assignment.

Do not wait until the last minute to start your homework. Plan your study time to include enough time to do all of your work carefully. Studying in the proper environment is extremely important. Locate a table large enough to spread out your materials. Take inventory—be sure you have everything you need before you begin. Hopping up and down to get other materials wastes time and energy.

Survey your assignments and "chart your course" for your evening's work. It may be a good idea to do the most mentally demanding tasks first before you begin to tire. When you are ready to begin, take time to ask the Lord's blessing on your efforts.

Reading Assignments—This text uses bold headings and subheadings. As you read the material under each heading, concentrate on the relationship of the material to the heading. Take special note of terms that are also printed in bold type. Pay particular attention to the names of people because people are an important part of history. Do not ignore the maps, charts, graphs, diagrams, and captions under the illustrations. These have been included in the text to add interest as well as to increase your understanding of the information.

Answering Questions—Read the question carefully before you begin to look for the answer. When you think you have found the answer, reread the question to be sure you are responding properly. Write down the complete answer neatly. In parentheses, write the page number on which you found the answer to the question.

Maps—As you work on a map assignment, concentrate on the purpose of the map and how each step relates to the subject matter being covered. In other words, whether you are coloring, labeling, or reading a map, relate what you see and do to the purpose or theme of the map.

Studying for Quizzes and Tests

When preparing for a quiz or a test, each individual must find the method that is right for him. Some students read the material to be tested several times. Many do not find that rereading is a profitable use of their time. Those individuals need to try other methods until they find the method that works for them.

Studying from an Outline—Underline or use a highlighter to draw your attention to important details. For instance, select one color for people, another for terms, another for battles, another for important dates, and so on. When studying from an outline, always remember that subheadings relate to main headings. Never study each bit of material as an isolated fact.

As you initially read the chapter, fill out note cards on important people, events, dates, terms, and so on. This will help to organize your material as well as provide a method for quick review.

Question-Answer Method—As you study from an outline, from the text, or from cards, ask yourself questions. Ask the same question in several different ways. Do not go on to the next fact until you can answer the question accurately. Work your way through the material by asking questions, going back to review the previous questions, and then going on to the next questions.

Be wary of studying with a friend unless you are a well-disciplined individual. Too often, "studying" with a friend can become a social time, and little is accomplished. Do not allow yourself to become frustrated. If you have special difficulty, see your teacher. He may be able to suggest just the right thing to help you along.

2

Settling the Thirteen Colonies

In the early 1600s Spain and France held or claimed most of North America. With the defeat of the Spanish Armada, however, England gained new boldness to challenge their claims. Although plagued by hardships, early attempts at settlement inspired other Englishmen to cross the Atlantic. England brought to the New World her customs, laws, and language; and she established thirteen colonies that would later separate from her to become the United States of America.

A. To Build a Colony

The Spanish and French had restricted those who could go to their New World colonies. The Spanish sent mainly noblemen, soldiers, slaves, and priests to their colonies, while the French permitted only approved citizens to go to New France. (Non-Catholics such as the Huguenots were among those that could not go.) In contrast, the English allowed almost anyone who wanted to leave to go to its North American colonies. This opened up the New World to Englishmen who had many reasons for starting a life in that new land.

Reasons the English Came

There were many motives for the founding of the English colonies. In Jamestown and other settlements, the desire for profit was a major concern. Like the Spanish and French, many Englishmen came to the New World hoping to find gold and silver. Investors, with the same desire for personal gain, paid the expenses of new colonies settled by their countrymen. These Englishmen hoped that raw materials from the colonies would repay their investment and return to them a healthy profit.

Another reason for settlement was the chance to own land. In England, wealthy families held most of the land, and tradition kept a family from selling it to anyone else. Thus unless Englishmen inherited land from relatives, they had little hope of owning any. Many were forced to rent farmland or work for a large landholder. In America, however, there was plenty of land. The opportunity to own land of their own drew many farmers to the New World.

Still another motive was the desire for employment. About the time the colonies began, many English landowners started turning their farmland into pastures for sheep. The farmers who had rented these lands were kicked out, and they found themselves with neither homes nor jobs. Many of these men found a new life in America, where they could farm or practice a trade without worrying about landlords.

The desire for political freedom was another important reason for English colonization. The English had gained some voice in their government. The *Magna Carta,* a document signed by King John in 1215, had limited the power of the English monarch and had guaranteed certain basic rights to the English people. In later years the English people had gained many more freedoms from their kings, and they had elected representatives to serve in the English Parliament, or legislature. However, in the early 1600s two kings, James I and Charles I, tried to strengthen royal power and restrict some of the people's freedoms. As a result, many Englishmen went to America, where they could be far away from the strict rule of these kings.

Although many of the earliest settlers desired political freedom, even more came to America in search of religious freedom. It was this reason for settlement that helped to give the colonial heritage of the United States a great distinction. English monarchs had established the Church of England, or Anglican church, as the official church of the land. Everyone in England supported that church with taxes, and everyone was supposed to belong to it. The Church of England had embraced the Protestant Reformation and had renounced the authority of the pope, but it kept some of the Roman Catholic practices. A number of Englishmen were dissatisfied with the church

Original pages from the Fundamental Orders of Connecticut, an early document that helped to set the pattern of political freedom in America

because they believed it did not fully follow Biblical practice. Those who refused to support or belong to the church lost many privileges, and some were severely persecuted for their beliefs. Consequently, these Englishmen looked on the New World as a haven where they could freely worship God according to their beliefs.

One more reason that some of the English settlers came to America was a desire for adventure. The fact that the New World was unknown and there was much to explore made it attractive to some. However, the hardships usually overshadowed the excitement. As it turned out, many of America's early settlers who came to begin a new life found plenty of adventure, whether they wanted it or not.

Difficulties of Colonization

Moving to a new American colony in the 1600s and early 1700s was not easy. The men and women who decided to go had to face many challenges. Not only did they have to find a way to finance their voyage, but also they had to survive the long and uncomfortable trip across the Atlantic. Many had to endure hardships such as hunger and sickness while they were finding a way to make a living in a land that was still a wilderness. The early settlers also had to establish law and order among themselves and their colonial neighbors. Although promoters sometimes billed America as a paradise on earth, those who were led to the colonies by such promises soon found that the new land held many difficulties.

Financial Support and Colony Organization—Founding a new colony was not a cheap activity. It was not easy to raise the money needed for ships and supplies. For example, Sir Walter Raleigh risked his personal fortune to found a colony at Roanoke. In the end he had nothing to show for his efforts. Such prospects made the wealthy reluctant to sponsor colonization.

To provide a solution for the financial needs involved in settling a colony, English investors began to form **joint-stock companies.** These businesses, the forerunners of our modern corporations, were specifically developed for the purpose of helping colonies get started. Groups of Englishmen pooled their money to form a company. To get even more money, they allowed others to invest in the company by buying "shares of stock" at a certain price. Then they invested the money from the sale of stock in a colonization attempt in hopes that the colony would prosper and make money for the investors. This idea not only helped provide the initial cost of setting up the colony, but it also provided money to maintain the settlement for a while. If the venture failed, each investor lost only the amount he had put in. If it became profitable, the profits were split among the investors according to the number of shares each held.

One joint-stock company was the Virginia Company, formed by a group of Englishmen who wanted to get raw materials from the New World. The company was divided into two parts: the London group and the Plymouth group. It was the London group that financed Jamestown, the first permanent English settlement in North America. The Plymouth group never established a colony.

The king gave joint-stock companies a charter for establishing their colonies. The charter, which contained the regulations governing where the colony would be

THE AMERICAN COLONIES		
COLONY	**SETTLED**	**TYPE**
Virginia	Jamestown, 1607	Charter; became royal colony, 1624
Plymouth	Plymouth, 1620	Charter; absorbed by Massachusetts, 1691
Massachusetts	Salem, 1628 Boston, 1630	Charter; became royal colony, 1686
Rhode Island	Providence, 1636	Charter
Connecticut	Hartford, Wethersfield, & Windsor, 1635-36	Charter
New Hampshire	Odiorne's Point, 1623	Proprietary (John Mason); absorbed by Massachusetts, 1641; made separate royal colony, 1679
New York	Settled as New Netherland by Dutch, Fort Orange (Albany), 1624 conquered by English, 1664	Proprietary (Duke of York); became royal colony
New Jersey	A part of New Netherland early settlement by Swedes	Proprietary (John, Lord Berkeley and Sir George Catteret); became royal colony, 1702
Maryland	St. Marys, 1633	Proprietary (George Calvert, Lord Baltimore; transferred to his son, Cecilius Calvert)
Pennsylvania	Philadelphia, 1682	Proprietary (William Penn)
Delaware	Settled as New Sweden by Swedes Fort Christina (Wilmington), 1638 annexed by New Netherland, 1655 conquered by English, 1664	Proprietary (the Duke of York transferred it to William Penn, 1682); separated from Pennsylvania, 1704
North Carolina	Settlers from Virginia moved near Albemarle Sound, 1654	Proprietary (eight English nobles received grant, 1663); separated to form two colonies, 1712; both became royal colonies, 1729
South Carolina	Charles Town (Charleston), 1670	
Georgia	Savannah, 1733	Proprietary (James Oglethorpe) became royal colony, 1751

located and how it would be administered, was the official permission for founding the colony. Thus, colonies founded under these conditions were called **charter colonies.** There were also two other kinds of colonies. **Proprietary colonies** were those which had been given to individuals or groups by the king. The men who received these colonies from the king were called pro-prietors, and they could govern their colonies much as they pleased. The king took control of some of the colonies. These **royal colonies** fell under the direct supervision of the king.

Hardships of the Early Settlers—If the colonist survived the hazardous voyage to America, he probably faced many dangers in the new land. Food and shelter were his immediate needs. Those who lacked adequate nourishment and protection often did not survive the long and cold months of winter. Over half of the original Jamestown colonists in 1607 died of scurvy, fever, or exposure before they had spent three months in the New World. Casualties such as these were common in the early years of settlement.

Indians were another problem. Although some were friendly, many began to turn against the white man when they saw he was taking their land. In 1622 an Indian attack wiped out over three hundred settlers around Jamestown, and in 1675-76 Indians raided and burned many settlements in Massachusetts and surrounding colonies. The Indian threat was over in the more populous colonies by 1700, but regions in the southern colonies and along the western frontier remained in danger.

With these dangers came many other difficulties as the colonists learned to support themselves in the new land. But as these people learned to deal with the challenges of life in the colonies, they developed their own culture and abilities. Separated from life in England, these Americans would one day found their own new nation.

Section Review

1. How did English colonists generally differ from those that went to Spanish or French colonies?
2. List six reasons that English colonists went to America.
3. What was a joint-stock company? How was it used to found colonies?
4. List at least three hazards faced by the early colonists.

B. The New England Colonies

Religious freedom was the dominant factor in the founding of the New England colonies. Many English Christians were unhappy with the Church of England. They believed that it was still too much like the Roman Catholic church, whose practices they thought were un-Scriptural.

Among those who disagreed with some of the practices of the Anglican church were the **Puritans.** They called themselves *Puritans* because they hoped to purify the church from various Roman Catholic practices and ceremonies. They believed that laymen should be able to participate in the governing of the church, and they stressed the authority of Christ over that of the church. A second group, called **Separatists,** did not believe that the Anglican church could be "purified." As a result, they chose to separate themselves from the church and to hold their own worship services.

Plymouth Colony

Because of persecution, a group of Separatists left their village in Scrooby, England, and went to the Netherlands, where their religious beliefs would be tolerated. Led by their pastor, John Robinson, they settled in Leyden, Holland, in 1609. After a few years the parents in this group became concerned that their children were learning the worldly ways of the Dutch children and were losing sight of their English heritage.

These Separatists, who are known in history as the Pilgrims, decided to go to the New World, where they could live as Englishmen but still have religious freedom. Too poor to finance such a venture themselves, they arranged for financial support from a group of English businessmen. These businessmen were to receive any profits the

Statue of a Pilgrim in Plymouth, Massachusetts

colony made in its first seven years. The Pilgrims were also to receive permission from the London group of the Virginia Company to settle in Virginia, just north of Jamestown.

In September, 1620, the Pilgrims set sail from Plymouth, England, in a ship named the *Mayflower.* With them went other Englishmen who wanted to share in founding the new colony. Since these people were not Separatists, the Pilgrims called them "Strangers." The two groups got along fairly well because both the Pilgrims and the Strangers believed in religious freedom and because both groups had skills the colony needed in order to survive.

After more than two stormy months at sea, the *Mayflower* arrived in America. Because of the storms, however, it had landed far north of its destination. Instead of being just north of Jamestown, it was off Cape Cod in what is today Massachusetts. The Pilgrim leaders were troubled, for they had no authority to settle that far north. With winter coming on, there was no time to sail south to where they had originally intended to settle. So before leaving the ship to begin their new colony, the men gathered to write and sign an agreement calling for a government to be formed in Massachusetts. Called the **Mayflower Compact,** this agreement became the first document providing for self-government in the New World. Thus it was an important contribution to the heritage of the American republic that would later arise.

After electing one of their leaders, **John Carver,** to be governor, the Pilgrims began to build their colony. They named it **Plymouth,** after the port in England from which they had sailed. Like those at Jamestown, the Plymouth settlers had a difficult first winter. Since they had landed at Plymouth in December, there had been no time to plant crops. Weak, sick, and hungry, nearly half the colonists, including Governor Carver, died the first winter.

When spring came, however, things began to improve. An Indian named Squanto (SKWON toh), who had learned English from coastal fishermen, showed the Pilgrims how to plant corn and squash. He helped them start a trading industry with the other Indians, who were of the Wampanoag (WAM puh NOH ohg) tribe. For times when the Indians were not so friendly, Miles Standish, one of the Strangers, trained the men to defend their colony.

Despite hardships, the Pilgrims had much to be thankful for by the end of their first year in Plymouth. They had survived and prospered. Their new governor, **William Bradford,** called for a celebration of thanksgiving to God, following the Biblical example set forth in Deuteronomy 26:10—"I have brought the firstfruits of the land, which thou, O Lord, hast given me." They invited the Indians to this feast, and for three days the settlers and their Indian friends rejoiced together.

Why did Plymouth do so much better than Jamestown in its first year, despite the greater harshness of the winter? One reason was that entire families came to Plymouth, whereas Jamestown had only men for its first twelve years. The presence of families forced the colonists to make the area livable for women and children, thus civilizing the colony more quickly; also, the men had to work to provide not only for themselves but also for their wives and children. Another reason was that the Pilgrims were all used to hard work; none of them refused to work, as some of the "noblemen" at

Jamestown had. But the most important reason was the motives of the colonists. Those at Plymouth had come for religious freedom; they had devoted their lives to God, and they lived to be His servants. They wanted this new land to be their home, where they could serve and worship God. Those at Jamestown were not so dedicated, and they let their selfish desires hinder the colony's welfare.

By 1627 the Plymouth Colony was doing well. The settlers had repaid their debt to the English businessmen who had sponsored them. They were finally on their own, and their labor in agriculture and business was supplying their needs.

Scenes of thatching a roof at Plymouth Plantation, the re-created village displaying Pilgrim life

Plymouth was never a large or rich colony. In fact, after seventy years it became part of its larger neighbor, the Massachusetts Bay Colony. As a result, Plymouth did not become one of the colonies that formed the United States. However, the Pilgrims became a major part of America's heritage because of the example they set. They practiced religious toleration; they set up a responsible self-government; and they worked hard, persevering through difficult times. For these reasons, Americans should be grateful for these forefathers.

Massachusetts Bay

Puritan attempts to reform the Church of England met with little success. Weary of the rising tide of persecution and increased taxation, twenty-six Puritan businessmen decided to follow the example of the Pilgrims. They formed a company, the **Massachusetts Bay Company,** to establish a colony in America. After receiving a charter from the king, the leaders of the Massachusetts Bay Company began recruiting settlers.

In 1630 a fleet of seventeen ships carrying nearly one thousand settlers arrived in Massachusetts Bay. These settlers joined other Puritans who had previously founded the town of Salem. Soon new towns and villages such as Boston, New Towne (later called Cambridge), Watertown, and Dorchester began to thrive. The colony grew rapidly during the 1630s as over fifteen thousand new colonists arrived, giving this period in the colony's history the title, "the Great Migration."

Like the Pilgrims, the Puritans came to the New World seeking religious freedom, and they wanted to make a good home for themselves and for their children. For the most part the Puritans who came were wealthier and better educated than the Pilgrims. Learning from the mistakes of others, they were able to bring many supplies with them from England. Among those who came were merchants and craftsmen, doctors and preachers. Because the Puritans believed the Bible to be the Word of God and stressed that God spoke to men through it, they valued education as a means of learning to read and obey Scripture. They had more college-educated settlers than did any other colony. Most of the colonists, however, were farmers.

The charter gave to the stockholders, or "freemen," full powers to govern the colony. Of the original twenty-six stockholders, only twelve were actually interested in going to America. Those twelve bought the shares of the other fourteen and took the charter and control of the colony with them to America. Thus all those in charge of the company governed the colony from America, and England did not interfere during the early years of the colony.

Not everyone who eventually settled in the Massachusetts Bay Colony was a Puritan. Puritans were not even in the majority. Yet it was the Puritans who established the

A portion of John Winthrop's Journal

government, built the churches, and set up the schools. The Puritan leaders had a high goal for their settlement. They wanted to establish an ideal state based on Biblical principles, one that would be a model for other governments. Their leader, Governor **John Winthrop,** hoped that Massachusetts would be "a city set upon a hill" to bear witness to all the world of the wisdom of Biblical government as they interpreted it.

Because of this aim, church and state leaders worked closely together. The state, in an attempt to assist the church in promoting godliness in society, required everyone to attend church—even non-Puritans. Likewise, the state enforced a strict standard of moral conduct on everyone in the community, on the unsaved as well as the saved.

The leaders of the colony did not want to let control of the colony fall into the hands of the ungodly. Thus only church members were given the right to vote. Others were free to live in the community as long as they did not disrupt Puritan teaching or authority. In 1634 the colony became too big for all the voters to participate effectively in every decision. It was decided that each town would elect two delegates to attend the General Court, which governed the colony. This representative body functioned much like the House of Burgesses in Virginia.

Puritanism, firmly planted in Massachusetts Bay, soon spread to other areas of New England. As the population increased, many settlers went out from this colony to establish new ones. Some left to seek better farmland, where they could enjoy greater prosperity; others left to find more religious liberty. They did not wish to, or were not allowed to, remain in the Massachusetts colony because they disagreed with the way

The Governor's Wife

She described herself in a letter as "a fierce spirit, unwilling to submit to the will of God." Yet two sentences later she honestly asserted her fervent desire that the will of God be done. Such was Margaret Winthrop, the wife of John Winthrop, the first governor of Massachusetts.

Margaret was born in England in 1591. When Margaret was twenty-six, her father was murdered. The next

the colony was run. As new colonies were established, however, they could not help resembling in some way the "mother" colony of Massachusetts Bay.

Rhode Island

One of the first to disagree openly with the Puritan leaders was **Roger Williams,** a pastor in Salem, Massachusetts. Although he was generally a Puritan in belief, Williams disagreed with them on three points. First, he believed that the church and state should be separate; that is, that the government should not try to force a particular year—on the heels of that tragedy—Margaret married John Winthrop, a lawyer who was no stranger to sorrow himself. At the age of thirty-one, he was already twice a widower. His second wife had died after less than a year of marriage. Along with her husband, Margaret gained a country estate in England called Groton Manor. She also gained four children from John's first marriage, children she would love as her own. She and John also had eight more children, but only four lived to adulthood.

Life at Groton Manor was prosperous but lonely. John's law practice kept him in London most of the time. The love letters the two exchanged give us great insight into the times in which they lived. In fact, Margaret's letters have made her famous. In them she beautifully expresses the proper foundation for love: "I have many reasons to make me love thee, whereof I will name two, because thou lovest God, and secondly because that thou lovest me. If these two are wantinge all the rest would be eclipsed."

As John contemplated moving to the New World, Margaret constantly assured him of her support and of her willingness to give up all the wealth, security, and familiarity of home. When he did finally decide to go to Massachusetts, Winthrop left his wife behind for a year until he could get settled.

On November 4, 1631, Margaret arrived in Boston. She was greeted with a six-cannon salute and a day of feasting and thanksgiving. Margaret Winthrop would spend the last sixteen years of her life in Massachusetts. During most of that time her husband was governor of the colony. There were no doubt many difficult and exciting times. Her duties as the governor's wife were numerous, not to mention her duties as a mother. Yet she seems to have handled it all exceedingly well. Those who knew her best—her husband and children—never recorded a word of complaint. Often they wrote to her seeking advice and aid. Always, it seems, she was ready to help.

In 1647, after one day of illness, Margaret Winthrop died. In less than a year John Winthrop passed away too. God had obviously provided John Winthrop with the right wife for the challenge of establishing a Puritan colony in the New World. In her life Margaret had learned to submit her will and could say with confidence, "As for God, his way is perfect" (Ps. 18:30).

religion on society. This idea ran directly against the whole purpose of the Massachusetts Bay Colony. The Puritan leaders wanted their colony to be governed by the Bible as they interpreted it. Second, Williams believed that the Indians owned all the land in the colonies. Thus the colonists had no right to stay unless they paid the Indians for the land. This, too, most Puritan leaders denied. Finally, he believed that the Puritans should not try to "purify" the Church of England from within, but, like the Pilgrims, should leave the church.

In 1635 Williams was brought to trial for "newe and dangerous opinions." To preserve the peace, the Puritans exiled him from Massachusetts. Puritan leaders offered to let him stay through the winter. But fearing that he would be kidnaped and sent back to England, he left.

He spent the bitterly cold winter with the Narragansett Indians, who considered him a friend. In the spring he traveled south to Narragansett Bay, where he bought a tract of land from the Indians and founded a village. He named it Providence as a testimony of God's protection, guidance, and comfort in his time of trouble. Williams was determined that his settlement would have religious freedom, including separation of church and state. He welcomed all, regardless of their religion, to settle nearby. Several of the people from his old church in Salem joined him.

By 1644 the English Parliament recognized four settlements, including Providence, as the colony of Rhode Island. Soon the colony drew up a constitution guaranteeing that the government would have authority "only in civil [nonreligious] things."

Connecticut

Unlike that of Rhode Island, the settling of Connecticut did not arise from controversy. Despite the strict rule in Massachusetts Bay, settlers kept arriving, and that colony was soon crowded. As a result, several settlers decided to move west to the fertile Connecticut River Valley. There they settled Windsor (1634) and Wethersfield (1635). In 1636 **Thomas Hooker,** a pastor in New Towne, Massachusetts, received permission to move. He journeyed with his congregation to Connecticut and founded the town of Hartford. In 1639 these three newly settled villages merged to form the colony of Connecticut, naming Hartford as its capital. Connecticut, like Massachusetts and Rhode Island, would survive as a colony and later help form the United States.

In 1639 the settlements in Connecticut adopted a plan of union called the **Fundamental Orders of Connecticut.** This document is usually regarded as the first written constitution, or plan of government, drawn up in America. According to the Orders, the authority behind government lay in the "free consent of the people." For the most

part, Connecticut's government copied that of Massachusetts. One main difference was that the Orders did not make church membership a requirement for voting. The Orders became a model for future state constitutions and the United States Constitution of 1787.

New Hampshire

Besides moving south and west into Rhode Island and Connecticut, Massachusetts colonists also moved north into New Hampshire and Maine. These areas were proprietary colonies for a while, but they experienced little success. As the number of Puritans increased in this region, Massachusetts extended its control over the settlements established there. In 1679 sev-

The New England Colonies

eral towns received a royal charter for New Hampshire, making it a separate colony from Massachusetts. Thus New Hampshire was one of the four New England colonies that would later become one of the thirteen original states of the new nation. Maine did not become a separate colony but remained a part of the Massachusetts colony until 1820, when it became a state. Vermont, also in this New England area, was largely under French influence until New York and New Hampshire were able to gain some control. Like Maine, Vermont never became one of the thirteen English colonies, but in 1791 it became the first state added to the union.

Section Review

1. What was the main reason for the founding of the New England colonies?
2. How did the Puritans and the Separatists differ?
3. Why did the Pilgrims believe it necessary to write the Mayflower Compact? Why is this document so important?
4. How did Puritan leaders hope to prevent the colony from falling into the hands of the ungodly?
5. List the three criticisms that Roger Williams made concerning the way the Massachusetts Bay Colony was run. What colony was formed as a result of his belief, and what was its first settlement?
6. What plan of government is considered the first written constitution drawn up in America? What was an important difference between the government it created and that of Massachusetts?
7. List the four New England colonies that eventually became part of the original thirteen states of the United States.

C. The Middle Colonies

New England was primarily settled by the English, who shared a common heritage. Unlike New England, several of the middle colonies were influenced first by other nations. The Dutch and the Swedes had claimed and settled part of this region decades before the arrival of the first Englishmen. By the time England gained control, there was a diversity of language, ideas, religion, and culture in these colonies. However, they did share the common goal of carving out a civilization from the wilderness. Gradually their differing cultures blended into a common American culture.

New York and New Jersey

An Englishman named Henry Hudson explored for both the Netherlands and England. While sailing for the Netherlands in 1609, Hudson discovered the river that now bears his name, and he sailed up it to the present site of Albany, New York. His exploration gave the Dutch claim to the region that became the colony of New York, although they called it **New Netherland.**

Dutch efforts to settle in the New World were primarily directed by government-approved companies. Merchants organized these companies to establish settlements from which they hoped to profit.

In 1624 a Dutch ship brought thirty families from the Netherlands to America. They landed on Manhattan Island (now part of New York City), but most settled up the Hudson River near the present site of Albany. Two years later a settlement was begun on Manhattan Island. The governor of the colony, **Peter Minuit** (MIN yoo wit), purchased Manhattan from the Indians. The town that grew there, later called New

Swedish and Dutch Colonies 1654

The Middle Colonies

Amsterdam, became the capital of New Netherland.

The Dutch promised large grants of land to anyone who could bring fifty settlers to the New World. Those who received these large grants were called **patroons.** People who could not bring fifty settlers received as much land as they could farm themselves. Although many of the farmers were successful, the development of the new land did not bring as much profit as the Dutch investors had hoped. Soon the Netherlands began to neglect its colony, sending few new colonists and offering little aid.

The English Take Control—The Dutch settlements along the Hudson River, however, made the English envious. At New Amsterdam, the Dutch had one of the finest harbors on the Atlantic coast. Moreover, New Netherland stood between New England and the southern colonies, thereby preventing England from controlling the entire Atlantic coastal region.

John Cabot had claimed the Atlantic coast of North America for England in 1497. Before long, England pressed her claim that New Netherland was her rightful territory. In 1664 the king of England gave the land that was the Dutch colony to his brother, the **Duke of York,** as a proprietary colony. The duke sent warships to capture the colony. The settlers in New Amsterdam, who were already dissatisfied with the Dutch administration, saw the fleet and decided to surrender. Thus this Dutch colony passed peacefully into the hands of the English, who renamed it New York.

The Founding of New Jersey—The Duke of York gave the southern portion of his new territory to two of his friends: **Sir George Carteret** and **Lord John Berkeley.** In order to attract settlers to their new colony of New Jersey, they offered cheap land, full religious liberty, and a measure of self-government. Trouble plagued the colony for a time, and it was divided into East and West Jersey. It was later reunited as a royal province under the direct rule of the English king. The name "New Jersey" comes from the island of Jersey in the

English Channel, of which Sir George Carteret had become governor.

Pennsylvania

Pennsylvania, like Plymouth, was established because of religious persecution in England. The Society of Friends, commonly known as the **Quakers,** separated from the Church of England. They believed in and practiced few of the accepted religious ceremonies of the Church of England, but they did practice many "good works." They viewed all men as equal regardless of race, color, or social status. They opposed war and refused to take oaths. Unfortunately many trusted in these works for their salvation, and they believed that they had an "inner light" which told them God's will apart from the Bible. These beliefs made them unpopular both in England and in the American colonies.

One Quaker, **William Penn,** came from a wealthy English family. King Charles II owed Penn's father a large sum of money. When Penn's father died, the debt was to be paid to William. In 1681 the king agreed to pay Penn by giving him a large piece of land in America. Penn called it "Sylvania," Latin for "woodland"; the king called it "Penn's Sylvania." Although the land was Penn's by royal grant, Penn wisely bought the land from the Indians. In doing so he made friends with them and avoided the attacks that plagued other colonies.

Penn hoped to use the proprietary colony to provide a haven for himself and his persecuted Quaker friends. He referred to his colony as a "Holy Experiment." His goal was to establish a colony ruled by "brotherly love," the fruit of which would bring peace and prosperity. He began by setting up laws granting religious freedom to all who believed in one God. There was no established church to obstruct people from worshiping

Top: *Old Quaker Meeting House in Lincoln, Rhode Island*
Bottom: *Title page of the* Bay Psalm Book *and William Penn making a treaty with the Indians*

God in their own way. This freedom attracted other persecuted religious groups from Europe. Many of the people who came to Pennsylvania were from Germany. They called themselves *Deutsche* ("Germans"). Others, however, called them the "Pennsylvania Dutch."

With many industrious people and more fertile land than that of New England, Pennsylvania became the most prosperous colony in North America. By 1776 its capital city, Philadelphia ("city of brotherly love"), was a bustling city. Only one city in the entire British empire, London, was larger.

Delaware

Penn's land also included what is now Delaware. This region had originally been settled by the Swedes. In 1638 they founded Fort Christina (now Wilmington, Delaware) and named it after the Swedish queen. Their colony, known as **New Sweden,** later passed into the hands of the Dutch and then to the English. The Duke of York granted this territory to Penn in 1682. Although the settlements of Delaware were later allowed a separate assembly, they remained under the governor of Pennsylvania until 1776.

Section Review

1. How were the people that settled the middle colonies different from those in New England?
2. How did the Dutch colony of New Netherland become the English colony of New York?
3. Name the two men to whom the Duke of York gave New Jersey.
4. How did William Penn acquire territory in the New World that he used as a haven for Quakers?
5. What colony's control passed from the Swedish to the Dutch to the English?

D. The Southern Colonies

The five southern colonies—Virginia, Maryland, North Carolina, South Carolina, and Georgia—were, like New England, settled mainly by the English. While they shared some concerns and characteristics with the middle colonies and New England, the southern colonies developed differently.

Virginia

In the last chapter we looked at the early English attempts to settle Virginia. The first permanent settlement was Jamestown, but this settlement did not live up to the high expectations of its financial backers. Instead of providing quick profits, the colony became a financial burden for the profit-minded company. Hunger, disease, dissension, and Indian attacks drained the life from the colony.

From the Indians the Virginia colonists learned how to grow tobacco. John Rolfe, the husband of an Indian maiden named Pocahontas, cultivated tobacco and sold it in England, where tobacco products were popular. (People in that day were less concerned with the health dangers of tobacco, although it had already been called "a noxious weed.") As the demand for tobacco

The marriage of Pocahontas and John Rolfe

products increased, the tobacco industry grew. Tobacco became the one major crop of the Virginia colonists and eventually was so valuable that it sometimes served as money for payment of taxes and wages.

By the 1620s Virginia was a prospering colony. However, bickering among the leaders of the London Company made the king of England displeased with the way the colony was being managed. As a result he revoked the company's charter and made Virginia a royal colony. The king then took control and appointed a colonial governor and council. However, he allowed the House of Burgesses (the colonial representative assembly) to continue to meet.

Throughout the seventeenth century, settlers branched out from the original Jamestown settlement. New towns and plantations were established. When fire destroyed much of Jamestown toward the end of the century, the capital of the colony

was moved to Williamsburg, just a few miles away. This colonial city became a leading center of government and culture among the thirteen colonies.

Scenes of Williamsburg: the George Wythe House (left), *the Governor's Mansion* (top right), *and a display of colonial weaving* (bottom right)

MARYLAND

Baltimore

VIRGINIA

St. Marys

Williamsburg

Jamestown

Chesapeake Bay

NORTH CAROLINA

Roanoke Island

SOUTH CAROLINA

GEORGIA

Charles Towne (Charleston)

Savannah

The Southern Colonies

St. Augustine (Spain)

0   50   100   200

Scale of Miles

Maryland

Roman Catholics, as well as Separatists, Puritans, and Quakers suffered persecution in seventeenth-century England. However, Charles I, the English king who ruled from 1625 to 1649, was sympathetic to the Catholics. He gave the land of Maryland as a gift to his friend **George Calvert,** known as Lord Baltimore. Calvert, a Roman Catholic, wanted a place where other Catholics could be free from the persecution they faced in England. He also wanted to make money by investing in a colony in the New World. The king named the territory Maryland in honor of his queen, Henrietta Maria.

George Calvert died before he could begin his settlement, but his son **Cecilius Calvert,** also called Lord Baltimore, led the first settlers across the Atlantic. In 1634 they founded a town called St. Marys. According

to the king's charter, Calvert was to be the proprietor of Maryland, but all the land-owners were to have a part in making the laws.

Soon Protestants also began to settle, and eventually they outnumbered the Catholics three to one. The Catholics began to fear that they might face new persecution in their own colony. So in 1649 the law-makers passed the Act of Toleration, which guaranteed religious freedom to all who believed in the Trinity. This was the first written law of religious freedom in the colonies, although Rhode Island already had unwritten laws of religious freedom.

The Carolinas

After a period of turmoil and civil war in England, Charles II came to the English throne. He wished to reward those who had been loyal to the royal family during the time of trouble. In 1663 he granted to eight English noblemen a tract of land that they named Carolina after the king, whose name in Latin was *Carolus.*

In 1670 a large group of settlers began the settlement of Albemarle Point. Ten years later they moved to a better site nearby, founding the port city of Charles Towne (now Charleston, South Carolina). Because of its fine harbor, the city became an important colonial commercial center. Soon other settlers were attracted to the region. French Huguenots, Scots-Irish, and Englishmen from the islands in the West Indies moved to the new colony.

A much smaller group settled on the Carolina coast far to the north, next to Virginia. These distant settlements grew, but they had little in common. In 1712, less than fifty years after receiving its charter, the colony of Carolina was divided: the northern portion became North Carolina; the southern portion, South Carolina.

Both of the Carolinas followed Virginia's example of raising a large cash crop. Tobacco became that crop in North Carolina, but South Carolina found its coastal lands and climate to be suitable for growing rice. **Indigo,** a plant from which a popular blue dye could be made, added a second cash crop for South Carolina.

Top: *Charleston, South Carolina, has been an important port since colonial times.*
Bottom: *Indigo*

Georgia

Georgia, the last of the thirteen colonies, had an unusual beginning. Because the English government worried about the Spanish forts in Florida, Parliament wanted to use the land between the Carolinas and Florida as a buffer zone, to keep the Spanish at a distance. While Parliament was considering this idea, a wealthy English general named **James Oglethorpe** (OH gul THORP) asked for permission to found a colony. He was unhappy with the way debtors were treated in England. If a man owed a debt, he could be thrown into prison until he paid. But if he were in prison, he could not work to pay off the debt. Oglethorpe thought that such men should be allowed to work and have an opportunity to repay their debts. King George II finally gave Oglethorpe and some other trustees title to the new colony of Georgia, which could both serve as a new home for debtors and provide protection for the colonies that lay farther north.

Parliament agreed to Oglethorpe's plan, and it even contributed money for the project. The first settlers arrived in 1733 and founded the city of Savannah under Oglethorpe's direction. Oglethorpe worked hard to insure the colony's success. He built forts along the coastal islands for protection from Spanish attack, and in 1739 a Georgia force defeated a small Spanish force that came against them. Realizing that the Creek Indians, a powerful tribe in West Georgia, might also be a threat, Oglethorpe sought to maintain peace with them.

Only a few debtors ever settled in Georgia, defeating Oglethorpe's original purpose, but other Europeans did come to the colony. After only a few years Georgia became a royal colony and began to resemble the other southern colonies.

Section Review

1. What crop became the staple crop of Virginia?
2. What city became the center of government in Virginia after Jamestown?
3. Who was the proprietor of Maryland? What was the first settlement?
4. What was the first written law of religious freedom in the colonies? For what colony was it written?
5. Eight English noblemen were the proprietors of what colonies?
6. For what two reasons was Georgia founded? By whom was it founded?

Summary

The English colonists came to America for many reasons—profit, land ownership, employment, political freedoms, religious freedoms, and adventure. They established the original colonies as either charter colonies, proprietary colonies, or royal colonies.

The first colony in New England was Plymouth, established by Separatists in 1620. Plymouth eventually merged with Massachusetts, a strong colony built with Puritan leadership. Colonists from Massachusetts helped to build three other New England colonies: Rhode Island, Connecticut, and New Hampshire.

The Dutch originally settled New York and New Jersey as their own colony of New Netherland, and Swedes settled Delaware as New Sweden. However, the English took control of these colonies in 1664. They, along with William Penn's Pennsylvania, became the middle colonies.

The southern colonies found much of their prosperity by growing cash crops of tobacco or rice and indigo. Jamestown, Virginia, was the first permanent English settlement in North America, and Lord Baltimore founded Maryland as a colony that would welcome Roman Catholics. North Carolina and South Carolina were one proprietary colony until their division in 1712, and James Oglethorpe tried to make Georgia a refuge for debtors.

Chapter Review

Do You Remember?

■ Name these twos and threes.
1. Three kinds of colonies
2. Three regions of colonies
3. Two religious groups that settled in the Massachusetts area
4. Two important documents for colonial government
5. Two countries that colonized the middle colonies before England
6. Three important southern colonial crops

■ Match these men with the appropriate colony.

7. Cecilius Calvert	a. Plymouth
8. James Oglethorpe	b. Massachusetts
9. William Bradford	c. Rhode Island
10. Roger Williams	d. Connecticut
11. John Winthrop	e. Maryland
12. Thomas Hooker	f. Georgia

■ Name the colony most closely associated with the following:
13. Quakers
14. Roman Catholics
15. patroons
16. Separatists
17. debtors
18. many German immigrants

Why Is It So?

1. Why did the English come to America?
2. How did the joint-stock company help to finance American colonization?
3. How did the Puritans and Separatists differ?
4. Why was the Fundamental Orders of Connecticut significant?
5. How did John Rolfe influence the southern colonies?
6. For what two reasons was Georgia colonized?

What Do You Think?

1. How was the joint-stock company like modern corporations?
2. Why was Plymouth Colony important to America's heritage even though it did not survive as a separate colony?
3. How did Quakers believe God reveals His will to man? In light of I Corinthians 2:14, what could you conclude about this belief?

3

Colonial Society and Government

A North Carolina farm scene

People of all kinds left Europe to come to the British colonies. Preachers, paupers, wealthy landowners, merchants, thieves, and plenty of farmers were among the thousands who sailed the ocean to find their new home. The average crossing took over four months, and the passengers usually spent their time in crowded, damp conditions. No doubt many of these new colonists took their minds off their present discomforts by thinking about the new land that awaited them. What would life be like in the colonies?

A. Occupations: How the Colonists Made Their Living

Some settlers came prepared for what they found in the New World. Those who settled in Plymouth and Massachusetts Bay, for example, generally brought necessary materials, tools, and supplies. They found the land and climate of New England similar to that of their home in England. Most of those enroute to America, however, were unaware of the variety of land and climate that the colonies would hold. Plains and mountains, forests and grasslands, warm

Physical Map of the Thirteen Colonies

and cold climates—all were available in this land they were to settle. In many areas of the colonies, these people had to learn to adjust to a land that was different from their homelands in Europe.

The climate and resources of the land were very important to the early settlers. Today at our local grocery store, we may buy foods brought from many parts of the country or even imported from other countries. In our department stores, we may buy merchandise manufactured all over the world. The colonists, however, had to depend mainly on what would grow on their own land or what they could make from other available materials to meet their other needs. This was especially true for the farmers, who made up over ninety per cent of the colonists. The vast majority of these were **subsistence farmers** who were able to raise just enough crops and livestock to provide their families with adequate food and clothing. Even colonists who were not farmers themselves had to depend on locally grown food, and many also used local resources for their work—carpenters and shipbuilders used trees from nearby forests, and smiths often used metals from nearby deposits.

Because geography influenced the lifestyle of the colonists, definite patterns arose in the three colonial regions we have already learned about—New England, the middle colonies, and the southern colonies. As we learned in Chapter 2, colonies within each of these regions shared some similar features in their founding and settlement. They also shared some similarities in the climate and resources that influenced the activities of the colonists. Although all three regions would eventually band together as the United States, they developed their own special characteristics.

The New England Colonies

The geography of New England is rough and cold in comparison to the other regions. Although a wide coastal plain extends along most of the Atlantic coast, all but a narrow piece disappears in New England. As a result, the remaining landscape bulges with hills and low mountains. The region lacks not only flat farmland but also fertile and abundant soil. It has only a thin, rocky cover of soil that makes farming difficult. In addition, New England has only a short growing season and long, cold, and snowy winters.

Because New England's geography was not favorable for extensive farming, nearly all the colonists who were farmers were

subsistence farmers. With little hope for profit in agriculture, many New Englanders looked to the ocean for other work. Fishing opportunities along the New England coast and codfish off the Grand Banks of Newfoundland soon made fishing an important industry. The fish were caught, salted, and exported to the middle colonies, the West Indies, and Europe. Whaling also became important to New England. Whales were processed for their oil and bone, and New Bedford, Massachusetts, and Nantucket, Massachusetts, became busy whaling ports.

At first, fishermen and whalers sailed on British ships, but soon the Americans began building their own and even supplying ships for England. The region had plenty of timber for the shipbuilding industry. By 1776 nearly one-third of the British trading ships were made in the colonies. Most of the products the ships carried were raw

A whaler ready with his harpoon

materials from America or manufactured articles from England. Although New England settlers manufactured some products at home during the winter, most produced only enough for their own family's use. The colonies did not export many manufactured products until some time later.

Almost all of the early settlers of New England were British, and so it was natural for them to take up many of the industries that were common in the mother country. Britain, as an island country, had built much of its wealth in sea trade and related activities. New Englanders, with their limited land resources, also made sea activity profitable. Because these colonists looked to the sea, harbors became important points of settlement and centers of trade.

The Middle Colonies

Life in the middle colonies was influenced by its diverse peoples and its geography. These colonies were "melting pots." Immigrants from many different European countries, not just the British Isles, came to this region, and the colonists blended their various cultures. Pennsylvania, although opened to settlement by English Quakers, also became the home of Scots-Irish Presbyterians from northern Ireland. Moravians had come from Czechoslovakia by way of Germany; Mennonites from Switzerland. The Pennsylvania "Dutch" settled from Germany. New York had descendants of the Dutch as well as Englishmen within her borders. New Jersey's settlers were mostly Dutch or Swedish. As a result of such diverse cultures, the settlers in the middle colonies were less strictly bound to British traditions.

Geography offered two other strong influences on the middle colonies. One was the abundance of navigable rivers. The

Hudson River helped settlers move to inland New York and New Jersey. On the banks of the Delaware River, Philadelphia grew from four thousand people in 1690 to more than forty thousand by 1775. The Susquehanna (SUS kwuh HAN uh) and Allegheny (AL ih GAY nee) rivers also opened paths into Pennsylvania. These and other rivers served as water highways to inland settlements and farms, providing transportation routes for trade.

The second geographic advantage was that the middle colonies had rich, thick soil. Although the region had plenty of hills and mountains, it also had fertile coastal and river plains. Settlers could grow an abundance of cereal grains like corn, oats, barley, and wheat. For this reason the middle colonies were also called the **bread colonies.**

Farming became the major activity in the middle colonies. And, although most farmers raised food primarily for their own needs, some were able to sell extra farm produce for profit. Abundant pasture lands fed cattle and horses, and livestock became

An Amish wedding in Lancaster, Pennsylvania

an export. Other industries arose to meet the needs of the farmers. Coopers and wainwrights used lumber from the forests to produce barrels and wagons. Merchants in the towns bought the farmers' produce and sold them all kinds of needed supplies.

Settlers in the western areas of the colonies, where few whites lived, trapped animals for their fur and traded with the Indians for more furs. Those settlers could then trade in the towns and make large profits. Albany, New York, became an early fur-trade center because of its location on the Hudson and its closeness to the Iroquois Indian tribes.

The Southern Colonies

The rich soil and long growing seasons of the southern colonies prompted agriculture to become the dominant activity. Although some corn, wheat, and other basic food crops were grown, the colonists found other more profitable crops. They could grow and export tobacco, rice, and indigo because those crops were in demand in Europe. Since greater profits could be made if these crops were raised in large fields and tended by unskilled laborers, large farms called **plantations** became a major part of southern culture. A few port cities and river towns grew to meet the transportation and trading needs for the plantations and other farms, but few other industries grew.

The geography of the southern colonies suited plantation agriculture. A wide coastal plain gave these colonies plenty of flat farmland, and the money crops thrived in the warmer climate. Most of the early colonists were English, and the wealthy planters set up their plantations to resemble the large country estates in Britain. Far more of the southern colonists, however, were not so wealthy. Because their small farms could not compete with the plantations, many of them became subsistence farmers in the inland "Piedmont" or foothills of the Appalachian Mountains.

Southern Money Crops—Tobacco became the first important money crop for the southern colonies, despite some discouragements. From the bitter experience of starvation at Jamestown, the colonists had learned that it was more important to grow food than tobacco. Furthermore, the English recognized that tobacco contained some type of habit-forming drug. Nonetheless, economic gain finally overruled better judgment, and tobacco production increased rapidly. Although tobacco was difficult to grow and depleted the soil, it became the leading cash crop in Maryland, Virginia, and North Carolina.

Rice was raised in the **tidewater** (areas along coastal rivers and inlets), where tides could be used to raise and lower water levels in rice fields. At high tide farmers opened floodgates to cover the fields with water. Later as the tide ebbed, the floodgates were opened again to lower the water level. The fields were flooded twice each season, and the rice was finally dried for harvest in September.

Indigo proved a good second crop because it grew off-season from both rice and tobacco. Thus the workers could stay busy all year. Harvested indigo was laid in vats to ferment. When the leaves had decayed enough, the water was drained out and the plants beaten. Limewater was added to bring out the indigo's rich blue color. One drawback of handling indigo was that the fermenting leaves gave off an unpleasant odor. Indigo and rice were especially important crops in South Carolina.

Corn—The largest and most important food crop in all the colonies was corn, also known as maize. The Indians had taught the colonists to grow this valuable New World plant. Corn could grow almost anywhere, was easy to hoe and weed, and grew quickly. It could be ground into meal for johnny cake or corn pone, cooked with lima beans to make succotash, sweetened with sugar to make Indian pudding, or roasted in unshucked cobs. Soaked in lye, it became hominy; dried hominy was ground to make grits, a favorite in the South. Dried corn could be stored until needed; corn stalks could be used to stuff mattresses, make children's toys, or to feed to livestock. Dried cobs could be used to kindle fires. Virtually every part of the corn plant was put to some practical use.

Scenes of colonial architecture and foods

The Frontier

All the early settlements in the colonies were on or near the Atlantic coast, and settlement moved inland slowly. The Appalachian Mountains, which lie inland from the coast, helped to form a western barrier for the British colonies for over one hundred years. Even so, all three colonial regions constantly had a frontier. The **frontier** was the undeveloped area at the edge of the settled areas. As settlements moved west, the frontier moved west, too. Easterners also called the frontier the "back country."

Most frontier people were hard-working and God-fearing. But they were joined by others, the riffraff of society—people whom Easterners wanted out of the way. Wife-deserters, escaped convicts, and debtors running from bill collectors came to live on the edge of society. Some of the riffraff remade their lives; others failed again. But on the frontier few questions were asked. Men and women worked at backbreaking tasks for hours to keep themselves fed and clothed. Only a few became wealthy.

The frontier settler claimed land almost anywhere he wished. Since the land had to be cleared, few farms exceeded two hundred acres. The farmer grew a patch of corn and perhaps some peas, potatoes, and wheat. He had a cow or two and a hog—animals that lived off the land. The farmer did not have time to clear land to grow food for the animals. Because he was a subsistence farmer, he had little to sell—perhaps a little flax, wheat, tobacco, or indigo. With the money he could buy a new sickle, a cooking pot, some salt, or some cloth for his wife to make a dress. He lived on pork and hominy, ate from wooden "trenchers" (platters), and drank from wooden "noggins" (mugs).

Despite the frontier's problems and dangers, its population grew. The Wilderness Road, begun in 1769, enabled people to cross the Appalachians more easily than before. The Great Wagon Road, stretching seven hundred miles from Salisbury, North Carolina, to Lancaster, Pennsylvania, became the main north-south highway. Parliament made it illegal to settle beyond the Appalachians after 1763, but by 1776 more than 250,000 settlers had found their way to the frontier. A few brave souls headed even farther west.

Section Review

1. What was the occupation of most of the colonists?
2. Why was farming not the primary source of profit in the New England colonies?
3. What three occupations provided a major source of income to the New England colonies?
4. What two geographic characteristics were advantages to the middle colonies?
5. What was the nickname of the middle colonies? What gave them this name?
6. List three major money crops in the southern colonies.
7. What was the frontier?

B. Social Classes: Who Was Who in the Colonies

The colonists were much more concerned about a person's social class than we are today. John Winthrop, the first governor of Massachusetts Bay, wrote, "God Almighte in his most holy and wise providence hath soe disposed of the Condicion of mankinde, as in all times some must be rich, some poore, some highe, and eminent in power and dignitie; others mean and in subjection." Even the young students were affected by colonial class structure. Students were called on to recite not by academic grade or alphabetical arrangement, but by the father's income and social class. Diplomas were given out in the same manner. Even so, class structure was less permanent in the colonies than in England. If a man started out in a "lower" class, he could work his way into a "higher" class if he made the effort.

Aristocrats

All three colonial regions had their **aristocrats** or upper-class people. In New England the upper class generally included merchants, traders, and clergymen. Names

The George Wythe House in Colonial Williamsburg

like Mather, Winthrop, Faneuil (FAN yul), and Hancock meant wealth. In the middle and southern colonies the upper classes were those who owned large pieces of land. A few gained their positions by holding high government offices or by marrying someone wealthy. In colonial New York the Roosevelts (ancestors of two presidents) and the Van Rensselaers (VAN REN-suh-LEERZ) were in the upper class. Plantation owners in the South included the Byrds, Lees, and Pinckneys.

In all three regions, the upper-class families enjoyed more comforts and luxuries than the lower classes. Usually the upper class imported much of their clothes, furniture, and other possessions from Europe. Their sons received good educations. Servants helped the family perform the household chores. Most of these wealthy colonists, however, were not at all lazy. They worked hard to earn their money, and they worked hard to keep it.

The Middle Class

The middle classes were those colonists who were neither wealthy nor poor. Many

Craftsmen in Colonial Williamsburg

had gradually made their way up the social ladder in the New World. They generally owned some land and had a reasonably comfortable home. But they lacked the servants and the luxuries that the aristocrats could afford. The middle classes included small independent farmers, clergy, shopkeepers, ship captains, carpenters, and blacksmiths.

The Lower Classes

The colonies had few extremely poor people. Land was available to almost everyone, and a good effort at farming would usually feed and clothe a family. Nonetheless, there were a good number of servants who, while they served, owned no land and had few material possessions. And at the very bottom of the social scale were the growing numbers of slaves.

Servants—The two bottom rungs on the social ladder in white society were occupied by redemptioners and indentured servants. **Redemptioners** usually came from continental Europe rather than the British Isles. They brought their families and possessions. Because they could not pay for all of their passage, they hoped to find a relative or friend to pay the remaining fees after they arrived. If they did not, the fees were paid by some wealthy colonist who required two to four years of service as repayment.

Indentured servants were usually single men from ages eighteen to thirty. Most agreed to be servants to gain passage to the colonies, but a few became servants to repay debts or to learn a trade. By the year 1636 indentureships were so common that those who applied received a printed form with blanks to be filled in. The master paid the servant's passage to America, and then the indentured servant in return worked for the

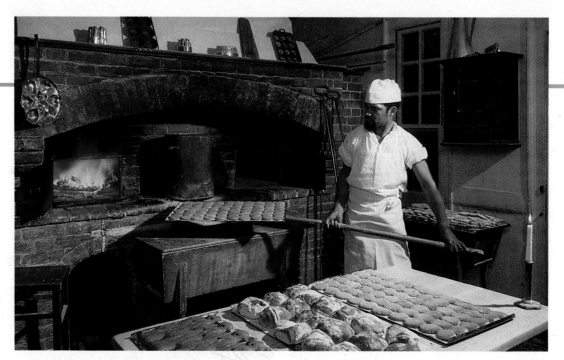

Baking bread in a colonial manner

master for four to seven years. A servant could not marry without his master's consent. Few masters consented, for they would have to pay the cost of rearing children that might result from such a marriage. Indentured servants who ran away from their masters usually paid with additional years of service. Sometimes they were whipped as well. Some of the servants lived in relative comfort, but others lived difficult lives.

When his service was completed, the indentured servant received land and his "freedom dues"—a new suit, an ax, a hoe, and even cash. Most of these people moved quickly into the middle classes, and some indentured servants became quite successful. For example, Charles Thomson of Pennsylvania became the secretary of the Continental Congress, and Matthew Thornton signed the Declaration of Independence for New Hampshire.

Slaves—The first blacks in the mainland colonies were brought to Jamestown in 1619 by the Dutch. They were received as indentured servants, not slaves. Before long, however, the practice of not releasing the

black servants became common. As the supply of indentured servants from Europe failed to meet the demand for laborers in America, the colonists began to want more and more of these Africans. The average slave cost about five times as much as an indentured servant, but the slave would work for the master for the rest of his life.

Most estimates say that about nine or ten million slaves were sent from Africa to the New World, but only about half a million were sold in what became the United States. By 1730 thirty per cent of the population south of Pennsylvania was black. By 1760 South Carolina was sixty per cent black. The numbers of slaves grew higher in the South because large numbers of workers were needed there to farm the cash crops. The smaller farms in New England and the middle colonies rarely used slaves, but the blacks were often used as household servants in upper-class northern homes.

Although those in other groups could move up the social ladder and benefit from English policies and a free economic system, slaves could not. By 1760 slavery was usually associated with blackness, and a freed black in the South had to carry papers to prove he was free. Slaves lacked many privileges: land ownership, occupational and religious choice, a normal marriage relationship, education, voting, and holding office, among other things.

Most slaves worked six days a week, fifteen to sixteen hours a day in the summer, and fourteen hours a day the rest of the year. Although this may seem very harsh to us today, most free workers in those days kept similar hours—even the masters. The maximum hours slaves could work were set by law in most colonies, but it was the common sense and compassion of the masters that really determined how well slaves were treated. George Washington wrote to his overseer:

> To request that my people may be at their work as soon as it is light, work till it is dark, and be diligent while they are at it can hardly be necessary, because the propriety of it must strike every manager who attends to my interest . . . or who, on reflecting, must be convinced that lost labor is never to be regained. The presumption is, that every laborer does as much in twenty-four hours as his strength, without endangering his health or constitution, will allow.

Section Review

1. Name four groups that probably were part of the aristocratic class in the colonies.
2. Define these terms:
   a. redemptioners
   b. indentured servants
   c. slaves
3. Why were there more slaves in the southern colonies?

C. Government: Establishing Law and Order

Because of man's natural selfish desires, God ordained that governments should rule over man to keep him from doing evil to his neighbors. The early colonists recognized their need for government, and they set up their own governments when leadership from Europe was not provided. The principles of their colonial and local governments were a pattern for the later establishment of the government of the United States.

Colonial Governments

We have already learned that colonies were established and governed under three different plans of authority. One was the royal colony, where the king kept control; one was the proprietary colony, where the king gave the colony to one or more proprietors; the third was the charter colony, where the king signed a charter, which gave permission and regulations for a joint-stock

Weapons from the colonial era

company or other group to establish a colony. These different colonies had different types of government.

Governors and Legislatures—Some governments were more powerful than others. The charter colonies (Massachusetts, Connecticut, and Rhode Island) elected their own government and legislature. They had the least interference from Britain. In proprietary colonies such as Pennsylvania and Carolina, the governor was appointed by the proprietor or his heirs, if the king approved. In royal colonies—sometimes called crown colonies—the king chose the governor himself. Often the governor stayed in England and sent a lieutenant governor to rule for him. In most colonies the governor served five years. He was responsible to members of the British government. Sometimes the colonists tried to influence those officials in Britain to give them a new governor or force the old one to be more cooperative. Benjamin Franklin, for example, lived in England for several years while he served as an agent for Pennsylvania, Massachusetts, New Jersey, and Georgia.

In all but the charter colonies, the governor was quite powerful. He could veto laws that the legislature passed, regulate land grants, and command the local army, called the **militia.** But the legislature had **"the power of the purse"**—they paid the governor's salary and financed government activities. If the governor did not do what they wanted him to do, they could refuse to pay for his programs or even refuse to pay his salary. All the colonies developed their own legislatures or assemblies similar to the House of Burgesses in Virginia. All free men in the colonies who owned some property were generally able to vote for representatives to these colonial assemblies.

A colonial militia might have looked like this as they trained for action.

The House of Burgesses in Williamsburg

on how much he owned. Some colonies had poll taxes that citizens paid before they could vote. A Massachusetts poll tax required every voter to pay except for the governor and lieutenant governor; the president, faculty, and students at Harvard; and ministers, school teachers, and invalids. A poll tax in New York in 1702 was a graduated tax—that is, wealthier people had to pay more than poorer people. For example, those who wore wigs, a common fashion for the rich in colonial times, paid more. Other forms of taxes were tried, but eventually property taxes became the main source of income for the government in all the colonies.

Local Governments

Most of the colonies were divided into counties. These areas of a colony, along with the communities that developed, needed their own special organizations of government. Although the British government sometimes exerted some control in the colonial government, the colonists ran their own town and county governments with little interference from England.

In New England the basic unit of government was the **township**. At announced times all the **freeholders** (property owners) attended town meetings. The town meeting was the purest form of democracy, or direct government, by the people in America. The average citizen had his own say in a town meeting, and he did not have to rely on an elected representative to speak for him. Some towns still use this system today.

At a town meeting local issues were settled by majority vote. Each new settler was given citizenship and allowed to own land in the township by vote of his fellow townsmen. Other issues were settled as well.

Thus a representative or republican government became an early feature of American life.

The Courts—Most of the ideas for the colonial court systems came from England, but they were changed to meet local needs. Governors appointed **justices of the peace** to try those accused of crimes and to settle disputes between citizens. The justices also collected taxes, granted licenses, recorded deeds to property, and served other public needs. Sometimes the justices even conducted the elections. This system usually worked well because the justices knew the people in their communities. They rendered justice to each individual person, guided by the spirit of the law.

Taxes—The colonists paid for their governments by paying taxes. The main tax was a property tax. Anyone who owned land or other valuable property paid a certain amount to the colony, depending

For example, the citizens appointed night watchmen to protect the town. At first all able-bodied men over sixteen were expected to take turns serving night watch. Wealthy people who did not want to serve paid someone to serve for them. Besides patrolling the streets, the watchman was sometimes expected to call out the time of night and tell the state of the weather.

At a town meeting citizens also considered ways to help the poor. The simplest type of relief was to send a poor person "round the town" to live several weeks with each family. Another was "putting out"— a single family provided food and shelter and received money from the town for giving it. If a poor person could work at all, he was bound out like an indentured

Election Day in the Colonies

In New England the rights to vote and hold office were usually given only to free adult male church members who owned property (usually fifty acres or fifty British pounds of personal property). If a colonist met qualifications such as these, he could participate in the elections.

Voting in a colonial election was very different from going to the polls today. If the candidate had no opposition, he might be elected "by view" at a meeting. The voters just raised their hands, in the same way that we often "vote" on simple matters in the classroom.

When there was more than one candidate, the sheriff or justice of the peace opened the polls on election day by standing in front of the door and reading the official notice of election. When each voter came in, his name was called out, and the sheriff cried, "How vote ye?" The voter then answered aloud, and the town clerk recorded the vote. Sometimes each candidate stayed at the polls. When someone voted for him, he stood, bowed, and thanked the voter. When the sheriff thought all the voters had come, he went to the door and called, "Gentlemen, freeholders, come into the court and give your vote, or the poll will be closed."

Election day was often a day of celebration. Those who lived far from the voting place had to travel some distance to vote; so they often took care of other business in town as well. They stayed part of the day, visiting friends, gathering news, and perhaps celebrating the results of the election.

servant. He then worked for the person who paid for his care. Larger towns built almshouses, where both the "honest poor" and the criminals lived. Most people considered poverty a shame and had to be totally desperate before asking for help. The town wasted little sympathy on the lazy or beggars. Idlers were indentured, jailed, or even whipped and expelled from the town.

In the southern colonies, where there were fewer towns and the population was mostly rural, local government was organized more by counties. Sometimes, however, counties were divided into smaller areas called parishes. Elections were generally held to elect officials for the counties and parishes, and the prominent plantation owners were usually the winners. Then these officials acted on most of the matters of local government themselves. The middle colonies had local governments similar to both those in New England and those in the southern colonies.

Section Review

1. List the three types of colonies and tell who had the authority to establish a government for each type.
2. What official was in charge of holding court in the colonies?
3. What tax was the main source of government income in the colonies?
4. What is a poll tax?
5. Why was the town meeting considered the purest form of democracy in America?
6. Who usually had the right to vote and hold office in the colonies?

Summary

The English colonies shared many similarities, but they also had geographic and cultural differences that affected their development. The New England colonists, who lacked good farmland and a warm climate, turned to sea industries for most of their livelihood. The middle colonies used their good farmland to grow much grain, and the southern colonies grew large money crops on their plantations.

Although the colonists respected social class, opportunities for people to climb into the middle and upper classes were common. Hard work was respectable and necessary in the colonies. Unfortunately, the practice of black slavery developed because of the need for even more workers.

Governors and legislatures provided government for the colonies. Most of the colonies set up legislative assemblies that represented the people and their wishes. However, colonial power was kept in check in the royal and proprietary colonies by appointed governors. Even so, all the colonies were able to establish their own local governments without British interference.

Chapter Review

Do You Remember?

■ Tell whether each of the following statements best describes New England, the middle colonies, or the southern colonies:

1. also known as the bread colonies
2. large amounts of certain crops were grown for sale
3. had a variety of cultures
4. had the most slaves
5. developed many sea industries
6. could also be called "plantation colonies"
7. grain crops were important
8. soil was thin and rocky

■ What do you call the things described below?

9. the basic area ruled by a local government in New England
10. property owners who were allowed to vote in town meetings
11. a colonial army
12. the kind of farmer who raised only enough food for his family
13. the kind of servant who worked for a master for a limited time
14. power which the colonial legislatures had over the governors
15. upper-class people
16. large, southern farms
17. people who worked as servants to pay for their passage to America

Why Is It So?

1. How did geography affect colonial activity?
2. Why was corn important?
3. Why was it easy for many colonists to rise socially?
4. How did slavery begin in the colonies?
5. How did colonial legislatures gain power over governors?

What Do You Think?

1. Why do you think so many people were subsistence farmers in colonial times?
2. How would you explain the fact that the frontier moved west?

4

Life in the Colonies

A colonial kitchen in Charleston, South Carolina

Life in colonial days lacked many of the conveniences we take for granted today. There were no electric lights, only the light of a fireplace, candles, or perhaps a whale-oil lamp. Of course there were no airports, train stations, or superhighways, but there were not many roads either. Those that did exist connected only major towns, and they were made of dust or mud, depending on the weather. The fastest way to travel between two towns like Boston and Philadelphia was by ship along the coast, but that took over a week. Today we can make the three-hundred-mile trip by car in a few hours.

Life has changed greatly from colonial times to today, but the people themselves were just like us today. The colonists had spiritual needs as well as a desire for learning and for expressing themselves through their arts and crafts. As they pursued these interests, they added much to the heritage of America.

A. Religious Backgrounds of the Colonies

Religion was important in the early colonies. It was, after all, the reason some of the colonies had been founded. But religious beliefs in the colonies varied greatly, mainly because the colonists had different religious backgrounds.

Puritan New England

In New England the Puritan groups were most influential. Most of the Puritans came to be called **Congregationalists** because the members of the congregations had more say in church affairs. (Anglican, Presbyterian, and other churches had bishops, elders, or other leaders who ruled in church affairs.) The Puritan religion dominated every aspect of life and society. Their emphasis on diligent work (the work ethic) and the need for godly education set a good example for future Americans. They tried to build their government on Biblical principles, but they soon found that they could not force unwilling colonists to abide by godly standards.

The Puritan Congregationalists faced the same problem found in some Christian homes today: not all their children accepted Christ. These unsaved young people grew up, married, and reared their own children. They continued to attend services, but inwardly many were unconcerned about spiritual truths. Church membership was important in most of the New England colonies because only church members could vote in colonial government elections. Each Puritan was accepted for church membership after his conversion when he "proved up" (showed evidence of his conversion before his pastor and congregation). But what about these growing numbers of unsaved in the church? Should they be allowed to vote even if they did not prove up?

The Puritans tried to solve this problem by adopting the **Halfway Covenant** in 1662. They decided to accept the children of church members even if the applicants or

their parents were not saved. But only the genuinely converted could take communion. The clergymen hoped that the "halfways" might be saved if the church accepted them. This unfortunate compromise did not succeed. The church reformed few sinners, but the sinners affected the churches. Eventually some unsaved men became part of the clergy, and the influence of Puritanism steadily declined. When Massachusetts was rechartered as a royal colony in 1691, Puritan leaders lost control of the colony, and the Anglican church became the established church. The decline of Puritan influence definitely created a need for revival.

The Southern Colonies

The Church of England, or the Anglican church, was the official church in every southern colony. The Bishop of London was the Anglican church leader who was

The First Congregational Church in Lynn, Massachusetts, was built in 1682.

responsible for the churches in America. Although he never came to the colonies himself, he appointed *commissaries,* or official substitutes, to report on the conditions, advise American pastors, and promote education. The two best-known commissaries were Thomas Bray and James Blair. Bray is noted for his work in establishing good libraries for churches in Maryland, and Blair helped establish William and Mary College in Virginia.

The Anglican church was strongest in the cities. Each church served a neighborhood or area called a parish, but there were too few ministers to serve in the colonies, especially in all the rural areas. The Anglican rector, or pastor, received the use of a home and sometimes a small farm; he also received a small salary collected from taxes (usually on tobacco), as well as wedding and funeral fees. South Carolina raised money by taxing non-Anglicans. North Carolina collected so little money that it could pay the salaries of only two Anglican clergymen.

The early English settlers were the ones who attended the Anglican churches in the southern colonies. Many of the members were the planters, merchants, and other wealthy colonists. As other Europeans moved in—Germans, Scots-Irish, French Huguenots, and others—they increased the numbers of non-Anglican colonists. Although it had few members, the Anglican church did little recruiting among these other peoples. It remained the church of the "upper class." In 1701 King William III did charter the Society for the Propagation of the Gospel in Foreign Parts to support Anglican missions among Indians, slaves, and non-Anglican whites, but it met little success in the American colonies.

The Supernatural

Colonial Christians were much more conscious of God's working than most Christians today. They looked for direct evidence of God's working, both in nature and in themselves. Thomas Prince, a Puritan preacher in Boston, said:

> God does not confine himself to act according to his common Course of Nature, but most wisely and justly reserves the Liberty of acting otherwise on all Occasions when he sees most fitting. . . . In this Manner, he may in the most proper Seasons send both Droughts and Rains, and Sicknesses and Health, to particular Places; he may point his Lightnings to particular Persons; he may raise a storm to disperse a fleet, and give additional Powers to a Gust of Wind to overset a Vessel, or to the waves to break her. . . . And so in Multitudes of other Cases.

Unusual events usually gained considerable attention. In 1646, after a calf was born with three mouths, three noses, and six eyes, John Winthrop confessed, "What these . . . portend [mean] the Lord only knows, which in due time he will manifest." Comets in 1665 and 1666 caused great excitement. Thunderstorms and crop failures were considered warnings of God's displeasure. Earthquakes in 1727 and 1755 caused some to examine their hearts. The events, interpreted as signs of God's judgment, brought changes in some lives, but most of the changes were short-lived.

Other religious groups were permitted to settle in the South as long as they paid taxes to the state church and followed certain rules. The Scots-Irish on the frontier were strongly Presbyterian. Baptists also settled there. Huguenots were numerous on the Carolina coast. Most Huguenots were skilled artisans, refined and industrious people who contributed greatly to colonial life.

Another interesting religious group in the colonies was the **Moravians,** followers of the early reformer John Huss. The group was called *Moravians* after Moravia, the place in Eastern Europe where Huss's early followers had lived. Searching for refuge from religious persecution, the Moravians had settled in Germany. When they met persecution there, they came to Georgia in 1732. They were not well received in Georgia, however, because they did not believe in fighting wars, even against the Indians. Consequently many of the Moravians moved on to Moravian settlements in North Carolina and Pennsylvania, where the group grew and prospered.

The Moravians wanted to come to America to do missionary work among slaves, Indians, and German settlers, many of whom had no religion at all. Probably no other Christian group of the colonial era made as great a missionary effort as did the Moravians. The Moravians also influenced American church music. They used string, brass, and woodwind instruments in their services. Benjamin Franklin described a visit to a Moravian church: "I was entertained with good musik, the organ being accompanied with violins, hautboys [oboes], flutes, clarinets, etc." A beautiful Moravian service took place every Easter morning when the Moravians gathered at their cemeteries, "God's acres." There, with appropriate festival music, they were reminded that Christ will resurrect those who have died in Him.

Buildings in the Moravian settlement of Old Salem, North Carolina

Huts of Peace, Huts of Grace

The story of the Delaware Indians shows the dramatic influence the gospel can have on people. The missionary work of a Moravian named David Zeisberger (ZICE berg ur) encouraged this group of Indians to accept Christ and abandon their savage customs, and even to adopt the unpopular Moravian conviction that a Christian should not bear arms. These Indians refused to go against their beliefs, even after many years of severe persecution from Indians and white men alike.

In 1743 Zeisberger established a mission in Shamokin, Pennsylvania, where sixty-three Indians were soon converted. However, within months the first of many political difficulties disrupted the Christian community. The British, fearing French influence, closed the work until the end of King George's War in 1748. They then required the Indians to take an oath of allegiance, which the Indians refused on religious grounds. The angered Englishmen promptly moved them. The Indians went west and built two successful villages called Friedenhutten ("huts of peace") and Gnadenhutten ("huts of grace").

However, the outbreak of the French and Indian War brought more threats to the new Moravian villages. In January 1754 the French burned Gnadenhutten. The Indians did not retaliate; instead, they quietly rebuilt their homes. When peace finally came, the illegal westward movement of whites stirred up local Indians led by Chief Pontiac of the Ottawas. The Moravian Indians, caught between, were easy targets for the whites who said, "The only good Indian is a dead Indian." In 1763 soldiers guarding a traveling Indian party got drunk and murdered the Indians they were guarding. Citizens in the area, fearing reprisals, threatened to destroy all the villages. The Christian Indians, influenced by Zeisberger's preaching, did not fight back as expected. Instead they fled to a stockade at the village of Bethlehem. Then they willingly gave up their fields and weapons to travel under guard to Philadelphia. As they passed through cold November rains, angry village mobs hurled insults, stones, and garbage at them. Yet the Moravian Indians sang hymns and prayed for their enemies.

The colonists placed them in filthy, crowded buildings on Providence Island, where, despite everything, the men knelt and gave thanks to God for their safety. By December public pressure forced them to leave on a three-week pilgrimage through New Jersey and New York. But neither state received them. So they returned home in a savage January snowstorm, praising God for their opportunity to spread the

The tombstone of an Indian buried at Bethlehem, Pennsylvania, a town founded by the Moravians

gospel. A group of white people proved the tribe's innocence and allowed them to stay in their village. After a long year and a deadly smallpox epidemic, the Indians decided to move west. On the banks of the Ohio River, they built the first Protestant schoolhouse and the first Protestant church west of the river. The "Golden Age of Indian Work" followed. For ten years Indians visited from all over, many were saved, and everyone marveled at the town's strict discipline.

Hopes of lasting peace ended with the coming of the War for Independence. When the Delaware Indians refused to "take up the hatchet" against the colonists, the British offered rewards for the scalps of their leaders and missionaries. In 1781 the British destroyed their fields and took the people prisoner. Zeisberger went north to Detroit to face trial as a spy. When the troops guarding him were called away, he proceeded faithfully on to the trial on his own. The judge released him when the guarding officer returned and vouched for his innocence.

Nevertheless, a bitterly cold winter brought the Indians to the point of starvation. They had to send a relief party south for supplies. Before returning, the party offered to share their goods with some American militia in the area. Little did they know that the soldiers wanted revenge for the recent murder of a white family by Indians of another tribe. The soldiers took the weapons from the unsuspecting Indians and voted to kill them. After a time of prayer and preparation, the innocent Indians went two by two to their deaths. Ninety-six died in the massacre. The event actually brought a revival among the remaining Indians because they searched their hearts to see why God had spared them.

After the war a government commission showed that the Moravians had done more with the Indians in a few years than the government had been able to do in two hundred. The new Confederation Congress offered to pay for the wrongs of the war by granting the Delawares a tract of land. The Indians returned to the Ohio and built the town of Goshen. But the aging Zeisberger could no longer protect them from evil influences. Liquor entered and morality declined. Eventually the Delaware moved, intermarried with the Cherokee, and lost their national identity. But their story remains a living testimony of what the gospel can do: God's power was able to transform a tribe of Indians into Christians with the character and conviction to endure great affliction for their beliefs.

The Middle Colonies

The middle colonies had the greatest religious diversity. Most of the traditional denominations and some sects were found there. Anglicans, Lutherans, Dutch Reformed, Presbyterians, and Quakers all settled in the middle colonies.

Jews also migrated there, but their freedoms were limited. Because the Jews were not "Christians," the Protestants of early America treated them as pagans. Although the Jews could trade and buy land, they could not be shopkeepers or skilled tradesmen. At first they could not meet in their own synagogues. One influential Jewish family was the Levys. Along with nineteen other families, Asser Levy helped set up a synagogue in New York and also influenced Jewish settlements in Baltimore and Philadelphia in the mid-1700s.

Pennsylvania, a Quaker colony, allowed more religious toleration than any of the other middle colonies. The Schwenkfelders (SHWENK fel durs), a mystical group, settled in Philadelphia in 1734. Amish Mennonites settled in large numbers in Lancaster County. The Dunkers (a German group) founded a secluded colony at Ephrata (EF ruh tuh) in 1745. Some of the Dunkers, including those at Ephrata, denounced marriage, kept Saturday as the sabbath, and baptized by triple immersion, face forward. Christopher Sauer, a German printer and Dunker leader, printed America's first Bible in a continental European language in 1743. He also edited and printed the first German newspaper in America.

A group of Moravians from Georgia bought land at Nazareth, Pennsylvania, and began settling in the area. On Christmas Eve, 1741, the Moravians named their most important settlement in the Pennsylvania colony Bethlehem.

Section Review

1. What religious group dominated every aspect of life and society in New England? Why was its name changed to Congregationalist?
2. What was the reason behind the Halfway Covenant? What happened to Puritanism because of it?
3. What church was strongest in southern cities? How was it usually supported?
4. What group followed the teachings of John Huss? In what three colonies did they settle?
5. What colonial region had the greatest religious diversity? Name some groups that settled that region.

B. The Great Awakening

As the years passed in the colonies, the people suffered more and more spiritual poverty. Puritan churches had lost their spiritual strength, and fewer churches in the southern or middle colonies preached the gospel. Many ministers were unsaved; colleges lost their spiritual emphasis; the people grew less interested in spiritual things. The nation stood in need of revival. That revival began in the 1720s. It was so powerful that even non-Christian historians call it **"The Great Awakening."**

Leaders of the Great Awakening

The revival first came in New Jersey. There Theodore Frelinghuysen (FREE ling HIGH zen) preached in Dutch Reformed churches, and William Tennent and his son Gilbert preached to Presbyterians. Gilbert and fifteen other young men had been trained by William Tennent in a log cabin later called "the log college." The log college graduates became God's instruments to spread revival throughout the middle colonies, especially New Jersey and Pennsylvania. The revival also spread to the South when William Robinson, a log college graduate, preached in western Virginia and North Carolina. Samuel Blair also preached in the South, but the greatest figure in the southern Great Awakening was probably **Samuel Davies** in Virginia.

Jonathan Edwards played a key role in the Great Awakening. Edwards, who was from Massachusetts, entered Yale at the age of thirteen. In 1727 he became associate pastor of his grandfather's Congregational church in Northampton, Massachusetts. Two years later he became the pastor.

Edwards described the conditions in the town of Northampton:

> Licentiousness [lie SEN shus ness; lack of moral restraint] for some years greatly prevailed among the youth of the town; there were many of them very much addicted to night walking and frequenting the taverns, and lewd practices wherein some by their example exceedingly corrupted others. It was their manner to get together in assemblies of both sexes, for mirth and jollity, which they called frolics; and they would often spend the greater part of the night in them, without regard to order in the families they belong to; indeed family government did too much fail in the town.

In 1737 Edwards began preaching sermons on justification by faith. Conversions began first among the young and later among the older people as well. Within two years over three hundred were saved. The New England revival reached its peak in 1741. That July, Edwards preached what is probably the best-known revival sermon of all time, "Sinners in the Hands of an Angry God." As he calmly and clearly preached the judgment of God, the listeners' guilt increased. Conviction of sin was so great that Edwards had to stop several times when the cries of the people threatened to drown out the sermon. In all his preaching Edwards stressed not only the love of God to save men, but also the wretchedness of sin in the light of God's holiness. A hatred for sin brought genuine repentance and godly living.

Edwards later served as a missionary to the Indians, and then in 1757 he became president of the College of New Jersey (later Princeton University). But after only a few months at the college he died from smallpox. Historians have ranked Edwards with Benjamin Franklin as "one of the two most outstanding minds in America of the early eighteenth century." One author says that as a philosopher and theologian, Edwards "had no peer [equal] in his own time."

One other important preacher of the Great Awakening was not an American but an Englishman. **George Whitefield** (WHIT feeld) had attended Oxford, where he had been a close friend of John and Charles Wesley. Whitefield became an evangelist, and his evangelistic preaching brought him across the Atlantic seven times in his thirty-four-year ministry. It is estimated that he preached at least eighteen thousand times (an average of once every seventeen hours). He was often forced to preach in open fields because established churches refused to let him use their pulpits. But his resonant voice reached greater crowds outdoors than could have gathered in even the largest church

Jonathan Edwards

buildings. Once he preached to a crowd of twenty thousand without even a megaphone. When Benjamin Franklin heard him preach in Philadelphia, he estimated that thirty thousand people could have heard him at one time.

Whitefield was concerned for all men, but he had a particular burden for children. In 1740 he founded what is today America's oldest orphanage, Bethesda (meaning "house of mercy"), near Savannah, Georgia. He preached to slaves, wrote a gospel tract for American Indians, and had an indirect influence in starting several colleges. Whitefield died during a preaching tour of New England. He is buried beneath the pulpit of a church in Newburyport, Massachusetts.

Enemies of the Great Awakening, then and since, have attacked preachers such as Edwards and Whitefield because they preached the Scriptures plainly and emphasized the truths of the gospel. We should not forget that unsaved men who are not spiritually discerning usually fail to grasp spiritual truths. "The natural man receiveth not the things of the Spirit of God: for they are foolishness unto him: neither can he know them, because they are spiritually discerned" (I Cor. 2:14).

Effects of the Great Awakening

The Great Awakening produced far-reaching results. It has been said that the Great Awakening knew no boundaries—political, social, or geographic. The most obvious result was the great number of converts. Between 1740 and 1742 more than thirty thousand were added to churches in New England alone—out of a total population of only three hundred thousand.

Second, the Great Awakening increased the number of American missionary works. The best known missionary to the Indians following the Great Awakening was David Brainerd, who worked in New York, New Jersey, Pennsylvania, and Massachusetts. He died from tuberculosis in 1747 at the age of twenty-nine. Brainerd's diaries have continued to inspire others to devote their lives to missionary service.

Another missionary, Samuel Kirkland, began his work in 1764 with the Iroquois tribes. Simon Horton, a Presbyterian, worked among the Indians on Long Island. The Moravians carried on works among the Indians throughout the colonial era.

Third, the Great Awakening affected American higher education, for as orthodox Christians parted company with religious unbelievers, they established new schools to train their pastors and missionaries. The College of New Jersey (Princeton)—an outgrowth of Tennent's "log college"—was

Samuel Kirkland, missionary to the Iroquois

established by Presbyterians in 1747, Kings' College (Columbia) by Anglicans in 1754, Queen's College (Rutgers) by the Dutch Reformed in 1766, and Brown University by the Baptists in 1764. Dartmouth was founded in 1770 to train young men to reach the Indians.

Fourth, the Great Awakening helped increase the gap between church and state. Roger Williams and others had already helped establish the principle of separation between church and state. Now many people realized that their churches could exist without the support of government. Although a few government-sponsored churches remained in some colonies, the end of established state churches would come after the War for Independence.

Fifth, the revival increased the colonists' desire for political freedom. Pastors and evangelists stressed man's worth and personal responsibility before God. If individuals were so important in God's plan that Christ died for them, then they were important enough to the state to be equal under the law. If an individual man was responsible to accept or reject Christ, then

Nassau Hall, the first building constructed on the present Princeton University campus, was completed in 1756.

Samuel Davies and the Southern Great Awakening

Samuel Davies, a major leader of the Great Awakening in the southern colonies and perhaps the greatest American pulpit orator of his day, was born to Welsh parents on November 3, 1723. His mother gave him the name "Samuel" because, like Samuel of the Bible, he had been "asked for of the Lord." Davies' mother had prayerfully dedicated her son to the Lord to preach. However, Davies related that until the age of fifteen he was "not particularly concerned with things of a religious nature." But while studying at St. George, Delaware, under an itinerant preacher, Davies awoke "to solemn thoughtfulness and anxious concern about [his] eternal state." Saved shortly thereafter, he began to make a practice of secret prayer and ended his prayers with the plea that he might be "suitably prepared to enter the gospel ministry."

That preparation was aided by a gift of money made to William Robinson, a Presbyterian preacher who was serving in Hanover County on Virginia's frontier. There was no regular minister, and out of grateful hearts for the services Robinson had held, the people gave him a gift of money. Robinson did not feel right about accepting it for himself but told the group,

he should also be responsible to guide his own government. It is significant to note that in atheistic communistic countries, the individual is not important and is subjected to the wishes of the government.

Finally, the Great Awakening strengthened the moral fiber of the American people. This strength helped them to withstand the perils of two upcoming wars.

There is a very promising young man, now studying divinity . . . whose parents . . . find great difficulty in supporting him at his studies. I will take this money and it shall be given him to help him through—and when he is licensed, he shall come and be your preacher.

After finishing his training, Davies was ordained as "an evangelist to all congregations without preachers in Virginia but especially in Hanover County." Except for a fourteen-month interval when Davies went to England to raise money for the College of New Jersey (Princeton) and a two-year period when he served as its president just before his death, he devoted all his preaching years to this needy area.

For almost twelve years Davies held services in seven churches in five different counties and traveled by horseback over the whole state of Virginia organizing revival meetings. He also gave young preachers practical training, traveled from plantation to plantation preaching to slaves, organized his church members to teach slaves to read so that they would be able to study the Scriptures, and served as a distributor of books to frontier homes and slave dwellings. He also influenced the founding of two schools in the Hanover Presbytery: Hampden-Sydney College and Washington (later Washington and Lee) College.

Moreover, because the Anglican church was still the established church in Virginia, he worked for more freedom of religion in the colony. He told his people that loyal patriotism would encourage government leaders to give them more religious liberty, and the Virginians found his advice to be sound.

In his pastorate Davies was always conscious to challenge his people by example. He sought to have balance in his ministry and in his preaching. He preached to meet men's needs. He said that preaching "had to help the people in the things that most affected them; it had to help them solve the problems of life and ever prepare them to face death."

Opponents of the Great Awakening

The Great Awakening changed the religious thinking of many Americans, but it was not the only influence on eighteenth-century minds. Many Americans, especially those educated in Europe, were influenced by a movement called the **"Enlightenment."** This movement exalted rational thinking and critical reasoning. Unfortunately, man's ability to think often became more important than God's truths as revealed in Scripture. If a man could not understand God's truths, he discarded them. Although such men prided themselves in casting off "old prejudices," they merely showed man's inability to understand the wonders of God. "Hath not God made foolish the wisdom of this world?" (I Cor. 1:20).

Deism—One important philosophy that grew out of Enlightenment thinking was **Deism.** Deists taught that God created the universe in a perfect and balanced manner. But then He left the world to function under certain laws of nature and never intervened in man's affairs again. Deists pictured God as the great Watchmaker who made the watch (the earth), started it running, but then just let it run without touching it again. Thus there was no way to know God or have fellowship with Him. God was just a distant power without any concern for man's present needs. But according to the Bible, God does intervene in our lives. His Holy Spirit convicts of sin, and He offers salvation through His Son, Jesus Christ. God also guides and protects us day by day.

Deism argued that miracles in the Bible did not take place because they violated the "unchangeable laws" of God's created universe. For instance, Christ could not have walked on the water as Matthew 14:25 states, because a man is heavier than water and will sink. Such a belief, however, fails to recognize that a powerful and wise God who could create the world and the basic laws of nature can also overrule those laws when it suits His divine purpose. Nevertheless, Deists denied the inspiration of the Scriptures. They believed that their own reason showed them all they needed to know about God and their own moral duties. By the end of the colonial era, many prominent men—Benjamin Franklin, Thomas Jefferson, Ethan Allen, and others—were Deists. Although their view of God was un-Biblical, many Deists did have high moral principles that aided them as they helped to found a new American nation.

Unitarianism—A second un-Biblical philosophy that originated during this time was **Unitarianism.** This religious movement asserted the "unity" of God by denying the doctrine of the Trinity. Unitarians denied the deity of Jesus Christ, insisting that He was only a great man. Although Unitarians claimed to believe the Bible, they denied man's need of salvation through the blood of Christ. According to Unitarianism, people needed only to live a moral life. The influence of Unitarianism continued to grow even after the War for Independence. Unitarianism became especially strong among some American intellectuals, and it influenced American writers for many years.

False teachings have always been part of history. Studying such teachings, however, can remind us of our responsibility to test the new ideas of every age to be certain that they are consistent with the Word of God. Paul cautions us to "beware lest any man spoil you through philosophy and vain deceit, after the tradition of men, after the rudiments of the world, and not after Christ" (Col. 2:8).

Section Review

1. In what decade did the Great Awakening begin?
2. What Puritan preacher played a key role in the Great Awakening in New England?
3. What English preacher was also instrumental in the Great Awakening?
4. List the six major results of the Great Awakening.
5. What movement exalted rational thinking and critical reasoning? What was the danger of this type of thinking?
6. What is Deism?
7. What is Unitarianism?

C. Colonial Education

In seventeenth- and eighteenth-century Europe, education belonged almost exclusively to the rich. Common people rarely had access to schools or books. They labored at their occupation from the time they were children until they died, without having time or money to learn about the world around them. In the American colonies an education was still a privilege. But Americans, especially those in New England, began to want all the children to go to school. They should have the opportunity to learn about God by reading the Bible and to learn about His world by reading other books.

Grammar Schools

Grammar schools were something like our elementary schools. Children learned to read and write, but they learned far more at a grammar school in the colonial era. Older students learned to read Greek and Latin. These subjects, along with math and natural philosophy, were difficult, but they disciplined the mind. The upper social classes also believed that correct grammar, acceptable accent, fluency in Greek and Latin, and some knowledge of ancient classical literature set them and their children apart from average people. Grammar school studies took seven grueling years. If a student did well and had the financial support, he might be able to enter college while still in his early teens.

Spelling was not on the list of subjects for grammar school. Since Noah Webster's *Blue-Backed Speller* was not published until 1783, there was no consistent model for spelling words. The way people spelled sometimes depended on how they felt at the time or on how much reading they had done. Some schoolmasters used the King James Version of the Bible as the spelling model.

Most colonial children first learned to read from a hornbook, a printed sheet posted on a board that looked much like a paddle. It was called "hornbook" because it was covered with a thin transparent sheet of animal horn. Hornbooks always had the alphabet on them; sometimes they also contained a list of vowels, some syllables to sound out, or the Lord's Prayer. Upper-class children sometimes had fancy hornbooks engraved on brass or pewter plates. As they learned from their hornbooks, a common way for students to practice forming their letters was to trace them with a stick in the hearth sand. (Sand was put in front of the fireplace to catch sparks and prevent fires.)

A hornbook

If you had lived in colonial days, you might already be preparing for your graduation exercises. And graduations *were* exercises! You gave memorized speeches in Latin or Greek and then debated, using all the knowledge you had gained in grammar school.

Schools in New England—In the earliest colonial days parents were responsible to teach their children to read and write at home. By 1647 there were only eleven grammar schools in New England. In 1642 the Massachusetts General Court passed a law ordering parents to teach their children "to read and understand the principles of religion and the capital laws of the country." If a child did not learn to read, his parents could be fined. Parents sometimes gave the task of education to widows or single ladies, who established simple schools in their homes. These were called **"dame schools."**

In 1647 the General Court passed an act "to prevent that Old Deluder Satan" from keeping men "from the Knowledge of the Scriptures." The act required all towns of fifty or more families to appoint a schoolmaster to teach the children to read and write. Other New England towns gradually began to follow Massachusetts's example and establish town schools.

By 1750 Latin grammar schools were being replaced by academies. In addition to keeping the emphasis on Latin and Greek, these schools also included English composition and literature, math, modern languages, and natural science. Private schools taught much the same subjects but also included skills such as letter writing, civil government, navigation, gunnery, and even fencing and shorthand.

Schools in the Middle and Southern Colonies—Some of the middle colonies established public schools, but most of the schools were organized by church groups. The Dutch Reformed church established some schools in New Netherland, and the Quakers founded seventy schools in Pennsylvania, admitting students from all the social classes.

In the middle and southern colonies, however, there were fewer schools than in New England. Because long growing seasons required children to help on the farms during many months of the year, schooling was difficult. Government officials did not value education either. In 1671 Governor Berkeley of Virginia noted that "there are no free schools nor printing in Virginia . . . for learning has brought disobedience, and heresy, and sects into the world, and printing has divulged them, and libels against the best government. . . . God keep us from both!"

Some planters or wealthy farmers joined to hire a schoolmaster and provide a school for several families. Others could afford private tutors for their children. Either way, only the children of the upper classes were usually able to receive such an education.

Higher Education

The first chartered institution of higher learning in the colonies was **Harvard College** in Cambridge, Massachusetts. Puritans founded it in 1636 "to advance learning and perpetuate it to Posterity." The Puritans did not want "to leave an illiterate Ministry to the Churches when our Present Ministers shall lie in the Dust." Three years later the college got its name when John Harvard, a young minister in nearby Charlestown, died of tuberculosis. He left half of his estate and his handsome library of four hundred books to the young school. Although the sum Harvard left was not large, the high cost of books and the purchasing power of the money made his donation important and led to the college's taking the name of its early benefactor.

College students followed a strict schedule. Their days frequently began at 5:00 A.M.

and included study, prayers, lectures, recitations, chapels, and meals along with two short breaks daily. To enter college, students had to be able to write, speak, and translate in Latin since college books were written in Latin and lectures contained much Latin. There was no definite end to a class; a course of study ended when the tutor believed that his students had mastered the subject. Students and teachers often lived in the same building, ate their meals together, and studied and worshiped together.

Yale and Dartmouth were started when New England Puritans saw that Harvard had been affected by the liberal ideas of the Enlightenment. Other schools were fostered by the Great Awakening. Although they were begun primarily to teach preachers of the gospel, they did not keep their original godly goals. Today these schools have a totally secular emphasis.

William and Mary, founded in 1693, was the only college in the southern colonies for many years. Many southern planters and other wealthy people from all the colonies, however, continued to send their sons across the Atlantic for college education. This practice helped keep Americans

Harvard University in Cambridge, Massachusetts, as it appeared in the early 1800s

interested in the current discoveries and fashions in science and thought in Europe.

Vocational "Schools"

Formal schooling was not the only way for colonial young people to learn. Farm and shop training were also valued. The **apprenticeship** system was used to teach trades. Apprenticeships usually lasted seven years or until the apprentice turned twenty-one. The apprentice was supposed to be moral and serve his master faithfully.

Benjamin Rush, future doctor and signer of the Declaration of Independence, was apprenticed to a Philadelphia physician, Dr. John Redman. He had little free time. In 1766 Rush wrote that during a five-and-a-half-year apprenticeship, "I was absent from Redman's business but eleven days and never spent more than three evenings out of his house." Apprenticeships were often means to wealth, and men who completed them were able to reach positions of high esteem. In addition to Rush, several other signers of the Declaration of Independence had once been apprentices. Roger Sherman of Connecticut began as a shoemaker's apprentice; George Taylor had served as an iron maker in Chester County, Pennsylvania; and Benjamin Franklin had been a printer.

Section Review

1. What were the early elementary schools called? What languages did these schools teach?
2. What was a hornbook?
3. Which colonial region had the most schools and the most emphasis on education for all children?
4. What was America's first college and when was it founded?

D. Colonial Arts and Crafts

Although many colonists enjoyed artistic beauty, making a living in a new and rugged land allowed little time for such enjoyment. One New Englander summed it up by saying, "The plowman that raiseth grain is more serviceable to mankind than the painter who draws only to please the eye." Nonetheless, the colonists often expressed artistic ideas in their daily lives—in dishes, furniture, and architecture. If a colonist had to make something, he often made it attractive as well as practical.

Glassware

The first glassworks in America was in Jamestown, Virginia. It was started in 1608, just one year after the colony was founded. By the late 1630s glass factories in Massachusetts and New York made window glass and bottles that compared favorably with European glass. Two German immigrants established glassworks in Pennsylvania. Caspar Wistar (WIS tur), who had come in 1717, established his in Philadelphia; Henry William Stiegel (STEE gul) established one at Manheim in 1764. Stiegel made a rich, deep blue glass that is still admired. Glassware became the first manufactured product to be exported from America.

Metalworking

Pewter, which the colonists called "poor man's silver," was an alloy of tin, lead, and copper. Pewter was used to make plates, mugs, and porringers (shallow bowls). During the War for Independence, pewter became scarce because lead supplies were needed for bullets.

The first recorded American silversmith was Thomas Howard, who lived in Jamestown in 1620. Although Boston boasted twenty-four silversmiths by 1776, including the famed Paul Revere, much of the silver in America's early years was imported from England. But over the years Americans began to produce more silver. Silverware soon replaced wooden and pewter tableware because it lasted longer. The first American forks had two tines, but by 1725 four-tine forks were in use. The "teaspoon" dates from the early 1700s, when British traders introduced tea drinking to the colonists.

Local ironworks were usually located near sources of bog iron. They produced pots, kettles, cooking cranes for fireplaces, nails, and hinges. Colonists on the frontier sometimes pounded nail heads into their doors to protect them from Indian tomahawks. They arranged the nail heads in geometric designs to make decorative doors. Hinges could be simple or ornate. Wind vanes also gave the ironmaster or blacksmith a chance to show his artistic talents. Joseph Jenkins, sometimes called the "father of the iron industry," invented the boot scraper, which colonists used to clean the mud from their shoes before entering buildings. Since there were no paved roads or sidewalks, this device was much appreciated. Two famous early ironworks were the Saugus Iron Works in Lynn, Massachusetts, and Hopewell Forge in Pennsylvania. The Saugus (SAW gus) works, begun in 1640, employed 185 men—ironworkers, miners, woodcutters, and boatmen. Just eight years later Governor John Winthrop noted, "The Furnace runnes 8 tun per weeke, and their barre Iron is as good as Spanish."

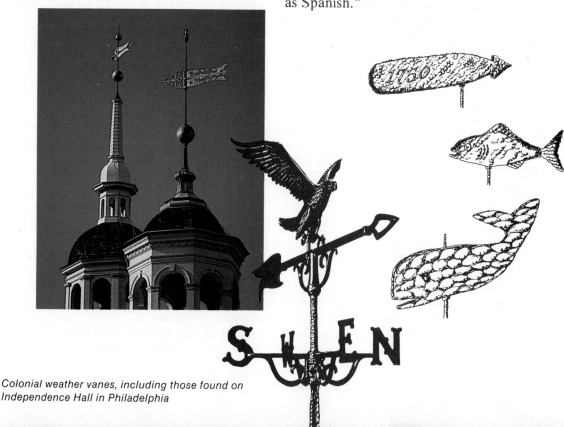

Colonial weather vanes, including those found on Independence Hall in Philadelphia

Clocks

Colonists made and repaired all kinds of clocks. Since most people did not use bedside tables, alarm clocks were made to be fastened to the high bedposts. Because of the cost of producing metal pieces for clocks, Eli Terry invented a clock with all wooden workings. In 1807 he formed a partnership with Seth Thomas and Silas Hoadley to mass produce clocks. They harnessed nearby waterfalls for power and in three years produced four thousand clocks. Eventually Seth Thomas founded his own company at Thomaston, Connecticut. His thirty-hour clock originally sold for $15.00, but by efficient production methods and high sales, he brought the price down to $5.00. His company still exists today.

Three brothers, sons of seventeenth-century clock maker Simon Willard, settled in Roxbury, Massachusetts. They specialized in church, hall, and gallery clocks. Willard clocks were so finely made that some are still working today, after two hundred years. The banjo clock, so called because of its shape, was probably the most unusual Willard clock.

Furniture

Most settlers made their own furniture. They usually did so in winter, when they could not work in the fields. They made cupboards ("hutches"), chests, tables, chairs, and other needed items. Ever eager to save time, some enterprising settlers fashioned bedsteads with cranks on the footboards. By tying the quilt to the crank and rotating the crank in the morning, one could tidy up the bed quickly.

By the late 1600s furniture craftsmen became established. Although native American woods were often used, mahogany

came into use for construction of the best furniture. The strength of mahogany permitted a refinement of style. Duncan Phyfe (FIFE) was probably the most famous furniture maker. He made furniture of top-quality mahogany, sometimes paying up to $1,000 for a single log. His furniture commanded high prices, but much of it has lasted for generations.

Architecture

Colonial houses varied in style, depending on the climate, the type of building materials at hand, the builder's training, and the money available. The most common early style was that built by most English

Colonial furniture and clocks

settlers.
It had a large
central chimney
with a kitchen on
one side and a parlor
or living room on the other.
An overhead loft, reached by a ladder, held two sleeping rooms. A lean-to might be added in back to store farm implements. Some houses had clapboard siding, made of split logs.

Log cabins, introduced by the Swedish settlers along the Delaware River, proved practical because they did not require any nails, which were always rare. Brick was used where clay was abundant, especially in areas where fire had devastated earlier dwellings. Boston had a disastrous fire in 1679 and was rebuilt mostly of red brick.

Georgian architecture became popular from 1725 to 1750, during the reigns of Kings George I and George II. Georgian houses had a balanced arrangement of windows and doors. Inside there were cornices over the windows, paneling on some of the walls, and fancy mantlepieces. The houses were usually rectangular and were two or three stories tall. Most were plain on the outside and more ornate inside.

Painting

Early painters, called "limners" (from the word *illuminate*), usually painted in a style called American Primitive—a simple style unaffected by European styles of the day. Most pursued art as a sideline while they worked at some other trade for a living.

They produced three main types of works: portraits, landscapes, and historical scenes. Since cameras had not been invented, portraits were especially popular. While religious art was popular in Europe, not much of it was done in America. Puritans believed that divine things were understood by the mind rather than pictured to the eye. Here more people could read the Bible for themselves and did not need pictures.

This cut-away drawing of a common style of colonial house reveals the details of its construction.

blind in one eye, John Trumbull also painted battle scenes, including *The Battle of Bunker Hill.* Four of his paintings hang in the rotunda of the United States Capitol. Benjamin West lived in England during the War for Independence, but he became one of the most well-known American painters. Gilbert Stuart is remembered most for his "unfinished portrait" of George Washington—the portrait that appears on the one-dollar bill.

Five of these American painters are especially well known. **John Singleton Copley** has been called "the greatest painter ever to work in colonial America." He created a famous painting of Paul Revere. Charles Willson Peale traveled with the army during the War for Independence and painted many battle scenes, including *Cornwallis's Surrender at Yorktown.* Although

Section Review

1. What inexpensive metal was used to make the utensils used by many colonists?
2. Who was one of the best furniture craftsmen in the colonies?
3. Who first built log cabins in the colonies?
4. List the five well-known colonial painters.

Summary

Religion was an important part of life in the colonies. In New England the Puritan Congregationalist influence was greatest, while the Anglican church was established in most of the southern colonies. The middle colonies saw many religious groups settle in the region. Although many of the colonists were very religious, many were far from God in the early 1700s. But the Great Awakening brought a revival to parts of the colonies, and many were saved. Even so, other Americans turned away from God to the ideas of the Enlightenment, embracing Deism and Unitarianism.

Educational opportunities grew, especially in New England, where grammar schools and colleges multiplied. Many colonists served as apprentices to learn trades. America soon developed many talented craftsmen and educated leaders.

John Trumbull's painting The Battle of Bunker Hill

Chapter Review

Do You Remember?

■ Match the philosophy or religious group with its description.

1. Congregationalists
2. Deism
3. Moravians
4. Unitarianism

a. supported much missionary activity
b. believed God was not personally concerned with man
c. denied the Trinity
d. members of the Church of England
e. Puritans

■ Who was he?

5. The English preacher of the Great Awakening
6. "The greatest painter ever to work in colonial America"
7. Preacher in Hanover County, Virginia
8. Famous Boston silversmith
9. Preached "Sinners in the Hands of an Angry God"
10. Famous furniture maker

■ Fill in the blanks in the following paragraph with the appropriate words.

Not everyone could receive an education in the colonies, but some children were able to go to _(11)_ where they learned to read, write, and study literature. Some schools were operated by single ladies or widows and called _(12)_. As the students learned to read, they used a _(13)_ that contained the alphabet and other simple information. Instead of going to school, some colonial young people became _(14)_ so that they might learn a trade from a master.

Why Is It So?

1. Why didn't the Halfway Covenant work?
2. How did the Great Awakening affect America?
3. Why were the ideas of Enlightenment thinkers dangerous?
4. Why did the Puritans want their children to learn to read?
5. Why did it take some time before great artists arose in America?

What Do You Think?

1. Would you say that Enlightenment ideas are still common today? Why or why not?
2. What are some of the differences between education in colonial times and education today? Was a good education as important then as it is today? Why or why not?

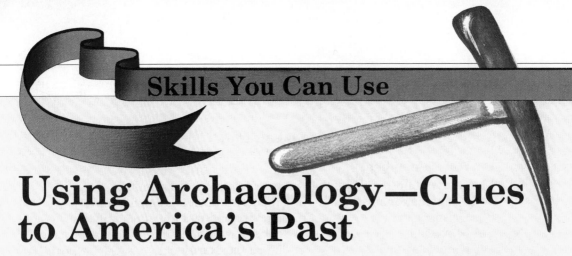

Using Archaeology—Clues to America's Past

Most students associate archaeology with some scientist's excavating an ancient city or burial site in Greece or Egypt. The Americas, however, also have their share of great archaeological finds, such as the remains of the civilizations of the Aztecs, Incas, and Mayas. Archaeology has also provided us with a great deal of information about the first North Americans—the American Indians. Scientists have uncovered tools, weapons, bones, pottery, household utensils, and mounds throughout North America.

Before an archaeologist actually begins his painstaking work of digging for evidence, much research is done to insure the exact location of the building, town, settlement, or fort in question. This information may be obtained through letters, journals, documents, maps, inventories, or a previous find. When he has established the location of the site, he begins digging and mapping the area. Workers remove soil in small quantities and wash it through screens to reveal even the smallest pieces of evidence. As the archaeologist begins to find evidence of the past, he works with small tools such as garden trowels, brushes, and dental picks to prevent the destruction of any evidence found. Scientists record and number all *artifacts* (manmade objects from the past) that they find.

The restored town of Williamsburg, Virginia, is an excellent example of archaeological excavation of the Colonial American period. Many buildings were carefully restored to their previous appearance based on the evidence accumulated by archaeologists and other researchers. The Governor's Palace is an excellent example. Workers unearthed the original cellars where archaeologists found remains of the original building materials of the structure as well as several artifacts. Other information supplemented what the archaeologists found. A floor plan drawn by Thomas Jefferson gave room dimensions. Inventories compiled by various governors gave valuable information as to the interior furnishings of the palace. All of the evidence used together produced an authentic reproduction of the original palace.

You do not have to become an archaeologist to find evidence of America's past. A walk through an old church or family graveyard will provide hours of interesting reading. A tour of an old city will take you through American history as you observe changes in American architecture. Cities such as Boston, Philadelphia, Charleston, and New Orleans may contain structures from colonial times through the present. Open your eyes; your archaeological "dig" may be right around the corner.

Consider, for example, the story of Bruce Mellor and his shoe box full of junk. Bruce was twelve years old in 1966 when he and a friend dug up a quantity of burned animal bones, some handmade iron nails, a gunflint dated before 1800, pieces of a broken blue and white bowl, and some salt-glazed stoneware. Bruce deposited his great finds in an empty shoe box and put them on a shelf in his closet. Every year he had to rescue the box from his mother who, during the annual spring cleaning, would throw out "that old box of trash," as she called it.

In 1978, when Bruce was a graduate student at the University of Minnesota, he took his box to the office of Dr. Douglas Birk, an archaeologist. Dr. Birk specialized in Minnesota's presettlement history. When Bruce took the lid off his shoe box, Dr. Birk tried to contain his excitement. He recognized the blue and white pieces of dish as *faience,* a special kind of eighteenth-century porcelain that had been brought to France from China. Faience is commonly associated with French sites. The stoneware pieces looked as if they had come from narrow-necked pitchers from the early 1700s. Such pitchers were used by Frenchmen of notable social status. Dr. Birk

thought that his visitor "had dug into one of the earliest European habitation sites yet found west of Lake Superior."

Historical records said that a French trader-diplomat, Joseph Marin, had built an outpost in 1752 somewhere in Central Minnesota. The records had not been clear as to the exact location of the outpost. Historians and archaeologists had given up all hope of finding the site. A preliminary dig of Bruce's site proved promising and in July 1983, a full-scale excavation of the site of Bruce's "treasure" began.

After getting the right to dig on the property, the archaeological team made a series of maps of the land. They first made a contour map that used lines to show the location of every ridge, hill, or ditch on the property and also to show (in feet) the exact rise or fall of the land. Then the team drew up site maps, which were divided into *hundreds,* that is, small numbered squares. Each square stood for a square yard or a square foot. When the digging is done, each of those squares appears on a separate piece of paper and what is found within the square is labeled on it. In this way those who study the results could see exactly where Bruce had found, for example, the broken blue dishes.

The study of sites such as the "Shoe-Box Fort" (as the archaeologists affectionately called the site) can provide a wealth of information for historians. Digging can help discover how the French utilized their storage space and what foods they ate and how they prepared them. Archaeologists can discover this and more from locations, and they owe their discoveries at the Minnesota dig to a boy's interest in an "old shoe box full of junk."

5

American Colonies in the British Empire

Britain's power was growing in the 1700s. It was expanding its empire in the Americas and in India. It was also acquiring islands in the Pacific and on the continent of Australia, as well as many other lands that would become a part of the British Empire. The thirteen American colonies, as a part of this empire, were allied with Britain in its growth and development. Yet while Britain attended to other needs in its empire, it had given the thirteen colonies much independence in handling their own affairs.

Although the colonists were still willing to fight side by side with the British against common enemies, they were not willing to give up the liberty they had enjoyed.

A. The French and Indian War

At the outset of the eighteenth century, France and Britain were the two leading European powers. Both nations were actively involved in building overseas empires. By establishing new colonies, they hoped to increase their wealth and power. The

A re-enactment of a British army march

intense rivalry between the two led to a series of wars.

Background to the Struggle

North America was important to both the French and the British. French colonists had settled along the St. Lawrence River, in the Great Lakes region, and by the Mississippi River, while British colonists had settled along the Atlantic seaboard. Both, however, laid claim to the whole continent. Both wanted control of the fur trade in the vast, unsettled territory west of the Appalachian mountains. In addition, they both wanted control of the rich fisheries off the coast of Newfoundland. It was not long before their rival interests led to open conflict.

French Advantages and Disadvantages—The French had many advantages in their struggle against the British. Their government exercised strong and unified control over her colonists. Furthermore, the French were actively building forts at strategic spots along America's inland waterways. They also had a well-trained army and the support of many Indian tribes who hated the British. Despite these advantages, however, the French had one major weakness: New France was a vast territory with widely scattered and sparsely populated French settlements. To defend such a large region was difficult.

British Advantages and Disadvantages—The British colonies had a few advantages as well. They had nearly fifteen times the population of New France. In addition, they had the support of the **Iroquois** (ir uh KWOY), the strongest confederation of Indian tribes in America. The English navy was also the strongest in the world.

French & British Claims in North America c. 1750

Perhaps Britain's greatest weakness was a lack of unity among the colonists. There was no central colonial organization, and there was little cooperation among the thirteen colonies or between the colonies and the British government. Each colony preferred to protect its own special interests rather than the interests of the colonies as a whole. When faced with the threat of Indian uprisings and French expansion, many colonists did not want to help unless they themselves were immediately threatened. Only then were they willing to take action to defend their homes, families, and livelihood.

Earlier Wars—Between 1689 and 1763 the rivalry between France and Britain led to four wars. The first three conflicts broke out in Europe and spread to America. (They were "King William's War," 1689-97;

"Queen Anne's War," 1702-13; and "King George's War," 1744-48.) The results of these three wars were indecisive; neither side was able to gain an upper hand. The fourth war, however, decided who would control the North American continent. In this last war fighting broke out in America two years before it began in Europe. Europeans named it the "Seven Years' War." The American colonists called it the **"French and Indian War"** because the French and Indians joined forces against the British.

The Outbreak of War

The immediate cause of the French and Indian War was a struggle for control of the Ohio Valley. The British hoped to open the region to settlement. This alarmed the French, who feared that British settlers would disrupt their fur trade. Furthermore, if the French could gain control, they could stop further British expansion and keep the British colonists hemmed in along the Atlantic coast.

The key to the region was the point where the Allegheny and Monongahela (muh NON guh HE luh) rivers joined to form the Ohio River (the present site of Pittsburgh, Pennsylvania). Here in 1754 some Virginians began building a fort. The governor of Virginia sent a force under the leadership of **George Washington** to protect them. But before they arrived, the French attacked the unfinished fort and drove off the Virginians. The French completed the fort and named it Fort Duquesne (doo KANE) in honor of their new Canadian governor.

As Washington and his troops advanced to the fort, they met and defeated a small French force. Learning of a larger French force nearby, Washington fell back and hastily constructed a stockade called Fort Necessity. A much larger French force was sent out to meet the British colonial troops. After a valiant defense Washington's outnumbered men were forced to surrender. The French allowed them to return to Virginia. This fighting on July 3, 1754, marked the beginning of the French and Indian War.

Early War Activity

During the early years of the war, the French successfully drove the British from the Ohio Valley. Indian tribes in league with the French used a style of fighting that was effective in the wilderness. They hid behind trees and brush, ready to ambush the British. In contrast, the British went to battle in European style, dressed in full uniform and marching in rank. These rows of colorfully dressed soldiers made easy targets for Indians hiding in the forests.

The Albany Plan of Union— Both the British and the colonists were concerned about the Indian threat to the colonies. In particular they were afraid that the Iroquois Indians would also join the French in their fight. A meeting was called to deal with this problem, and in June of 1754 delegates from several American colonies met at Albany, New York. At this Albany Congress these leaders met with some of the chiefs and persuaded the Iroquois to support the British.

The congress was more important for another reason, however. During the conference the delegates adopted a plan of union to submit to the colonies. The **Albany Plan of Union,** primarily the work of Benjamin Franklin, called for the creation of a grand council made up of delegates from all the colonies. The assembly would be empowered to raise an army, build forts, and govern Indian affairs. Nevertheless, both Britain and the colonial legislatures rejected the plan. Britain feared that such a union would threaten her control of the colonies. Individual colonies likewise feared that they might lose some of their freedom to such a union. Even so, the plan was significant because it was the first attempt of the American colonies to unite.

Braddock's Road—The first major step the British took in the war was an attempt to capture Fort Duquesne. British General **Edward Braddock** took about fifteen hundred British soldiers and about a thousand colonials in his march northward from Virginia. George Washington served as an aide to Braddock on the mission. Braddock moved his men slowly, clearing a roadway and building bridges as they marched. When Braddock's forces finally met the French near Fort Duquesne on July 9, 1755, Braddock suffered not only a defeat but also a fatal wound. The loss discouraged the British and left the colonists uncertain about future British support. However, it did leave the colonists with a new road that would be useful in future settlement of the frontier.

William Pitt's System—In 1756 the war broadened into a world-wide conflict, with British and French troops battling on three continents: North America, Europe, and Asia. To meet the new challenges, the struggling British placed the war effort in the hands of **William Pitt.** His energetic leadership brought a dramatic change in the war. Pitt turned Britain's half-hearted, defensive tactics in America into aggressive action. He named young, talented generals to replace older, incompetent ones appointed because of their social and political standing. Pitt also agreed to pay for the outfitting of colonial soldiers to aid the British. Now backed with the full support of the British government, British troops, teamed with American colonials, began their assault on French strongholds in America.

One by one French posts began falling to the British. Late in 1758 a British force ousted the French from Fort Duquesne. The British rebuilt the badly damaged fort and renamed it Fort Pitt. The following year the British began preparation to capture Quebec, the crucial blow planned by Pitt to defeat the French.

Top: *To amuse the French, who thought all Americans were backwoodsmen, Benjamin Franklin wore a coonskin cap while posing for this drawing.*
Bottom: *Drawing of battle in the French and Indian War*

An eighteenth-century engraving of the fort at Quebec

The Battle of Quebec

Quebec was the strongest city of New France. Perched high above the St. Lawrence River and protected by steep cliffs, it was a seemingly invincible fortress. The British, under the command of General **James Wolfe,** laid siege to the city. The French, however, were content to stay within the safe confines of their stronghold and wait out the siege.

After several unsuccessful attempts to take the city, General Wolfe decided on a daring plan. Under cover of night, British troops crossed the river downstream from the fort. By morning on September 13, 1759, more than four thousand British troops had silently scaled the cliffs protecting Quebec. They took up battle positions on a plain called the "Plains of Abraham" a short distance from the fortress. When the surprised French commander **Marquis de Montcalm** (mar-KEE deh mont-KAHM) learned what the British had done, he ordered an immediate attack hoping to

defeat the British before they could become entrenched. But the British routed the French and their Indian allies. Both Wolfe and Montcalm were mortally wounded in the battle. With their commander dead and their troops disorganized, the French surrendered Quebec.

Results of the War

Although the British would not capture Montreal until a year later, for all practical purposes the fall of Quebec spelled the defeat of New France. The struggle for North America was over, but the war in Europe continued until 1763. In that year the Peace of Paris was negotiated. France gave up her claim to all territory east of the Mississippi River except New Orleans. Britain retained control of Canada and also received Florida from Spain, a French ally. To compensate Spain for the loss of Florida, France gave her the Louisiana Territory.

Section Review

1. Why did France and England both want North America?
2. What war settled the question of who would have control? What was this war called in Europe?
3. What advantages did the French have in fighting the war? What advantages did the English have?
4. What river valley did both countries seek to control?
5. What did the Albany Plan of Union seek to do?
6. What man's leadership turned the tide, helping the British win?
7. What battle became the turning point of the war, giving the British certain victory?

Hudson Bay

St. Lawrence River

Quebec

Montreal

Albany

Boston

Atlantic

SPANISH

Allegheny R.

Ft.
Duquesne
(Ft. Pitt)

New York

Philadelphia
Wilmington

Ocean

River

Ohio River

Monongahela R.

LOUISIANA

Mississippi

French & Indian War
and Results

Line of 1763-67

British

Taken from France
by Britain—1763

Spanish

Charleston

Savannah

WEST FLORIDA

EAST FLORIDA

0   100   200   300

Scale of Miles

New Orleans

Gulf of Mexico

B. New British Policies

Britain emerged from the war as the strongest nation in the world. Her colonial empire reached from India to America. To administer such a large empire, Britain sought to tighten her hold on her colonies, including those in America. An added reason for tightening control on these colonies was that many leaders in Britain were upset that the colonies had only half-heartedly provided troops and supplies to assist in the war effort. Likewise they were angered that colonial merchants had traded with Britain's enemies during the war. Some members of Parliament decided that the colonies had been allowed too much independence, and they enacted policies aimed at bringing America under the closer supervision of the mother country. These policies took many forms, including trade regulations, the closing of western lands, and new taxes. What members of Parliament failed to recognize was that they had previously fostered the colonists' attitude of independence by allowing them to handle their own local affairs. The new imperial policy created growing tension between Britain and its American colonies.

The Closing of Western Lands

After the war the colonists thought the frontier would be safe to settle. Consequently some trappers, settlers, and speculators moved into the region. But **Pontiac,** an Ottawa Indian chief, had organized the tribes from Canada almost to the Gulf of Mexico to stop the entrance of the white man. The Indians captured British forts and terrorized settlers along the frontier. The British, who finally put down Pontiac's revolt, took steps to prevent further problems in the West.

The king issued the **Proclamation of 1763,** forbidding colonial settlement west of the Appalachian Mountains. The British government did not want traders or settlers stirring up unrest among the Indians; therefore, it closed this region to colonial settlement. Settlers already there were asked to leave. Trappers and traders were allowed into the region only with official licenses. Such actions angered the colonists. They had fought to open the frontier to colonial expansion. Besides, Britain had violated colonial charters that promised the colonies the land from the Atlantic to the Pacific.

Quartering British Troops

To defend her holdings, Britain left ten thousand troops in America. This force could put down Indian uprisings and enforce British policies if the colonists refused to obey. The colonists viewed the presence of these troops as a violation of their rights. Many saw the British troops as a greater threat to their liberty than either the French or the Indians. Objections grew when the Quartering Act of 1765 ordered colonists

Pontiac, the Ottawa Indian chief

Mercantilism

Throughout the 1600s and 1700s, most European nations were guided by an economic system known as **mercantilism** (MUR kun tee LIZ um). According to this system, wealth was measured by the amount of gold and silver a nation possessed. Competing for control of the world's wealth, European nations tried to become self-sufficient. They disliked purchasing goods from rival countries because this drained their own supply of gold while enriching their rivals. Most European nations sought to remedy this problem by establishing colonies and building empires.

Mercantilistic countries viewed their colonies as a source for raw materials for the industry of the mother country. They also viewed their colonies as markets where goods from the mother country could be sold, increasing the homeland's wealth and power. By regulating the economies of their colonies, the mother countries profited—but often at the expense of the colonies. By strictly controlling the trade of the colonies and by heavily taxing colonial trade and activities, the mercantilistic country could reap large short-term gains from its empire.

to house the troops, provide them with firewood, salt, and drink, and pay for a share of the cost of their housing. Colonies where large numbers of British troops were kept were especially outraged because of the extra expense they suffered.

Navigation and Trade Acts

The **Navigation and Trade Acts** were one series of Britain's mercantilistic policies. These acts regulated trade between the colonies and Britain's foreign competitors. Such regulations were supposed to help British manufacturers and raise revenue for the British treasury. The acts were not effective, however, and were quickly outdated. Also, the British did not enforce these acts strictly, a fact that encouraged colonial merchants to smuggle in goods from other countries.

Following the French and Indian War, British officials changed their habits and began enforcing the colonial trade laws strictly. Such trade not only had helped Britain's enemies during the war but also had deprived Britain of badly needed revenue. Realizing this, the British sent customs officials with **writs of assistance** (general

search warrants) to search for smuggled goods anywhere—even in homes. Several colonial leaders protested these writs that gave British officials unlimited authority to search private property. James Otis, a Boston attorney, held that these searches violated the rights of Englishmen, arguing that a man should be "as secure in his house, as a prince in his castle."

Taxes

The colonists had been paying taxes to support their colonial and local governments, but they had not been required to pay taxes to the British Parliament. This policy also changed as the British began to impose taxes on the colonies.

The Sugar Act—In April 1764 Parliament passed the **Sugar Act.** Through it Britain sought to gain money to help pay for protecting the colonies. The Sugar Act placed **duties** (taxes on imported goods) on such items as sugar, molasses, coffee, silks, and indigo. The American colonies were importing these items from the West Indies.

The Stamp Act of 1765—To raise additional revenue for the defense of the colonies, Parliament proposed another tax—

a stamp tax. It differed from the duties on imported goods because it directly affected colonial businesses, and therefore every colonist. The **Stamp Act** of 1765 required colonial businessmen and lawyers to purchase special stamps and place them on items that were taxed. This in turn raised the price that the colonists had to pay for these items. Among the items taxed were legal documents, newspapers, calendars, and playing cards. Without a stamp, such items were considered illegal.

Opposition from the Colonists

A storm of controversy erupted in the colonies over the Stamp Act. The protest was not over the amount of the tax, for the new tax amounted to only a few pennies per colonist. Compared to their counterparts in England, who had paid the tax for some time, the colonists were paying little.

Some of the stamps whose use was required by the controversial Stamp Act

The issue was whether Parliament had the right to tax the colonies at all. The colonists argued that since they had no representation in Parliament, Parliament could not tax them. "No taxation without representation" became a colonial rallying cry. Taxing lawyers and printers, the most vocal of the colonists, proved to be an unwise policy for Britain, as these colonists spread their views quickly.

Throughout the colonies groups called Sons of Liberty organized and held rallies to protest the Stamp Act. These groups, however, often resorted to intimidation and violence to obtain their ends. They threatened to tar and feather stamp agents, hoping to force them to resign. Sometimes those agents who refused to resign had their homes destroyed by rioting mobs. Of course, use of violence was not a proper response even to injustice.

A more conservative protest arose from an assembly commonly known as the **Stamp Act Congress.** This general colonial congress met at the urging of Massachusetts's **Samuel Adams.** In 1765 delegates from nine colonies gathered in New York. They sent a petition **King George III** and affirmed their loyalty to him. However, they insisted on their rights as English citizens to be taxed by their own representative bodies. When the king did not grant their requests, they responded by advocating a boycott.

Throughout the colonies; people refused to buy English merchandise. Colonial merchants would not unload goods from British ships. This boycott hurt British trade, and as a result, many factories in England closed and workers were laid off. Soon British merchants and workers joined the colonials in calling for the repeal of the Stamp Act.

In response to the mounting opposition, Parliament finally did so. The repeal brought rejoicing in both Britain and the colonies, and trade between the colonies and their mother country was quickly restored.

Section Review

1. How did the British attitude toward the colonies change after the French and Indian War?
2. Why did the British issue the Proclamation of 1763?
3. What were writs of assistance?
4. What tax act led to the strongest protest in the colonies?
5. What action did the colonists take against Britain to ruin her trade when the king did not give in to their requests?

Samuel Adams, a colonist who loudly opposed British injustices

C. The Breach Widens

The Townshend Acts

The storm of controversy seemed to have ended with the repeal of the Stamp Act. But a change in the leadership of Parliament brought renewed efforts to tax the colonies. Parliament passed the **Townshend Acts** in 1767, placing new duties on such items as glass, paper, lead, and tea. Once again the colonists protested by boycotting British goods.

Again some colonial merchants sought to avoid the new duties by smuggling goods past British customs agents. The British in turn stepped up their efforts to find the smugglers by widening the use of writs of assistance. Resentment between colonial merchants and British agents mounted. Sam Adams and the Massachusetts legislature denounced the act as a violation of their rights. Adams wrote a circular letter urging united colonial action, and this letter was sent to all the colonial legislatures. In several port cities British troops were called in to maintain order, but the presence of troops only deepened colonial resentment.

The Boston Massacre

Distrust between the colonists and British soldiers was especially evident in Boston. Here two regiments of British soldiers were called in to try to calm what was already a hotbed of colonial resistance. The citizens resented having British troops stationed in their city. They showed their resentment by booing the troops as they marched down the streets. Some patriots even dared to throw rotten eggs and seashells at the soldiers.

The situation came to a climax on the night of March 5, 1770. A crowd of men and boys began taunting seven soldiers by throwing snowballs and stones at them. The troops fired into the mob, killing five people and wounding six others. It is still uncertain who gave the command to fire. Their leader, Captain Preston, defended by lawyer John Adams, was later cleared of all charges. Two soldiers were branded on the hand, and the rest were acquitted.

News of the incident quickly spread throughout the colonies. Most accounts of what happened, however, were exaggerated by radicals who hoped to rouse public sentiment against the British. They labeled

America's Last King and Queen

America's last king, George III, came to the throne in 1760 at the age of twenty-two. He married Charlotte Sophia, who remained loyal to him throughout his life. Early in their marriage he purchased Buckingham Palace for her, and there they reared their fifteen children.

When George III came to power, he had three goals: to curb the power of the Whigs (one of the major political parties), to cleanse British politics of corruption, and to restore royal powers that had been lost. As a result of these goals, his early years as king upset British politics, and his court, because of the very high moral standards it had, was known as "the dullest court in Europe"—a fact of which King George was proud.

King George tried to bring the American colonies under tighter rule. His insistence that the British not give in prolonged the War of Independence that was to come. The defeat of his armies and the independence of the colonies was a great embarrassment to him because they thwarted his dreams of restoring the power of the monarchy. When William Pitt came on the scene, the king withdrew from politics for the most part and left the government in Pitt's hands.

From 1786 on he survived several assassination attempts. His forgiving spirit toward some of the attackers gained him some measure of popularity. But he began having periods of madness around 1788, and by 1810 was permanently insane. Many believe the insanity was a hereditary condition. His son—whom he despised because of his loose living and poor moral character—took over the throne in 1811.

How do historians sum up the character of America's last king? He was a man of great personal bravery, calm in a crisis, sincere, and highly principled. America's last queen was just as highly principled and was faithful to her husband. Charlotte, North Carolina, and Charlottesville, Virginia, today bear her name.

the incident the **"Boston Massacre"** and praised those killed as patriot "martyrs."

"Harboring Resentments"

Faced with renewed colonial opposition, Parliament repealed the duties on everything but tea. The British hoped this would restore peace in the colonies. But this action only divided the colonists. Some thought that Britain had conceded enough. Others, however, raised again the cry "no taxation without representation."

The Committees of Correspondence— Samuel Adams, perhaps the most prominent leader of colonial opposition, urged Boston to adopt a **Committee of Correspon-**

dence. Soon eighty Massachusetts towns followed Boston's example. These committees were organized to promote opposition to Britain and became important in alerting the colonists to British threats on liberties throughout the colonies.

The Tea Act of 1773 and a Tea Party— Little happened to stir up the public for about three years. But then Parliament passed the Tea Act of 1773. This act gave the struggling British East India Company a monopoly on tea trade to America. The monopoly enabled the company to bring cheaper tea to the colonies in spite of the tax on tea. This was a blow to American tea merchants, who could not compete with such a monopoly. The Committees of Correspondence joined the protests of the merchants.

When the first tea ships arrived, the colonists refused to unload them. In Boston a group of fifty or sixty men dressed like Indians boarded the ships and threw the tea overboard. A crowd along the shore watched this **"Boston Tea Party"** in silence.

Passage of the Intolerable Acts

News of the Boston Tea Party angered the British. They viewed the incident as an act of defiance. Many believed the colonists had gone too far and called for swift retaliation. This retaliation came through passage of several parliamentary acts.

The Boston Port Act and the Quartering Act—During 1774 Parliament passed a series of acts, which the colonists called the **Intolerable Acts,** designed to punish unruly Massachusetts. The Boston Port Bill closed the port of Boston until the destroyed tea was paid for. Parliament also made changes in the colony's charter, giving British officials more control over the government.

Top: *An artist's conception of the Boston Massacre*
Bottom: *The "Boston Tea Party"*

Massachusetts colonists lost their right to conduct town meetings, elect representatives, name judges, and select juries. Another act allowed royal officials charged with crimes to be tried in London or in another colony to insure a fair trial. Parliament also passed a new Quartering Act. This gave colonial governors power to requisition whatever supplies or buildings were needed to house British troops in America.

The Quebec Act—In that same year Parliament passed the **Quebec Act.** This act was not meant to punish the colonists, since it dealt with the newly acquired territory in Canada, not the colonies. Nevertheless, many colonists viewed this act as even more "intolerable" than the others. Not only did it allow French law to be used in civil cases, but it extended the borders of Quebec south to the Ohio River. The colonists feared that this would further shut off westward expansion. Parliament also gave Roman Catholicism, the leading religion in Quebec, a recognized status. The colonists resented Parliament's granting favored status to French law and Roman Catholicism. If Parliament could do that in Quebec, what would stop it from doing the same in America?

Section Review

1. What goods were taxed by the Townshend Acts of 1767?
2. How did the merchants avoid the tax?
3. What New England city expressed great distrust and resentment toward the British actions?
4. If the taxed tea was cheaper, why did the colonists and merchants protest it?
5. What three acts did the British pass following the Boston Tea Party? What did each act do?

D. The Colonies Unite for Action

The tide of discontent over the "intolerable acts" spread beyond the port of Boston. Other colonies became concerned that their liberties would be taken away too. The Virginia House of Burgesses declared the day the port of Boston was to be closed as a day of fasting and prayer. Angered by this show of sympathy for the "rebels" in Massachusetts, the royal governor of Virginia dissolved the House. Its members, however, gathered at the nearby Raleigh Tavern in Williamsburg, where they called for a general colonial congress to address the complaints of the colonies.

First Continental Congress

On September 5, 1774, more than fifty delegates, men from every colony except Georgia, gathered at Carpenter's Hall in Philadelphia. The delegates were united in their opposition to the Intolerable Acts but were divided in deciding what action to take against the British. Those who wanted to retain the benefits of British protection and trade urged conciliation. Others, however, believed that to yield would be to lose their right of self-government.

Sessions of this **First Continental Congress** lasted more than a month. The delegates adopted a formal statement of protest, a Declaration of Rights and Grievances. This declaration voiced their objections to the recent acts of Parliament, which they called "unjust, and cruel, as well as unconstitutional, and most dangerous and destructive of American rights."

The congress also organized the Continental Association. Its members pledged not to import any goods from Britain after December 1, 1774, nor to export any goods to Britain after September 10, 1775. They also refused to participate in the English

Liberty or Death

It was March 23, 1775. Some one hundred and twenty delegates from across Virginia had gathered at St. John's Church in Richmond to discuss what action Virginia should take in pressing the controversy with Britain. Among the delegates was George Washington, who had distinguished himself as a military leader in the recent French and Indian War. Also in attendance was the young Thomas Jefferson. But they were not the center of attention on this day.

A tall, stooped gentleman in the third pew rose to his feet. With a commanding voice and bold gestures he addressed the convention: "They tell us, sir, that we are weak—unable to cope with so formidable an adversary. . . . Three millions of people armed in the holy cause of liberty, and in such a country as that which we possess, are invincible by any force which our enemy can send against us."

He viewed the events of recent months with great alarm and wished to motivate the convention to action.

> There is no retreat, but in submission and slavery! . . . The war is inevitable—and let it come! . . . Gentlemen may cry, peace, peace—but there is no peace. The war is actually begun. The next gale that sweeps from the North will bring to our ears the clash of resounding arms! Our brethren are already in the field! Why stand we here idle? What is it that gentlemen wish? What would they have? Is life so dear, or peace so sweet, as to be purchased at the price of chains and slavery? Forbid it, Almighty God! I know not what course others may take; but as for me, give me liberty or give me death!

The speaker took his seat. His words, however, lingered on in the hearts of the delegates. Their complacency now turned to action as they, too, became willing to say with **Patrick Henry,** "Give me liberty or give me death!"

slave trade. The delegates affirmed: "We do solemnly bind ourselves . . . to adhere to this association, until such part of the several acts of Parliament passed since the close of the last war . . . are repealed."

Throughout the congress the delegates declared their loyalty to the king. They sent him their petitions hoping he would correct the injustices of Parliament's actions. The congress, however, called for another meeting for the spring of 1775 if their pleas went unheeded.

The colonists fully expected Britain to repeal the Intolerable Acts. After all, Britain had responded to earlier colonial protests by repealing the Stamp Act and the Townshend Acts. But this time Britain was determined to force the "rebellious" colonists to submit. Additional troops were sent to Boston. Further restraints were placed on colonial trade. King George III wrote to his chief minister, "The die is now cast; the Colonies must either submit or triumph; I do not wish to come to severer measures, but we must not retreat."

"The British are Coming!"

In rural towns surrounding Boston, the colonists began storing arms and ammunition in case armed resistance against the British became necessary. The British commander, General Thomas Gage, learned of a stockpile in nearby Concord and ordered a detachment of British soldiers to destroy it. He also gave orders to arrest two colonial leaders in nearby Lexington: Samuel Adams and John Hancock.

On the night of April 18, 1775, British troops left Boston and began their march toward Lexington and Concord. They hoped to surprise the colonists, but their departure did not go unnoticed. William

Dawes and **Paul Revere** rode through the countryside warning that the British were coming. As the soldiers marched, the alarm was spread—bells rang and guns fired. Early the next morning the soldiers reached **Lexington.** In the middle of the town square, they encountered about seventy colonial militiamen, or Minutemen. No one knows who fired first, but shots rang out. Eight colonials lay dead; ten more were wounded. The rest of the militiamen scattered.

The British continued to **Concord,** where they destroyed what military supplies they could find. But more Minutemen gathered

A statue of Paul Revere in Boston

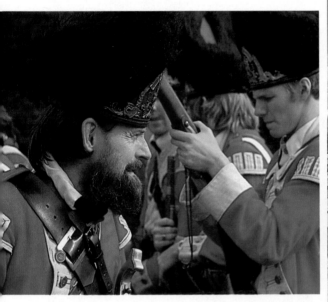

and another brief skirmish occurred at Concord Bridge. The British advanced no further but began a retreat to Boston. All along the way colonial Minutemen from other towns harassed the British. They fired at the British "Redcoats" from behind trees, buildings, and fences. The British made it back to Boston but suffered heavy casualties.

The skirmishes at Lexington and Concord mark the beginning of the War for Independence. The British force suffered 273 casualties, nearly three times that of the colonials. Word of the conflict spread quickly throughout the colonies. Colonial militiamen from other colonies rallied to Massachusetts's aid. They set up a siege around Boston. But they could not drive the British out. The first shots had been fired, and a war that neither side wanted—nor was prepared to fight—had begun.

British and colonial soldiers in a modern re-enactment of a battle of the Revolutionary War

Section Review

1. Why did colonies other than Massachusetts become concerned about the Intolerable Acts?
2. Where did the delegates meet to decide what to do about British actions? What was the body called?
3. What did the colonists expect the British to do?
4. For what two reasons did Thomas Gage send British soldiers out toward Lexington and Concord?
5. What was the group of patriots called who came to stop the British on short notice?

Summary

During the French and Indian War (1756-1763), British and colonial troops fought side by side to defeat their French and Indian enemies. They won control of most of North America for Britain. But shortly after the war, Britain began tightening its control over the colonies. The colonists resented the threat to their liberty, and soon a conflict was in the making between the colonies and the mother country.

Chapter Review

Do You Remember?

■ Choose the word or words that make each of these statements true.
1. The (Iroquois/Pontiacs) were Indian friends of the British.
2. Another name for the French and Indian War was (Queen Anne's War/the Seven Years' War).
3. Both the British and the French wanted to build a fort where the (St. Lawrence River/Ohio River) formed.
4. The Albany Plan of Union was (accepted/rejected).
5. The British won the French and Indian War by defeating the city of (Quebec/Toronto).

■ Match these men with their description.

6. George Washington
7. Edward Braddock
8. Samuel Adams
9. William Pitt
10. Paul Revere

a. most prominent leader of colonial opposition
b. defeated by the French at Fort Necessity
c. British general who built a road
d. rode to warn the colonists of approaching troops
e. British leader who organized the war effort

■ Match these events to the time line.
11. The Boston Massacre
12. The Battles of Lexington and Concord
13. Proclamation closed the West to settlement
14. Meeting of the Stamp Act Congress
15. The Boston Tea Party

Why It Is So?

1. Why was the Albany Plan of Union significant?
2. Why were the colonists upset about the use of writs of assistance?
3. Why did the Stamp Act fail?
4. Why were the Intolerable Acts considered intolerable?
5. Why were the colonists concerned about the Quebec Act?

What Do You Think?

1. What do you suppose would have happened if the French had won the French and Indian War?
2. What do you think the British could have done to keep the colonies a contented part of their empire?

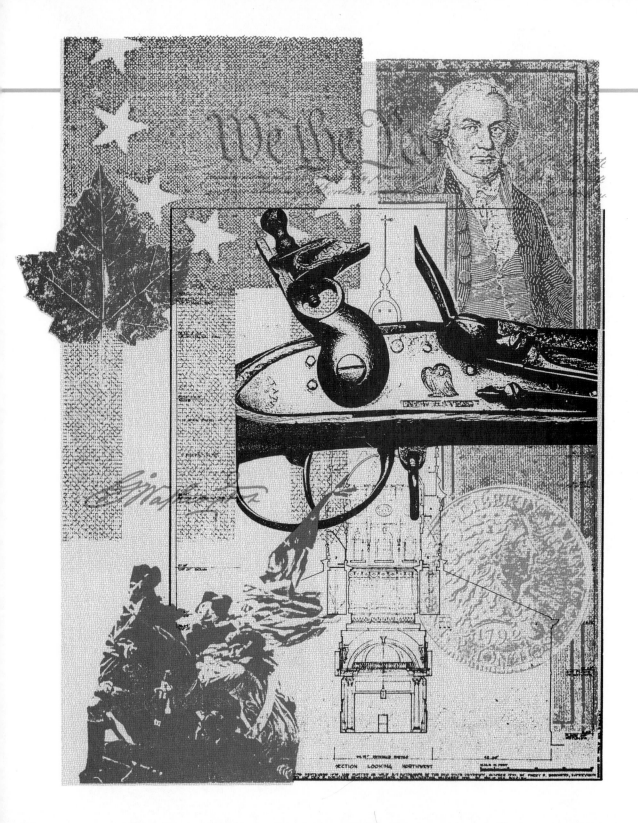

6

America Gains Its Independence

Two days after the incidents at Lexington and Concord, twenty-two thousand angry Americans gathered at Cambridge near Boston. They were ready to put a stop to any British actions. Gage's force of four thousand English redcoats seemed isolated in Boston. A conflict was in the making, and Americans were ready to take action.

A. Moving Toward Independence

Although the colonists' determination to stand up and fight against British assaults was growing, there was not yet a confirmed desire for total independence. Most still hoped to convince the king and Parliament that the colonies wished to be a loyal part of the British Empire. They only wanted their rights as Englishmen to be acknowledged. Events would soon prove, however, that America would separate from its mother country.

The Second Continental Congress Meets

On May 10, 1775, the **Second Continental Congress** convened in Philadelphia.

The delegates first sent a letter to the king to ask him to preserve their rights as Englishmen. The tone of the petition was so conciliatory that it became known as The Olive Branch Petition. (The olive branch is a symbol of peace.) However, the Second Congress was not optimistic and went ahead preparing for war.

The Continental Congress put the army at Boston under their command and asked the colonies for war supplies and troops. The Congress decided to call the troops the **Continental Army** and made George Washington of Virginia its commander-in-chief.

The king refused to receive the colonial agents bearing the Olive Branch Petition from the Congress. Instead he ordered the army to suppress the rebellious colonists, asserting that peace could be restored only when they were willing to submit. Compromise was impossible.

To make matters worse, Parliament— at the urging of the king—issued the Prohibitory Act. This act cut off British trade to the colonies and stated that Britain would no longer protect them. Colonial ships were now subject to capture, and their cargo became the "lawful prize" of the captors.

Early Military Action

Even before the Congress had met, the colonists were stirred by the events in Boston and the stubbornness of the king and Parliament. Many were ready to take up arms, and some did.

Fort Ticonderoga and Crown Point— The news of Lexington and Concord had quickly traveled to western New England. There, **Ethan Allen,** the leader of the Green Mountain Boys—a unit raised to defend the New Hampshire land grants—decided to capture the British outposts of Fort Ticon-

deroga (tie KON duh ROE guh) and Crown Point. Since these forts were on Lake Champlain, getting them into American hands would prevent the British from cutting off New England from New York state and the rest of the colonies.

Meanwhile, **Benedict Arnold** (who later became a traitor) had set out from Massachusetts on the same mission. Allen and Arnold met en route and argued about who should lead the expedition. Unable to decide, they both served as commanders. These unwilling partners captured **Fort Ticonderoga** without a shot at dawn on the same day that the Second Continental Congress first met. In addition to gaining a strategic location, they seized the fort's artillery. The following day the same forces captured Fort Crown Point, clearing the way for an invasion of Canada.

*The Battle of Bunker Hill—*Meanwhile, back in Boston, the conflict continued to grow. While the Second Continental Congress debated proposals vital to the American

Ethan Allen

Northern Campaigns
1775-1776

Colonial Victory
British Victory

0   50   100
Scale of Miles

cause, the Boston patriots took possession of Bunker and Breed's hills on the Charlestown peninsula, just across the bay from the city. Colonel William Prescott then ordered his men to build trenches in case of attack.

The British general Gage wanted to force the Americans from these hilltop positions. Reinforced by **William Howe** and his three thousand men, Gage ordered Howe to capture the hills. The first two assaults were driven back. On the third attempt the colonists ran out of ammunition and were forced to retreat. Howe had won, but his casualties were heavy.

The British were determined to put a stop to colonial resistance, and they quickly stepped up their military action. To prevent any trade of weapons and supplies between colonies, the British ordered a blockade of New England. They also hired several thousand troops to help them. These hired soldiers, or **mercenaries** (MUR suh NAIR eez), were called Hessians after the German region from which most of them came.

British "redcoats" in the re-enactment of a Revolutionary War battle

A Canadian Invasion—The colonists hoped that they could rally Canadians to the patriot cause and thus win Canada easily. If the British lost Canada as a base for their operations, it would be harder for them to attack elsewhere. The colonists were optimistic about Canadians coming to their aid for two reasons. Some Canadians were French and had never liked the British. Others had suffered many of the same injustices the colonists had suffered.

Congress approved a two-front approach. General Philip Schuyler (SKY lur) was to advance along Lake Champlain northward to take Fort St. John and Montreal. While Schuyler was moving, Benedict Arnold was to trek across Maine and southern Canada to Quebec. Schuyler would then join Arnold at Quebec for an assault on that city.

During November Schuyler became ill, and Richard Montgomery, a former British officer, assumed command and captured Fort St. John and Montreal. Crippled by cold and hindered by the freezing waters of the Kennebec (KEN uh BEK) River, Arnold's forces did not reach Quebec until late December. Montgomery joined Arnold for an attack on Quebec on New Year's Eve. The Americans waged the attack—a disastrous failure—in a driving snowstorm. Montgomery was killed, Arnold was severely wounded, and one-third of the American force was captured. Smallpox also broke out among the troops, forcing them to pull back to Fort Ticonderoga. The Americans had gained a healthy respect for the British army, and although reinforcements came in the spring, the Continental Army never again attacked Canada.

Common Sense

As the months passed, more and more people saw that they would have to choose either to submit to the British or to fight against them. One factor that influenced their thinking was a pamphlet written by **Thomas Paine** called ***Common Sense.*** Although Paine had been in America less than two years, he had quickly embraced the American cause. Here he saw a land of greater opportunity and less poverty than England. He believed that America was a

place where the eighteenth-century ideas about a just society could work.

In one of the most influential political tracts in history, Paine built a case for American separation from Britain. He tried to convince the masses that Britain had become unfit to rule them. He noted tyrannical acts of the king and Parliament and used these facts to show that to separate from Britain was the "common sense" thing to do. Within six months after the publication of *Common Sense,* the Declaration of Independence was signed.

Later Paine wrote a second pamphlet called *The American Crisis.* This essay was first read to Washington's troops on December 10, 1776. The pamphlet rallied the men amid their hardships to complete or even stay beyond their enlistments. These men then went on to win victories in New Jersey. Thus they proved that they were not the mere "summer soldiers" or "sunshine patriots" the pamphlet had scorned.

Thomas Paine

Freeing Boston

During the winter of 1775-76, American efforts centered on getting the British out of Boston. Colonel Henry Knox, a Boston bookseller turned soldier, performed one of the most amazing feats of the war. Using forty-two sledges pulled by eighty teams of oxen, the twenty-five-year-old Knox and his men hauled sixty tons of artillery (cannon and ammunition) from Fort Ticonderoga to Boston. They did it in forty-seven days over mountains, snow, and ice, covering a distance of about three hundred miles. The Americans placed the cannon on Dorchester (DOR chuh stur) Heights overlooking Boston on the night of March 1.

When the British army saw the cannon looming over them, they evacuated the city and sailed south to New York on March 17. About a thousand **Loyalists**—colonists who favored the British cause—also left Boston and sailed to Halifax, Nova Scotia, where they settled.

Declaring Independence

During the fall of 1775 and the winter of 1776, the Continental Congress took some steps toward declaring independence from Britain by creating an American navy, purchasing more war supplies, and welcoming unofficial French aid. On May 15th Virginia's House of Burgesses endorsed a resolution for independence. The other colonies were also ready to make such a move. Only Pennsylvania and New York were reluctant.

On June 7 Richard Henry Lee of Virginia introduced a resolution to the Continental Congress "that these United Colonies are, and of right ought to be, free and independent states." A committee of five men was appointed to write the declaration.

(Other committees were to design a plan of union, or confederation, and to consider making foreign alliances.) On July 2 the resolution came up for a vote. All the delegations except New York's voted for the declaration. The document, written primarily by **Thomas Jefferson,** was polished for two days. On July 4, 1776, the Congress unanimously approved the **Declaration of Independence.**

Section Review

1. Why did the Second Continental Congress meet?
2. What two commanders led their men in the strategic capture of the British Forts Ticonderoga and Crown Point?
3. What was the British response to the Olive Branch Petition?
4. What was Thomas Paine's role in America's fight for independence?
5. When did the Continental Congress finally approve a declaration of America's independence?

The Continental Congress committee drafting the Declaration of Independence

B. Battling for Independence

The Declaration of Independence forced Americans not already committed to the cause to declare themselves either patriots or Loyalists. The number of patriots grew toward the end of the war, but throughout most of the struggle, from about one-third to one-half of the colonists were in this group.

Another one-fourth to one-third of the population were Loyalists, sometimes called Tories after the British party that was strongly loyal to the crown. Around a hundred thousand Loyalists were either uncomfortable enough or unsure enough about the future that they fled the colonies and went to England, Canada, or the British West Indies. Most Loyalists stayed behind, probably because they did not want to risk losing valuable properties. To stay out of trouble, they often kept their opinions to themselves. Other Tories, about fifty thousand, fought directly for Britain, especially during periods when Britain seemed to be winning. These colonists aided the British by selling them food and supplies. Some even led Indian parties raiding the settlements. Others became spies or propagandists.

There were good men on both sides. Many Loyalists, seeing the king as God's authority over them, believed it wrong to rebel against the British Empire. On the other hand, many patriots believed that Britain had relinquished her authority over the colonies and that they should thus "be subject" to the colonial government.

The remaining colonists were indifferent. Some were neutral for business reasons, fearing financial hurt if they chose sides. Others lived in remote areas and were not greatly concerned with the conflict.

Middle Colonies' Campaigns 1776-1778

Ft. Ticonderoga

Saratoga

Albany

Connecticut River

Hudson River

Delaware River

West Point

Harlem Heights

Princeton
Trenton
Valley Forge
Brandywine

Germantown

Philadelphia

New York
Monmouth Court House

Colonial Victory ●
British Victory ●

0   50   100
Scale of Miles

Washington's Action

With Boston secure in American hands, Washington moved his army south to New York in April. The Americans assumed that New York would be the British target and committed troops to its defense. Because of its sea access, islands, and rivers, however, New York proved impossible to defend. Throughout July seven hundred British ships brought an army of 34,000 from Nova Scotia to New York under General Howe's command.

Trouble in New York—Outnumbered four to one, Washington could not defeat the British. However, he could outmaneuver them in battle. If he did not, he would lose his army. Howe had broken through the American outer defense on Long Island, forcing the Americans to flee to Brooklyn Heights by the East River. There seemed to be no way of escape for the colonial army. But Alexander McDougall, one of Washington's aides, hurried across the East River to New York City and returned with a motley fleet of fishing boats, rowboats, and sailing ships. A rainy night followed by a heavy morning fog permitted the American army to be ferried to temporary safety on Manhattan Island.

After losing the battle of Harlem Heights on Manhattan, Washington managed to get most of his troops across the Hudson River to relative safety in New Jersey and later across the Delaware to Pennsylvania.

Washington Attacks Trenton and Princeton—Howe settled down in New York for the winter but sent Hessian soldiers to Trenton, New Jersey, to keep an eye on Washington. Since the Americans had been forced out of New York and had not won a major battle in seven months, their morale was low. Moreover, the troop enlistments were to expire December 31, 1776. If these men left, Washington would have only fourteen hundred men—unless, of course, he gained some new recruits. He needed a victory to attract more men to the cause.

Responding to the challenge, he and his men crossed the ice-filled Delaware River on Christmas night, surprised the Hessians at **Trenton** the next morning, and captured over nine hundred of them.

The British responded quickly and sent a superior force under **Charles Cornwallis** to confront Washington. Washington left decoy campfires burning, slipped out of

camp, went around Cornwallis's camp, and marched north to Princeton. There he overcame a small British force.

He then turned toward Morristown, the location selected for his winter headquarters. His daring, unconventional moves had freed most of New Jersey from British occupation and had given new hope to Americans. A British observer wrote, "A few days ago they had given up the cause for lost; . . . now they are liberty mad again."

Victory at Saratoga

Because the British believed that a mere show of force might end the colonial rebellion, they had not been overly aggressive in 1776. In 1777, however, they developed a plan of attack that they thought would quickly end the war.

According to the British plan, General **John Burgoyne** (bur GOIN) would lead an army south from Montreal into New York while General William Howe went up the Hudson River from New York City. General Barry St. Leger (SAINT LEJ-ur) would go down the St. Lawrence from Montreal to Lake Ontario and then cut east across the Mohawk River Valley. The three generals were to meet at Albany. Their offensive, had it been successful, would have cut off

George Washington leading his men at Trenton

Nathan Hale: The Schoolmaster Who Gave His Life

One problem Washington faced in New York was that he desperately needed information about the British plans and troops on Long Island. When officers were asked to volunteer for this dangerous task, there was only one volunteer: a school teacher from East Haddam, Connecticut, named **Nathan Hale.**

Hale had no special training for such a mission. He did have his Yale diploma, however, which enabled him to travel as a schoolmaster. He was thus able to work his way south from Connecticut to Long Island in a few days.

But Hale had no sooner gotten information on Long Island when Howe forced the Continental Army across to Manhattan. Because his information about Long Island would now be of less value, Hale pursued the British army up Manhattan Island. There, on the night of September 21, he was captured. The information he was carrying implicated him, and Howe ordered him hanged the next morning without even a trial.

On his way to the gallows, Hale supposedly said, "I only regret that I have but one life to lose for my country." It is not certain if Hale indeed said these words. It is possible, however, for

they were a paraphrase from *Cato,* an eighteenth-century play by Joseph Addison. It is reasonable to assume that a schoolmaster of Hale's caliber could readily recall the quotation. In any case, Captain Frederick Mackenzie, a British officer who described Hale's death, wrote, "He behaved with great composure and resolution." He added that Hale's last words were, "It is the duty of every good officer to obey any orders given him by his commander-in-chief."

New England and upstate New York, centers of colonial resistance, from the rest of the colonies.

In trying to execute their plan, the British made disastrous mistakes. Instead of moving up the Hudson, Howe sought the war minister's permission to pacify Pennsylvania. Washington met him unsuc-cessfully at Brandywine Creek west of Philadelphia and at Germantown. Howe then wintered in the luxury of Philadelphia and missed the fall action at Albany.

St. Leger made some initial progress, but as he worked his way east, he found New York militiamen to be tougher than he expected. St. Leger's force was made up of about two thousand Indians and Tories, and the Indians were difficult to control. When Benedict Arnold's carefully planted rumors about American strength reached their ears, many Indians deserted. Because his force was crippled by the desertions and by an American attack, St. Leger retreated to Lake Ontario.

Marching southward, Burgoyne recaptured Ticonderoga on July 5th. From that point on, however, his progress was slowed. First, General Philip Schuyler's men felled trees and dammed streams to block him. Soon Burgoyne ran short of supplies and draft animals. He sent a foraging party of seven hundred men—mostly Hessians—east to Bennington, Vermont, where he heard there was a stockpile of American military supplies. But his soldiers were met by a force of more than fifteen hundred New Hampshire militiamen under John Stark. They had been angered by the shooting and scalping of Jane McCrea, a settler's wife, and Burgoyne's pardon of her murderer. The patriots captured all of the foraging party and most of the relief party sent to rescue the British troops.

Burgoyne needed either to crush the Americans speedily or to wait for rescue by Sir Henry Clinton, who was in New York City. On September 19 he attacked the Americans under Horatio Gates at Freeman's Farm near Saratoga (SEHR uh TOE guh). The British suffered heavy casualties. Thinking that Gates would divide his forces to go after Clinton, Burgoyne took the offensive a second time three weeks later at Bemis Heights. Again Burgoyne lost heavily. Low on supplies, he surrendered on October 17, 1777.

This battle of **Saratoga** knocked one British army out of the war and forced Britain to give up any hope of taking the northern colonies. Alarmed, the British changed their strategy. They would now focus on the South, where the population was more scattered and where there were supposedly more Loyalists. Meanwhile, in the North they would only continue the naval blockade and make coastal raids.

Besides giving renewed hope to Americans, the battle at Saratoga officially brought France into the war on the American side. French military and financial aid proved helpful as the war continued.

The Bad Winter of 1777-78

Although the victory at Saratoga offered Americans new hope, it did little to change the physical condition of Washington's men. Acute supply problems had left them hungry, cold, ill-clothed, and sick at **Valley Forge,** Pennsylvania, in late 1777 and early 1778. Baron Von Steuben (STOO bun), a drill master from Prussia, gave military training to those who were well enough. The pride and skill he instilled helped the men to focus less on their hardships and more on the cause.

A re-enactment of the battle of Saratoga

Joseph Brant: Mohawk Loyalist

Joseph Brant, a Mohawk chieftain, first gained recognition during the French and Indian War, when he fought under Sir William Johnson against the French. After the war Johnson sent Brant to Eleazar Wheelock's Indian school in Lebanon, Connecticut, where Brant became a devout Christian. During Pontiac's Rebellion, Brant again fought with the British. In the meantime he had been serving as a missionary to his people.

When the War for Independence began, Brant sided with the Loyalists. In his opinion as a Christian, the colonies were wrong to rebel against the king, whom God had placed in power. His influence brought many other Indians to the Loyalist cause as well. Commissioned a captain, he led several raids on American settlements in the Cherry Valley. The colonists soon feared his men.

After the war Brant encouraged peace. For his help during the war, the British gave his people land and money to settle in Ontario. Brant returned to his missionary work and translated the gospel of Mark into the Mohawk language. He never took up arms again.

As an Indian statesman he negotiated treaties with other tribes and traveled in the American West in an effort to form an all-Indian confederacy.

Joseph Brant was a man who gave his all to whatever cause he believed to be right. He was an Indian whom even modern historians are forced to recognize as a devout Christian, a man of convictions.

A new army quartermaster, General **Nathanael Greene,** tried to solve the supply problem, but it improved little. Congress had no power to tax and little money for purchasing supplies. Those supplies sent by the states often never reached the men because of poor transportation or theft. Collapse of the paper money system also added to the financial crisis. Eventually some New Jersey troops mutinied, two Connecticut regiments demonstrated, and Pennsylvania troops marched off to the state house to negotiate their pay.

The slim pocketbook of the Continental Army was replenished by some donations. Robert Morris, head of the Department of Finance, was able to ask for money and supplies from the states and for a loan of four million dollars from France. Morris also used the banking system to stretch the government's resources.

In June 1778, **Sir Henry Clinton,** who took Howe's place in the North, moved from Philadelphia toward New York, hoping to use its harbor as a base for sea raids. Washington followed him and attacked at Monmouth Court House, New Jersey. The American effort was unsuccessful, however, and the British army made it to New York. Washington and his men spent the winter

Valley Forge, Pennsylvania

of 1778-79 at White Plains, New York, hoping at least to keep Clinton in the area.

The War in the West

The British, Loyalists, and Indians were also active in the West. In 1778 some settlers in the Wyoming Valley of Pennsylvania and Cherry Valley, New York, were massacred. General John Sullivan drove the Tories back to their base at Fort Niagara, but he never gained the fort itself.

Settlements in the Ohio River Valley were also raided. British colonel Henry Hamilton, who had been nicknamed "Hair Buyer" because he paid bounties for American scalps, was responsible. **George Rogers Clark** organized a force of 175 men to go into the Ohio Valley to drive Hamilton out. Braving dark forests, swamps, and icy rivers as well as the threat of Indians and Tories, Clark captured two frontier outposts—Kaskaskia (kus KAS kee uh) in Illinois and Vincennes (vin SENZ) in Indiana. This meant that later the United States could lay claim to lands bordering the Mississippi River.

Women at War for Independence

There were several women who contributed to the patriot cause on the field of battle. Some helped in a moment of crisis; others fought throughout the struggle. From the front lines to the frontier, however, these women of the War for Independence took the call to arms seriously. They were not afraid to fight for the cause their family and friends believed in—no matter what the danger or the cost.

Margaret Corbin: This young lady went to war with her husband. At the British attack on Fort Washington, she began firing a cannon when the man working it was killed. Then her husband, who was firing the cannon next to her, was killed. Margaret took over his position and continued firing until she was shot and wounded. Her wound was so severe that she was an invalid for the rest of her life.

Mary Ludwig Hays McCauley: This woman warrior became known as Molly Pitcher. She served as a water carrier for her husband and the other patriot soldiers during the Battle of Monmouth.

When her husband was wounded, Mary took charge of his cannon and fired it for him.

Betty Zane: In an Indian and Loyalist attack on Fort Henry, the patriot defenders found themselves running low on gunpowder. They knew that some was available in a cabin about one hundred yards away. To go after the

The War at Sea

Throughout the war America was involved in fighting at sea. America did not have a navy at the beginning of the war. The early navy consisted mostly of **privateers,** merchant vessels outfitted to fight.

Since Great Britain had a strong navy, Americans faced an almost impossible task on the seas. After France came into the war, the Americans hoped that French sea power would come to their aid. The United States could, and did, use French ports as a base of operations and even used French ships to attack the British.

The most famous American naval officer was **John Paul Jones.** A Scotsman by birth, Jones gained his greatest fame by defeating the British ship *Serapis* (SEHR up pis) in the North Sea. He used a French ship rechristened the *Bonhomme Richard* (BON-om RICH-urd), after Benjamin Franklin's *Poor Richard's Almanac.*

powder appeared suicidal, but Betty Zane convinced the men that she could make it. She reasoned that since she was a woman, the Indians might be more interested in capturing her than in shooting her. Leaving the stockade, Betty calmly walked across the line of fire to the cabin. There she put the powder into a tablecloth and headed back. On her return trip the Indians and Loyalists saw what she was doing and began firing at her. Running all the way, she arrived safely at the fort.

"Mad Anne" Bailey: This adventurous woman served as a scout and messenger for the patriots on the frontier. She was given her nickname by the Indians because they thought that either she had special protection from the Great Spirit or she was insane. Her husband had been killed in an Indian attack. Once, when being chased by Indians, she hid in a hollow log. After the Indians left, she trailed them to their camp and that night took back everything they had stolen from her. Several times she traveled alone through areas infested by the Indians to get gunpowder for a fort running low on it.

Nancy Hart: The Indians fighting for the British in Georgia called her the "War Woman." Once she helped a patriot escape from several Loyalists by having him gallop right through her house so he wouldn't leave a trail. When the six Loyalists returned from their futile search, they forced Nancy to prepare a meal for them. While doing so, she sent her daughter for help. Then while they were eating, she took their muskets, killed two of the men, and held the rest at gunpoint until help arrived.

Section Review

1. What is the difference between the patriots and the Loyalists (Tories)?
2. What two victories virtually freed New Jersey from British occupation and gave new hope to Washington's men?
3. What American victory forced the British out of the North?
4. What American leader won important victories in the West?
5. Who were the privateers and what part did they play in the War for Independence?
6. Who was the most famous American naval officer in the War for Independence?

When asked to surrender by the captain of the Serapis, *John Paul Jones answered, "I have not yet begun to fight!"*

C. Winning Independence

After the loss at Saratoga, the British turned their interest toward the South. In the fall of 1778, Clinton's force set sail for the major southern port city of Savannah, Georgia. It was captured easily, as was Augusta, Georgia. In 1780 the British besieged Charleston, South Carolina, from March until May, when it also fell. Clinton believed that the British could recover everything back up to the Hudson "unless a superior fleet shows itself."

Southern Successes

The Continental Congress sent Horatio Gates south from Saratoga. He engaged Lord Cornwallis at Camden, South Carolina, and suffered a crushing defeat. Gates then fled to Charlotte, leaving his men behind. He was soon replaced by General Nathanael Greene. British colonel Banastre Tarleton used his forces to harass the southern soldiers as they tried to regroup. Although the situation seemed bleak for the patriots, success would soon come.

In October, 1780, British colonel Patrick Ferguson demanded that frontiersmen of the Carolina Piedmont come to **Kings Mountain,** South Carolina, and lay down their arms. Those who had been indecisive about freedom were now furious. The Scots-Irish settlers from east Tennessee and the western Carolinas came to Kings Mountain ready to fight. These "over-mountain men," as the patriots were called, met Ferguson's challenge by killing or capturing the entire force of a thousand Tories. Ferguson himself was killed and buried on the battlefield.

Nathanael Greene then divided the small patriot army in the South and had Daniel Morgan fake a retreat. Banastre Tarleton took the bait and came after him. On

Southern Campaigns 1779–1781

Baltimore

Yorktown

Guilford Court House

Kings Mountain

Cowpens

Camden

Colonial Victory ●

British Victory ●

Charleston

Savannah

0   50   100   150

Scale of Miles

January 17, 1781, at **Cowpens,** South Carolina, Morgan and his men killed or captured most of Tarleton's force.

Greene lured Cornwallis northward away from Morgan and crossed the Dan River, faking a move into Virginia. Then on March 15, 1781, he dropped back down to challenge Cornwallis at Guilford Court House near Greensboro, North Carolina. Although Cornwallis won the battle, his victory proved expensive, and the cost of the "win" contributed to his ultimate defeat.

British Surrender at Yorktown

As Cornwallis moved across the Carolinas chasing Greene, his supply lines lengthened. Guerilla fighters—such as Francis Marion, Thomas Sumter, and Andrew Pickens—attacked those lines and harassed British troop movement at every turn. A frustrated Cornwallis pulled out of the Carolina midlands and Piedmont and headed for coastal southeastern Virginia. There, he reasoned, the British navy could keep him supplied, and he could devise a new strategy. Cornwallis believed he could subdue Virginia, the source of patriot supplies. Then his troops could menace the South once more. The only threat to Cornwallis seemed to be a twenty-four-year-old French volunteer, **Marquis de Lafayette** (mar-KEE deh LAH-fee-ET) whom Washington had sent to the area with troops. Cornwallis met little resistance from these troops as he headed for Yorktown, where he planned a well-fortified base. British general Clinton, a rival, did little to help him.

Cornwallis was unprepared for what happened next. The patriots had pleaded repeatedly for French naval help. Suddenly Admiral de Grasse (GRAHSS), now in the West Indies, was ready to help with his twenty-eight ships. The British did not expect this show of strength, and they thought that when an attack did come it would be at New York City rather than at Yorktown.

Washington slipped out of New York with most of his forces to help trap Cornwallis in Virginia. De Grasse's French troops arrived to reinforce Lafayette's and Washington's men and help prevent Cornwallis's escape. Eight additional French warships prevented any of the remaining British ships from leaving for New York. Now Cornwallis was trapped at **Yorktown** without the hope of support from the British navy. Outnumbered more than two to one, Cornwallis offered only brief resistance, and on October 18, 1781, he surrendered. With his surrender came the British recognition that the Americans had won.

Although the British had formally surrendered one army, they still occupied some American territories. They were especially active in the Northwest and still controlled some forts there. The conflict between Loyalists and patriots continued for some time.

Treaty Negotiations

Since France had been America's major ally, the peace talks were held in Paris. Benjamin Franklin, John Jay, and Henry Laurens were chosen as the American negotiators. While on his way to Paris, Henry Laurens was captured by the British and imprisoned in the Tower of London. He arrived only in time for the signing. Franklin, meanwhile, suffered a kidney stone attack, leaving John Jay as the chief negotiator.

Left: *The field where Cornwallis surrendered at Yorktown*
Right: *Washington at the siege of Yorktown*

The **Treaty of Paris,** signed September 3, 1783, ended the eight-year war with Britain. It formally granted the United States of America its independence and gave the new nation all lands that had not already been occupied east of the Mississippi. It also set the northern boundary from the Great Lakes to Lake of the Woods.

The fighting between the United States and Britain had stopped in April 1783. The last British troops left New York City on November 25, 1783. The war was officially over. But now, as an independent nation, the United States faced enormous problems. Independence would bring change—and many new challenges.

Section Review

1. What brought the "over-mountain men" out to fight the battle of King's Mountain?
2. What battle did Cornwallis "win" that was so costly it ultimately contributed to his defeat?
3. Where did Cornwallis surrender?
4. What treaty officially ended the war with Britain?

Summary

Although the War for Independence had begun with the Battles of Lexington and Concord in 1775, the colonies did not officially declare their independence until a year later. The early years of the war brought only a few victories to the Continental Army, but the British defeat at Saratoga in 1777 began to turn the tide. Victories for the United States in the South led to the eventual entrapment of Cornwallis's British army at Yorktown in 1781. After that, only scattered resistance remained until the peace treaty was signed two years later. America's independence was won.

Chapter Review

Do You Remember?

■ Supply the name of the missing man or location in these statements.
   1. Ethan Allen and ____ captured Fort Ticonderoga from the British.
   2. General Gage and ____ defeated the colonists at Bunker Hill.
   3. General Henry Knox brought cannon from ____ to drive the British from Boston.
   4. ____ crossed the Delaware River to defeat the Hessians at Trenton.
   5. The Americans defeated General Burgoyne at ____.
   6. Washington spent a hungry, cold winter with his men at ____.
   7. ____ defeated "Hair Buyer" Hamilton in the West.
   8. America's most famous naval officer was ____.
   9. The Americans trapped the British general ____ at Yorktown.
■ For each of the following pairs of terms, write a sentence or two explaining the connection between them.
   10. George Washington/Continental Army
   11. mercenaries/Hessians
   12. Thomas Paine/*Common Sense*
   13. Declaration of Independence/Thomas Jefferson
■ Match the following terms to their descriptions.
   14. Marquis de Lafayette
   15. Treaty of Paris
   16. privateers
   17. Second Continental Congress
   18. Loyalists

   a. established the Continental Army and issued the Declaration of Independence
   b. trading ships equipped for warfare
   c. officially ended the War for Independence
   d. backed the British in the war
   e. Frenchman who aided the Americans

Why Is It So?

1. Why did the Second Continental Congress send the Olive Branch Petition?
2. Why did the Americans expect Canada to side with them against the British?
3. Why was the battle of Trenton important to the Americans?
4. How did British strategy change after the Battle of Saratoga?
5. How was Cornwallis trapped at Yorktown?

What Do You Think?

1. What do you think would have happened if Canada had sided with the Americans?
2. Why do you suppose the patriots won their victory at Kings Mountain?

7

Confederation

SIGNERS
OF
THE
DECLARATION
OF
INDEPENDENCE

Before and during most of the War for Independence, the First and Second Continental congresses along with state assemblies governed the colonies. Although the people had been reluctant to grant extensive political power to any centralized government, the crisis convinced the patriot leaders that they needed a more permanent form of government. Cooperation among the colonies in financing and fighting the war was essential. Many colonial leaders questioned whether the Continental congresses even had the authority to wage war. Consequently, a committee was appointed

The Portrait Gallery in Independence Hall, Philadelphia

in 1776 to submit a new plan for an improved system of government. The new form suggested was a **confederation,** a loose association or league of states.

A. Organization and Achievements of Confederation

The new plan, drafted in 1777, was called the **Articles of Confederation** and was largely written by Delaware's John Dickinson. Under this plan the government had one governing body, a congress, whose members were to be elected yearly.

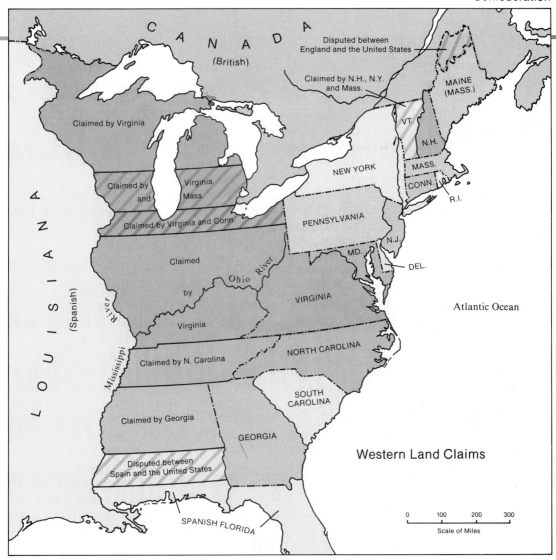

Western Land Claims

Adoption of the Articles of Confederation

Before the articles could become law, however, each state had to **ratify** them (give them formal approval). The articles were presented to the states in November 1777, but it took almost four years to complete the ratification process. There were several roadblocks to adoption. The biggest problem was the power given to the Congress to control and dispose of western lands. Some states objected to this idea for two main reasons. First, the states with western land claims did not want to give them up. Second, influential land speculators, men who had already purchased lands at low prices with plans for reselling them at huge profits, saw their dream of quick riches vanishing.

The states compromised. The Confederation Congress gained control of the western lands, but in return each state, no matter how small, was given an equal vote in the Congress. Also, to satisfy the large southern states, tax assessments in the slave states were based on the value of improved lands rather than on the population. Still, Virginia, the state with the largest western land claim, held out. Its small neighbor, Maryland, also withheld approval, waiting for Virginia to reverse its position. The dispute was finally resolved when Virginia accepted the plan in March 1781.

Under the new plan laws could be passed when nine of the thirteen states approved them. The Articles themselves could be changed only with the unanimous consent of the states.

The Powers of Congress

Although the Confederation Congress lacked some crucial powers, especially the power to tax, it did have more powers than the makeshift Continental congresses. For example, the Confederation Congress could raise and maintain an army, declare war, make treaties with foreign countries, manage Indian affairs, establish a postal system, and borrow and coin money. These powers, however, were not held exclusively by Congress. The states, without congressional consent, could also coin their own monies, issue bills of credit, deal directly with foreign governments, and even make war.

In addition, certain powers were held only by the states. The states, for instance, controlled both domestic and foreign trade; the right to act in economic matters involving debts, contracts, and family affairs; and the right to tax citizens.

The states also agreed to cooperate in some matters. First, they agreed to give full faith and credit to public civil acts of other states. Thus each state would respect the others' birth, marriage, and death certificates, and wills. Second, they agreed to return, at the request of a state's governor, criminals and runaway slaves who crossed state lines. Third, they agreed to settle their differences by arbitration. This meant that two states involved in a dispute would let a mutually acceptable third party help them reach a solution.

Lasting Achievements

Although the Confederation government lasted only eight years, it did take some legislative actions that are noteworthy. Several important ideas of government were established, some of which are still being followed today.

Probably the most important legislation passed by the Confederation Congress dealt with the western lands. Until 1890 the West was a constantly changing land area. In the 1780s the term *West* meant the land west of the thirteen colonies. Thomas Jefferson, who penned most of the Declaration of Independence, also drafted two pieces of legislation dealing with these lands: the Northwest Ordinance of 1785 and the Northwest Ordinance of 1787.

The Northwest Ordinance of 1785—The Confederation Congress had first gained control of the lands that lie north of the Ohio River and between the Mississippi and the Appalachian Mountains. The Congress quickly made provision for the settlement of this land, which was called the **Northwest Territory.** The **Northwest Ordinance of 1785** provided for surveying and selling the western lands that the Articles of Confederation had placed under the Congress's control. This government land totaled almost a quarter billion acres of excellent land and was eventually divided into five states.

The ordinance provided for the land to be divided into six-mile square areas called **townships.** Each township was then divided into thirty-six smaller parcels (each one-mile square) called sections, with each section containing 640 acres. (See the illustration.) Second, the ordinance provided for the sale of the land at auctions. The minimum acceptable price was one dollar an acre, and the buyer had to purchase at least one section, or 640 acres.

Although Congress could have made more money by setting a higher price or by using a different method of sale, it wanted to give people of modest means the opportunity to purchase the land for family farms. Many did, but others either could not raise the necessary $640 or saw no need to purchase parcels so large. Consequently, Congress, ever short of cash, sold the land at wholesale prices to several large land companies, the Ohio Company being probably the best known.

Another condition placed on the sale of the land was that Congress had to have clear title to the land before selling it. That is, Congress had to make treaties with the Indians to buy the lands they claimed before

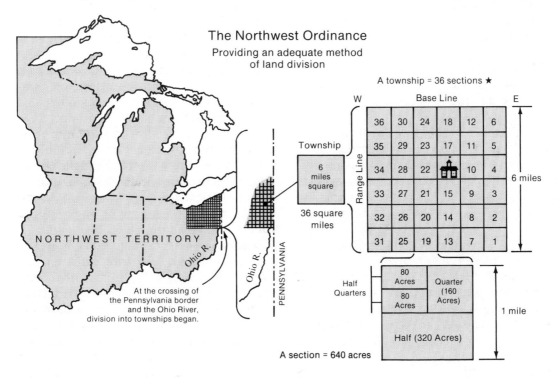

The Northwest Ordinance
Providing an adequate method
of land division

At the crossing of the Pennsylvania border and the Ohio River, division into townships began.

A township = 36 sections ★

A section = 640 acres

★ Four sections of each township reserved for future disposition

 Section 16 reserved for support of education

any of that land could be sold. Congress hoped this would prevent Indian uprisings like Pontiac's Rebellion (1763-1766).

The orderly, practical system established by the Ordinance of 1785 has had a lasting effect on America. Not only were the states of the Northwest Territories surveyed according to its demands but also other new territories and states. A look at the map of the fifty states (see the map of the United States in the front of the book)

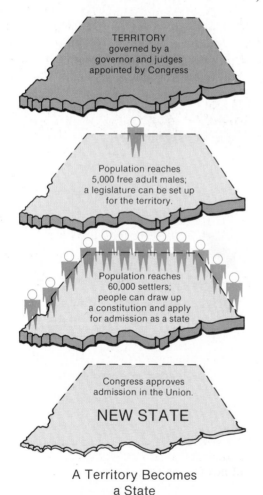

TERRITORY
governed by a
governor and judges
appointed by Congress

Population reaches
5,000 free adult males;
a legislature can be set up
for the territory.

Population reaches
60,000 settlers;
people can draw up
a constitution and apply
for admission as a state

Congress approves
admission in the Union.

NEW STATE

A Territory Becomes
a State

shows that unless there was a natural waterway like a river or lake to form a boundary between states, the boundaries were usually drawn as straight lines. In addition, a flight over land west of the thirteen colonies shows an almost checkerboard arrangement of farms, with the roads running as straight lines with right angle turns. The Land Ordinance of 1785, with its system of surveying western lands, is responsible for both of these features.

The Northwest Ordinance of 1787—A second piece of legislation, the **Northwest Ordinance of 1787,** provided a means for governing these large tracts of western land. Originally, the ordinance applied only to those lands in the Northwest Territory, an area bounded on the east by the original thirteen colonies, on the west by the Mississippi River, on the north by the Great Lakes, and on the south by the Ohio River.

Under this ordinance the land was divided into territories. Each one had a governor to preside over its affairs, three judges to handle the courts and legal matters, and a secretary. All these officers were appointed by Congress, and the people living in the territory had no voice in their government.

When the population of any territory reached 5,000 adult white free males of voting age, however, that region could elect its own territorial legislature, but Congress would still select its governor. This governor, like governors in colonial days, had the power to approve or veto acts of the legislature.

When the population in a territory grew to 60,000, the people could write a constitution and submit it to Congress. If they submitted a constitution that guaranteed a republican form of government, they could

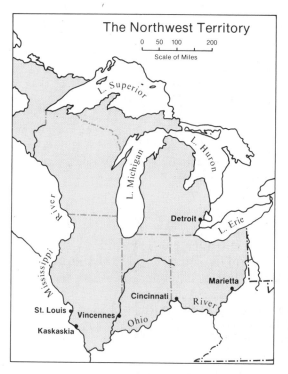

The Northwest Territory

0   50   100   200
Scale of Miles

L. Superior

L. Michigan

L. Huron

L. Erie

Detroit

Mississippi River

Marietta

Cincinnati

Ohio River

St. Louis

Vincennes

Kaskaskia

The legislation was wise. It allowed new states to come into the Union on an equal footing with the old. Instead of becoming an empire controlled by the original states, the United States became one growing republic with the new states gaining a full representation in the government. As a result the legislation helped unite the nation and did more to further the ideals of the union than any other political document except the Constitution.

Other Helps for the Nation—The Confederation Congress also set other important examples for future government. For example, it published its proceedings, an official record of what was done in the Congress. Started as monthly publications, these journals developed into today's *Congressional Record.* Congress also used the decimal system for the money it coined. This system, based on tens and hundreds, is the basis of the money system Americans use today.

be accepted as a state. Each new state would have the same powers and rights as the old states.

The Northwest Ordinance allowed Congress to accept no fewer than three and no more than five states from these western lands. A look at the map shows that five entire states and part of a sixth (Minnesota) came out of the Northwest Territory.

The Northwest Ordinance also included what one historian called "a mini-bill of rights." For example, this legislation guaranteed freedom of religion. Perhaps the most surprising point was that the ordinance forbade slavery in the Northwest Territory, thereby making the Ohio River the dividing line between slave states and free states.

Section Review

1. What two groups were responsible for governing the colonies before and during the Revolutionary War?
2. What convinced the leaders of the need for a more permanent form of government?
3. Who wrote much of the Articles of Confederation?
4. What roadblock held up the states' ratification of the Articles of Confederation?
5. What did the Ordinance of 1785 provide for western lands?
6. What did the Ordinance of 1787 provide for western lands?
7. What steps did a region go through as it moved toward statehood?

B. Weaknesses of Confederation

The Confederation Congress had not only several notable accomplishments but also a few failures. However, most of these failures resulted from the weaknesses in the Articles of Confederation themselves, not from what Congress did or did not do.

Organizational Weakness

The primary organizational weakness of the Articles was that the Confederation Congress did not have any power to enforce the laws that it made. There were no executive or judicial branches to enforce or interpret the laws, allowing the national government's decrees to be ignored or disobeyed with little chance of punishment.

Economic Weaknesses

There were serious economic weaknesses as well. For example, Congress could not levy taxes. The Confederation Congress could, and did, ask the states for help. However, the states seldom complied. Because Congress lacked the power to tax, it lacked the necessary funds to run the government and to pay war debts. This meant that debts owed to soldiers, to foreign nations, and to those who had bought war bonds, all went unpaid.

Congress also lacked the power to regulate domestic and foreign trade. France eagerly waited to pick up the foreign trade the British had lost, while the states argued over whether they should tax one another's imports.

In addition, Congress did not have the sole authority to coin money or to regulate its value. Gold and silver, needed for coinage or to back the paper money in circulation, were scarce. As a result, states printed paper money with so little backing

that it was almost worthless. When this money was not accepted by creditors, people who owed debts couldn't repay them. In some places creditors got control of state legislatures and levied heavy taxes to pay off state debts. When the small farmers could not pay the taxes, the courts moved in and took their property.

Poor Foreign Relations

A lack of respect for the political power of the new government produced more problems for the Confederation Congress both at home and overseas.

Problems with Britain—Although the Treaty of Paris, signed in 1783, called for all British troops in the colonies to return to England, the British kept their troops in western forts that they had held before the war. The British reasoned that since Americans could not pay the debts they owed British subjects, Britain would continue her fur trade in America as a way to collect the money owed. Moreover, since no American army was available to dislodge the troops, Britain saw no real need to call them home.

The Treaty of Paris had also required the fair treatment of Loyalists. Many Americans, however, were still bitter toward those who had supported Britain, and they did

Six dollar Continental note issued by the United Colonies

not treat them well despite the provisions of the treaty. The patriots sometimes kept Loyalist property and even lynched some Loyalists. The British government was justifiably annoyed.

In addition, before the war American shipping enjoyed the protection of a strong British navy because America was a part of the British Empire. Now the British navy was stopping American ships, especially those who still used old British trading routes. Since the American navy was small, it could not rescue these ships. The only option was to find new trade routes where the British did not operate. On their own, however, American ships had little protection from pirates. This was particularly true in the Mediterranean, where the Barbary pirates thrived by preying on unprotected shipping and by forcing the payment of tribute (money paid to protect the ships from harassment as they passed by). Such treatment was an insult to the United States because it implied that the country was too weak to protect itself.

Problems with France and the Netherlands—Since France had been an ally during the war, the United States continued to court her friendship. But with the states' failure to supply the money requested by the Congress, the United States could not pay even the interest owed on its debt to France. When Americans turned to France for more loans, they were refused. As a result, French merchants who thought they would gain from the decline in America's trade with the British were disappointed.

The United States also owed the Netherlands, which had given financial aid to the war effort. Although the Dutch pursued claims with less vigor than others, the debt did not decrease through silence.

Problems with Spain—Relations with Spain had been uneasy for years. Although Spain fought against Britain in the war, she could hardly be labeled a close ally. Spain still held land in North America, and it now eyed the new nation nervously. Because American expansion into the Southeast was a direct threat to Spanish holdings along the Mississippi River and in Florida, Spain retained its forts in the Southeast. Spain easily convinced the local Indians that the Americans would deprive them of their lands and urged them to raid American frontier settlements. Spain hoped these raids would discourage further American settlement so that it could keep the land.

Another dispute with Spain involved American use of ports on the lower Mississippi for exporting. American flatboats floated down the rivers to New Orleans regularly. The Americans expected to have the **right of deposit,** the freedom to stockpile goods until ships came to transport them overseas, but Spain wanted to deny them that privilege. Congress gave its experienced treaty maker, **John Jay,** the task

John Jay

of working out the problem. But the Spanish minister had been told not to yield on the right of deposit. The resulting treaty pleased no one, and Congress did not *ratify* (approve) it. Americans retained the right of deposit, but they paid dearly for it with high **tariffs** (charges on imported goods).

Spain also disputed the placement of America's southern boundary. The Americans drew the boundary at the 31st parallel; Spain placed it one hundred miles farther north. Disputes with Spain flared until 1795, when the Pinckney Treaty officially settled them.

Lack of Respect

The Confederation Congress had not gained much respect at home either. In the summer of 1786, discontent rose markedly among the farmers of western Massachusetts. The pledge of the Massachusetts Assembly to repay war debts meant levying heavy taxes on the state's citizens to raise the funds. Since crop prices at the time were low, the tax burden was heavier than many farmers could bear. Some fell behind on their taxes; others were forced into bankruptcy. A state law also required that business transactions, even small ones, be recorded by the courts and an appropriate fee paid to the court official for his efforts.

By late summer farmers in four western counties had organized angry mobs that kept the county courts from convening. Despite the state's efforts to lift the tax burden, the mobs continued to show the same spirit they had shown in earlier years against the redcoats. **Daniel Shays,** a veteran officer of the Continental Army, led the mob. As the news of their movement spread eastward, citizens feared that the government would be thrown into turmoil, and many began to panic. The state's governor raised a militia to subdue Shays, who by this time had marched his men toward Springfield, where a federal arsenal (a storage place for weapons) was located. Instead of taxing the people to pay for the militia, rich Bostonians gave to what might be termed a "fright fund." Shays' mob of twelve hundred met the state troops in January, 1787. One volley of shots dispersed the rebels, and there was no property damage or loss of life.

Recognition of Weaknesses

Nevertheless, **Shays' Rebellion** underscored the weakness of the Confederation. When George Washington heard of it, he was "mortified beyond expression," for he believed it made the young nation look "more contemptible" than ever. Congress voted to call a convention to create a government better able to cope with such difficulties. The result was the **Philadelphia Convention**—a meeting that would settle the question of what kind of government America should have.

The government of the United States under the Articles of Confederation was in severe trouble. Something had to be done to strengthen it, and most of America's leaders recognized the need. Their concern would lead to the Philadelphia Convention and a new Constitution. Before this action came, several other meetings laid the groundwork for the Philadelphia Convention.

Preparation for Change—The first important step leading to change came in 1785, when delegates from Maryland and Virginia met at Mount Vernon (George Washington's home). They met regarding the use and navigation of the Potomac River and Chesapeake Bay. Encouraged by their success, they issued an invitation to

When the Philadelphia Convention opened, however, scarcely a dozen men had arrived. Eleven uneasy days went by until finally the delegates from seven states, a bare majority, showed up, and the meeting was convened on May 25.

Eventually fifty-five delegates attended the meeting, coming from twelve states. Only Rhode Island failed to send representatives. The meeting was held in Independence Hall, the same building in which the Declaration of Independence had been signed. George

Pennsylvania and Delaware to join them. They hoped to discuss tariffs on imports, the use of paper money, and other common commercial problems. Some Virginia legislators who were more open to a stronger union seized the opportunity and called for a meeting of all the states to be held at Annapolis in September 1786.

Because only five states showed up, the **Annapolis Convention** did not resolve any commercial disputes as its leaders had hoped. Yet with a vision of a better union that went beyond the moment, three delegates—New York's Alexander Hamilton, Virginia's James Madison, and Delaware's John Dickinson—persuaded the others to ask the Confederation Congress for a convention of the states to be held on May 14, 1787 in Philadelphia. The purpose of the Philadelphia convention would be to revise the Articles of Confederation so that the national government would be strong enough to govern the country.

Left: *Mann's Tavern in Annapolis, Maryland, site of the Annapolis Convention*
Right: *Independence Hall in Philadelphia*

Washington, already respected because of his leadership during the war, was elected convention chairman. The delegates wisely decided to keep their discussions secret. This gave them the freedom to speak their minds, and also to change them, without fear of public criticism. It also helped avoid the pressures of special-interest groups whose members might have besieged the delegates had they been aware that important matters were being discussed. The secrecy also made it more likely that the states could ratify the document when it was presented to them, for had the people been aware that the delegates had not been in unanimous agreement on the content, their faith in the resulting Constitution might have been shaken.

Top: *James Madison*
Bottom: *The interior of Independence Hall, where the Constitutional Convention was held*

Men Who Brought Change—God in his wisdom brought the right men to Philadelphia at the right time. Rarely in American history has such a talented, brilliant group of men been assembled in one place. Major William Pierce, a delegate from Georgia, called it "the wisest council in the world" and believed he was greatly privileged to be able to serve with men of such outstanding ability. Proverbs 15:22 reminds us, "Without counsel purposes are disappointed: but in the multitude of counsellors they are established."

George Washington led the Virginia delegation. Some have said that his presence at Philadelphia made the convention a success. As chairman he provided the control and balance necessary. His colleague, **James Madison,** who is called "America's first political scientist," was the single most influential member of the convention and he has often been called the "father of the Constitution." Madison, a lawyer by profession but also a keen student of government, kept a diary of the proceedings that is the most accurate source of information about the event. Still another Virginia delegate, George Mason, had written the constitution and bill of rights for Virginia. The preamble of that bill had served as a model for the preamble of the Declaration of Independence.

The leader of the Pennsylvania delegation was the philosopher-scientist **Benjamin Franklin.** At age eighty-two, he was the oldest delegate and his sense of humor helped relieve tension. One of Franklin's Pennsylvania colleagues was James Wilson. Major William Pierce wrote of him, "Government seems to have been his peculiar study; all the political institutions of the world he knows in detail, and can trace the causes and effects of every revolution from the earliest stages . . . down to the present time." Wilson's broad knowledge of history and government made him a great asset to the convention. A third noteworthy Pennsylvanian was Gouverneur Morris. He was a captivating speaker and persuasive debater. His gifts as a writer gave the Constitution much of its literary grace.

Alexander Hamilton led New York's delegation. Hamilton favored a strong central government, "one," he said, "that could stand like a Hercules." He believed that the states should have little power and that the national leader should appoint the governor for each state.

The youngest delegate, twenty-six-year-old Jonathan Dayton from New Jersey, later became a proprietor of the Ohio Land

Alexander Hamilton

Companies. Today the city of Dayton, Ohio, bears his name.

Some of the men who were key leaders during the War for Independence were absent from the convention. Thomas Jefferson was serving as minister to France, while John Adams was minister to Great Britain. Thomas Paine was in England seeking to interest the British in his design for iron bridges, and Samuel Adams had not been selected for his state's delegation. Well-known patriot leaders John Hancock and Patrick Henry had not been selected either. Some stayed away because they believed the convention had become an upper-class conservative effort. The more "radical" elements from the war years were less welcome as ideas had mellowed.

Section Review

1. What was the organizational weakness that caused most of the failures of the Confederation Congress?
2. What was to be the source of income to run the government under the Articles of Confederation? What was the result of the Congress's insufficient income?
3. Why were Massachusetts farmers not satisfied with the taxation process in 1786? What was the result?
4. What two meetings prepared the way for the Philadelphia Convention?
5. When did the convention in Philadelphia begin? Where was it held? Who was the chairman? What was its original purpose?
6. For what two reasons did members of the convention decide to keep their discussions secret?
7. Name six notable men who were at the convention.

C. Stepping Beyond a Confederation

The men who met at Philadelphia soon realized that the Articles of Confederation could not be changed to make an effective government. Edmund Randolph suggested that what was needed was the creation of a completely new plan of government. The others agreed, and they set about to devise a new government for the United States by writing its Constitution.

Points of Agreement

As the process of writing the Constitution got underway, there were several items on which the delegates agreed. They agreed that a stronger central government was needed. They reasoned that a stronger federal government could be given the power to handle certain matters while allowing state and local governments to solve those problems affecting only their citizens. Thus there would be a division of powers to limit the power of the federal government.

They also agreed that the government established would be a **republic.** In a republic, elected representatives govern the people. The power of these representatives, as well as that of the government as a whole, is limited by the Constitution. (Many people mistakenly refer to the United States government as a democracy, which is rule by the people directly.)

The writers believed in the separation of powers, that no branch or level of government should have all the power. They had learned this principle while suffering under the tyrannical rule of Parliament and the king. Most of the delegates also knew of *Spirit of the Laws,* a work written by the French philosopher Montesquieu (MON

Why Not a Democracy?

Why did the leaders who wrote the Constitution choose to form a republic rather than a democracy? They had learned from their many experiences in colonial, revolutionary, and confederation days that what the people wanted could change and that their wants could be easily manipulated. The writers did not want the wishes of small groups to be overrun by the changing attitudes of the majority. In other words, they did not want a government based on mob rule. Thus they specified in the Constitution what each branch of the government could and could not do. These men knew that in a true democracy the rules for governing could change whenever the wishes of the majority changed. But in a republic the rules could be changed only by changing the Constitution. Consequently these early leaders concluded that a republican form of government would best insure the freedoms of all the American people. The republican form of government they developed was different from all the forms of government tried before. Their new American republic, however, would become a model for many governments that followed.

tuh SKYOO). In his book Montesquieu outlined three branches of government: the executive, legislative, and judicial. Each of these branches had specific functions.

As Montesquieu had also suggested, these men desired a balance of power. They wanted each branch of government to have powers that would balance and control the powers delegated to the other branches. In this way no one branch of government could become more powerful than the others.

As had been evident in the Declaration of Independence, these men wanted to preserve the rights of the individual and his property. And finally, the delegates realized that in order to produce a document acceptable to all the states, compromises would be necessary. The convention members adopted so many compromises in writing the Constitution that it has sometimes been called "a bundle of compromises." Yet even with its compromises, William Gladstone, a prime minister of Britain in the nineteenth century, deemed it "the most wonderful work ever struck off at a given time by the brain and purpose of man." As Christians we realize that the Constitution was no accident.

Convention Compromises

The disputes at Philadelphia involved two groups. First, the large and small states disagreed about the number of votes each state should have in Congress. Second, the northern and southern states argued over slavery and commerce.

The Great Compromise—Two different plans were submitted in an effort to solve the controversy over voting and representation. Edmund Randolph, a delegate from Virginia, submitted Madison's **Virginia Plan** (also called the Large State Plan). According to this plan, the new government would have two legislative houses with membership in both of them based on a state's population.

Meanwhile, the small state of New Jersey proposed a plan written by William Paterson. (It became known as the **New Jersey Plan** or the Small State Plan.) This plan advocated one legislative house with all the states having the same number of representatives.

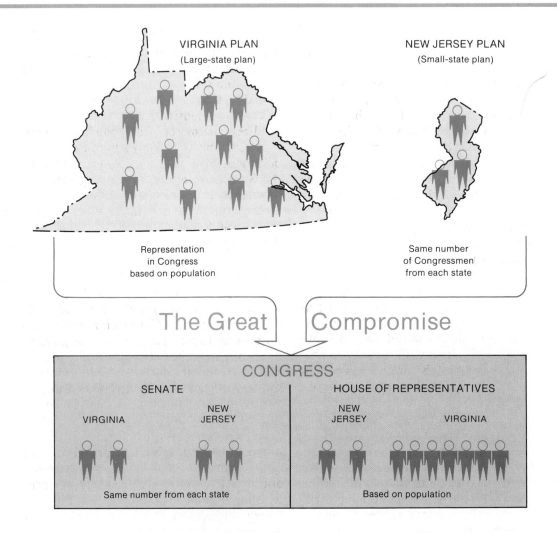

VIRGINIA PLAN
(Large-state plan)

NEW JERSEY PLAN
(Small-state plan)

Representation
in Congress
based on population

Same number
of Congressmen
from each state

The Great Compromise

CONGRESS

SENATE

VIRGINIA

NEW
JERSEY

Same number from each state

HOUSE OF REPRESENTATIVES

NEW
JERSEY

VIRGINIA

Based on population

During the debate, Roger Sherman of Connecticut proposed the **Great Compromise** (or Connecticut Compromise). The compromise provided for two legislative assemblies. In the upper house, called the Senate, all states would be equally represented, with two senators per state. In this way the power of the small states would be preserved. In the lower house, called the House of Representatives, representation would be based on population. The larger the population of a state, the larger would be its representation. This part of the compromise favored the large states. Every ten years the federal government would determine the population of the states by taking a **census,** a count of the population. The people would elect the members of the lower house, while the state legislatures would elect the senators.

The Three-Fifths Compromise—The differences over slavery revolved around how the slaves should be counted for taxation and representation. Since a state's taxes were levied according to population, if the census included the slaves, the South's tax burden would be heavy. The North, of course, was not upset by this prospect. On the other hand, when figuring the number of representatives each state would have, the South, by counting the slaves, could have a greater influence than the North in the House of Representatives.

The matter was settled through the **three-fifths compromise.** A slave would be counted as three-fifths of a free person in figuring both taxes due and the number of representatives. Unfortunately, the compromise also included a promise that for twenty years Congress would make no laws interfering with slavery. But many people believed slavery was becoming less profitable, and many hoped that it would die out by itself. Therefore, the delegates agreed to the three-fifths compromise, believing it to be only a temporary measure.

The Commerce Compromise—The commerce disputes centered on whether the nation needed to pass navigation and tariff laws. The northern states wanted Congress to pass such laws to protect their industries from foreign competition. The South, on the other hand, had few factories and produced mostly raw materials. Hence Southerners believed that navigation and tariff laws would lead to higher prices on goods the South needed to buy. Southerners reasoned that countries would have less money to buy the South's raw materials if tariffs made it more difficult for those countries to sell their products in the United States.

Consequently, the South wanted to require a two-thirds vote to pass navigation laws or tariffs. Since the southern states totaled five of the thirteen, they figured that they would be able to block any laws that would be to their disadvantage.

The Commerce Compromise favored the North by allowing navigation laws to be passed by a simple majority. It favored the South by forever forbidding states to levy taxes on one another's exports. This insured the development of a large home market and made the United States less dependent on foreign trade.

Ratifying the Constitution

Instead of amending the Articles of Confederation, the men at the Philadelphia or "Constitutional" Convention had drawn up a remarkable new plan for the government of the United States. On September 17, 1787, the delegates gathered for their last session and signed the Constitution. (Because the Constitution was signed on this day, it has been called Constitution Day.) The delegates then returned to their home states with a big job, promoting the new Constitution so that the states would approve it. Three of the delegates—George Mason, Edmund Randolph, and Elbridge Gerry—refused to sign the Constitution because they wanted a Bill of Rights to be added first.

Those who favored the adoption of the Constitution were called **Federalists.** They persuaded their states to ratify through a series of newspaper essays, the *The Federalist Papers.* Written by Alexander Hamilton, John Jay, and James Madison, this collection of essays stated the most common objections to the Constitution and then systematically refuted them.

Roger Sherman:
Big Man from a Small State

It was Roger Sherman of Connecticut who seconded a motion by Franklin for prayer as they began the Philadelphia Convention. The second oldest delegate at the convention, the tall, lean, brown-eyed man had an outstanding reputation. John Adams spoke of him as "that old Puritan, honest as an angel." Jefferson told a visitor to the Congress, "That is Mr. Sherman of Connecticut, who never said a foolish thing in his life." Sherman had learned the lesson of Proverbs 29:11—"A fool uttereth all his mind: but a wise man keepeth it in till afterwards."

Born in Massachusetts, Sherman was apprenticed to his father, a shoemaker and farmer, as a youth. Although his formal education was only that given by the grammar schools, Sherman acquired a love of books. Patrons of his shoe shop said there was always a book lying on the cobbler's bench. He showed special interest in mathematics, law, and politics. His most enduring interest, however, was the Bible, and

he read it constantly. He had a deep interest in theology and studied the works of Richard Baxter, an important Puritan writer. Cautious in making big decisions, Sherman did not join the Congregational Church until he was twenty-one. From that time on he was active in church work and served many years as a deacon.

After his father's death, Sherman left Stoughton, Massachusetts, and walked about two hundred miles to New Milford, Connecticut, carrying his tools on his back. He had learned surveying and hoped to make that his living, but it took several years before he prospered. He joined his brother in a country store and continued to run it after his brother's death. He gathered information and published a series of almanacs. Sherman pursued his study of law and was admitted to practice in 1754. He was elected to local offices, including town clerk, mayor, and superior court judge. He was also elected to the legislature and later to Connecticut's upper house.

After moving to New Haven, Connecticut, he became actively involved in the affairs of Yale University, including giving and raising money for the Yale University Chapel. The War for Independence next demanded his time. Although he had monetary reasons for supporting the war, his biggest concern was a religious one: he believed that if the British won, his church would have to submit to Anglican bishops.

He represented Connecticut in the Continental Congresses, was on the committee of five who drafted the Declaration of Independence, and was selected for the committee on the Articles of Confederation. Although his ideas for the articles were commendable, few were accepted. This was probably because he pushed for a strong currency system, for Congress to have the power to tax, and for a supreme court. Although these ideas were unpopular at the time, all were included in the United States Constitution some ten years later.

In 1787 he went to the Philadelphia Convention "disposed to patch up the old scheme of government." But soon he too saw the need for an entirely new system. Although he favored a strong national government, he was the leading member of the compromise group. On June 11 it was he who introduced the famous Connecticut Compromise. Sherman signed the Constitution and the other two great documents of America's early history: the Declaration of Independence (1776) and the Articles of Confederation (1777).

He returned to Connecticut and there led the campaign to have the new Constitution ratified. In the new government he served first in the House and then in the Senate. Sherman died

on July 23, 1793. Because of the years of service he had given his state and nation, sometimes with little or no pay, Sherman never gained much worldly wealth. Historian Clinton Rossiter, in judging the wealth of the delegates, listed Sherman as a man "of very modest means" and among the three poorest delegates. But to Sherman, honest devotion to God-given duty was more important than any material gain. His epitaph aptly described him as "a man of approved integrity; a cool, discerning judge; a prudent sagacious [wise] statesman; a true, faithful, and firm patriot."

A number of American leaders opposed the Constitution because they believed it would rob the states of their power. These people worked against ratification and were called **Anti-Federalists.**

Nine states were required to accept the Constitution before it could be approved. New Hampshire became the ninth state to ratify, in July 1788. Although the large states, New York and Virginia, had not ratified by this time, they did so before the new government met.

Elections for the new republic were held early in 1789. In January the **electoral college,** the system established by the Constitution to elect the president, unanimously named George Washington as president and John Adams as vice president. Not long after, the new Congress passed the **Bill of Rights,** a specific listing of the personal and civil rights and freedoms of every citizen. The Bill of Rights became the first ten amendments to the Constitution, and it went into effect on December 15, 1791.

Among other freedoms, the Bill of Rights has given Americans a freedom to worship God and to preach the gospel. As Christians we should be very thankful that the writers of the Constitution wisely added these amendments.

Section Review

1. What is a republic?
2. What two principles of government were suggested by Montesquieu?
3. What was the difference between the Virginia Plan and the New Jersey Plan?
4. Who proposed the Great Compromise and what was his proposition?
5. What was the three-fifths compromise?
6. Why did the North and the South have different views on navigation and tariff laws?
7. Who were the Federalists? Who wrote the *The Federalist Papers,* and what did they contain?
8. Who were the Anti-Federalists, and why did they take this position?

Gilbert Stuart's famous "unfinished portrait" of George Washington

Summary

With independence declared and a war to maintain that independence in progress, the new country needed a plan of government. The Articles of Confederation served to unite the states in a loose confederation. Unfortunately, the national government under this plan was kept weaker than the state governments. With no power to enforce its laws and no taxes to finance the nation's debts and operations, the Confederation government was doomed. Finally, the nation's leading statesmen met at Philadelphia in 1787. They realized the articles could not be revised satisfactorily, and so they drew up a new plan of government for the country. That plan was the United States Constitution.

Chapter Review

Do You Remember?

■ Fill in the blanks with the appropriate words or phrases.

After the United States declared its independence, its leaders drew up a new plan of government called the __(1)__. Although the plan was used for several years, it kept the national government very weak. To strengthen the government, a convention was organized in 1787 in the city of __(2)__. There leaders decided to abandon the old plan and to write a new __(3)__. This new plan was written and presented to the states for ratification. Those who supported it were called __(4)__. Some Americans refused to accept it until certain freedoms were guaranteed by a __(5)__ . The first ten amendments were added to satisfy this need.

■ Match the following terms to what they did.

6. Annapolis Convention
7. electoral college
8. *Federalist Papers*
9. Northwest Ordinance of 1785
10. Northwest Ordinance of 1787
11. Spain
12. Virginia Plan

a. established the method for territories to become states
b. wanted to deny right of deposit
c. divided lands into townships
d. prepared for the Constitutional Convention
e. favored large states with representation based on population
f. tried to encourage adoption of the Constitution
g. elected the new president

■ Answer these.

13. What are charges or taxes paid on imported goods called?
14. A delegate from which state devised the Small State Plan?
15. What is an official count of the population called?
16. What three men composed the *Federalist Papers?*
17. Who was the oldest delegate at the Constitutional Convention?
18. What kind of government did the Constitution give the United States—a democracy or a republic?

Why Is It So?

1. Why did the United States need a plan of government in 1776?
2. In what ways was the Confederation Congress weak?
3. How did the Great Compromise come about?
4. Why did the Anti-Federalists oppose the Constitution?

What Do You Think?

1. How would the Confederation government have been different if the Congress had had the power to tax?
2. Why was the Shays' Rebellion in Massachusetts a disgrace for the United States government?

8

The Constitution of the United States

The two most important documents in American history are the Declaration of Independence and the Constitution with its Bill of Rights. The Declaration of Independence stated that the United States would no longer be under British rule and affirmed the rights and universal principles of justice on which the new republic would be built. The Constitution put these principles into practice and is the written law by which the United States has been governed ever since.

A. America's Amazing Document

The United States Constitution is now more than two hundred years old. No other nation's constitution has lasted as long. Nearly two-thirds of the approximately one hundred and sixty national constitutions in the world have been adopted or revised since

1970 alone. Only fourteen were written before World War II. While Norway's 1814 constitution is the second oldest constitution in continual use, it has not had the influence outside its own borders that America's Constitution has had. One law professor said, "The United States Constitution is this nation's most important export." The constitutions of many other nations have been modeled after it. The Constitution is remarkable not only because it has lasted but also because it has worked so well with so few changes. Although others have copied its ideas, few have been able to make the principles work so effectively.

Reasons for Its Success

One reason that the Constitution has been successful is that its writers included some Biblical principles and practices. Even though their debt to Scripture may not have been known to them or may not even have been intended in every case, they saw from experience which principles worked. Bible principles work and make life operate more smoothly even for unbelievers.

A second reason for success was that Americans put forth much patient effort to make the Constitution work. They decided to abide by its laws and follow its precepts. When certain parts of the Constitution did not seem to work as planned because they were flawed or circumstances outdated them, Americans did not throw out the document and revolt. They modified the document through a formal amendment process. If America's form of government is to continue, it is essential that the laws be respected and followed. Disrespect for authority and government undermines any form of government.

A third reason for the success of the Constitution is that while it outlines broad principles and some specifics, it has also been flexible enough to deal with changing times. The Constitution is a living, working document. In the past two hundred years, there have been only twenty-six times that the Constitution was amended. Ten of the amendments were passed as the Bill of Rights in 1791, so there have been only sixteen changes since that date. Of course, some changes in the interpretation of the Constitution have also been made through court decisions.

Principles in the Constitution

It is important, as our study of this document begins, to recognize some of the principles that the writers used to form it. Because these ideas are important and are seen throughout the document, not just in one specific item, they will be listed and described here. But as you read the Constitution, you will want to note where they appear and how they are applied.

Written Law—Under the Constitution, rule is by written law. The powers of government leaders cannot be changed by their own desires. The Constitution has limited those powers, establishing what government may and may not do. Thus the Constitution gives the United States a limited government that may not step beyond the powers given to it. The only ways the written law of the Constitution can be changed are by amendment or by a change in interpretation by the courts. Because these changes are somewhat difficult to bring about, major changes in constitutional law are rare.

The written law of the Constitution helps to protect Americans from the rise of cruel dictators as well as from unconstitutional governmental action. This protection depends, however, on the constitutional knowledge of American citizens. If Americans are unaware of the limitations of government, they may unknowingly allow the government to overstep them. This thought should motivate us to study the Constitution carefully.

Separation of Powers—As we learned in Chapter 7 (p. 122), the powers that government does have are divided among three branches: the executive, legislative, and judicial. With this **separation of powers,** no one branch has too much power. Congress, which is the legislative branch, makes the laws. The executive branch, led by the president, is responsible for enforcing the laws. And the courts of the judicial branch interpret the laws as they apply them to specific cases. These are the major, separate responsibilities of the three branches of government.

Checks and Balances—There is also a system of **checks and balances** that keeps each of the three branches of government

LEGISLATIVE BRANCH   EXECUTIVE BRANCH   JUDICIAL BRANCH
(The Courts)

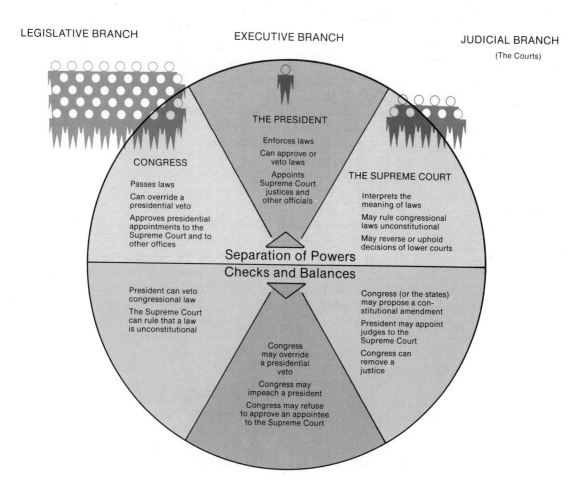

THE PRESIDENT
Enforces laws
Can approve or veto laws
Appoints Supreme Court justices and other officials

CONGRESS
Passes laws
Can override a presidential veto
Approves presidential appointments to the Supreme Court and to other offices

THE SUPREME COURT
Interprets the meaning of laws
May rule congressional laws unconstitutional
May reverse or uphold decisions of lower courts

Separation of Powers
Checks and Balances

President can veto congressional law
The Supreme Court can rule that a law is unconstitutional

Congress may override a presidential veto
Congress may impeach a president
Congress may refuse to approve an appointee to the Supreme Court

Congress (or the states) may propose a constitutional amendment
President may appoint judges to the Supreme Court
Congress can remove a justice

from going beyond its powers. Each branch has been given one or more powers that limit or check the powers of the other two branches. Such a safeguard is useful because government leaders may be tempted to take added powers for their own selfish purposes. These checks, however, keep the powers of each of the branches balanced or in proportion to those of the other branches.

A Federal System—Under the Articles of Confederation, the states operated almost as though they were independent nations. The government allowed them to keep most powers for themselves, while the Confederation Congress had only a few powers. The Constitution sought to strengthen the power of the national government, but it did not intend to take away all the powers of the states. To do this, the Constitution established a **federal system** that divided the powers of government between those given to the national government and those reserved for the states.

Under a federal system the duties and powers of government are assigned to the level of government best equipped to handle them. No single level has total power. Under the federal Constitution, the national government is given powers over things of importance to the whole nation. For example, waging war and providing for the common defense involve the whole nation and are powers given to the national government. Other powers, such as many of those relating to health, safety, education, most election regulations, and punishment for most crimes, are left to the state and local governments. You would not call the White House, for example, to report a stolen bicycle.

The system of national, state, and local government, each with its own powers, is called a federal system. However, you should not be confused if you hear the term used in another way. The national government in Washington, D.C., is often called the federal government, and things that are related to the national government are also described as "federal." Federal employees, federal regulations, and federal agencies are some examples.

A Republic

When Benjamin Franklin left the final meeting of the convention, someone asked him, "What have you given us?"

He answered simply, "A republic, if you can keep it."

The old statesman knew that the ideas of the Constitution were good, but it would be up to the American people to make them work. Although the ideas of the Constitution have proved to be sound for over two hundred years, it still remains the responsibility of the American people to continue to make them work.

Section Review

1. What two documents are the most important in American history?
2. What is meant by the statement: "The United States Constitution is the nation's most important export"?
3. What are the two ways of making changes in the Constitution?
4. Why is it important that the Constitution is written law?
5. What keeps one branch of government from getting too much power?
6. What system divides the powers of government between the national government and the state governments?

THE CONSTITUTION OF THE UNITED STATES

Preamble

We the people of the United States, in order to form a more perfect union, establish justice, ensure domestic tranquillity, provide for the common defense, promote the general welfare, and secure the blessings of liberty to ourselves and our posterity, do ordain and establish this Constitution for the United States of America.

The **Preamble** introduces the Constitution. First it states the source of government's power: "We the people." Second, the Preamble lays out six purposes of government: (1) to form a more perfect union (a workable united government), (2) to establish justice (fairness), (3) to insure domestic tranquillity (keep peace within the nation), (4) to provide for the common defense (protect from enemies), (5) to promote the general welfare (benefit the people), and (6) to secure the blessings of liberty . . . to our posterity (the generations that follow us).

Article I: The Legislative Branch

Section 1. All legislative powers herein granted shall be vested in a Congress of the United States, which shall consist of a Senate and House of Representatives.

Article 1 deals with the legislative branch of government, whose primary function is to make laws. This power belongs to Congress, which has two houses, an upper house called the Senate and a lower house called the House of Representatives. A two-house legislative system is called a **bicameral system.**

Section 2. The House of Representatives shall be composed of members chosen every second year by the people of the several states, and the electors in each state shall have the qualifications requisite for electors of the most numerous branch of the state legislature.

Members of the House are elected every two years and serve two-year terms. The House has always been elected directly by the people.

No person shall be a representative who shall not have attained to the age of twenty-five years, and been seven years a citizen of the United States, and who shall not, when elected, be an inhabitant of that state in which he shall be chosen.

Qualifications: members of the House of Representatives must be (1) at least twenty-five years old, (2) American citizens for at least seven years, (3) residents of the state they represent.

Representatives and direct taxes shall be apportioned among the several states which may be included within this Union, according to their respective numbers, which shall be determined by adding to the whole number of free persons, including those bound to service for a term of years, and excluding Indians not taxed, three-fifths of all other persons. The actual enumeration shall be made within three

The number of representatives each state receives is determined by its population. Also, any direct federal taxation of the states must be distributed according to population. Amendment 16, however, makes the income tax an exception to this rule. Special arrangements were made for counting slaves, indentured servants, and Indians in the population; but these rules no longer apply since the end of slavery and the beginning of Indian citizenship. Today the House membership has been set at 435. A counting of the population, called a census, is taken every ten years to determine how many of these representatives each state receives.

years after the first meeting of the Congress of the United States, and within every subsequent term of ten years, in such manner as they shall by law direct. The number of representatives shall not exceed one for every thirty thousand, but each state shall have at least one representative; and until such enumeration shall be made, the state of New Hampshire shall be entitled to choose three, Massachusetts eight, Rhode Island and Providence Plantations one, Connecticut five, New York six, New Jersey four, Pennsylvania eight, Delaware one, Maryland six, Virginia ten, North Carolina five, South Carolina five, and Georgia three.

When vacancies happen in the representation from any state, the executive authority thereof shall issue writs of election to fill such vacancies.

The House of Representatives shall choose their speaker and other officers; and shall have the sole power of impeachment.

Section 3. The Senate of the United States shall be composed of two senators from each state, chosen by the legislature thereof, for six years; and each senator shall have one vote.

Immediately after they shall be assembled in consequence of the first election, they shall be divided as equally as may be into three classes. The seats of the senators of the first class shall be vacated at the expiration of the second year, of the second class at the expiration of the fourth year, and of the third class at the expiration of the sixth year, so that one-third may be chosen every second year; and if vacancies happen by resignation, or otherwise, during the recess of the legislature of any state, the executive thereof may make temporary appointments until the next meeting of the legislature,

Vacancies are filled by special elections called by the state governors.

The head of the House is called the Speaker of the House; he is elected by the House members. The House has the sole power of **impeachment**— the filing of charges against a major federal official.

Each state has two senators, who serve six-year terms. Originally, state legislatures elected senators. Since the passage of Amendment 17 in 1913, the people have directly elected senators.

One-third of the senators are up for election every two years. By this method, there are always experienced people in the Senate.

which shall then fill such vacancies.

No person shall be a senator who shall not have attained to the age of thirty years, and been nine years a citizen of the United States, and who shall not, when elected, be an inhabitant of that state for which he shall be chosen.

Qualifications: senators must be (1) at least thirty years old, (2) citizens for at least nine years, (3) residents of the state they represent.

The Vice President of the United States shall be President of the Senate, but shall have no vote, unless they be equally divided.

The head (president) of the Senate is the vice president of the United States. He votes only in case of a tie.

The Senate shall choose their other officers, and also a president pro tempore, in the absence of the Vice President, or when he shall exercise the office of President of the United States.

The Senate also elects its own **president pro tempore** (PROH TEM-puh-ree), who serves as leader of the Senate when the vice president is absent.

The Senate shall have the sole power to try all impeachments. When sitting for that purpose, they shall be on oath or affirmation. When the President of the United States is tried, the chief justice shall preside: and no person shall be convicted without the concurrence of two-thirds of the members present.

The Senate acts as a trial court for impeachment cases. Two-thirds of the senators must vote for conviction in order to remove the official from office. If the president is impeached, the chief justice of the Supreme Court presides over the trial rather than the vice president.

Judgment in cases of impeachment shall not extend further than to removal from office, and disqualification to hold and enjoy any office of honor, trust or profit under the United States: but the party convicted shall nevertheless be liable and subject to indictment, trial, judgment and punishment, according to law.

When the House impeaches an official and the Senate tries and confirms the charges, Congress may punish him only by removing him from office and barring him from holding any government offices in the future. Even so, the person can be tried in a regular civil or criminal court afterwards and be sentenced to further punishment if found guilty.

Section 4. The times, places and manner of holding elections, for senators and representatives, shall be prescribed in each state by the legislature thereof; but the Congress may at any time by law make or alter such regulations, except as to the places of choosing senators.

State legislatures have the right to administer congressional elections in their states, but they must follow any regulations established by Congress. For instance, national law requires that secret ballots be used in these elections. Congressional elections are held on the Tuesday following the first Monday in November in even-numbered years.

The Congress shall assemble at least once in every year, and such meeting shall be on the first Monday in December, unless they shall by law appoint a different day.

Congress is to meet at least once a year. Originally it began its meeting on the first Monday in December. Now it first meets at noon on January 3, as the date was changed by the Twentieth Amendment.

Section 5. Each house shall be the judge of the elections, returns and qualifications of its own members, and a majority of each shall constitute a quorum to do business; but a smaller number may adjourn from day to day, and may be authorized to compel the attendance of absent members, in such manner, and under such penalties as each house may provide.

Each house judges its own elections. A *quorum* (KWAWR um) is the minimum number needed to transact business, and a simple majority (just over one-half the members) is a quorum.

Each house may determine the rules of its proceedings, punish its members for disorderly behavior, and, with the concurrence of two-thirds, expel a member.

A disorderly member can be expelled by a two-thirds vote of the body he has served in.

Each house shall keep a journal of its proceedings, and from time to time publish the same, excepting such parts as may, in their judgment, require secrecy; and the yeas and nays of the members of either house on any question shall, at the desire of one-fifth of those present, be entered on the journal.

Each house keeps a journal or record of what it does each day. Today this is called *The Congressional Record.* A written record of the vote is kept if one-fifth of those present request it.

Neither house, during the session of Congress, shall, without the consent of the other, adjourn for more than three days, nor to any other place than that in which the two houses shall be sitting.

Since the houses work together to pass legislation, one cannot adjourn (go out of official session) for more than three days without the permission of the other.

Section 6. The senators and representatives shall receive a compensation for their services, to be ascertained by law, and paid out of the Treasury of the United States. They shall in all cases, except treason, felony and breach of the peace, be privileged from arrest during their attendance at the session of their respective houses, and in going to and returning from the same; and for any speech or debate in either house, they shall not be questioned in any other place.

Senators and representatives are public employees paid salaries by the U.S. Treasury. They cannot be arrested going to or from the House or Senate, nor can they be arrested for what they say on the floor of the House or Senate. This precaution gives congressmen the freedom to voice even unpopular ideas without fear of being arrested to prohibit their participation in Congress.

No senator or representative shall, during the time for which he was elected, be appointed to any civil office under the authority of the United States, which shall have been created, or the emoluments where-

A congressman must give up any other federal offices he holds to become a congressman. He cannot take any federal office created by his house of Congress until his term is ended, and until his term is expired, he cannot take an office for which Congress has increased the pay during his term. This precaution prevents Congress from giving themselves offices with increased salaries.

of shall have been increased during such time; and no person holding any office under the United States, shall be a member of either house during his continuance in office.

Section 7. All bills for raising revenue shall originate in the House of Representatives; but the Senate may propose or concur with amendments as on other bills.

Bills dealing with money must start in the House, but the Senate may make changes if it desires.

Every bill which shall have passed the House of Representatives and the Senate, shall, before it becomes a law, be presented to the President of the United States; if he approves, he shall sign it, but if not, he shall return it with his objections to that house in which it shall have originated, who shall enter the objections at large on their journal, and proceed to reconsider it. If after such reconsideration, two-thirds of that house shall agree to pass the bill, it shall be sent, together with the objections, to the other house, by which it shall likewise be reconsidered, and if approved by two-thirds of that house, it shall become a law. But in all such cases the votes of both houses shall be determined by yeas and nays, and the names of the persons voting for and against the bill shall be entered on the journal of each house respectively. If any bill shall not be returned by the President within ten days (Sundays excepted) after it shall have been presented to him, the same shall be a law, in like manner as if he had signed it, unless the Congress by their adjournment prevent its return, in which case it shall not be a law.

In order for a bill to become a law, it must be passed by both houses and signed by the president. This is a part of the system of checks and balances. If the president opposes the bill, he may return it to the body where it started, stating his objections. This is a **veto.** Congress may override the president's veto with a two-thirds vote of both houses, and the bill becomes law. If the president does not sign a bill that comes to him and does not veto it, it becomes law in ten days as long as Congress remains in session. If he does not sign a bill and Congress adjourns within ten days, it is vetoed automatically. This is called a **"pocket veto."**

Every order, resolution, or vote to which the concurrence of the Senate and House of Representatives may be necessary (except on a question of adjournment) shall be presented to the President of the United States; and before the same shall take effect, shall be approved by him, or being disapproved by him, shall be passed by two-thirds

All other acts requiring approval of both houses of Congress (except the decision to adjourn Congress) require the signature of the president or the passing over his veto by a two-thirds vote of both houses.

of the Senate and House of Representatives, according to the rules and limitations prescribed in the case of a bill.

Section 8. The Congress shall have the power to lay and collect taxes, duties, imposts and excises, to pay the debts and provide for the common defense and general welfare of the United States; but all duties, imposts, and excises shall be uniform throughout the United States;

To borrow money on the credit of the United States;

To regulate commerce with foreign nations, and among the several states, and with the Indian tribes;

To establish a uniform rule of naturalization, and uniform laws on the subject of bankruptcies throughout the United States;

To coin money, regulate the value thereof, and of foreign coin, and fix the standard of weights and measures;

To provide for the punishment of counterfeiting the securities and current coin of the United States;

To establish post offices and post roads:

To promote the progress of science and useful arts, by securing for limited times to authors and inventors the exclusive right to their respective writings and discoveries;

To constitute tribunals inferior to the Supreme Court;

These are the enumerated (numbered and listed) powers of Congress; they are specifically stated.
(1) *It has the power to tax.* Congress can lay (impose the amounts or system) and collect taxes, duties (taxes on imports), imposts (taxes on duties), and excises (internal taxes on production, sale, or consumption of certain items such as telephones).

(2) *It has the power to borrow money.* The government usually borrows money by selling *bonds* (certificates that it pledges to repay with interest).

(3) *It has the power to regulate trade with foreign nations, within the country, and with the Indians.* Indians were dealt with as independent nations.

(4) *It has the power to regulate naturalization and bankruptcy laws.* **Naturalization** is the process by which a foreign-born person gains citizenship. **Bankruptcy** is the way a debtor is declared unable to pay his creditors. These laws must be uniform so that it is not easier or harder to gain citizenship or declare bankruptcy in one state than in another.

(5) *It has the power to control the nation's currency and the standard weights and measurements.* These values need to be the same throughout the nation.

(6) *It has the power to punish those who illegally interfere in the currency system.* **Counterfeiting** means making copies of something (often money) and using them illegally.

(7) *It has the power to provide needed offices and roads for the postal service.* Post roads are roads for delivering the mail. They became the basic roads of the U.S. highway system.

(8) *It has the power to issue copyrights and patents.* **Copyrights** protect authors or their heirs from having their works copied by another person. (Today the length of the copyright is the lifetime of the author plus fifty years). **Patents** protect inventors from having their ideas taken by another person for use or profit.

(9) *It has the power to establish federal courts other than the Supreme Court.*

To define and punish piracies and felonies committed on the high seas, and offenses against the law of nations;

(10) It has the power to determine what acts committed at sea are crimes and to commit offenders to federal courts for trial. "Offenses against the law of nations" include piracy, terrorism, and hijacking.

To declare war, grant letters of marque and reprisal, and make rules concerning captures on land and water;

(11) Congress alone has the power to declare war. Letters of marque and reprisal permitted private citizens to outfit vessels to fight in wartime and to capture enemy goods and people. Such permissions are no longer granted.

To raise and support armies, but no appropriation of money to that use shall be for a longer term than two years;

(12) Congress may create an army, but it cannot vote to use money to support the army more than two years ahead of time. The limit of two years helps prevent a takeover or misuse of power by the military.

To provide and maintain a navy;

(13) It has the power to create a navy and to vote for money to support it.

To make rules for the government and regulation of the land and naval forces;

(14) It has the power to make the rules for the armed services.

To provide for calling forth the militia to execute the laws of the Union, suppress insurrections and repel invasions;

(15) It may call the state militias (now the National Guard) into service for the national government under certain conditions.

To provide for organizing, arming and disciplining the militia, and for governing such part of them as may be employed in the service of the United States, reserving to the states respectively, the appointment of the officers, and the authority of training the militia according to the discipline prescribed by Congress:

(16) It has the power to organize, arm, and discipline the militias, while the states appoint the officers and train these troops. When called into national service, however, the militia is under federal control as a part of the armed forces.

To exercise exclusive legislation in all cases whatsoever, over such district (not exceeding ten miles square) as may, by cession of particular states, and the acceptance of Congress, become the seat of the government of the United States, and to exercise like authority over all places purchased by the consent of the legislature of the state in which the same shall be, for the erection of forts, magazines, arsenals, dock yards, and other needful buildings; and

(17) It has the power to make laws for the District of Columbia and for all federal properties such as military installations or bases. This also includes historic sites, national cemeteries, national forests, and parks and fisheries.

To make all laws which shall be necessary and proper for carrying into execution the foregoing powers, and all other powers vested by this Constitution in the government of the United States, or in any department or officer thereof.

This "necessary and proper clause" of the Constitution lets Congress do what it believes is necessary and proper to carry out any listed power. This clause is sometimes also called the **elastic clause.** To borrow money, for example, it can sell bonds and even create a bank. The Supreme Court can check this power by deciding whether the laws Congress passes by this authority are really necessary and proper.

Section 9. The migration or importation of such persons as any of the states now existing shall think proper to admit, shall not be prohibited by the Congress prior to the year 1808, but a tax or duty may be imposed on such importations, not exceeding ten dollars for each person.

Powers Forbidden to the Federal Government:
(1) *Congress could not interfere with slavery until after 1808.* Nor could it tax slavery out of existence by levying heavy taxes on slaves.

The privilege of the writ of habeas corpus shall not be suspended, unless when in cases of rebellion or invasion the public safety may require it.

(2) *Congress may not take away a person's right to the writ of **habeas corpus** except in times of extreme danger.* Habeas corpus, Latin for the first words in the writ, forces authorities to charge a person with a crime if he is held in jail. Because of this right, a person cannot be held prisoner unless a charge of a crime is made against him.

No bill of attainder or ex post facto law shall be passed.

(3) *Congress cannot pass a **bill of attainder,** which permits punishment without a trial, or an **ex post facto law,** which makes a law retroactive.* Acts that were legal when they were done cannot be made illegal afterwards.

No capitation, or other direct tax shall be laid, unless in proportion to the census or enumeration hereinbefore directed to be taken.

(4) *Congress cannot levy a direct tax that is not equal for all citizens.* For example, it could not make Californians pay a special tax of one hundred dollars when people from Ohio have to pay only fifty dollars. Amendment 16 made the income tax an exception.

No tax or duty shall be laid on articles exported from any state.

(5) *Congress cannot tax the exports of the states.* (This means that neither goods exported to other nations nor those exported to other states may be taxed.)

No preference shall be given by any regulation of commerce or revenue to the ports of one state over those of another: nor shall vessels bound to, or from one state, be obliged to enter, clear, or pay duties in another.

(6) *Congress cannot give preference to any port or state through its laws, and it cannot tax trade between the states.*

No money shall be drawn from the treasury, but in consequence of appropriations made by law; and a regular statement and account of the receipts and expenditures of all public money shall be published from time to time.

No title of nobility shall be granted by the United States: and no person holding any office of profit or trust under them, shall, without the consent of the Congress, accept of any present, emolument, office, or title, or any kind whatever, from any king, prince or foreign state.

Section 10. No state shall enter into any treaty, alliance, or confederation; grant letters of marque and reprisal; coin money; emit bills of credit; make anything but gold and silver coin a tender in payment of debts; pass any bill of attainder, ex post facto law, or law impairing the obligation of contracts, or grant any title of nobility.

No state shall, without the consent of the Congress, lay any imposts or duties on imports or exports, except what may be absolutely necessary for executing its inspection laws: and the net produce of all duties and imposts laid by any state on imports or exports, shall be for the use of the treasury of the United States; and all such laws shall be subject to the revision and control of the Congress.

No state shall, without the consent of Congress, lay any duty of tonnage, keep troops, or ships of war in time of peace, enter into any agreement or compact with another state, or with a foreign power, or engage in war, unless actually invaded, or in such imminent danger as will not admit of delay.

(7) *Money from the treasury can be spent only if Congress approves, and a record of income and expenditures must be published.*

(8) *The United States cannot grant titles of nobility (duke, earl, baron, etc.), nor can our citizens accept titles or honors from foreign countries without the permission of Congress.*

Powers Denied to the States:
States are forbidden from doing many of the things the federal government can do. They are also given some of the same prohibitions that the federal government has. By limiting state powers, the Constitution makes the central government stronger and produces a more united government. In addition to the topics already described in Section 9, states are forbidden to keep troops or ships (except a state militia), make alliances with foreign powers, or declare war. However, states may respond to attacks if invaded.

Questions on Article I
1. What is the primary function of the legislative branch?
2. What is a bicameral system?
3. What are the two houses of Congress called?
4. How much older does a senator have to be than a representative?
5. Who is the head of the House? Who selects him?
6. How many senators does each state have? How long are their terms?
7. Who is the head of the Senate? How often does he vote?
8. What function does the Senate play in impeachment? What is the punishment (judgment) for impeachment?
9. When can a pocket veto be used?
10. What federal areas or properties does Congress control?
11. What is another name for the "necessary and proper clause"?
12. What is a writ of *habeas corpus*?
13. In addition to the things forbidden Congress, list four things that states are forbidden to do.

Article II: The Executive Branch

Section 1. The executive power shall be vested in a President of the United States of America. He shall hold his office during the term of four years, and, together with the Vice President, chosen for the same term, be elected as follows.

Each state shall appoint, in such manner as the legislature thereof may direct, a number of electors, equal to the whole number of senators and representatives to which the state may be entitled in the Congress; but no senator or representative, or person holding an office of trust or profit under the United States, shall be appointed an elector.

The electors shall meet in their respective states, and vote by ballot for two persons, of whom one at least shall not be an inhabitant of the same state with themselves. And they shall make a list of all the persons voted for, and of the number of votes for each; which list they shall sign and certify, and transmit sealed to the seat of the government of the United States, directed to the president of the Senate. The president of the Senate shall, in the presence of the Senate and House of Representatives, open all the certificates, and the votes shall then be counted. The person having the greatest number of votes shall be the President, if such number be a majority of the whole number of electors appointed; and if there be more than one who have such majority, and have an equal number of votes, then the House of Representatives shall immediately choose by ballot one of them for President; and if no person have a majority, then from the five highest on the list the said House shall in like manner choose the President. But in choosing the President, the votes shall be taken by states,

Article II deals with the executive branch of government. Its primary function is to carry out the nation's laws. Both the president and vice president serve four-year terms.

The president is still elected by this electoral college. The original design was modified by the Twelfth Amendment in 1804.

The Senate and House of Representatives oversee the counting of the electors' votes. When no candidate receives a majority of the votes, the House of Representatives votes by state to choose the new president.

the representation from each state having one vote; a quorum for this purpose shall consist of a member or members from two-thirds of the states, and a majority of all the states shall be necessary to a choice. In every case, after the choice of the President, the person having the greatest number of votes of the electors shall be the Vice President. But if there should remain two or more who have equal votes, the Senate shall choose from them by ballot the Vice President.

The Congress may determine the time of choosing the electors, and the day on which they shall give their votes; which day shall be the same throughout the United States.

Congress determines the time for the president's election. Election day is the first Tuesday after the first Monday in November.

No person except a natural born citizen, or a citizen of the United States, at the time of the adoption of this Constitution, shall be eligible to the office of President, neither shall any person be eligible to that office who shall not have attained to the age of thirty-five years, and been fourteen years a resident within the United States.

Qualifications: the president must be (1) a natural-born citizen, (2) at least thirty-five years of age, and (3) a resident of the U.S. for at least fourteen years.

In case of the removal of the President from office, or of his death, resignation, or inability to discharge the powers and duties of the said office, the same shall devolve on the Vice President, and the Congress may by law provide for the case of removal, death, resignation, or inability, both of the President and Vice President, declaring what officer shall then act as President, and such officer shall act accordingly, until the disability be removed, or a President shall be elected.

Presidential Succession: In 1948 Congress established the present line of succession: (1) the vice president (as stated in the Constitution), (2) the Speaker of the House of Representatives, (3) the president pro tempore of the Senate, and (4) members of the president's cabinet in order of the creation of their departments. The State and Treasury Departments are the two oldest.

The President shall, at stated times, receive for his services, a compensation, which shall neither be increased nor diminished during the period for which he shall have been elected, and he shall not

The president's salary stays the same throughout his term.

receive within that period any other emolument from the United States, or any of them.

Before he enter on the execution of his office, he shall take the following oath or affirmation:—"I do solemnly swear (or affirm) that I will faithfully execute the office of President of the United States, and will to the best of my ability, preserve, protect and defend the Constitution of the United States."

The president's oath of office is dictated by the Constitution. The word "affirm" is offered because some religious groups object to the use of the word "swear." (See Matt. 5:34.) George Washington added the words "so help me God" to the end of the oath, and that addition has become a tradition.

Section 2. The President shall be commander in chief of the army and navy of the United States, and of the militia of the several states, when called into the actual service of the United States; he may require the opinion, in writing, of the principal officer in each of the executive departments, upon any subject relating to the duties of their respective offices, and he shall have power to grant reprieves and pardons for offenses against the United States, except in cases of impeachment.

Powers and Duties of the President
The phrase "in each of the executive departments" became the basis for the president's cabinet. **Reprieve** means a temporary postponement of punishment; **pardon** means a complete forgiveness of a crime and its consequential punishment.

He shall have power, by and with the advice and consent of the Senate, to make treaties, provided two-thirds of the senators present concur; and he shall nominate, and by and with the advice and consent of the Senate, shall appoint ambassadors, other public ministers and consuls, judges of the Supreme Court, and all other officers of the United States, whose appointments are not herein otherwise provided for, and which shall be established by law: but the Congress may by law vest the appointment of such inferior officers, as they think proper, in the President alone, in the courts of law, or in the heads of departments.

Treaties must be approved by a two-thirds majority of the Senate. The president appoints ambassadors, ministers (usually to foreign countries), consuls, judges, and other officers as allowed by Congress with approval of the Senate.

The President shall have power to fill up all vacancies that may happen during the recess of the Senate, by granting commissions which shall expire at the end of their next session.

The president can fill vacancies in offices without Senate approval if the Senate is out of session.

Section 3. He shall from time to time give to the Congress information of the state of the Union, and recommend to their consideration, such measures as he shall judge necessary and expedient; he may, on extraordinary occasions, convene both houses, or either of them, and in case of disagreement between them, with respect to the time of adjournment, he may adjourn them to such time as he shall think proper; he shall receive ambassadors and other public ministers; he shall take care that the laws be faithfully executed, and shall commission all the officers of the United States.

Section 4. The President, Vice President, and all civil officers of the United States shall be removed from office on impeachment for, and conviction of, treason, bribery, or other high crimes and misdemeanors.

Duties of the President
(1) The information the president gives Congress is called the State of the Union message. It is usually given near the end of January.
(2) The president can suggest that Congress pass certain legislation. He can influence opinion.
(3) He can convene (call into official session) both houses. This has been done to deal with national emergencies.
(4) If the House and Senate cannot agree on adjournment, the president can intervene.
(5) Receiving ambassadors and public ministers is important to the presidential power in foreign affairs. If the president fails to recognize diplomats of a certain country, it may mean the United States is about to declare war.

The Process of Impeachment
The president can be impeached—have charges filed against him with the intention of removing him from office—for treason (aiding an enemy), bribery (giving or accepting money, gifts, or favors illegally), high crimes (felonies such as murder and arson), or misdemeanors (lesser misdeeds).

Questions on Article II
1. What is the primary function of the executive branch?
2. How long does the president serve?
3. What are the qualifications of the president of the United States?
4. Concerning treaties and appointments, what check does the Senate have on the president?

Article III: The Judicial Branch

Section 1. The judicial power of the United States shall be vested in one Supreme Court, and in such inferior courts as the Congress may from time to time ordain and establish. The judges, both of the Supreme and inferior courts, shall hold their offices during good behavior, and shall, at stated times, receive for their services, a compensation, which shall not be diminished during their continuance in office.

Section 2: The judicial powers shall extend to all cases, in law and equity, arising

The function of the judicial branch is usually defined as "to interpret the law." This function is not listed in the Constitution; it was established through the court case *Marbury* v. *Madison* under Chief Justice John Marshall. The nation's highest court is the Supreme Court. Inferior or lower courts may be and have been created by Congress. They include Circuit Courts of Appeal and Federal District Courts as well as tax, claim, and military courts. Federal judges do not have specific terms of office and may serve as long as they behave—usually for the rest of their lives unless they resign.

This section lists the cases that the federal courts must decide. No other courts can have jurisdiction in these cases.

under this Constitution, the laws of the United States, and treaties made, or which shall be made under their authority; to all cases affecting ambassadors, other public ministers and consuls; to all cases of admiralty and maritime jurisdiction; to controversies to which the United States shall be a party; to controversies between two or more states; between a state and citizens of another state, between citizens of different states, between citizens of the same state claiming lands under grants of different states, and between a state, or the citizens thereof, and foreign states, citizens or subjects.

In all cases affecting ambassadors, other public ministers and consuls, and those in which a state shall be party, the Supreme Court shall have original jurisdiction. In all the other cases before mentioned, the Supreme Court shall have appellate jurisdiction, both as to law and fact, with such exceptions, and under such regulations as the Congress shall make.

Original jurisdiction (JOOR is DIK shun) means that this court has first opportunity to hear and decide the case. With **appellate** (uh PEL it) **jurisdiction** the case, which has already been brought to trial at least once, is sent up from a lower court, and the court hears the case on appeal.

The trial of all crimes, except in cases of impeachment, shall be by jury; and such trial shall be held in the state where the said crimes shall have been committed; but when not committed within any state, the trial shall be at such place or places as the Congress may by law have directed.

Trials for crimes occur where the crime was committed, unless the person cannot get a fair trial there. (If a fair trial is considered unlikely at the location of the crime, a *change of venue* can be obtained, and the trial will be moved to another location.) The common method for trial is by jury.

Section 3. Treason against the United States shall consist only in levying war against them, or in adhering to their enemies, giving them aid and comfort. No person shall be convicted of treason unless on the testimony of two witnesses to the same overt act, or on confession in open court.

Treason is defined specifically so that no one can be accused unjustly. To be convicted of treason, the accused must either confess to it or have two people who saw it testify in an open court.

The Congress shall have power to declare the punishment of treason, but no attainder of treason shall work corruption

The punishment for treason extends only to the life of the person himself, not his family.

of blood, or forfeiture except during the life of the person attained.

1. What is the primary function of the judicial branch?
2. What is the nation's highest court and the only one specifically established by the Constitution?
3. What branch of government was given the power to create inferior or lower courts?
4. How long is the term of a federal judge?
5. Where is a case normally tried?
6. Except in impeachment cases, what is the method of trial?
7. To prevent unjust accusations, what is necessary to convict a person of treason?

Article IV: Interstate Relations

Section 1. Full faith and credit shall be given in each state to the public acts, records and judicial proceedings of every other state. And the Congress may by general laws prescribe the manner in which such acts, records and proceedings shall be proved, and the effect thereof.

Full Faith and Credit among States: Each state is to respect the public civil acts of other states. Thus items like marriage licenses, wills, and contracts are respected among the states. This clause does not apply to police acts; thus each state can control its own long-term licensing for drivers as well as for occupations such as barbers, beauticians, lawyers, teachers, and doctors.

Section 2. The citizens of each state shall be entitled to all privileges and immunities of citizens in the several states.

Mutual Duties of States: If a person passes through another state or moves there, he still has all his rights as an American citizen.

A person charged in any state with treason, felony, or other crime, who, shall flee from justice, and be found in another state, shall on demand of the executive authority of the state from which he fled, be delivered up to be removed to the state having jurisdiction of the crime.

A governor can request that a criminal who flees to another state be returned to the state where the crime was committed to stand trial. The process of returning the criminal is called **extradition.**

No person held to service or labor in one state under the laws thereof, escaping into another, shall, in consequence of any law or regulation therein, be discharged from such service or labor, but shall be delivered up on claim of the party to whom such service or labor may be due.

Runaways—applied to slaves—could be returned to their owners.

Section 3. New states may be admitted by the Congress into this Union; but no new state shall be formed or erected within the jurisdiction of any other state; nor any

New States
(1) Congress admits new states to the Union.
(2) If a state is formed out of another state or by the combination of two states, the legislatures of those states involved must approve.

state be formed by the junction of two or more states, or parts of states, without the consent of the legislatures of the states concerned as well as of the Congress.

The Congress shall have power to dispose of and make all needful rules and regulations respecting the territory or other property belonging to the United States; and nothing in this Constitution shall be so construed as to prejudice any claims of the United States, or any particular state.

Congress regulates the territories. (Today this applies to Puerto Rico, Guam, and other American possessions.)

Section 4. The United States shall guarantee to every state in this Union a republican form of government, and shall protect each of them against invasion; and on application of the legislature, or of the executive (when the legislature cannot be convened) against domestic violence.

When it submits its constitution, each state is to have a republican form of government. The federal government will protect the states from invasion or handle riots or domestic violence when a state legislature, a governor, or the president requests it.

Questions on Article IV
1. With what does Article IV deal?
2. Give some examples of public civil acts that are respected from state to state.
3. What branch of government admits new states to the Union?
4. What kind of government are new states required to have?

Article V: Amending the Constitution

The Congress, whenever two-thirds of both houses shall deem it necessary, shall propose amendments to this Constitution, or, on the application of the legislatures of two-thirds of the several states, shall call a convention for proposing amendments, which in either case, shall be valid to all intents and purposes, as part of this Constitution when ratified by the legislatures of three-fourths of the several states, or by conventions in three-fourths thereof, as the one or the other mode of ratification may be proposed by the Congress; Provided that no amendment which may

Two-thirds of both houses of Congress or two-thirds of the states in convention propose amendments. *Ratification*—approval to put an amendment into effect—requires a vote of three-fourths of the state legislatures or three-quarters of the states in conventions.

be made prior to the year 1808 shall in any manner affect the first and fourth clauses in the ninth section of the first article; and that no state, without its consent, shall be deprived of its equal suffrage in the Senate.

1. What groups have the power to propose amendments?
2. How much support is required to propose an amendment?
3. How much approval is needed to ratify an amendment?
4. What provision can never be changed unless a state would consent to it?

Article VI: Constitutional and National Supremacy

All debts contracted and engagements entered into, before the adoption of this Constitution, shall be as valid against the United States under this Constitution, as under the Confederation.

This Constitution, and the laws of the United States which shall be made in pursuance thereof; and all treaties made, or which shall be made, under the authority of the United States, shall be the supreme law of the land; and the judges in every state shall be bound thereby, anything in the constitution or laws of any state to the contrary notwithstanding.

The senators and representatives before mentioned, and the members of the several state legislatures, and all executive and judicial officers, both of the United States and of the several states, shall be bound by oath or affirmation, to support this Constitution; but no religious test shall ever be required as a qualification to any office or public trust under the United States.

The United States Constitution is the supreme (highest) law of the nation. The order of authority in the United States is (1) the American Constitution (as interpreted by the Supreme Court), (2) the laws of the U.S. Government (Congress), (3) constitutions of the states, (4) state laws, and (5) local laws (city and county).

All national and state officers affirm to support the Constitution. Holding specific religious beliefs is not a qualification for holding public office.

Questions on Article VI
1. What is considered the supreme law of the land?
2. What was to happen to debts contracted before the adoption of the Constitution?
3. How does the adoption of the Constitution assure that state officers will support it?

Article VII: Ratifying the Constitution

The ratification of the conventions of nine States shall be sufficient for the establishment of this Constitution between the States so ratifying the same.

Done in convention by the unanimous consent of the states present the seventeenth day of September in the year of our Lord 1787, and of the independence of the United States of America the twelfth. In witness whereof we have hereunto subscribed our names.

George Washington, President
and Deputy from Virginia

Nine of the thirteen states had to ratify the Constitution to start the new form of government.

New Hampshire
John Langdon
Nicholas Gilman

Massachusetts
Nathaniel Gorham
Rufus King

Connecticut
William Samuel Johnson
Roger Sherman

New York
Alexander Hamilton

New Jersey
William Livingston
David Brearley
William Paterson
Jonathan Dayton

Pennsylvania
Benjamin Franklin
Thomas Mifflin
Robert Morris
George Clymer
Thomas Fitzsimons
Jared Ingersoll
James Wilson
Gouverneur Morris

Delaware
George Read
Gunning Bedford, Jr.
John Dickinson
Richard Bassett
Jacob Broom

Maryland
James McHenry
Daniel of St. Thomas Jenifer
Daniel Carroll

Virginia
John Blair
James Madison, Jr.

North Carolina
William Blount
Richard Dobbs Spaight
Hugh Williamson

South Carolina
John Rutledge
Charles Cotesworth Pinckney
Charles Pinckney
Pierce Butler

Georgia
William Few
Abraham Baldwin

Questions on Article VII
1. How many states had to ratify the Constitution before it became the law of the land?
2. On what day was the Constitution signed?

Amendments to the Constitution

The first ten amendments, known as the Bill of Rights, went into effect December 15, 1791. House member James Madison introduced these amendments, and they were ratified two years and three months later. The immunities listed in the Bill of Rights were already in existence, but the amendments insured them. The Constitution and Bill of Rights made the people's liberties secure. The amendments illustrate the principle of limited government.

Amendment I: Five Freedoms

The First Amendment insures five freedoms: religion, speech, press, assembly, and petition. At first the limitations in the Bill of Rights applied only to the central government and not to the states. For example, Massachusetts levied state taxes to support a state church until 1833.

Congress shall make no law respecting an establishment of religion, or prohibiting the free exercise thereof;
or abridging the freedom of speech or of the press;

Congress cannot establish any church or denomination as a state-sponsored church. But people are free to worship as they choose.

Freedom of speech is important to our political system because it permits criticism of misdeeds of those in power. Freedom of speech is not, however, unlimited. *Slander,* defaming a person by word of mouth, or *libel,* defaming a person in writing, are not protected.

or the right of the people peaceably to assemble, and to petition the government for a redress of grievances.

Without the right of assembly, there could be no clubs, churches, or other private organizations except those approved by the government. People would be unable to unite to change the government by legal means. Lack of the right to assemble often leads to dictatorships. Communist countries do not have this freedom.

Amendment II: The Right to Bear Arms

A well regulated militia being necessary to the security of a free state, the right of the people to keep and bear arms shall not be infringed.

This amendment forbids Congress from infringing on the right of citizens to keep weapons.

Amendment III: No Quartering of Troops

No soldier shall, in time of peace, be quartered in any house, without the consent of the owner, nor in time of war but in a manner to be prescribed by law.

This amendment protects the people from military intrusion into their homes. In colonial days, Americans resented being forced by Britain to take soldiers into their homes during times of war.

Amendment IV: No Unreasonable Searches

The right of the people to be secure in their persons, houses, papers, and effects, against unreasonable searches and seizures, shall not be violated, and no warrants shall issue, but upon probable cause, supported

This amendment guarantees the privacy of homes from illegal searches. It does not keep authorities from conducting legal searches or seizures with search warrants.

by oath or affirmation, and particularly describing the place to be searched, and the persons or things to be seized.

Amendment V: Rights of the Accused

No person shall be held to answer for a capital, or otherwise infamous crime, unless on a presentment or indictment of a grand jury, except in cases arising in the land or naval forces, or in the militia, when in actual service in time of war or public danger; nor shall any person be subject for the same offense to be twice put in jeopardy of life or limb; nor shall be compelled in any criminal case to be a witness against himself, nor be deprived of life, liberty, or property, without due process of law; nor shall private property be taken for public use without just compensation.

A grand jury determines whether there is enough evidence against a person to warrant a jury trial for guilt or innocence. This amendment insures that no citizen can be forced to give evidence against himself. It protects citizens from being tortured or brainwashed to force information from them.

Jeopardy means danger or risk. No person can be tried twice for the same crime.

A person cannot be imprisoned, have his property taken away, or be sentenced to death without a fair and proper trial (due process of law).

Private property can be "condemned [taken] for the public good," but it has to be paid for. For instance, government can take land needed for the building of a new highway, but it must pay the owner a fair price for that land.

Amendment VI: Rights of the Accused in Criminal Trials

In all criminal prosecutions, the accused shall enjoy the right to a speedy and public trial, by an impartial jury of the state and district wherein the crime shall have been committed, which district shall have been previously ascertained by law, and to be informed of the nature and cause of the accusation; to be confronted with the witnesses against him; to have compulsory process for obtaining witnesses in his favor, and to have the assistance of counsel for his defense.

Because some political trials in England had been held in secret and lasted for years (and the accused remained in jail for that time), the Bill of Rights guaranteed the right to a speedy public trial. An accused person has the right to see and face his accuser and his witnesses. The court will require witnesses to appear by serving a subpoena (suh PEE nuh), a document requiring a person to appear in court as a witness. A counsel for the defense (lawyer) is provided even at public expense.

Amendment VII: Rights of Citizens in Civil Trials

In suits at common law, where the value in controversy shall exceed twenty dollars, the right of trial by jury shall be preserved, and no fact tried by a jury shall be otherwise reexamined in any court of the United States, than according to the rules of the common law.

A litigant in any court case involving money or property of twenty dollars' value or more can demand a trial by jury.

Amendment VIII: Cruel, Unusual, and Unjust Punishments

Excessive bail shall not be required, nor excessive fines imposed, nor cruel and unusual punishments inflicted.

Bail, money held by the court to insure an accused person's appearance at a court of trial, may be required, but it is not to be excessive. Unusual punishments included whipping, hanging by the heels, branding, and stocks. Such abuses were here outlawed for federal offenses. The courts decide when bail and fine are excessive and punishments cruel or unusual.

Amendment IX: Unlisted Rights

The enumeration in the Constitution of certain rights shall not be construed to deny or disparage others retained by the people.

Amendment X: Unlisted Rights Go to States or to the People

The powers not delegated to the United States by the Constitution, nor prohibited by it to the states, are reserved to the states respectively, or to the people.

The fact that the Constitution does not list a specific right does not mean the right does not exist. For example, the rights to move and settle somewhere and to choose an occupation are unlisted rights, yet we still have them.

The states or people have any rights that the Constitution does not forbid them to have. The federal government cannot take such rights away from them.

Questions on Amendments 1-10
1. What are the first ten amendments usually called?
2. With what do these amendments deal?
3. What five freedoms are included in the First Amendment?
4. What are three rights you have if accused, according to the Fifth Amendment?
5. Why was a speedy public trial important?
6. What does the Eighth Amendment insure about any punishments or fines?
7. To whom do rights not listed in the Constitution go?

Amendment XI: Suing States (1798)

The judicial power of the United States shall not be construed to extend to any suit in law or equity, commenced or prosecuted against one of the United States by citizens of another state, or by citizens or subjects of any foreign state.

Amendment XII: Separate Ballots for President and Vice President (1804)

The electors shall meet in their respective states, and vote by ballot for President and Vice President, one of whom, at least, shall not be an inhabitant of the same state with themselves; they shall name in their

Sixteen other amendments have been passed since 1791. Some amendments have corrected problems or more fully explained subjects touched upon by the Constitution. Some of the amendments are related to one another, such as those passed during Reconstruction, and they deal with problems or ideas from a given time. Others deal with single issues or ideas.

The Eleventh Amendment states that a citizen of another state or a foreign country may not sue a state in a federal court without that state's consent. Suits must be in the state's own courts.

Instead of electors' voting for two persons, electors are to vote separately for the president and vice president. Thus the possibility of a tie between the president and vice president, such as had occurred in 1800, was eliminated.

ballots the person voted for as President, and in distinct ballots, the person voted for as Vice President, and they shall make distinct lists of all persons voted for as President and of all persons voted for as Vice President, and of the number of votes for each, which lists they shall sign and certify, and transmit sealed to the seat of the government of the United States, directed to the President of the Senate; the President of the Senate shall, in the presence of the Senate and House of Representatives open all the certificates, and the votes shall then be counted; the person having the greatest number of votes for President, shall be the President, if such number be a majority of the whole number of electors appointed; and if no person have such majority, then from the persons having the highest numbers not exceeding three on the list of those voted for as President, the House of Representatives shall choose immediately, by ballot, the President. But in choosing the President, the votes shall be taken by states, the representation from each state having one vote; a quorum for this purpose shall consist of a member or members from two-thirds of the states, and a majority of all the states shall be necessary to a choice. And if the House of Representatives shall not choose a President, whenever the right of choice shall devolve upon them, before the fourth day of March next following, then the Vice President shall act as President, as in the case of the death or other constitutional disability of the President. The person having the greatest number of votes as Vice President shall be the Vice President, if such number be a majority of the whole number of electors appointed, and if no person have a majority, then from the two highest numbers on the list, the Senate shall choose the Vice President; a quorum for the purpose shall consist of two-thirds of the whole number of senators, and a majority of the whole number shall be necessary to a choice. But no person constitutionally ineligible to the office of President shall be eligible to that of Vice President of the United States.

Amendment XIII: Slavery (1865)

Section 1. Neither slavery nor involuntary servitude, except as punishment for crime whereof the party shall have been duly convicted, shall exist within the United States, or any place subject to their jurisdiction.

Section 2. Congress shall have power to enforce this article by appropriate legislation.

Amendments 13-15 were all ratified during or just after the Civil War and deal with problems of that era. Amendment 13 abolished slavery. It restricted the states as well as the national government.

Amendment XIV: Citizenship (1868)

Section 1. All persons born or naturalized in the United States, and subject to the jurisdiction thereof, are citizens of the United States and of the state wherein they reside. No state shall make or enforce any law which shall abridge the privileges or immunities of citizens of the United States; nor shall any state deprive any person of life, liberty, or property, without due process of law; nor deny to any person within its jurisdiction the equal protection of the law.

All persons, regardless of race or former status as slave or free, born in the United States or naturalized, are both American citizens and citizens of the state in which they live. A state cannot deprive any person of life, liberty, or property without due process (a fair trial based on just laws). States that deny voting rights could have their representation in Congress denied, but this has never been done.

Section 2. Representatives shall be apportioned among the several states according to their respective numbers, counting the whole number of persons in each state, excluding Indians not taxed. But when the right to vote at any election for the choice of electors for President and Vice President of the United States, representatives in Congress, the executive and judicial officers of a state, or the members of the legislature thereof, is denied to any of the male inhabitants of such state being twenty-one years of age, and citizens of the United

Sections 2, 3, and 4 deal with restrictions and provisions made for the states that were in the Confederacy during the Civil War as they took back their responsibilities in the national government.

States, or in any way abridged, except for participation in rebellion, or other crime, the basis of representation therein shall be reduced in the proportion which the number of such male citizens shall bear to the whole number of male citizens twenty-one years of age in such state.

Section 3. No person shall be a senator or representative in Congress, or elector of President and Vice President, or hold any office, civil or military, under the United States, or under any state, who having previously taken an oath, as a member of Congress, or as an officer of the United States, or as a member of any state legislature, or as an executive or judicial officer of any state, to support the Constitution of the United States, shall have engaged in insurrection or rebellion against the same, or given aid or comfort to the enemies thereof. But Congress may by a vote of two-thirds of each House, remove such disability.

Section 4. The validity of the public debt of the United States, authorized by law, including debts incurred for payment of pensions and bounties for services in suppressing insurrection or rebellion, shall not be questioned. But neither the United States nor any state shall assume or pay any debt or obligation incurred in aid of insurrection or rebellion against the United States, or any claim for the loss or emancipation of any slave; but all such debts, obligations, and claims shall be held illegal and void.

Section 5. The Congress shall have power to enforce, by appropriate legislation, the provisions of this article.

Amendment XV: Black Voting Rights (1870)

Section 1. The right of the citizens of the United States to vote shall not be denied or abridged by the United States or by any

Race, color, or past service as a slave should not prevent any citizen from voting.

state on account of race, color, or previous condition of servitude.

Section 2. The Congress shall have power to enforce this article by appropriate legislation.

Amendment XVI: Income Tax (1913)

The Congress shall have power to lay and collect taxes on incomes, from whatever source derived, without apportionment among the several states, and without regard to any census or enumeration.

Amendments 16-19 are sometimes called the Progressive Amendments because they were passed at the height of the progressive era (1900-1917).

Rather than using state apportionment to set a tax base so that each state paid a tax equal to the percentage of its population, Congress was given the power to tax incomes.

Amendment XVII: Direct Election of Senators (1913)

The Senate of the United States shall be composed of two senators from each state, elected by the people thereof, for six years; and each senator shall have one vote. The electors in each state shall have the qualifications requisite for electors of the most numerous branch of the state legislature.

When vacancies happen in the representation of any state in the Senate, the executive authority of such state shall issue writs of election to fill such vacancies; *provided,* that the legislature of any state may empower the executive thereof to make temporary appointments until the people fill the vacancies by election as the legislature may direct.

This amendment shall not be so construed as to affect the election or term of any senator chosen before it becomes valid as part of the Constitution.

The people rather than the state legislatures gained the right to elect their two senators. Anyone who is qualified to vote in a state house of representatives election is also qualified to vote in a United States Senate election. Senate vacancies may be filled by special election or by a state governor who can appoint a senator if state law allows it.

Amendment XVIII: Prohibition (1919)

After one year from the ratification of this article, the manufacture, sale, or transportation of intoxicating liquors within, the importation thereof into, or the exportation thereof from the United States and all territory subject to the jurisdiction thereof, for beverage purposes is hereby prohibited.

Prohibition refers to forbidding the manufacture, sale, or transportation of liquor. Congress passed the Volstead Act to define "intoxicating liquor" and to enforce the amendment. The Twenty-first Amendment repealed the Eighteenth in 1933.

The Congress and the several states shall have concurrent power to enforce this article by appropriate legislation.

This article shall be inoperative unless it shall have been ratified as an amendment to the Constitution by the legislatures of the several states, as provided in the Constitution, within seven years from the date of submission hereof to the states by Congress.

Questions on Amendments 11-18
1. According to the Fourteenth Amendment, who besides the federal government cannot deprive a person of life, liberty, or property without due process of law?
2. What is meant by "due process of law"?
3. What amendment makes income taxes constitutional?
4. What amendment gives voters rather than state legislators the right to elect senators?
5. What does the Eighteenth Amendment prohibit? When and by what amendment was this repealed?

Amendment XIX: Women's Suffrage (1920)

The right of citizens of the United States to vote shall not be denied or abridged by the United States or by any state on account of sex.

The Congress shall have power to enforce this article by appropriate legislation.

Women were hereby given the vote. The right to vote is also called **suffrage.**

Amendment XX: Lame Duck Amendment (1933)

Section 1. The terms of the President and the Vice President shall end at noon on the 20th day of January, and the terms of Senators and Representatives at noon on the 3rd day of January, of the years in which such terms would have ended if this article had not been ratified; and the terms of their successors shall then begin.

Section 2. The Congress shall assemble at least once in every year, and such meeting

The dates for starting terms for the president, senators, and representatives to take office were changed. Presidential terms begin on January 20 every fourth year; terms for senators and representatives begin on January 3 and are six and two years respectively. This amendment shortens the length of time between the November elections and the taking of office.

shall begin at noon on the 3rd day of January, unless they shall by law appoint a different day.

Section 3. If, at the time fixed for the beginning of the term of President, the President-elect shall have died, the Vice President-elect shall become President. If a President shall not have been chosen before the time fixed for the beginning of his term, or if the President-elect shall have failed to qualify, then the Vice President-elect shall act as President until a President shall have qualified; and the Congress may by law provide for the case wherein neither a President-elect nor a Vice president-elect shall have qualified, declaring who shall then act as President, or the manner in which one who is to act shall be selected, and such person shall act accordingly until a President or Vice President shall have qualified.

Section 4. The Congress may by law provide for the case of the death of any of the persons from whom the House of Representatives may choose a President whenever the right of choice shall have devolved upon them, and for the case of the death of any of the persons from whom the Senate may choose a Vice President whenever the right of choice shall have devolved upon them.

Section 5. Sections 1 and 2 shall take effect on the 15th day of October following the ratification of this article.

Section 6. This article shall be inoperative unless it shall have been ratified as an amendment to the Constitution by the legislatures of three-fourths of the several states within seven years from the date of its submission.

If the president-elect dies before taking office, the vice president-elect takes his place until another president qualifies.

Amendment XXI: Repeal of Prohibition (1933)

Section 1. The Eighteenth Article of amendment to the Constitution of the United States is hereby repealed.

Section 2. The transportation or importation into any state, territory, or possession of the United States for delivery or use therein of intoxicating liquors in violation of the laws thereof, is hereby prohibited.

Section 3. This article shall be inoperative unless it shall have been ratified as an amendment to the Constitution by conventions in the several states, as provided in the Constitution, within seven years from the date of the submission thereof to the states by the Congress.

This amendment repealed prohibition, but states and territories could prohibit the sale of alcohol within their borders.

Amendment XXII: Presidential Terms (1951)

No person shall be elected to the office of the President more than twice, and no person who has held the office of President, or acted as President, for more than two years of a term to which some other person was elected President shall be elected to the office of the President more than once.

But this article shall not apply to any person holding the office of President when this article was proposed by the Congress, and shall not prevent any person who may be holding the office of President, or acting as President, during the term within which this article becomes operative from holding the office of President, or acting as President during the remainder of such term.

This article shall be inoperative unless it shall have been ratified as an amendment to the Constitution by the legislatures of three-fourths of the several states within seven years from the date of its submission to the states by the Congress.

Presidents can be elected for only two terms in their own right. If elevated from the vice-presidency during the second half of a previous president's term, a vice president who becomes president could serve a maximum of ten years.

Amendment XXIII: Voting for Washington, D.C. (1961)

Section 1. The District constituting the seat of Government of the United States shall appoint in such manner as Congress may direct:

A number of electors of President and Vice President equal to the whole number of Senators and Representatives in Congress to which the District would be entitled if it were a state, but in no event more than the least populous state; they shall be in addition to those appointed by the states, but they shall be considered, for the purpose of the election of President and Vice President, to be electors appointed by a State; and they shall meet in the District and perform such duties as provided by the twelfth article of amendment.

Section 2. The Congress shall have power to enforce this article by appropriate legislation.

Residents of the District of Columbia can vote in presidential elections, and the district has three electoral votes.

Amendment XXIV: No Poll Tax (1964)

Section 1. The right of citizens of the United States to vote in any primary or other election for President or Vice President, for electors for President or Vice President, or for Senator or Representative in Congress, shall not be denied or abridged by the United States or any State by reasons of failure to pay any poll tax or other tax.

Section 2. The Congress shall have the power to enforce this article by appropriate legislation.

The payment of a poll tax to a state in any federal election was forbidden. A **poll tax** was a tax some states charged people before they let them vote.

Amendment XXV: Presidential Succession (1967)

Section 1. In case of the removal of the President from office or of his death or resignation, the Vice President shall become President.

Section 2. Whenever there is a vacancy in the office of the Vice President, the

If the vice-presidency becomes vacant, the president can appoint a new vice president with the approval of both the House and the Senate.

President shall nominate a Vice President who shall take office upon confirmation by a majority vote of both Houses of Congress.

Section 3. Whenever the President transmits to the President Pro Tempore of the Senate and the Speaker of the House of Representatives his written declaration that he is unable to discharge the powers and duties of his office, and until he transmits to them a written declaration to the contrary, such powers and duties shall be discharged by the Vice President as Acting President.

The president can transfer his duties to the vice president when he is unable to perform them. He may do this, for example, when he is undergoing surgery and therefore under anesthetic and unable to make decisions.

Section 4. Whenever the Vice President and a majority of either the principal officers of the executive departments or of such other body as Congress may by law provide, transmit to the President Pro Tempore of the Senate and the Speaker of the House of Representatives their written declaration that the President is unable to discharge the powers and duties of his office, the Vice President shall immediately assume the powers and duties of the office as Acting President.

If an executive or congressional panel declares that the president is unable to fulfill his duties, the vice president assumes them until the president is again declared capable.

Thereafter, when the President transmits to the President Pro Tempore of the Senate and the Speaker of the House of Representatives his written declaration that no inability exists, he shall resume the powers and duties of his office unless the Vice President and a majority of either the principal officers of the executive department or of such other body as Congress may by law provide, transmit within four days to the President Pro Tempore of the Senate and the Speaker of the House of Representatives their written declaration that the President is unable to discharge the powers and duties of his office. Thereupon Congress shall decide the issue, assembling within forty-eight hours for that purpose if not in session. If the Congress, within twenty-one days after receipt of the latter written declaration, or, if Congress is not in session, within twenty-one days after Congress is required to assemble, determines by two-thirds vote of both Houses that the President is unable to discharge the powers and duties of his office, the Vice President shall continue to discharge the same as Acting President; otherwise, the President shall resume the powers and duties of his office.

Amendment XXVI: Eighteen-Year-Old Vote (1971)

Section 1. The right of citizens of the United States, who are eighteen years of age or older, to vote shall not be denied or abridged by the United States or by any state on account of age.

Section 2. The Congress shall have power to enforce this article by appropriate legislation.

Eighteen-year-olds were given the right to vote. (Previously the voting age was twenty-one.)

Questions on Amendments 19-26
1. Who was given the right to vote in each of the following?
   a. Amendment 15
   b. Amendment 19
   c. Amendment 26
2. According to the Twentieth Amendment, when is the president to be inaugurated?
3. What section of the country got the right to vote for president in 1961?
4. If the vice president becomes president, who picks a new vice president, and how is he approved?

Summary

The United States Constitution has served as the foundation of American government for over two hundred years. It has provided a written law for the land, and it contains features that have helped it to adjust and endure as the nation and its governmental needs have changed through the years.

Chapter Review

Do You Remember?

■ Match the following constitutional terms to their best description.

1. appellate jurisdiction
2. bicameral system
3. bill of attainder
4. counterfeiting
5. elastic clause
6. extradition
7. habeas corpus
8. impeachment
9. naturalization
10. pardon
11. patent
12. reprieve
13. suffrage
14. veto

a. prevents imprisonment without a criminal charge
b. temporary postponement of punishment
c. a foreigner's becoming a citizen
d. presidential rejection of a bill
e. protection for inventors and their inventions
f. Congress can do anything "necessary and proper"
g. a legislature with two houses
h. file charges against a major federal official
i. making phony money
j. document permitting punishment without a trial
k. complete forgiveness of a crime
l. court's right to hear a case already tried in a lower court
m. returning a criminal to the state in which he committed his crime
n. the right to vote

Why Is It So?

1. Why is the Constitution an amazing document?
2. What are four principles contained in the Constitution, and why are they significant?

What Do You Think?

What do you think will be necessary for the continued success of the Constitution?

Men Who Shaped America's Constitution

Fifty-five delegates attended the Constitutional Convention at Philadelphia in 1787. Forty-two of those men were present on September 17, and thirty-nine were willing to sign their names to the document they had produced. Their efforts devised a workable government for the new republic.

The Doctor in the House

There were actually two doctors in the house at the Constitutional Convention: Hugh Williamson and James McHenry. Both of them had served as surgeons for the Continental forces in the War for Independence. Williamson, who was from North Carolina, was recognized as a leading scientist as well as a physician. He had even assisted Ben Franklin in his studies of electricity. His special scientific interest was the weather.

McHenry, from Maryland, went on to politics. During the war he served under Washington and later under Lafayette. After the war he rose to the position of secretary of war under John Adams. Fort McHenry, of national anthem fame, was named for this Maryland doctor-politician.

The Judge

Oliver Ellsworth of Connecticut helped Roger Sherman, his fellow state delegate, put together the Connecticut Compromise that became part of the Constitution. After the Constitution's ratification Ellsworth became one of Connecticut's first senators. He was largely responsible for writing the Judiciary Bill of 1789, which established the federal judicial system. Later he served as the third chief justice of the Supreme Court and as a commissioner to France.

The Large State Champion

Edmund Randolph of Virginia had been the man who presented the large-state plan to the convention. His father had been a Loyalist who fled to England at the outbreak of the War for Independence. Randolph had served in the Continental Army as Washington's aide and then as the governor of Virginia. Although the Constitution contained many of the ideas present in the large-state plan, Randolph's first reaction to the compromise version was vigorous opposition. Later, however, he changed his mind and supported its adoption. Under the new government he served as the first attorney general of the United States and as the secretary of state. Falsely accused of seeking bribes from the government of France, Randolph was forced by Washington to resign. It took many years for him to clear his name. He finished his life as a lawyer in Virginia.

The Man with a Proxy

Before the war John Dickinson of Delaware had often been accused of being a Loyalist. He had opposed Ben Franklin's point of view on several issues, had openly opposed the idea of violent resistance to the king, and had refused to sign the Declaration of Independence. Still, when war broke out, Dickinson had served in the patriot army. After the war he became a political leader in Delaware. His *Letters from a Farmer in Pennsylvania,* which ably attacked British policy, had made him well

known among the colonists. He had presided over the Annapolis Convention, which had led to the formation of the Constitutional Convention. Dickinson was a vigorous supporter of the Constitution. Although he could not be present at the signing of the document, he insisted that George Read act as his proxy, or substitute, and sign Dickinson's name to the Constitution. He wanted everyone to know that he strongly supported the new form of government produced by the convention.

The New Hampshire Patriots

Nicholas Gilman and John Langdon were both delegates from New Hampshire who had been military officers during the War for Independence. Both of them served in the first Congress: Gilman in the House of Representatives, and Langdon in the Senate as the first president pro tempore. Later Gilman served in the Senate as well.

In his youth Langdon served as an apprentice and later became a wealthy ship owner. During the war he served as New Hampshire's naval agent, outfitting privateers and building regular warships. He also financed the New Hampshire militia that served at Saratoga. Initially a Federalist, he became a Jeffersonian and even received that party's nomination for vice president in 1812 but declined it because of his age.

The Pastor-Educator

Abraham Baldwin was a clergyman and tutor at Yale before the War for Independence began. During the war he served as chaplain for the Continental Army. At the convention he pushed for a compromise between the large-state men and the small-state men. His change of vote forced a tie between the supporters of each plan and caused the delegates to form a committee to seek a compromise. After the convention he served in both the House and the Senate and then helped to found the University of Georgia. He was the author of the university's charter and served as its president for a time.

The Pinckney Cousins

Two of the delegates from South Carolina were cousins: Charles Pinckney and Charles Cotesworth Pinckney. Charles was the younger of the two—by about ten years—but he submitted a plan for the Constitution that influenced the thinking of many of the delegates. Later he served in both the House and the Senate, as a minister to Spain, and as the governor of his home state.

Both of the cousins had been captured during the war and had spent time in prison, but Charles Cotesworth had been exchanged for several British prisoners, while Charles had remained in prison until the conclusion of the war. This older cousin served as

minister to France and gained recognition for his refusal to use bribes to court the favor of the French. Later he was an unsuccessful candidate for president and for vice president on the Federalist ticket.

The Virginia Dissenter

George Mason of Virginia was one of the three delegates who refused to sign the Constitution. Many of his ideas in the Virginia Declaration of Rights had been used by Jefferson in the writing of the Declaration of Independence. He had also been a long-time friend of Washington and had served with him as far back as the French and Indian War. Yet Mason refused to support the Constitution because he opposed a strong central government, he wanted a Bill of Rights, and he opposed the compromise that allowed the continuation of slavery—"a disgrace to mankind." He and Patrick Henry fought hard in Virginia to defeat ratification of the Constitution, and they almost succeeded. Consistent with his opposition, he refused his election to the first Senate. That first Congress, however, took many of Mason's ideas and arguments and incorporated them into the Bill of Rights— the Constitution's first ten amendments.

9

Establishment of the New Government

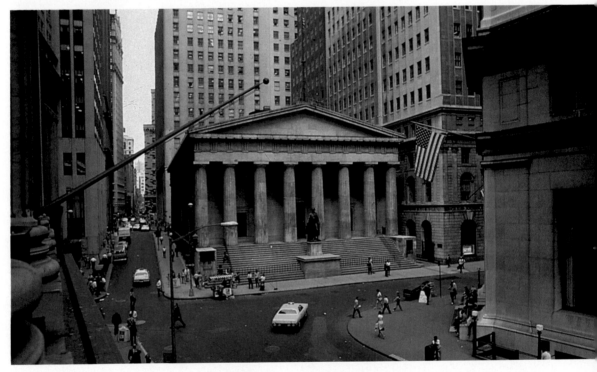

Just before noon on April 30, 1789, a solemn George Washington stepped out on the balcony of Federal Hall on the corner of Wall and Broad streets in New York City, the capital at that time. Washington's **inauguration,** the formal ceremony that officially begins a president's term, began precisely at noon. He placed his left hand on the Bible and raised his right hand to take the oath of office. He then repeated the thirty-five words required by the Constitution:

"I do solemnly swear that I will faithfully execute the office of President of the United States, and will to the best of my ability preserve, protect, and defend the Constitution of the United States."

At the end of the oath, Washington added a phrase of his own: "so help me God." He realized that he could not do his job without God's help. The oath of office taken, he entered the Senate Chamber to give his inaugural address before both houses of Congress.

A statue of George Washington stands in front of Federal Hall in New York City where he took his oath of office.

Washington had good reason to be solemn. At that time the United States had only four million people, seven hundred thousand of whom were slaves. Other world governments were ruled by kings unfriendly to the United States and her new form of government. The nation had no money in its treasury and lacked a strong army and navy. The Constitution had outlined a framework for the new government but lacked many of the exact details.

A. Challenges of the New Government

The government that Washington was going to supervise was completely new. No country had a working republic to act as an example for Washington and the other leaders. They had to find out how to make this new government work, and so Washington began to build an administration that could help him meet the problems that would come. Setting up a cabinet was his first challenge.

Establishing a Cabinet

Although Article II, Section 2 of the Constitution (see p. 146) provided for executive departments to give advice, nothing was said about how to pick leaders or how to organize the departments. Washington benefited from the counsel of James Madison, his unofficial administrative assistant. Washington established four departments of government and placed men he trusted at their heads. The department of state was headed by Thomas Jefferson, the treasury by Alexander Hamilton, that of defense by Henry Knox, and what has come to be called the justice department by Attorney General Edmund Randolph. He also appointed

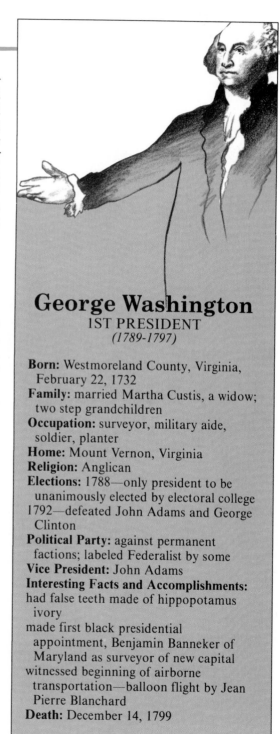

George Washington
1ST PRESIDENT
(1789-1797)

Born: Westmoreland County, Virginia, February 22, 1732

Family: married Martha Custis, a widow; two step grandchildren

Occupation: surveyor, military aide, soldier, planter

Home: Mount Vernon, Virginia

Religion: Anglican

Elections: 1788—only president to be unanimously elected by electoral college 1792—defeated John Adams and George Clinton

Political Party: against permanent factions; labeled Federalist by some

Vice President: John Adams

Interesting Facts and Accomplishments: had false teeth made of hippopotamus ivory

made first black presidential appointment, Benjamin Banneker of Maryland as surveyor of new capital

witnessed beginning of airborne transportation—balloon flight by Jean Pierre Blanchard

Death: December 14, 1799

The First President and His Cabinet

GEORGE WASHINGTON
President

THOMAS JEFFERSON
Secretary of State

ALEXANDER
HAMILTON
Secretary of the Treasury

HENRY
KNOX
Secretary
of War

EDMOND RANDOLPH
Attorney General

Samuel Osgood to head the post office. These department leaders became Washington's cabinet, advising him on policies and problems of the government.

National Finances

There was little federal income. This meant that there was almost no money to pay for government. The cost of operating the government in 1789 seems ridiculously low to us today. Washington's annual salary was to be $25,000, but he agreed to serve for his expenses. The members of the House and Senate received $6.00 per day. The Speaker of the House received $12.00 per day. Cabinet members made $3,500 annually. At first the government had much difficulty paying these salaries because the government had not organized its finances. The war debts owed to individuals and states could not be repaid either. Even the interest owed on those debts was not paid. Of course, the government's inability to meet its obligations caused lack of respect for the government, just as a Christian's inability to fulfill obligations leads to lack of respect for Christianity in the eyes of the world.

Hamilton's Plan—Secretary of the Treasury Alexander Hamilton designed a financial program to make the new nation capable of paying its debts and meeting its obligations. First, the government would have to levy (impose and collect) taxes to obtain the needed revenue. A tariff of eight per cent was levied on foreign imports, and an **excise tax** (a tax paid for the manufacture or sale of certain goods and services within a country) was levied on whiskey to raise money.

Second, the government would repay the money borrowed during the Revolution. To settle this debt, it had to repay Americans who had purchased bonds to finance the war. The Continental Congress had not been able to pay this debt, and most of the bond owners doubted that they would ever be repaid. However, news of possible repayment by the new government leaked to speculators who began to purchase many bonds. Because some of the owners thought the bonds to be worthless, they sold them to the speculators for a fraction of their value. When the Funding Bill of 1790 passed, it arranged for repaying the bonds at their printed value plus interest. Some innocent citizens who had sold bonds for small sums were hurt. Nonetheless, the act helped the government stand by its promises. The debt was paid.

Third, Hamilton wanted the federal government to take over responsibility of repaying the debts of the states. Thereby it was hoped that the states' loyalty to the federal government would be increased because the federal government would be repaying citizens rather than just their states. This idea resulted in the Assumption Act of 1790.

Precedents

Washington knew that "many things which appear of little importance in themselves and at the beginning, may have great consequences." He wrote James Madison: "At the first everything . . . will serve to establish a precedent. It is devoutly wished on my part, that these precedents may be fixed on true principles."

Even the way in which Washington took office became a precedent for other presidents to follow. Presidents since Washington have continued to put their hand on the Bible and say "so help me God." Washington realized the importance of being a good example even in little things.

That first government faced many problems. His solutions to them set precedents—models for doing things—that were so wise they have been followed ever since.

Congress argued over what to call the new chief executive. Vice President Adams suggested "His electoral Highness." The Senate suggested "His Highness, the President of the United States of America, and Protector of their Liberties." The House's idea was "President of the United States." Although their idea was adopted, and this is the way the president is introduced, it became the custom to call him simply "Mr. President."

Washington established a **cabinet,** a group of executive advisors, to help him with his responsibilities. Other presidents have since used and expanded the cabinet and their executive departments. Washington also traveled through the country as president and gave many Americans the opportunity to see him.

Washington served the United States as president for two four-year terms. No president served more than two terms until Franklin Roosevelt violated that tradition almost a hundred and fifty years later. Belatedly, seeing the wisdom of Washington's precedent, Congress passed the Twenty-second Amendment to the Constitution. When it was ratified in 1951, it made the two-term tradition law.

Fourth, the federal government should establish a **national bank.** The bank could hold the tax money the government collected in one place, and the nation's financial transactions could be handled through the bank. The major share of the bank would be owned by private citizens while the federal government would retain only a twenty per cent interest. Thus the bank was largely a private business operation. Accordingly, Congress set up the Bank of the United States in 1791.

Differing Views—Several of Hamilton's ideas brought widespread disagreement, particularly the assumption of state debts and government involvement in banking. A group opposed to both emerged under Thomas Jefferson's leadership. He and many Southerners opposed the assumption of state debts because the southern states had already paid most of their debts. They did not wish to help pay those of the northern states. They also opposed the national bank because its business operations would help northern industries but not southern agriculture.

Despite this opposition, Hamilton's plan was implemented. The Assumption Act was passed because of a compromise. In return for Jefferson's and southern support of the debt assumption, the federal capital would be located in the South. Maryland and Virginia gave land along the Potomac River for a federal district to be named after Columbus and George Washington. Today's Washington, D.C., is built on the land given by Maryland. Regardless of the criticisms, Hamilton's plan did work, and the nation's credit and reputation were restored.

Although Washington himself had expressed hope that there be no political parties, the groups that had formed around Hamilton and Jefferson during the debates over Hamilton's plans eventually became the basis of America's two-party political system. Hamilton's party was called the **Federalist Party;** Jefferson's received the name **Democratic-Republican.** (Its members were called "Republicans" for a few years, but later they became known as the "Democrats.")

The Whiskey Rebellion

The excise tax on whiskey led to a controversy that tested Washington and the federal government. On the western frontier, in addition to being used as a foodstuff for man and animals, corn was fermented and then distilled into whiskey. Because there was a shortage of money and a desire for whiskey, some people used whiskey in place of money. Westerners resented the tax that affected many of their purchases. If a man paid for a pig with a gallon of whiskey, he was still charged the tax on the whiskey. If he refused to pay the tax and was arrested, he had to go to a federal court for trial. The federal courts were sometimes miles away in cities close to the coast.

In the summer of 1794 in western Pennsylvania, a federal marshal sought to serve papers on a whiskey distiller who had not paid the tax. Angry farmers attacked the marshal, burned the home of a tax inspector, and tarred and feathered other officials. Soldiers arriving to stop the violent outbursts gave up when they met armed resistance. President Washington tried to get the state of Pennsylvania to handle the problem, but the state's governor refused. Washington offered the rebels amnesty, a group pardon, if they would agree to abide by law, but his offer was ignored. The president then called about thirteen thousand militiamen out as a federal force, and he commanded the rebels to disperse by September 1 or the militia would move in.

Washington moved forcefully. A larger group of volunteers than he had ever had at his command during the Revolution rode with the president himself on September 30, 1794. He told the troops to "combat and subdue all who may be found in arms in opposition to the national will and authority." Washington, then sixty-two, soon realized he was too old to sit in a saddle all day, but he went almost halfway before he decided to return to Philadelphia. When the rest of the troops arrived at the scene, some rebels were arrested; two of them were condemned to death, but Washington later pardoned them. In using federal force to put down the **Whiskey Rebellion,** Washington established another precedent and let the public know that he would allow no disobedience of national laws.

Establishing the Federal Court System

Although Article III, Section 1 (see p. 147) of the Constitution had established by

This courthouse in Williamsburg, Virginia, was built in 1770.

name only one court, the Supreme Court, it did give Congress the power to set up lesser courts. Under the Judiciary Act of 1789, Congress provided the mechanics of a working court system. The Supreme Court would have five associate justices and one chief justice. Washington appointed John Jay as the first chief justice.

There would also be thirteen federal district courts, one per state. Most cases involving violation of federal laws could be tried in these courts. Three circuit courts were set up to hear cases sent up and appealed from the district courts and state supreme courts. Today's federal court system follows this pattern, with only the number of courts being expanded.

Ratification of the Bill of Rights

The Philadelphia Convention had already discussed a bill of rights. They rejected it because they believed that the rights listed in it already belonged to the people and that the federal government really had no power over such matters. Yet others had been uneasy and believed that failure to guarantee rights might lead to their loss. As a result in the struggle to ratify the Constitution, the Bill of Rights became an issue. Four states had agreed to ratify it only if the first Congress would give adoption of the Bill of Rights first priority.

When the first Congress convened, a debate erupted over the Bill of Rights. The bill left the House with sixteen amendments. By the time the Senate finished with it, there were fourteen left. A House-Senate Conference Committee agreed on twelve, and on September 25, 1789, they released them to the states. In December of 1791, ten were ratified.

Fighting Indians on the Frontier

Americans desired to move into the lands of the Old Northwest but found such desires blocked by Indians. The British in the Northwest Territory had been urging the Indians to attack whites. Sometimes the Indians were openly promised British help if they would halt the spread of American settlements.

The government made several unsuccessful attempts to put a stop to the Indian attacks. Finally in 1794, war hero **Anthony Wayne** and a well-trained force moved into what is now northwestern Ohio. They soundly defeated a band of Indians and their allies at **Fallen Timbers,** near modern Toledo, Ohio. Following the defeat the Indians came to a peace conference at Fort Greenville in 1795. There they gave up their claim to about one-half of the state of Ohio in return for gifts and annual payments.

Despite the fear of hostile Indians and other obstacles, pioneers went west. Three new states met congressional standards for admission as outlined by the Northwest Ordinance of 1787 during the 1790s: Vermont (1791), Kentucky (1792), and Tennessee (1796). Also Ohio and the western sections of New York, Pennsylvania, and Georgia made population gains during this decade.

Section Review

1. Give three reasons Washington may have been solemn on his inauguration day.
2. Why did so much responsibility rest on the first president, congress, and the courts?
3. What did Washington do to organize and thus strengthen the executive branch of the government?
4. List the four parts of Hamilton's financial program and the purpose of each.
5. What brought about the origin of the first political parties in the United States?
6. What three states were admitted to the Union in the 1790s?

Anthony Wayne

George Washington entertaining French generals at Mount Vernon during the War for Independence

B. Foreign Threats to the New Government

Although the United States had established its independence with its victory in the Revolution, other world nations were not sure of its strength. European powers doubted that the United States would be able to protect its rights. The young country had yet to prove that it could not be bullied.

America and the French Revolution

By late summer of 1789, word reached American shores that the French had revolted against the government of King Louis XVI. Americans cheered, identifying with the French slogan "Liberty, Equality, and Fraternity." They liked the French because the French had aided America during the War for Independence, and at first they gave approval to the French revolutionaries. Lafayette, who temporarily served as the French leader, even sent George Washington the key to the Bastille Prison. The fall of the prison had symbolized the start of the French Revolution. But by 1793 Americans were horrified. Lafay-

ette had been imprisoned, and France was bathed in blood. The French governments, although professing to be republics, were highly unstable, and citizens suffered from a reign of terror. Furthermore, the French campaigned against religion, and infidel thinkers became popular. During that riotous time, France and Britain became involved in a war.

America's Position of Neutrality—The Americans had joined the French in 1778 in a "perpetual" Treaty of Alliance and a trade pact. The Federalists now urged Washington to denounce both. A Federalist from Massachusetts named Fisher Ames denounced revolutionized France as "an open hell, still ringing with agonies and blasphemies, still smoking with sufferings, and crimes in which we see . . . perhaps our own future state." The Democratic-Republicans, however, agreed with the more liberal Thomas Jefferson, who said that he was willing to see "half of the earth devastated" to insure "the liberty of the whole." But when it appeared the devastated half might include the American portion of the sphere, even the secretary of state gave in to Washington's desire to announce neutrality. On April 22, 1793, Washington issued his **Neutrality Proclamation** urging Americans to be "impartial" toward all possible foreign foes and to cease actions that would involve the United States in foreign wars.

Citizen Genêt—Meanwhile, a young French diplomat decided to test the proclamation. **Edmond Charles Genêt** came to Charleston, South Carolina to set up a base for French land and sea operations against Spain and England. Genêt unwisely tried to hire war hero George Rogers Clark and other veterans to fight Spain in Spanish-owned Florida and Louisiana. He also out-fitted American private ships to attack Spanish and British shipping. When the president refused Genêt's pleas to call Congress into special session to vote aid for France, he announced that he would go over Washington's head and appeal to the American people. Since the American press did not agree on the matter, he was sure that he would find a sympathetic audience.

Genêt managed to equip twelve priva-teers who captured eighty British vessels before Jefferson could see Washington's point that this citizen was dragging the United States into "war abroad and anarchy at home." Washington asked France to recall Genêt, and Congress passed laws to prevent other foreign agents from causing such trouble. However, just as Genêt was to be deported, the French government changed hands. Since the new faction said that it would behead Genêt, Washington kindly let him stay in America.

But the end of the Genêt affair also meant the end of Jefferson's career as sec-retary of state. Ever locked in disputes with Hamilton and pressing Washington and the newspapers to take sides, Jefferson finally resigned his position.

Trouble with the British

Although the Neutrality Proclamation and the silencing of Genêt may have helped calm England's fears of America's siding with France, the threat of another United States war with Britain continued. The nations disagreed over what rights neutral countries—namely the United States— might have at sea. The United States, with an ever-growing trade fleet, had opened up trade with the French West Indies and France, Britain's enemies. To retaliate,

Britain invoked an old law, the "Rule of 1756," which said that trade not open in peace could not be opened in war. Thus she seized two hundred and fifty American ships with their cargoes and crews.

Impressment—The British also were of-fended when their own sailors, who had been subjected to bad food and harsh discipline, jumped ship in ports where American ships were also docked. These sailors deserted to American ships for higher pay and better treatment. To regain their lost sailors, the British retaliated by seizing American sailors and forcing them to serve the British, a practice called **impressment.** Although these disputes led to a session around a peace table in 1795, they really were not settled by that treaty. Instead, they were factors that would lead to a war in 1812.

The Jay Treaty—To avoid war, Washington appointed Chief Justice John Jay to head a peace mission to Britain. Since Britain was a strong world power and the United States was a small new republic, Jay was at a disadvantage from the start. The United States agreed to limit trade with France, Britain's enemy, and to pay British citizens what Americans owed them. The British agreed to abandon their forts in the Northwest, pay the United States for ships seized, and open some ports in the British West Indies to American trade.

The **Jay Treaty** did not really settle the issues of neutral rights at sea or of Indian attacks. Congress and the American public were angry with it and with Jay; but since there was no other option open except war, the Senate ratified the treaty. The House of Representatives tried to block the treaty by voting down monies needed to carry it out. President Washington stepped in, insisting that a treaty ratified by the Senate was already law and had to be honored. The House was silenced, and ever since, presidential treaties have been free of House influence. But the public called Jay "an archtraitor worse than Benedict Arnold." Jay remarked that he could have found his way across America by night using the light from the many burning effigies of himself.

Settling Differences with Spain

Spain still controlled Florida, and it had temporary control of the Louisiana Territory (the land west of the Mississippi River; see map on p. 111). Spain's interference in America's frontier regions remained an unsettled issue. Now Westerners clamored for the government to solve their problems. If the government did not help them, the settlers announced, they would take matters into their own hands and make their own treaty with Spain.

Washington responded by sending Thomas Pinckney of South Carolina to Spain to negotiate the dispute. Pinckney successfully made a treaty with Spain in 1795 that gave the United States the right of deposit at New Orleans and made the thirty-first parallel of latitude the southern boundary of the United States. The treaty, called the **Pinckney Treaty** in America, was also called the Treaty of San Lorenzo. Unlike the Jay Treaty, the Pinckney Treaty was popular, and Pinckney became an instant hero.

Section Review

1. Why did American enthusiasm over the French Revolution cool as time passed?
2. For what two reasons did Britain seize American ships and impress American sailors?
3. What precedent did Washington set when the House tried to block the treaty by refusing to allocate funds to carry it out?
4. What two issues were settled by the Pinckney Treaty and with what country was that treaty made?

John Jay

C. Continuation of the Government

Washington's presidency was a time of great trials for the new government, but the young nation survived. Now it was time for a new administration to take over and continue what Washington had begun.

Washington's Farewell

On September 19, 1796, six months before he officially left office, Washington gave what is now called his "Farewell Address" to David Claypoole, a newspaper publisher, to print. Although some people thought that Washington should run again, Washington said that two four-year terms were enough.

In addition to asserting the two-term tradition, the address gave advice for future years. Washington warned against disputes that would divide both politicians and people into factions. He urged caution in making any permanent alliances with foreign countries. This warning helped lead the United States to a century-long policy of isolationism. He encouraged maintaining the nation's credit and implied that America should stay out of debt.

Washington was sixty-six years old when he returned home to his beloved Mount Vernon. After eight years of the pressures of the presidency, the Washingtons enjoyed the change. But they had only a little over two years to enjoy their retirement. Washington died December 14, 1799, when his throat swelled shut from infection. He had been further weakened by doctors who bled him, a common medical practice of the time.

The country mourned him. His name and memory were greatly honored. He is the only American for whom a state was named, and seventy other places bear his name—the most places named for any individual. In addition, his image appears on many postage stamps and other national emblems and memorials. George Washington is, in the words of fellow-Virginian Henry Lee, still "first in war, first in peace, and first in the hearts of his countrymen."

Left: *Mount Vernon in Fairfax County, Virginia*
Right: *Martha Washington by an unidentified artist, National Portrait Gallery, Smithsonian Institution, Washington, D.C.©*

The Election of 1796

Since Washington had faced no opposition, had not campaigned for office, and had not had to deal with political parties in his elections, there were no real precedents to follow for the election of 1796. There were, however, political parties. The party leaders met and chose their candidates. Everyone expected the Republicans to choose Thomas Jefferson, and they did, with Aaron Burr to run as vice president. The Federalists, however, disagreed on their choice. The High Federalists, or pro-Hamiltonians, favored Thomas Pinckney, while the moderates of the party selected John Adams.

John Adams won the most votes in the electoral college. But the split in the Federalist votes allowed Jefferson to come in second and to win the vice-presidency. This meant that the president and vice president were from different parties, a situation that hindered the creation of a unified administration.

John Adams, second president of the United States

In Washington's Shadow

Few presidents came to office as well equipped as John Adams. A lawyer and a diplomat, he had never really sought or expected popularity, but his service in both of the Continental congresses had won him the respect of other legislators. In addition, his twelve years as minister in France and England had won the new nation respect overseas and had equipped Adams to deal with foreign affairs. As the nation's first vice president, John Adams called that office "the most insignificant ever contrived by man." His only constitutionally stated duties were to preside over the Senate, where he cast votes only in case of ties. Yet he did use his office to observe the problems of the new government firsthand. It was natural that when Washington decided not to run for a third term, Adams was suggested as his successor.

Following Washington as president, however, was no easy matter. On the day he took office, the cheering for Washington was louder than that for him. There were tears of sadness in people's eyes for a great man that was leaving and little praise for another that had arrived. On what was probably the biggest day of Adams's life, his inauguration day in Philadelphia, his wife Abigail was not there to share it. Fearing public criticism, Abigail had stayed home on their farm in Massachusetts. Thus his "dearest and best friend," as John called her in his letters, shared the experience only by letter.

Adams did not appoint a new cabinet but left Washington's cabinet in office. Although he did not know it, the cabinet was consulting with Alexander Hamilton, who was no longer in office, before they made decisions that sometimes opposed the

Abigail Adams

If any president ever found the perfect woman for his needs, it was John Adams, the second president. His wife, Abigail Smith Adams, loved him unfailingly through fifty-four years of marriage. She would do anything for him. He was often gloomy and uncompromising, but her charm would cheer him up and soothe his impatience. She sacrificed her personal pleasures for the good of his career and the benefit of their estate. She stood by him when all others were against him. She was a humble, dutiful wife but certainly no mindless slave. Her husband always delighted in her wit and opinions. Her many letters addressed him in all seriousness as "my dearest and best friend."

From their first meeting, he loved her ability to talk on a wide range of issues. Although she never had a formal education, she became one of the nation's best-educated women. She took every opportunity to learn, whether from her father's library or from the rigging on a ship. She would not let any obstacle keep her from marrying John. Her parents disliked him because he was nine years her elder, because he was born into a poor, lowly family, and because he was a lawyer. She, on the other hand, could claim a long line of noble ancestors. Her father was a parson, and he considered law a dishonest and unworthy profession. Nevertheless, he agreed to let them marry after a three-year courtship had proved their love. He chose for his wedding sermon the amusing text: "For John came neither eating bread nor drinking wine, yet ye say 'He hath a devil.'" The nineteen-year-old bride moved to a cottage in Braintree, Massachusetts. For ten years she managed the farm and raised five children while her husband rode his circuit of courts.

She wrote him often during this time. But it was not until John entered the political activities of the War for Independence that her writing was in earnest. It was at this time she proved to be the most outstanding woman correspondent of the period. The first of several separations came in 1774, when John left home to represent his state in the Continental Congress at Philadelphia. Her letters were essential sources of encouragement when he became disheartened by the course of the war and by his loneliness. She discussed politics as well as life on the farm. Her letters, written as often as three times a day, kept him up to date on the military and political situation at home. She was a keen observer, and she fully realized the historical importance of all she wrote. She kept up his faith in the colonies; she told her husband to declare a complete break from Britain.

She did not let the hardships at home depress her. She sacrificed her energy in running the farm, caring for needy American soldiers, and ordering the household. She never failed, despite outbreaks of smallpox in the area and her own poor health. She took great care in the raising of her children. She prodded her talented son John Quincy to make the most of himself. She learned Latin because she believed she should teach it to him. When he became gloomy later in life, she would remind him: "These are times in which a genius would wish to live. It is not in the still calms of life . . . the great characters are formed."

John returned home briefly in 1778, but he was soon sent to France as an ambassador. She did not try to stop him: "I found his honor and reputation dearer to me than my own pleasure and happiness." She let him take the ten-year-old John Quincy because she believed that the boy would profit from the experience. For six years, except a short leave in 1779, the couple was separated. Her many letters reveal much about her wide scope of interests. She scolded her husband when he failed to write or when his letters were too short. When she joined him in 1784, they had to send their son back home to Harvard. She kept in constant contact with John Quincy, showering him with motherly advice.

The house of John Adams in Quincy, Massachusetts

The next year, John took his wife with him to London as the first ambassador from the colonies. She rejoiced when he resigned in 1788 and they returned to Braintree: "I have learned to know the world and its value. I have seen high life. I have witnessed the luxury and pomp of state, the power of riches, and the influence of titles. Notwithstanding this, I feel that I can return to my little cottage and be happier . . . and if we have not wealth, we have what is greater—integrity." But in nine short months, national duty again called her husband away to New York to be vice president under Washington. He presided over the Senate and shared everything with her. When he was away, which was often, he said that her letters kept him going: "There is more good thoughts, fine strokes, and mother wit in them than I hear in the whole week." She and her friend Martha Washington helped their husbands to work well together.

When Abigail became the First Lady following John's election in 1796, she was better suited for her role than any woman has been since. She had traveled around the world, had been active in politics from the beginning, and took her duties very seriously. Experienced with running a large estate, she knew how to spend money wisely. Her receptions were smaller than those that the Washingtons had been able to afford, but the atmosphere was more informal and pleasant. She dressed modestly, but with the dignity befitting a president's wife. Her day started at 5:00 A.M. She kept the family budget, directed thirty servants, read, wrote, planned entertainments, received visitors, dined, and made public appearances.

Four months before John was to leave office, he decided to move into the unfinished building called the Executive Mansion (later called the White House). She agreed to join him, although she knew the stay was temporary and only six rooms were completed. The stairs were unfinished, the plaster was not up, and she had to yell for her servants because the bells had not yet arrived. Every day thirteen fires were kept burning in a vain attempt to dry out the walls. She even had to use the audience chamber to wash and hang the family wash. Yet she was a perfect hostess. She prepared the drawing room for a New Year's reception, the first of its kind given in the White House.

The couple left Washington and politics to spend sixteen years together at their farm. It had become a great success due to Abigail's wise management. The year she died, her son John Quincy had been appointed secretary of state. The future president wrote of his mother, "She had been fifty-five years the delight of my father's heart, the sweetener of all his toils, the comforter of all his sorrows, the sharer and heightener of all his joys."

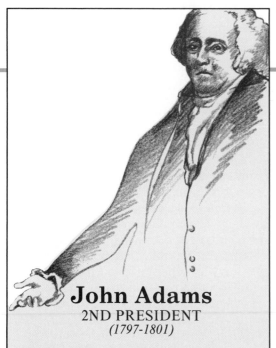

John Adams
2ND PRESIDENT
(1797-1801)

Born: Braintree, Massachusetts, October 30, 1735
Family: married Abigail Smith; one daughter and four sons
Occupation: lawyer
Home: Peacefield, Quincy, Massachusetts
Religion: Unitarian
Election: 1796—defeated Thomas Jefferson
Political Party: Federalist (first election under real two-party system)
Vice President: Thomas Jefferson
Interesting Facts and Accomplishments:
graduate of Harvard
could read seven languages
first president to live in White House; Washington, D.C. became the new capital
lived to age ninety-one, older than any other president
his son, John Quincy Adams became sixth president (only father-son presidents)
Death: July 4, 1826 (fiftieth anniversary of the Declaration of Independence and same day as Thomas Jefferson's death)

new president's wishes. This opposition frustrated many of Adams's policies. Criticisms from his political adversaries throughout his term of office caused Adams to lose the admiration of many Americans. Even though John Adams sought the best interest of his country in his actions as president, he could never be as popular as George Washington.

To people outside his own family, Adams often seemed reserved and aloof. Had he perhaps made an effort to be more outgoing with the American people, Adams's presidency might have been more effective. However, he did have a strong sense that it was his God-given duty to serve others, regardless of the personal cost. This idea he passed on to his own children. His descendants have continued to serve their nation, state, and city for over two hundred years.

Although Adams's one term as president was not particularly impressive in some matters, it was very important in one respect. The new government, which was passed from the "Father of Our Country," George Washington, to Adams, was safely kept and passed on to be continued to our day.

Section Review

1. When he left office, in what three areas did Washington advise that caution should be exercised?
2. Name the Federalist and the Democratic-Republican candidates for president in the election of 1796.
3. What was unusual about the outcome of the election of 1796?

D. Difficulties for President Adams

Even though George Washington had set a good example as first president and though the country was growing stronger, Adams still had a difficult job ahead of him.

The XYZ Affair

Although the British were still seizing American ships when Adams took office, the greatest problem faced came from America's recent ally, France. A new French government, angered by the Jay Treaty with Britain, became hostile. The French ordered their navy to raid American shipping. They seized more than three hundred American sailors found on British ships. Moreover, the French said they would hang the impressed American sailors they found. To add to the insult, they refused to receive Charles Cotesworth Pinckney, the American minister to France.

American Envoys Meet French Agents—Although some Federalists believed Adams should break relations with France and perhaps even declare war, he first chose to try negotiating. He sent John Marshall and Elbridge Gerry to assist Pinckney. The trio sought a hearing with Talleyrand, the French minister of foreign affairs, but after nine months they had yet to see the man. However, the Americans did meet his three agents. The agents implied that the Americans could have recognition if they would give a $250,000 bribe and insure a $10 million loan for France.

Adams, still a lawyer at heart, went to Congress to expose this insult to the United States. He laid out every piece of evidence before an open session of Congress. To protect the three American envoys, Adams substituted the letters *X, Y,* and *Z* for the names of the French agents. Soon the whole episode was dubbed **"the XYZ Affair."**

A Call to Arms—Congress was angered by the evidence and took measures to arm the country for action against France. They voted, over Republican opposition, to make the navy a separate department, and to build forty ships, a far cry from the three-vessel fleet of Washington. The most famous of the new frigates was the U.S.S. *Constitution.* The size of the army was tripled. Washington, still alive at that time but reluctant to lead an army again, was recalled as commander-in-chief. He asked for Alexander Hamilton, Thomas Pinckney, and Henry Knox—to be ranked in that order—as his commanders.

Although open war was never declared, by the fall of 1800, ninety French vessels had been captured while the Americans had lost but one ship. (Because there was some actual fighting, this conflict is sometimes called a "quasi-war.") The public cheered the victories and pressured for real war. But Adams was hesitant. He believed a full-scale war unwise and the United States unprepared to fight.

War Avoided—Meanwhile the French formed still another government; Napoleon Bonaparte took over in 1799. Napoleon, who could see that the United States might be a stronger enemy than was commonly thought, grew nervous. With France's defeat by Lord Nelson at the battle of the Nile and the entrapment of its army in Egypt, Napoleon sent word he would move to a peace table.

The Capitol in Washington, D.C., as it appeared around 1800

Although Adams wanted Napoleon to pay the damages, he settled for the signing of a new agreement called the **Convention of 1800.** Adams had avoided war. But few of his countrymen recognized the benefit. Dismayed Federalists now sided with the Republicans and denounced him. But Adams considered this his single most important contribution to America. He requested that his epitaph (the engraving on his tombstone) read: "Here lies John Adams who took upon himself the responsibility of peace with France in the year 1800."

Federalist Opposition to Adams

Adams, who responded to duty and was a statesman rather than a politician, had done little to win the favor of the Federalist party leaders on domestic matters. Adams began to pay a high price for his restraint even before the conflict with France became

Napoleon Bonaparte, ruler of France in the early nineteenth century

an issue. In 1798 Adams angered the majority of his party when he disagreed with them on some of their legislation.

The Alien and Sedition Acts—In 1798, against Adams's wishes, some of the Federalists passed four laws called the **Alien and Sedition Acts.** Although the Federalists claimed that the laws would help the whole country, the acts were aimed to harm the Democratic-Republican party and to keep it from gaining power.

The first of the laws, the Naturalization Act, extended the time required to gain American citizenship from five to fourteen years. Since most immigrants joined the Democratic-Republican party, the supposed party of the "common man," this act would keep them from voting. However, because states controlled their own elections, and the Republicans had control in many states, the law had little affect.

The Alien Enemies Act and the Alien Act allowed the president to imprison or expel any foreigners deemed "dangerous to the peace and safety of the United States." The first act gave this power during times of war or invasion, and the second allowed him to deport any aliens thought to be dangerous even if war had not been declared. The laws were purposely though dangerously vague. "Peace and safety" were not defined, nor was "war." Adams, aware of the dangers of the acts, never enforced them.

The last act, the Sedition Act, however, was enforced. It said that any person found guilty of saying, writing, or publishing anything false or malicious against the government or its officials could be fined $2,000 and imprisoned up to two years. The Republicans rightly saw this act as an attempt to stop both their mouths and pens. They protested that the law was a violation of the freedom of the press and speech. Although numbers of people were arrested under this law, only twenty-five were brought to trial, and scarcely a dozen were convicted.

Opposition to the Alien and Sedition Acts—The Republicans worked hard to overrule the Alien and Sedition Acts, and a few Federalists sympathized. Republicans James Madison and Thomas Jefferson wrote **Virginia and Kentucky Resolutions** for those two state legislatures. Each set of resolutions asserted the right of **nullification,** the ability of a state to nullify, or declare void, any federal law within its boundaries. Jefferson and Madison held that the union of states had come from an agreement in which the states freely gave up their independent rights to a central government. But the states were still sovereign, holding powers of their own. This fact should allow states to rule on whether actions of the federal government were constitutional in their opinion. Supporters of nullification based their thinking on Article 6 of the Constitution. (See p. 151.) However, those who opposed nullification read the same article to mean supremacy of the national government over the state.

Although the Kentucky and Virginia Resolutions were never put into effect, the idea that they expressed, nullification, resurfaced several times over the next sixty years. Eventually it led to the temporary breakup of the federal union and a civil war. Their immediate effect, when coupled with the Alien and Sedition Act, was a Republican victory at the polls in 1800.

The Disputed Election of 1800

Despite their dislike of Adams, the Federalists chose him to run for reelection in 1800, and they selected Charles Cotesworth Pinckney of South Carolina as his vice-presidential running mate. The Republicans chose Thomas Jefferson for president and **Aaron Burr** of New York to run with him.

However, the ballots for that election did not state which man was running for which office. This omission had caused a problem in 1796, and it did again in 1800. Each of the electoral college members was allowed to cast two votes. When the 1800 vote came in, Jefferson and Burr both received equal numbers of votes, more than Adams or Pinckney, but there was no designation that Jefferson was the one who was supposed to be president.

The Constitution stated (see p. 144) that in tie cases the president would be selected by the House of Representatives. Each state was to have one vote, and the winner was to have a majority of votes cast (nine at that time).

Burr, ever a political opportunist, refused to defer to Jefferson and say he was

Monticello, home of Thomas Jefferson

Thomas Jefferson

really running for vice president. Many of the Federalists decided to vote for Burr. They believed that if they helped him win, he would later be more favorable to their party. Some also believed that if there was a deadlock, Adams or Pinckney might win as a compromise candidate.

The states voted: Jefferson took eight states, but he did not get the needed majority. The election dragged on for a week and through thirty-five ballots. Finally on the thirty-sixth ballot, James Baynard of Delaware shifted his vote to Jefferson.

Section Review

1. How did the French react to Jay's treaty with England?
2. What steps did the Americans take to prepare for war with France?
3. Why did Napoleon seek peace with the United States?
4. What was the purpose of the Sedition Act? Why did the Democratic-Republicans feel this law unfair?
5. What power did the nullification theory give to the states?

E. Strengthening the Courts

One of John Adams's accomplishments was the appointment of a new chief justice for the Supreme Court. His appointment had far-reaching effects on the power of the court.

The Appointment of John Marshall

During Adams's term the health of Oliver Ellsworth, chief justice of the Supreme Court, failed. Ellsworth resigned shortly before Adams left office, giving him the rare opportunity of appointing a new chief justice and extending the influence of his administration far beyond his term as president. On January 20, 1801, Adams nominated **John Marshall,** and the Senate confirmed Marshall a short time later.

John Marshall agreed with Alexander Hamilton, who had earlier called the judicial branch "the weakest of the three departments of power." Marshall believed the national government's power could be made stronger through the courts. He believed the nation's future was closely tied to the Constitution's ability to adapt to changes in American life. The courts could be guardians of the past as well as guides of future change.

Marshall wasted no time in starting to strengthen the court system. First, he believed the Supreme Court looked weak in the eyes of the people. Every justice had been writing his own ideas on each case rather than issuing a group opinion for the majority. Marshall unified the court by having the justices hold private conferences, and by having them issue one opinion to support their decision, usually called the majority opinion. If some justices disagreed, they could still write dissenting opinions telling why.

The Judiciary Bill and the Midnight Judges

Just six days before Adams left office, Congress passed the Judiciary Act of 1801. Until this time the Supreme Court justices had been serving as circuit court judges, too. This required them to move from place to place, as the cases demanded. The new act created sixteen new circuit judgeships to aid in administration of the law. It also cut the number of court justices from six to five and allowed a number of justices of the peace to be appointed.

Since John Adams signed the commissions that appointed some fifty-eight judges to full-time positions late the night before he left office, the judges have often been called "the midnight judges." Although the Republicans were highly critical and later repealed the act, Adams was within the law in naming his judges. Moreover, the Senate had to approve his choices, and so he would have their backing for these appointments if they were accepted.

Marbury v. Madison

Federalist William Marbury had been appointed as one of Adams's midnight judges. The commission for his job was not delivered before Adams left office, however, and James Madison, the Republican secretary of state, refused to release it. Marbury sued for his job, believing that it was Madison's duty to deliver that commission.

Chief Justice Marshall decided the case of *Marbury* v. *Madison.* He realized that if he gave Madison the order to deliver the document, he would probably ignore it. This would weaken the image of the Supreme Court. Instead Marshall ruled that Madison did not have to deliver the commission because the section of the federal law which granted such power was unconstitutional. Although the Supreme Court had earlier declared state laws to be unconstitutional, this was the first time the court had declared a federal law unconstitutional. Thus the court took the power of **judicial review,** which the Constitution provided for state laws, and applied it to federal laws as well. This was an extension of the court's power.

Despite the favorable decision in *Marbury* v. *Madison,* Jefferson probably would have challenged Marshall's use of judicial review in later cases in an attempt to reduce Marshall's power. Marshall, however, outfoxed him. He never again used the power himself, and it would be 1857 before another chief justice would assert judicial review.

Section Review

1. Whom did Adams nominate to be the chief justice of the Supreme Court?
2. How did the new chief justice strengthen the power of the judicial branch of the government?
3. What was the significance of the *Marbury* v. *Madison* case?

Summary

As first president of the United States under the Constitution, George Washington helped to establish a sound government for the young nation. His administration overcame foreign and domestic threats to the country's stability and passed a functioning government on to the second president, John Adams. Although not a popular figure like Washington, Adams also provided needed leadership to steer the government through the problems of the era.

Chapter Review

Do You Remember?

■ Identify each of the following people or terms.
1. This French citizen hoped to gain American support for France.
2. The president is "advised" by this group of presidential advisors.
3. Marbury tried to get his commission from this secretary of state.
4. This political party reflected Hamilton's views.
5. Adams appointed these judges at "the last minute."
6. The British forced American sailors to serve in their navy by this method.
7. This war hero stopped Indian attacks in the Northwest Territory.
8. Some claimed that states had this right to declare a federal law to be void.
9. Adams appointed this man to be chief justice of the Supreme Court.
10. This secretary of the treasury planned the nation's finances.
11. John Marshall used this type of review to declare a federal law unconstitutional.
12. This dipolmat made a popular treaty with Spain
13. This formal ceremony begins a president's term.
14. Anthony Wayne defeated the Indians here.

Why Is It So?

1. Why was establishing a good financial system for the nation an important issue?
2. Why did two political parties develop during Washington's administration?
3. Why did the United States need to remain neutral in the war between France and Britain?
4. Why was the XYZ Affair an insult to the United States?
5. Why was the election of 1800 called a disputed election?
6. Why was the court case *Marbury* v. *Madison* significant?

What Do You Think?

1. Why do you think George Washington became such a distinguished and respected president in America's history?
2. Why do you think John Adams's presidency was not considered to be as successful as that of Washington's?
3. Why was the Sedition Act dangerous?

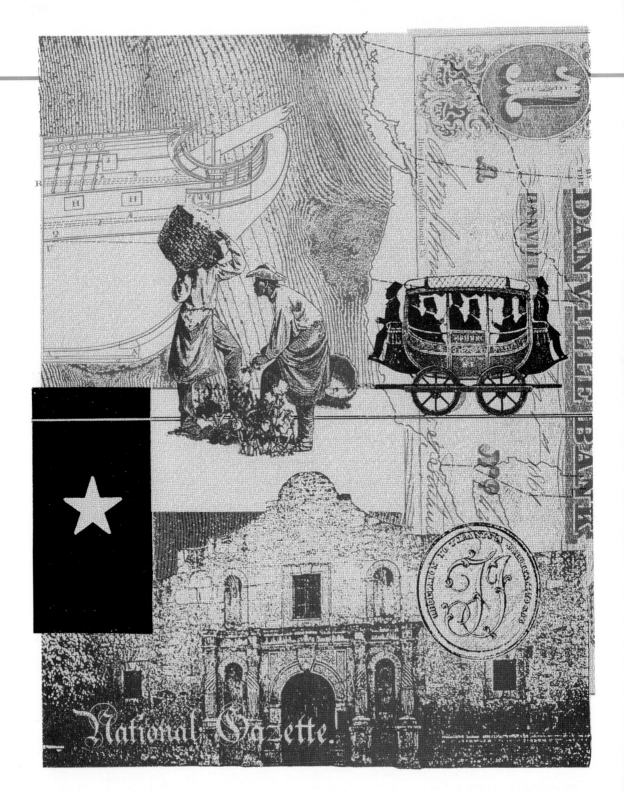

10

Growth of a Nation

Captain William Clark wrote in his notes on November 7, 1805, "Ocian in view! O! the joy." After nearly fourteen months of hardship, toil, and peril, William Clark, Meriwether Lewis, and their band of rugged adventurers had crossed through America's western wilderness to the Pacific. The Lewis and Clark Expedition was only one of the challenging experiences that the early years of the nineteenth century held in store for the United States.

Raising the flag at Fort McHenry

A. Triumphs of a Growing Nation

The election of 1800 had brought the Democratic-Republican party into power. Many Americans believed that the Federalists had used the government for the greater benefit of the Northeast's wealthy merchants and industrialists. Thomas Jefferson's presidency was thought to be a victory for the common people.

Thomas Jefferson took his oath of office on March 4, 1801. He was the first president to be inaugurated in Washington, D.C., the nation's new but still unfinished capital. New York and Philadelphia, the two previous capitals, were older, elegant cities. Washington, D.C., in 1801, however, did not look like the beautiful city we know today. For example, the mall in front of the partly finished Capitol was a forest. Members of Congress reached the White House by using a muddy track though the trees. There were no paved streets labeled with street signs. The new city was almost wilderness.

Although some historians have suggested Jefferson's presidency meant great change—a Jefferson Revolution—for the common man, such suggestions are overblown. The new president stressed simplicity and informality, but this may have resulted from necessity more than design. In his inaugural address, President Jefferson seemed eager to bind the nation's factions together. "Let us then fellow-citizens unite with one heart and one mind. . . . We have called by different names brethren of the same principle. We are all [Democratic-]Republicans, we are all Federalists."

Reversing Federalist Policies

During his first term Jefferson increased his popularity in a variety of ways. He began by ousting only those Federalists who had abused their powers, especially those who had enforced the Sedition Act.

Rather than having the Alien and Sedition Acts repealed, Jefferson let them expire in 1801. He pardoned those jailed under the Sedition Act and wrote personal letters of apology to the victims. The five-year residence requirement for citizens was restored, thus repealing the Naturalization Act, which had required a citizenship of fourteen years.

Thomas Jefferson
3RD PRESIDENT
(1801-1809)

Born: Albemarle County, Virginia, April 13, 1743
Family: Married Martha Wayles Skelton, a widow; six children, two daughters survived
Occupation: lawyer, architect, inventor
Home: Monticello, Charlottesville, Virginia
Religion: Unitarian
Elections: 1800—elected by House of Representatives on 36th ballot
1804—defeated Charles Cotesworth Pinckney
Political Party: Democratic-Republican
Vice Presidents: first term—Aaron Burr; second term—George Clinton
Interesting Facts and Accomplishments:
wrote the Declaration of Independence
designed his home, Monticello
became founder and first president of the University of Virginia after leaving office
first president to take the oath of office in Washington, D.C.
Death: the same day as John Adams—July 4, 1826

Gallatin, Jefferson's secretary of the treasury, was a frugal financier. He and Jefferson wanted to rid themselves of the debt incurred when the nation's defenses were increased during the XYZ affair. Jefferson opposed a strong standing army and navy, fearing they could be sources of too much federal power. Instead he chose to rely on state militias that were cheaper to maintain because they were part-time and because they were not federally funded. By doing this, he decreased the national debt by one-half, which in turn allowed him to abolish the whiskey tax.

At Jefferson's request Congress reversed itself and repealed the Judiciary Act of 1801. Consequently, many of the midnight judges never served. Jefferson then attacked the Federalist courts from another angle. According to the Constitution, judges were to be appointed to office for life. But the Constitution also said that judges could be impeached for "Treason, Bribery, or other high Crimes and Misdemeanors." Before taking power the Jeffersonians had claimed to take the Constitution literally; now they wished to use the language loosely.

First, the Jeffersonians impeached John Pickering, a district court judge from New Hampshire. Because Pickering was both an alcoholic and insane, they were able to get the House to file the charges and two-thirds of the Senate to vote to remove him.

But the next target, Federalist Supreme Court Justice Samuel Chase, was another story. Although Chase was not a great jurist, his attacks on Republicans were hardly a crime. The Senate, sensing that Jefferson was threatening to destroy the Supreme Court's power and independence, refused to remove Chase. Jefferson's attacks on the judiciary probably made some judges more

responsive to public opinion, but after this defeat Jefferson never again attacked the courts.

Retaining Federalist Benefits

Jefferson was wise enough to leave some Federalist policies alone. Although he had opposed the founding of a national bank, he now left it intact because it was working well. He also retained the Federalist plan for repaying war debts. Jefferson, who had charged others with hypocrisy in earlier years, now began to see how difficult it was to be a truly consistent politician. Although he had often denounced the growth of the government's power when Washington and Adams were president, he came to realize that power was not necessarily bad, if used for good ends. Since he believed his ends were good, he became skillful in his use of presidential powers. He soon extended presidential powers farther than his predecessors had.

The Barbary Pirates and the Tripolitan Wars

A foreign challenge came to America from the small Muslim countries in North Africa known as the Barbary States. These countries gained money by charging tribute to ships that sailed on the Mediterranean. This piracy hampered trade in the Mediterranean Sea. While he had been secretary of state, Jefferson had suggested that the United States organize an international blockade to shatter the system. But the two-million-dollar annual tribute seemed small compared with the cost of a possible war.

Now, however, the Barbary States increased their tribute fees, and Jefferson refused to pay them. The pasha (ruler) of Tripoli then declared war. Jefferson sent Commodore Richard Dale and later Stephen

Decatur to the region to protect American interests and deal with the terrorists. Dale tried a local blockade. On February 16, 1804, Decatur boldly sailed into Tripoli's harbor and seized the American frigate *Philadelphia,* which had been run aground and captured. Rather than let Tripoli have the ship, he burned it. Over the next decade Decatur led other expeditions in the area. The tribute dispute was settled in 1815, when a combined British-American force moved in on the pirates.

The **Tripolitan War** increased the respect of foreign countries for the United States. It also allowed American naval commanders to stay in practice and to be prepared for the much larger conflict with England that was soon to come.

The Louisiana Purchase

The port of New Orleans was of great importance to American settlements west of the Appalachians. Three-eighths of American trade in 1800 passed through this port in Spanish-owned Louisiana Territory. In 1800 Spain ceded Louisiana back to France, its original owner. France, however, was no longer the ally who had helped win American independence. In the years since the French Revolution, she had given up republican ideals and was under the rule of Napoleon. Jefferson correctly suspected that Napoleon, who had been forced into a temporary truce with Britain, was planning a New World empire. Napoleon's brother-in-law, Charles LeClerc, and large numbers of troops had arrived in Haiti, an easy launching point for an invasion of North America. At the same time another French force moved to a Dutch port to await the signal to embark across the Atlantic.

Jefferson told Robert Livingston, the American ambassador to France, to try to buy New Orleans and East and West Florida. Jefferson then put the nation on war footing. Secretary of War Henry Dearborn set up recruiting centers for soldiers, rushed troops to Fort Adams near Natchez, Mississippi, and sent more guns and ammunition to battle LeClerc's forces.

A series of events forced Napoleon to reconsider. First, a yellow fever epidemic doubled his heavy war losses in Haiti. Second, winter ice stranded his other army in Holland. At the same time he was told that Jefferson did not want the Louisiana Territory because it would divide the American nation into eastern and western factions. (This was an idea that Jefferson had purposely planted.) Napoleon reasoned that he should defeat Britain first. If England was soundly defeated, he could control the seas and then handle a divided America. Besides, the money he needed to fight Britain could come from the sale of Louisiana.

Initially, Napoleon's foreign minister Talleyrand had rejected Livingston's offer for New Orleans. Then, nine months later, in May 1803, Talleyrand suddenly asked the American if he wanted to buy the entire Louisiana Territory. After several bargaining sessions, Livingston settled on $15 million for what was later discovered to be 529,911,680 acres—making the cost only 2.8 cents per acre. Livingston and the other envoys working on the negotiations nervously wrote Jefferson to inform him of "a truly noble acquisition." They hoped Jefferson would not be angry because they had exceeded their original instructions.

Jefferson's feelings about the **Louisiana Purchase** were mixed. There were over fifty thousand French and Spanish Creoles in Louisiana. Would his action make them citizens? Did he have the right to make them citizens without their consent? Did he have the right to buy land for the nation when the Constitution did not give him the power?

Jefferson hesitated, but only briefly. His first thought was to ask Congress to pass an amendment making such a land purchase legal. This would insure the bargain and preserve his principles. But he feared that the restless Napoleon might change his mind before three-quarters of the states approved the amendment. Jefferson decided to call Congress into special session, ask for the purchase, and not bring up any of the constitutional questions concerning the bargain. In doing so, Jefferson again extended governmental powers beyond those that the Constitution specifically gave. The Senate approved the purchase, and rushed the money to France on the fastest ship available. On December 20, 1803, the Stars and Stripes were raised over Louisiana.

The Western Expeditions

The Lewis and Clark Expedition—Even before the Louisiana Purchase was made, Jefferson was interested in learning more about the West. He recruited his private secretary, **Meriwether Lewis**, to lead the first of two expeditions to explore the West. Lewis chose **William Clark,** under whom he had fought in the Indian wars in the Northwest Territory, to go with him. Although Clark lacked the classical education of Lewis, Clark's wilderness experience and interests made him a good surveyor, mapmaker and naturalist. Lewis and Clark went west to seek the source of the Missouri River and to explore lands of what became ten western states.

Jefferson sent Lewis a detailed letter of instructions and advice. Lewis and Clark were to make careful studies on the geology, botany, and zoology of the region, and to gather detailed information on any natives they met. They were to search for the source of the Missouri River, report on any commercial possibilities, and seek for evidence of British soldiers or forts in the vast area.

Lewis hurried to Philadelphia where he took crash courses under five leading scientists. He learned celestial navigation, geology, and medicine. He even learned to perform emergency surgery.

Congress approved an expense of $2,500 for the expedition to buy the needed supplies and to pay men who were out twenty-eight months, covering more than nine thousand miles. The trip actually cost $39,000. For repeatedly risking their lives during more than three years of work, Lewis and Clark each received 1,600 acres of public land.

Meriwether Lewis and William Clark

Westward Expansion
and Exploration

←——→ Lewis & Clark
———— Zebulon Pike

0   100   200   300
Scale of Miles

The party left St. Louis on May 14, 1804 (five months after the Louisiana Purchase had been made), using a fifty-five-foot keelboat and two flat-bottomed dugouts. The keelboat had a cannon mounted at the bow and lockers whose heavy lids could be raised to protect the men. But when the Missouri River became shallow further upstream, all the boats were abandoned.

There were twenty-nine men in the official party, along with seven soldiers and nine river men who acted as guards. York, Captain Clark's personal slave, came with his master. Among the Indians he was an object of curiosity. Some of them had seen white trappers and fur traders before, but none had ever seen a black man. They wanted not only to look at him but also to feel him. The Indians thought York was painted and tried to scrub his skin.

The trip west took the group from St. Louis on the Mississippi River to the site of Astoria, Oregon, on the Pacific Coast. The men followed the Missouri, Snake, and Columbia rivers most of the way. At Fort Mandan, in what is now North Dakota, a French fur trapper named Charbonneau (shahr bohn NOH) joined the expedition. His wife, Sacajawea (sak uh juh WEE uh), also came along. She was a Shoshone Indian who had been stolen from her tribe as a child. When the explorers had no means of transportation and desperately needed horses, they met a group of Shoshones, including Sacajawea's long-lost brother, now a chief. They received thirty horses from the Shoshones. Eventually they had to kill some of the horses for food. Sacajawea helped the expedition through the Bitterroot Mountains with her guiding abilities and her skills as an interpreter.

The expedition usually moved ten miles a day, sometimes less. The scenery was breathtaking. The trip to discover the falls of the Missouri was worth the view, but it meant carrying their boats and everything else for sixteen miles. Clark nearly lost his life when he ran into a bear that was more than seven feet tall. Ten shots were needed to bring it down. He named it the "grizzly" bear. Later Lewis was mistaken for an elk, shot in the leg, and had difficulty continuing the journey. The party split up to explore the two branches of the Missouri on their return trip. Lewis navigated the upper Missouri while Clark's group followed the Yellowstone. The group met on the Missouri above Fort Mandan, and the trip back to St. Louis was completed uneventfully on September 23, 1806.

Lewis and Clark were celebrities of their day. They were acclaimed just as aviators and astronauts have been in the twentieth century. In their explorations, the team had discovered twenty-five varieties of fish (including the anchovy), six kinds of birds, five reptiles, and four amphibians. Clark used his artistic talent to illustrate the flowers, plants, animals, and Indians he had seen on the trip. Their journals did much to stir interest in western settlement. Lewis and Clark were also among the last white men to contact western Indians who were mostly unaffected by the white man's way of life. They found the Indians to be friendly and curious. In a few years the western

A statue of Sacajawea, the Indian woman who accompanied Lewis and Clark on their expedition, stands in a park in Portland, Oregon.

Indians would have reason to become suspicious of, if not openly hostile to, whites.

The Pike Expedition—The second expedition, under **Zebulon Pike,** was accomplished in two different trips. On the first, in 1804, Pike followed the Mississippi in search of its source. He also let the British know that the American flag would fly over the Louisiana Territory, although he did not have enough military force to oust the British from their forts.

Pike's second trip, in 1806-1807, went up the Arkansas River into Spanish-held territories. He explored the Rockies of Colorado and sighted the peak that today bears his name. He used the Rio Grande for his return trip but was captured by the Spanish. They imprisoned him and took his diaries, but he was later released. Other explorers followed him into the region in preparation for the later settlement of these mountainous lands.

Section Review

1. What was unique about Jefferson's inauguration? What did he stress in his inauguration speech?
2. Why did the United States pay tribute fees to the Barbary States?
3. Why was the city of New Orleans vital to the settlers west of the Appalachian Mountains? What did Jefferson fear might happen to this area?
4. How did the Louisiana Territory finally become part of the United States? Why did Jefferson hesitate to take advantage of this bargain?
5. List the accomplishments of the Lewis and Clark expedition; of the Pike expeditions.

B. Troubles of the Growing Nation

In his reelection in 1804, Jefferson and his new running mate, New Yorker George Clinton, carried every state but Connecticut and Delaware. Burr, who had alienated Jefferson in the election of 1800, had been ignored most of the first term and was dropped as his running mate.

Neutral Rights at Sea

During Jefferson's second term as president, the defense of neutral rights at sea again troubled America. The years to come held many of the same frustrations faced earlier by Washington and Adams. France and Britain were again at war. Americans, determined to make money from the war, traded with both war powers. Huge stocks of goods from French colonies in the West Indies found their way to American ports. The British also found a ready market in growing America. While the warring countries were busy fighting each other, they did not bother American shipping.

With Lord Nelson's victory over the French fleet at Trafalgar on October 21, 1805, Britain kept her supremacy at sea. Napoleon's armies, however, controlled much of Europe, having defeated Austria, Prussia, and Russia. By 1807 the war was a stalemate. Both countries now planned to win by destroying the economy of the other. The United States was soon caught in the middle of this strategy.

British and French Actions—The British blockaded all French-controlled European ports, and they proclaimed their **Orders in Council** in 1807 to make it illegal for neutral nations to trade in European ports unless they first stopped in England

Whatever Happened to Aaron Burr?

Aaron Burr, a grandson of Jonathan Edwards, had risen to fame through his heroism and service under Washington during the War for Independence. Some predicted a promising career for the man, and he did achieve the vice-presidency in 1800. It would not have been surprising for him to become president. But further glory never came for Burr.

Because Burr had tried to usurp the presidency in the election of 1800, Jefferson ignored Burr while he was vice president. Burr resented his exclusion and believed that his talents were not being recognized.

In 1804, while still vice president, Burr decided to run for governor of New York. Alexander Hamilton campaigned for Burr's rival, and the two men became bitter enemies. Biting words from both appeared in the press. Burr demanded Hamilton take back his statements. When Hamilton refused, Burr challenged him to a duel. Burr killed Hamilton in the duel, and many considered it murder because Hamilton fired into the air.

Scorned in the East, Burr fled west, while he was still vice president. He became involved in a scheme to set up an empire in Louisiana. Some think that he planned to conquer Mexico and become its emperor. Jefferson had him charged with treason. Burr was brought east to face trial, but he was acquitted (cleared of charges) because there was only one witness who would attest to his treason in open court.

After the trial Burr became an outcast, suffering personal loss and rejection. Burr could not win respect in America, and he also failed in England. Burr could have served his country with distinction; instead he died disgraced. His life was ruined by his inability to deal with his pride. He was not willing to wait until people recognized his genuine talents but pushed himself into positions and used people. He had not learned the truth of I Peter 5:6-7: "Humble yourselves therefore under the mighty hand of God, that he may exalt you in due time: casting all your care upon him; for he careth for you."

for inspection. Britain hoped that limiting European trade with America would cause so much dissatisfaction that the conquered nations would revolt against Napoleon.

France meanwhile hoped to keep Britain from getting necessary supplies, forcing her surrender. To stop the flow, the French ordered a blockade of British ports. In 1807 Napoleon issued the **Berlin and Milan Decrees,** which stated that neutral ships trading with Britain or obeying the Orders in Council could be seized.

The potential profits were so high, however, that Americans risked defying both powers. If only one of three trade vessels got through, the ship owner still made a profit.

The Chesapeake and the Leopard— Both Britain and France seized ships and cargoes. The British also seized American sailors, as they had in the 1790s. More than ten thousand Americans were impressed by the British. (See p. 178.) Although forty per cent were released once they arrived in England, the practice was greatly resented.

Things worsened because the British believed American officials were encouraging His Majesty's sailors to desert. Many of the desertions took place around Chesapeake Bay, where the many inlets gave the deserters refuge. A few even enlisted in the United States Navy. One deserter, Jenkin

The Jefferson Bible

He saith unto them, But whom say ye that I am? And Simon Peter answered and said, Thou art the Christ, the Son of the living God. (Matt. 16:15-16)

In 1804 Thomas Jefferson began work on the first of two of his own editions of the Bible. Among many other things Jefferson had studied religions and religious figures of the past. He wrote, "Of all the systems of morality, ancient or modern, which have come under my observation, none appear to me so pure as that of Jesus." Although he was impressed by

Ratford, served on the U.S.S. *Chesapeake,* based at the Norfolk navy yard. The British found out where he was when he insulted his old officers, who were on shore leave in Norfolk.

When the *Chesapeake* left harbor on June 1, 1807, the British were on the lookout for her. The British ship H.M.S. *Leopard* ordered the frigate to stop to be searched. The captain refused. The *Leopard* then fired three broadsides (all the guns on one side of the ship firing together) at the *Chesapeake,* leaving three dead, eighteen wounded, and a nation incensed. Ratford and three other deserters were forcibly removed.

The ***Chesapeake* affair** stirred a desire for war, but Jefferson, like Adams, took a more moderate course. Since Jefferson had just disarmed the navy and the army to reduce his budget, he really had few options. He chose an economic option, believing that if the United States withheld

the precepts of Jesus, he did not believe Jesus to be the Son of God.

It was this erroneous view of Jesus that led Jefferson to put together his own editions of the Bible. His first work was a forty-six-page extract called *The Philosophy of Jesus of Nazareth.* It contained the moral teachings of Jesus in nugget form, organized by topic. Believing it suffered from being "too hastily done," he then started on a fifteen-year project to distill the gospel of Jesus—what he thought Jesus actually did and said, rather than what others in Scripture said about Him. He sent to Ireland for two English New Testaments, and he also used Greek, Latin, and French translations. He then assembled them in columns, each language side by side.

Jefferson did not believe the miracle stories, nor could his reason grasp supernatural events. Thus in Jefferson's Bible there are no verses telling of Jesus' walking on the water, healing the sick, or being raised from the dead. Thomas Jefferson's gospel ends with Jesus in the tomb. Jefferson also omitted references to the Holy Spirit. His rendition of the Christmas story deletes the shepherds, angels, and references to the glory of God, and it does not make Jesus the Saviour who is Christ the Lord. Although his scissors-and-paste Bible denies by omission the hope of life after death that God's Word assures us, Jefferson did believe in a vague personal immortality. Perhaps that was because his wife and child had preceded him in death; at least he talked of being reunited with them.

Jefferson cut everything out of the Bible that he did not believe and pasted the rest together. We know, however, that "all scripture is given by inspiration of God" (II Tim. 3:16). Jefferson's shortened gospels show us that we cannot expect the natural man—then or now—to receive the things of the Spirit of Christ, "for they are foolishness unto him" (I Cor. 2:14). In all Jefferson's dealings with Scripture he ignored Revelation 22:19—"If any man shall take away from the words of the book of this prophecy, God shall take away his part out of the book of life."

goods and closed her ports to trade, Britain and France would soon be begging for American goods.

The Embargo Act of 1807—Jefferson asked Congress to place an **embargo,** a stop on all exports from the United States, and to forbid imports from Europe to be carried on American ships. Since foreign ships could not carry any exports, there was little reason for them to come. Domestic coastal trade was still allowed. Clever shippers found the loopholes and turned to smuggling, but when the Giles Enforcement Act of 1809 closed some of the loopholes, American trade ceased.

Although the people had complained about impressment and ship seizures, the lack of any trade at all angered them more. Farmers who sold foodstuffs and raw materials to Europe saw prices plunge because there were no buyers for their goods. Merchants and those dependent on them were hurt, too. Sympathy toward Britain grew, especially in Federalist New England, the area most affected. The Embargo Act did little to hurt the British, but its effect on America was great.

The law came under attack from both parties, and just before leaving office in March 1809, Jefferson signed a new act. The Non-Intercourse Act lifted the embargo somewhat and permitted trade with foreign nations except France and Britain.

James Madison Meets More Difficulties

Thomas Jefferson declined a third term. His secretary of state, James Madison, ran for the Republicans in 1808 and defeated Federalist C. C. Pinckney. Madison had secured his place in history before becoming president. He brought a wealth of experi-

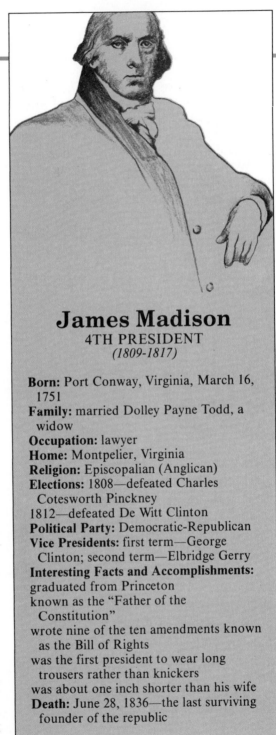

James Madison
4TH PRESIDENT
(1809-1817)

Born: Port Conway, Virginia, March 16, 1751
Family: married Dolley Payne Todd, a widow
Occupation: lawyer
Home: Montpelier, Virginia
Religion: Episcopalian (Anglican)
Elections: 1808—defeated Charles Cotesworth Pinckney
1812—defeated De Witt Clinton
Political Party: Democratic-Republican
Vice Presidents: first term—George Clinton; second term—Elbridge Gerry
Interesting Facts and Accomplishments:
graduated from Princeton
known as the "Father of the Constitution"
wrote nine of the ten amendments known as the Bill of Rights
was the first president to wear long trousers rather than knickers
was about one inch shorter than his wife
Death: June 28, 1836—the last surviving founder of the republic

ence to his office and was one of America's most intelligent presidents. His two terms in office, however, proved both difficult and frustrating. He was indecisive in both peace and war, and when he finally did act, he always seemed to do the wrong thing.

Since the Non-Intercourse Act put too much strain on trade, Congress replaced it with the Macon's Bill Number 2. This act offered to open trade with Britain and France if those countries ceased to attack American ships.

Napoleon's foreign minister responded by saying that the Berlin and Milan Decrees had been lifted. But the same day that he "repealed" the decrees, he signed a new order confiscating American ships in French ports. Nevertheless, America began trading again with the French. Naturally, England was upset.

Indian Stirrings

By the spring of 1810, there were sporadic Indian attacks on settlements in the western Indiana Territory. Settlers blamed the English or the Canadians for inciting the Indian raids. But the truth was that America was now reaping the consequences of unfair treaties that had robbed the Indians of millions of acres of choice land.

The Indians were now unwilling to give up any more land and united their forces in an Indian Confederation under a Shawnee chief, **Tecumseh** (tih KUM suh). In late 1811 General **William Henry Harrison** marched on Prophetstown, Tecumseh's Indian capital beside the Tippecanoe River. Although he failed to capture Tecumseh, who was elsewhere, Harrison burned the village and became "the hero of Tippecanoe." Tecumseh joined the British cause in Canada and died in 1812 in the battle of the Thames (TEMZ) River.

Section Review

1. When the war between England and France reached a stalemate, how did each country plan to defeat the other?
2. How did the British and French treat American ships? Why did American ships continue to sail under these conditions?
3. Explain the Embargo Act of 1807. What effect did it have on Americans?
4. How did Jefferson's Non-Intercourse Act of 1809 differ from his Embargo Act of 1807?
5. Who was the leader of the Indian Confederation in the West? Why did the Indians unite their forces?

Left: *Montpelier in Orange County, Virginia, the home of President Madison*
Right: *An artist's conception of William Henry Harrison's meeting with Tecumseh*

C. The War of 1812

Work of the War Hawks

Although the battle of Tippecanoe had somewhat lessened their fears, Westerners did not believe they could be really safe until the British were out of Canada. Besides, they blamed the British for the surplus of grain that Americans in the West could not sell. In Congress a group of forty western and southern representatives, united by their strong nationalism and desire to be free of English influence, formed a **coalition** (a temporary alliance of groups) under the leadership of Kentucky's **Henry Clay.** Called the **War Hawks,** these men successfully elected Clay as Speaker of the House and placed their supporters on important congressional committees. From such positions they denounced Britain and pushed for a stronger defense.

War Is Declared

Relations with Great Britain worsened throughout 1811 and early 1812. The British, angered by the embargo, now blockaded the American coast more than ever, and they continued to stop American ships to remove suspected British deserters. Madison asked the British to suspend their Orders in Council in April of 1812. When they refused, Congress gave the president the power to activate state militias for six months.

Weakened by the loss of trade, Britain was soon ready to suspend the Orders in Council and did so on June 16, 1812. But since there were no quick means of communicating across the Atlantic, word did not reach the United States until June 18, after the United States had declared war. The resulting war with Britain lasted two and a half years, and it is known as the **War of 1812.**

American Handicaps

The United States was unprepared for the war it faced. The army had only 6,700 men, most of whom were in western forts. Although Congress allowed an increase in the size of the army and allowed for calling out a militia of 100,000, some states, especially those in New England, had not wanted war and refused to commit their troops. In addition, the navy was small—it had only sixteen vessels. But Britain had two hundred frigates, and most had twice the number of mounted guns as the seven seaworthy American ships.

Financing was a problem, too. In 1811 Congress had voted against rechartering the National Bank. Now there was no bank to borrow from or to transfer funds to pay for war supplies. In addition, reduced trade had cut tariff income, curtailing funds even more. The public, divided over the war, refused to buy war bonds to support it.

Poor communications and transportation systems also troubled the American cause. Few roads had been built to the West. With the coast blockaded and the West isolated, it was hard to move men and supplies to the places where they were needed. Sometimes the president had little idea where his armies really were.

America's generals also handicapped the war effort. Most of the generals Madison chose were older men who had not fought actively since the War for Independence. The first year of fighting was a disaster.

Fighting the War in the North: the War in 1812

The war plan was to attack Canada since it was close by and sparsely populated. Also, since some Canadians were French and therefore were lukewarm to British rule,

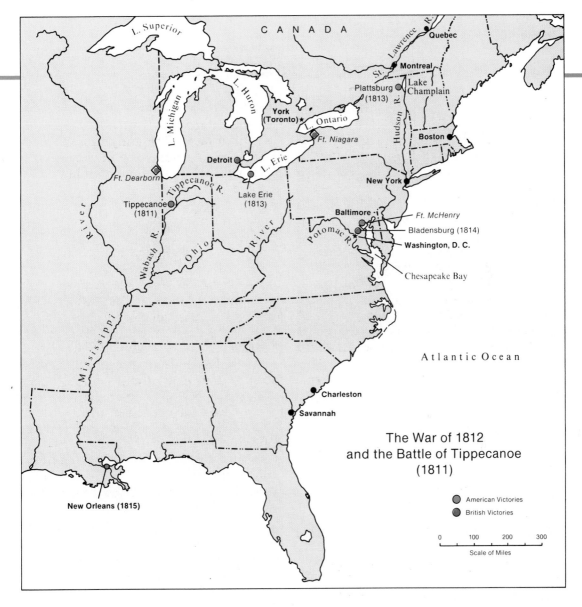

The War of 1812
and the Battle of Tippecanoe
(1811)

● American Victories
● British Victories

0   100   200   300
Scale of Miles

Americans believed that they might have some support there.

In August of 1812, Major General William Hull, on his way to attack the British at Ontario, surrendered in disgrace to General Isaac Brock at Detroit. William Henry Harrison's attempt to regain Detroit failed, resulting in the loss of much of the Northwest. Fort Dearborn (modern Chicago) also fell to the British.

In October an American force moved to take the Niagara peninsula. But the Americans attacking Queenstown, New York, were thrown back, as was an attack on Fort Niagara. A second attack on Fort Niagara met defeat because the New York militia refused to cooperate and move across the border. Instead they stood by and watched the British defeat the American regulars.

During the first year of the war, the only American successes were at sea. The American frigate *Constitution* defeated the *Guerrière* (GEHR ih EHR), and the *United States* victoriously battled the *Macedonian* (MAS ih DOH nee un).

In November 1812 Madison won reelection. Despite the war disasters, most electors stuck with Madison rather than changing leaders in the middle of a crisis.

Fighting for the Great Lakes: The War in 1813

The second year of the war did not go much better. Harrison and his lesser commanders lost land battles around the Great Lakes. Finally the Americans realized that the British were probably winning because they controlled the Great Lakes. **Oliver Hazard Perry,** a twenty-seven-year-old dynamo, spent almost a year preparing to win control of Lake Erie. This was no easy task. Perry built a naval base on Erie's south shore by bringing artillery and ammunition hundreds of miles over rough roads and unbridged streams. He instilled pride into local militias, entrusting them with the job of keeping local outposts and shipyards from falling into British hands. He built two new frigates, the *Lawrence* and the *Niagara,* especially for use on the Great Lakes. In September of 1813, Perry's new ships were ready to meet the British. The *Lawrence,* Perry's flagship, was heavily damaged early in the attack. Perry, in a small boat, crossed to the *Niagara* and refused to surrender.

The U.S.S. Constitution *earned the name "Old Ironsides" by surviving the War of 1812 and winning more battles than any other early American warship. Today she is moored in Boston, manned by sailors dressed in the style of 1812.*

An hour later the tables turned. Perry wrote General Harrison: "We have met the enemy and they are ours!" The British abandoned Fort Detroit and their interest in the Northwest. They then decided to launch a three-pronged attack on the Northeast, the Chesapeake Bay, and the Mississippi Valley.

Invasions in the East: the War in 1814

The defeat of the French in Europe freed the British to fight much harder against America. They massed troops at Montreal and then moved southward using Lake Champlain as a gateway. Their goal was to take New York City and to cut off New England, but they were defeated on September 11 at Plattsburg, New York.

A second British prong shoved into Chesapeake Bay, a hideaway of American privateers. They easily routed a small American militia at Bladensburg, Maryland, on August 23. This left the capital open to attack the next day. Congress fled across the Potomac to Virginia, as did the president, whom the British were hoping to make their prisoner.

The president told his wife, Dolley, to leave too. She had crammed two trunks full of papers belonging to her husband and cabinet members and had packed much of the silver. These things were sent to Virginia in the only wagon she could commandeer at the time. The last thing Dolley paused to take was a full-length portrait of George Washington done by Gilbert Stuart. It was screwed to the wall, and her servant French John could not get it down. Dolley then told him to cut out the canvas and roll up the portrait. The portrait she saved hangs today in the East Room of the White House.

At six o'clock the same evening, the British marched into Washington. First

Admiral Cockburn and his army went up Capitol Hill to the House chamber. He stood in the speaker's chair, rapped the gavel for order, and asked his men if the Capitol should be burned. "Aye! Aye!" they cheered. Heaping furniture, files, and the books from the Library of Congress in the middle of the floor, they soon set the building afire.

By 9:00 P.M. Admiral Cockburn had made his way to the president's house on Pennsylvania Avenue. He bowed in front of the mirror in the drawing room and took a pillow and one of Madison's hats for souvenirs. His soldiers roamed the building seeking objects for keepsakes. They again piled up the furniture, using it as kindling to torch the building. They burned all the government buildings except the Patent Office.

A gentle summer rain began to fall about midnight. It soon turned into a heavy downpour that put out the flames and kept the buildings from heavier damage. The Capitol and the president's house could be rebuilt because the outside walls were in good condition. However, the sandstone on the president's house was so darkened by smoke that the house was repainted white. Over a period of years, people started to call it the White House.

The famous message of Oliver Hazard Perry: "We have met the enemy and they are ours."

Because the capture of Washington had been so easy, the British now decided to launch a joint land-sea attack on Baltimore, Maryland, the nation's third largest city. American troops, however, kept the British army out. The British navy opened its guns on Fort McHenry, the harbor fortress, but Fort McHenry stood, and the British soon retreated.

The third prong of the British attack came at New Orleans. **Andrew Jackson** had rushed south from Baton Rouge to attempt to save the city. The British attacked twice in January of 1815, but Jackson's men threw them back, killing more than two thousand.

The **battle of New Orleans** was the biggest American victory of the war. Had the Americans lost, it is possible that the British would have tried to take the Louisiana Territory. Oddly, though neither force knew it, the battle of New Orleans was fought after the war had officially ended.

The Treaty of Ghent

In February of 1815, Americans got word that the **Treaty of Ghent** (GENT) ending the war, had been signed on December 24, 1814. Sometimes called "the Treaty of Christmas Eve," the treaty took its name

"And the Flag Was Still There"

Almost everyone knows the story of Francis Scott Key, but few know the story of the flag that "was still there." The flag had been made by a widow named Mary Young Pickersgill. She had sewn it the year before when Fort McHenry was being renovated. The flag was gigantic; four hundred yards of cloth were needed to make the thirty- by forty-two-foot flag. Each of the fifteen stars were twenty-six inches across; the fifteen stripes were all two feet wide. The flag was visible from several miles away on a clear day. Major Armistead, the man in charge of the fort, clipped part of it to give away after the thrilling victory. Today the original flag hangs in the Smithsonian's Museum of History and Technology, protected from temperature and humidity by special controls.

Top: *Fort McHenry at Baltimore*
Bottom: *The flag that "was still there"*

The battle of New Orleans

from the city of Ghent in neutral Belgium, where it had been signed. John Quincy Adams, son of an earlier president, headed the American delegation. The treaty failed to settle the key issue over which the war had been fought: neutral rights at sea. However, it did provide for special commissions or groups of men to settle disputes in later years.

Results of the War of 1812

Although the Treaty of Ghent made some Americans unhappy, and no territory was gained, the War of 1812 did have important results. First, the United States gained respect in the eyes of other nations. They saw that the United States was ready to fight for what she believed was right—freedom of the seas—and to protect her honor. Second, the war inspired a greater sense of **nationalism.** People were proud to be Americans and had a strong feeling for their country. They saw that they could compete and win. This gave them more self-confidence. Third, new heroes emerged from its fields of battle. Americans were willing to follow Andrew Jackson and William Henry Harrison and would later elect them as presidents.

Fourth, Americans developed much of their own industry during the war. Because they could not get goods from England and France, they had to make their own. After the war the need to rely on foreign countries almost disappeared. Americans continued to increase their output to keep pace with the needs of a growing country. Fifth, Napoleon's defeat in Europe and Britain's rebuff in North America ended the long struggle between France and Britain for colonies in North America and for supremacy in Europe. The war brought America nearly a century of freedom from European conflicts. It enabled Americans to focus on their own affairs. Instead of fighting wars, they fought and tamed the vast American wilderness. Sixth, the War of 1812 affected both political parties. The Federalist party, already declining, was ruined beyond all hope of recovery because of its opposition to the war. The Republican party changed its stand slightly on some issues. It had opposed efforts to strengthen and centralize the federal government. Now its leaders began to favor it at times.

Section Review

1. What sections of the country did the "War Hawks" represent? Who was their leader in Congress?
2. List several ways the United States was unprepared for war with England, thus making the first year of fighting a disaster.
3. List the three areas the British planned to invade in 1814. What was the purpose and the outcome of each?
4. What was unusual about the battle of New Orleans?
5. List six results the War of 1812 had on the United States.

Summary

The early 1800s were a time of growth for the United States. Not only did the young nation add the vast area of the Louisiana Purchase to its territory, but it also added to its stature among the countries of the world by its actions in the Tripolitan War and the War of 1812. Thomas Jefferson continued to extend the powers of the government, but the Supreme Court under John Marshall kept presidential power in check. New leaders in Congress and in the military began to arise to take charge of the continued development of the nation. The United States was beginning to mature.

Chapter Review

Do You Remember?

■ Complete each of these statements about Thomas Jefferson.
1. The political party to which Thomas Jefferson belonged as president was the ____.
2. Jefferson refused to pay tribute to the ____.
3. Jefferson bought from France the large western area called the ____.

4. To explore the source of the Missouri River, Jefferson sent out
_____.

5. For his second term, Jefferson chose a new vice president instead
of _____.

6. Despite the *Chesapeake* affair, Jefferson avoided a war with _____.

■ Match each of the following terms to their definition or significance.

7. embargo
8. coalition
9. War Hawks
10. Treaty of
    Ghent
11. nationalism

a. made peace with Britain
b. a temporary alliance of groups
c. a people's pride in and support for their
   country
d. forbidding exports to and imports from a
   foreign country
e. Congressmen who wanted to take action
   against Britain

■ Who was the man who did each of the following things?

12. He went with Meriwether Lewis to the West.
13. He was victorious on Lake Erie in the War of 1812.
14. He won the battle of Tippecanoe.
15. He was a leading War Hawk.
16. He won the battle of New Orleans.
17. He was a Shawnee chief who fought against the Americans.
18. He explored Colorado, followed the Rio Grande, and was
    captured by the Spanish.

Why Is It So?

1. How did Jefferson increase his popularity during his first term?
2. Why was the Louisiana Purchase a questionable action for
   Jefferson?
3. Why were the British Orders in Council and the French Berlin and
   Milan Decrees upsetting to Americans?
4. How did the Embargo Act backfire for Jefferson?
5. How was the United States handicapped during the War of 1812?
6. Why was the battle of New Orleans an unnecessary battle and also
   an important battle?

What Do You Think?

1. Why shouldn't people accept just parts of the Bible as the Word of
   God as Thomas Jefferson did?
2. What can you learn from the life of Aaron Burr?

The Era of Good Feelings

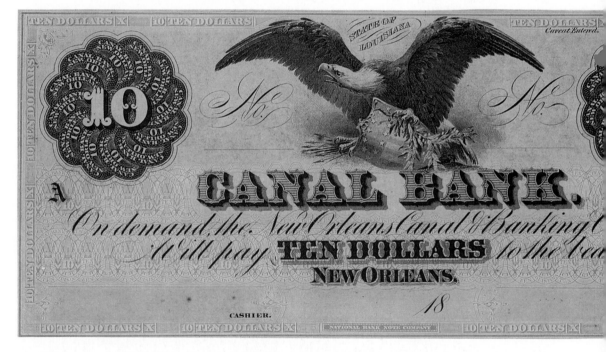

When President James Monroe visited Boston in 1817, a local paper reported the event in an article and spoke of an "Era of Good Feelings" that the nation was enjoying during the Monroe presidency. It was true that the United States was experiencing a brief period of relative harmony. Political rivalries were not intense. The North, the South, and the West all had their particular needs, desires, and opinions, but sectional differences were in a temporary calm. No great national crisis, such as the War of 1812, was arising, and the great trials that were to come over slavery and its related issues were as yet only smoldering.

"Good feelings," whether between men or nations, are often hard to maintain, and Monroe and his successor, John Quincy Adams, soon saw the harmony begin to break up. The problems of national government began to loom again as the United States recognized its position in world affairs and also as it began to deal with its own expansion.

Currency issued by a canal company in Louisiana

A. Monroe Begins the Era

Madison's secretary of state during the War of 1812 had been **James Monroe.** By the summer of 1816, the governors of twelve states and the senators and congressmen from fourteen had signed a petition asking Monroe to run for president. Madison also urged him to run. Monroe was hesitant, but he agreed to accept the nomination on two conditions. First, he would not be tied to a single political party. Second, he would not wage an active campaign. He would run on his own record, as he had for an earlier seat in Congress and for governor of Virginia.

Winning the Election

While his opponent, Rufus King, toured the country making speeches, Monroe stayed in Washington performing his duties in the state department. "If they want me, they'll vote for me if I don't make a single speech or open a single county fair," he said. The voters sensed Monroe's sincerity, and he won the election.

Although the major political parties did not clash nationally during the **"Era of Good Feelings"** (Monroe's two terms in office), some rivalries still existed on the state level. Voter turnouts were small, however, because people had little influence in choosing the national and state candidates. Most candidates were picked by party **caucus,** a closed meeting of party leaders. For president, the parties usually nominated the **incumbent,** the current office holder, to run again. If he had served his two terms, they chose the secretary of state. The position of secretary of state thus seemed to be the stepping stone to the presidency. Things were so cut and dried that the voters lost interest for a while.

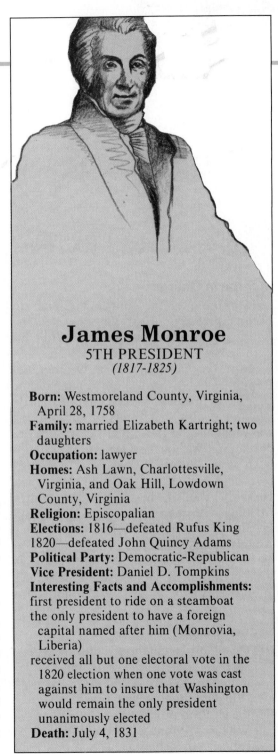

James Monroe
5TH PRESIDENT
(1817-1825)

Born: Westmoreland County, Virginia, April 28, 1758
Family: married Elizabeth Kartright; two daughters
Occupation: lawyer
Homes: Ash Lawn, Charlottesville, Virginia, and Oak Hill, Lowdown County, Virginia
Religion: Episcopalian
Elections: 1816—defeated Rufus King
1820—defeated John Quincy Adams
Political Party: Democratic-Republican
Vice President: Daniel D. Tompkins
Interesting Facts and Accomplishments:
first president to ride on a steamboat
the only president to have a foreign capital named after him (Monrovia, Liberia)
received all but one electoral vote in the 1820 election when one vote was cast against him to insure that Washington would remain the only president unanimously elected
Death: July 4, 1831

Monroe in Charge

Monroe was the fourth Virginian to become president. He broke precedent by not giving an inaugural address. After his oath he simply said: "I will do my best."

Monroe was basically a Democratic-Republican, but he was also sympathetic to some of the ideas of the Federalist party, which was now dying out. In addition, he was ready to hear the varied views that were developing within the Democratic-Republican party. Monroe's ideal of not being tied to a single party was reflected in his cabinet. He said "I want the best men in the country working with me regardless of their party beliefs." He chose such men as **John Quincy Adams** (who would later run against him in 1820 as an Independent Republican) as his secretary of state and South Carolina's young war hawk, **John C. Calhoun,** as his secretary of war.

Section Review

1. On what two conditions did Monroe agree to accept the presidential nomination?
2. Why had many voters lost interest in the election process?
3. Why were Monroe's choices for cabinet posts significant?

The birthplace of James Monroe in Westmoreland County, Virginia

B. International Concerns

Although Monroe did not totally neglect affairs at home during his terms, he is most noted for championing American interests abroad. With the war over, the United States now faced different challenges which centered on Latin America. These lands south of the border were so named because the languages brought there by Portuguese and Spanish colonizers had come from Latin.

The Florida Purchase

Florida was the first challenge. Over the years Spain's power had been weakening, and she had nearly lost control of Florida. For example, in 1810 Americans in West Florida, the part of Florida extending to the Mississippi River, had revolted against Spanish rule and had asked to become a part of the United States. Spain did nothing to stop them. Then in 1814 Creek Indians who had gone on the warpath from their base in West Florida were defeated by Andrew Jackson in the battle of Horseshoe Bend in Alabama. Because the Indian menace was lessened and Spain was doing little to develop the area, Americans, particularly cotton farmers, moved into the Deep South region. By 1817 Mississippi had enough people to apply for statehood, and by 1819 so did Alabama.

Trouble along the Border—In 1818 trouble developed in East Florida and the small part of West Florida still under Spanish rule. Southern slaves fled to Florida by the hundreds if not by the thousands. Some runaways fled to the Seminole Indian settlements while others started farms, plantations, or ranches. The Indians and their runaway slave allies frequently crossed over the border and attacked largely unprotected American settlements. Then they would retreat to Florida, defying the few soldiers along the frontier to go after them. Moreover, Florida had also become a haven for smugglers of European goods.

Andrew Jackson Invades Florida—Secretary of State Adams complained to Spanish leaders and warned them that if they could not control their own territory, the United States would take action. When the Spanish did nothing, Secretary of War Calhoun gave General Andrew Jackson control of the Tennessee and Georgia militias. Jackson was to go to the border and stop the smugglers. Jackson chose to interpret his order liberally rather than literally and invaded Florida. His actions surprised the Indians and enabled him to defeat them, capture towns, and even depose the Spanish governor.

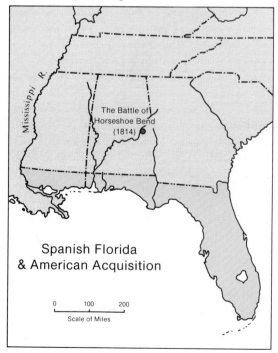

Mississippi R.

The Battle of Horseshoe Bend (1814)

Spanish Florida & American Acquisition

0   100   200
Scale of Miles

Spain soon demanded money for damages and asked for the punishment of Jackson. Monroe refused both demands and even allowed Jackson to stay in Florida until Spain sent enough men to end the abuses. Lacking funds and troops, Spain soon decided it would be better off selling Florida. In 1819 the United States made a treaty with Spain, purchasing East Florida for $5 million and keeping American ownership of the lands already taken in West Florida. The Spanish boundary west of the Mississippi was also defined. Spain kept control of Texas and her other western lands.

Revolutions in Latin America

Spain's inability to control its other Latin American colonies resulted in their loss as well. In these colonies Spanish-born settlers had the most political power and social status. The Creoles, those born in Latin America but of European descent, were thought inferior. But because they were men of wealth and education, they had the means and leadership ability to take action. Of course mestizos (those who were half-Indian and half-European), Indians, and blacks, regarded even lower on the Spanish social scale, did not object. The Creoles resented Spanish control of their economy. Spain got profits that the colonists believed they should be enjoying. Furthermore, the colonists felt no loyalty to their new king, who was not Spanish but French. (In 1808 Napoleon had named one of his brothers, Joseph Bonaparte, king of Spain.)

Mexico tried to overthrow Spanish rule as early as 1810 and in 1821 finally gained her independence. Mexico's success encouraged the other countries of Central America to revolt. Then South America followed, led by two inspiring Creoles, **Jose de San Martín** (ho-ZAY duh SAN mahr-TEEN) in the northern areas, and **Simón Bolívar** (SEE mohn BOH-luh-VAHR) in the southern areas. Most of the new republics modeled their constitutions after that of the United States. But the poor economic conditions, the high illiteracy, the tradition of **autocracy** (government by one powerful ruler), and the power of the Roman Catholic church weakened these new republics. Strong military leaders easily took control, and foreign powers were also tempted to intervene.

President Monroe feared the latter. He and his fellow Americans were sympathetic to the new republics; so with the approval of Congress, Monroe established diplomatic outposts in those countries. Britain recognized the new lands, too, but some of the other European rulers did not. Austria, France, Prussia, and Russia planned to resist revolutions and republican forms of government wherever they emerged. Although Britain at first cooperated with these countries in an alliance, it later voiced objections to their plans.

Other Foreign Threats

Monroe also had reason to eye Russia closely. The Russians owned Alaska, where they had developed a profitable fur trade. They began to move down the coast seeking greater profits. By 1812 they had built a fort only a short distance north of San Francisco. By 1821 they had laid claim to Pacific lands on what is now the west coast of Canada. Some of this land lay within the lands that the British and the United States had already jointly claimed.

Then in early 1823 the president learned that the French were preparing to send shiploads of troops to Latin America. In August of 1823, Lord George Canning, the British Foreign Secretary, contacted John Quincy Adams. He suggested that the United States and Britain issue a joint declaration to warn the other European nations to stay out of the New World.

Since Monroe did not want to make a mistake that would have long-range consequences, he waited. He asked Jefferson, Madison, and John Quincy Adams to come to the capital to advise him. Although few realized it at the time, it was a historic occasion. Four men—past, present, and future presidents—met together to discuss the matter.

Several weeks later Monroe told Adams: "When a weak nation accepts partnership with a stronger, she places herself at the mercy of her ally." By fall, Monroe decided to issue a declaration separate from any made by Britain. John Quincy Adams wrote the statement, and President Monroe included it in his annual message to Congress on December 2, 1823. This statement has been called the **Monroe Doctrine.**

The Monroe Doctrine

The Monroe Doctrine added three new basic principles to America's foreign policy. First, "the American continents . . . [were] not to be considered as subjects for future

John Quincy Adams

colonization by any European powers." In other words, European nations could not set up new colonies in the Americas. Second, the United States would not interfere in European affairs or wars unless its rights were "invaded or seriously menaced" when it would then "make preparations for [its] defense." Third, the United States "should consider any attempt . . . to extend their system to any portion of our hemisphere as dangerous to [its] space and safety" and to be an unfriendly act. The Monroe Doctrine simply told the Europeans not to meddle with Western Hemisphere countries while it promised that the United States would not get involved unnecessarily in European affairs.

The Monroe Doctrine did stop the immediate threat of European intervention in the Americas. Some believe this was because European powers feared the British navy, not because they feared the United States. In future years, however, the importance of the Monroe Doctrine increased. In fact, it became a foundational element of American foreign policy.

Section Review

1. What two groups of people were using Florida as a haven to avoid capture and possible punishment?
2. When Spain did not solve Florida's problems, what American was given authority to take action?
3. Why did many people in Spain's Latin American colonies resent Spanish control?
4. What two countries approved and recognized the new republics in Latin America?
5. What three principles were included in the Monroe Doctrine?

C. Internal Affairs Under Monroe

Although the nation avoided foreign problems during the Era of Good Feelings, it could not avoid some problems at home.

The Economic Crisis of 1819

The War of 1812, by creating greater demands for raw materials, caused an economic boom. Since farmers were getting higher prices for their crops, more and more people went west and bought farmland. In addition, Europe was again producing her own agricultural products. Soon, because so many farms were producing crops, there was a surplus in America, and prices of farm products began to drop.

The charter of the National Bank, although allowed to lapse briefly, had been reissued. Meanwhile, state banks had grown in number. They had begun to issue their own bank notes even when they lacked silver and gold to back them up. When the new National Bank called in loans from western banks, the state banks could not pay them, and the economy collapsed. The collapse was especially hard on southern and western farmers. They called this crisis "The Panic of '19."

The Marshall Court's Nationalist Decisions

The Panic led to a major Supreme Court decision. Since the states tended to dislike national banks, some states began to tax their national branches, hoping that the increased costs would make people less likely to use them. When Maryland required the Baltimore branch to issue bank notes on paper bought from the state, the bank refused. Maryland then sued the federal cashier, James McCulloch. The case soon reached the Supreme Court.

This was one of several cases in which Chief Justice John Marshall asserted the power of the national government over that of the states. In *McCulloch* v. *Maryland,* the court ruled that a state could not tax the federal government because the "power to tax includes the power to destroy." Marshall based his decision on the supremacy clause of the Constitution. He asserted that when the national government performed a function permitted by the Constitution, it could not be threatened by the states.

In other cases Marshall declared certain state laws to be unconstitutional. Thus the Supreme Court and the federal government were given definite authority over state governments. Another case settled by the Supreme Court gave the federal government power to regulate **interstate commerce** (selling and transporting of goods from one state to another).

Slavery and the Missouri Compromise

The original northern states had already abolished or were in the process of abolishing slavery. The newer states formed out of the Northwest Territory had never had it. Of course, slavery was still allowed in the southern states. By 1819 there were twenty-two states in the Union. Eleven were free; eleven were slave states. There was almost a straight line between the two sets of states.

Although slavery had not yet become a moral issue, it now produced an economic and political squabble. The nation had continued to grow, especially in a westward direction, and in 1819 Missouri asked to join the union as a slave state. Northerners could see that if Missouri came in as a slave state, the balance between slave and free would

be upset. James Tallmadge of New York added an amendment to Missouri's statehood bill saying that no more slaves could be brought into Missouri and that all children born to slave parents would be freed when they reached the age twenty-five. Southerners protested loudly. The House passed the bill, but the Senate refused it.

The possibility of a compromise arose in late 1819 when Maine, earlier a part of Massachusetts, applied for statehood. If Maine came in free and Missouri came in slave, then the balance would be maintained. This seemed fine on the surface, but it did not settle the problem of what would be done in the future. Would slavery be permitted in the rest of the Louisiana Purchase? When Florida grew in population and applied for statehood, would it be slave? If Texas gained its independence from Mexico, what would its status be? If more slaveholders moved into northern states such as Indiana and Illinois, could they change the free status of those states? If the Supreme Court could rule on the legality of a national bank, could it also abolish slavery? The debates over these questions were long and heated.

The deadlock was finally broken when Henry Clay of Kentucky, a border state, worked out the **Missouri Compromise.** Maine's admission would be tied to Missouri's, keeping a balance of slave and free states. Slavery would be forbidden north of 36° 30′ north latitude, Missouri's southern boundary. Slavery would be permitted, although not necessarily protected south of the invisible line. The bill passed by a slim margin. Monroe said he would veto it but was talked out of it at the last minute. The emotion involved in discussing slavery made it obvious that feelings on the subject ran

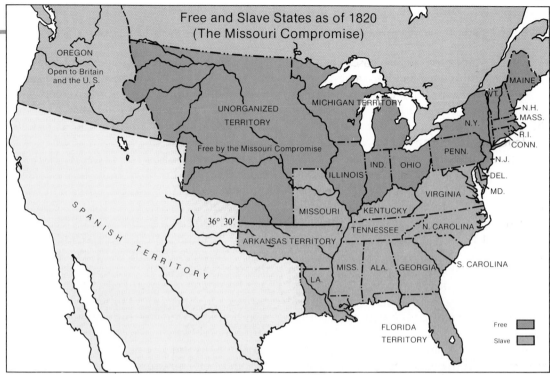

Free and Slave States as of 1820
(The Missouri Compromise)

OREGON
Open to Britain
and the U. S.

UNORGANIZED
TERRITORY

MICHIGAN TERRITORY

MAINE

VT.

N.H.

MASS.

N.Y.

R.I.

CONN.

Free by the Missouri Compromise

PENN.

N.J.

ILLINOIS   IND.   OHIO

DEL.

MD.

VIRGINIA

SPANISH TERRITORY

MISSOURI   KENTUCKY

36° 30'

TENNESSEE

N. CAROLINA

ARKANSAS TERRITORY

MISS.   ALA.   GEORGIA   S. CAROLINA

LA.

FLORIDA
TERRITORY

Free

Slave

deep. John Quincy Adams wrote: "I take it for granted that the present question is a mere preamble—a title page to a great tragic volume." Former President Jefferson called it "a firebell in the night . . . which awakened and filled me with terror. I considered it at once as the knell of the Union."

Section Review

1. Why did many western banks collapse in 1819?
2. What was the strategy behind the state's taxation of the national bank?
3. Name the Supreme Court decision that reinforced the idea that the national government was supreme over state governments.
4. Why were northern and southern states concerned by Missouri's request to join the Union?
5. What were the terms of the compromise that settled this issue?

D. A Disappearance of Good Feelings

There had been few major problems for the nation during the Monroe administration. But as these years passed, new challenges were ready to surface.

A Candidate Collection

In 1824 the Democratic-Republican party defied tradition. Rather than choosing the current secretary of state as their candidate, the Republicans chose William Crawford, who drew most of his support from the southern states. His thinking was close to Thomas Jefferson's. He disliked protective tariffs, which would increase the price of goods for southern planters and western farmers. He opposed federal support of internal improvements because they would have to be paid for by taxes.

Crawford, however, lacked national support. Furthermore, he had been briefly paralyzed by a stroke in 1823, and some thought he might not be able to face the rigors of office.

The remaining candidates were selected by state legislatures. Massachusetts chose John Quincy Adams, a career diplomat. Kentucky nominated Henry Clay, the Speaker of the House, believing he would be elected because the new western states backed him. The views of Clay and Adams were close on many issues. For example, both were strong nationalists, favoring a strong central government. Neither feared the federal government's playing an active role in the nation's economy. Hence, they favored the rechartering of the national bank and a high tariff. They believed tariff monies could pay for internal improvements such as roads, canals, and harbors. Such projects, in their opinion, would help the nation to grow and would benefit their sections of the country—New England and the West.

Tennessee's candidate was Andrew Jackson. Although he had been a lawyer and United States senator, his fame had been gained as the hero of New Orleans, and as an Indian fighter in Spanish Florida. Jackson's slogan became "Old Hickory, the Nation's Hero, and the People's Friend."

The Election Goes to the House

Jackson won more votes than anyone else in both the electoral college and the popular vote. He surprised many with his national following by carrying some states from each section. Adams came in second. Crawford was a distant third with Clay just behind him. But with so many candidates, no man won a majority of the electoral vote (131 votes in 1824). This meant that the election went to the House of Representatives. The Twelfth Amendment had given each state one vote and said that the states must choose from among the top three candidates.

Jackson's followers believed that the House had a moral responsibility to pick the man with the largest vote. The most important factor in the House's decision, however, turned out to be Henry Clay, who had to drop out of the race. Whoever Clay chose to support with his votes would be the winner. Since his views were close to Adams's and he disliked Jackson, Clay chose to support John Quincy Adams. Clay also believed that he stood a better chance of following Adams into the White House.

When John Quincy Adams became president he kept most of Monroe's cabinet because he believed they were qualified. He replaced only three men. One position he had to replace was his own, secretary of state. Although Monroe told him that making Henry Clay secretary of state might be an unwise political move, Adams picked Clay because of his qualifications and experience. This decision did prove to be a downfall for Adams.

Jackson's followers angrily charged that Adams and Clay had made a "corrupt bargain." They thought that Clay had made a deal with Adams in which Clay supported Adams for president in return for the high political appointment. John Quincy Adams was both hurt and horrified. His strong moral conscience and devotion to duty would never have allowed it. An angry Andrew Jackson resigned his Senate seat and set out for Tennessee. But before he left, Jackson allowed his supporters to start organizing for the 1828 election. They plotted Adams's political demise and made his presidency the most miserable experience of his life.

The Presidency of John Quincy Adams

John Quincy Adams, the son of John Adams, had been in public service thirty-six years before becoming president. He had served in the Department of State during every presidential administration. Probably the best-educated man of his day, he had an enviable record. But in an era when other politicians used their personalities to draw support, John Quincy Adams appeared cold, aloof, plain, and unexciting. While other politicians awarded jobs to those who would follow them, Adams refused to do so. He did his best work behind the scenes. Although he would have appreciated praise and honor from others, he would not seek either.

Ideas and Opponents—Adams's single term of office turned into a series of unending disasters. For one thing, his talents did not make him sensitive to either opinions or trends. In addition, his program was highly nationalistic, designed to improve the national economy at a time when people were trying to protect the interests of their own section of the country. Henry Clay suggested an American system, a high tariff package rewarding all sections of the nation with projects paid for out of the monies collected. Adams endorsed it. After the public debt was repaid, the monies left from the tariff and the sale of public lands could be used to build roads and canals to aid the communication "between distant regions and multitudes of men." He also wanted to build lighthouses along the coast to aid shipping, a national university to improve

John Quincy Adams
6TH PRESIDENT
(1825-1829)

Born: Braintree, Massachusetts, July 11, 1767
Family: married Louisa Catherine Johnston; three sons, one daughter
Occupation: lawyer
Home: Quincy, Massachusetts
Religion: Congregationalist
Election: 1824—by the House of Representatives following an election with no candidate receiving a majority; defeated Andrew Jackson, William Crawford, and Henry Clay
Political Party: no major party affiliation
Vice President: John C. Calhoun
Interesting Facts and Accomplishments:
served as secretary to his father when his father was foreign minister in Russia and France
graduated from Harvard University
wrote the Monroe Doctrine
helped establish the Smithsonian Institution
only president who was the son of an earlier president
kept a personal diary for over sixty years
earliest president to be photographed (after he left office)
Death: February 23, 1848, from a stroke while in the House of Representatives

the minds of Americans, and an observatory to view the skies. His critics made fun of his "lighthouses in the sky" as well as his suggestion that Congress promote art, literature, and science. His ideas were not well accepted, and in the 1826 elections he lost most of his support in Congress.

The moderate tariff he had favored was revised upward (had its rates raised). Southerners called the tariff of 1828 **"the tariff of abominations"** and threatened to leave the Union. Yet Adams signed the bill. He further angered those who promoted states' rights by standing up for the Indians, threatening to use federal troops to protect the Creeks and Cherokees from invasions by Georgians.

Adams Deals with Latin America— Even in foreign affairs where Adams had vast experience, he made little headway. Simón Bolívar called a Pan-American Conference. Adams, hoping to strengthen ties with Latin America, sent the Senate the names of two delegates. Southerners delayed approving them because the American delegates would have to mix with black delegates from Haiti. Finally the delegates left for Panama. One died en route; the other arrived after the meeting had ended. Even though it suffered this failure, the administration did make some

The home of John Quincy Adams in Quincy, Massachusetts

commercial treaties with the major nations of Europe and Latin America. Adams also enlarged the American navy and pushed for a naval academy.

The Election of 1828

By the end of Adams's term, two political parties existed once again. John Quincy Adams and his running mate, Richard Rush, were selected by a party called the National Republican party. Jackson and his running mate, John C. Calhoun, were named by the Tennessee legislature and then placed on the ballot by supporters in state legislatures in other states. Jackson's group, composed largely of former Democratic-Republicans, was called the **Democratic party.**

Old Man Eloquent: The President Who Never Retired

John Quincy Adams's career continued after he left the White House. In 1830 he was persuaded to run for Congress for his home district in Massachusetts. He had the attitude of a servant. The position did not matter nor did the pay. (He received $8.00 a day for his services.) Serving the people, however, did matter. He wrote: "No person could be degraded by serving the people. . . . If the people elected me town selectman, I would consider it an honor."

In Congress he was highly respected for his many accomplishments. His speech-making was so skilled he was soon nicknamed "old man eloquent." In 1832 he led the fight to revise the tariff downward (lowered the rates). The new tariff has sometimes been called "the Adams tariff."

The election of 1828 was unique for other reasons, too. For the first time, many techniques of mass campaigning appeared. Broadsides (posters), banners, editorials, testimonials, barbecues, banquets, and torchlight parades were all used to win voter support.

Such techniques brought out more voters than ever before, as did changes in voting requirements. Some states had already lifted the requirement that voters own property. Most new western states had constitutions that allowed white manhood suffrage or at least gave the vote to male taxpayers, which was almost the same thing. This expansion of suffrage in some states plus the addition of new states into the

A lifelong foe of slavery, he forced the House to repeal the Gag Rule, which had forbidden antislave petitions to be submitted to the House. He predicted correctly that wars would be fought if the issue of slavery was not settled. He introduced a constitutional amendment to abolish slavery in 1839. His antislavery speeches were not just idle talk. When a freed slave named Nathan Jones saw his family sold into slavery, John Quincy gave him money and the names of friends to contact to raise the funds needed to secure their freedom.

He helped establish the United States Naval Academy at Severn, Maryland, and led an eleven-year drive to found a national museum, the Smithsonian. James Smithson, a British chemist, had willed one-half million dollars to the United States for such a purpose, but Congress wanted to divert the money to other causes.

In 1846 a tall, slim, Whig congressman from Illinois was elected to the House. In his initial meeting with John Quincy, Abraham Lincoln praised the veteran congressman for what he had done to repeal the Gag Rule and help slaves. The old patriarch looked at Lincoln and slowly said, "There is much yet to be done."

On February 21, 1848, when Adams rose for a roll call vote in Congress, he collapsed from a stroke. He was carried into the cloakroom. Too sick to be moved, he died there two days later. Abraham Lincoln represented the House and rode the funeral train back to Massachusetts. John C. Calhoun, who was often opposed to Adams, served as a pallbearer. Daniel Webster wrote his epitaph. Adams had devoted fifty-eight years of his life to directly serving his nation. He has been called "the president who never retired."

John C. Calhoun of South Carolina served as vice president to both John Quincy Adams and Andrew Jackson.

Honorable Murder

Duels—fights to the death to preserve one's honor—unfortunately, were not uncommon during the early history of the United States. Thousands of them were fought in the name of honor. This was particularly true in the West and South, although America's most famous duel (the one between Hamilton and Burr) took place in Weehawken, New Jersey. Duels were even fought during the Civil War between officers on the same side.

There were rules to be followed when one was involved in a duel. The person being challenged chose what weapons would be used. The seconds, or alternates, usually decided the manner in which a duel was to be fought. It was also their duty to try to negotiate a peaceful settlement of the argument in order to avoid actual combat. The first thing that had to be decided—after the choice of weapons—was how far apart the two combatants were to stand. Then a decision had to be made on who would give the command to fire. Also a time limit had to be set unless the two parties involved agreed not to have a time limit at all. Usually the duelists would face each other at the arranged distance with the pistols pointed down or straight up. On command the duelists would commence firing. If there was a time limit, the command would be spoken very fast: "Fire! One, two, three!" If someone had not fired by then, it was too late. One shot was normally all the duelist was allowed, although in the last recorded duel, one of the men shot six times—and missed. Misses or slight wounds were common because the

weapons were of poor quality. In one duel involving two women—over a man, of course—both women missed. The man, however, who was standing in the crowd watching, was shot in the head and killed.

Of the two most famous duels in American history, that of Burr and Hamilton, has been a source of controversy among historians for years. Some suggest from Hamilton's last letter and dying words that he had no intention of shooting at Burr at all. Witnesses at the scene, however, describe Hamilton's actions as giving every indication that he did mean to shoot at his opponent. The bullet from Hamilton's gun lodged in a tree limb some twenty feet or so above the ground—too high but not straight up. There was some argument among the three witnesses concerning who fired first. Burr and his second claimed that Hamilton did. Hamilton's second claimed Burr did. Either way, Burr killed Hamilton and although all the rules of dueling had been observed, Hamilton became a martyr, and Burr a scoundrel.

The other famous duel involved Andrew Jackson and a man named John Dickinson. This duel nearly cost "Old Hickory" his political career. Allegedly Jackson's duel was fought because Dickinson had insulted Mrs. Jackson. Dickinson was the favorite to win the duel because he was an expert marksman. Supposedly he could hit a string with a bullet at a distance of twenty-five feet or even farther. Jackson, however, showed up at the duel in a heavy overcoat and twisted his body as much as he could beneath it. He resolved to let Dickinson shoot first and then to shoot him. Because of Jackson's contortions, Dickinson's shot barely missed "Old Hickory's" heart. Jackson then aimed—and after one misfire—gave his opponent a mortal wound. The public considered it a cold-blooded execution. Jackson, who could have regained his honor by simply wounding Dickinson, should not have fired again when the first shot misfired. Only Jackson's crushing victory over the British at the battle of New Orleans during the War of 1812 restored him to public favor.

Eventually dueling became unacceptable to the public. Some men in the eighteenth and nineteenth centuries valued their honor or the honor of someone dear to them more than they valued life itself. For others dueling indicated faulty reasoning. They dueled in an effort to seek revenge. Although dueling was (and is) illegal, many people exhaust countless hours trying to express their hatred toward others in more subtle ways. They succeed only in wasting time and embittering themselves. They do not realize that "whosoever hateth his brother is a murderer" (I John 3:15).

Union caused the number of voters to more than double between 1824 and 1828. By 1840 virtually all adult white males could vote. Moreover, three-quarters of those eligible did so, a much higher percentage than in elections today.

The election of 1828 was also one of the worst in terms of **mudslinging** (making malicious statements about opponents). The Democrats claimed that John Quincy Adams was a snob who displayed fancy foreign manners. Because he had a billiard table in the White House, he was charged with being a gambler. He was even accused falsely of immorality.

Adams's followers fought back. They claimed Jackson was a murderer since he had killed at least one man in a duel and had sentenced others to death while in the military. They also accused him of adultery. Jackson had married Rachel Donelson Robards, believing her divorce was final. Later he discovered it was not and had another marriage ceremony. Jackson loved his wife and defended her honor. Unfortunately, Rachel died on November 22, 1828, after reading a pamphlet that slandered her. Jackson took office only a few weeks later and the rest of his life, he blamed the National Republicans for causing Rachel's death. Although the candidates themselves were not directly involved in the mudslinging, they did not use their authority to stop it. They allowed the evil to continue when they could have used their leadership to prohibit it.

Section Review

1. Why did Jackson not win the election of 1824 if he had the largest number of votes?
2. Why did Adams choose Clay to be his secretary of state, and how did Jackson's followers interpret this action?
3. What were some of the ideas included in Adams's nationalistic program?
4. What two aspects of the election of 1828 made it different from other elections?
5. For what two reasons did the number of voters more than double between 1824 and 1828?

Summary

America enjoyed an "Era of Good Feelings" after the War of 1812 ended. Relations with foreign nations were peaceful, and problems within the nation were minimal. Yet the troubles of the years to come were developing—especially the sectional rivalry between regions of the country. These differences grew during the presidency of John Quincy Adams, and his main opponent, Andrew Jackson, played on these sectional differences to promote his own popularity.

Chapter Review

Do You Remember?

■ Fill in the blanks.

James Monroe's presidency has often been called the __(1)__. During that time the United States purchased __(2)__. It also issued a warning to European nations interested in American lands. This warning, called the __(3)__, was largely written by __(4)__, who followed Monroe into the presidency. The nation faced a major decision when the number of free and slave states might have lost their balance, but Henry Clay worked out the __(5)__ to settle the issue for that time and allow the entrance of two new states to the union.

■ Answer these who, what, or when questions.

6. What is a meeting of political party leaders who choose a candidate called?
7. Who defeated the Indians at the battle of Horseshoe Bend?
8. Who were the two men who led much of South America to independence?
9. When did the United States buy Florida?
10. What court case was used to strengthen the federal government's power over that of the states?
11. Who was said to have made a "corrupt bargain" with John Quincy Adams?
12. What was Andrew Jackson's political party?
13. Who was the incumbent presidential candidate in 1828?
14. What state came into the union as a free state as a result of the Missouri Compromise?

Why Is It So?

1. Why was James Monroe's presidency called "the Era of Good Feelings"?
2. Why did Monroe fear that European countries would interfere in the Americas?
3. Why did the Panic of '19 occur?
4. Why did slavery affect the addition of states to the Union?
5. Why did John Quincy Adams receive the presidency in 1824?
6. Why did Southerners generally dislike high tariffs?

What Do You Think?

1. Why is it hard for a nation to maintain an "Era of Good Feelings"?
2. Do you think a candidate with Monroe's attitude toward campaigning could win a presidential election today? Why or why not?
3. What effect does mudslinging have on a political election?

12

The Jacksonian Era

Outside Nashville, Tennessee, stands a stately southern mansion called the Hermitage. This beautiful home of Andrew Jackson was a far cry from the log cabin in which the president was born. But the self-taught lawyer and Indian fighter who lived there became an inspiration to many Americans who wished for a similar chance to better themselves.

Jackson's log cabin birthplace was in South Carolina. His parents had been linen weavers in Ireland before coming to America. His father died shortly before Jackson's birth. Then his mother and brother died of smallpox when he was

Andrew Jackson's home, the Hermitage, in Nashville, Tennessee

fifteen, leaving him totally on his own. Made bitter by these early experiences, he lived a wild life for a time. Eventually, however, he studied law and moved to Tennessee. There he became a lawyer, judge, land speculator, politician, Indian fighter, and planter. The battle of New Orleans brought him national fame.

Jackson was the first president elected from a state west of the original thirteen states and the first president from a poor family. His was a new formula for political success: log cabin to the White House. However, this did not mean he was a crude frontiersman at the time of his election (although his political enemies worked hard to portray him so). He owned over a hundred slaves and much land, and he was one of the richest planters in Tennessee. Yet he was able to make his causes those of the common people.

Coming into office at a time of great advantages for a president, Jackson became the symbol of the age. More and more western lands were opening, and new states were joining the union. Industry and agriculture were expanding at a rapid pace with the introduction of many inventions and ideas of the Industrial Revolution. In addition, immigration was helping the population grow at an amazing rate, and more people had the vote than ever before.

A. Jacksonian Democracy for Some

Andrew Jackson came to office in 1829 as a champion of the common man—particularly the western farmer and the eastern worker. His rise from humble beginnings to wealth, influence, and the presidency gave Americans an example of the possibilities of achievement in their land. The common man elected Jackson, and he intended to represent their interests by molding his form of democracy for the country.

After Jackson took office, he boldly made changes that he believed the people wanted. He was a strong president who used the powers of the presidency more than they had ever been used before. Jackson made friends—and enemies—easily. He also translated his thoughts into actions so swiftly that he sometimes appeared reckless and unthinking. He had a short temper, which he never really learned to control. As a result his actions did not always benefit the nation.

Andrew Jackson
7TH PRESIDENT
(1829-1837)

Born: Waxhaw, South Carolina, March 15, 1767
Family: married Rachel Donelson; one adopted son
Occupation: lawyer, planter, soldier
Home: The Hermitage, Nashville, Tennessee
Religion: Presbyterian
Elections: 1828—defeated John Quincy Adams
1832—defeated Henry Clay
Political Party: Democratic (sometimes called Jacksonian Democrat)
Vice Presidents: first term—John C. Calhoun; second term—Martin Van Buren
Interesting Facts and Accomplishments:
joined the South Carolina militia at age thirteen and was captured by the British during the War for Independence
opened the White House to the crowds attending his inauguration, but had to escape their misbehavior by exiting through a window
first president to ride a train while in office
lived most of his life with a bullet lodged in his chest
first president to have an assassination attempt made on his life (but the gun of the assassin did not fire properly)
Death: June 8, 1845

Jackson and the Spoils System

At the beginning of his administration, Jackson replaced hundreds of capable government workers with his followers. This method of handing out government jobs to loyal followers is known as the "spoils system." The spoils system for jobs was not new. It had been used on both national and state levels earlier, but Jackson used it on a wider scale.

Jackson and his followers defended the spoils system, claiming that workers of already proven loyalty would do a better job than uncaring holdovers. The spoils system was a way to get rid of officials who might not go along with the desires of the new administration. They also held that giving new people jobs gave the government fresh vigor and gave the people a chance to see how government really worked. This, they argued, would make them more useful citizens. In reality, the spoils system gave the party in power more political muscle.

The spoils system also had disadvantages. It did not encourage efficiency or the hiring of highly qualified workers. In later years it sometimes even caused corruption because people paid bribes to get high-paying jobs. It also aided the growth of **political machines,** organized groups of politicians who sought to control government. These political machines used their power to keep themselves in office and to gain profits from public funds. Such politicians often joined parties not for what they could give but for what they could get.

Since many of the government jobs in the Jacksonian era did not require special skills or a high level of training, the effects of the spoils systems were only slight. Many of the common people to whom Jackson gave offices had the good qualities nurtured on the frontier: determination, honesty, hard work, and common sense. But though less than twenty per cent of the workers were replaced, Jackson's actions set an unwise precedent. Other presidents extended the system until Congress stopped it in 1883 by adopting a civil service system.

Jackson's Kitchen Cabinet

Jackson appointed men to cabinet posts as he did to other government jobs. He used the positions as rewards for party loyalty. Although Jackson had a formally appointed cabinet, he rarely consulted it as a group. Instead he consulted informally with another group of men who were his close friends. These men were known as Jackson's **"Kitchen Cabinet."** The kitchen cabinet members were really the idea men. Jackson asked for their ideas and also discussed his own ideas with them.

Jackson and the Indians

Jackson sought to involve the common man in government, and the new emphasis of his administration brought some attention to the needs of others. Active crusades to free the slaves and give women more rights were launched—although real changes were not to come for many years. The Indians, however, received nothing but mistreatment during the Jackson years and gained no benefit from Jacksonian Democracy.

Attitudes and Policies—Jackson's policies toward the Indians were harsh, but they reflected the thinking of many people in that era. They did not see Indians as real people, as individuals. They did not understand Indians because the Indians did not live or think as they did. White men wanted the Indians to become civilized and to live as the white man did. They also believed that because they had purchased

Indian lands through treaties, the Indians should leave and let them use what was now the white man's private property.

The Indians, on the other hand, believed that most white men were greedy, always wanting more goods, money, and land. The Indians did not own land as private property in the sense that the white man did, and they often did not understand that they were giving up all rights to the land by signing treaties. Because some whites had victimized the Indians and lied to them in the past, many Indians resisted any further advance by the white man. The mistreatment of the Indians by some encouraged many of the Indians to react with hostility. Unfortunately, the misunderstandings between white men and Indians led to many confrontations as the frontier was settled.

Jackson believed that the Indians were "subjects of the United States, inhabiting its territory and acknowledging its sovereignty." Yet almost one hundred treaties were signed with Indians under Jackson. These actions clearly showed that the United States treated the Indian tribes as foreign nations. As a result the Indians had an uncertain status within the United States.

Trouble in Georgia—In 1827 the Creeks ceded their lands in Georgia to the government, but the **Cherokees** refused to give up their lands. The Cherokees were highly civilized Indians. They had copied both the white man's political and agricultural systems. They wrote a constitution declaring that they were an independent nation. They did not want their lands to be taken by the United States, but in 1828 gold was discovered at Dahlonega, Georgia, bringing miners who coveted the Cherokee lands. The Georgia legislature then passed laws making any whites in Cherokee areas sub-

ject to Georgia's laws rather than Cherokee laws. They also made all Cherokee laws void after 1830.

In 1831 a white missionary, Samuel A. Worcester, was convicted for his refusal to take an oath of allegiance to the state of Georgia. He held that Georgia had no authority over Cherokee lands. The next year the Supreme Court agreed with him. Chief Justice John Marshall in *Worcester* v. *Georgia* ordered Georgia to release the missionary and told the president to send troops into Georgia to remove white men from Cherokee lands. Both Georgia and Jackson, assuming a states' rights position, ignored the court. Jackson said: "John Marshall has made his decision. Now let him enforce it." The Cherokees, under their elected chief, John Ross, held out, but by 1838 they were worn down from dealing with the government. Those that had not gone West to Indian Territory (now Oklahoma) were moved forcibly by the U.S. Army. Ironically it was the Cherokees who had taken Jackson's side and fought with him against other Indian tribes in the battle of Horseshoe Bend. Yet they received no help from Jackson as they tried to keep their own lands.

By the middle of the 1830s the best lands in the Mississippi Valley had been taken by the white men, and the Indians had been moved to supposedly permanent homes across the Great River, the Mississippi. In 1837 John Quincy Adams judged the Indian policy and found it wanting. "We have done more harm to the Indians since our Revolution than had ever been done to them by the French and English nations before. . . . These are," he said, "crying sins for which we are answerable before a higher jurisdiction."

Sequoyah: Cherokee Scholar

One Indian who made a name for himself in history never fought a single battle. Sequoyah earned such a reputation as a Cherokee scholar that the California redwoods were given his name. (The tree name, *sequoia*, is the Latin feminine form of his name.)

Sequoyah, whose father was a white man, was recognized among his Cherokee tribesmen as an excellent silversmith. His work excelled that of most of the silversmiths in the area, both white and Indian. A hunting accident had left him crippled, but he did not waste his mental powers in feeling sorry for himself. Instead he decided to develop a Cherokee alphabet.

Despite opposition from some of his own people, Sequoyah completed the work, and it was an unqualified success. Using his alphabet, he taught many of the Cherokees, not only in the East but also in the Indian Territory, how to read. No doubt due partly to his teachings, the Cherokee became leaders among the Indian nations. Eventually they published a weekly newspaper in Oklahoma and even printed parts of the Bible.

In his later years Sequoyah served as an envoy to Washington. He also studied the languages of other tribes and tried to come up with a single Indian language. In addition, he attempted to trace the history of his own people, the Cherokees. Sequoyah was a man with a host of discouraging circumstances surrounding him, who, nevertheless, used the gift he had—a ready mind—to accomplish great things.

ᏏᏉᏯ = si kwo yah

The Black Hawk War—Although the Indians lacked the power to resist the advancement of the white settlers, they tried. One Indian who fought against the Americans was **Black Hawk,** an Indian leader among the Sac and Fox tribes. Black Hawk had fought with the British in the War of 1812 and was a friend of Tecumseh. Forced off their land by a treaty with the United States, Black Hawk and his followers found themselves facing starvation. Consequently, in 1832 Black Hawk and about four hundred Indians returned to their lands to try to find food. The settlers in the area panicked and viewed the return as an act of war. The army was called out, and a force of militiamen organized to battle Black Hawk's band.

After battling with those who assembled against him, Black Hawk fled with his band to the swamps of Wisconsin. The army and the militia pursued. Trapped once at the battle of Wisconsin Heights, Black Hawk retreated across a river to safety. Finally, the militia cornered him again and attacked. Almost all of his followers were killed at the Bad Axe Massacre. Black Hawk escaped but surrendered himself to a band of Winnebago Indians who turned him over to the authorities.

Section Review

1. What factors contributed to making Andrew Jackson a symbol of his age?
2. What was the spoils system?
3. What was the view of many whites toward Indians?
4. How did Indians typically view whites?
5. Why did settlers want the Cherokee lands in Georgia?

B. The Nullification Controversy

One of the most important issues that arose during the Jackson presidency concerned the states and their rights in relation to the power of the federal government. This **states' rights** issue sprang to the forefront as Congress considered the imposition of tariffs.

Tariff Troubles

The idea of a tariff, a tax on goods coming into the country, was not new. Congress had passed a **revenue tariff**—a tariff designed to raise money—during Washington's administration. But by Jackson's time, different sections of the country sharply disagreed on the value of tariffs.

Reasons for Tariffs—One reason for this disagreement stemmed from the fact that the purpose of tariffs had changed. Initially, tariffs were used simply to raise money. Later they were also used to limit the import of foreign goods. The latter type of tariff, called a **protective tariff,** protected businesses and manufacturers from foreign competition, but it also raised the price of foreign goods.

American industries had developed rapidly in the years just before the War of 1812. The Embargo Act of 1807 and other acts that limited trade from Europe had forced people to buy American goods. Then the British blockades during the War of 1812 required Americans to build their own factories to make needed products. Most of these factories were in New England or in the Middle Atlantic States of New York, Pennsylvania, and New Jersey. These areas had ample waterpower and capital (money) available for investment. They also had plenty of manpower to work in the factories. The South, on the other hand, attracted

---

The Tariff

Cost of British hat before tariff: $3.00

Cost of British hat with 8% revenue tariff: $3.24

Cost of British hat with 28% protective tariff: $3.84

Cost of American hat: $3.50

Effects of revenue tariff: Revenue tariffs add money to federal treasury. Since the British hat maker can still undersell his American competitor, he will bring his hats to America. The government will make money. The American hat maker, however, is in trouble. He can't compete unless he becomes smarter and uses more efficient methods or new technology so that he can sell his product for a lower price.

Advantage: British manufacturer and federal treasury

Effects of protective tariff: Now the British manufacturer cannot compete. He will probably quit sending hats to America. The American hat maker will have the market to himself. But the federal treasury will not collect as much money. The American manufacturer may also become more complacent, less competitive, and not as open to improvements.

Advantage: American manufacturer

---

few factories since much of its money was tied up in slaves and cotton. Also few immigrants went to the South because slaves provided much of the labor.

Despite rapid industrial growth in the North, most new American industries—often called infant industries—wanted protection from foreign competition. They wanted a protective tariff.

The Tariff of Abominations—In 1816 Congress responded to the demands of protectionists and levied a higher tariff. In 1824 the tariff was revised upward and more products were put on the tariff list. Four years later in 1828 the tariff was raised again. Some Americans had objected to the earlier tariffs, but the 1828 tariff drew wide protest. Most of the protests came from areas and states that had little industry. They believed this "tariff of abominations" raised the price on almost everything they bought or manufactured.

Because the South had remained agricultural, it needed to buy most of its manufactured goods either from the North or from foreign countries. The Southerners depended on the profits they made from their crops to pay for those goods. Because the high tariff forced the South to buy American-made products, it increased their costs and decreased their trade with foreign countries. Selling cotton became more difficult as the trade decreased, and cotton prices fell. In addition, increased competition from new cotton states in the Southwest complicated the problem. In hopes of selling more cotton, Southerners were farming more acres. This meant they needed more slaves—and slave prices went up steadily. Thus, while the price for cotton fell, production costs rose. Southern planters began to blame their troubles on the high tariff.

John C. Calhoun, Defender of States' Rights

These economic troubles, along with worry over the slavery questions, increased political tensions. The troubles also brought a stronger defense of states' rights.

South Carolina's John C. Calhoun, Jackson's vice president, became the leading defender of the idea of states' rights. The South Carolina legislature had formed a committee to study the tariff problem and had asked Calhoun to write the final report.

The report said that the people of South Carolina—or anyone else in the minority—could protect themselves from tariffs or any other laws that might hurt them by nullifying them. According to this theory of nullification, a state could declare a federal law harmful and thus unconstitutional and not enforceable in the state. Calhoun thought that nullification would satisfy the South by allowing it to protect itself from the ever-growing North while not limiting his appeal in the North and West. He hoped that this would help him gain the presidency after Jackson and protect the outnumbered Southerners. (Remember that nullification had been proposed earlier by Thomas Jefferson in the Virginia and Kentucky Resolutions, p. 188.)

Webster vs. Hayne

When Jackson did not pursue tariff reform, the South decided to seek it by bargaining with the West. They pushed the West to support a lower tariff in return for southern support of a free land policy. (Westerners wanted more western lands opened to settlement without cost, but Northerners opposed the idea because they feared that their workers would move away to the free lands.) In the Senate debate that followed, Calhoun's doctrine of nullification came under attack.

In an 1830 speech, South Carolina Senator **Robert Y. Hayne** defended nullification and state sovereignty. Hayne noted that the states had voluntarily joined the union and that the Constitution protected their authority by granting them their reserved powers. Hayne argued that the Constitution did not give the national government the power to pass laws hurting one group of people while helping another.

Since such laws violated the Constitution, the state had the right to nullify and refuse to obey them.

Senator **Daniel Webster** of Massachusetts attacked nullification point by point, carefully defending the Constitution and the federal union. Webster argued that the people, rather than the states, had established the Union, making the Constitution and the Union superior to state governments. He said that nullification would lead to the end of the Union. Webster argued that if anyone believed that a law was unconstitutional, he should take his case before the Supreme Court. But a state, he said, did not have the right to disobey federal law. He closed his speech pleading, "Liberty and Union, now and forever, one and inseparable!"

Daniel Webster, one of America's greatest statesmen

Calhoun and Jackson Clash

Jackson had not taken sides. He had a deep respect for states' rights and believed the South was justified in its complaint about the tariff. But to Jackson, nullification was out of the question.

On April 13, 1830, the Democrats gathered for a dinner in honor of the birthday of their party's founder, Thomas Jefferson. A series of toasts—speeches in honor of someone—was a regular part of such gatherings. When the president rose to make his toast, he looked squarely at John C. Calhoun and in a clear voice said only: "Our Federal Union: it must and shall be preserved!" After all had sat back down John C. Calhoun responded: "The Union! Next to our liberty most dear!"

This incident was but one of many in a growing rift that eventually led John C. Calhoun to resign the vice-presidency. Calhoun then went to the Senate, where he led the fight for states' rights.

A Time of Crisis

The issue of states' rights simmered dangerously for another two years until it boiled over in 1832. Congress passed a new tariff. The tariff of 1832 gained some support in the South and West because it was a bit lower than the 1828 tariff. But it retained high tariffs on textiles and iron. Nullifiers saw that Congress was still pro-tariff; therefore, they felt the tariff of 1832 was a direct challenge. When Jackson signed the tariff, they believed all hope was gone.

South Carolina legislators called a state convention late in November and declared both the tariff of 1828 and 1832 "null, void, and no law, nor binding upon the State; its officers or citizens." Their Ordinance of Nullification forbade state and federal officers from collecting tariffs after February 1, 1833. If there was any federal attempt to use force in South Carolina, the state would issue an order of **secession**—it would leave the Union.

Jackson met the crisis head on. He sent a warship and a revenue cutter (a federal boat that collected tariffs in ports) to Charleston, said he would personally take the field if it came to an armed clash, and threatened to hang John C. Calhoun. In December 1832 he told the people of South Carolina that he understood their plight but that nullifying a federal law defied both the spirit and letter of the Constitution. He also told them that they could not leave the Union. "The dictates of a high duty oblige me solemnly to announce that you cannot secede. The laws of the United States must be executed. . . . My duty is emphatically pronounced in the Constitution."

Congress supported Jackson by passing a Force Bill allowing the president to use the army and navy to enforce the laws. Meanwhile, South Carolina looked for allies. The state called a national convention to support nullification. To its surprise, not one state responded.

The Compromise of 1833

Henry Clay, who always seemed to find a compromise that would settle disputes, believed South Carolina might want a way of escape. He also knew Jackson wanted to avoid violence. Clay talked with Calhoun and worked out the details for a compromise tariff. This tariff lowered duties gradually. By 1842 no tariff was to be over twenty per cent. This plan gave the infant industries in the North time to grow stronger before they lost their protection. Congress adopted this **Compromise of 1833** on March 1 of

that year. Two weeks later South Carolina withdrew its nullification of the tariff. But it still held the Force Bill null and void. Jackson, however, ignored this action. Although Jackson and Clay had managed to keep the Union together, the question of states' rights remained unsettled. Many Southerners still believed they could leave the Union if they wanted to.

Section Review

1. What are the two basic purposes of a tariff?
2. Why were Southerners and unindustrialized areas against the tariff?
3. Who became the South's spokesman and leading defender of states' rights?
4. What senator attacked nullification, and what did he fear would happen to the Union if nullification were carried out?
5. What brought the states' rights issue to a crisis in 1832?

Andrew Jackson in his later years

C. Jackson and the National Bank

The election of 1832 differed from the 1828 election. There was no mudslinging, and there was an issue—the future of the National Bank. The bank had been rechartered for twenty more years in 1816. Thus it would cease to exist after 1836 unless Congress renewed its charter and the president endorsed the action.

Banker Nicholas Biddle

Nicholas Biddle, a talented, wealthy Philadelphian, had handled the bank skillfully. Its twenty-nine branches regulated the nation's finances and had helped the country tremendously. It was powerful because it controlled one-fifth of all bank notes and one-third of bank deposits and coins. Since four-fifths of its stock was held by private parties, most of whom were rich Easterners, the bank was responsible to them. The bank did earn a profit. Biddle courted Jackson's favor by making loans to Jackson supporters and suggesting that the national debt be repaid on the anniversary of Jackson's victory at New Orleans.

Although such a goal was dear to Jackson's heart, Jackson was not won over. He made it known that he disliked banks—not just Biddle's but all banks. But Jackson vented his dislike only on the National Bank. Moreover, Jackson thought the bank unconstitutional. Although the Supreme Court had already upheld the bank, Jackson was not impressed. "I have read the opinion of John Marshall," he said, "and could not agree with him." Although Jackson's supporters pursued wealth and economic power as eagerly as Eastern merchant and factory owners, they made it sound as if the Easterners were interested only in special privilege and maintaining a monopoly.

Jackson also had the support of state bankers. He led them to believe that Biddle would destroy state banks by calling in their notes. Although Biddle had never used the bank's power to this end, he did hold this threat over them. The threat had forced the state banks to be more careful in their lending. In addition, New York bankers whose wealth was growing from the Erie Canal trade, joined the antibank group out of jealous resentment. If Biddle's bank was not rechartered, New Yorkers thought the business might be thrown their way.

The Election of 1832

Aware of the feelings of Jackson and others, Biddle could have played a waiting game. But in 1832 Henry Clay thought he saw a way to win the presidency for himself and save the National Bank at the same time by making the bank the central campaign issue.

Nicholas Biddle

The Bank of the United States in Philadelphia

Although Biddle hesitated, Clay introduced the bill for the bank's recharter in 1832, four years ahead of its scheduled renewal. Congress passed the bill with strong support from Jackson's own party, but Jackson angrily vetoed it. More of the voters supported Jackson's view in the presidential election that year, and he won 219 electoral votes to Clay's 39. Congress did not override Jackson's decision.

Jackson and His "Pet Banks"

Jackson's veto meant that there would be no National Bank after 1836. But to Jackson that was not enough. He was now out to kill the bank and ruin his enemy Biddle. Jackson ordered the secretary of the treasury to quit depositing government money in Biddle's bank. Instead, the government revenues from taxes and land sales would go into newly opened accounts in eighty-nine different state banks. These soon became known as Jackson's **"pet banks."** Fearing an economic panic, the secretary refused to follow Jackson's orders, and Jackson fired him. Jackson then went through three secretaries before he found one willing to do his bidding. Since the law required current bills to be paid out of national bank deposits, the balance dropped $17 million in a year's time. Lacking funds, Biddle was forced to call in loans owed by state banks. Unfortunately that recall caused hundreds of state banks to fail and the savings of thousands of Americans were wiped out. What Jackson had feared would happen was now a reality—and the president was partly to blame for it.

Biddle soon responded to pressure from bankers and businessmen. Rather than calling money in, he lent it out in an effort to save more banks from failure. In the West this sudden influx of money led to a new problem: speculation in western lands. Money became freely available to almost anyone who wanted it.

Congress, with Jackson's approval, added to the instability of western banks.

It passed a Distribution Bill providing state governments with $37 million to be spent for internal improvements. In response, with more money being spent in the states, more state banks were founded hoping to profit from such windfall spending. Between 1830 and 1837, the number of state banks increased from 330 to about 800.

The Specie Circular

The rising inflation alarmed Jackson—especially the great rise in prices for western lands. Since he would not use the bank to settle prices down, Jackson requested the Treasury Department to issue a **Specie Circular.** This act required anyone who bought government lands to pay for them in **specie** (gold or silver coins) rather than paper money.

The Circular did cut down on bank loans issued. But at the same time, it meant that borrowers, including speculators, could no longer pay back their debts. Soon people did not trust paper money at all. More banks failed and more farmers lost their lands. With no money for people to spend and no banks to borrow from, businesses failed. The economic crisis grew worse. By the time Jackson's hand-picked successor took office, the nation was suffering from an economic depression that was to last five years.

Section Review

1. What was the major issue in the election of 1832?
2. How did Jackson view the bank?
3. Where did Jackson order federal monies be placed?
4. What did Jackson do to drive prices down?
5. How did the Specie Circular affect the economy?

D. Effects of the Jackson Administration

Although Jackson left office in 1837, his strong imprint remained. He had greatly increased the powers of the executive branch. When challenged by advocates of states' rights on the tariff, he had staunchly defended the Union. But when Indian policy was the issue, he had favored the states and deprived the Indians of their lands. He claimed to follow the Constitution strictly yet refused to enforce Supreme Court decisions. He said he believed in free enterprise; yet he caused an economic panic by undermining a bank that was largely privately owned. He promised to return the government to that "simple machine which the Constitution created." But by cutting the government's role, he also created many problems for the national government to deal with in later years.

The Election of 1836

Martin Van Buren, who had served as Andrew Jackson's vice president since 1832, was Jackson's hand-picked choice for the Democratic candidacy in 1836. The new opposing party, the **Whigs,** were eager to restore the proper constitutional balance of power. They unified several diverse groups into one party, and the biggest element uniting the groups was opposition to Jackson. The Whigs wanted the national government to promote a strong economy by restoring the national bank and sponsoring a protective tariff as well as internal improvements.

Also the ideals of Democrats and Whigs seemed to differ. The Democrats did not make as many statements as the Whigs about religion and morals. The Whigs applauded Sunday closing laws, and some wanted to outlaw alcohol. The Democrats held that such matters were more personal than they were public. The northern Whigs saw slavery as sinful. The Democrats said it was not the North's concern because they could not solve the problem. As a result of the issues, evangelical Protestants tended to favor the Whigs. The hands-off approach of Democrats attracted more Catholics, Episcopalians, and free thinkers. Since many of the newer immigrants, especially the Irish, were Catholic, they joined with the Jacksonian Democrats, giving them an added advantage in upcoming elections.

The Whig strategy was to try to throw the election into the House by running strong sectional candidates. In Tennessee they ran Hugh L. White, who had broken with Jackson; in the mid-Atlantic and western states, General William Henry Harrison carried the Whig banner. In Massachusetts Daniel Webster was the choice. The Whig strategy backfired. Fifty-one per cent of the popular vote went to Van Buren, and his margin of victory in the electoral college was comfortable.

The Van Buren Years

Van Buren was the first president not to have been born a British subject. His family was Dutch and never gained prominence. Denied the education acquired by other national politicians, he mastered the practical: he learned how to unite men, motives, and issues into a plan of action. Although not always right, Van Buren learned from his mistakes. He was a masterful politician who retained personal principles.

The first problem that Van Buren faced was an economic depression that began in

Martin Van Buren
8TH PRESIDENT
(1837-1841)

Born: Kinderhook, New York, December 5, 1782
Family: married Hannah Hoes; four sons
Occupation: lawyer
Home: Lindenwald, Kinderhook, New York
Religion: Dutch Reformed
Election: 1836—defeated William Henry Harrison, Hugh L. White, and Daniel Webster
Political Party: Democrat
Vice President: Richard M. Johnson
Interesting Facts and Accomplishments:
first president not born a British subject
discarded crimson upholstery in the Oval Drawing Room of the White House and created the Blue Room by changing everything to blue
initials of his campaign nickname, "Old Kinderhook," brought the expression "o.k." into use
ran for president on the Free Soil party ticket in 1848 to take a stand against slavery
Death: July 24, 1862

1837. British trade and investments dropped off sharply. Cotton prices went down to six cents a pound from an earlier high of fifteen cents. With no money, the canal and road building stopped, throwing thousands of men out of work. Van Buren called Congress into special session to deal with the crisis. He suggested that government end all contact with banks, both central and pet banks. "The less government interferes with private pursuits, the better for the general prosperity," he said. In Massachusetts and Pennsylvania, state legislatures took over the building of roads and canals. But nine other states **defaulted** (did not repay the money they owed) on their bonds.

Van Buren proposed an **independent treasury** system that would consist of a number of separate federal vaults and depositories. The treasury could collect and spend from these subtreasuries without using any banks. Gold and silver would be the medium for all federal business. Congress adopted Van Buren's plan in 1840.

Chief Justice John Marshall had died in 1835, allowing Jackson to appoint **Roger B. Taney** (TAW nee) to his position. Jackson had appointed four new associate justices in his term as well. Van Buren was also able to appoint two justices when vacancies occurred in 1837. With all these new appointments, Taney now had control of a new court. Whigs were panic-stricken. They feared that the Democratic court would reverse all Marshall's nationalist decisions. As it turned out, Marshall's decisions stood and few dramatic changes occurred, but the court did move to protect states' rights in business, banking, and commerce. Its greatest impact came in the late 1850s when it moved strongly for states' rights as the Civil War approached.

William Henry Harrison

When the election of 1840 came, Van Buren was again the Democratic choice. Convinced that Clay would not attract Eastern voters, the Whigs turned to William Henry Harrison, a man not closely identified with either party. Harrison, however, was a Southerner by birth and could attract Democratic votes in the South. He was a military hero, too, known for his victory at Tippecanoe and his efforts in the War of 1812. Since his political views were not known, they could not hurt him. A careless comment by a Democrat—that if Harrison were given a log cabin and a barrel of hard cider, he would retire on a pension—played directly into Whig hands. They soon pictured Harrison, who was really wealthy, as a simple man of common tastes, and they labeled Van Buren as a snobbish aristocrat.

The Whigs campaigned with gusto. Dressed as Indians, they played up "Tippecanoe's" victory over Tecumseh. They served gallons of cider to voters and put on parades complete with bands, banners, and flags. Voter turnout increased sixty per cent over 1836. This, when added to his war fame, helped Harrison and his running mate, **John Tyler,** to win nineteen of the twenty-six states and fifty-three per cent of the popular vote. With campaign slogans such as "Tippecanoe and Tyler Too!" "Van, Van, Van is a used-up man!" and "To guide the ship, We'll try old Tip!" the Whig ticket put Van Buren out of office.

No sooner had the 68-year-old Harrison taken office than disaster struck. While making the longest inaugural address in the nation's history (an hour and forty minutes) Harrison caught cold. Before Congress could even convene, Harrison's cold turned into pneumonia. Just four weeks

William Henry Harrison
9TH PRESIDENT
(1841)

Born: Charles City County, Virginia, February 9, 1773
Family: married Anna Tuthill Symmes; ten children
Occupation: soldier, planter
Home: Grouseland, Vincennes, Indiana
Religion: Episcopalian
Election: 1840—defeated Martin Van Buren
Political Party: Whig
Vice President: John Tyler
Interesting Facts and Accomplishments:
his father was Benjamin Harrison, who signed the Declaration of Independence
served the shortest presidential term—one month
at age 68, he was the oldest president to take office until Ronald Reagan took office at age 69 in 1981
Death: April 4, 1841

after he took office, he died, the first president to do so while in office.

Tyler Too

John Tyler, the first vice president to reach office through the death of a president, was a Virginian. He was a Whig because he disagreed with Jackson on nullification and the removal of bank deposits. Clay told Tyler that since he had not really been elected as president, Tyler should let a congressional committee of Whigs make crucial decisions. Clay, of course, intended to head the committee. Tyler, however, had a mind of his own, and he knew what the Constitution said. He was unquestionably the rightful president.

Man Without a Party—The Whig program went before Congress with Henry Clay in charge. It abolished the independent treasury system. Clay also pushed through a new land act. The Pre-Emption Act of 1841 allowed **squatters**—settlers on western lands without titles to the land—to buy those lands when they came up for public sale. Moreover, the act allowed them to buy the land at a low price—$1.25 an acre for a minimum of 160 acres. This "log cabin" bill also said that monies from the sale of lands could be distributed to the states as long as the tariff stayed under 20 per cent. This would help the states out of debt. Tyler had little say over this program.

When the national debt increased, Tyler was forced to sign a bill to raise the tariff back to its 1832 level. Clay then submitted a bill establishing a new national bank. Tyler vetoed it, holding it to be unconstitutional and of greater benefit to the Northeast than to the rest of the nation.

John Tyler
10TH PRESIDENT
(1841-1845)

Born: Charles City County, Virginia, March 29, 1790

Family: married Letitia Christian and, after her death, Julia Gardiner; fifteen children

Occupation: lawyer

Home: Sherwood Forest, Charles City County, Virginia

Religion: Episcopalian

Election: 1840—as vice president, succeeded to the presidency upon the death of Harrison

Political Party: Whig

Vice President: none

Interesting Facts and Accomplishments:

graduated from William and Mary College

almost killed in two accidents while he was president—when a cannon exploded on a ship, and when a horse ran wild at the funeral for those who were killed in the previous accident

first wife died while he was president in 1842; became the first president to marry while in office when he married his second wife

had the most children of any president—fifteen

was elected to the Confederate Congress at the beginning of the Civil War, but died before he could take office

Death: January 14, 1862

The Whigs, who were already calling Tyler "his accidency" because of how he had gained office, now turned on the president and expelled him from the party. All the Whigs in Tyler's cabinet resigned except Daniel Webster. Tyler became "a man without a party."

The Webster-Ashburton Treaty—In foreign affairs the Tyler administration faced problems with Britain, primarily as a result of the vaguely drawn northeastern border with Canada. Daniel Webster and Lord Ashburton, the British minister, met to resolve matters. The resulting treaty, the **Webster-Ashburton Treaty** of 1842, was a compromise. The United States gave a portion of Maine to Canada. The United States gained additional land in northern New York and Vermont as well as lands on Lake Superior in northeastern Minnesota. The undefined portion of the boundary line between the United States and Canada was drawn from Lake of the Woods east to the Atlantic. As soon as the Senate had ratified the treaty, Webster resigned, joining the other Whig leaders in their protest against President Tyler.

The End of Tyler's Term—When Tyler's cabinet resigned, he created a power base of his own by placing southern Whigs in the vacant cabinet seats. Tyler worked to add Texas to the Union partly because he believed Texas would aid his reelection. His early efforts failed. Texas remained outside the Union, and **James K. Polk** won the election of 1844. In the time that remained between the election and Tyler's leaving office, he kept pushing his ideas. (A president during the time between election and leaving office is called a **lame duck** because he does not have as much support and political power as the president-elect, who

The Webster-Ashburton Treaty—1842
(Maine Boundary Settlement)

St. Lawrence River

Quebec

Maine

Bangor

N. H.

Portland

U. S. Claim _____

British Claim _____

Present Boundary —··—··—··—

has just won the election.) When the Senate refused to ratify a treaty by the required two-thirds vote to annex Texas, Tyler proposed Texas be admitted by a joint resolution. The resolution, requiring only a simple majority vote, passed.

Harrison had been elected in 1840 because of the popular opinion against Jackson's policies and those of Van Buren, his successor. By the end of Tyler's administration, however, many Americans were clamoring for another strong leader like Jackson.

Section Review

1. What was the Whig strategy in the election of 1836?
2. What problem did Van Buren face right after he became president?
3. What did Van Buren substitute for the regular banking system?
4. What techniques did Harrison and Tyler use to win votes in their election?
5. What part of the American boundary line was drawn by the Webster-Ashburton Treaty line of 1842?

Summary

As the first "log cabin" president, Andrew Jackson did much to change the influences on the national government. The "common man," especially the poor western farmer, gained as great a voice in government as that of the eastern industrialist or the southern planter. Jackson's policies helped to open land for the farmers and to create business opportunities for those outside of the industrial Northeast. Although he was committed to the preservation of the Union, some of his actions were rash and harmful to the country. Financial problems resulted in the Van Buren administration that followed, and other presidents faced the growing sectional and political differences without the help of permanent solutions.

Chapter Review

Do You Remember?

■ Match each of the following items or descriptions with the man or men with whom they are most closely related. Answers may be used more than once, and questions may have more than one answer.

1. helped make the Compromise of 1833
2. most prominent defender of states' rights
3. had "pet banks"
4. first president to die while in office
5. participated in a debate over nullification
6. "his accidency"
7. helped make a treaty with Britain
8. served as president of the United States
9. Bad Axe Massacre
10. Chief Justice
11. National Bank president
12. vice president under Jackson
13. first vice president to become president at the death of his predecessor
14. formed a "Kitchen Cabinet"
15. first Whig president
16. wanted to form an independent treasury
17. became a hero as a soldier
18. resigned the vice-presidency

a. Andrew Jackson
b. Black Hawk
c. Robert Y. Hayne
d. Daniel Webster
e. John C. Calhoun
f. Henry Clay
g. Nicholas Biddle
h. Martin Van Buren
i. William Henry Harrison
j. Roger B. Taney
k. John Tyler
l. James K. Polk

Why Is It So?

1. Why was Andrew Jackson considered the champion of the common man?
2. Why was the spoils system not beneficial for the government?
3. Why was the South opposed to protective tariffs?
4. Why would nullification have been beneficial to the South?
5. Why did Jackson's dealings with the National Bank prove harmful for the economy?
6. Why did Tyler lack power as a president?

What Do You Think?

1. Do you think the hostilities between the Indians and the white man could have been avoided? Explain your answer.
2. Is states' rights an issue in government today? Why or why not?
3. Why do you suppose Jackson did not make South Carolina recognize the Force Bill?

13

Means of Transportation and Communication

A river steamboat called the Bridgeport

Most of America's early settlements were located along the coast because water made transportation easy. Over the years, however, the nation acquired vast areas of new land. Explorers and traders told of the value of these western lands, and some Americans wanted to go settle there. They faced a serious problem, however. The distances were great, and there were no good roads to the West. Because of poor transportation and communication, people who left for the frontier knew that they might never see or hear from their friends and relatives in the East again.

A. Roads in the Early 1800s

Colonial America had few roads, most of which were in the East, and they were no more than dirt paths or muddy ruts. Many of them were initially paths that animals and Indians had used to get to streams or clearings. Settlers later cut back the bushes and trees a few feet to widen the roads.

A few roads linked major cities. The Boston Post Road between Boston and New York was usually passable year around. It took three days to travel the ninety miles between New York and Philadelphia in a

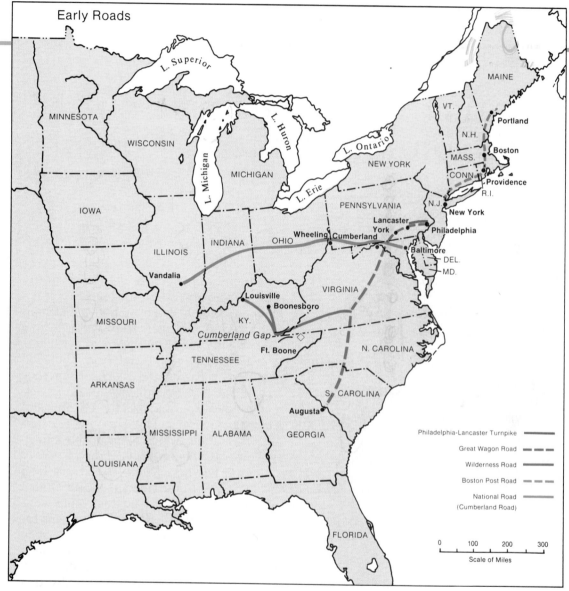

Early Roads

MINNESOTA

L. Superior

WISCONSIN

L. Huron

MICHIGAN

L. Michigan

IOWA

ILLINOIS

INDIANA

OHIO

L. Erie

L. Ontario

NEW YORK

MAINE

VT.

N.H.

MASS.

CONN.

R.I.

Portland

Boston

Providence

N.J.

New York

PENNSYLVANIA

Lancaster
York

Philadelphia

Wheeling Cumberland

Baltimore

DEL.

MD.

Vandalia

VIRGINIA

Louisville
Boonesboro

KY.

Cumberland Gap

Ft. Boone

MISSOURI

TENNESSEE

N. CAROLINA

ARKANSAS

S. CAROLINA

Augusta

MISSISSIPPI

ALABAMA

GEORGIA

LOUISIANA

FLORIDA

Philadelphia-Lancaster Turnpike ————
Great Wagon Road — — —
Wilderness Road ————
Boston Post Road — — —
National Road ————
(Cumberland Road)

0   100   200   300
Scale of Miles

covered wagon. By 1766 "flying machines"—stagecoaches—cut the time by a day (when the weather was good). Because the South had a fairly good water transportation system, few roads were built there.

New Roads Improve Transportation

Three major roads provided transportation routes for thousands of intrepid early Americans, their stock, and their products. These roads stretched into the frontier to help open new areas of settlement.

The Great Wagon Road—The Five Nations of the Iroquois, all eastern woodland tribes, had traveled through the Appalachian Mountains long before the white man. These Indians used a road, called the Great Warrior's Path, that ran north and

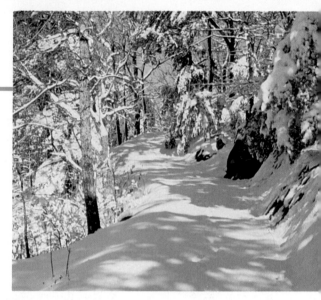

Transportation and Communication Timeline

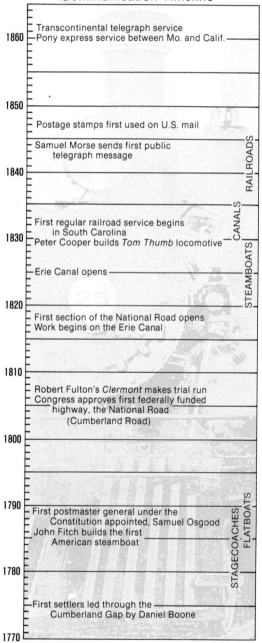

1860 — Transcontinental telegraph service
— Pony express service between Mo. and Calif.

1850

— Postage stamps first used on U.S. mail

— Samuel Morse sends first public
    telegraph message

1840

RAILROADS

— First regular railroad service begins
    in South Carolina
1830 — Peter Cooper builds *Tom Thumb* locomotive

CANALS

— Erie Canal opens

STEAMBOATS

1820

— First section of the National Road opens
— Work begins on the Erie Canal

1810

— Robert Fulton's *Clermont* makes trial run
— Congress approves first federally funded
    highway, the National Road
    (Cumberland Road)

1800

1790 — First postmaster general under the
        Constitution appointed, Samuel Osgood
      — John Fitch builds the first
        American steamboat

STAGECOACHES   FLATBOATS

1780

— First settlers led through the
    Cumberland Gap by Daniel Boone

1770

south along the western slope of the mountains. In 1744 the English took control of the Warrior's Path through a treaty. Freed of Indian dangers, hardy Germans and Scots-Irish farmers from Pennsylvania followed the road southward to settle less crowded lands. They went from Philadelphia to Lancaster and York. Then they crossed the Potomac to Virginia and eventually moved south across the Carolinas to Augusta, Georgia. Thousands of settlers used this route, which came to be known as the **Great Wagon Road.**

The Wilderness Road—In 1775 a land speculator, Richard Henderson, purchased twenty million acres of Kentucky and western Virginia from the Cherokee Indians for $44,500. Henderson summoned woodsman **Daniel Boone** to handle final details with the Indians and to cut a road into Kentucky. This road was a westward extension of the Great Wagon Road. Boone and his thirty axe men started in March 1775. Their route took them through the **Cumberland Gap,** a natural passage through the mountain barrier. Thomas Walker had discovered the gap in 1750. Their **Wilderness Road** finally reached Boonesboro in east central Kentucky—over two hundred miles from their starting point.

The Wilderness Road winds through the Cumberland Gap.

The National Road—Despite opposition to using government funds, Congress approved the first federally funded highway in 1806. Construction began in 1811 at Cumberland, Maryland. The first section of the road, reaching to Wheeling (now in West Virginia), was opened in August 1818. Because of the need for drainage, the road was raised with ten-foot shoulders and ditches sloping from each side. The twenty-foot roadbed was dug into the ground a foot deep on the sides and a foot and a

---

Road Construction: How Roads Were Built

By our standards the tools used for road building were primitive—carts, picks, shovels, and crude blasting tools. In 1831 a "sulky scraper," a simple horse-drawn board device, was used to scrape dirt from the ditch to the center of the road. In 1843 a horse-drawn roller system was introduced to pack road surfaces.

One type of road—a stone railroad—used stone slabs for wheel tracks and cobblestone in the center. From 1845 to 1855, plank roads became popular. Workers laid two parallel rows of stringers or log pieces; space between was covered with earth. The builders then nailed a plank floor eight to twelve feet wide to the stringers. This type of road was a great improvement and the smoothest surface available until blacktop and concrete were introduced. But the toll companies found that at $2,000 a mile the plank roads were expensive to build and maintain.

In other areas logs were laid side by side to form a rough road surface. These "corduroy roads" provided a bumpy ride, but they could be hastily constructed to help travelers avoid being stuck in mud holes. They were also used in swampy areas.

From England came the idea of macadamized roads of crushed stone placed in a pre-dug road bed. These roads multiplied when in 1858 an American, Eli Whitney Blake, invented a stone crusher operated by a belt from a steam engine.

Few of America's early roads were designed by engineers. Roadbuilding was considered nonprofessional and highly dangerous work. Engineers were called on only for bridge construction. Irish immigrants were often hired for the other jobs. Eager for work and used to poverty, these newcomers were willing to take the low-wage, high-risk jobs of building roads.

half in the middle. All stones for the bottom layer were to be passed through a seven-inch ring while those for the surface had to go through a three-inch ring. The original **National Road,** or Cumberland Road as it was sometimes called, cost $1.7 million or about $13,000 a mile. Later the road extended westward to Vandalia, Illinois.

Turnpikes

Additional roads called **turnpikes** were built by private companies hoping to make a profit. Their name came from the sharp sticks guarding the entrances to the road. On payment of the toll or charge to use the road, the sticks were turned down into a grate. While up, the fence-like pikes kept animals from wandering onto the roads. The Philadelphia-Lancaster Pike, built of stone in 1792, was the nation's longest pike. Turnpikes became a business rage in the early 1800s. In Connecticut in the 1830s, fifty turnpike companies were incorporated. Pennsylvania ranked first in mileage; Maryland was second. Unfortunately builders did not make the profits they had planned on, and some projects were phased out. Generally individual states then inherited the responsibility of keeping up the roads.

Section Review

1. Why had there been little inland settlement up to this time?
2. What three major roads provided routes to the frontier?
3. Who cut a westward extension of the road that led into Kentucky, and what natural passage through a mountain barrier did this road use to its advantage?
4. What was the first federally funded highway called?
5. Who paid for turnpikes?

B. Water Transportation

While colonial America had built up a valuable coastal trade and sailing ships crossed the Atlantic and later the Gulf of Mexico to New Orleans, there had been little development of inland waterways.

Upstream Without a Paddle

The early river craft included canoes of all sizes, flatboats, keelboats, and barges. Moving downstream with these vessels was relatively easy because they could float with the current. Moving upstream, however, required extra effort. Paddling a canoe upstream was not too difficult, but paddles could not propel the larger craft against river currents. Winds would sometimes push boats with sails, but winds were unreliable. Some keelboats and barges could be poled upstream if the water was not too deep and the current not too strong. Animals along the shore could also tow boats upstream with a rope. Because of the difficulties and expenses involved, many boats never returned upstream. Instead they were dismantled and used for lumber or firewood.

Passenger and freight rates were high; it cost $160 in 1800 to take a flatboat down the Ohio and Mississippi rivers from Pittsburgh to New Orleans. Freight shipments cost $6.75 per hundred pounds.

Steamboats Furnish a Vital Link

Steamboats, which could easily paddle upstream, quickly became a vital part of America's transportation system. Although early experiments with them took place on the Atlantic seaboard, the greatest possibility for their use came later on western inland waters. In the East they made the Hudson, Potomac, and Delaware rivers busy waterways. Steamboats helped settlement along western rivers like the Ohio and the Mississippi. By 1839 tonnage on the western rivers was two times that of all Atlantic ports. Major cities—such as New Orleans, St. Louis, Cincinnati, and Pittsburgh—grew up along steamboat routes.

Steamboats made going west to settle much easier. Settlers within reach of steamboats no longer faced isolation. Letters, newspapers, and books as well as manufactured goods flowed west. Trade between the East and the West also became more profitable. The West was full of opportunities for the immigrants who were swelling eastern cities, and steamboats were ready to transport new settlers to those lands.

Robert Fulton is credited with building the first commercially successful steamboat in 1807. But as early as 1790 five other steamboat pioneers had built and operated steam-driven vessels. Very little attention was paid to their trial runs. Shore-bound spectators laughed at their efforts to race against currents. Probably the best known of this group of disappointed inventors is John Fitch.

John Fitch Experiments with Steamboats—John Fitch's life was problem-plagued from his early years. His father was a tyrant; his wife was a nag; and his great idea—for which he thought he should be remembered forever—was twenty years ahead of its time. Fitch had been a clock maker and a silversmith, but during an attack of rheumatism in his knee he had the idea to make a "steam carriage" to help him get around. However, he soon abandoned the steam carriage as impractical and drew a plan for a steamboat.

Fitch brought his idea to Philadelphia and asked prominent statesmen to finance the craft. But even Benjamin Franklin had doubts that Fitch's craft would work. Fitch

did not give up. He met a watchmaker, Henry Voight, who had the mechanical knowledge that Fitch lacked. Their first boat wallowed in the Delaware River while boatmen laughed. His second craft was a partial success. It went three to four miles per hour against the current. Then he built the *Perseverance,* a seven-ton boat with twelve paddles. Fitch demonstrated it for some delegates to the Philadelphia Convention of 1787, but they were too skeptical to help.

In 1790 Fitch built a boat that could go eight miles an hour. By fall Fitch's boat had logged three thousand miles and had carried over a thousand passengers. Fitch claimed that he and Voight "reigned as Lord High Admirals of the Delaware, and no boat in the River could hold its way with [them]." But his boat could carry only seven passengers per trip because the engine took up so much space. Although the boat ride was more comfortable than being bounced in a stagecoach, it also took longer. Speed seemed more important to the public than comfort; the company lost money. Then the *Perseverance* was destroyed by a storm. In

An early steamboat

1798 a dejected Fitch took an overdose of opium and ended his life.

***Robert Fulton and his* Clermont—** About the same time Fitch was making trial runs on the Delaware, a young artist-turned-engineer named Robert Fulton entered the contest. He had just built a submarine, the *Nautilus,* which he thought the French Navy could use to blow up British vessels in the English Channel. In Paris Fulton met Robert Livingston, American minister to France. Fulton told Livingston of another idea he had—a steamboat. Livingston had the money, the right to navigate the Hudson, and the political clout to help Fulton's idea become a reality.

Fulton got his steam engine from England. Because the British did not want other countries to outdo them, they tried to keep any inventions from leaving the country. But Fulton was not to be denied. A suave diplomat, he convinced Boulton and Watt, the inventors of the engine, to sell him one for $2,600. Returning to America with it, he built a vessel, installed his engine, and named the vessel the *Clermont* after Livingston's home on the Hudson. On August 17, 1807, the boat made its first public trial. The lone newspaper to cover the event said the boat was "invented with view to the navigation of the Mississippi upward." The steamboat line paid off and paid well. Fulton and Livingston made $16,000 their first year. By 1825 steamship travel was so common, no one could even remember scoffing at it. Fulton became a national hero.

Canals

Although Europe had been building useful canals for years, America's great canal age began in 1817, with the construc-

tion of the Erie Canal, and lasted until about 1840. A **canal** is a shallow, manmade water highway that connects two bodies of water. Most canals were thirty-six to forty feet wide at the top, twenty-four to twenty-eight feet wide at the bottom, and four feet deep. Canals used a system of **locks** (water compartments that can be opened and shut) and dams to keep a constant water level. Most of the brightly colored canal boats and barges on the canals were privately owned. Their owners paid tolls to the construction companies to use the canals. The most famous canal, the **Erie Canal,** opened in 1825. It connected Albany, New York, on the Hudson River, with Lake Erie. Boats could enter the Hudson River at New York City and sail to Albany to reach the canal. This made water transportation possible between the Atlantic Ocean and the Great Lakes.

Other states, quick to follow New York's example, built their own canals to compete.

Robert Fulton made the steamboat a success.

In Ohio, the Ohio and Erie Canal linked the Ohio River to Lake Erie. The Miami and Erie Canal connected the Miami and Ohio rivers with Lake Erie. Indiana's Wabash and Erie Canal tied Indiana to the trade system. The Chesapeake and Ohio brought trade to Washington, D.C., and the James River and Kanawha Canal linked Richmond to interior Virginia.

When the Illinois and Michigan Canal, connecting Chicago on Lake Michigan and LaSalle on the Illinois River, was completed in 1848, a system of water travel was complete that made it possible to travel by inland waterway from New York City to New Orleans. Farmers in the Mississippi Valley could now market their livestock and grain in the East. They, as well as railroad builders, could get from the Northeast the lumber they needed to build on treeless western prairies.

Not all the canals that were built turned out to be so useful. Pennsylvania's canal system was much harder to build than those in flat areas. Because its terrain was much hillier, not only were dams and locks used but also a horse-drawn railroad to carry loads over the highest points. Although ingenious, the Penn State Canal proved both costly and impractical.

At its height in the 1840s, the canal craze produced a water highway network of 3,326 miles. But because canals were expensive to build and to keep up and because they were closed in the winter due to freezes, the canal era soon drew to a close. The greatest problem for canals, however, was competition from the new railroads. Nevertheless, for a time the canals had reduced freight rates, opened new areas to settlement, and helped America to expand its activities. A few continued to give useful service.

The Big Ditch

"You must have heard of it," wrote Herman Melville, referring to the Erie Canal in 1851 in *Moby Dick*. The Erie Canal became so famous that most foreign tourists wanted to see it. Called "the eighth wonder of the world," the Erie Canal became the perfect example of Yankee ingenuity.

The drive to build a state-financed canal linking New York City with the Great Lakes was led by Governor DeWitt Clinton. He believed that a canal would make New York the nation's leading port by diverting traffic from a then more prosperous New Orleans. The water connection would also give New York City an edge over Philadelphia and Baltimore in the race for western trade.

The 363-mile-long Erie Canal connected Albany on the Hudson River with Lake Erie and cost $7 million to build. The finished canal had a series of eighty-three lift locks and eighteen aqueducts. Locks were used to raise and lower the water level. Each lock was just long enough to hold a canal boat. Giant gates at both ends of the lock opened and closed to let the water in or out. When a canal boat entered a lock on the lower end of an upward slope, gates closed behind it. Water poured into the lock from the canal above until the boat floated at a higher level, a level even with that part of the canal. The canal gates at the far end then opened and the boat continued upstream. When boats came the opposite direction, the locks were gradually drained to lower the levels.

The canal was the brainchild of three men, James Geddes, Benjamin Wright, and Charles Broadhead, all self-made engineers. The canal became their school of practical civil engineering. They had to dig their canal through all types of terrain: mosquito-infested marshes, river valleys, and rock walls. Sometimes solid rock had to be blasted away with gunpowder.

Travel along the canal was slow. Speeds ranged from one and a half to three miles per hour. Mules or horses walking on narrow tow paths beside the canal dragged the freight barges or passenger canal boats. If a boat did not offer sleeping quarters or food, the charge for a passenger was only one cent per mile—far less than the fares for stagecoaches, which ran as high as ten cents a mile. Larger packet boats with bunks and food charged only five cents a mile.

The canal's completion on October 25, 1825, was marked by huge celebrations. The Erie Canal paid for itself through tolls within seven years, and the cost of shipping a ton of freight dropped by ninety-five per cent from one hundred dollars a ton to about five dollars. New York City, where boats bound for the canal entered the Hudson River, soon became the nation's busiest port and most prosperous city.

Section Review

1. How were river vessels propelled upstream before the steamboat?
2. Where did steamboats prove to be most valuable in their use?
3. Who built the first commercially successful steamboat?
4. What canal became most famous, and what two points did it join?
5. For what two reasons was the canal era short-lived?

C. Railroads

Steam engines that could run on tracks had developed in Britain shortly after 1800. The first American locomotive on a railroad track was one built in 1825 by John Stevens in Hoboken, New Jersey. Another locomotive was used briefly by a Pennsylvania canal company in 1829, but the first major trial of a railroad was that made by **Peter Cooper** in 1830.

Railroad developments such as the iron rail, the flanged or rimmed wheel, and the steam locomotive helped Cooper's invention to be a success. In the next twenty years railroads added a new dimension to American travel. The railroad was a faster and cheaper type of transportation than the canal. Moreover, railroads were not much affected by weather. Winter ice, spring floods, or summer drought did not keep railroads from operating as they did canals. Since railroads were not dependent on water, they could go into areas where canal construction would have been impractical.

The first regularly scheduled service in the United States began in 1831. It was the largest railroad in the world at the time— 136 miles—and it ran from Charleston to Hamburg, South Carolina. Although the railroad's locomotive, called *Best Friend,* was the first to pull a train of cars in regular service and was successful, the South was slow to build more track. Ten years later there was no new track in South Carolina, and by 1850, track miles had only been doubled.

Northeasterners were quick to see the potential value of railroads for moving their manufactured goods and raw materials. In the New England states the 1840s brought a five-fold increase in railroads. Better technology also made the locomotives safer

Main Railroads by 1860

0   50 100   200   300

Scale of Miles

and more powerful. "Railroad fever" swept the nation. Many railroads were financed by private investors, who bought stocks and bonds from railroad companies. State governments and local communities also furnished money, and the federal government underwrote some of the costs with land grants.

More than two-thirds of the total mileage was in the North and West. This tended to unite the economic interests of those regions, a factor that would be of great importance when the nation was later torn by the Civil War.

"TOM THUMB"

The Little Engine That Couldn't

Peter Cooper, a New York glue maker and part-time inventor, thought he could build a steam locomotive—and he did. Cooper's engine, named the *Tom Thumb* because of its small size, was more often called "a tea kettle on a track" by passers-by. Cooper himself ran the locomotive on its first round trip from Baltimore to Endicott, Maryland, and back. The train reached the unheard-of speed of eighteen miles per hour. Cooper's triumph, however, turned to shame on the return trip. A stagecoach company challenged the *Tom Thumb* to race the last eight miles back to Baltimore. The train gained the lead, but a pulley slipped off the train's drum, causing the engine to lose power. Cooper cut his hands trying to tug it back on, but the horse-drawn stagecoach won the race. The victory for the stagecoach was short-lived. Soon even presidents took the train; Andrew Jackson was the first in 1833.

Section Review

1. What four advantages did railroads have over other forms of transportation?
2. When did regular rail service begin?
3. What sections of the country built the most railroads, and why?

D. Communications

In early colonial times news generally spread by word of mouth. Colonists often gathered in local businesses to hear the latest news brought by travelers. Sometimes special messengers were sent to take important news to someone, but that type of communication was reserved mostly for the wealthy.

Postal Service

Ships arriving at a port in America might carry written messages from people in Europe or other American ports. These letters might be delivered by friends and neighbors, but there was no real postal service. Then in 1639 Massachusetts Bay Colony gave Richard Fairbanks permission to use his home in Boston as a post office. Mail for people in the area would be brought from the ships to his house for distribution, and people could leave letters with him to be sent by ship to other places. Similar situations developed in other colonial areas, but service was irregular and unreliable. The king authorized a colonial postal system in 1692, but the colonists disliked it. A high postage rate was charged, and letters could be opened if the authorities wished to check for disloyalty to the king.

Benjamin Franklin became the first postmaster general of the United States, serving under the Continental Congress. He helped organize a working postal service for the new nation. The Continental Congress helped make this service more useful to Americans by prohibiting postal authorities from opening or delaying private letters. Some roads were built or improved as "post roads," roads necessary for the delivery of the mail.

When the government was organized under the Constitution in 1789, Samuel

Early U.S. postal covers, 1852-53

Osgood became the postmaster general. The young country had less than seventy-five post offices at that time, but the postal system grew. Ships, stagecoaches, and later railroad trains carried the mail from place to place. As settlement spread westward, the service expanded as quickly as possible.

Perhaps the most exciting activity for the nation's postal service was the operation of the **pony express.** Beginning on April 3, 1860, riders carried mail on horseback from St. Joseph, Missouri, to Sacramento, California. The trip took eight to ten days as young riders rode about seventy-five miles before turning the mail over to another rider. They changed horses at relay stations every ten to fifteen miles along the route. Although the pony express was successful, it ended on October 24, 1861

after only a year and a half of service. The reason for its end was the success of another system of communication—the telegraph.

The Telegraph

The telegraph was invented to meet a serious need that railroads had. Lack of communication presented a difficulty in running trains and later steamships. There was a simple system for communicating on the train itself: bell cords were installed for the workers to pull. Different rings carried different meanings to the engineer in the cab. Signal lanterns were also used along the tracks and by trainmen. However, early railroads did not have two sets of tracks— one for trains going each direction. There were sidings or pull-offs at specific spots for trains to stop to let others pass, but head-on collisions were always a danger. What the railroads really needed was a dependable way for the train stations to communicate with each other and keep track of the moving trains.

An American artist, **Samuel F.B. Morse,** solved the communication problem by inventing the telegraph. By stopping and starting electrical impulses, he could send messages over long distances in just a few seconds through a wire. In 1837 Morse applied for government funds to develop his idea, but Congress did not grant the money until 1843. Morse was down to thirty-seven cents when he got the news. The grant—$30,000—was to be used to build a telegraph line from Washington, D.C., to Baltimore, Maryland. In fourteen hectic months, forty miles of copper wire was strung between trees and poles. Broken bottle necks served as insulators. On May 24, 1844, Morse was at a telegraph key in the Supreme Court room of the Capitol.

Soon telegraph poles were placed alongside railroad tracks. Cities and towns were linked by a giant network of telegraph communication. Railroad stations could relay information that could keep the trains operating more safely and on schedule. The Western Union Telegraph Company combined many of the independent telegraph companies that had grown to form a more unified service for the country in 1856. By October 24, 1861, telegraph wires had been strung all across the continent. Because California could receive communication almost instantly by wire, there was little need for the pony express. California sent the first telegraph message across the continent on that day in 1861. It notified Abraham Lincoln that California would be loyal to the Union.

Section Review

1. Who was the first postmaster general of the United States?
2. What was the pony express?
3. What device did Samuel F.B. Morse invent that helped rail travel?
4. Between what two cities was the first telegraph message sent?
5. When did telegraph communication first stretch across North America?

A crowd of judges, senators, and congressmen stood by. Morse's first message, part of a Bible verse, was "What hath God wrought!" The next day news of James K. Polk's nomination for president was sent from the Democratic Convention in Baltimore using the telegraph.

Summary

Traveling and communicating across colonial America had been very difficult because of the lack of roads and technical abilities. In the early 1800s, however, transportation and communication changed rapidly as new inventions and better methods of doing things came into use. New roads and canals opened up some regions of the nation to better transportation, and railroads and steamships became important new carriers of people and goods. Communications also improved through better-organized postal services, and telegraph wires eventually linked all the regions of the nation with immediate service.

Top: *Samuel F. B. Morse*
Bottom: *An early telegraph machine*

Chapter Review

Do You Remember?

■ Tell whether each of the following men or items is most closely associated with roads, water transportation, or railroads in the early 1800s.

1. locks
2. Robert Fulton
3. John Fitch
4. turnpikes
5. Daniel Boone
6. canal
7. Peter Cooper
8. Cumberland Gap

■ Match each of these transportation routes with its description.

9. Great Wagon Road
10. Wilderness Road
11. National Road
12. Erie Canal

a. provided a route across New York state
b. also known as the Cumberland Road
c. the Great Warrior's Path made by the Iroquois
d. built through the Cumberland Gap

Why Is It So?

1. Why were the new roads important to American Settlement?
2. Why were steamships such an important improvement in river transportation?
3. In what ways did the railroads prove to be a better form of transportation than canals or roads?
4. Why were most railroads built in the Northeast and West?
5. Why did the pony express die out so quickly?
6. How did the telegraph affect railroad transportation?

What Do You Think?

1. How did transportation and communication improvements in the early 1800s help the United States to grow?
2. What could you learn from the life of John Fitch?
3. Why do you suppose the Erie Canal helped New York City to grow?

14

Changing American Life

Brooklyn, New York, in the early 1800s

The changing means of transportation and communication helped to bring many more changes to American life. New ideas and inventions spread quickly around the country as businessmen saw opportunities to make a profit from these advances. Farming, manufacturing, and trade benefited from the innovations as America experienced its own Industrial Revolution.

A. American Agriculture

In 1800 most Americans were still farmers who owned and worked their own lands with the help of large families. By using simple tools and working hard, the farmer raised enough food for his own family. He sold or traded any surplus for items that could not be grown or made on the family farm.

Between 1815 and 1860 the Industrial Revolution profoundly affected not only the American factory worker but also the American farmer. The use of new farm machinery enabled the farmer to improve his methods and lower his costs, thereby increasing his profits. Since fewer farmers were needed to produce the same amount of food, some farmers were free to join the growing urban work force in factories, shipyards, banks, and other businesses.

Farming Before 1800

Before new laborsaving machines were invented, American farmers used tools similar to those used centuries before. They still plowed with oxen as Elisha had done (I Kings 19:19). If there were hard lumps left after the plowing, farmers used a harrow, a device with teeth or later disks, to break up the soil. Sometimes they simply used a hoe. At harvest time the farmers used a scythe or a sickle to gather the grain, just as in the time of Moses (Deut. 23:25) and Christ (Mark 4:26-29). After the grain had been dried by the sun, it was picked up for threshing. Sometimes wealthy farmers hired a crew of reapers to harvest their crops, as Boaz did (Ruth 2). When grain was threshed, it was beaten with a flail (stick) until the kernels fell out of the husks. Then the farmers hauled their grain to a mill, where it was crushed between rotating stones to produce meal. All the farmers' toil usually produced only a meager amount of food to feed their families.

When most crops ripen and are ready for harvest, they must be gathered in quickly or they will rot in the fields. For this reason farmers had to be careful not to plant more than they could harvest successfully. In many areas plantings were limited or staggered to avoid harvesting problems. But as new farm machines were developed, the farmers found it easier to plow and plant more acres and to harvest their crops more quickly and efficiently. In addition, new machines made some farm products easier to process. As a result America's farm production increased rapidly.

Agricultural Advances

The new farm implements produced by inventors during the Industrial Revolution greatly improved the life of the farmers. With all the new equipment and the demand for food in eastern cities, farmers could increase their production, meet the needs of their own families, and still make a profit by selling the extra grain in eastern markets. American grain even became an important export to Europe after crop failures and political disputes there created

Agriculture Time Line

1855	
	Double-walled milk can developed
1850	
1845	
1840	Joseph Dart installed first grain elevator / Cyrus McCormick invented reaper
	John Deere developed first steel plow / Thresher invented
1835	
1830	
1825	
1820	Jethro Woods developed an iron plow with replaceable parts
1815	
1810	
1805	
1800	
1795	Charles Newbold developed a cast-iron plow / Eli Whitney invented the cotton gin
1790	

food shortages and a demand for American grain. Three particular inventors and inventions played important roles as America developed its agricultural production.

John Deere's Plow—By 1838 a young blacksmith named **John Deere** realized that the common iron plow needed improvement. One great problem with the iron plow was that the soil stuck to the blade. While visiting a saw mill, Deere noted that a steel blade shone when it had been polished by friction. He thought that steel might clean itself, too, when cutting earth. Using an old circular steel blade, he made a plow. He cut twelve smooth, straight furrows nonstop while a group of Illinois farmers looked on in amazement.

Deere began to build plows for sale, and his first plows sold for ten dollars each. Seeing the possibilities of his product, Deere built a plow factory in Moline, Illinois. He went into commercial plow production using high-grade steel from Pittsburgh. His plows made a humming sound and were popularly called "singing plows." Almost every wagon going west carried a John Deere plow. The steel plow was important in opening and conquering the prairies of the West.

Cyrus McCormick's Reaper—Planting more grain, however, was of little value if it could not be harvested quickly enough. In the 1820s **Cyrus McCormick,** son of a Virginia blacksmith, started work on a **reaper,** a machine for cutting or harvesting grain. By 1831 he had invented a reaper that cut six acres of oats in one day. Pulled by four horses, this reaper could do the work of six men. In 1841 McCormick sold two reapers, and the next year he sold seven more.

By 1844 he was ready to turn his back on the East and go west to the heartland with sixty dollars in his pocket. Since his reaper could cut twenty acres of wheat per day, he knew that sales would flourish when the vast prairies were plowed into wheat fields. He picked Chicago for his headquarters, where in 1851 he built and sold a thousand reapers. He then entered his reaper in the London Exposition, where it won first prize and made him an instant celebrity. By 1857 his profits were $1.25 million.

Eli Whitney's Cotton Gin—Tobacco had been a profitable crop for the South since colonial days, but the appeal of that product was limited. Since the English were using new machines to make cloth, selling them raw cotton seemed like a good activity for the South. But cotton was not a profitable crop except on the Sea Islands off the coast of South Carolina and Georgia. Sea Island cotton, which would not grow on the mainland, had seeds that could easily be removed from its long fibers. Upland cotton, grown on the mainland, had shorter staples (fibers) and the seeds were difficult to remove. If a workman cleaned seeds from this short-staple cotton for an entire day, his yield would be just one pound of cleaned cotton. Even when slaves were put to the task of cleaning the fibers, farming upland cotton just did not pay until **Eli Whitney** appeared on the scene.

Eli Whitney's **cotton gin** could clean the short-staple cotton quickly and efficiently. It suddenly made growing cotton more profitable. In 1793, the year he invented the gin, 138,328 pounds of cotton were exported. Within one year, exports reached 6,276,000 pounds. By 1825, 176 million pounds of cotton were exported to Britain, and 100 million more pounds were sent to northern mills. By 1850 cotton made up seven-eighths of all American exports. It was little wonder that Southerners believed that cotton might be king, not only in the South, but throughout America.

Southern Agriculture and Slavery

Both cotton and tobacco could be grown profitably only on large plantations worked by gangs of unskilled laborers. Because the many workers could be supervised by one man and the tasks involved were simple, plantation owners believed that slaves were the ideal laborers for them. Slavery, a practice that many Americans had thought would die out, was now a growing, profitable way of life in the South, thanks to the cotton gin.

Although slavery became important to the South during the early 1800s, it did not

The *Armistead*

In 1806 Britain became the first country to abolish slavery. In 1808 the American Congress followed with a law that forbade American vessels from taking on slaves. Unfortunately, because profits were high—more than $100,000 per load—and because men were evil, the law was not strictly enforced. As late as 1847 the United States Navy had seven ships patrolling Africa's Guinea Coast and the British had twelve. They did little to slow the vicious traffic.

Because there was a shortage of slaves for sugar plantations in Cuba, American ships carried slaves there. In 1839 thirty slaves from Liberia were held captive on the *Armistead,* bound for Cuba. Several Africans managed to cut their chains. Under the leadership of Singbé Piéh, called Cinq by the Spaniards, the slaves killed the ship's captain and cook but spared two Cubans to navigate them back to Africa. By day the Cubans sailed east, but by night they doubled back and

edged north, reaching Long Island, New York, where they beached their ship. The Coast Guard stumbled on four blacks wandering on shore near Sag's Harbor, Long Island.

Since the slaves were from Mendi in northern Liberia and spoke no English, there were problems. A linguist at Yale helped identify their language so that someone could decide what would be done with them. Under American law slavery was still legal, and so the slaves would have been returned to Cuba to be sold. It was then that former president John Quincy Adams took on their case and cause. He saw the case through the Supreme Court. On March 9, 1841, the court declared the Mendi captives free on the basis that the laws of Spain allowed such an act. With this victory, Adams was inspired to continue his fight for the appeal of the Gag Rule. In 1842 he suggested an amendment to end slavery. His suggestion was eventually adopted as the Thirteenth Amendment in 1865.

A cotton gin

become common for most Southerners to own slaves. Only about one-fourth of all southern families owned slaves before the Civil War. The majority of those slaveholding families owned fewer than ten slaves, and probably only a little over five thousand planters in the entire South had fifty or more slaves. Yet the cotton and other crops produced on plantations by slave labor were an important part of the South's economy. Lacking other industries, the South increasingly depended on the money earned from its cotton exports.

Section Review

1. What was farming like prior to the 1800s?
2. What were the inventions of John Deere, Cyrus McCormick, and Eli Whitney?
3. What were the two major crops grown by southern farmers?

The hold of a slave ship, which brought slaves to the New World

B. American Industry

While the ideal place to build mills for weaving cotton into cloth would have been near southern cotton fields, few mills were built in the South. There were several reasons the southern textile industry failed to develop at this time. First, the South lacked an adequate power supply. It had few fast-flowing rivers for turning water wheels. Also, since Southerners knew that they could make money easily through agriculture, they were not eager to work in factories. It seemed illogical to waste capital and energy on factories when plenty of money could be made growing cotton. As a result, industrial growth bypassed the South and took hold in other areas of the country, especially New England.

The Factory System

With the Industrial Revolution came the factory system. Before machines became available, most work was done in homes. Other items were made in craftsmen's shops. The **factory system,** however, collected many workers in one place, where many like items could be turned out in one day. Schedules rarely varied, and the workers did not come and go as they wished. Usually they performed only one step of a many-staged process. In other words, there was a division of labor. One person, a group of men, or numerous investors owned the building, the machinery, and the tools. The workers received a fixed salary, with the owners receiving the profits.

The idea of the factory system came from England. Some Americans had tried to start factories in the 1780s, but they had failed because the machinery was not adequate and because most Americans still preferred British imports. Some states were so eager to have factories that they offered rewards to get them started. They even advertised in British newspapers to get men to come. The British feared that if the United States gained access to their men and machines, they would soon lose their industrial advantage. To protect the textile industry, the British forbade the export of their machinery and the emigration of the men who could build and operate it.

Samuel Slater's Factory

An English mechanic named **Samuel Slater** saw one of the American advertisements. He had been an apprentice to the partner of Richard Arkwright, father of the English factory system and inventor of the water frame, a waterpowered textile machine. Knowing the risks he was taking by leaving the country illegally, Slater did not even tell his own family he was going. He had no plans for machinery on paper, but

he had learned how to use and repair every machine in the Arkwright system.

Once in the United States he was told about Moses Brown, a famous Quaker merchant who had just built a textile mill in Rhode Island. Brown was seeking a manager; so Slater wrote him a letter telling of his experience and applying for the position. Brown offered Slater the job and all the profits once the cost and interest on the machinery were subtracted. Slater had applied for the job by letter and got the entire plant by return mail!

Slater went to the factory in Pawtucket. Seeing the machines, he wrote: "These will not do. They are good for nothing in their present condition." Slater then built a whole series of machines from memory. The yarn plant got off to a slow start, but ten years later Brown and Slater were ready to open a second factory.

Slater ran his factory using children as young as seven years old, as was done in England. He broke with British tradition by giving the children meals and more humane treatment. Since American children on farms went to work when they were very young, using such young laborers was not considered improper, and most people rated his factory highly. Parents were happy to

Old Slater Mill in Rhode Island

have their children in such a place. Slater's factory with its simple machines was ideally suited to a young country that would have a shortage of skilled labor for the next seventy-five years. Although it was not ideal, the system provided work that helped to feed and clothe people and give them more than they had ever had before.

Further Development of Industry

Other developments of machinery and methods of production helped to boost American industries in the early 1800s.

The Sewing Machine—Another invention, the **sewing machine,** aided the growth of the factory system. The sewing machine allowed seamstresses to cut drastically the time needed to sew garments and other textile products. Thus the textiles flowing from the new yarn and weaving machinery could quickly become clothing and other products for consumers at home and abroad. Sewing factories soon sprang up, with hundreds of sewing machines humming as the operators turned out the products.

Although Walter Hunt had invented a sewing machine in 1838, he never sought a patent for it. Because it was believed that machinery took jobs away from the laboring class, especially women, Hunt withdrew his invention. Little did anyone know that during the Civil War the sewing machine would permit women to enter the work force in ever-increasing numbers.

The credit for inventing the sewing machine has gone to **Elias Howe,** who patented it in 1846. Like many inventors, Howe made little money while trying to perfect his invention. His family suffered terribly; Howe had to borrow from his father to get to the bedside of his dying wife. He fared little better in England while promoting his

machine because he was cheated out of his royalties.

In 1851 a third inventor, **Isaac Singer,** also patented a sewing machine. Differing from Howe's, Singer's machine used a foot treadle rather than a hand crank so that the operator's hands were left free. The needle operated vertically rather than horizontally and could sew a curved seam. However, like Howe's it did use an eye-pointed needle, and Singer was charged with violating Howe's patent.

Howe won the case, and Singer was forced to pay damages for every machine that had infringed Howe's rights. Heeding the adage "if you can't beat them, join them," Singer quickly suggested combining ideas. The result was the first patent pool in American history, uniting seven sewing machine companies into one. Singer was above all a genius at promoting his idea. His was the first company to spend a million dollars a year on advertising. Believing that

An early sewing machine

Isaac Singer

every American home would want a sewing machine if the price were within range, he sold machines on the installment or time-payment plan.

Eli Whitney's Influence on the Factory System—Besides inventing the cotton gin, Eli Whitney also played an important role in improving the factory system through the development of **interchangeable parts.** He and other men used the idea of assembling products, guns in particular, by producing large numbers of each part. In the past each gun was assembled individually from parts made specifically for that gun by skilled craftsmen. Whitney instead made molds that could form large numbers of each part. The interchangeable parts could then be assembled quickly by less skilled workers to make large quantities of guns. This idea led to the **mass production** of many other products.

New England Industry—The factory system grew quickly in New England, where fast-moving streams provided needed power for turning the water wheels. When steam power superseded waterpower, New England was still in the running because her vast forests could be cut down to provide fuel. Since New England soil was too poor for most heavy agriculture, New Englanders willingly tried other ways to make their livings.

New England's banking system also financed new industry. Even when the Bank of the United States went out of existence, state banks offered loans to build mills. Some of their state governments also underwrote internal improvements, fostering transportation to aid new industries.

New England was also an ideal place for factories because a labor force was readily available. Her cold climate allowed only a short growing season and long winters without work, and subsistence farmers often could not support larger families. Therefore, the youth of New England were attracted to factory work. Although sometimes families and single men went west or to other cities seeking better opportunities, young women were often available for employment. **Francis Cabot Lowell,** a New England cloth maker, organized a mill town for girls in Waltham, Massachusetts. The factory provided their room and board and strict supervision, and the girls received one to two dollars a week for long hours of labor in the mill. Of course, a dollar was a lot of money in those days.

Results of the Rise of Industry

Industrialization influenced the lives of many Americans. The new inventions made work easier for many. Money enabled some to enjoy a higher living standard. People moved from farms to cities, where new jobs were available. Factories were placed near sources of waterpower, and towns and cities grew up near these sites. The factories also gave many immigrants the opportunity for a new life in America.

Although the factory system contributed much that was positive, there were some aspects that would be hard for us to accept today. For example, workers labored six days a week, seventy-five hours a week. Most had only half an hour for lunch, and wages were low. Thus it was necessary for several people in a family, including children, to work just to provide enough money to live. In 1818 a factory in Paterson, New Jersey, reported the following weekly wages: men, $5.00; women $2.37; children, $1.37. By the early 1850s, pay for some common laborers and factory workers reached a new high of $6.00 a week.

Often both working and living conditions were miserable. Factories were stuffy, cramped, and noisy. Machines were not equipped with safety devices, and injuries resulted. Besides the fear of injury, workers feared losing their jobs to new machines that were brought in. Factory towns were usually crowded and drab. Working families were squeezed into one-room tenements as the urban population more than doubled between 1820 and 1860. Because many children worked, few children could attend school, even free public schools. To combat these problems, some workers joined labor organizations.

The Rise of Labor Unions

In 1827 the first **labor union** was organized. Called the Mechanics' Union of Trade Associations, the group united skilled craftsmen in Philadelphia. In 1828 the Workingmen's party, a labor party, began. This party started the country's first labor newspaper, *The Mechanics' Free Press,* to promote labor goals.

The labor groups concentrated on broad reforms, not just specific changes. Among their goals were free public education, the end of imprisonment or seizure of tools for failure to pay debts, a ten-hour work day, and the end of child labor.

Although the federal government did give the workers a ten-hour day in 1840 and more towns started schools, the unions' successes were limited. When the nation prospered, so did unions. When depressions came, the unions failed. Workers were willing to accept wage cuts and feared being fired in hard times. Many Americans believed that if they applied the work ethic and used their God-given talents and abilities, they could succeed without unions. Where they could not, they could leave and try to seek a new life somewhere else in the country.

Immigration also worked against the unions. Most newcomers were eager to work and knew they were better off than they had been in Europe. Many of them held factory jobs for only a few years. As soon as they had learned the language and could go elsewhere, they did.

Section Review

1. List two reasons for the slow development of the South's textile industry.
2. Briefly describe the factory system.
3. In what section of the country did the factory system especially flourish?
4. List some of the negative effects of the factory system.
5. What prompted the rise of labor unions?

C. Expanding Sea Trade

The Industrial Revolution also affected overseas trade. Americans had been involved in shipping and trade from its earliest days. After the War for Independence Americans sought new markets overseas. Trade with European countries expanded. France, Prussia (Germany), the Netherlands, and countries with Baltic and Mediterranean ports all traded with the United States. Americans traded their surplus goods, like cotton, tobacco, and lumber, for things unavailable or scarce in America, such as hemp, raisins, olive oil, and iron.

New Asian Markets

Americans also surveyed markets in Asia. Americans had heard of Europeans gaining riches by trade in China and did not want to be left out. In 1784, only a year after the War for Independence had ended, a ship was refitted for a trading expedition to China. New York merchants hired John Green, assisted by Major Samuel Shaw, to captain the *Empress of China.*

China had shown little interest in foreign products and had insisted that goods be paid for in gold and silver coin. But there was one product the Chinese wanted to buy: a root called ginseng. The Chinese believed that ginseng had some medicinal qualities. The *Empress of China* carried thirty tons of ginseng.

The *Empress* sailed across the Atlantic to Africa, around the Cape of Good Hope, and across the Indian Ocean. A French vessel, the *Triton,* helped guide it across the reef-filled South China Sea. The ship finally reached Whampoa, the Chinese port fourteen miles below Canton, where foreigners were allowed to drop anchor.

The Chinese welcomed the Americans, and the *Empress* brought home tea, spices, silk, chinaware, and stories of its profitable trip. Upon Shaw's return, he was named as the consul, a special trade minister, to China. By 1786 Shaw had opened America's first trading company in Canton itself.

The Chinese also liked furs. The first American to engage in the new fur trade was Captain **Robert Gray,** whose trinket-laden ship sailed around South America to what is now Oregon to buy furs from the Indians. There they learned that the Indians now desired iron and copper tools and weapons more than trinkets. Aboard ship for the winter, the crewmen made chisels that were worth eight otter skins.

After trading for the furs, Gray's ship, the *Columbia,* headed for Hawaii, the first American ship to visit those islands. After taking on fresh fruits, hogs, and water, the ship crossed the Pacific to China. The homeward trip took Gray west through the Indian Ocean, around Africa, and across the Atlantic. Gray and his crew returned to Boston in the summer of 1790. His profits were disappointing, but Gray had made Americans proud by becoming the first American to circumnavigate the earth. He had also established an American claim to Oregon territory by going up the Columbia River and had set up a three-corner trade route that skippers, the so-called "lords of the China trade," followed. Hardware from

Commodore Matthew Perry opening trade with Japan

the East Coast was carried to the Pacific Coast and traded for furs. Once the Pacific crossing was made, the furs were exchanged for Chinese tea, dishes, and silk.

On these voyages the Americans also found the source of the Dutch pepper trade in Sumatra. They soon cornered that trade for themselves. Touching on the coast of Brazil, they brought back coffee. The coffee soon became a favorite beverage. Americans began, and continue, to drink more coffee than the people of any other country.

The most important new Asian market for America was Japan. For centuries the Japanese had rejected any kind of contact with the outside world. In 1852, however, President Fillmore ordered Commodore Matthew Perry to take several warships to Japan and attempt to secure a trade treaty. Perry arrived in 1853 and told the Japanese of his mission. He then went to China to give the Japanese government time to consider his offer. When Perry returned in 1854, the Japanese agreed to allow the United States to begin trading with their nation.

Fishing and Whaling

Fishing had been an important way of making a living from America's earliest years. Cod were harvested from Newfoundland's Grand Banks, and herring and lobster were caught off the Atlantic coast. Whaling cruises to the Bering Sea, though long and treacherous, attracted other venturers. There were profits to be made from whale oil burned to give light. Sailors spent the long hours aboard ship on the way home carving on whalebone or whale ivory, producing a new and exquisite art called scrimshaw.

The Age of the Yankee Clipper

Over the years the United States had developed a highly productive shipbuilding industry. Shipyards dotted the eastern coast. American shipbuilders were not afraid to try new things, and in the 1840s they developed a new type of sailing vessel designed for increased speeds. The **clipper** was invented by John W. Griffiths, but Donald McKay surpassed him in both fame and design with his clipper ships. In contrast to earlier ocean-going vessels, the clipper had a much sharper point on her bow that could "clip" into the waves. The bow or front portion of the ship curved inward. But what caught the eye and excited people the most were the sails. Some clippers had as many as thirty-five sails; the area of the canvas sails was one and a half acres, equal to one and a half football fields.

Clippers reached their heyday after 1848 when gold was discovered in California. They carried the many gold seekers west. (Sometimes, though, they had problems coming back; the crews deserted to go to the gold fields.) The clipper ship era lasted only about fifteen years. It came to an end by the mid-1850s, when new advances like railroads and steamships outdated them.

An example of scrimshaw

Off to the Races

Clippers often raced each other carrying cargoes from New York to San Francisco or New York to Canton, China. The first great race to San Francisco, in 1850, pitted seven clippers against each other and was won by Donald McKay's *Sea Witch*. His *Flying Cloud* soon set a record, making the run from New York to San Francisco in 89 days 2 hours, a record that has never been bettered by any sailed ship. The record for a day's run, 495 miles, was set by the *Sovereign of the Seas*. Another clipper, *Lightning*, set a record of thirteen and a half days from New York to Liverpool.

Section Review

1. List several surplus goods Americans exported to European countries.
2. What one product did the Chinese especially want to purchase from America?
3. Name some goods the Americans bought from China.
4. What is scrimshaw?
5. What eventually made the clipper ships obsolete?

Donald McKay and the Flying Cloud

D. America's Spiritual Life

America experienced many changes during the early decades of its independence. New inventions and techniques brought advancements in agriculture, industry, and trade. And the nation's government was growing stronger and adapting to the new needs of Americans. Religious ideas were also changing. Nevertheless, the spiritual needs of the people remained the same.

American religious life in the early 1800s was marked by two contrasting movements. On the one hand was a tremendous revival known as the **Second Great Awakening.** On the other was Unitarianism, a movement that denied many truths of the Christian faith.

The Second Great Awakening

Following the War for Independence, American churches entered a period of spiritual deadness. John Marshall, chief justice of the Supreme Court, declared sadly

Timothy Dwight

that the church was "too far gone ever to be revived." At this low point in America's spiritual life, God sent a sweeping revival to the young nation. Called the Second Great Awakening, this revival transformed the lives of cold church members and saw thousands won to Christ who had never before professed any interest in religion.

The revivals in the East centered in the colleges and individual churches. Although most American colleges had been founded by godly men, the schools had grown increasingly non-Christian. At Yale, for example, the students debated over whether Christianity was true, and they delighted in calling each other by the names of famous infidels.

Into this appalling situation came minister **Timothy Dwight,** who became president of Yale in 1795. Dwight dealt directly with this unbelief. He debated students on questions such as "Is the Bible the Word of God?" and he won. Dwight also began preaching a series of sermons on the true Biblical faith. After seven years of his lecturing and preaching, Yale experienced a revival in which a third of the students professed faith in Christ. This was the first of several Yale revivals. Other colleges experienced similar revivals.

In the churches in the East, members were stirred to new life through the preaching of faithful men like evangelist Asahel Nettleton. Fearful of the excessive emotionalism of some earlier revivals, Nettleton always insisted on calm, orderly services. When inquirers came to him under conviction of sin, Nettleton would talk and pray with them at great length. Such evangelists wanted to be sure that converts knew what they were professing and were not being pressured into quick decisions.

On the frontier the revival took a different form. "Out West," which at this time meant areas like Kentucky and Tennessee, revivals usually came in the form of **"camp meetings."** Hundreds or even thousands of people would gather in some central location to listen to preachers and to sing camp meeting songs such as "Brethren, We Have Met to Worship."

The most famous camp meeting was held in 1801 at Cane Ridge, Kentucky, not far from the city of Lexington. The crowd numbered at least ten thousand people and may have been as large as twenty-five thousand. The camp meetings seemed to have a positive effect on frontier life.

Unitarianism: The Unbelieving Religion

While these revivals were sweeping across America, Unitarianism was also making an impact on the country, especially in New England. (We discussed the teachings of Unitarianism in Chapter 4. See p. 62.) The first church in America to become Unitarian was King's Chapel (formerly an Anglican church) in Boston in 1785. The movement became much stronger in the 1800s, especially when Harvard became Unitarian. The movement did not found churches itself. Instead it took over churches that had formerly believed the Bible.

The Unitarians were usually intellectual men, and the movement provided many political and educational leaders. Probably its most famous minister was **William Ellery Channing,** a persuasive preacher and writer in Boston. Through his sermons, books, and articles, Channing promoted Unitarianism throughout the East. Orthodox, Bible-believing men opposed the movement, however, and founded new churches and schools to replace the ones the Unitarians had taken over. Nevertheless, the faith of many Americans was being eroded by unbelieving preachers, even in that day. As the years passed, more and more people followed the teachings of such men instead of supporting the preachers who continued to stand for the truth of God's Word.

Section Review

1. What two contrasting religious movements marked the early 1800s?
2. Name two men influential in the revival of the early nineteenth century.
3. What was the first Unitarian church in America?
4. Name one famous Unitarian leader.

Summary

While means of transportation and communication were changing during the early 1800s, so too were agriculture, industry, and trade. New inventions and methods of production helped America's farms and factories to produce much more than they had in colonial days. American traders were ready to ship the nation's products for sale abroad. While these changes affected the way Americans made their living, their religious ideas affected the way they lived. Some people were influenced by the Second Great Awakening and its emphasis on the Scriptures. Other Americans allowed Unitarianism to destroy their faith in Jesus Christ and God's Word.

Chapter Review

Do You Remember?

■ Match these men with their invention or accomplishment.

1. William Ellery Channing	a.	the steel plow
2. Timothy Dwight	b.	the reaper
3. John Deere	c.	leader of Second Great Awakening at Yale
4. Robert Gray	d.	credited with inventing the sewing machine
5. Elias Howe	e.	cotton gin and interchangeable parts
6. Francis Cabot Lowell	f.	set up a textile mill in Pawtucket, R.I.
7. Cyrus McCormick	g.	formed a large, successful sewing machine company
8. Isaac Singer	h.	organized factory work for girls in Massachusetts
9. Samuel Slater	i.	circumnavigated the earth
10. Eli Whitney	j.	leading Unitarian

■ Explain the significance of each of the following inventions or accomplishments.

11. steel plow
12. reaper
13. cotton gin
14. sewing machine
15. factory system
16. interchangeable parts
17. mass production
18. clipper ships

Why Is It So?

1. How did agriculture change in the early 1800s?
2. Why did the invention of the cotton gin affect slavery in the South?
3. Why did many factories arise in New England?
4. Why were labor unions not very effective during the early 1800s?
5. Why were camp meetings a means of revival on the frontier?

What Do You Think?

1. How do you suppose American history would have been different if the cotton gin had not been invented?
2. Why was Asahel Nettleton's method of evangelism wise?
3. Why do you suppose Unitarianism could take over churches that once believed the Bible?

Maps

Maps in a history text add to the student's understanding of history by illustrating the location of specific events and geographical information. In order to use maps effectively, you need to have a basic, general knowledge about maps. Understanding the language of maps is of prime importance in obtaining necessary information from a map. Look at the maps in the front of the book and at a globe as you consider the definitions below.

Hemisphere: the northern or southern half of the earth divided by the equator, or the eastern or western half divided by the meridian.

Equator: a great circle of the earth that is everywhere equally distant from the North Pole and the South Pole and that divides the earth's surface into the northern and southern hemispheres.

Meridian: an imaginary circle on the earth's surface passing through the North and South poles.

Prime Meridian: the meridian of 0° longitude from which other longitudes are reckoned east and west.

Longitude: distances measured by degrees or time east or west from the prime meridian.

Latitude: distance north or south from the equator measured in degrees.

Political Map

Scale: a divided line or a statement on a map or chart indicating the length (such as an inch) used on the map or chart to represent actual distances on earth (usually in miles or kilometers).

Different types of maps can be used in order to indicate different kinds of information about an area. For example, a *political map* indicates political features such as national, state, and local boundaries; capital cities; cities; towns; and so on. *Topographical maps* (also called physical maps) portray natural and man-made features of an area for the purpose of indicating their position and elevation. Differences in elevation can be illustrated by using contour lines to connect points that have the same elevation, by using shaded colors, or by *raised relief* (texturing a map to indicate elevation).

The *transportation map* is probably the most familiar kind of map. Your family has, no doubt, used road and city maps when planning a vacation. Two less familiar transportation maps are those used for air and water navigation. These are generally called charts.

Thematic maps illustrate information on a specific subject. Population distribution, industrial and agricultural distribution, and territorial growth are all examples of thematic maps.

The reading of maps is usually not difficult if you study the legend or key carefully. Once you understand the symbols and scale, the rest is easy.

Topographical Map

Thematic Map

15

The Era of Manifest Destiny

When Washington took office in 1789, there were four million people in the United States. Almost all of them lived east of the Appalachian Mountains. However, by 1830, when the population had grown to 12.8 million, four million Americans lived west of the Appalachians. And by 1850, one-half of the 31.4 million people lived in the West.

A.   Westward Movement

For over a hundred years, moving west was an almost constant process in America's development. Over the Appalachians into Kentucky, Tennessee, and the old Northwest Territory, and on past the Mississippi River, Americans moved to begin their new lives and to expand their nation. By the 1840s many Americans believed that God intended for them to have all the western lands to the shores of the Pacific. This expansion was their **"Manifest Destiny."**

Reasons for Going West

Americans had many reasons for moving westward, and western areas had much to offer. Some settlers found good farm land; others found mineral riches. Plenty found endless toil and many hardships, but the hardy pioneers succeeded in building the American West.

Western Colorado, one of the areas of the United States that benefited from the settlement of the American West

The Mood of the Day—The mood of the day encouraged people to go west. Americans believed that the West was theirs to claim. Many saw neighbors and relatives pack up and head west with great optimism. It was easy to catch the excitement and the dreams of others. The leaders of the day, especially President James K. Polk, encouraged expansion, and the people willingly followed.

The Lure of the Land—The West had a nearly irresistible attraction for American farmers. Planters whose soils had been worn out felt certain that the rich acreage near the Mississippi River could restore their prosperity. Poor farmers who could not compete with large plantation owners, but could afford to buy the cheap new western lands, thought they could improve their lives by moving west. The land could also become a refuge for thousands of immigrants seeking to escape the troubles of other countries. Political disturbances, low wages, high taxes, lack of economic opportunity, religious persecution, and famine encouraged immigrants from Ireland, Germany, and later the Scandinavian countries to come to the American West.

Desire for Wealth—Riches were available in the West in many forms. With the discovery of gold in California in 1848 and silver in Colorado and Nevada, many men went west seeking their fortunes. A few did become rich by mining, but others sought wealth in land. Land speculators took the risk of buying land at low prices from the government. They hoped that they could then develop settlements and resell the lands at a profit. Some lost money; others broke even; a few made fortunes. Real wealth out west was also made by those who built new businesses and made large profits by taking risks in business ventures such as railroads and supply companies.

Adventure and a New Start—Some restless Americans moved west seeking adventure. Such challenges as taming the land, facing hostile Indians, and starting new local and state governments rarely disappointed them. Some people went west because they wanted a new start, a chance to put the past behind them. A few left bills, jail sentences, wives, or criminal records behind them—but no forwarding addresses.

Religious Reasons—The desire to spread the gospel to both Indians and new settlers caused a few Easterners to go west as missionaries. In 1833 *The Christian Advocate and Journal* printed a letter about the arrival of four Indians in St. Louis who had come seeking the "white man's Book of Heaven."

When some Methodist and Presbyterian groups read of the request, they rallied to the challenge. Some Indians, especially the Nez Perce (NEZ PURS) and Flatheads, reasoned that the white man's power centered in his religion. Because they wanted a share of the power, they concluded that they needed to learn about Christianity. The new religion might bring them enough guns and goods to defeat their enemies. Missionaries grieved over these so-called converts whose responses to the gospel were self-centered and short-lived. However, because of the power of the Word of God and the faithfulness of the missionaries, some Indians were genuinely saved.

One religious group called the **Mormons** saw the West as a refuge from the persecution they were experiencing in the East. Their movement to Utah was responsible for much of the settlement in the Great Basin area.

The Mormons

The Mormons started out in Palmyra, New York. There **Joseph Smith,** the cult's founder, supposedly received tablets containing the *Book of Mormon.* This book and another called *Pearl of Great Price* contained additions to God's Word and are the basis for some of Mormonism's false doctrines. The Mormons believed they were to gather the elect together and build their Zion. The first attempt to build Zion, in Kirtland, Ohio, failed because of a shortage of funds. Next they moved to Missouri, where they were forced from two sites by unfriendly neighbors. In 1838-39 attitudes became so hostile that a Mormon War broke out and forty lives were lost. The next city of refuge was Nauvoo, Illinois. There the Mormon practice of polygamy, having more than one wife, angered the local population. Smith and his brother were murdered while being held in jail in nearby Carthage.

The Mormons were forced to leave Illinois in February in subzero temperatures. A new leader, **Brigham Young,** emerged. After reorganizing at a temporary winter headquarters near Omaha, Nebraska, the Mormons again trekked west. Two days after sighting the valley of the Great Salt Lake in Utah, Young declared, "It is enough. This is the right place!" By the time Young died in 1877, about 140,000 had made their way to Utah on what came to be called the Mormon Trail.

Trails to the West

Once American pioneers moved west of the Mississippi, they temporarily bypassed the vast Great Plains region. As yet, its dryness and its Indians discouraged settlements. The riches of western trade, California gold, and Oregon farms tempted many to make long journeys to reach their western goals. Finding ways to get to the far West proved to be a challenge. But over a period of years, several major westward routes were established.

The Santa Fe Trail—The first American route west of the Missouri River was the **Santa Fe** (SAN-tuh FAY) **Trail.** This route was primarily a trade route and was used

Some of the later Mormon emigrants arriving by covered wagon in the 1870s

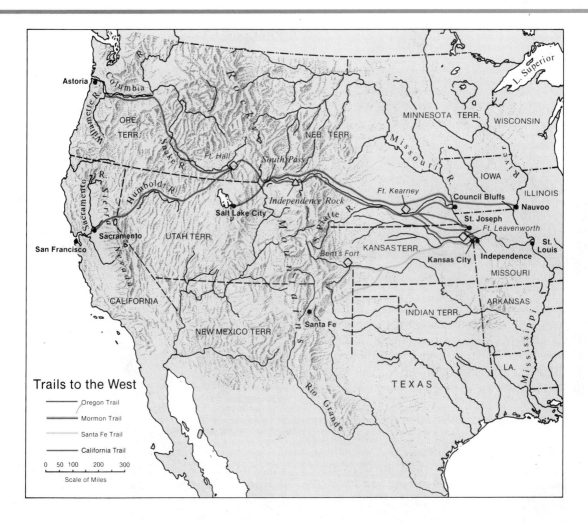

Trails to the West

— Oregon Trail
— Mormon Trail
— Santa Fe Trail
— California Trail

0 50 100 200 300
Scale of Miles

less by settlers than other trails. When explorer Zebulon Pike, who had made it to Spanish-held Santa Fe, returned, he told Americans of the high prices that goods were bringing there. The only problem was that Spain wanted to keep the trade profits to herself. Consequently, the members of an 1812 American expedition to Santa Fe were all captured and held in a lice-infested jail for eight years. But when Mexico broke free of Spain in 1821, changes came. Trade was permitted, but the Mexican government imposed high taxes, sixty per cent, on imported goods. Still, $35,000 worth of goods—cotton, wool, tools, and needles—could be sold for $185,000 once the ten- to twelve-week journey on the Santa Fe Trail was completed.

To insure safety on the trail and to ward off Indian attacks, the traders all gathered at one spot, usually Independence, Missouri, and made a single annual caravan

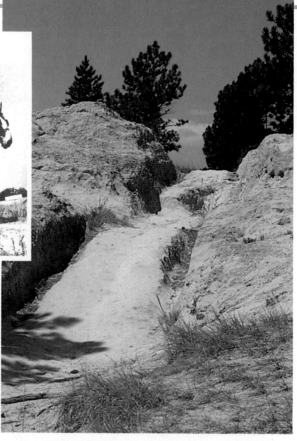

from there. All the men in the caravan, including hired hands, voted for a captain to lead them. Other positions included a wagon boss, a pack train boss, a chief scout, lieutenants for divisions, and wranglers for the loose livestock being taken along. The caravan traveled in three to four parallel columns to aid in defense. The heavily laden wagons formed a square at night. Horses and mules were tethered in the middle since one of the favorite and most deadly Indian strategies was to stampede the animals and scatter them. Without any animals for travel and with water frequently miles away, the traders could not last long.

William and Charles Bent, two brothers who used the Santa Fe Trail and later founded a trading outpost called Bent's Fort, discovered that oxen could out-travel mules and were safer from Indian raids. The Bents also took a cannon on the trail. The Indians, familiar by now with musket and rifle fire, had little fear of either. Cannon fire was another matter, however. Because the Indians tended to treat anything unknown as supernatural, cannon fire usually scattered them.

In 1827, with the establishment of Fort Leavenworth, Kansas, the military began patrolling the Santa Fe and later the Oregon Trail. The Santa Fe Trail had two branches: one, the Cimarron Cutoff, though shorter by one hundred miles, exposed the travelers to acute danger from hostile Indians and took them far from reliable water sources. The other route stretched more than a thousand miles. Sticking closer to the Arkansas River, it went to Bent's Fort. The route then turned more sharply south through steep mountain terrain and Raton Pass.

With the start of the Mexican War in 1846, the Santa Fe Trail took on more importance. It was used to move both troops

Covered wagons carried settlers to the West. In the photograph on the right, wagon ruts are still visible along the Oregon Trail.

and supplies to Mexico and California. But in later years, as parts of the Atchison, Topeka, and Santa Fe Railroad were finished, the trail shrank in both length and importance. When the last miles of track opened on February 14, 1880, a Santa Fe newspaper headline told the final story: "The Old Santa Fe Trail Passes into Oblivion."

The Oregon Trail—The **Oregon Trail** was first traced by a mountain man, a representative of a fur company sent out to deal with the Indians. Robert Stuart led fur trappers from Astoria, Oregon, to Missouri by way of South Pass in 1812-1813. But the trail was largely forgotten until 1824, when **Jedediah Smith** rediscovered it. The Oregon Trail became an important route for settlers and missionaries going west. Because the trail had several starting points—St. Joseph, Missouri; Independence, Missouri; Fort Leavenworth; and Council Bluffs—as well as several ending spots, depending on one's destination in Oregon, one writer has described the trail "like rope twisted hard in the middle and raveled at both ends."

In the spring settlers wanting to follow its two-thousand-mile route gathered at the starting points. Organized much the same way as the trade caravans on the Santa Fe Trail, the wagons traveled twelve abreast across the expanse of the Great Plains. This enabled the captain to keep more wagons going if one wagon broke down. Others could continue and time would not be lost. Since the Oregon Trail crossed America farther north than did the Santa Fe, time was always a factor. If the wagons did not reach Independence Rock by July 4th, they ran the risk of being caught in the mountains by early snow and cold. One observer at Fort Kearny reported that all the traffic passed in a fifteen-day period. The Great Emigration of 1843 left Kansas on May 22 and arrived at Oregon City on October 27th, more than twenty-two weeks later.

In 1841 less than one hundred settlers set out for Oregon, an area claimed jointly by both the United States and Great Britain at that time. But soon the trail traffic increased. As every new wagon with settlers started to Oregon, British efforts to hold Oregon became less certain. In 1844, fifteen hundred emigrants made the trip—some walked most of the way because of the jolts and ruts—and the next year more than three thousand people used the trail. In 1847 emigration swelled to four thousand.

Wagons drawn by oxen provided slow travel along the western trails.

The settlers on the trail faced many hardships. Missionary Narcissa Whitman rejoiced at being able to wash clothes near Parma, Idaho. It was only the third time she had been able to do so in fifteen hundred miles of travel. Diaries tell of travelers with cracked lips and dry nostrils in the dry lands. Near or just west of the 100th meridian of longitude, the turf changed to bunch grasses, and the colors shifted from greens to browns and tans. Even the animals were different. Bison (buffalo), jack rabbits, prairie dogs, and horny toads surprised the travelers. Rattlesnakes struck at both livestock and humans. Their venom was fatal to animals although it did not always kill people. Bolts of lightning zig-zagged across the sky and touched the earth as late-afternoon thunder showers struck. Sleepy children fell off wagons and were run over by iron-shod wagon wheels. Rolled into almost every mile on the trail are little-known stories of self-reliance, determination, courage, and answered prayers.

The California Trail—The **California Trail,** a cutoff from the Oregon Trail, extended south and west. Blazed by mountain men in 1846, it gained importance as a route for gold seekers and settlers. This trail followed the Oregon Trail for twelve hundred miles. When it cut south from Fort Hall, few travelers had any idea of what lay ahead over the next eight hundred miles. The wagons faced the challenge of the rugged Rockies, weeks of wading in loose, warm desert sand, and days with only the water that could be carried in barrels hanging on hoops on the backs of wagons. A four-hundred-mile stretch along the Humboldt River provided the wagon trains with needed grass and water before they faced the forty-mile desert or a murderous ascent through the Sierra Nevada (see-EHR-uh nuh-VAH-duh). Despite the horrors of the trail, 165,000 pioneers risked their lives to reach California between 1846 and 1858.

Growth of Towns

Usually the first men to arrive in a new western area were trappers and traders. After they had worked an area for a while, pioneer farmers would begin to arrive. When they cleared the land, the number of game and fur-bearing animals decreased. As this happened, the trappers and traders moved on.

As more and more settlers came into an area, it became more civilized. Settlers established county governments. Often a church was the first nonresidential building to be built in an area. As in colonial days, the church met both the spiritual and social needs of a community. Circuit-riding preachers served some of the churches. Until a store was built in the area, itinerant or traveling peddlers brought goods to sell. Their horses and wagons carried pots, pans, tools, cloth, thread, and other goods to meet the needs of pioneer families. Eventually settlers built stores and other businesses such as forges and mills. The resulting towns emerged, usually located on transportation arteries or near power sources. Most western towns grew slowly.

Section Review

1. Define the term "Manifest Destiny."
2. List four reasons for westward expansion.
3. What group settled in Utah and why?
4. Name the first trail route west of the Missouri.
5. What other famous trail cut off from the Oregon Trail?

B. Acquiring Texas and the Southwest

The Spanish had explored Texas and the Southwest in the 1500s and 1600s. Spain later tried to cement its claim by setting up missions in these areas. Because the Indians were hostile, however, this system did not work well in Texas. Thus by 1800 there were only three prominent Spanish settlements in Texas: San Antonio, Goliad (GO LEE ad), and Nacogdoches (NAK uh DOH chiz). Unrest in Spanish Mexico spread over the border into Texas after 1810. When Mexico gained its freedom from Spain, Texas and the Southwest came under Mexican control.

American Settlement of Texas

The Mexicans then decided to allow a limited number of Americans to enter Texas. In 1821 a Missouri promoter named Moses Austin secured a permit to bring three hundred families to Texas. When he died, his son Stephen took over the project. Each family received at least 640 acres at low cost along with six years of freedom from taxation, the right to have slaves, and protection from suits to collect any debts they owed back in the States. In return the settlers had to pledge allegiance to Mexico and become Roman Catholics. Because of the great opportunity offered and the expectation that Mexico would not enforce its religious policies, the settlers willingly agreed to come.

Although the American colonists helped Texas to prosper and to control the Indians, they were not absorbed into the Spanish population as Mexico had hoped. By the end of the 1820s, more than thirty thousand Americans had poured into Texas. Although they became Mexican citizens, some of the new settlers were hot-tempered firebrands who stirred up trouble and pushed the weak Mexican government to the limit. Consequently, in 1830 Mexico reversed its policy, closed its borders to immigrants, and restricted its trade. The few Mexican soldiers who patrolled the borders, however, could not control the flood of incoming Americans. When **Stephen Austin** went to Mexico City in 1833, he asked the Mexican officials to let the American-settled area become a separate Mexican state. He also advised his colonists to become a state even if his mission failed. As a result, he spent eighteen months in jail on charges of treason.

Meanwhile Mexico's president, **Antonio Lopez de Santa Anna,** decided to use force against Texas and sent troops there under the command of his brother-in-law, General Martin Cos. Texans grabbed their rifles and muskets and manned cannons on town plazas. Although the United States government sent no official aid, some southern states sent help secretly. Three hundred volunteers from Georgia and two companies from New Orleans joined the Texan forces. The thought of thirty thousand Texan colonists facing the might of a nation with seven million subjects inspired Americans.

Texas Battles for Independence

The Texans were tough and determined. On October 2, 1835, a Mexican military detachment arrived at Gonzalez and demanded surrender of the town's brass cannon. The cannon fired a shot, the Mexican forces retreated, and the skirmish became "the Lexington of the Texas Revolution."

The Texans declared that they were fighting to gain the republican rights that the Mexican constitution promised. Texans easily took Goliad, a Mexican supply base,

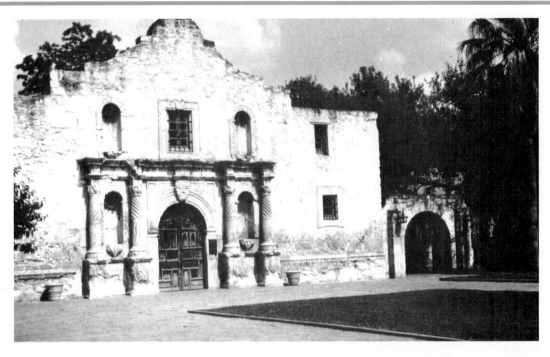

The Alamo in San Antonio, Texas

and then took control of San Antonio. Some of the American volunteers believed the war was over, but **Jim Bowie** and **Sam Houston,** two of the American commanders, knew otherwise. They correctly believed that Santa Anna would try a winter invasion.

Houston believed that the Americans stood a chance of winning if they fought in the field. They knew the terrain, and American rifles were more accurate than Mexican muskets. The last place Houston wanted to fight a battle was at San Antonio's huge abandoned mission, **the Alamo.** Since it was never meant to be a fort, it would be difficult to defend. He ordered the Texans to abandon the mission before the Mexicans arrived.

"Remember the Alamo!"—But when Houston's order to abandon the fortress came, Jim Bowie decided against it. In his opinion, the Alamo kept Mexico from in-

vading all of Texas. Although the resources at hand were limited, the men used them well. They secured the three-acre mission as well as possible with wood and earthen barricades, and they positioned cannon for their defense.

When Lieutenant Colonel William Travis arrived, he assumed command. He vowed to hold the mission and to fight until "victory or death." Davy Crockett arrived from Tennessee, carrying his country fiddle and a long rifle named Betsy. The defenders fully expected more help. But no more came. Only 183 men were left to defend a quarter mile of makeshift walls.

Santa Anna crossed the Rio Grande and moved toward San Antonio. Once there, he sent the Alamo a demand for unconditional surrender. He said that every man would be "put to the sword in case of refusal." The defenders answered with a cannon shot, and on February 23, the historic siege by more than four thousand Mexican troops began.

As the siege dragged on, the supply of powder and cannonballs dwindled. On March 3, Travis told the defenders to expect no aid. He drew a line on the ground with his sword and asked all who would stand by him to cross it. Every man crossed. Jim Bowie lay on a cot, too ill to move, suffering from tuberculosis and typhoid-pneumonia, but he asked his comrades to lift him across the line.

The thirteenth day of the siege, Santa Anna, aided by fresh reinforcements, attacked. His gun batteries opened two holes in the walls, and his men placed ladders at other points. The fighting became hand to hand as Texans clubbed any attackers who made it over the walls. But the enemy burst through the holes, opening up an attack from both sides.

Travis was slumped over a cannon, shot through the forehead. Davy Crockett's right arm was broken by a bullet. He fired with his left until the stock of his rifle was shattered. He went down only when a knife was buried in his chest. Five Texan prisoners were paraded before the victorious army before being cruelly bayoneted.

Oil was poured over the mound of bodies, and they were burned. The only American survivors were Sussanah Dickerson, wife of a soldier, her daughter Angelina, and a black slave sent along to escort her as she carried back the gruesome news to the Texan forces.

To Santa Anna the battle was "but a small affair." But to Americans and Texans, it had tremendous impact. To Texans the only alternative now was freedom; enraged, they wanted revenge.

Goliad and San Jacinto—The feelings of rage deepened when a group of soldiers under James Fannin surrendered to the Mexicans near Goliad. They believed they would be treated as prisoners of war, but when they arrived at Goliad, the Mexicans killed over three hundred of the prisoners, all of them unarmed.

Texas's last hope was Sam Houston, with his army of eight hundred men. Houston planned carefully for one last battle on the plain where the San Jacinto (SAN juh-SEN-toh) River ran into Galveston Bay. The forces made a surprise attack on Santa Anna, yelling, "Remember the Alamo!" as they charged. In twenty minutes the **battle of San Jacinto** was history. Almost the entire Mexican Army of fourteen hundred was either killed or captured. Houston kept the Texans from murdering Santa Anna so that he could hold him hostage to prevent further attacks on Texas.

Sam Houston, leader of the Texan army and first president of the Lone Star Republic

The Lone Star Republic

Houston recrossed the river and returned to Texas. Only a few days before the fall of the Alamo, Texans had met in a convention, issuing a declaration of independence and writing a constitution. Sam Houston was elected the first president of their provisional government by a landslide. Texas first applied for admission into the Union in 1836 but was refused because Mexico threatened war with the United States if action were taken on statehood. Hence, Texas stood alone for nine years as the **"Lone Star Republic."**

Other attempts at **annexation** (the formal process of being added to the Union) were refused, not only because of fear of war with Mexico, but also because of slavery. Rumors that supporters of slavery were planning to carve five or six states from Texas brought strong protest from opponents of slavery.

Texas Gains Statehood

By 1844, a presidential election year, the dispute between Britain and the United States over Oregon had resurfaced. The Whig candidate, Henry Clay, vowed to keep Texas out of the Union, as did Martin Van Buren, the Democratic front-runner. Ex-president Jackson astutely read public opinion. He told "Young Hickory," **James K. Polk,** a fellow Tennessean, that he could win both the nomination and the presidency by promising "All of Oregon, All of Texas." This pledge lured both Northerners and Southerners into the Democratic fold, made James K. Polk, the Democratic dark horse (an unexpected winner), president, and led to statehood for Texas in 1845.

Top: *Flag of Texas, "the Lone Star State"*
Bottom: *Currency issued by Texas while it was an independent republic*

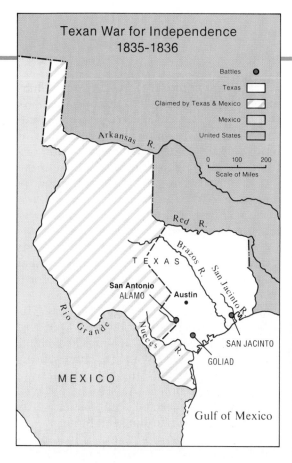

Texan War for Independence 1835-1836

Battles ●
Texas
Claimed by Texas & Mexico
Mexico
United States

0   100   200
Scale of Miles

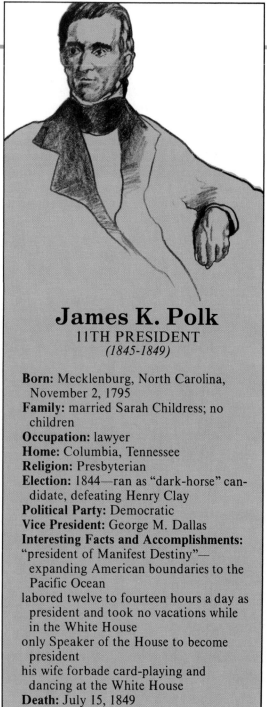

James K. Polk
11TH PRESIDENT
(1845-1849)

Born: Mecklenburg, North Carolina, November 2, 1795

Family: married Sarah Childress; no children

Occupation: lawyer

Home: Columbia, Tennessee

Religion: Presbyterian

Election: 1844—ran as "dark-horse" candidate, defeating Henry Clay

Political Party: Democratic

Vice President: George M. Dallas

Interesting Facts and Accomplishments:

"president of Manifest Destiny"—expanding American boundaries to the Pacific Ocean

labored twelve to fourteen hours a day as president and took no vacations while in the White House

only Speaker of the House to become president

his wife forbade card-playing and dancing at the White House

Death: July 15, 1849

The Mexican War

Just three weeks after Polk took office, Mexico broke off relations with the United States. President Polk sent General **Zachary Taylor** and fourteen hundred troops across the Gulf of Mexico to land at Corpus Christi in case war broke out. While he expected war, he also sought a peaceful settlement. He sent John Slidell to Mexico City, Mexico's capital, to offer to buy California and New Mexico, but the Mexicans refused to meet with Slidell.

Mexico held that the southern border of Texas was the Nueces (noo AY sis) River. Therefore, Mexico held that the presence of American troops south of that river was an act of war. Polk and Taylor chose to believe the Rio Grande was the border and cared little about what Mexico thought. For two weeks the two armies taunted each other across the river.

On May 8, 1846, the Mexican general Mariano Arista slipped across the border and launched a surprise attack on Taylor at Palo Alto. After staunch American resistance, the Mexicans withdrew to a dry thorny river bed called Resaca de la Palma. American sharpshooters routed them. Happy Americans celebrated with torch-light parades and even talked of making Zachary Taylor the new president.

War is Declared—When Taylor's reports reached Washington, President Polk asked Congress to declare war on Mexico. The declaration was signed May 13, 1846, and Congress authorized the president to call fifty thousand volunteers. More volunteers came forward than were needed; in some places they drew lots to see who would get to go to war.

The **Mexican War,** however, was not universally popular. Many New Englanders believed the war was a well-planned attempt by Southerners to grasp more land to create new slave states. The war was especially unpopular in the American intellectual community. For example, an American writer, Henry David Thoreau (thuh ROH), went to jail rather than pay a poll tax, part of which might go to support a war that he believed unjust.

Nonetheless the war was fought with patriotic fervor. A press corps followed the armies; using Samuel Morse's new telegraph, reporters wired back descriptions of American bravery to an eager public. For the first time Americans had a chance to follow a war closely.

Old Rough and Ready—Taylor's volunteer army was shaped into seasoned regulars through training and hardships. Their camp at Corpus Christi contributed its share of hardships. The area was infested with rattlesnakes and malarial mosquitoes, and the water caused dysentery. The rations were almost inedible: the bacon was spoiled, the hardtack was wormy, and the flour was maggot-laden.

Although Taylor was not a brilliant strategist, he was a brave soldier. He had no love for military pomp; his field uniform included a wide-brimmed straw hat, a soiled white linen jacket, and baggy trousers. His nickname, earned in the Seminole War, was "Old Rough and Ready." His men loved him.

By September, Taylor had marched his troops into Mexico toward Monterrey. Mexican resistance in Monterrey was stronger than expected, but the city was captured by house-to-house fighting.

Taylor then faced a period of inactivity. Polk believed that Taylor's popularity had

Zachary Taylor

increased enough to make him a presidential competitor. To take the focus off Taylor, Polk appointed several Democrats as brigadier generals, hoping that one would outshine Taylor. In the meantime, the Americans grew careless and did not send out patrols. Santa Anna's army captured a half-dozen outposts, then wheeled into position to take Taylor's army from the rear. Taylor retreated to a sheep ranch called Buena Vista (BWAY-nuh VEE-stuh). He had to burn tons of supplies to keep them from capture.

Twice the American troops were pushed back. A severe thunderstorm halted the Mexicans, allowing the Americans to stiffen their line and prepare for a counterattack. Taylor was outnumbered three to one, but he still won the battle.

The Santa Fe and California Campaigns—While the Mexican War progressed, Polk saw opportunity for the dream of Manifest Destiny to be fulfilled. The Mexican provinces of California and New Mexico were tempting prizes that soon became a war objective. Polk made plans to seize both territories, and Americans already in those areas were ready to show the American government that they were loyal.

The scheme to conquer California was shrewd. Captain **John Charles Frémont,** called "the Pathfinder" because of his western explorations, came to California with sixty soldiers clad in buckskin. He said they were making a geographic survey. Frémont's secret orders, however, were to help the United States Pacific Squadron if war came. Commodore John Sloat had brought several warships to California to guard the American interests. Sloat proclaimed California American territory and

turned the command over to Commodore Robert Stockton, who headed south with a land force. Learning of the war with Mexico, Frémont led his band and some American settlers in what was called the **"Bear Flag Revolution."** Thus California fell easily into American hands.

In the meantime, Colonel Stephen Kearny was leading an army to California from Fort Leavenworth, Kansas. The first leg of Kearny's trek to San Diego took him to Santa Fe. But the Mexicans in Santa Fe fled their positions, allowing Kearny to take the town without firing a shot. He left Colonel Alexander Doniphan (DON ih fun) and nine hundred men to complete the conquest of New Mexico and to seize Chihuahua (chee WAH wah), a province in northern Mexico.

John C. Frémont, "the Pathfinder"

The Battles of Veracruz and Mexico City—General **Winfield Scott** was placed in command of the Veracruz operation, the closing campaign of the war. Scott was just about everything Zachary Taylor was not.

Scott was a six-foot-four-inch handsome man who had a taste for dress uniforms and who expected his men and others to adhere to military regulations. His liking for discipline and pomp had won him the

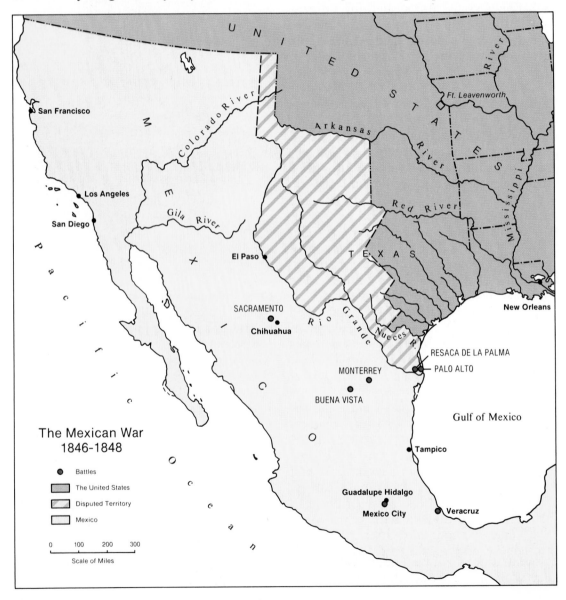

The Mexican War
1846-1848

- ● Battles
- ▨ The United States
- ▨ Disputed Territory
- ☐ Mexico

0   100   200   300

Scale of Miles

nickname "Old Fuss and Feathers," but he was a skilled soldier. Scott and his troops left New Orleans, traveled to Veracruz by steamer, and took the city.

Despite the losses at Buena Vista and Veracruz, Santa Anna did not concede defeat. He reorganized his army for a last stand, but Scott found a route around the mountains and attacked from behind. Santa Anna's army panicked and fled to Mexico City. Four more minor battles were fought before Mexico City finally surrendered in September of 1847.

The Treaty of Guadalupe Hidalgo—By the terms of the **Treaty of Guadalupe Hidalgo** (GWOD-ul-OOP ee-*TH*AL-gaw), the fighting was ended; the Rio Grande became the boundary of Texas; California and a large area called the **Mexican Cession** became part of the United States. The United States agreed to pay Mexico $15 million for the land and canceled all debts Mexico owed to the United States.

Results of the Mexican War

The Mexican War made the expansionists' dream of "Manifest Destiny" a reality. It also made a hero of Zachary Taylor, soon putting him into the White House.

But the Mexican War reopened the old controversy over slavery. Would the new lands of the Mexican Cession be slave or free? The South wanted the new cession to be open to slavery; the North wanted it to be free. "The United States will conquer Mexico," author Ralph Waldo Emerson wrote, "but it will be as the man who swallows the arsenic which brings him down in turn. Mexico will poison us."

The Mexican War served as a training ground for the Civil War, which was to come thirteen years later. Many of the men who

became famous leaders in the Civil War gained valued experience in this earlier conflict. Jefferson Davis, Robert E. Lee, U. S. Grant, Thomas "Stonewall" Jackson, George C. Meade, and George McClellan were among the many army officers who fought in Mexico.

The lands gained in the Mexican War proved to be valuable. Already in 1848 Americans realized the value of California's fine harbors. These could be used to aid Pacific trade. Soon after the war, gold was discovered in California, and in later years major sources of silver and uranium were also found in these lands. Although much of the land was desert or at least semiarid, through the use of irrigation some of the lands became valuable even for farming.

The Gadsden Purchase

Just five years after the war had ended, the United States realized its need for

Winfield Scott, "Old Fuss and Feathers"

another section of Mexican land on the border of New Mexico and Arizona. The United States wanted this narrow strip of land as a possible southern transcontinental railroad route. Mexico agreed to sell the land, and diplomat James Gadsden arranged the American purchase for $10 million. This **Gadsden Purchase** completed the acquisition of territory for the forty-eight contiguous United States.

Section Review

1. What part did Stephen Austin play in the settlement of Texas?
2. What was the significance of the Alamo?
3. What American politician used the issue of Texas statehood to win a presidential election?
4. How did the Mexican War contribute to the fulfillment of the dream of "Manifest Destiny"?
5. What treaty ended the Mexican War?

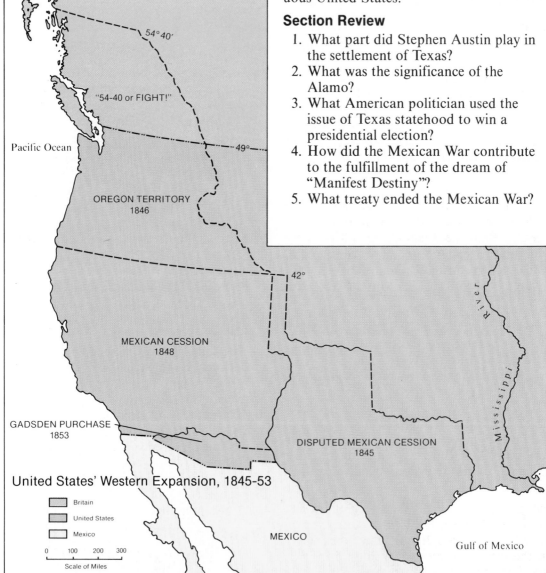

54° 40'

"54-40 or FIGHT!"

Pacific Ocean

49°

OREGON TERRITORY
1846

42°

River

MEXICAN CESSION
1848

GADSDEN PURCHASE
1853

DISPUTED MEXICAN CESSION
1845

Mississippi

United States' Western Expansion, 1845-53

Britain

United States

Mexico

0   100   200   300

Scale of Miles

MEXICO

Gulf of Mexico

C. The Settling of Oregon and California

The far western lands of Oregon and California held many treasures for Americans, and the 1840s and 1850s saw the great rush of settlers and miners to these areas.

Opening Oregon

Great Britain and the United States both claimed Oregon, and in 1818 they agreed to a joint occupation of the area. This was extended indefinitely after 1827. The first lure to Oregon Territory was furs. After trapping first in the coastal areas, the traders turned eastward to the Rocky Mountain region. More fur trading companies became involved in the area, joining the Hudson Bay Company, a company that had been active since its founding in 1670 and still exists today. John Jacob Astor, a German immigrant, set up the American Fur Company in 1811. The Rocky Mountain Fur Company, directed by three trappers—Thomas Fitzpatrick, James Bridger, and Milton Sublette—also entered the region.

Each year beginning in the early 1820s, the fur companies in the area hired parties to go west from St. Louis to meet the **mountain men.** About six hundred in number, these men lived in the Rockies and trapped furs themselves or bought pelts from the Indians. Each summer all the mountain men, many Indians, and several company agents gathered in one place. They usually met at Green River Flats, Wyoming, near Fort Laramie (LAHR uh mee). There the trappers traded their furs for goods and caught up on the year's events. The rendezvous (RAHN day voo), or coming together, also brought out some of the worst in the mountain men; gambling, drinking, and fighting were commonplace.

The mountain men did provide valuable services, however. They marked the best routes, explored the courses of the rivers, and found major passes through the mountains. The most useful pass, South Pass, was located by Jedediah Smith, whose Christian life made him notable among the mountain men. South Pass greatly aided western caravans and enabled missionaries to bring the gospel to the West. Mountain men like Joe Meek and Kit Carson also served as guides for the wagon trains.

The first Americans to seek permanent homes in Oregon were Methodist missionaries. Although their primary purpose had been to bring the gospel to the Indians, their work was soon frustrated by the arrival of great numbers of whites who got "Oregon fever." Reports of cheap fertile land in the Willamette (wuh LAHM it) Valley drew thousands west. Every American settler

Jedediah Smith, Christian mountain man

helped to reinforce the United States' claim to the territory. Although Polk's use of "54° 40′ or fight" during his presidential campaign had made that slogan a battle cry, the British were willing to compromise. (54° 40′ was the extreme northern boundary of the disputed Oregon Territory.) Since most of the furs had been trapped in the region near to and south of the Columbia River, and since more Americans were in that region, the British base was moved north to Vancouver (van KOO vur) Island. Therefore, in 1846 the boundary line was set at the 49th parallel, stretching from Minnesota's Northwest Angle west to Puget (PYOO jit) Sound.

California

When the Spanish explorer Cabrillo (kah BREE lyaw) claimed California in

Mountain Man of Faith

As a group the mountain men were rough, profane, ungodly men, determined to make their fortune as trappers and traders in the unsettled West. Their yearly rendezvous was a time of gambling, violence, and drunkenness.

Yet perhaps the greatest of these trappers, Jedediah Smith, stands in stark contrast to the common image of a mountain man. Smith rediscovered the Oregon Trail and thus paved the way for the host of pioneers who settled in that territory. He was the first white man to travel by land to California. He was the first to cross the Sierra Nevada mountain range from the west and the first to cross the arid Great Basin. In the history of America, Jedediah Smith takes his place among the greatest of the explorers.

His personal courage is also unquestioned. Fearlessly he explored lands unknown to white men. Often he battled Indians; once only he and three companions escaped a massacre at the hands of the Umpqua. Early in his explorations he was almost killed by a grizzly bear. The bear had bitten him on the head, and as Smith lay on the ground bleeding, he calmly supervised a friend who sewed up his wounds. Such courage soon established Jedediah Smith as a leader of men.

But as a man of faith, Jedediah Smith excelled all of the other mountain men. He never drank, smoked, or swore. Along with his trapper's gear he carried his Bible, a hymnbook, a set of Matthew Henry's commentaries, and other theological texts. When a fellow trapper died, Jedediah insisted on having a service and reading from his Bible. As fellow trapper, William Waldo, testified, "No one who knew him well doubted the sincerity of his piety." He had been raised in a Christian home, and despite the hostile environment of the mountains and the ungodly influences of the other men, Jedediah Smith never turned back from service for His Lord. His own testimony was, "How often ought we on our bended knees to offer God our grateful acknowledgments for the gift of His dear Son."

At the age of 32, while scouting for a group of pioneers, Jedediah Smith was attacked and killed by a party of Comanches. The testimony of his Christian character, however, lives on today.

1540, the Spanish shared it with the "digger Indians." Those Indians lived by seed-gathering or digging for shellfish along the Pacific Coastal Plain. Franciscan missionary priests moved into the area, but it was only after 1769, when the British and Russians threatened to move into the area as well, that the Spanish settled there in earnest. Gaspar de Portolà (pawr taw LAH) established a settlement at Monterrey in 1770, and Junípero Serra (HOO-nih-peh-roh SEHR-ah) set up a mission system along the coast. After Mexico declared its independence from Spain, Californians declared allegiance to Mexico. Trading opportunities and the Frémont expeditions west stimulated the American interest in California. The area became an American possession following the Mexican War and the Treaty of Guadalupe Hidalgo.

Discovery of Gold—On January 24, 1848, just ten days before the signing of the treaty, an event that would drastically shape the history of California occurred at Sutter's Fort. **John Sutter,** a Swiss immigrant who had left his wife and family behind in Europe, had secured a fifty-thousand-acre grant from the Spanish. On this land he had set up his own community called Sutter's Fort. Sutter had hired a mechanic, **James W. Marshall,** to build and operate a sawmill. The site Marshall chose for the mill was by the American River, forty miles upstream from the fort, in a valley that the Indians called the Columa, meaning "Beautiful Vale." Marshall tried to deepen the river channel and divert the channel to form a fast-running millrace to drive the mill's water wheel.

While making his daily inspection of the lower part of the channel in January of 1848, Marshall saw a sparkling object in the mud and sand. Using a tin plate, Marshall washed out the dirt, leaving yellow particles "about as much as would cover a dime." He found more metal the next morning. Since no one was sure whether it was real gold, he performed several tests. Marshall returned to Sutter's Fort to share the news with his employer. Sutter also tested the metal and was convinced that it was gold. It was impossible to keep the news secret. When one of Marshall's workmen tried to pay off a bill in gold bits, the creditor asked for confirmation. The word was out, and the **California Gold Rush** was on.

The Forty-Niners—The argonauts, as the men who searched for gold called themselves, were hard-working men who set out for California full of hope and energy. In 1849 alone over eighty thousand men came to California, and they came to be called **"forty-niners."** Thirty-nine thousand came by sea on the four- to five-month journey around Cape Horn. Some sailed to Panama, crossed the isthmus by foot or horseback, and got on a ship on the other side. More than forty thousand made the trip by land using trails.

Hard physical labor in the gold fields was the key to wealth. Since all the men worked with their hands, there was little snobbery. Most of the miners dressed alike, wearing colorful shirts, broad-brimmed hats, and trousers stuffed into high boots. Mining camps grew up wherever gold was being found. Pans, rockers, troughs, and sluice boxes were used to separate the gold from the dirt. As miners accumulated their wealth, crime became rampant in many of the camps. Claim disputes, robberies, and murders were common.

About half of the would-be miners chose to pursue wealth another way. They became farmers, ranchers, and storekeepers and provided the miners with needed goods and services.

By the fall of 1849, Californians had written a state constitution. Since its writers voted to prohibit slavery in California, Congress delayed California's request for statehood. California became a state on September 9, 1850 because of a compromise made in Congress.

Section Review

1. What two countries agreed in 1818 to occupy Oregon jointly?
2. Who were the first Americans to seek permanent homes in Oregon?
3. The Americans took possession of California during what war?
4. What incident at Sutter's Fort greatly affected the settlement of California?

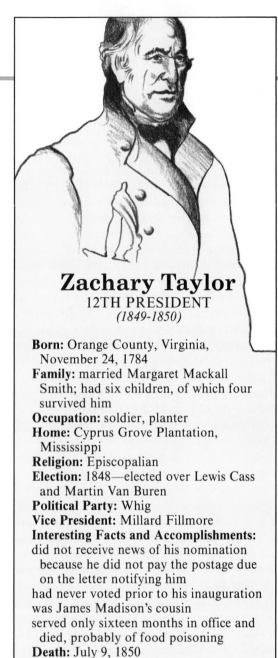

Zachary Taylor
12TH PRESIDENT
(1849-1850)

Born: Orange County, Virginia, November 24, 1784
Family: married Margaret Mackall Smith; had six children, of which four survived him
Occupation: soldier, planter
Home: Cyprus Grove Plantation, Mississippi
Religion: Episcopalian
Election: 1848—elected over Lewis Cass and Martin Van Buren
Political Party: Whig
Vice President: Millard Fillmore
Interesting Facts and Accomplishments:
did not receive news of his nomination because he did not pay the postage due on the letter notifying him
had never voted prior to his inauguration
was James Madison's cousin
served only sixteen months in office and died, probably of food poisoning
Death: July 9, 1850

D.   Sectional Rivalry Increases

With the acquisition of the new western lands, the slavery issue boiled. The South wanted to keep the lands open to slavery while most Northerners wished to ban slavery from these territories. When California sought admission to the union as a free state, debate raged for months.

The Compromise of 1850

Henry Clay and other leaders in Congress proposed a compromise. They hoped that these measures would allow California entrance and give the South some satisfaction while the compromise addressed the problems at hand. Preserving the Union became most important as the tensions between North and South grew.

In the **Compromise of 1850** California was admitted as a free state. The rest of the land gained through the Mexican Cession was divided into New Mexico and Utah territories. In both territories the people were allowed to decide whether or not they wanted to have slavery. This was called **popular sovereignty** (SAHV er in tee). In addition, a stricter Fugitive Slave Law requiring all federal government officials to help return runaway slaves was included to please Southerners, and slave trade was outlawed in the District of Columbia. Finally, Texas was paid for giving up some of its land.

Taylor and Fillmore

Meanwhile, 1848 had been an election year. Zachary Taylor, the hero of Buena Vista, was elected president over Michigan's Lewis Cass. Although Taylor was a Southerner and a slave owner, he had taken little interest in politics before 1848, and Northerners did not think he was a strong supporter of slavery.

Taylor stunned Southerners by encouraging Californians to apply directly for statehood as a free state. When California statehood was linked to other legislation,

Millard Fillmore
13TH PRESIDENT
(1850-1853)

Born: Cayuga County, New York, January 7, 1800
Family: married Abigail Powers and after her death, Caroline C. McIntosh, a widow; two children by first marriage
Occupation: lawyer
Home: East Aurora, New York
Religion: Unitarian
Election: none, succeeded to the presidency upon the death of President Taylor
Political Party: Whig
Vice President: none
Interesting Facts and Accomplishments:
installed first bathtub and kitchen cook stove in the White House
refused an honorary degree from England's Oxford University because he did not feel he deserved it
both his children died unmarried
ran as a third-party candidate in the 1856 election for the Know-Nothings, an anti-immigrant party
Death: March 8, 1874

Taylor refused to back the whole bill. He believed that the Texans should not be paid any money. However, after only sixteen months in office, Taylor died in 1850.

Taylor was succeeded by his vice president, **Millard Fillmore,** who was a Whig and a supporter of the compromise. By splitting Clay's measures into five separate bills that could individually gather enough support to be passed, **Stephen Douglas** got the compromise through. Fillmore approved the compromise even though it proved to be political suicide since the Whig Party strongly opposed the Fugitive Slave Law.

Doughfaces

By 1850 Congress and the nation were changing. The Great Compromisers—Clay, Calhoun, Webster, and Thomas Hart Benton—were passing from the scene. New, younger leaders were of a different frame of mind. Charles Sumner of Massachusetts, William H. Seward of New York, Thaddeus Stevens of Pennsylvania, and Salmon P. Chase of Ohio bitterly fought against slavery in Congress while Southerners fought to protect it. The only ones willing to compromise on the problems of the 1850s were Stephen Douglas and a group of Northern Democrats called **Doughfaces.** The Doughfaces seemed more moderate because they did not oppose the pro-slavery position. They were willing to concentrate on other political issues and let the South handle its own affairs.

War hero Winfield Scott was the Whig nominee for president in 1852. Because he lost votes to Democrats in the South and Free Soilers in the North, Scott lost the election to **Franklin Pierce,** a Doughface Democrat.

Section Review

1. What was the significance of the Compromise of 1850?
2. What president was elected in 1848 and died after sixteen months in office?
3. What was a *Doughface?*

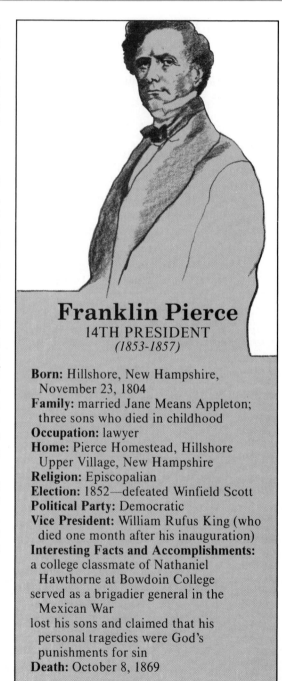

Franklin Pierce
14TH PRESIDENT
(1853-1857)

Born: Hillshore, New Hampshire, November 23, 1804
Family: married Jane Means Appleton; three sons who died in childhood
Occupation: lawyer
Home: Pierce Homestead, Hillshore Upper Village, New Hampshire
Religion: Episcopalian
Election: 1852—defeated Winfield Scott
Political Party: Democratic
Vice President: William Rufus King (who died one month after his inauguration)
Interesting Facts and Accomplishments:
a college classmate of Nathaniel Hawthorne at Bowdoin College
served as a brigadier general in the Mexican War
lost his sons and claimed that his personal tragedies were God's punishments for sin
Death: October 8, 1869

Summary

The United States expanded to fulfill its "Manifest Destiny" before the Civil War. Trails west carried traders and settlers who sought new opportunities in Oregon, California, Utah, and the Southwest. Texas, heavily settled by Americans, won its independence from Mexico and later joined the Union. The resulting Mexican War gave the United States opportunities to gain California and the rest of the Southwest for its own. These acquisitions, along with settled boundaries for the Oregon Territory, made the United States a land that stretched from coast to coast.

Chapter Review

Do You Remember?

■ What were these people often called?

1. miners who rushed to California
2. followers of Joseph Smith
3. moderate northern Democrats who did not fight against slavery
4. fur trappers and traders who blazed trails in the West

■ Who am I?

5. James W. Marshall
6. Zachary Taylor
7. Stephen Douglas
8. Jim Bowie
9. Brigham Young
10. Jedediah Smith
11. Stephen Austin
12. John Charles Frémont

a. I was called "the Pathfinder."
b. I led the Mormons to Utah.
c. I discovered gold in California.
d. I led American settlers to Texas.
e. I supported the Compromise of 1850.
f. I fought at the Alamo.
g. I rediscovered the Oregon Trail.
h. I was a Mexican War hero and a president.

Why Is It So?

1. How did the United States fulfill its "Manifest Destiny" during the 1840s and 1850s?
2. What was the significance of the Alamo?
3. Why was a compromise needed in 1850?

What Do You Think?

1. Why was the skirmish at Gonzalez called the "Lexington of the Texas Revolution"?
2. Is it necessary for Congress to make compromises on some political issues? Why or why not?

16

One Nation, Now Divided

A cannon emplacement at Fort Sumter, where the war began

In the 1850s, the United States experienced new growth and, except for a brief financial panic in 1857, prosperity. The population reached thirty-one million, a thirty-five per cent increase in just ten years. Production of foodstuffs and manufactured goods reached new heights. The resources that God had given the United States, vast acres of unoccupied land, a network of navigable rivers, and huge amounts of timber, would allow the country to sustain progress. But this economic boom was only a part of the picture of the United States at that time. Greater problems were about to rend the nation in two.

A. Differences Between the North and the South

There were several key issues that led to a division between the North and the South. Although the issues were not new, more people were beginning to see the issues as matters of right and wrong instead of as mere regional preferences. There was no longer much room for compromise between the two regions of the country.

Differing Economies and Lifestyles

There were major economic differences between the North and the South. The South was agricultural. Towns and villages were few—cities, scarcer yet. Furthermore, nearly all of the South's cities, such as Charleston, Richmond, and Savannah, were relatively small, having populations under 40,000. Only New Orleans, with its population of 150,000, compared to northern cities in size and diversity. Instead of factories, the South had plantations and farms that raised cotton and other crops for sale. Much of the business of southern cities revolved around the trade of agricultural materials and crops.

In the South, the upper class, one per cent of the population, was made up of planters owning large plantations and many slaves. This top one per cent was the ruling class politically, socially, and economically. More white farmers owned only a few slaves (generally less than ten). A much larger part of the southern white population, however, owned no slaves at all. (Small farmers and other Southerners without slaves made up three-quarters of the white population.) Yet the way of life of all Southerners was greatly influenced by the needs and desires of the slaveholders.

In contrast to the agricultural, slaveholding South, the North was industrialized and had few slaves. Its many cities were crowded and noisy. Some grew so quickly that it was hard for them to handle the growth. New York City's population soared to over 800,000. When Chicago became incorporated in 1837, it had only 4,170 people. In 1860 the census takers counted 112,000 Chicagoans.

One reason for the great population increase in the North was immigration.

More than 2.8 million immigrants had come to America, and seven out of eight settled in the North or West. Initially many were forced to live in filth and misery in the cities while laboring long hours for low wages. The working and living conditions of some northern workers were so poor that Southerners called them "wage slaves." But soon many foreigners adopted American ways and raised their standards of living. Many held political offices. In Boston, New York, and Philadelphia, Irish voters were influential, and in St. Louis, Cincinnati, and Milwaukee anyone running for office had to consider the wishes of the German residents.

In the North small farmers, merchants, and increasing numbers of factory workers made up most of the population. Four-fifths of the nation's factories were in the North. Although most people were still farmers, mechanized agriculture helped them to pro-

Several generations of a slave family on a South Carolina plantation in 1862 duce food for nearby towns. Railroads carried food to the ever-growing cities and returned to rural areas carrying manufactured goods. Owners of factories, railroads, and other businesses and industries became the wealthy and influential people in northern society.

Differing Political Views

The differing economies and lifestyles produced differing political views as well. Generally the North favored a strong central government. Northerners tended to be more willing to pay higher taxes to provide local and state goods and services. The North also had more wage earners to help pay for such costs.

Many Southerners feared a strong central government. They still believed in Jefferson's ideal that the best government was local and state government. Little money was spent on local services because few of the Southerners lived in cities and towns where services such as police protection or city building projects were needed. Since education was considered a private matter, there were few public schools in the South at this time. Neither did most southern taxpayers wish to pay large amounts of taxes to the federal government for spending on improvements and benefits that often chiefly aided the more populous areas in the North.

The two sections also sharply disagreed about what level of government (federal or state) should possess more authority. Most Northerners believed that the Constitution was the nation's highest law under God and that the Constitution and federal law overruled any conflicting state and local laws. They based their view on Article 6 of the Constitution.

Many Southerners disagreed, arguing that the federal government could not overrule the rights of the states. They emphasized the idea that government was an agreement between a ruling body and those ruled. When those rulers exceeded the power given to them by the people, the people had the right to nullify unacceptable laws. In this way states' rights could be upheld over national sovereignty or authority.

The South feared being in the minority, and every time a new state applied to join the Union, the South's fears resurfaced. Every new free state in the Union meant more votes against the southern views. If the North gained too large a majority, it might force the South into submission.

Another political issue dividing the North and South was the tariff. The North generally favored a high protective tariff to protect its industries from foreign imports. The South opposed it not only because it had little industry of its own, but also because it needed foreign imports and trade to support its livelihood. The South was, in effect, being forced to pay the tariff to support northern industry.

In addition to the other differences, the issue of slavery was widening the rift between the North and South.

Section Review

1. What were the differences between the economic activities of the North and South?
2. How did northern and southern lifestyles differ?
3. List four political differences between the North and South, and briefly explain the reasons behind each difference.

B. Slavery: America's Peculiar Institution

We learned about how slaves first came to America and how slavery developed there in Chapter 3 (see pp. 44-45). Because slavery in the United States was limited to the black race, was usually a permanent condition for the slave, and was promoted by slave traders seeking profits, it has often been called America's "peculiar institution." Although slavery is nearly as old as the human race, these conditions were not common in other times and places.

Slavery came about largely because of the need for labor, especially in the South. In that region many laborers were needed to produce the profitable crops of the region—tobacco, indigo, rice, cotton, and sugar cane. Few whites sought low-paying, hard field jobs on southern plantations when they could easily acquire land to farm for themselves. The forced labor of black slaves became a solution. In northern and western areas, farms were smaller, and large money crops had not developed. Not needing large numbers of field hands, and with immigrants to supply labor for many factories, the North did not need slaves. The few slaves that were kept in northern areas were usually household servants. Slavery was, no doubt, an injustice, but it developed with little protest under the disguise of a "needed" and "acceptable" institution in early America.

By the 1830s, however, many Americans were realizing that slavery was not just another system of labor. The question of whether it was morally right or wrong became a great debate. Those who depended on slavery had to defend the institution. Some justified slavery on religious grounds.

They said that bringing the uncivilized slave to the new world helped him to be Christianized. Some praised it as "a positive good," as had a college professor, Thomas R. Dew, in 1832. He wrote that instead of being an evil, slavery was a positive good when compared to other labor systems. Dew used religious, historical, cultural, racial, and sociological arguments to support his "positive good" theory. John C. Calhoun and other Southerners used these arguments to defend slavery against rising attacks. Nonetheless, opposition to slavery increased as its wrongs were exposed by zealous whites and free blacks.

How Slaves Were Acquired

Most slaves came from the nations on Africa's western coast. Some slaves were captured in raids and sold to traders. Some were prisoners of war captured by warring African tribes. These tribes were sometimes guilty of selling their enemies into slavery for personal profit. Men, women, and children were captured, chained together, and driven like cattle to the seacoast, where slave traders bought them with liquor and various utensils and trinkets. In early colonial days Europeans and New Englanders provided most of the slave ships that then carried the captives to the New World.

While slaves were treated inhumanly from the moment of capture, the slave's worst experience was crossing the Atlantic to America. This crossing was called the "**middle passage.**" (The first passage took the slave to the coast of Africa; the third passage involved their final sale to slave owners in America.)

Since slave traders knew that even under the best conditions many captives would die, they tried to pack their ships with as

A slave auction

many as possible. Crowded into shelf-like decks, the Africans were then chained and shackled wrist-to-wrist and ankle-to-ankle. Poorly fed, the captives usually received gruel and water twice a day. Disease spread quickly because of poor sanitation. Some captives broke down under the stress of the voyage and killed themselves and others. There is no way to estimate the number of Africans who died on the middle passage. It may have been as low as one in seven or eight, or as high as one in four.

In 1808 the United States became the last major western nation to ban foreign slave trade. (See Article I, Section 9 of the Constitution.) Some slave smuggling did continue, but after 1808 the slaves already in the country were living long enough and having enough children to meet most of the demand for slaves in the South. Most of the northern states had abolished slavery by the end of the War for Independence.

Some Southerners, moved by the ideals of America's independence, spoke out against slavery. As late as the 1820s a few Quaker-sponsored emancipation (ih MAN suh PAY shun) societies campaigned for gradual **emancipation,** or freeing of the slaves. Some also pushed for an overseas colony for freed American blacks. Low tobacco prices and worn-out soil caused some to predict that slavery was a dying institution. But the invention of the cotton gin and the opening of new fertile lands in the West revived the plantation economy and made slavery profitable. When the first American census of the population was made in 1790, there were about 750,000 slaves in the United States. By 1860 the slave population had reached three and a half million; one out of every three Southerners was a slave. The price of an average field slave rose from about $600 in 1810 to $1,800 in 1860.

The Northern Viewpoint

Since there was little slavery in the North, the practice had little direct effect on the region. Most Northerners in the early 1800s were not concerned with its existence in the South, either. The prospect that brought the issue of slavery to the attention of the North was its possible spread to new areas in the West. The North did not want more western states to gain the same interests and political views as the South.

Northern feelings also began to change with the growth of **abolitionism** (AB uh LISH uh NIZ um), a movement to do away with slavery completely. Abolitionists supported emancipation, either gradually or immediately. Some favored **compensated emancipation,** whereby the slave owner would be paid for the loss of his property. One of the most vocal and militant abolitionists, **William Lloyd Garrison,** began a newspaper in Boston called *The Liberator*. Garrison strongly advocated immediate abolition of slavery without compensation.

While most Northerners embraced antislavery views, their attitudes towards blacks were generally prejudiced. Few northern states allowed free blacks to vote or offered them public education. Northerners also restricted blacks from many occupations and public offices, and blacks were often assigned separate areas in many churches and other establishments. Some of the western states avoided blacks altogether by prohibiting their settlement.

The Southern Viewpoint

The more abolitionists attacked slavery, the more Southerners rallied to defend it. Even those who were not slave owners supported it; some hoped one day to own slaves themselves. Because many of the South's

Bond Slave of Jesus Christ

John Jaspar was the youngest of twenty-four slave children. As a young man he became embittered when his wife was taken from him on their wedding night, and he never saw her again. He turned to a wild lifestyle, with no time for God.

The turning point in his life came when he was sold to a Christian slaveholder. The witness and prayers of his godly owner led to his salvation. When he told his owner of his conversion, Jaspar was given the day off to "go and tell it." He soon became a minister to his fellow slaves, but his preaching was so good that whites in town came to hear him too. Set free after the Civil War, Jaspar started a church of his own

businesses relied on cotton produced by slave labor, the prosperity of the entire region seemed to be dependent on the institution. Some whites might have been opposed to slavery, but they saw it as a necessary evil for keeping the cotton culture going.

On the other hand, struggling white farmers on the fringes of the Appalachians in western Virginia and in North Carolina, and some farmers in eastern Kentucky and Tennessee, opposed slavery. Ownership of slaves gave the large plantation owners most of the influence in state government. Many people from these highlands would later side with the North on the issue of slavery.

Treatment of Slaves

How slaves were treated varied from plantation to plantation. Since slaves were an economic investment, keeping them fit and treating them well made sense. They in Richmond, Virginia, where he ministered faithfully for thirty-five years. By 1883 the average attendance at his church was over a thousand each Sunday.

were generally assured of receiving food, clothing, and shelter, and care in childhood and old age was expected. The slave's food, like that of most Southerners, was plain: cornmeal mush or cornbread, fatback (fat pork from the back of a hog), beans or field peas or vegetables from the slaves' own gardens. Slaves who did their work well were sometimes rewarded with an extra day off, better food, or even a little cash. The promise of a bigger Christmas celebration or a marriage to someone on a nearby plantation also motivated the slaves. Some slaves became almost like members of the family. As a rule, house slaves were treated better than field slaves, and the smaller the plantation, the closer the slaves were to their master.

Some slaves were badly treated. A few were treated little better than farm animals. Public whippings for laziness and disobedience sometimes took place. Slaves who were continual troublemakers might be sold to another plantation. Such a sale might

mean parting with loved ones. The typical slave faced being sold once in a lifetime. Especially dreadful was being "sold down river" (down the Mississippi) to sugar plantations. Cutting sugar cane was extremely hard work; some slaves were actually worked to death.

Black Responses to Conditions on Plantations

Slaves were not slaves by choice. Strict slave codes in every southern state kept slaves in bondage. In some states if a slave gained his freedom, he was not even allowed to stay in the state.

The Underground Railroad—Hundreds of slaves ran away from their masters to find freedom. The **"Underground Railroad"** offered slaves who could reach the border states a reasonably good chance to escape. This "railroad" was actually just a network of people who aided runaway slaves. These people hid the slaves by day from captors. Then they aided their night travels to the next stop, where others on this escape route helped the runaways move farther north. When the Fugitive Slave Law of 1850 required northern states to return runaways, the "railroad" extended its route. Ontario, Canada, became the final destination for many slaves seeking freedom.

Slave Rebellions—Some slaves, such as Nat Turner in Virginia and Denmark Vesey (VEE zee) in South Carolina, led revolts. All of them failed, and the slaves involved were hanged. While the hangings made other slaves less likely to rebel, the revolts panicked the whites. They slept with guns and enacted even stricter laws to control the blacks. Several southern states even made it illegal to teach slaves to read and write. They feared that ideas of revolt would spread uncontrollably if blacks possessed these skills.

Black Leaders Against Slavery—Among the blacks who worked against slavery in the troubled years before the Civil War were **Frederick Douglass** and **Harriet Tubman.** Douglass, the leading black abolitionist, escaped from slavery in 1838. Because he was a talented speaker, he lectured against slavery in the North and in Britain. He also wrote an influential biography and edited an antislavery newspaper. Harriet Tubman escaped from slavery in Maryland. She returned to slave territory nearly twenty times to help runaway slaves. During these ventures she guided about three hundred blacks along the Underground Railroad northward.

Section Review

1. Why was slavery called America's "peculiar institution"?
2. Describe the "middle passage."
3. Contrast the northern and southern viewpoints on slavery.
4. What was the "positive good" theory concerning slavery?
5. How did those who opposed slavery show their dissatisfaction?

The capture of Nat Turner, leader of a slave revolt

C. Final Eruptions of the Slavery Issue

The nation had made attempts to deal with the spread of slavery at different times. However, attempts such as the Missouri Compromise and the Compromise of 1850 never really solved the problem. All they did was postpone facing the problem. Even today it's easy for the Christian to react to sin much like Americans reacted to slavery. Some go on the defensive; some blame others; some ignore the sin problem, hoping it will go away. Others make half-hearted attempts to solve the problem. But the sin problem returns, bigger than ever before, and haunts the Christian until it is squarely faced and resolved. Slavery was just like that on a national scale.

Uncle Tom's Cabin

The plight of slave families and run-aways was brought to public attention in a unique way in 1852. **Harriet Beecher Stowe,** a preacher's daughter from Connecticut, had lost a young son to cholera in 1849. Believing she now understood how slave mothers felt when their children were taken from them, she vowed to do something on their behalf.

Since the Stowe family had lived for a while in Cincinnati, Ohio, across the Ohio River from the slave state of Kentucky, Mrs. Stowe had glimpsed something of slavery and the plight of fugitive slaves. From 1850 to 1851 she submitted a novel in installments to the *National Era,* an antislavery paper. When the novel was released in book form, *Life Among the Lowly,* or **Uncle Tom's Cabin,** sold 300,000 copies within a year. Although the book seems emotional and artificial to us today, *Uncle Tom's Cabin* became one of the most influential existing political parties. As soon as the **Kansas-Nebraska Act** passed, both pro-slavery and antislavery groups urged their supporters to go west. Naturally the two sides clashed, especially in Kansas, where open fighting took place between those supporting each side. The territory soon earned the nickname *Bleeding Kansas*. The bloodshed there was a foretaste of what would soon happen nationwide.

The Founding of the Republican Party

By 1852 the Whig Party had split into two factions over the slavery issue—the Cotton and the Conscience Whigs. After the passage of the Kansas-Nebraska Act, the Cotton Whigs joined with southern Democrats because of their stand for slavery. The Conscience Whigs and northern Democrats, angered by the Kansas-Nebraska Act, now joined with Free Soilers, those against the spread of slavery to new lands. In 1854 these antislavery groups formed a new political party, the **Republican Party.** The party grew with startling speed, electing Congressmen its first year. In 1856 John C. Frémont became the first Republican to run for president. He was defeated, however, by the Democratic candidate, **James Buchanan.**

pieces of propaganda ever written. The story reached an even wider audience when performing troupes of actors toured the country giving it as a play. Soon the tragic sufferings of Little Eva and of the slaves Uncle Tom and Eliza tugged at the heart-strings of readers and audiences. The novel rallied antislavery opinion in the North, but the implication that southern society was evil naturally angered Southerners. The book was soon banned in the South.

The Kansas-Nebraska Act

When Kansas and Nebraska sought acceptance as new territories, the government again faced the slavery issue. Senator Stephen Douglas applied the idea of popular sovereignty to these territories in 1854. The Illinois senator designed a compromise dealing with these western lands that allowed the settlers there to decide for or against slavery for themselves. Feelings ran so deep, however, that the bill produced rifts in the

Top: *Harriet Beecher Stowe, author of* Uncle Tom's Cabin
Bottom: *Schoolhouse in Ripon, Wisconsin, where the first meeting of the Republican party was held in 1854*

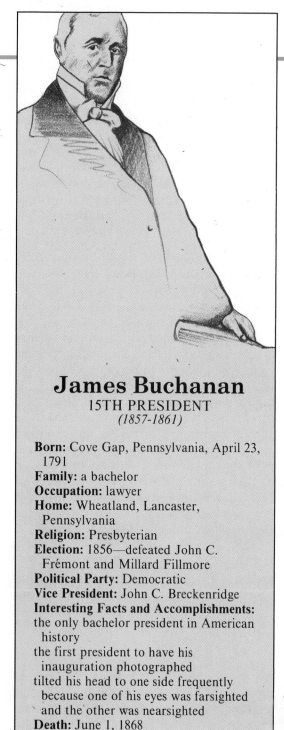

James Buchanan
15TH PRESIDENT
(1857-1861)

Born: Cove Gap, Pennsylvania, April 23, 1791
Family: a bachelor
Occupation: lawyer
Home: Wheatland, Lancaster, Pennsylvania
Religion: Presbyterian
Election: 1856—defeated John C. Frémont and Millard Fillmore
Political Party: Democratic
Vice President: John C. Breckenridge
Interesting Facts and Accomplishments:
the only bachelor president in American history
the first president to have his inauguration photographed
tilted his head to one side frequently because one of his eyes was farsighted and the other was nearsighted
Death: June 1, 1868

The Dred Scott Decision

For three years after the Kansas crisis, the nation experienced a relative calm. But two days after President Buchanan took office in 1857, the quiet ended when the question of the legal status of slavery in the territories came before the Supreme Court.

At stake was the freedom of an elderly black man, **Dred Scott.** Scott, born a slave, had been owned by an army doctor, John Emerson of Missouri. Emerson took Scott with him to military posts in the state of Illinois and to the Wisconsin territory, where slavery was outlawed. In 1838 Scott returned with Emerson to Missouri. After Emerson's death, local antislavery lawyers helped Scott sue Emerson's heirs for his freedom on the grounds that living on free soil had made him free. Finally the case reached the Supreme Court, where the chief justice at that time was Roger B. Taney, a Southerner.

The majority of the court ruled against Scott, and Taney stated that since Scott was a slave and black, he was not a citizen. Hence, he had no right to sue in the nation's courts. Further, Taney ruled that Scott was not free as a result of having lived on free soil. Taney reasoned that the Fifth Amendment forbade the government from depriving a person of life, liberty, or property without due process of law. He ruled that the Missouri Compromise had deprived citizens north of 36° 30′ of property, their slaves, and was thus invalid.

The consequences of the **Dred Scott decision** were serious. The South temporarily rejoiced in the fact that slavery had been upheld and could lawfully expand into new territories. The Supreme Court, however, had made the national conflict more

Dred Scott

serious. Politically the decision wrecked any chance for future political compromise. The Republican stand against the spread of slavery into new territories had suffered a setback, but antislavery forces were not to be quieted. Now the question of slavery expansion lay in the hands of the new settlers who would vote on it. No one knew if the North or the South would be willing to abide by the outcome in the West.

Loss of the Compromisers

Compromise to solve problems became even less likely after the men who had accomplished it in earlier years died. Henry Clay, John C. Calhoun, and Daniel Webster, giants of the first half of the century, were all dead by 1852. Most of their successors had less experience, less wisdom, and less patience. Men such as Millard Fillmore, Franklin Pierce, Stephen Douglas, and James Buchanan were not strong enough leaders to provide needed and acceptable solutions to the nation's problems.

John Brown: Slavery's Avenger

One settler who set out for Kansas to aid antislavery forces was **John Brown.** An unstable man with little schooling, Brown had failed at many business ventures, including farming, tanning, land speculation, and stock breeding. His intense hatred for slavery, however, led him to become a fanatical leader and a martyr for the antislavery cause.

Brown wanted to do great harm to slaveholders, to "smite them for God." As is typical of some extremists, Brown used Scripture wrongly to justify his acts. He often quoted Hebrews 9:22—"Without shedding of blood is no remission," implying that the verse meant that slaveholders would pay for the sin of slavery with their blood. Despite his wild temper, he won a following. "Wherever he spoke, his words commanded earnest attention," said black abolitionist Frederick Douglass. "His arguments seemed to convince all; his appeals touched all, and his will impressed all."

Brown's first effort in his war against slavery was waged at Pottawatomie (PAHT uh WAHT uh mee), Kansas in 1856. In one night of terror, Brown and four of his seven sons butchered five proslavery men and added to the turmoil of "Bleeding Kansas."

His most daring move was an attempt to deliver a death blow against slavery. He armed a small band, including four of his own sons and two slaves he had freed, in an effort to free all the slaves. His plans were to raid a federal arsenal, or storage place for weapons, at Harper's Ferry, Virginia. On October 16, 1859, Brown and his twenty-one-man army rode into Harper's Ferry. They captured the watchman at the arsenal by surprise and took prominent local slave owners, including George Washington's great-grandnephew, as hostages. Brown thought this action would stir slaves into rebellion. He hoped that thousands of slaves would revolt and rally to him; no such revolt occurred.

Word of Brown's presence at Harper's Ferry leaked out. Soon military action was taken against him. Lt. Col. **Robert E. Lee,** home on leave in Virginia, was called into active service to put down the raid. He left for Harper's Ferry without even donning his uniform and commanded the Marine assault force in civilian garb.

Brown, injured in the raid, faced trial only ten days after his capture. Before and during the trial he won many admirers. The Virginia jury, however, convicted him of murder, and he was hanged. Southern whites now feared a slave revolt more than ever. Although the revolt never came, Brown's trial and death made him a martyr. Soon Yankee soldiers marched off to war singing: "John Brown's body lies a-mouldering in the grave, . . . His soul goes marching on."

Section Review

1. What famous novel prompted a wave of sympathy for the abolitionist cause? Who wrote the novel?
2. In what way did the Kansas-Nebraska Act foreshadow the conflict of the Civil War?
3. Who was Dred Scott?
4. What was the significance of the Dred Scott decision?
5. How did John Brown try to avenge slavery?

D. The Election of 1860 and Secession

The Election of 1860 was to have great consequence on the nation. The turmoil was displayed in the disruption of traditional ties in the political parties. The new regional bonds that formed were to remain for decades to come.

A Republican Victory

The South was clearly worried about the election of 1860. Southern extremists, called **fire-eaters,** threatened **secession,** to leave the Union, if the Republicans won. The views of the Republicans on almost all issues were in opposition to the interests of the South. Not only views on slavery, but also positions on states' rights and the tariff were placing the Republicans at odds with most Southerners.

The best chance for defeating the Republicans lay in the Democrats' picking a moderate candidate acceptable to both the South and the North. Illinois Senator Stephen Douglas was such a moderate. But in 1860 fire-eaters, who had undue influence, thought him their enemy. Rather than uniting to stand behind Douglas, the southern Democrats left the nominating convention. Their split foreshadowed the Civil War. The divided party led to a divided nation. The Democrats no longer accepted "compromise" presidents like Pierce or Buchanan. While the northern Democrats nominated Douglas, the Southerners chose **John C. Breckenridge** of Kentucky. Their **platform** (statement of what they stood for politically), based on the Dred Scott decision, called for Congress to enact a federal slave code to protect slavery in all the territories.

With the Democrats divided, the Republicans had real hopes for victory. In an effort the Constitutional Union party. They were trying to buy time, hoping that the fire-eaters would see there was no real future in their position.

Southerners believed that a Lincoln victory would put southern states at a disadvantage in Washington and might even spark more raids like John Brown's. They said that if Lincoln were elected, they would leave the Union and form their own nation. President Buchanan did nothing to discourage them.

Lincoln carried the northern and western states, enabling him to win more popular votes than any other candidate. Douglas came in second in popular votes, followed by Breckenridge and Bell. Lincoln's victory, however, was far from overwhelming. Douglas and Bell's vote total exceeded that of Lincoln's, and combined with the Breckenridge vote, these candidates won over sixty per cent of the vote. In addition, Lincoln had failed to carry a single southern state. The circumstances of the election put Lincoln at a disadvantage. Bell had carried the border states; so no one knew what side they would take in the secession controversy. If Lincoln had been able to take office right away, however, he might have been able to save the Union.

The Confederacy Takes Shape

Fearing that its rights as a state could not be maintained, South Carolina voted to leave the Union on December 20. The nation waited for President Buchanan to react. Although he believed secession was illegal, he was unwilling to use either his influence or force to halt it. Instead he left Lincoln to face the problem.

But before Lincoln could take office, other southern states called conventions.

to keep the Union intact, they chose a moderate rather than an abolitionist or Free Soiler. Their choice was an Illinois lawyer, **Abraham Lincoln.**

In the Illinois senate election in 1858, Lincoln had challenged Stephen Douglas, the Democratic candidate, to a series of seven debates. Although Douglas won the election, the debates gave Lincoln and his views public exposure. Although Lincoln was not an abolitionist and was not opposed to slavery where it already existed, he was against the spread of slavery to new territories. This stand, however, was not acceptable to the southern fire-eaters.

The Whigs from the border states of Delaware, Maryland, Virginia, and Kentucky were not eager to leave the Union. They decided to pick an alternate candidate, **John Bell** of Tennessee, who stood for staying in the Union. Their party was called

Campaign banner from the election of 1860

Abraham Lincoln
16TH PRESIDENT
(1861-1865)

Born: Hodgenville, Kentucky, February 12, 1809
Family: married Mary Todd; four sons
Occupation: lawyer
Home: Springfield, Illinois
Religion: no formal affiliation, attended a Presbyterian church
Elections: 1860—defeated Stephen Douglas, John C. Breckenridge, and John Bell
1864—defeated George McClellan
Political Party: Republican
Vice Presidents: Hannibal Hamlin—first term, Andrew Johnson—second term
Interesting Facts and Accomplishments:
largely self-educated
worked as a farmer, store clerk, and ferry pilot
first Republican to be elected to the presidency
lost an 1858 Senate race in Illinois to Stephen Douglas, but beat him in the presidential race two years later
only president to have a patent issued; invented a hydraulic device that could lift ships over shoals
Death: April 15, 1865; first president to die by assassination

Mississippi, Florida, Alabama, Georgia, Louisiana, and Texas all followed South Carolina's example. South Carolina summoned the other slaveholding states to a convention held in Montgomery, Alabama, on February 1, 1861.

Delegates from these seven states formed the **Confederate States of America.** They wrote their own constitution. It was like the American Constitution, except that it recognized the "sovereign and independent character" of the states and guaranteed states' rights. It also promised that no law against slavery could ever be passed, allowed cabinet members to take part in legislative debates, and gave the president a single six-year term.

Next, the Confederacy had to choose its leaders. Fire-eaters chose moderates, hoping to win the support of Southerners who were still unsure about splitting from the Union. **Jefferson Davis** from Mississippi became president. Alexander Stephens, a Georgian who had firmly opposed secession, took the vice-presidency.

The Confederacy sent out commissioners seeking to increase the size of the Confederacy. But the border and upper southern states took a "wait-and-see" position.

Section Review

1. Name the four presidential candidates in 1860 and their parties.
2. What was Lincoln's attitude toward slavery?
3. Which state was the first to leave the Union?
4. Who became president of the Confederacy?

E. Fort Sumter and War

The South, realizing that the Union was a voluntary organization of the states, believed that it could withdraw its membership in the Union by secession to form the Confederacy. Lincoln believed that secession was not possible—the Union was permanent, and no state could pull out once it had joined. The Civil War resulted to determine if the South's view or President Lincoln's view of the Union would prevail.

On March 4, 1861, Abraham Lincoln took office. In his inaugural address he appealed to the people, "In your hands, my dissatisfied fellow-countrymen, and not in mine, is the momentous issue of civil war." Lincoln held that the Union was still whole; it was, he held, indivisible and indissoluble (not able to be dissolved or split up). He hoped to reconcile the sections, but he would fight, if he had to, to preserve the Constitution and the Union. He stated that he would use the power of government "to hold, occupy, and possess the property and places belonging to the government."

By property Lincoln meant the two federal forts in the South where the Stars and Stripes still flew: Fort Pickens at Pensacola, Florida, and Fort Sumter in South Carolina's Charleston harbor. To retain control of these forts, however, it would be necessary to send them supplies.

Firing on Fort Sumter

In January South Carolina had already shown it was unlikely to allow the government to land supplies at the fort. When a merchant ship, *The Star of the West,* approached **Fort Sumter** with supplies and troops, it was fired on and was turned away.

Lincoln reasoned that if he let the Confederates have Fort Sumter, he would have to invade the South to preserve the Union, and an invasion would probably drive the border states into the Confederate fold. The

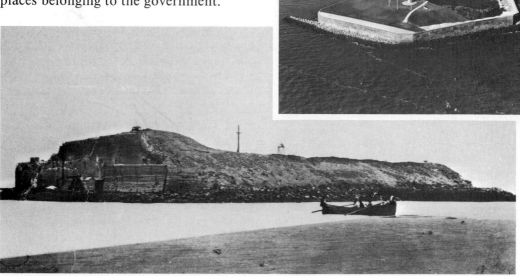

Bottom: *Fort Sumter, Charleston harbor, April 1865*
Top: *Fort Sumter today*

South might react to the Union's keeping its hold on Fort Sumter in one of two ways: either rejoining the Union or shelling the fort. If the Confederates shelled Sumter, they would be the ones who started the war. Then if Lincoln had to call for federal troops to quell the rebelling Confederates, his action could be defended.

Lincoln sent a note to F. W. Pickens, the governor of South Carolina, telling him that a supply ship but no troops would be coming to Sumter. (Lincoln chose to write Pickens, the lawful governor of the state, rather than Jefferson Davis. He held that writing Davis meant recognizing the Confederacy.) Pickens contacted Davis, who gave orders to prevent all efforts to resupply Fort Sumter. When the federal supply ship came to Charleston harbor on April 12, 1861, the batteries (rows of guns) in Charleston harbor fired on the fort. After enduring a forty-hour Confederate bombardment, the Union troops surrendered the fort.

Across the Confederacy church bells rang and people celebrated. A pastor in Charleston confidently told his flock that "Providence is fast uniting the whole South in a common brotherhood of sympathy and action, and our first essay in arms has been crowned with perfect success."

The Call for Troops

Lincoln, meanwhile, sent out a call for 75,000 troops. Any reluctant border or southern states now had to take sides. Davis was especially eager to have Virginia join the Confederacy because it was the South's most populous and richest state. Virginia joined, as did Arkansas and Tennessee, although neither was especially eager to do so. Since North Carolina was now encircled by Confederate states, it was forced to join the Confederacy.

The people in fifty counties of western Virginia had long resented the tidewater area's greater influence in their state. This was their chance to strike back. They boldly set up their own state government and sought statehood. Since Virginia had left the Union, they held that they hardly needed her permission to become a state. In 1863 West Virginia came into the Union.

Lincoln took action to keep the four border slave states (Kentucky, Missouri, Delaware, and Maryland) in the Union. People in these states were divided in their loyalties. Some favored secession while others wanted to stay in the Union.

If Kentucky had become Confederate (and it did have a Confederate governor for a time), the North's access to the Ohio River would have been threatened. Its population, lukewarm to the Confederacy, was kept in the Union through persuasion and force. In Missouri, Union troops moved to key areas, preventing secession there. Missourians against the Union were carefully isolated and ignored, except when ruffian bands carried on warfare within the state.

There was little concern about Delaware, whose culture and location aligned her with other Middle Atlantic States more than with the South. But Maryland presented a real problem. If it joined the Confederate camp, Washington, D.C., could end up there, too. Lincoln sent federal troops to Maryland and then closed bridges keeping others out. Potential Confederate leaders were held against their will. Lincoln justified his actions, the use of martial or military law, since a grave emergency existed. Maryland had little choice but to stay in the Union.

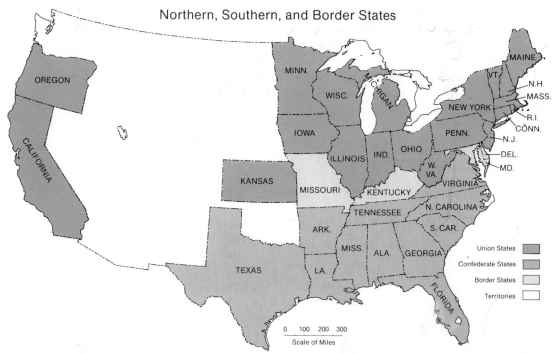

Northern, Southern, and Border States

Union States
Confederate States
Border States
Territories

0 100 200 300
Scale of Miles

Northern Advantages

Looking at the resources available to the North and the South, it's obvious that the North had a great advantage. The North had both the means and the manpower to industrialize. This tremendous industrial capacity was the Union's most significant advantage, even more so as the war wore on. The South produced only ten per cent of the nation's manufactured goods, and had only 110,000 industrial workers. The North, meanwhile, had 120,000 factories. Consequently, the South had to buy overseas what it could not produce at home. Only at the outset of the war would she have the capital and the freedom to do this. The lack of southern sea power to maintain its trade routes would soon greatly hinder its war effort. In addition, the North was adding 300,000 immigrants a year to its population, almost as many as the total number of northern troops killed in the entire war.

Why the South Stood a Chance

With so many disadvantages, why did the South believe it could win? First, the southern goal was a simple one: to set up and to maintain a separate independent nation, the Confederate States of America. To do this, the South did not need to conquer the North; it had only to defend its own territory. Also, the South was immense. The North would need long supply lines to attack and hold so vast an area.

Second, the average Southerner was more deeply involved in the war than was the average Northerner. The Southerner was fighting for his home and way of life. The Northerner, perhaps an immigrant, was

General Robert E. Lee

Robert E. Lee, the son of Lighthorse Harry Lee, a hero in the War for Independence, went to West Point. There Lee's behavior and academic excellence soon placed him at the top of his class. During the Mexican War Lee distinguished himself for bravery and leadership. After the Mexican War, Lee continued in the service, and while home in Virginia on leave, the army called on him to lead the small force that recaptured Harper's Ferry from John Brown and his group of fanatics.

When the Civil War broke out, Lee had a choice to make. His stand on slavery was well documented: "Slavery as an institution is a moral and political evil in any country." Yet, he was a loyal Virginian. His dilemma was increased when he was offered the position of commander-in-chief of the Union army. Torn between loyalties, Lee decided for Virginia and was appointed commander of the Army of Northern Virginia. His methods were unconventional, but brilliant. Constantly outnumbered, he managed time and again to defeat the northern armies. Only the tenacity of U. S. Grant and the Union's numerical supremacy in men and equipment eventually defeated Lee.

After the war Lee accepted the presidency of Washington College—now Washington and Lee. His presidency was an enormous success as the college grew and prospered. He was buried at a site on the university campus. The South greatly loved and honored him; the North also highly esteemed him. He is, perhaps, history's most admired losing general.

supposedly "fighting for the Union." The North would lose if its people lost the desire to stay on the offensive. It could win only when it destroyed the Confederate desire and ability to fight.

Third, the Confederacy believed it would get foreign help. Since it was the source of much of Britain's cotton, the Confederacy believed that the British would be at least sympathetic, if not supportive.

Fourth, the South had an almost endless coastline. Even though the Confederacy had no real navy at the start, the North would need thousands of ships to block the entire coast from supply ships.

Fifth, the Confederacy believed its soldiers were better. Confederates had little respect for Yankees as fighting men, and the South did have better commanders, at least in the beginning. Most of the Confederate

Left to right: *General Robert E. Lee; the "Stars and Bars," the Confederate battleflag; and a Confederate veteran's reunion medal*

In 1960 as Dwight D. Eisenhower's second term neared its end, the president received a critical letter from a citizen. The citizen was upset that a picture of Robert E. Lee, a Confederate, was included among the Eisenhower mementos in the White House. Eisenhower had gained an interest in Lee as a fellow graduate of West Point. This was Eisenhower's reply to the citizen:

The White House
Washington, DC
August 18, 1960

Dear Dr. Scott:

General Robert E. Lee was, in my estimation, one of the supremely gifted men produced by our nation. He believed unswervingly in the constitutional validity of his cause, which until 1865 was still an arguable question in America; he was a poised and inspiring leader, true to the high trust reposed in him by millions of his fellow citizens. . . .

From deep conviction, I simply say this: A nation of men of Lee's calibre would be unconquerable in spirit and soul. Indeed, to the degree that present-day American youth will strive to emulate his painstaking efforts to help heal the nation's wounds once the bitter struggle was over, we, in our time of danger in a divided world, will be strengthened and our love of freedom sustained.

Such are the reasons I proudly display the picture of the great American on my office wall.

Dwight D. Eisenhower

officers were well trained; many were West Point graduates. And no one argued about Robert E. Lee's abilities. Lee had been Lincoln's first choice to be commander-in-chief of the Union armies. But because he believed that his duty was to his native state of Virginia, Lee declined. President Lincoln, on the other hand, had to go through seven different commanders before finding the one who could win the war, Ulysses S. Grant.

Section Review

1. What part did Fort Sumter play in the growing conflict between the North and South?
2. What state in particular did Jefferson Davis want to join the Confederacy?
3. What advantages did the North have over the South?
4. What factors gave the South a fighting chance despite the North's advantages?

Summary

Political issues of the early 1800s came to a boil in the 1850s. The North's and South's differing views on states' rights, the tariff, slavery, and other topics led to great controversy. When Abraham Lincoln won the 1860 election for the Republicans, the South lost hope for a continued federal government tolerant of its views. The South then broke its ties with the Union by seceding. Whether the South could secede from the Union was the issue that would pull the nation into the Civil War. With the firing on Fort Sumter in April of 1861, the war had begun.

Chapter Review

Do You Remember?

■ Fill in the blanks in the paragraph below with the following terms or names. Not all will be used.

Middle Passage	John Brown
emancipation	Frederick Douglass
abolitionists	William Lloyd Garrison
compensated emancipation	Dred Scott
Underground Railroad	Harriet Beecher Stowe
Uncle Tom's Cabin	Harriet Tubman

As the problem of slavery troubled America, __(1)__ began to work to put an end to slavery. They wanted __(2)__ for the slaves, although some supported the idea of __(3)__ , reimbursing the slaveholders for their loss. __(4)__ was a vocal supporter of abolitionism in Boston where he published a paper called *The Liberator*. Other abolitionists helped runaway slaves follow the __(5)__ to freedom in the North or in Canada. __(6)__ was an escaped slave, who helped many other slaves follow that route. Another influence against slavery was the book, __(7)__, written by __(8)__. __(9)__ , a black abolitionist, also spoke out against slavery in speeches and publications. The most daring antislavery action was probably that taken by __(10)__ , who tried to spark a slave rebellion by capturing a federal arsenal.

■ Define the following terms.

11. fire-eaters
12. secession
13. party platform

▪ Make two columns on your paper. Over one write *United States of America,* and over the other write *Confederate States of America.* Then answer these questions for each.

14. Who became its president in 1861?
15. Who was its leading general?
16. What advantages did it have as the war began?
17. What disadvantages did it have as the war began?

Why Is It So?

1. How was life in the North and South different?
2. How were the political views of the North and South different?
3. Why were Southerners afraid of the Republican party?
4. Why was the Dred Scott decision important?
5. Why did the Republicans win the 1860 presidential election?
6. Why did Lincoln try to keep control of Fort Sumter?

What Do You Think?

1. Why was slavery a difficult problem for Americans to deal with?
2. What do you suppose would have happened if southern Democrats had supported Stephen Douglas in the 1860 election? Why?

Reading Graphs

As we consider the conditions of the North and the South at the time of the Civil War, we realize that there are many important differences between the resources of the two sections. Reading statements about those differences may be very helpful, but such information becomes more understandable when we see it as a picture. Graphs help us in this way by presenting numeric differences in picture form.

Another kind of picture graph illustrates the fact that the North had much more money in its banks than did the South.

A very simple picture graph may use a difference in the size of figures to show that the North had far more factories than the south.

A circle or pie graph shows the divisions of a whole. With this graph we notice that the South had less than one third the total railroad mileage of the North and South.

To compare the population of the North and South, we can easily use this bar graph to see that the North had a definite advantage in total population.

NORTH

SOUTH

A line graph can help us understand numerical changes over a length of time. With this line graph we see that the North had the advantage of more soldiers throughout the war.

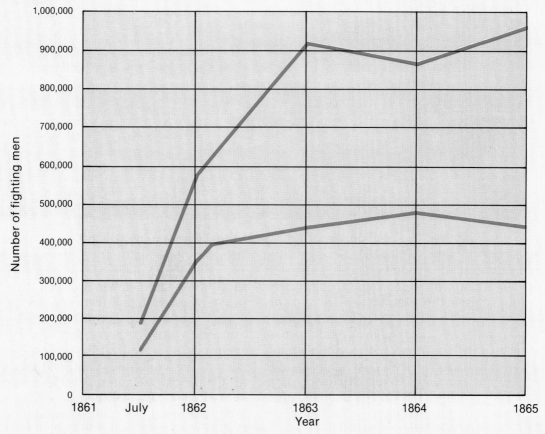

17

The Civil War

As war had loomed ahead after the election of Lincoln in 1860, Senator John Crittenden of Kentucky had led one last vain attempt to preserve the Union peacefully. Despite his passionate pleas and stirring speeches, Crittenden's compromise plan failed to win enough support to pass the Senate. The defeat became doubly bitter for Crittenden when his own family divided over the issue of secession. His son George became a major general in the Confederate army, while his son Thomas became a major general in the Union army. After George took his stand with the South, a newspaper editor who opposed Crittenden roundly criticized the senator for his son's action. The editor must have been embarrassed a short while later, however, when his own son went south to join the Confederacy.

All through the country families split over the war. Brother sometimes fought against brother and father against son in the four years of bloody conflict. In his plea for the Union, Lincoln echoed Jesus' words in Matthew 12:25—"A house divided against itself shall not stand." When families fought against each other, what hope could there be for the nation?

Late afternoon, Gettysburg National Battlefield

A. Gearing up for War

The firing on Fort Sumter in April of 1861 ignited the flame of civil war between North and South. Billy Yank and Johnny Reb were soon to struggle through the triumphs and tragedies of four years of bitter conflict. Not only the soldiers but also many civilian Americans came to know the hardships and the death and destruction that was part of this war to save the Union.

Turning Men into Soldiers

Thousands of young recruits, responding to the patriotic fervor, joined the armies. Union recruits poured into Washington, D.C., or newly built camps in the West. At the same time southern patriots were gathering in Confederate camps.

Life in the camps, however, was far from exciting. A soldier spent sixty per cent of his time in camp, thirty per cent marching or bivouacking (BIV WAK ing; camping temporarily in the open air), and only five per cent of his time fighting. Some soldiers assigned to forts never fired a shot.

At the beginning of the war, both sides relied totally on volunteers. But soon volunteers became too scarce to supply the needed troops, and thus both Lincoln and Davis resorted to drafting men to fill their armies.

Raising Northern Forces—President Lincoln's Fourth of July message in 1861 called for 500,000 volunteers to enlist for three years. The next year Congress called "all able-bodied male citizens between the ages of eighteen and forty-five" into state militias. At this point drafting was a state function. Most of the states also offered a large sum of money, a bounty, for those who joined.

In March of 1863 Congress passed a law drafting a national army. The North had a harder time motivating the people to join its forces. While the South could appeal to the men to protect their own land and honor, the North's cause of fighting to preserve a nation was not so personal. This lack of personal concern for the northern cause led many northern men to join the army reluctantly or halfheartedly.

All men between the ages of twenty and forty-five were subject to regular army service. Those who were physically or mentally unfit were exempted, as were certain office-holders. A draftee was also allowed to hire a substitute or to pay $300 for an exemption. (Recent immigrants, who were not subject to the draft, often served as substitutes to earn money.) The system did not work well. At first over twice as many men bought substitutes as entered the army themselves. Others ran away from service. Furthermore, the law caused ill will. Believing that the new draft law was unfair, penniless Irish immigrants, already harmed by runaway wartime inflation, rioted for four days in New York City. The rioters' hatred was vented on local blacks. The mob resented that they were being drafted to free the blacks while blacks stayed home. Most of the 128 people killed in the riot were black.

Raising Southern Forces—The South had more of a fighting spirit than the North. Further, some of West Point's best students had been Southerners. One-third of all West Pointers joined the Confederate command, providing able leadership for that army.

At the outset the South had no problem getting enough men to fight. In fact, there were more volunteers than the South could equip and train. But such enthusiasm was short-lived. When the first one-year enlistments were up and no special benefits were

Since blacks were fighting for freedom for their own people and capture would mean almost certain enslavement, they had good reason to fight hard, harder perhaps, than some whites. Yet it wasn't until after the Emancipation Proclamation was issued and the number of northern recruits dwindled that blacks were allowed to join the army.

Black soldiers, however, were not treated the same as white soldiers. Until 1864 black soldiers served at lower wages than white soldiers. Blacks also had medical care far below the norm. As a result the death toll for blacks ran thirty-seven per cent higher than for whites. Blacks were also given the most mundane tasks. Because Northerners were unsure of how well blacks could lead, none were appointed as officers. Instead, black regiments had white officers.

In the South blacks served in the army in noncombatant (nonfighting) positions such as cooks, wagon drivers, laborers, and personal servants to officers. By March of 1865, however, when there was an extremely severe manpower shortage, the Confederate Congress passed a bill to draft 300,000 blacks. The first two black companies astounded southern whites with their skill at arms. But no blacks fought for the Confederacy; the southern war effort ended before blacks could take the field.

offered, the number of recruits declined. In April 1862, the South had to resort to drafting all men aged eighteen to thirty-five. Later the upper limit was extended to fifty, and men up to sixty-five could be placed in a home guard.

The southern system was not foolproof either. There were so many ways to get out of the war that a War Department clerk joked: "Our Bureau of Conscription ought to be called the Bureau of Exemptions." The most disputed feature of the law was the so-called "Twenty-Negro-Law," which exempted any planter or overseer with more than twenty slaves. Its supporters claimed that these men were needed at home to keep the blacks from rioting. But poor Southerners who were drafted resented this exemption for the rich. Understandably, when the southern army began losing, getting recruits became even more difficult.

Blacks in the War—As early as 1861, Indiana blacks offered to serve the Union.

Civilian Preparations

The Civil War was a total war; it involved both the military and civilians. Hardly anyone escaped at least some of its effects.

In the North—The North had begun to widen its industrial base even before the war. The North drew its workers from among women, who were new to the work force, and from a pool of 800,000 immi-

Private James Allen Oakes, 38th Virginia Infantry, C.S.A., died at Gettysburg from wounds received in Pickett's Charge.

grants who came to America between 1861 and 1865. When war came, uniforms, boots, shoes, hats, blankets, tents, rifles, swords, cannon, revolvers, ammunition, wagons, canned foods, lumber, shovels, steamboats, and surgical instruments all went from northern factories into the war effort.

Industrialism also had a positive effect on farm production. Even though thousands of men left their farms to fight in the war, farm production did not decline. Instead, as the demand for food products increased, farmers began to mechanize. As many harvesters, reapers, and mowers were bought in one year as had been bought in the previous decade. In addition to feeding the northern army, these farms began to feed Europeans. For example, forty per cent of England's wheat and flour now came from the North.

The war also made private volunteer groups stronger. Private groups, sometimes called commissions, helped to purchase medicines and to supply Bibles and other reading materials. These commissions sent money home to a soldier's family and even secured food, shelter, and clothing for slaves who had fled from behind Confederate lines.

In the South—In the first months of the war, life changed little for most Southerners. Confident of their cause, they believed they would win and win quickly. Early victories at Fort Sumter and Bull Run seemed to confirm that belief. As the war continued, however, life began to change. The Union navy kept many needed imports from arriving in the South, and the small number of southern factories could not produce enough materials to supply the South and its armies. Soon there were severe shortages of some goods. Southerners also had to pay high prices for what goods they could get.

Coffee, tea, sugar, butter, lard, flour, and fresh fruits became expensive. Then such things disappeared altogether, along with household items such as candles and oil.

Substitutions became common. Okra seeds, rye, sweet potatoes, and even peanuts were used to make coffee. As the need for medicines grew, the woods became the South's medicine chest. For example, Southerners could no longer import quinine to treat malaria, a disease that was a problem in swampy areas; so a less effective mixture of red pepper, table salt, and tea took its place.

Since cotton could be neither sold nor eaten, Jefferson Davis waged a crusade to get planters and farmers to grow corn. One Georgia newspaper said: "Plant corn and be free, or plant cotton and be whipped!" *Corn* and *patriotism* became synonyms.

Farmers and planters often struggled more than others. The Confederate government took livestock, mules, horses, and carriages as well as tools and buckets for the war effort. Southerners had to use what they had available or do without. The longer the war lasted, the greater was the sacrifice required.

As real and counterfeit currency flooded the South, inflation occurred. Prices soared. By 1864 bacon sold at $20.00 a pound and flour for $100 a barrel. Some people used a barter system, trading goods for food. To fight inflation and provide needed war materials, the South used **taxes in kind.** Such taxes required the producers to send one-tenth of their products—hogs, corn, or whatever—directly to the Confederacy.

Southern farmers did produce enough food. But hampered by a poor transportation system, they could not always get it to those who needed it.

Military Methods

Because of the development of industry and technology and because of improved weapons, tactics, and strategies, the Civil War was really the first modern war.

Modern Warfare—For the first time the army was able to use the railroad to move goods and soldiers from place to place. In addition, the government could use the telegraph for its communications. Almost every evening before President Lincoln went to bed, he walked over to the War Department to read the war dispatches from the front lines. The telegraph helped him to make military decisions and to stay in close contact with his generals.

Mines, trench warfare, wire barricades, and other methods of fighting or hindering the enemy were put to use. Rifled guns and cannon were also used. These weapons spin the bullet or shell as it is fired to give it a straighter path, thus making it more accurate in hitting its intended target.

Tactics of the war progressed on land, in the sea, and also in the air. Much use was made of cavalry (mounted troops) for reconnaissance, or information gathering.

On the sea, ironclad ships proved their superiority in warfare. The fight between the *Monitor,* a Union ironclad, and the *Merrimac,* a Confederate ironclad, was decisive in the future of fighting vessels. Balloons were first used in the Civil War for observing troop movements. In that way aerial reconnaissance began even before the invention of the airplane.

Images of the Civil War, its death and destruction, linger with us today because of another innovation of that time—photography. Photography had developed twenty years before, but its use had been limited. Only a few photographs were taken of wars in the 1840s and 50s. In addition, the complicated processes and the large expenses involved in early photography prohibited its common use.

By the time of the Civil War, however, photography was becoming less expensive

Top: *Union sailors on the deck of the* Monitor
Bottom: *A lithograph of the* Monitor

and more common. Many soldiers had their pictures taken for their families or sweethearts. Photographers also followed the troops and captured images of war. One of these photographers was **Mathew Brady,** who kept his darkroom with him in a horse-drawn wagon. His many scenes of the war continue to offer revealing glimpses of that time of conflict.

Northern and Southern Strategy—As the South faced the task of making the North accept its independence, the North proceeded to show the South that the Union would not be dissolved. As each side approached its objective, it developed a strategy for winning the war that consisted of a few basic goals. Whichever side could accomplish its goals would emerge as the victor.

Confederate Strategy
1. Break the blockade.
2. Gain recognition from Britain and France. Cut off cotton shipments to Britain so that it would recognize its dependence on the South.
3. Fight a defensive battle.

Union Strategy
1. Impose a naval blockade to shut off southern ports from foreign trade and thus strangle the Confederate economy.
2. Take control of the Mississippi River, splitting the Confederacy in two and cutting off the states west of the Mississippi from their sister states.
3. Take Richmond, the new Confederate capital.
4. Protect Washington, D.C.

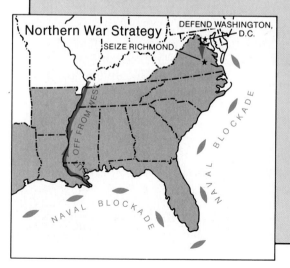

Northern War Strategy
DEFEND WASHINGTON, D.C.
SEIZE RICHMOND
CUT OFF FROM WEST
NAVAL BLOCKADE
NAVAL BLOCKADE

Section Review
1. Why was the draft initiated?
2. List several sacrifices that Southerners were forced to make as a result of the war.
3. List several factors that made the Civil War the first "modern war."
4. Compare and contrast the northern and southern strategies in the war.

Mathew Brady specialized in taking Civil War photographs such as the one above.

B. Marching into Battle

The fervor for war was on. After Fort Sumter Northerners were eager for something to happen. But the Union Army, under seventy-five-year-old Winfield Scott, was made up of rough, untried recruits. Since many Northerners believed they had a decided edge and could win the war and be home before harvest, the pressure to attack Richmond grew greater. Richmond, the Confederate capital, lay only about one hundred miles away from Washington, D.C. The press cried "On to Richmond!" so loudly and so often that Congress soon joined the refrain.

First Battle of Bull Run

In July 1861, the Union army moved south, now led by General **Irvin McDowell,** a good strategist from West Point. A Confederate force was encamped twenty miles to the south of Washington, D.C., at Manassas, Virginia, and McDowell planned to capture it. Congressmen, their wives, and northern journalists followed McDowell's forces down the Centreville Turnpike to admire "the greatest army in the world."

The Confederates learned of this advance, and Jefferson Davis ordered General Joseph E. Johnston to leave the Shenandoah Valley and come to aid the troops at Bull Run Creek.

At the outset Union troops fought well. The Confederate Army gave ground and appeared to be retreating. But the brigade under the command of **Thomas Jackson** stood fast against the attack. (This action won Jackson the nickname "Stonewall.") Newly arriving Confederate troops then staged a southern counterattack, which forced the Union to retreat. The orderly retreat turned into a rout when a small

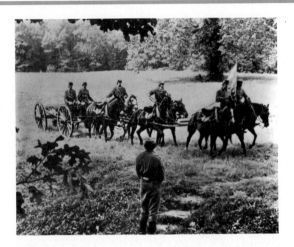

Confederate force attacked some troops on the turnpike and they panicked. Instead of having supper in Richmond, the Union soldiers threw down their guns and canteens and ran for Washington. Dazed Congressmen and reporters joined the exodus. In the resulting chaos, Washington was left unprotected, but the Confederate forces were just as disorganized as the Union troops, and they could not follow up their great victory.

Results of the First Battle

The **battle of Bull Run** (also called Manassas) affected both sides. The North realized that their troops were not yet ready to fight. **George B. McClellan** was called to the White House. Lincoln placed him in charge of all federal troops protecting Washington and told him to forge a new army to take Richmond. McClellan soon turned the army into a well-drilled machine. The troops sang: "For McClellan's our leader, he is gallant and strong! For God and our country, we are marching along." Meanwhile, the South had won so easily, just as Southerners had expected, that Bull Run made them overconfident.

Confederate soldiers moving a piece of artillery

Hesitation and Loss for the North

The North's goal of taking Richmond proved to be difficult. Slow progress in this "War in the East" frustrated Lincoln and most of the Union. Although McClellan claimed he needed more men and more time, Lincoln decided that McClellan had had enough time to ready the army.

McClellan finally tried a new approach. His army sailed down the Potomac River around the Virginia peninsula and debarked between the James and York rivers. Since the Confederacy had spent less time fortifying that area, McClellan chose to attack there.

Joseph E. Johnston, the Confederate commander, was caught totally off guard. That should have been to McClellan's advantage, but McClellan, believing he needed more men to win, stalled.

McClellan's troubles were only beginning. Because the Confederate commander, Johnston, was wounded in an indecisive battle at Fair Oaks, the Confederacy got a new commander for the Army of Northern Virginia, Robert E. Lee. Although his troops were outnumbered, Lee knew his men, his resources, and the area. In seven days (hence

the name Seven Days' Battle), Lee and Jackson attacked McClellan in five different places, and won every time. McClellan had been nine miles from Richmond on June 25th. Seven days later he was trying to pull his army out of the endless swamps that Lee had mired him in. McClellan's hasty retreat left twenty-five hundred sick and wounded soldiers behind in a field hospital.

Back to Bull Run

Lincoln quickly changed Union commanders and ordered McClellan back to Washington to join John Pope in a new land attack. But Lee decided the Confederacy could beat Pope before he gained strength.

Lee left half his force in Richmond and sent the other half north to keep John Pope busy. Meanwhile, J.E.B. Stuart, a dashing cavalry officer, raided Pope's headquarters

Left: *General George B. McClellan (fifth from the left) and his staff*
Right: *Confederate generals Thomas J. "Stonewall" Jackson, Joseph E. Johnston, and Robert E. Lee*

while Pope was gone. Seeking revenge because his favorite hat had been lost to Yankees in a skirmish several days before, Stuart collected Pope's war chest of $300,000, his dress coat, and the dispatch book that told where Union forces would be going. Of course, this gave Lee the offensive advantage he needed.

As the armies of the North and South converged, they took their stand once more on the battlegrounds of Bull Run. Stonewall Jackson's foot soldiers raced to aid Lee, covering sixty-two miles in less than forty-eight hours. The two day fight, the **Second battle of Bull Run** (Manassas Junction), ended with the Union troops back in Washington. Jackson said that the day had been won "by nothing but the blessing and protection of Providence." A disgraced Pope was sent off to Minnesota to fight Indians, and he was replaced by McClellan, who was now given a second chance.

This was probably the high tide of the Confederacy. Lee had defeated the army that faced him and the relief army that had come to aid them and had successfully switched the locale of fighting from Richmond back to Washington where it would do more damage to the Union than to the Confederacy.

Section Review

1. Why was the First battle of Bull Run significant?
2. What key city was the Union army striving to conquer?
3. What proved to be a major flaw in McClellan's leadership?
4. What exceptional Confederate leader overcame McClellan in the Seven Days' Battle?
5. What were the results of the Second battle of Bull Run?

C. Controlling the Waters

Two goals of the Union forces involved shutting off the South's major water transportation links. The North achieved these objectives with a minimum of delay and a better demonstration of leadership.

The Union Blockade

On April 17, 1861, only a few days after the fall of Fort Sumter, the Confederacy permitted privately owned ships to be outfitted to capture Union vessels. Two days later Lincoln issued orders for a naval **blockade** of the southern coast from South Carolina around to the Mexican border. Later he extended it northward to the Potomac River. Because of the shortage of ships, however, it was difficult at first for the Union to maintain a successful blockade. But the Secretary of the Navy started a giant ship-buying program, leasing or purchasing just about anything big enough to be armed. Once ready, the North concentrated the blockade on ten major southern ports, each of which had inland connections by rail or river.

The South tried to overcome the blockade with **blockade runners.** Because the runners had shallow drafts (little of the ship extended below the water line) they could dart into shallow inlets for cover. Since the Union ships needed deeper water to operate, they could not follow them. Runner ships had low profiles and were usually painted dull gray to blend with the seas. Most of them were steam-powered, and some could do eighteen knots (27 m.p.h.), enabling them to outrun any Union vessel. Their powerful engines burned hard coal because its smoke was less noticeable.

The easiest ports for blockade runners were those with more than one outlet, such as Wilmington, North Carolina. From these ports the out-going runners, loaded with cotton, usually headed south to British-held islands; Bermuda and the Bahama Islands were only about three days away. The goods were then shifted to ocean-going freighters that flew the flags of neutral countries. To overcome their ship and manpower shortage, the Confederates hired British ships and young captains from the Royal Navy. The chance for wealth made it worth the risks; a captain could make $5,000 in gold for one round trip, and the lowest crewman, $250. The Confederates made more than 8,500 successful trips through the blockade. Even in the closing months of the war, there was an even chance of evading the blockade.

In 1861 the chances of slipping through the blockade were high. Nine of every ten southern ships got through. But as the months went by, the Union increased its efforts. As various ports fell into Yankee hands, the blockade had more land bases to make it even more successful. In the spring of 1865, thirty-five fully laden runners carrying $15 million worth of goods sat in Nassau harbor with no ports of call open on the southern coast. Their provisions would never reach the starving South.

Although its effective rate at the war's end was only fifty per cent, the blockade took a huge toll on the Confederacy. In three years the South went from exporting ten million bales of cotton a year to shipping only one million bales. Drained of income, the South had to issue money backed only by faith in a cause. Its credit was undermined, and the foreign products it desperately needed became nearly unattainable, its foreign trade decreasing by two-thirds. While the outcome of the war was not decided on the blockade line but on the battlefield, it would have been a far different war if the Union navy had not guarded the southern coast.

Taking the Mississippi

The "War in the West" centered on the North's goal of gaining control of the Mississippi River. With control of the river, the North could separate Texas, Arkansas, and Louisiana and their resources from the rest of the Confederacy. They could also eliminate southern use of the important riverway and take advantage of its transportation opportunities for the Union. Instrumental in achieving this goal was the leadership of a Union officer named **Ulysses S. Grant.**

General Ulysses S. Grant

The Mississippi River Campaign, 1862-63

his troops moved down to the Tennessee border and captured two forts, Fort Henry and Fort Donelson. These forts defended the key waterways, and their fall, followed by the capture of Corinth and the battle of Shiloh in April, 1862, meant that the Union had control of the upper Mississippi and access to points south. The capture of these forts also made Grant a hero.

Gaining the Lower Mississippi—Next on the Union war agenda was gaining control of the lower Mississippi to prevent Confederate use of it. Two Confederate forts on a peninsula guarded the river. The Confederacy had also stretched two huge link chains across the Mississippi. The chains would be lifted to permit Confederate vessels to pass by and then lowered to snag any others that might try.

David Glasgow Farragut, a naval officer, devised a plan that with the aid of a land force, led by General Benjamin Butler, would take New Orleans. Farragut decided to bypass the forts and head for New Orleans. Under cover of night, an advance party unhooked the chains, and Farragut's fleet slipped past the forts despite heavy fire from the Confederates. Once past the forts, he scattered and disabled the Confederate fleet. New Orleans fell two days later. Butler's troops remained there to keep it under Federal control.

The Union navy then began moving up river, occupying first Baton Rouge, Louisiana, and then Natchez, Mississippi. By July of 1863 Federals had won control of the entire Mississippi River, except for a small area around Vicksburg, Mississippi, a prime Union target.

Vicksburg—Control of the Mississippi eluded the North because the Confederacy held **Vicksburg,** built high on the bluffs

Gaining the Upper Mississippi—Grant, who had given up soldiering earlier and had since failed at farming and business, rejoined the army in Illinois. He believed that the key to success west of the Appalachians was control of the Tennessee and Cumberland rivers. (These rivers emptied into the Ohio River, which in turn flowed to the Mississippi.) Leaving Cairo, Illinois, he and overlooking the river. Six times Confederate General Joseph Pemberton had repelled Union attacks on Vicksburg, each time inflicting heavy Union casualties.

Grant sought a new angle of attack. He designed a strategy that broke his army away from its own supply line. Grant announced his forces would "carry what rations of hard bread, coffee, and sort we can, and make the country furnish the balance." In a move that shocked Pemberton, Grant moved east to cut Confederate rail access to Vicksburg. Pemberton moved to cut off Grant's supply line only to find Grant had none. When Pemberton returned to Vicksburg, he was caught in a trap without an escape route. Now Grant could starve out Pemberton in the city. For six weeks, around the clock, the Union shelled Vicksburg. Short of goods, the people resorted to eating mules, rats, and even their own pets. Finally, with no food and no hope of relief, the Confederates surrendered Vicksburg. The date was July 4, 1863. It had taken Grant eighteen months to capture the Mississippi. A rising Union commander, William T. Sherman, had called it the "spinal column of America."

Section Review

1. Why was it initially difficult for the Union to maintain a successful naval blockade?
2. Why were the southern blockade runners so successful?
3. What did Grant believe to be the key to military success west of the Appalachians?
4. What Union naval officer was responsible for breaking through the Confederate chain in the lower Mississippi?
5. Why was the capture of Vicksburg by the Union army so significant?

D. The War in the East

While Grant found quick success in the West, the Union forces slowly moved from defeat to victory in the East. In September of 1862, Lee decided to take the offensive and move into Maryland, hoping to free it from Union control. Since it was early fall, the move would also free farmers in the rich granary of the Confederacy to harvest their crops. Moreover, Lee had reason to believe that a successful southern offensive would bring Britain in on the Confederate side.

Antietam

Lee divided his army, sending Jackson into the Shenandoah Valley. J.E.B. Stuart's cavalry was left behind to halt any Union attempts at pursuit. McClellan would have had little idea where Lee had planned to attack had it not been for an amazing discovery.

When McClellan was moving across an area recently vacated by Confederates, a Union corporal and a sergeant picked up three cigars. Wrapped around the cigars was a dispatch from Lee that a courier had lost, giving Lee's location and making it obvious that his army was divided. Using the information, McClellan moved to force Lee into a battle before Jackson could reach him. Lee found out about the lost dispatch less than twenty-four hours later and planned to pull back across the Potomac and change his strategy. But on September 17, 1862, McClellan's forces made massive attacks on Lee's lines. In one long ghastly day, three battles were fought. Just before dusk, though, Lee's reinforcements arrived. With one more attack McClellan might have defeated Lee, but the attack never came, only a stalemate. Rather than renewing the

The Eastern Campaigns, 1861-63

PENNSYLVANIA

New York

NEW
JERSEY

Sharpsburg
Antietam

Gettysburg

Philadelphia

Baltimore

Washington,
D.C.

Potomac

DEL.

Manassas
Bull Run

MD.

Shenandoah R.

Chancellorsville
Fredericksburg

Chesapeake Bay

1862

James R.

Richmond

York R.

Seven Days' Battle

Merrimac and
Monitor battle
inconclusively

1863

Union Movement

Confederate Movement

Union Victory

Confederate Victory

0   50   100

Scale of Miles

VIRGINIA

attack at daybreak, McClellan waited, permitting Lee to engineer an orderly retreat across the Potomac back into the safety of northern Virginia.

Since the Confederacy did not win at **Antietam** (an TEE tum), Britain stayed out of the war. Since the Union did not lose, Lincoln used the occasion to issue the Emancipation Proclamation.

Fredericksburg

Ambrose Burnside, the dashing officer Lincoln picked to replace McClellan, had no better success than his predecessor. On December 13, 1862, Burnside drove his refitted army across the Rappahanock to attack Confederates entrenched at Fredericksburg. Wave after wave of men failed to dislodge the Confederate forces, and the Union lost twice as many men as the Confederacy. Union morale dipped to the lowest point of the war. In twenty months the North had organized a grand army; yet no general seemed to be able to win with it. Lincoln now sent for "Fighting Joe" Hooker.

Chancellorsville

Hooker with 130,000 men now decided to strike Lee's army of 60,000 by going slightly west to **Chancellorsville.** The Union forces had an overwhelming advantage not only in numbers of men but also in supplies. An overconfident Hooker boasted, "May God have mercy on General Lee, for I will have none." Since the isolated crossroads was within easy reach of Richmond,

Lee risked a bold initiative. He split his army again and caught the Union by surprise. The battle, considered by many to be Lee's finest, raged for five days, and the fifth Union offensive for Richmond then failed.

Although the Confederate victory was probably the finest of the war, it cost the South dearly. The evening after the first day of battle, Stonewall Jackson was mortally wounded by some Confederate guards. In the darkness they failed to recognize Jackson, who was out scouting for information. When Lee heard of Jackson's wounds and the necessary amputation of his left arm, Lee sent word for Jackson to "make haste and get well, and come back to me as soon as he can. He has lost his left arm, but I have lost my right." However, Jackson died within the week. It was a loss that Lee and the Confederacy felt keenly. Because of his skill and unselfish cooperation, Jackson had been worth regiments to the Confederate cause.

Gettysburg

Buoyed by victory, Lee decided on a bold advance into Pennsylvania. This was his second and last invasion of the North. By capturing a Northern city like Harrisburg or Baltimore, Lee believed northern support for the war would be lost. He also thought that it would make Lincoln pull some troops out of the campaign along the Mississippi River and lessen pressure there. Lee also hoped his famished army could be resupplied as they passed through lush Pennsylvania farmlands.

Lee's Hopeful Advance—Lee started north early in June, going up the Shenandoah Valley, across the Potomac, across western Maryland, and then into Pennsylvania. Lincoln dispatched Hooker with an army of ninety thousand men to stop him, but Lee kept coming. In desperation, on June 28, Lincoln gave the army its fifth commander that year, George Gordon Meade. Although shy and scholarly, Meade was well qualified.

On July 1, Lee's advance troops came to a small town called **Gettysburg,** where they stopped to buy some badly needed shoes. There they unexpectedly met a Union scouting party. Both armies quickly pulled up to fight from two ridges. The Confederates were on Seminary Ridge; the Union forces stood on Cemetery Ridge about one mile away. At the southern end of Cemetery Ridge were two rocky points called Round Top and Little Round Top.

On the first day of the three-day battle, Lee's troops forced the Union lines back but did not break them. The next day, July 2, Lee attacked on the left end of the Union line near the Round Tops but was beaten back. That night Lee planned an attack on the Union center.

A Bitter Defeat for the South—The attack on July 3 began with the heaviest

Confederate dead from the battle of Chancellorsville

bombardment the South could deliver. Between one and two o'clock in the afternoon, fifteen thousand Confederate troops under General George Pickett gave the blood-curdling "rebel yell" and charged across an open mile-wide wheat field. Union fire power was murderous, and thousands of Pickett's men were killed in the courageous effort. "Pickett's charge" failed to break the Union lines.

Lee waited on July 4, poised for a counterattack that never came. Meade chose not to send his tired men across that open field. Thus he missed a golden opportunity to capture Lee and his forces. The next day Lee and his tattered troops rode back into Virginia in a torrential downpour. The Confederates and their baggage train were spread out over seventeen miles but returned without the slightest harassment from the Union army.

With Lee back in Virginia, the Union had no choice but to attack there. Since Meade showed no desire to follow through, Lincoln promoted a new general above him. On March 2, 1864, Lincoln brought Ulysses S. Grant from the West and made Grant his last supreme commander. **William T. Sherman** took Grant's place in the West.

Section Review

1. Why did Lee choose to take the offensive in Maryland?
2. What discovery prevented Lee from winning at Antietam?
3. What valuable Confederate leader was mortally wounded during the battle of Chancellorsville?
4. Who led the famous Confederate charge at Gettysburg?
5. Who became supreme leader of the Union forces following the battle of Gettysburg?

The Gettysburg Address

The battle at Gettysburg left thousands of dead soldiers who could not be returned to their homes for burial. Instead they were laid to rest on the battlefield at Gettysburg, where they had fought and died. President Lincoln came to dedicate the new cemetery there and delivered one of the shortest but most memorable speeches of all time:

Four score and seven years ago our fathers brought forth on this continent, a new nation, conceived in Liberty, and dedicated to the proposition that all men are created equal.

Now we are engaged in a great civil war, testing whether that nation, or any nation so conceived and so dedicated, can long endure. We are met on a great battlefield of that war. We have come to dedicate a portion of that field, as a final resting place for those who here gave their lives that that nation might live. It is altogether fitting and proper that we should do this.

But, in a larger sense, we can not dedicate—we can not consecrate—we can not hallow—this ground. The brave men, living and dead, who struggled here, have consecrated it, far above our poor power to add or detract. The world will little note, nor long remember what we say here, but it can never forget what they did here. It is for us the living, rather, to be dedicated here to the unfinished work which they who fought here have thus far so nobly advanced. It is rather for us to be here dedicated to the great task remaining before us—that from these honored dead we take increased devotion to that cause for which they gave the last full measure of devotion—that we here highly resolve that these dead shall not have died in vain—that this nation, under God, shall have a new birth of freedom—and that government of the people, by the people, for the people, shall not perish from the earth.

E. The War of Attrition and Destruction

Many Northerners, tiring of the war, wanted a negotiated peace. Lincoln and his cabinet planned definite steps to bring the war to a victorious end. They believed that freeing the slaves, destroying southern property, and winning the presidential election of 1864 might all help end the war.

Freeing the Slaves: The Emancipation Proclamation

President Lincoln had brought the nation into a war not to free the slaves, but to preserve the Union. However, as the war continued, it became obvious that ending slavery was necessary. The war-weary North needed a new cause to revive its fighting spirit, and so the proclamation was an important political move for Lincoln. In 1862 Congress had abolished slavery in Washington and in the new territories. Then in September 1862 Lincoln issued his **Emancipation Proclamation,** not to take effect until January 1, 1863. Even then it would free slaves only in Confederate-held areas, not in the border states or any other areas then under federal control. Also, if

Opposite page: *A statue on the battlefield at Gettysburg*
Top: *A scene from the battle at Gettysburg as depicted in the cyclorama there*
Bottom: *Lincoln reads the Emancipation Proclamation before his cabinet*

any Confederate states quit fighting before January 1, they could keep their slaves. Not one state, however, quit.

Encouraging the Confederacy to give up was but one reason for issuing the proclamation. It also gave the Union a positive, measurable goal. Instead of merely fighting for the Union, Northerners were now waging war "to make men free," in the words of Julia Ward Howe's new "Battle Hymn of the Republic." Third, since they would be fighting to end slavery, blacks were now given a real reason for joining the fight. More than 190,000 blacks fought on the Union side. Fourth, the proclamation hurt the South's war efforts because many slaves left their masters. As the word spread that slaves who reached northern lines would be freed, thousands deserted. Moreover, the proclamation paved the way for public acceptance of the total end of slavery, which came with the Thirteenth Amendment. Finally, it helped prevent Britain from entering the war on the South's side, because most of the British people opposed slavery.

Destroying the South

A war of attrition meant wearing down the South until it was too poor, too tired, and too hungry to fight. While the blockade cut off foreign supplies from the Confederacy, and Union control of the Mississippi prevented further aid from the West, Union armies now began to destroy provisions in the very heart of the Confederacy.

Sheridan in the Shenandoah Valley— Since Lee was aware of northern war weariness, he sent Jubal Early and his cavalry north. Although Lee did not expect Early to win any major battles, he hoped to create some anxiety. From his base in the Shenandoah Valley, Early's men raided Maryland

farms, stealing livestock. In July 1864, Early and his men rode to the outskirts of Washington. This action did keep some of Grant's troops in Washington for protection and out of the fight against Lee.

But Early's raid led Grant to make a decision that had a grave effect on the South. Grant decided to send **Philip Sheridan** to close down the Shenandoah Valley once and for all. Grant told Sheridan: "Leave nothing to invite the enemy to return. Destroy whatever cannot be consumed. Let that valley be left so that crows flying over it will have to carry their own rations."

Sheridan complied with grim efficiency. He not only defeated Jubal Early's outnumbered army three times but also laid waste to the valley that had fed Lee's army for three years. Sheridan's men rode out of nowhere, killing farm livestock and striking terror. They burned houses, barns, and crops. More than any one single battle, Sheridan's destruction marked the end of Lee's army. Now Lee's men lacked not only weapons but also food.

*Taking Tennessee—*Before Grant had been called to take control of the Union army, he had led his men from the Mississippi River eastward toward Chattanooga (CHAT un OO guh). There the Union general William S. Rosecrans had taken control of the city.

The Confederate forces, however, had moved south to Chickamauga (CHIK uh MAH guh), Cherokee for "river of death." Lee sent eleven thousand men to assist the Confederate commander, Braxton Bragg. Lee had no intention of letting the heartland go without a fight. On September 19, 1863, Bragg launched a hard counterattack that forced the Union forces to retreat to Chattanooga. Things looked grim for the Northern army while they were isolated there.

Then Grant and Sherman arrived. Union forces opened up the Tennessee River to get food in. On November 23 Grant gave the orders to attack. Sherman struck the Confederate right flank on Missionary Ridge while another force attacked Lookout Mountain. The combined Union armies dislodged the Confederates and regained

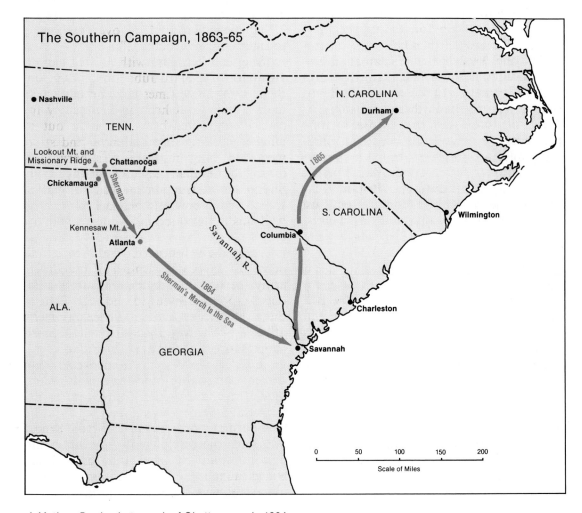

A Mathew Brady photograph of Chattanooga in 1864

Chattanooga. Their efforts cleared Tennessee of Confederate forces, sending Braxton Bragg south into Georgia.

Sherman's March to the Sea—Confederate troops lodged in north Georgia hoped to ride west into Alabama and slide back into Tennessee to attack Sherman again. Grant, leaving the western command to Sherman, told him to go after the Confederate Army, to "break it up, and to get into the interior of the enemy's country as far as you can, inflicting all the damage you can." And that Sherman did.

Moving southeast into Georgia, Sherman met staunch resistance from General Joseph Johnston. In a series of brilliant moves, Sherman attacked the flanks, or edges, of Johnston's troops. Every time Johnston was ready to take a stand, Sherman threatened to sweep around him, forcing Johnston to retreat still further. Finally, however, Johnston took his stand at Kennesaw (KEN ih SAW) Mountain, and the Union troops could not assault his defenses. Sherman then threatened the rear, forcing a retreat.

When Jefferson Davis became impatient with Johnston's slowness, he foolishly replaced him with the less able John Bell Hood. Hood lost heavily in Atlanta and by September 1 realized he could save his army only by evacuating the city. Sherman was more than willing to have Atlanta, a major railroad center whose loss devastated the southern cause.

Sherman saw, however, that keeping Atlanta might not be to his advantage. After all, he was now in the heart of the Confederacy and had moved far away from his supply base in Tennessee. His supplies were coming in by rail on a one-hundred-mile line that could easily be cut, placing his own men in grave danger.

Sherman, though, saw a way to change danger into triumph. Although Hood had already destroyed the supplies in Atlanta, Sherman got Grant's permission to destroy the city and leave only ruins behind. The civilians were told to leave, the city was torched, and Sherman cut the railroad back to Chattanooga. Thus he kept the Confederates from using it to counterattack him.

On November 10, 1864, Sherman's army moved out of Atlanta quickly to avoid fighting another major battle. Sherman divided his army into four groups and sent them toward Savannah on four roads across a sixty-mile-wide band of Georgia. They carried maps that carefully marked every village, path, and plantation. Their orders were "to forage liberally on the country during the march," keeping a ten-day supply on hand at all times. What was not needed was to be destroyed.

In the years since, many have wondered why Sherman was so destructive. Simply put, Sherman destroyed what was left to make it impossible for the Confederate army, now back under Johnston's command, to chase him. Second, this area of the Confederacy had yet to be physically affected by the war. By destroying the spirit and resources of this area, Sherman hoped to press Davis and the Confederates into surrendering more quickly. Finally, Sherman was under orders from Grant to destroy the area.

Sherman's orders stated, "Soldiers must not enter the dwellings of any inhabitant or commit any trespass" unless local bushwhackers molested them. Since the locals almost always did, wholesale destruction resulted. Confederate deserters called **bummers** and Union deserters, too, added to the problem, following the army and pillaging. Sherman did not try to stop them. As a result, Sherman's **March to the Sea** did cause a great deal of bitterness. To generations of Americans not used to war, this was war at its worst.

By December 10 Sherman's men had reached the port city of Savannah. The city fell easily; now supplies could not come by sea. Sherman presented Savannah to Lincoln as a Christmas present. Six weeks later he turned north to march across the Carolinas. His men devastated this area also. Sherman hoped to be able to join Grant in the final effort to defeat Lee.

The Election of 1864

Lincoln faced reelection in the fall of 1864. On August 23, 1864, Lincoln told his cabinet that he did not believe he would be reelected. Journalist Horace Greeley wrote that nine-tenths of all Americans were "anxious for peace, peace on almost any terms." The former Union general, George McClellan, running on a peace ticket, was Lincoln's opponent in the race.

Radical Republicans believed Lincoln was being too generous with the South, and northern Democrats criticized him at every turn. Yet they really could not see anyone else who could do better. Although he had not yet been able to end the war, Lincoln could not be faulted for lack of political skill. Lincoln used government jobs to increase his support; he picked cabinet members to appeal to different parts of the country and differing factions. He even picked a new running mate, a Southerner from Tennessee named **Andrew Johnson,**

who he believed could help him bring the South back into the Union more easily. Lincoln's experience also had taught him how to win political fights without making personal enemies of those he defeated. He was a man of force, ability, and vision.

The American public sensed this more than the politicians. Lincoln also had some men who helped to turn the tide for him. Their names were Sherman, Sheridan, and Farragut. Their victories in the fall of 1864 increased Lincoln's popularity and insured his win over McClellan.

Section Review

1. What were the provisions of the Emancipation Proclamation?
2. Who defeated the Confederate leader Jubal Early in the Shenandoah Valley?
3. What action of General Sherman's was specifically criticized as being excessively harsh? What was Sherman's reasoning for taking such action?
4. Who ran on the "peace ticket" in the 1864 election?

Mathew Brady took this photograph of President Lincoln in February 1864.

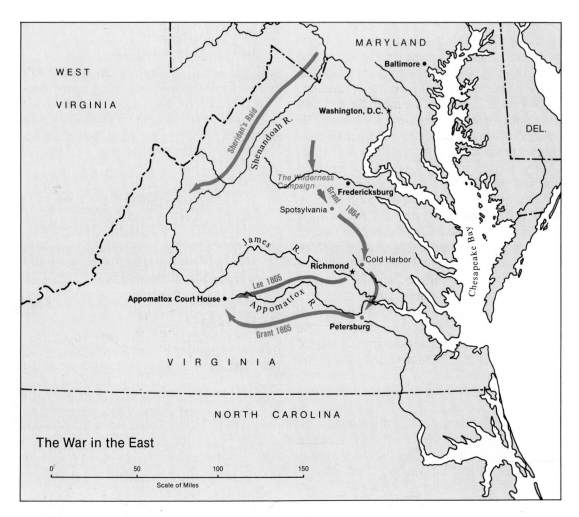

The War in the East

| 0 | 50 | 100 | 150 |

Scale of Miles

F. Appomattox and Aftermath

By May of 1864, Grant was ready to open a new Virginia campaign. His army moved into a heavily wooded area west of Fredericksburg called "The Wilderness." There Grant hurled a force of 100,000 men against Lee's smaller army. Although Grant suffered heavy losses, he knew he could replace his men while Lee could not. Grant believed that if he pressed Lee's army long enough and prevented Lee from maneuvering to fight him, he could wear Lee down and win.

The Road to Richmond

Despite his losses Grant rebounded, moving east and then south. Lee marched all night to head him off and caught him at Spotsylvania Court House. But Grant moved south again, and Lee had to throw himself and his troops between the Union army and Richmond. Grant lost more men at Cold Harbor (the dead covered five acres of ground), but his advance continued. By now Yankee newspaper editors were calling the North's leading general "the butcher." In one month he had lost more than 50,000 men. But Grant was wearing Lee down. He had no thought of changing his plans: "I intend to fight it out on this line if it takes all summer." Lincoln told his cabinet: "I cannot spare this man. He wins."

In June 1864, Grant crossed the James River, planning to attack Richmond from the south. To do this, the Federals needed to take Petersburg. Lee came to Petersburg's rescue. Grant settled in for a siege that did not end until April 1865. Eighteen trainloads of supplies came daily to Grant's aid while Lee's troops had less and less. The battle for Petersburg went on, and the South lost four thousand men but did not retreat. Lincoln told Grant: "Hold on with a bulldog grip and chew and choke as much as possible."

By March 1865 Lee realized he could not hold out much longer. On April 2 Lee moved the 54,000 men left in his army away from Petersburg. He hoped to lure Grant into open country and neutralize Union numbers with superior tactics. But outnumbered more than two to one, Lee had to fall back.

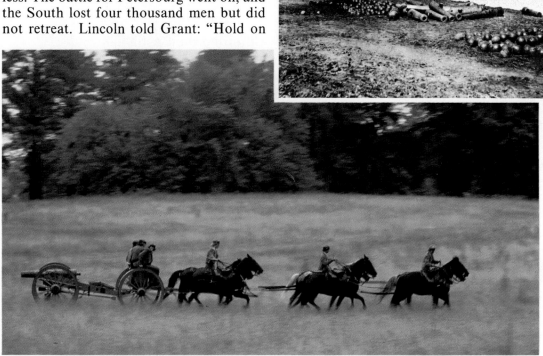

Top: *Richmond, Virginia in 1865*
Bottom: *Part of a re-enactment of the battle of Petersburg*

Chapter 17

Surrender at Appomattox

Lee feared having his army trapped in Richmond. He decided to destroy Richmond and bolt west. Johnston's army was in upper North Carolina, and Lee's last hope was to link with it for one last stand, but Sheridan blocked Lee's retreat to the Blue Ridge Mountains. On April 9, 1865, near Appomattox (AP uh MAT uks) Court House, the Confederacy made one final hopeless attack on Grant's line, hoping to buy time. When it failed, Lee asked for terms of surrender.

Only half of Lee's men had arms to stack when they laid down their weapons at **Appomattox.** Some were barefoot and most were hungry. With a nation to be reunited, Grant had been told to offer Lee generous terms. Officers could keep their revolvers and swords. Since horses were needed for farm work, the men were allowed to keep them. A local printer stayed up all night to print parole certificates. No prisoners would be kept. As soon as the soldiers signed a pledge not to take up arms again, they would be given enough provisions from Union and captured Confederate supplies to get them home.

Since Lee's army was the keystone of the Confederate army, it was only a matter

of time until the more scattered units surrendered. On April 18 Joseph Johnston surrendered to Sherman at the Bennett House in Durham, North Carolina. The last group of Confederates to receive the news, in Texas, gave up early in May.

Counting the Casualties

The Civil War was the most destructive war America has ever entered. About one-third of the approximately two million men who served in it were killed, injured, or captured. Practically every family lost at least one member or close friend in the war. In the South one-fourth of all manpower of military draft age never returned from war. By contrast, in World War II only one in sixteen was lost.

Of course, there had been great destruction of personal property, especially in the South. Unlike any other war since then, the Civil War was fought on America's own soil. Ruined homes, roads, businesses, and farmland were some of the material losses.

In addition, the war left deep bitterness. Mutual distrust and even hatred lingered between the North and South for decades,

Grant accepted Lee's surrender (right) *at the McLean House* (left) *at Appomattox Court House.*

Arlington National Cemetery

Across the Potomac River from Washington, D.C., stands a stately columned mansion on a hilltop. That mansion is the Arlington House, once called the Custis-Lee Mansion. Today the mansion is more often associated with Arlington National Cemetery, the site it overlooks, than with the families who once lived there.

In 1669 Governor Berkeley of Virginia deeded six thousand acres of land to a ship's captain. This was his pay for bringing over a shipload of colonists. Later the land was purchased by John Parke Custis, a son of Martha Washington by a first marriage. His granddaughter, Mary Ann Randolph Custis, married Robert E. Lee at the family mansion in 1831. In time Mary inherited the mansion and the surrounding lands.

When Mrs. Lee and her four children fled Arlington in 1861, the mansion fell into federal hands. Because of delinquent taxes, United States commissioners purchased the land in 1864. (Mrs. Lee had tried to pay the $92.00 due plus a fifty per cent penalty, but her emissary was sent back with the message that she would have to pay the taxes in person. As a result the government took the mansion.)

Washington's many hospitals had become crowded with wounded men. Because of poor medical conditions, many died. Some place was needed to bury them. Quartermaster Montgomery C. Meigs suggested that the grounds around Arlington be dedicated as a national cemetery so as to prevent Lee from ever returning to his family's home. Meigs even came up personally to insure that the graves

were placed as close to the house as possible. The burials were made throughout the war.

In 1866 the bones of 2,111 unknown Union soldiers were gathered from the battlefields of northern Virginia, brought to Arlington, and buried in a single mass grave right beside Lee's rose garden.

After the war Robert E. Lee's eldest son sued to regain his estate, and the Supreme Court ruled that it should be restored. But because thousands of soldiers were now buried on the estate, he settled quickly with the government for $150,000. Arlington National Cemetery was left to become America's most prestigious military cemetery.

A view of the Arlington House as it appears from the grave of President John F. Kennedy

A Letter of Consolation

The Civil War took a terrible toll on the lives of America's young men. One powerful example of the suffering endured by the mothers of soldiers was a poignant letter of condolence written by President Lincoln to a bereaved mother in Massachusetts.

Dear Madam,

I have been shown in the files of the War Department a statement of the Adjutant General of Massachusetts, that you are the mother of five sons who have died gloriously on the field of battle.

I feel how weak and fruitless must be any word of mine which should attempt to beguile you from the grief of a loss so overwhelming. But I cannot refrain from tendering to you the consolation that may be found in the thanks of the Republic they died to save.

I pray that our Heavenly Father may assuage the anguish of your bereavement, and leave you only the cherished memory of the loved and lost, and the solemn pride that must be yours, to have laid so costly a sacrifice upon the altar of Freedom.

Yours very sincerely
and respectfully
A. Lincoln

Mrs. Bixby
Boston, Massachusetts

because each blamed the other for losses or problems.

Lincoln's Assassination

There was still one casualty to come. It affected both sides, the South perhaps more than the North. On Good Friday, April 14, 1865, President and Mrs. Lincoln went to Ford's Theater to attend a play.

An actor who was also a fanatical Confederate sympathizer slipped into the president's box while the guard was away. **John Wilkes Booth** then shot Lincoln in the back of the head, and President Lincoln died the next morning. Booth was later trapped in a barn in Virginia. The barn was burned, and Booth either took his own life or was shot by one of his pursuers.

No one really knows what would have happened in the postwar years had Lincoln lived. However, Lincoln's second inaugural address had stressed "malice toward none," and his stated terms for re-entry of the southern states were quite generous. One writer said Booth's "trigger finger had done the South more harm than all the lawless bummers in Sherman's Army."

Lincoln's funeral train retraced the route that had taken him to Washington only a little more than four years earlier. He was buried in his hometown of Springfield, Illinois, on May 4, 1865. After the nation laid a president to rest, it soon awakened to problems it had never faced before. These problems would challenge our nation for a century.

Section Review

1. What was Grant's reason for continuing his pursuit of Lee despite the heavy losses Grant was suffering?
2. What strategic city did the Union soldiers need to take before attacking Richmond?
3. Where did Lee and his men lay down their weapons?
4. Why is the Civil War called the most "destructive war Americans ever entered"?
5. Who assassinated President Lincoln?

Summary

The Civil War began in 1861 between the North and the South. Although greatly outnumbered and lacking in materials, the Confederate armies successfully kept the Union armies from victory for four years. Eventually, however, the northern forces wore down the South's ability to fight until Lee finally surrendered to Grant in 1865. Four years of devastating struggle left much of the South in ruins and the nation in need of healing.

Chapter Review

Do You Remember?

■ Identify the following.
1. The fall of this city in the West gave the Union control of the Mississippi.
2. This is the name given to Sherman's devastating trip through the South.
3. This one location was the site of two early battles won by the South.
4. These two ironclad ships fought a major naval battle during the Civil War.
5. Lee surrendered at this site.
6. This term describes the North's effort to stop shipping along the southern coast.
7. This man shot Lincoln.
8. Lincoln hoped to make Union soldiers fight to free the slaves by issuing this document.
9. This man was a famous Civil War photographer.
10. This Pennsylvania battle was an important Union victory.

■ Identify each of the following men as Union or Confederate leaders, and then write a statement describing each man's role in the war.
11. Philip Sheridan
12. Thomas Jackson
13. Ulysses S. Grant
14. George B. McClellan
15. Irwin McDowell
16. Robert E. Lee
17. David Glasgow Farragut
18. William T. Sherman

Why Is It So?

1. Why was it often difficult for the North and South to recruit soldiers?
2. How did civilians in the North feel the effects of the war? How did those in the South?
3. What was the Union strategy for the war, and how did it prove effective?
4. Why was the South's victory at Chancellorsville also a loss for the Confederacy?
5. Why did Lincoln issue the Emancipation Proclamation?
6. Why did Sherman try to destroy the South on his march?
7. How did Grant finally make Lee surrender?

What Do You Think?

1. How did the first battle of Bull Run show that the people misunderstood what the war would be like?
2. Why did the North win the war?
3. What could have helped the South win the war?
4. Why was Lincoln's assassination untimely for the nation?

18

Reconstruction

Just weeks before the end of the weary conflict and his own tragic death, Lincoln had given his second inaugural address. Expressing his desire for the future of the United States, he said, "With malice toward none; with charity for all; with firmness in the right, as God gives us to see the right, let us strive on to finish the work we are in; to bind up the nation's wounds; to care for him who shall have borne the battle, and for his widow, and his orphan—to do all which may achieve and cherish a just, and a lasting peace, among ourselves, and with all nations."

A devastated Richmond, Virginia, in 1865

But as the Civil War ended and time progressed, more malice and less charity appeared than Lincoln would have liked. The wounds of the war were deep, and it would take years, even decades, before they would begin to heal. Some scars would linger for over a century.

A. Reconstruction and the South

The time following the Civil War is called **Reconstruction.** This was the time of reuniting the nation and attempting to solve the South's postwar problems.

The South's Need for Reconstruction

For many Northerners, life following the war changed little from life before the war. The North had lost thousands of men, and it felt that wound deeply, but industry had increased. Immigration continued to add to the northern population. Only a minor amount of northern property had been damaged in the war, and so returning soldiers could go back to their farms or jobs with little hindrance.

The situation in the postwar South, however, was entirely different. Not only had it lost many of its young men, but it also had lost its slaves. Thus its labor force was entirely disrupted, and no great wave of immigrants came to add to the working population.

In addition to lost lives, the South had suffered severe property damage. Many of its major cities—Atlanta, Columbia, and Richmond—lay in ruins. Many of the South's fields had been stripped bare, and its livestock confiscated or destroyed. Homes, businesses, and railroads had been demolished. After the war little remained with which the South could rebuild.

Not only was the South's plantation system dead, but also the money that remained was worthless. The South had almost no U.S. currency, and the paper Confederate money had no value. The South was bankrupt, and its accustomed means of making its living had been destroyed with little hope of rebuilding it.

The freed slaves, or **freedmen,** were another problem for the South. No longer controlled under slavery, over four million blacks were free to live in the South. They needed jobs for support, but white Southerners had no money to pay them. Neither were the freedmen particularly eager to return to the same work they had done as slaves. Slaves had been vital to the South's economy before the war, but the freedmen lacked an important role in the postwar South. Yet they were there, and they had to be given a place in southern society.

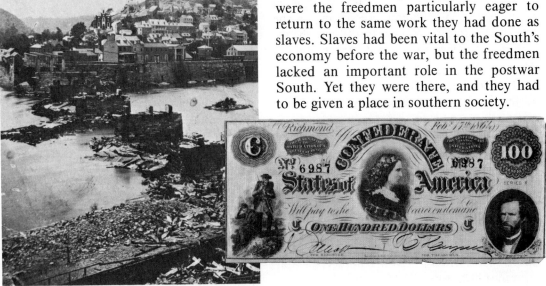

Left: *The war left many areas in ruins.*
Right: *A $100 bill issued by the Confederacy*

In addition to these problems was the need for the South to reestablish its state governments. Those governments in control during the Confederacy had been thrown out by the Union's victory. New governments had to be formed, and they in turn would have to deal with the conditions in the South.

All these problems of the postwar South were a major concern of the federal government. Presidents, Congress, and the states themselves would argue over their powers to control the methods of solving these problems of Reconstruction.

Phases of Reconstruction

Reconstruction is usually considered to be the twelve-year period from 1865 to 1877. During that time the federal government directly supervised the rebuilding of the South. In a larger sense, however, Reconstruction continued at least until the turn of the century as southern state governments continued to deal with the special problems of their region. According to the influences guiding Reconstruction policies, this larger period divides into three phases:

Phase 1 (1865-1867): Presidential Reconstruction or Self-Reconstruction
Phase 2 (1867-1876): Congressional Reconstruction or Radical Reconstruction
Phase 3 (1877-1900): Bourbon Restoration or Redeemers' Reconstruction

Section Review

1. List several of the South's economic, social, and political problems resulting from the war.
2. What was the postwar era called?
3. What was the purpose of this era? How long did it last?

B. Presidential Reconstruction

For just a short time, presidents Lincoln and Johnson directed the process of Reconstruction; this was the time of **Presidential Reconstruction.** Even before the war had ended, President Lincoln had developed a plan for bringing the seceded states back into the Union. Lincoln believed that the southern states, by illegally trying to secede, had committed an act of rebellion and had started an insurrection. As the commander-in-chief, his duty had been to quell their insurrection. Once this was done, he had the power given him under the Constitution to pardon their wrongdoing.

Lincoln's Ten Per Cent Plan and Congress's Reactions

In December 1863, Lincoln announced his **Ten Per Cent Plan** to reconstruct the areas of the South that had already come under Union control. This plan offered pardons to former Confederates who would swear an oath to support the Constitution and the Union. When ten per cent of the registered voters in 1860 in any state had taken the oath, the state could form a new government and be restored to the Union. They could even get seats back in Congress and elect senators and representatives. By the spring of 1864 three occupied states (Tennessee, Louisiana, and Arkansas) had met these "easy" terms and were ready to reenter the Union.

Radical Republicans Object—Lincoln's plan, however, met resistance from a group of Republicans known as **Radical Republicans.** They believed that the plan treated the South too kindly. They wished the South to be treated as a conquered foreign nation, not simply as erring brethren. They were not ready to forgive the South for the war. According to these Radical Republicans, the South should be punished severely or all the sacrifices of war would be worthless. They also believed that if Southerners were let off too easily, they would try to regain the influence they had possessed before the war. Although a minority, the Radicals won moderate Republicans to their side. Because the Radicals and moderates did not wish to see Confederates back in Congress before the war ended, they refused to let the three states back into the Union under the president's plan.

The Radicals also reacted to Lincoln's use of executive (presidential) powers during the war. Since war created many emergencies, the president had made decisions without asking Congress. The Emancipation Proclamation, for example, had not received the approval of Congress. The Radicals believed that Lincoln had gone beyond his powers as president.

The Wade-Davis Bill—In 1864 Congress responded with its own Reconstruction plan, the **Wade-Davis Bill.** Under this plan a state could reenter the Union when fifty per cent of the registered voters of the state in 1860 had taken the oath of allegiance. In addition, those who wished to vote or help govern their states had to swear that they had never supported the Confederacy voluntarily. The states also had to abolish slavery and repudiate (rih PYOO dee ATE; refuse to pay or acknowledge) their debts and their acts of secession.

The Wade-Davis Bill passed both houses. Congress was letting the president know that it alone, not the president, would be the judge for state readmissions and reseating members of the legislative branch.

In turn, Lincoln let Congress know he disagreed. Rather than vetoing the bill by sending a formal message to Congress listing his objections, Lincoln killed the Wade-Davis Bill by pocket veto. (See p. 139.)

The conflict between Congress and Lincoln had not yet been resolved when Lincoln was shot. Therefore, Andrew Johnson was left to battle with Congress for control of Reconstruction.

Andrew Johnson Takes Over

Vice President Andrew Johnson had been born in poverty in North Carolina. His wife, who was a teacher, had taught him to read and write. After moving to Tennessee, Johnson held his first political office. He moved up the local and state ladders to become a congressman and

Andrew Johnson

senator. When Tennessee seceded in 1861, Johnson opposed their action and was the only southern senator who did not resign his Senate seat. President Lincoln named him military governor of Union-held areas of Tennessee and later chose him as his running mate. Johnson's outspokenness (he once said that Jefferson Davis and other leading Confederates should be hanged) won him the support of Radical Republicans.

When Johnson took over the presidency, Congress was out of session. Since he did not reconvene Congress, he had from April through December to state his ideals and to put them into effect without its interference. Johnson shared Lincoln's belief that it was impossible for a state to secede. Thus, Confederate states were still in the Union. Even so, Johnson believed individuals in the states had left the Union, and they, rather than the states, deserved to be punished.

Johnson's Plan—Johnson began by offering **amnesty** or group pardon to Southerners who willingly took a loyalty oath to the Union. However, he excluded those whose taxable property was over $20,000. These people, mostly former planters, had to apply to him for a pardon. Unpardoned Southerners were unable to vote, hold office, or get back any property seized by the federal government.

Next, Johnson's plan provided for presidential appointment of provisional state governors to hold state conventions. Such state bodies would draft new state constitutions that repudiated Confederate debts and ratified the **Thirteenth Amendment,** the recent Constitutional amendment that had abolished slavery. When a state took this action and fifty per cent of its voters had

sworn loyalty, Johnson assumed Congress would readmit it.

By winter all of the former Confederate states except Texas had met most of Johnson's terms. But South Carolina refused to repudiate its war debt, Mississippi did not ratify the Thirteenth Amendment, and not one southern state offered voting rights to blacks. When Congress convened, it refused to seat southern representatives. Instead, moderate and Radical Republicans in the House and Senate formed their own Joint Committee on Reconstruction. They would determine if the southern states were really reconstructed. Unsurprisingly, they decided they were not.

Republicans React to the "Johnson Governments"—Several things offended northern Republicans. First, when southern states held their state and local elections, they voted former Confederates into office. Second, many Radicals, and others, believed that the government should take southern lands and divide them among the newly freed slaves, but this was not done.

Third, because most of the South's representatives and senators were Democrats, Republicans realized that seating them might cost them their power. The Republicans would be in the minority if northern Democrats sided with the Southerners to outvote them.

Fourth, some believed that to make the loss of life in the war worthwhile, black Americans had to receive full rights of citizens. "We must," one said, "see to it that the man made free in the Constitution . . . is a free man indeed . . . and that he walks the earth proud and erect in the conscious dignity of a free man." When the Joint Committee held hearings early in 1866, it found out that instead of being granted

Andrew Johnson
17TH PRESIDENT
(1865-1869)

Born: Raleigh, North Carolina,
  December 29, 1808
Family: married Eliza McCardle; three
  sons, two daughters
Occupation: tailor
Home: Greeneville, Tennessee
Religion: no formal affiliation
Election: none
Political Party: Democratic
Vice President: none
Interesting Facts and Accomplishments:
was taught to read and write by his wife
ran with a northern Republican in a
  presidential race even though he was a
  southern Democrat
wore black at all times in Washington
was the first president to be impeached,
  but was acquitted by one vote
was the first expresident to serve in the
  U.S. Senate after leaving the White
  House
Death: July 31, 1875

more rights, the former slaves were being denied them through **black codes.**

Black Codes—The black codes established after the war in the South were much like the old slave laws, although they did allow a few new basic rights. Black codes allowed blacks to sue, to be sued, and to testify in courts. They were also entitled to legalize their marriages and to marry within their own race. They could now buy, own, and transfer property. But in trying to control the large population of freed blacks, the codes were very restrictive. They placed blacks in an inferior position to whites, making them, in essence, second-class citizens. The codes were in some ways a replacement for slavery.

In some states, for example, blacks were allowed to work only as domestic servants or farmers. Some codes forbade blacks to live in towns or cities. Hence it seemed that the codes condemned many blacks to do the same field work they had done in slave days. Blacks who wanted to practice trades or do anything besides farming had to be apprenticed and often had to get licenses. Since few blacks had money, this closed trade doors to them. Blacks not usefully employed could be arrested for vagrancy (wandering around with no job). Blacks who could not pay fines for vagrancy or other crimes could be hired out to anyone who would pay their fines. Southern states forbade blacks to carry arms, and some codes told them where they could or could not own property. Southerners held that the black codes prevented the chaos that could have come from freeing four million slaves at once.

Johnson's Response to the Radicals—Although Johnson had worked hard to overcome poverty and a lack of formal education, he did not have the ability to be a strong but sensitive leader for the nation at that time. He was firm in his positions on Reconstruction, and when his policies were defied, he stubbornly refused to change and lashed back at those who opposed him. His stubbornness often forced his foes into harsher positions. Because Johnson refused to give any ground, his inflexibility disheartened moderates and drove them into the Radical camp. Soon, with the majority of Congress united against Johnson, Presidential Reconstruction was coming to an end.

Section Review

1. What was Lincoln's Ten Per Cent Plan?
2. How did Congress's plan differ from Lincoln's?
3. Who assumed the presidency after Lincoln's assassination?
4. How did the northern Republicans respond to Johnson's plan for Reconstruction?
5. What were the black codes?

Radical Republican leaders Charles Sumner (left) *and Thaddeus Stevens* (right)

C. Radical Republicans Take Over Reconstruction

Radical Republicans in the House were led by **Thaddeus Stevens** of Pennsylvania and Senate Radicals by **Charles Sumner** of Massachusetts. After refusing Southerners entrance into the House, they then took action to insure that the legislative branch, and not the executive, would control Reconstruction. However, President Johnson could and did use his power to veto their acts. The president retained his power until February of 1866, when the Radicals gained control of two-thirds of both houses of Congress and could override his vetoes.

Radical Republican Legislation

While Radical Republican strength grew in Congress, several pieces of legislation were brought forward to fight against the black codes and to aid the freedmen in the South.

The Freedmen's Bureau—In March of 1865 Congress had passed laws to set up a short-term agency to provide aid for refugees. The **Freedmen's Bureau** was the first federal relief agency ever established. It issued rations of surplus army food and clothing to freed slaves and to poverty-stricken whites. It also sent agents into the South to establish schools and hospitals for blacks of all ages. The bureau tried to locate jobs for the freedmen and to prevent employers from exploiting them. Because Congress assumed that state governments would soon be able to provide relief services, the bureau was to be federally funded for only one year. Since Congress refused to recognize the new state governments, it voted to keep the bureau going and even to extend its powers. President Johnson vetoed two versions of the bill, but the Republicans united to override his veto the second time. The Freedmen's Bureau then continued its work.

The Fourteenth Amendment—Next, Congress voted to give blacks legal citizenship through the Civil Rights Act of 1866. Because Johnson believed that the Constitution gave the states power over citizenship, he vetoed the act, but Congress passed it over his veto. However, Congress still feared that it would be declared unconstitutional. In June of that year Congress solved the problem of granting blacks citizenship by proposing the **Fourteenth Amendment.** The longest amendment to date, the Fourteenth Amendment was, and still is, significant.

First, the amendment made all persons citizens of both the United States and of the states where they resided. It also prohibited any state from depriving a person of his life, liberty, or property without due process of law (a proper trial). Moreover, a state could not deny equal protection of its laws to any person under its jurisdiction.

Second, a state's representation in Congress would be based on its whole population. This provision meant that blacks were no longer to be counted as three-fifths of a person. States that denied voting rights to blacks could have the number of representatives they had in Congress cut back.

Third, those who had engaged in insurrection or rebellion against the United States would be barred from voting or holding office unless Congress specifically pardoned them by a two-thirds vote. Finally, Congress refused to assume Confederate debts or accept claims for any costs of freeing the slaves.

When ratified, the amendment would cancel black codes in the southern states

The Plight of Robert E. Lee

★ ★ ★

Robert E. Lee, who had served as commander-in-chief of the Confederate army, was one of many Confederate soldiers and leaders affected by the government's policies for Reconstruction. Since he had served in the Confederacy, Lee had lost his American citizenship.

After the surrender Lee applied for pardon and restoration of his citizenship. General Grant endorsed his request and sent it on to President Andrew Johnson. Although Lee was not aware of it, he was also to have taken an oath of allegiance. On October 2, 1865, when he was sworn in as president of Washington College, Lee took that oath. Proof of the oath-taking was then sent to Washington. President Johnson had the power to issue pardons and restore citizenship until 1868. Either Johnson never received the oath or he chose not to sign it (perhaps because Grant, whom he saw as a political rival, had made the request).

In 1868 the Fourteenth Amendment changed the system. Congress was allowed to pardon Confederates who had lost their citizenship by a two-thirds vote of each house.

Treason charges against Lee, his sons, and fourteen other Confederates were dropped in 1869. Yet he died in 1870 without regaining his citizenship.

In 1971 a historian rediscovered Lee's petition among some Civil War papers in the National Archives. The Virginia State Senate asked Congress to pass a resolution restoring Lee's citizenship posthumously (POSS chuh mus lee; after his death). In April 1974 the Senate approved his request and by June the House had concurred. One-hundred and ten years after he had lost his citizenship, Lee's status as a man without a country ended.

as well as laws against blacks in some midwestern states. President Johnson urged southern states to vote against it. He held the amendment to be an invasion of states' rights. He traveled in the North and Midwest to give speeches against Radical Republicans running for fall election. Johnson's tour cost him support. His audiences rudely heckled him. Instead of ignoring them, Johnson lost his temper. Some people had rejected his plan for Reconstruction already because they feared it would put former Confederates back into power. Now many more were skeptical of his leadership.

The Radical Republicans swept the elections, electing enough men to insure the overriding of any presidential vetoes. When Congress convened in 1867, Reconstruction was wholly in Radical hands, and the phase of **Radical Reconstruction** had begun. By 1868 enough states had ratified the Fourteenth Amendment to put it into effect.

Further Radical Reconstruction Rule

Beginning in 1867 the Radical Republicans in Congress put their program into effect with great speed and little resistance. When the president vetoed their legislation, Congress quickly overrode his vetoes.

Reconstruction Act of 1867—The **Reconstruction Act of 1867** went far beyond the controls Lincoln and Johnson had wished to place on the South. This radical legislation put the area under military rule or "martial law," thus sending in the army to make sure that the South complied with the wishes of Congress. Naturally, Southerners resented this military occupation.

First, the act cut the South into five military districts, each ruled by a Union general. Second, it gave blacks the right to vote and hold office. At the same time the

act denied voting rights to those who had served in the Confederacy. Third, southern states wanting to reenter the Union were to hold open conventions with both black and white voting delegates. These conventions were to draw up new state constitutions using the guidelines given by Congress. The act also required the states to submit their documents to Congress for approval. Finally, to return to the fold, states would be required to ratify the Fourteenth Amendment. When these requirements were met, the troops would be withdrawn.

Scalawags and Carpetbaggers in the South—Few former southern leaders were eligible to hold public offices, because they had lost their citizenship by serving the Confederacy. And since Congress had opened politics to blacks by its Reconstruction acts, southern politics now underwent great change. New groups now took command of the South.

Northerners who came south to assist in Radical Reconstruction were called **carpetbaggers.** (They were supposed to have come south carrying their possessions in small suitcases made from pieces of carpet.) Most carpetbaggers were opportunists who came south seeking financial or political gain. Of course, Southerners resented them. A few carpetbaggers, however, were sincere men who came because they wanted to help the freedmen change the South. Some were Union soldiers who liked what they had seen of the South and decided to stay. Carpetbaggers took control of Southern politics for a while, but they also brought needed investment capital to a ravaged South.

White Southerners who supported Radical Reconstruction received the derisive name of **scalawag.** Some had been Unionists during the war and had no reason to change after. Others endorsed Radical Reconstruction because they honestly believed it was in the South's best interest. Some scalawags were prewar Whigs seeking a new party since theirs had collapsed. However, there were scalawags who did deserve their bad name. Many were those who saw a chance to get ahead with the help of Radical Republican support and military protection. Most Southerners looked on scalawags as traitors.

Although they did not control the government in any state, black freedmen did gain office in every southern state. Unfortunately since blacks had no earlier political experience, they were more susceptible to improper influence. Radical Republicans often used the black officeholders as puppets for their purposes. Some of the blacks were bribed to promote the interests of carpetbaggers and scalawags. Since southern whites already resented their former slaves, they were especially critical of any black corruption. Most of the blacks who held national political offices—for example, Mississippi senators Hiram H. Revels and Blanche K. Bruce, and South Carolina's

During Reconstruction some politicians used posters such as the one above to play upon the white voter's fears about blacks.

Robert Smalls—were well educated. Many blacks elected to offices served with dignity.

Congress Impeaches Johnson

Although the Congress passed its Radical legislation over Johnson's veto, he still enforced the laws that were passed. He carried out the laws because this was his constitutional duty. The Radical Republicans, however, were still unhappy with him and sought ways to limit what power he had. One executive power is to appoint officials. The Radicals feared that Johnson would remove those officials sympathetic to their views and replace them with his own men. Therefore, they passed the **Tenure of Office Act** in 1867. This act made it illegal to remove any presidential appointments approved by the Senate unless the Senate also approved their dismissal.

Johnson tested the law by removing **Edwin Stanton,** Lincoln's holdover secretary of war. (Stanton had never upheld Johnson's views and now openly sided with the Radicals.) Stanton refused to leave. He barricaded himself behind his office doors, accepted food through the windows, and cooked for himself. He even slept in his office. Congress now believed it had grounds for impeaching, or bringing charges against, Johnson so that they could remove him from office. (See p. 147.) In presidential impeachments the Constitution says that the House of Representatives is to file the charges; the Senate then serves as the trial court, and the chief justice of the Supreme Court presides as the judge. A two-thirds vote is required to remove the president. The basis for removal is "conviction of treason, bribery, or other high crimes and misdemeanors." A congressional committee did not believe President Johnson was guilty of such crimes, but the Radicals pressed on.

On February 24, 1868, the House voted to impeach Johnson. The president's trial under Justice Salmon P. Chase began March 13 and lasted until May 26. Johnson himself never attended the trial. He believed he had done nothing wrong and that his attendance would lend credence to his accusers' cause. Senators sold tickets to the affair, and at times the trial rivaled a theater performance.

Senators could not agree on whether the Tenure of Office Act was constitutional. Even if it had been, they did not know whether the act applied in Stanton's case. Stanton, after all, had been Lincoln's appointee before the Tenure of Office Act had ever been passed. The real issue was that Radicals were trying to get rid of the president because they disagreed with him politically, not because he was guilty of a crime. Removing a president for political reasons would have set a dangerous precedent. Some senators saw this danger, and others knew that if Johnson were removed, Ben Wade, an extreme radical, would be named the next president. Wade's views on public finance, labor, women's suffrage, and blacks were too shocking for most Americans to accept at that time.

When the final vote was taken, thirty-five Senators voted to convict the president; nineteen voted against. This was one vote short of the total needed to remove Johnson. Johnson finished his term; the presidency

Top: *The House impeachment council that brought charges against President Johnson*
Bottom: *A ticket of admission to the impeachment trial in the Senate*

was preserved. But Johnson's reputation was never the same. Years later, however, the Supreme Court completely cleared Johnson of any blame by declaring the Tenure of Office Act to be unconstitutional.

Johnson's Achievements in Foreign Affairs

Although Congress had kept Johnson's policies at home from working well, his achievements in foreign affairs were noteworthy. **William Seward,** his talented secretary of state, ably directed his foreign policy.

In 1864 Napoleon III, the emperor of France, had violated the Monroe Doctrine by setting up a puppet government in Mexico. Since the Civil War occupied America's attention at the time, Austrian Archduke Maximilian (MAK suh MIL yun) became Mexico's puppet emperor. Lincoln and

Secretary of State William Seward

Seward had reprimanded the French for their actions, but they could not send troops to evict Maxmilian at that time. In 1866, however, President Johnson moved against the French. He sent fifty thousand veteran troops to the border, and their presence forced the withdrawal of French troops.

Seward was also an expansionist. He signed a treaty of friendship and commerce with China in 1868. In 1867 he secretly negotiated a treaty with Russia to purchase Alaska for $7 million. When President Johnson sought Senate approval, cries of "Seward's Folly," "Johnson's Polar Bear Garden," and "Frigidia" flooded the press. But within ten days the treaty went through by a thirty-seven to two vote. Years later this purchase would prove to be a great bargain for the United States.

President U.S. Grant

By 1868 Andrew Johnson had lost almost all influence in the Republican party. For their presidential candidate in the election, the Republicans chose Ulysses S. Grant. The Democrats were still hampered by their ties to the old Civil War issues and by the Radical Republican takeover of the South, the party's former stronghold. Even so, Grant narrowly defeated the Democratic candidate, New York's governor Horatio Seymour. The support of a half-million new black voters helped bring about the Republican victory.

The Fifteenth Amendment—Once in office Grant disappointed the Radicals. He did reward black support, however, by calling for the passage of the **Fifteenth Amendment.** This amendment kept states from denying the vote to any person "on account of race, color, or previous condition of servitude" (see pp. 158-59). Passage of the amendment kept

Republicans in power by giving them more votes in northern states that still had anti-black laws. Since the southern states still had Republican governments that favored the blacks, the Fifteenth Amendment was ratified in less than a year. It took effect in 1870.

Grant was sympathetic to the plight of the South, and he limited the number of federal troops there. Six states—Alabama, Arkansas, Florida, South Carolina, North Carolina, and Louisiana—had been readmitted to the Union by the summer of 1868. (Tennessee had been readmitted in 1866.)

Ulysses S. Grant
18TH PRESIDENT
(1869-1877)

Born: Point Pleasant, Ohio, April 27, 1822

Family: married Julia Dent; three sons, one daughter

Occupation: soldier, farmer, clerk

Home: Galena, Illinois

Religion: Methodist

Elections: 1868—defeated Horatio Seymour

1872—defeated Horace Greeley

Political Party: Republican

Vice Presidents: Schuyler Colfax (first term), Henry Wilson (second term)

Interesting Facts and Accomplishments:
graduated from West Point

his Civil War success brought him acclaim despite his heavy drinking and his business failures before the war

earned the nickname "Unconditional Surrender Grant" because of his statement during an early Civil War campaign: "No terms other than an unconditional and immediate surrender can be accepted."

rated as one of the worst presidents, although he did lead the country through eight years of difficult Reconstruction

smoked up to twenty cigars a day and eventually died from cancer of the mouth and throat

Death: July 23, 1885

An 1868 campaign banner

Four remaining states—Georgia, Mississippi, Texas, and Virginia—held out until 1870. By the time they sought readmission, they were also required to ratify the Fifteenth Amendment.

The Grant Scandals—Ulysses S. Grant served two terms as president. Unfortunately he showed that a good general does not always make a good president. Both of Grant's terms in office were marked by political corruption. The corruption, largely the result of greed, was not the president's doing and existed on national, state, and local levels. But when the corruption was uncovered, the president allowed the dishonest to resign rather than face prosecution. He believed that prosecution would only divide the nation further. To distract the voters from the scandals, the party appealed to people to unite against the ex-rebels. Reviving these ill feelings, however, was not what the country wanted. The Radical Republicans, with their fierce hatred for the South, were losing power.

Section Review

1. What was the purpose of the Freedmen's Bureau?
2. List the provisions of the Fourteenth Amendment.
3. What was the significance of the Reconstruction Act of 1867?
4. Who were the scalawags, the carpetbaggers, and the freedmen?
5. The conflict between Johnson and the Radical Republicans came to a climax when Johnson attempted to remove whom from office? How did Congress respond to Johnson's action?
6. What significant contributions did Johnson make in foreign affairs?
7. Who won the election of 1868?

D. Bourbon Reconstruction Begins

Even while Grant was still in office, views toward Reconstruction were changing. Many Republican supporters were beginning to think that abandoning blacks and Southerners might be better than losing the whole country to the turmoil of Radical Reconstruction. They believed that peace in the South would certainly be better for business. The country was sick of bitter controversy and scandal. These attitudes paved the way for **Bourbon Reconstruction,** reconstruction led by conservative Southerners, or "Redeemers."

Liberal Republicans in 1872 persuaded Congress to pardon the remaining former Confederate leaders. A General Amnesty Act in 1872 pardoned all but a few hundred Confederate leaders. Those who had held federal offices at the time of secession were among those excluded. This action paved the way for many former southern leaders to regain their influence in government.

Although the blacks had gained rights on paper, the white Southerners did not find it easy to accept the changes that made blacks their legal equals. While blacks and Radicals were able to hang on to offices for a while, they soon found they could not match the organization and experience of Southerners who now sought to "redeem the South" from black rule. Southern states began the process of turning out blacks and Republicans and replacing them with southern Democrats. It was only in areas still occupied by Federal forces that Republican governments held on a bit longer. Grant, meanwhile, became more and more reluctant to send troops into the South to keep Republicans in power.

The Disputed Election of 1876

Since the Grant administration had been marred by one scandal after another, and since corruption existed in some state and local governments as well, both political parties chose honest reformers as candidates in 1876. When the results came in, Democrat **Samuel J. Tilden** of New York won the popular vote. He also had an electoral college vote of 184, compared to 165 for **Rutherford B. Hayes,** his opponent. But the votes of three southern states occupied by Federal troops—Florida, Louisiana, and South Carolina—were disputed. If the Democratic votes from those states were counted, Tilden would win easily. But if the Republican votes were accepted, Hayes would win, 185 to 184.

This was an unusual situation. Whose electoral votes should be counted? Finally Congress appointed a special electoral commission. Five senators, five representatives,

An 1876 campaign banner for the Democrats, Samuel Tilden and his running mate

Lemonade Lucy

Lucy Ware Webb Hayes was popular throughout her life for her moral uprightness and charity. When Lucy was only two, her father died while on a trip to Kentucky to arrange for the freeing of his slaves. Lucy's mother was a woman of strong convictions, and she shared them with her two sons and daughter. Lucy was trained in religious schools along with her two older brothers; she later attended Wesleyan Women's College (the first chartered college for women in the United States) at age sixteen and graduated with honors. Her commencement address was on "The Influence of Christianity on National Prosperity."

The young lawyer Rutherford B. Hayes was attracted by Lucy's beauty as well as by her reputation for religious devotion and intelligence. One year after her graduation, the two were engaged; and on December 30, 1852, they were married. She encouraged him as he defended fugitive slaves in court. In 1856 he first made a public stand against slavery by joining the new Republican party. With the coming of the Civil War, he believed it was his duty to join the Union army. Lucy did not discourage him, and when he was wounded in September of 1862, she joined him at the battlefront to nurse him back to health. Whenever she visited the Twenty-third Ohio Regiment, which he commanded, she spent much time encouraging the sick, writing for them, and tending to their needs. The grateful soldiers affectionately called her "Mother Lucy."

While still serving in the army, Hayes was elected to Congress. He served there from 1864 until he was elected the governor of Ohio in 1867. During his three terms in the Governor's Mansion, Lucy proved to be a perfect hostess and tremendous support to her husband. She was especially active in community services, and by her labors the Home for Soldiers' Orphans was started at Xenia, Ohio in 1869. She and her husband remained aloof from the scandals and waste of the Grant administration. When Hayes was elected president in 1877, he brought with him a wife who was well prepared for her role as First Lady.

From the day of the Inauguration, Lucy set a new trend of modesty and dignity in Washington. As the first First Lady with a college degree, she was hailed as a "new woman" in a new period of American history. The couple continued to have receptions and balls, but they were much more modest than the extravagant ones of the previous administration. The Hayes family was wholesome and God-fearing. The daily routine included after-dinner family gatherings in the Red Room to sing popular ballads and hymns. Afterward they retired to the Blue Room for family devotions and prayer.

The most noted trait of Lucy's stay in the White House was her insistence on abstinence from all gambling and liquor and from most dances. She was labeled as "Lemonade Lucy" and was criticized when she would not allow alcoholic beverages in the White House. But she was so gracious about her views that she gained the respect and good-humored support of the Washington officials. Her popularity did much to improve the popularity of her husband.

Two events during Hayes's administration are popular stories from White House lore. On Sunday, December 30, 1877, the couple held their twenty-fifth wedding anniversary in the Blue Room. Lucy dressed up in her original satin gown, many of the original guests were present, and the original minister led them in a renewal of their wedding vows. After the ceremony the two youngest children were baptized. The other event came on the following Easter, when Lucy came to the rescue of some children who were egg-rolling on Capitol grounds. When some Congressmen told them to leave, Lucy invited the children to the White House lawn. A similar invitation for Easter egg rolling has been given every year since.

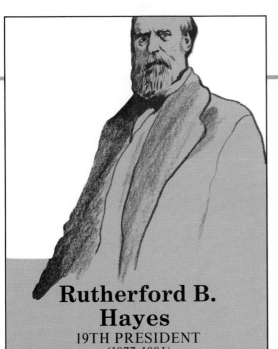

Rutherford B. Hayes

19TH PRESIDENT
(1877-1881)

Born: Delaware, Ohio, October 4, 1822
Family: married Lucy Ware Webb; seven sons, one daughter
Occupation: lawyer
Home: Spiegel Grove, Fremont, Ohio
Religion: no formal affiliation
Election: 1876—elected by an electoral commission over Samuel J. Tilden in a disputed election
Political Party: Republican
Vice President: William A. Wheeler
Interesting Facts and Accomplishments:
took oath of office privately and had no inaugural parade or ball because of national turmoil over his disputed election
first president to visit the Pacific Coast in 1880
first telephone installed in the White House while he was president
his wife was the first president's wife who was a college graduate; she received the nickname "Lemonade Lucy" because she served lemonade instead of liquor at White House receptions
Death: January 17, 1893

and five Supreme Court justices were picked for the commission. Seven of the commissioners were Republicans; seven were Democrats. Justice David Stevens was an independent. But he resigned rather than cast the deciding vote. His replacement, a Republican, voted to accept the Republican ballots, making Hayes the president.

The Hayes Presidency

Even though the Republicans won in 1876, the election was the final blow to the harsh Reconstruction of the Radicals. Rutherford B. Hayes had sought the support of southern whites, who favored his economic policies. To gain their support, he embraced policies that were to their liking. Undoubtedly his election was not contested because he had promised the South the freedoms it wanted. However, Hayes soon found that he had bargained away most of his presidential power. By the time he saw the real picture, it was too late to change his position.

Once in office Hayes pleased the Democrats more than he did his own party. In April of 1877, a month after taking office, Hayes withdrew the last federal troops from South Carolina and Louisiana. With troops no longer supervising elections, Democratic governors soon replaced the Republicans in power. With the military gone and white southern Democrats back in control in the southern states, Reconstruction now followed the dictates of these state leaders.

Section Review

1. What did the General Amnesty Act do?
2. What was unusual about the 1876 election?
3. What did President Hayes do to please Southerners?

E. Recovery in the South

While government tried to deal with the South's problems during the phases of Reconstruction, many unusual features developed in southern life. The South's people, economy, and political organization were molded by the pressures of Reconstruction.

Economic Aspects of Reconstruction

Because the Civil War had destroyed the South's plantation system, the freedmen were at once without jobs. Some hoped that the government would take over the old plantations and from them give every freed slave forty acres and a mule. Although some politicians supported such a plan, it never came to pass. While southern farmland needed laborers to grow its crops once again, there was no money to pay hired hands. To meet the needs of southern agriculture under such conditions, **sharecropping** became common.

Sharecropping—Blacks and poor whites became involved in this new economic system. Sharecroppers farmed small plots owned by planters and paid their annual rent for the use of the land with a part, or share, of their crop. Since sharecroppers had little money, especially at the beginning of the season, they borrowed for seed and provisions. Often the landlord was their creditor and owned the local store. When the harvest came in, the sharecropper squared up. If the sharecropper broke even, he was fortunate. He often started the next season in debt, however. The average sharecropper showed a profit only two years out of twenty-five. As a result the sharecropper was locked into a cycle of debt and poverty. The chances of breaking out of it were small indeed. Under such conditions, having the right to vote meant little. Most sharecroppers were more concerned about putting food on the family table.

Industry—During Reconstruction the Industrial Revolution finally reached the South. The Southerners had little money for industry, but many Northerners had capital and were eager to make profitable investments. These men saw the South as a place of opportunity. Consequently railroads, steelmaking, and the textile industry all expanded widely. As the need for laborers increased, Southerners moved from rural areas to factory towns and cities. The South's economy began to boom. By 1890 Southerners and Northerners spoke hopefully of a "New South" that would rival the North as an economic force.

One feature of southern industry was the **mill town.** Mill towns had some of the same features as plantations. The owner or investors built the housing, usually identical rows of houses near the factory site. The mill owners often built towns with churches and other community needs such as stores and doctor's offices. Often the workers bought needed items like food and clothing from company stores. Generally, employees in the textile industry hired whole families. Manufacturers of machines lowered the heights of their looms so that children could work them.

Political Trends

The prosperity of the nation through most of the era helped the Republicans control the presidency and usually Congress during most of the Reconstruction years. Stirring up war hatreds, or "waving the bloody shirt," also helped them stay in power, because Republicans were associated with winning the war and with freeing the slaves. The Republicans made inroads right after the war as the vote was given to blacks for the first time and ex-Confederate whites were barred from the polls. But when southern "Redeemers" got their power back, the Republican party declined dramatically in the South.

Because Southerners generally blamed the war and the hardships of Reconstruction on the Republicans, the South aligned itself with the Democratic party. For a century the South voted solidly for Democratic candidates almost without exception. Sometimes when people referred to the South's strong support of the Democratic party, they called it *the Solid South.*

In 1866 a secret organization, the **Ku Klux Klan,** was founded to frighten blacks and whites sympathetic to black interests away from the polls. Their least offensive tactic was to boycott businesses and force them to close. More unsavory were Klansmen dressed as white-hooded ghosts who rode through black communities at night, erecting burning crosses and even beating or killing blacks who tried to exercise their civil rights.

Southern moderates and many Northerners were upset by the Klan's activities. Congress passed two acts in 1870 and 1871, the Force Act and the Ku Klux Klan Act, to deal with Klan abuses. The acts outlawed the use of force to prevent people from voting and gave President Grant the power to place federal troops in polling places to insure everyone's voting rights. The Klan was officially disbanded, but in reality it went underground.

Civil Rights

Congress did pass two acts to give blacks citizenship and all of its privileges or civil rights. The Civil Rights Act of 1866, noted earlier, had granted freedmen the same rights and legal protection as whites regardless of local laws. A second act, the Civil Rights Act of 1875, guaranteed equal accommodations in public places, such as inns and theaters. It also said blacks could serve on juries. However, the bill did not provide any means of enforcing its provisions. The Supreme Court further weakened the legislation when in 1883 it declared the social provisions of the bill to be unconstitutional.

As the years passed, concern for the rights of the blacks lessened. The Civil Rights Acts were no longer enforced, although they did serve as precedents for the civil rights acts passed in the twentieth century. In the meantime blacks found little political equality.

Reforms in the South

Before the war the South had collected few taxes for public purposes. After the war both taxes and spending increased. Many people were critical of the high spending of southern governments, but in many instances the spending was justified. For the first time southern states began providing free public education. Prison systems were improved. Care for mentally and physically handicapped people developed, and imprisonment for debt was abolished.

Reconstruction Evaluated

Reconstruction was not a happy time for anyone. Northerners were not satisfied

Ku Klux Klan members in their white hoods

with its processes or results, and many Southerners remained bitter. The Civil War had caused a revolution, economically and socially, in the South. Not all the changes of Reconstruction, however, were ushered in smoothly. Some advances made were even lost. However, the postwar events and policies laid a foundation for change.

Some critics believe that Reconstruction was unduly hard on the South. It should be remembered, however, that the South had been defeated in a war, and the region was in disarray politically, economically, and socially. Recovery from such devastation could not be painless.

Some critics condemn Reconstruction as not having gone far enough. While it did insure that blacks got civil rights listed on paper, it is true that those rights did not become permanently established during Reconstruction. It must be remembered that the granting of such rights was a major step. Besides, not even Northerners were ready for the blacks in their region to gain significant social and political power. Reconstruction left many social, political, and economic problems for future generations to solve, but it also began the legislation and set an example for present Americans to follow or improve.

Reconstruction's chances for success were limited still further by great changes that America was undergoing at the same time. America was industrializing, and the industrial age brought a whole new set of problems. In both Reconstruction and the industrial era, people tried to solve these problems in new ways. Sometimes the solutions proposed were simply experiments. When they did not work, they should have been discarded.

Unfortunately, when people fail to assume their responsibility, government moves in. Some of the problems of Reconstruction should have been solved first by individuals willing to follow Biblical precepts on how to treat others. Some problems could have been solved by churches or private groups. But when they were not solved these ways, the federal government moved in. And life for Americans was really never the same again, as federal government powers began to increase.

Section Review

1. Describe the system of sharecropping.
2. How did the Industrial Revolution come to the South?
3. What was the purpose of the Ku Klux Klan?
4. How did Congress show its disapproval of the Klan's purpose and activities?

Summary

At the end of the Civil War the South's government, economy, and society were in disarray. Because of its condition, the South needed a time of Reconstruction. This Reconstruction did not come easily or smoothly, however, because of conflicting policies and desires in the nation. Presidents Lincoln and Johnson tried to restore the South quickly and with little punishment. Radical Republicans in Congress opposed these lenient policies and determined to make Reconstruction follow their strict guidelines. Eventually the Radicals lost their control, and Southerners were able to finish Reconstruction on their own terms.

Chapter Review

Do You Remember?

■ Match the accomplishment or related activity with the man responsible for it.

1. Ten Per Cent Plan
2. impeached president
3. secretary of war who refused to leave office
4. Alaska purchase
5. presidential scandals
6. lost the disputed election of 1876
7. was a leading Radical Republican
8. withdrew the last federal troops from the South

a. Ulysses S. Grant
b. Rutherford B. Hayes
c. Andrew Johnson
d. Abraham Lincoln
e. William Seward
f. Edwin Stanton
g. Charles Sumner
h. Samuel Tilden

■ Unscramble these letters to find the names of groups involved in Reconstruction.

9. TARGEBACSPREG (Northerners in the South)
10. DEFEMERN (slaves no longer)
11. DEMERRESE (Bourbons)
12. PRORRASHECEPS (poor farmers)
13. GACLASAWS (despised Southerners)

■ Match the following legislation and amendments with their effects.

14. Wade-Davis Bill
15. Thirteenth Amendment
16. Fourteenth Amendment
17. Reconstruction Act of 1867
18. Tenure of Office Act
19. Fifteenth Amendment

a. made all persons citizens
b. used to impeach Johnson
c. abolished slavery
d. Congress's unsuccessful attempt to override Lincoln's plan
e. gave blacks the vote
f. put the South under military rule

Why Is It So?

1. Why did the South need Reconstruction?
2. Why did Radical Republicans object to Presidential Reconstruction?
3. Why was Johnson impeached?
4. How was Johnson successful in foreign affairs?
5. Why did the Republicans win the election of 1876?

What Do You Think?

1. Why is *Reconstruction* a good name for the period of time following the Civil War?
2. How might Reconstruction have been different if Lincoln had lived?

19

Industrialism

When the United States entered the nineteenth century, it was a quiet land with family farms, small villages, and a few small cities on the Atlantic coastline. By the end of the century, however, crowded cities, busy factories, and mechanized farms stretched across the country. At the dawn of the twentieth century, the United States was on its way to becoming the greatest industrial nation in the world. Capitalism, America's economic system, along with new industrial techniques and American ingenuity (IN juh NOO ih tee; inventive ability or cleverness), were providing people with a host of products that made life easier. At the same time, America's population swelled. The population in 1800 was less than 5.5 million. The 1870 census counted 40 million, and by 1910 the population had reached 92 million. Immigration was the biggest single reason for that growth though the birthrate was high as well. Not only

The nineteenth century saw the United States emerge as a major industrial power, as is demonstrated by this carriage factory in Rochester, New York.

did the population increase but also the size of the country. In 1800 there were only sixteen states in the Union, but a hundred years later there were forty-five.

The late nineteenth century was a time of growth for the nation and especially for its industries. The land and its people were uniquely suited for its large industrial building project.

A. Materials and People

The United States was able to undergo such rapid changes for a variety of reasons. No single factor could have produced such change by itself. Two of the resources that helped the United States to produce goods for itself and the world were its supplies of raw materials and its labor force.

Natural Resources

One key to American industrial growth was its abundant natural resources. God endowed the nation with fertile soil and almost all the raw materials needed for important industries. After the purchase of Alaska in 1867, there was little geographic growth. Hawaii, Puerto Rico, and a few other areas were added. Yet the resources grew as new minerals were discovered and previously inaccessible regions were opened by new means of transportation.

Great lodes of gold, silver, and copper were found in the Rocky Mountains, the Far West, and Alaska. After the Civil War thousands of miners and businessmen streamed into the sparsely settled West. Towns with exotic or unusual names like Eureka, Paradise, Coarregold, Sloughouse, Dinkey Creek, and Whiskeytown, flourished briefly near the rich ore veins. When the ore was gone, most miners moved on, leaving behind some ghost towns. But some stayed in the West and found new ways to earn their living.

The rich iron ore deposits of northern Minnesota, the Mesabi (muh SAH bee) and Cayuna (kuh YOO nuh) ranges, provided raw materials for the growing iron and steel

Top: *An old mining town in Montana*
Lower right: *A deserted mining camp*

industries. Petroleum fuel resources added to America's wealth of natural resources. Tremendous coal deposits also provided an important fuel. And another source of energy, water power, would soon help the nation to produce electricity.

Another important American resource was its timber. Vast forests covering the Northwest and other areas of the country supplied timber for lumber, pulp, and other uses.

Immigration Provides Labor

Developing industries needed workers. Most of the American population was hard at work in the 1800s. For the country to expand its industrial production, it needed more workers. The growing tide of immigrants met America's need for laborers.

Immigrants Come to America—Before 1880 most of the immigrants came from northwestern European countries like Britain, Ireland, Germany, or the Scandinavian countries, and they were largely Protestant. Although immigrants continued to come from those countries, a greater proportion now came from eastern and southern European countries, and they were often Roman Catholics. Italians, Turks, Greeks, Slavs, Hungarians, and Rumanians all flocked to America. From northern Russia came Russians, Poles (Poland was then part of Russia), Finns, and Jews. Other immigrants came from Russia's Baltic States, Estonia, Latvia, and Lithuania. Between 1890 and 1914, the largest single group of immigrants was the Italians.

Most Europeans crossed the Atlantic by the shortest and cheapest routes. Many traveled first to Liverpool, England, or to Bremen or Hamburg, Germany, where the major steamship companies operated.

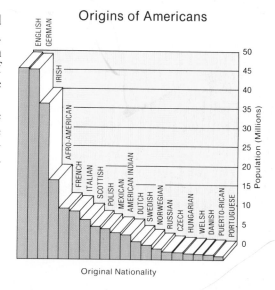

Steamship companies often used freighters to carry passengers over to the United States and then carried raw materials or manufactured goods back to Europe. Most immigrants bought the cheapest tickets available. These tickets gave them space in steerage, the noisiest, most crowded part of the ship, located underneath the deck and near the engine and rudder. Passengers brought their food with them in their bundles. Seasickness or disease often made the voyage a miserable experience, and some immigrants lost their lives. People from different walks of life were thrown together under strange conditions. In addition, many came from different countries and spoke different languages.

Some immigrants had been recruited in their homelands by agents of various American companies in need of laborers. It was common for companies to make contracts with immigrants. They agreed to pay their fares if the immigrants would agree to work a specified length of time for the employer. Other immigrants used most of their life's

This graph showing the heritage of Americans in 1980 gives us a clue to the diversity of American immigration.

savings to come to America. Still others had their trans-Atlantic tickets and even their rail tickets from the port where they landed paid for by relatives who had come earlier.

Employers were eager to hire immigrants. Because the recent immigrants were usually happy just to have a job, they were generally willing to work for cheaper wages than other Americans. Moreover, immigrants who complained risked losing their jobs. There were always newcomers waiting to be hired. Employers also liked hiring immigrants because most were hard working and reluctant to join the labor unions.

Ellis Island and Ports of Entry—The largest number of European immigrants came to America by way of New York harbor. Many were registered there at **Ellis Island.** It served as a temporary stopover for incoming immigrants who used its beautifully designed great hall, dining room, and hospital. Those who looked healthy enough to hold a job and who could prove they had the means to reach distant destinations usually took the ferry to New Jersey and rode a train inland. Others entered New York City totally bewildered. Public Health Service doctors assisted the immigrants who were ill. If they could be cured, they were treated and sent on their way as soon as possible. The immigrant center at Ellis Island operated from 1894 to 1943 and handled the entry of more than seventeen million immigrants. Often immigrants feared being turned back at Ellis Island, but of the millions who came, the total number rejected was under two per cent.

Some immigrants landed in Montreal; others, especially the Irish, came to Boston. New Orleans was a port of entry for many immigrants planning to go to the Midwest or the Far West.

Immigrants often settled in neighborhoods of cities where others of their nationality lived. Some of these neighborhoods came to be known by such names as "Chinatown" or "Little Italy." In later years after immigrants learned the language and saved enough money, many moved on to other areas of the city or suburbs and left the inner city to be occupied by newer immigrants.

Immigrants Work to Build America— While immigrants came from many lands, Ireland provided a large share in the 1800s. In the 1840s a potato blight spread slowly across Europe. The plant disease devastated Ireland, where the potato was the major

Ellis Island in New York harbor

farm crop and food. One-eighth of Ireland's population starved to death or died from diseases caused by malnutrition. Another three-eighths of the people, three million in all, left Ireland. Many of them came to the United States, primarily to Boston and New York City.

The Irish played important roles in the construction of America's canal and railroad systems. An early group of Irish immigrants provided the muscle to build the Erie Canal. Crews of Irishmen were also responsible for laying the track for western railroads. The Irish took these jobs despite a high risk of injury because they saw them as a means to escape their poverty.

Some Irishmen sought altogether different work. Because of previously unstable circumstances, they sought more stable jobs in civic service. Men became police or firemen, and Irish women became schoolmarms and domestic servants.

China also provided many immigrants for America. Because American ships were involved in the China trade, news of the discovery of gold in California soon reached China. Since China was overpopulated and her people faced flood and famine, the Chinese were easily attracted to America. Opportunities of the California gold rush brought them in great numbers. As was frequently the case with immigrants, the men came first. Once they had attained their riches, they hoped to return to China and find wives. Instead of mining for gold themselves, many of the Chinese founded businesses such as restaurants and laundries, providing needed services for others. Later, Chinese workers were hired to build western sections of the transcontinental railroad.

Chinese immigrants continued to come, and as long as there were jobs available,

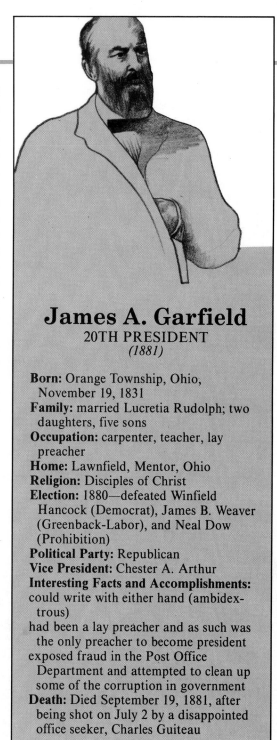

James A. Garfield
20TH PRESIDENT
(1881)

Born: Orange Township, Ohio, November 19, 1831
Family: married Lucretia Rudolph; two daughters, five sons
Occupation: carpenter, teacher, lay preacher
Home: Lawnfield, Mentor, Ohio
Religion: Disciples of Christ
Election: 1880—defeated Winfield Hancock (Democrat), James B. Weaver (Greenback-Labor), and Neal Dow (Prohibition)
Political Party: Republican
Vice President: Chester A. Arthur
Interesting Facts and Accomplishments:
could write with either hand (ambidextrous)
had been a lay preacher and as such was the only preacher to become president
exposed fraud in the Post Office Department and attempted to clean up some of the corruption in government
Death: Died September 19, 1881, after being shot on July 2 by a disappointed office seeker, Charles Guiteau

Americans did not object too much to their arrival. But when financial panics came, hostility grew. Californians claimed that the Chinese, who were willing to work for lower wages, were getting the jobs that whites deserved. They soon influenced politicians to pass the **Exclusion Act of 1882,** which cut off all legal Chinese immigration except for a few hundred per year. This act was passed over the veto of President Chester Arthur, who had assumed office after the assassination of James Garfield in 1881.

Northern Europe also sent many of its people to America. Political and religious unrest swept the German states during the 1840s. When the revolutions failed, people left that land. Many of these people had been landowners in Europe, and so they had enough money to buy land in the United States when they arrived. They often settled in the farming areas of America's heartland such as in Wisconsin. Others found work as lumberjacks in the northern woods, and then they bought farmland soon after.

Scandinavians—Norwegians, Swedes, and Finns—also came to America. They tended to settle whole towns or counties in Iowa, Minnesota, Wisconsin, and the Dakotas. They had their own newspapers and started their own colleges. Most were Lutheran and had come to America in protest of the policies of their churches back home. Some Swedes, Norwegians, and Finns worked in logging camps; others worked in the iron mines of northern Minnesota and the copper mines of Michigan.

The people of these and other ethnic groups contributed greatly to the American way of life. Inventions, works of literature and music, designs, and customs came with the immigrants. America would not be what it is today without the contributions these

citizens made to the developing culture of the nation.

Section Review

1. What were some of the changes the nation experienced during the nineteenth century?
2. What were two of the factors that helped the industries of the United States to grow?
3. List some of our nation's natural resources that aided industrial growth.
4. After 1880 many immigrants came from what countries?
5. What was the significance of Ellis Island?

Chester A. Arthur
21ST PRESIDENT
(1881-1885)

Born: Fairfield, Vermont, October 5, 1830

Family: married Ellen Lewis Herndon; one daughter, two sons

Occupation: teacher, lawyer

Home: Albany, New York

Religion: Episcopalian

Election: none; assumed office at the death of President Garfield

Political Party: Republican

Vice President: none

Interesting Facts and Accomplishments:

was a widower; his wife died about a year before he became president

often wore a flower in his buttonhole and a silk handkerchief in his vest pocket

had Robert Todd Lincoln, Abraham Lincoln's son, as his secretary of war

Death: November 18, 1886

B. Transportation and Technology

Two more American resources that helped the land's industries grow were its transportation networks and its technological developments. Promoting the development of these features became an important goal for the country.

Transportation and the Railroads

While steamships were improving transportation for trade with foreign countries, the railroads made it possible for America to conquer its immense territory. Railroads also moved America's raw materials to distant factories and distributed the manufactured goods to ready markets.

By 1860 there were 30,626 miles of track, but almost all of it was in the East. There were still no railroad bridges across the Hudson, Ohio, or Mississippi rivers. In addition, since different companies built the railroads, they failed to use a uniform gauge (width) of track. Different gauges kept lines from connecting, prohibiting transportation from area to area unless goods were transferred from one line to another. Such problems made it difficult to travel by rail or to send freight long distances. Chicago and New York had rails between them, but passengers and cargo had to change cars six times en route. The Civil War made the problems obvious and stimulated the building of more track and the development of more efficient and economical systems.

Consolidation Helps the Railroads— One means of making more efficient and more economical railroads was **consolidation,** combining small lines. Sometimes this was done through the friendly purchase of one company by another, but more often it was the result of ruthless pressure. Several men sought to gain control of large railroad networks. **Cornelius Vanderbilt** had the vision of connecting the Great Lake states to New York City by rail. He forced all his competition to sell out and gained a railroad empire. J. Edgar Thompson secretly bought up small lines in Pennsylvania and Ohio. Once he had a base, he cut his rates and drove his rivals out of business. Then he raised his rates.

Other men tried to make fortunes as they built railroad empires. Although small railroads were often hurt by the consolidation, the process did help the nation acquire an efficient railroad transportation network.

Government Policy Aids Railroad Building—A second factor leading to the development of a railroad system was government policy. Lincoln and the Republican party were committed to the idea of a transcontinental railroad. The outbreak of the war caused Congress to agree, and it chartered the **Union Pacific** and **Central Pacific** railroads in 1864. These two lines—the Union Pacific, building westward using Irish workers and war veterans, and the Central Pacific, building eastward using Chinese laborers—were linked on May 10, 1869. The official wedding of the rails took place at Promontory Point near Ogden, Utah, a short distance from the Great Salt Lake. The Central Pacific had faced the trial of crossing the steep Sierra Nevada Mountains. The Union Pacific gang had its problems, too. Because of a lack of wood, most of their ties had to be shipped long distances. A lack of water and the danger of attacks from fierce plains Indian tribes also hindered their work.

The federal government gave financial aid to the railroad builders but did not hand over sums of money directly. Instead, the government provided the builders with land. In 1862 and 1864 Congress developed a new land grant system. Each railroad got a strip of land four hundred feet wide for the right of way for its tracks. It also received two sections of land on alternating

The celebration at Promontory Point marked the completion of the first transcontinental railroad. As a result, the Union Pacific could offer passage from Omaha to San Francisco in four days.

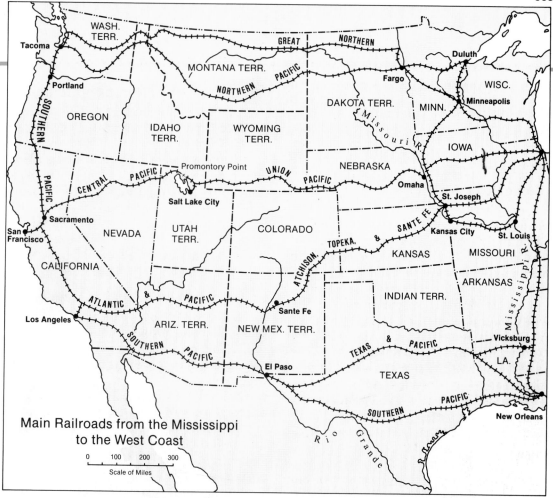

Main Railroads from the Mississippi
to the West Coast

0   100   200   300
Scale of Miles

sides of the tracks. The railroad could do whatever it wanted with the 1,280 acres of land it was given for each mile of track it laid. The railroads held on to some lands. More often than not, they sold the lands next to their tracks to eager settlers. The money from the sales helped pay for building the railroad.

The government's Homestead Act of 1862 also helped railroads. The alternate sections of land owned by the federal government were sold at low prices or made available free under the Homestead Act. Thus even more settlers, and land speculators, came into the region by means of the new railroad lines.

Building Other Lines—Because the men investing in railroads were accumulating enormous wealth, other people soon sought railroad land grants of their own. In 1864 Congress approved generous land grants for building a railroad linking Lake Superior and the Pacific Ocean. The Northern Pacific line, finished in 1883, joined Duluth, Minnesota, to Portland, Oregon, and also to Spokane and Tacoma, Washington.

In 1884 the Atchison, Topeka, and Santa Fe Railroad provided a more southerly route. The Texas Pacific Railroad built across Texas linked to the Southern Pacific at El Paso, Texas. When this route was finished, New Orleans was linked by rail with Los Angeles and San Francisco. Another transcontinental line was built with private funds by **James J. Hill.** His **Great Northern Railroad** included extensions into Canada to help provide transportation for farmers there.

Technology

Another important ingredient in American industrialization was technology—scientific inventions and improved methods for industry. The Yankee ingenuity at the dawn of the nineteenth century had, by the century's end, turned into a remarkable ability to innovate. Some inventions, like **Alexander Graham Bell's** telephone, led to whole new industries and big changes in American life. Other simple inventions—rivets for points of stress in Levi Strauss's blue jeans, for example—although minor, remain useful even today. The number of patents issued by the patent office shot up, averaging more than 21,000 a year through the 1880s and 1890s.

The increased use of electricity was especially beneficial to the advancement of both industry and technology. **Thomas Edison** promoted the generation of electricity for practical uses and also invented many electrical appliances. His incandescent light (light bulb) was among the most important. Hundreds of other inventors also made important contributions to American industry.

Section Review

1. How did the Civil War stimulate the growth of railroads?
2. Who was Cornelius Vanderbilt and what was he noted for?
3. List several government policies that aided railroad building.
4. Why were Bell and Edison important inventors?

C. New Ways of Doing Business

America's industries grew in size and produced more and more during the late 1800s. Competition, new technology, and better management helped to bring about this industrial growth. Companies were constantly looking for ways to improve their production, but improvements often required investment money or **capital.** To meet this financial need and other legal needs, businesses began to find new ways to organize and obtain capital.

Corporations for Increased Capital

In America's early years most businesses were either **sole proprietorships** or **partnerships.** Sole proprietorships were businesses owned by one person, while partnerships were owned by two or more people. Both worked well for small-scale operations. Proprietorships had the advantages of catering to individual needs. The owner got all the profit, but he also absorbed all the losses and often lacked the funds to expand his business.

Partnerships had the distinct advantage of increasing capital in a business and of sharing the losses of the business. **Andrew Carnegie** built a huge steel empire with the help of multiple partners. They provided him with expertise in areas where he knew little. He suggested that the epitaph on his tombstone should read: "Here lies a man who was able to surround himself with others far wiser than he." However, a big disadvantage to sharing the responsibility for all losses in a partnership was that those losses must be shared even when they resulted from the faults or failures of just one partner. It could lead to the financial ruin of all the partners unless protective measures were taken. Other disadvantages were

Andrew Carnegie

that all the partners must participate in the business's legal dealings, and if one partner died or pulled out, the partnership is ended and must be re-formed.

Another way to organize a business is to incorporate, a method that became very popular in the late 1800s. A **corporation** is formed when a business gains a legal charter and sells stock to many individual investors. Although the stockholders are essentially the owners, they can lose only the amount they invested in the stock if the corporation fails. If the business makes a profit, the stockholders receive dividends, or payments from that profit. Moreover, a corporation is considered a "person" in the eyes of the law, and it can carry on legal dealings without all of its stockholders being present. Nor is its existence ended by the death of a manager or single stockholder.

Because of advantages like these, more and more executives sought to incorporate in the years after the Civil War. Steel,

petroleum, and chemical manufacturers are but a few of the many who used the corporate form of business.

Sources of Corporate Money

Company executives realized that large amounts of capital were needed to finance the growth of their ventures. Some people with savings or other wealth became stockholders, buying stock with money that provided the corporation with capital. More capital, however, was raised in larger amounts from other sources.

The nation's banking system also helped provide industry with capital. As more Americans entered the work force and the number of businesses grew, the number of bank deposits increased. Banks invested their money in corporations to make more money and also offered credit to such corporations to cover the expansion of industry. Another large-scale source of capital came from life insurance companies that invested the premiums paid by policy holders.

Corporations Find New Ways to Organize

As the corporations grew larger, they needed better internal organization. America's early factories had had few executives, usually just managers and bookkeepers. Most new large-scale operations, however, required more management. Thus separate departments to handle each major phase of operations became normal. There were department heads for such responsibilities as purchasing, marketing, accounting, financing, and development. These specialized executives often helped to manage businesses more efficiently and profitably.

In 1882 oilman **John D. Rockefeller** and his associates formed the first **trust.** A trust

D. Effects of Industrial Expansion

The growth of industries brought many changes to the way Americans lived and to the government's attention to industry.

Changing American Life

First, America's trade increased greatly. American foodstuffs and factory products found their way to distant parts of the world. This trade also helped to make many more products available to Americans.

Second, urbanization occurred. Immigrants swelled city populations. In addition, as farming mechanized and farm production increased, fewer farmers were needed. Farmers—or at least several of the their children—often moved to towns and cities where work was available.

Industrialization emphasized urban problems. Pollution of air or water, overcrowding, and crime all became more obvious when concentrated in a single area.

Industrialism also meant that Americans began to have more leisure time. Machines freed people from some work, while other machines, labor-saving devices, made work easier. Americans soon found new ways to use the extra time. New spectator sports captured the public fancy. Others participated in already existing sports or tried the newly invented or popularized ones such as bicycling, tennis, or basketball.

In addition, industrialism affected American family life. Some women had gone to work outside the home during the Civil War. A few continued to work after the war. Some were recruited to work in expanding industries. And because inventions made housekeeping easier, some women were finding time to take other jobs. The number of women in the work force would continue to grow in the years that

combined several separate companies into one super-size corporation, such as Rockefeller's Standard Oil. The executives of the trust then had power to organize and manage all the companies involved as they wished. Other industries followed Rockefeller's example and set up trusts of their own in the 1880s.

Section Review

1. What are some advantages of a partnership over a sole proprietorship?
2. What is the difference between a partnership and a corporation?
3. How did corporations acquire capital?
4. What is a trust? Who formed the first business trust?

John D. Rockefeller made his enormous fortune in the oil industry followed, changing the lifestyle of more and more families.

Americans Focus on Capitalism

The United States had been founded with a capitalistic economy. **Capitalism** is an economy in which people are free to invest in businesses and make profits on their investments. Businesses are owned by private citizens instead of the government, and anyone is allowed to go into business, competing with others. Generally capitalism works well because it recognizes man's natural selfish desires. In competing for personal gain, businesses usually strive to sell good products or services so that the business can continue and grow. Poor products or services drive customers away. The competition of businesses created by a capitalistic system helped to bring Americans a high standard of living.

Nonetheless, industrialization revealed some weaknesses in the capitalistic system. The capitalistic system is not perfect, and man's evil nature caused some industrialists to run roughshod over their competitors. In some industries, workers labored long hours doing dangerous work at low pay while company owners became millionaires. The Biblical idea that "the labourer is worthy of his hire" (Luke 10:7) was sometimes ignored.

At that time of rapid industrial growth, a philosophy that justified harsh actions became popular. Charles Darwin's theory of evolution was used to defend piling up wealth by any means one wanted. Darwin's theory said that there was a constant struggle in nature. Only the fittest members of the species would survive. Applied to society, this thinking was called **social Darwinism**. Social Darwinists showed little mercy and no recognition of human weak-

nesses. In industry, social Darwinists held that driving weaker competitors out of business was just a part of the struggle for survival. Making a profit, according to their philosophy, should be accomplished by any means possible, even if others were hurt.

The ageless principles of God's Word shed light on this thinking. God's Word does not justify taking advantage of the weaknesses of others, even our enemies, for personal gain. The Bible reminds us often of the need to show mercy and love. Some industrialists gained wealth but ignored the principles of God's Word. "He that oppresseth the poor to increase his riches . . . shall surely come to want" (Prov. 22:16).

Closely tied to capitalism was the idea of *laissez-faire* economics. Most Americans believed that the best way for a capitalistic economy to develop was without any government interference or regulation. Those who supported *laissez-faire* policies argued that government regulation would disturb the fine balance between supply of products and the public's demand for those products. The economy might be ruined. Yet because individual men and some companies did not take on the responsibility to make changes, to right wrongs, and to correct imperfections in the system, people put more and more pressure on the government to do so. Americans were growing fearful that large corporations were going to control the nation. They generally preferred that their elected representative in Congress would take that control instead.

America's Government Begins to Regulate Business

Thus another result of industrialism was governmental regulation of business. Although the regulation at the time was probably meant to be experimental and was not as extensive as today's, a precedent was set. Government regulation of business and industry grew ever after.

The Interstate Commerce Act of 1887— Because the ruthless competition among railroads had hurt small shippers and western farmers, government regulation of railroad rates was demanded first. The first law regulating industry, the **Interstate Commerce Act** of 1887, was a reaction to such practices.

Initially, states set up commissions to regulate the rates railroads could charge. Midwestern states like Illinois and Iowa provided strong enforcement while in other states, like Massachusetts and Alabama, commissions gave only advisory opinions. Disputes grew as the rulings of the states affected railroad transportation in other states.

When the Supreme Court ruled that states could regulate railroads only within their own state boundaries and not those crossing state lines, Congress was pressured to act. In 1887 the Interstate Commerce Act was passed. It directed railroads to set "reasonable and just rates." It also prevented railroads from charging more for short runs where there was little competition than for long runs where the competition was stiff. An Interstate Commerce Commission was formed to examine complaints and take offenders to court.

But when the offenders came to court, the judges usually decided in favor of the railroads. Thus the ICC lost nearly every case filed from 1887 to 1906. Yet the act had an impact. It set a precedent for the government to organize other independent regulatory agencies. And in later years as the Supreme Court judges changed and reflected public opinion toward business practices more closely, court cases made more regulation effective.

A monopoly is the complete control of a certain business or industry so that free trade is discouraged. A trust or a holding company, for example, creates a monopoly. This 1881 political cartoon depicts a monopoly as a snake threatening America's liberty.

The Sherman Anti-Trust Act of 1890— The public viewed trusts with suspicion. They felt that their size and power gave them an unfair edge that harmed free enterprise. Large trusts such as Rockefeller's had driven small companies out of business by lowering prices. Once the competition was gone, prices reached new highs. By 1880 both political parties promised to regulate trusts.

In 1890 under Benjamin Harrison's presidency, Congress passed the **Sherman Anti-Trust Act.** The act said, "Every contract, combination in the form of trust or otherwise in restraint of trade or commerce . . . is illegal." But since "restraint of trade" was not defined and the courts still favored big business, the act had little effect at first. Its effects were also weakened when trusts devised ways to get around it. A new form of business consolidation, the **holding company,** came into being. The holding company gained control of companies by buying stock. While member companies retained their names, the holding company made decisions for them in the interest of the entire group as if it were one giant corporation. The holding company controlled the business as efficiently as the trusts had before them.

Abuses of Workers Lead to Labor Unions

The industrial era aided the rapid rise of labor unions. The abuses in some factories opened the door to unofficial and organized protests by the workers. Many began to organize in large groups or unions that could stand up against the management and ask for desired wages and working conditions. Although unions showed spurts of growth in this era, growth was often uneven. Competition for jobs among war veterans and immigrants plus economic depressions in 1873, 1882, and 1893 hindered their growth.

*The Knights of Labor—*The **Knights of Labor** began in 1869 under the leadership of Uriah P. Stephens. Its goal was the formation of one big union for all workers, skilled and unskilled, men and women. It sought equal pay for men and women, an eight-hour day for workers, safety features, and compensation (payment for loss) for injuries occurring on the job. In the year 1879 Terence V. Powderly took over the union's leadership. He was against strikes and believed that the union should not take sides politically. The membership rose from 9,000 in 1879 to 115,000 by 1884. By 1886 the Knights had a membership of 700,000.

Unfortunately for the future of the union, 1886 was a bad year. In Chicago about 80,000 workers, mostly Knights, struck for an eight-hour day. The police killed several workers when things appeared to get out of hand. Some anarchists, people who refused to obey the laws, staged a protest rally soon after. The police moved in to break up the meeting and someone threw a bomb into the crowd, killing a policeman and six spectators. A riot ensued, killing eleven more people. The Haymarket Square Riot, as it was called, hurt the unions since people then linked the union with violence. Membership dropped to just 100,000 in four years.

The American Federation of Labor— A second union, **the American Federation of Labor,** began in 1881. Its first president was a British-born cigar maker, **Samuel Gompers.** Gompers saw the problem in the structure of the Knights of Labor and set up his union on different lines. Only skilled workers could join; dues were high; women were not allowed. Workers joined local craft unions with those of the same skills. Local unions then affiliated or associated with state and national groups. Each local union, however, made its own decisions and handled its own funds. The national group provided guidelines. This union also pushed for an eight-hour day and for **collective bargaining** (the right of unions to represent workers in negotiations with owners and managers). This union did use strikes, and its high dues were spent supporting the workers during strike times. A violent strike over a wage cut at Carnegie Steel's Homestead Plant in 1892 greatly hurt this union's attempt to organize in other industries.

Responses to Unions—Employers were often unsympathetic to unions and their demands. They wanted the right to bargain with workers individually and deplored strikes because they hurt production. Courts did not favor unions either and often issued **injunctions,** official court orders, to stop strikes. The local press usually sided with employers too. Since most of the papers made their money from local advertising, they could ill afford to anger their advertisers. The general public reacted negatively to unions because they associated labor aims, like the distribution of wealth and agitation by lower classes, with socialism. Some also opposed collective bargaining because it could deprive an individual of his own worth.

In 1893 a group of employers joined together to form the National Association of Manufacturers. Its aim was to counteract unionism. In 1900 the National Civic Federation was formed. Its leaders, Frank Easley and Marcus Hanna, believed that labor unions were here to stay. The choice

The Johnstown Flood: The Nightmare of 1889

One of the great disasters in American history occurred in Pennsylvania in 1889. The victims were the mining town of Johnstown and some smaller towns to its north. Over two thousand people died. The killer was a flood resulting from the breaking of an old, neglected earthen dam. To some, however, the killer was actually the negligence of a group of millionaires who owned the dam and refused to make repairs they knew were necessary. These wealthy families were too busy enjoying the lake resort and the hunting and fishing spot created by the formation of Lake Conemaugh (KAHN uh MAW), at the time the largest artificial lake in the world.

The lake was three miles long, one mile wide, and in places one hundred feet deep. It contained twenty million tons of water. The earthen dam, located fourteen miles from Johnstown and at an elevation four hundred feet higher than the town, was thirty-seven years old. It stretched three hundred yards wide and seventy-two feet deep. It was wide enough at the top to have a two-lane dirt road there. To keep the fish in the lake, the spillways had been closed off. The overflow valves had clogged because of neglect. The few repairs that had been made on the dam had been done by stuffing tree stumps, leaves, and straw into the numerous leaks that had developed since the dam's construction. Several engineers had warned the owners of the dam's deteriorated condition. One company had even offered to pay half the cost of repairing the structure. Yet nothing had been done.

The people in the towns below had become indifferent as well. They had heard so many times that the dam was breaking that they had lost all concern. No one could convince them that the dam would someday actually break. And if it did break, they did not believe that the result would be disastrous.

At 3:10 P.M. on May 31, 1889, it happened. After a number of heavy storms, the dam burst. In thirty-five minutes, all twenty million tons of Lake Conemaugh came rushing down the valley in a wave forty feet high and traveling at forty miles an hour. At times it met an obstruction and the water piled higher, once up to ninety feet, and then it would burst through again to rush down on the towns below. Along the way it picked up debris that became as deadly as the wall of water itself: twenty-nine locomotives weighing up to eighty tons each, other railroad cars, boiling hot water from the iron works, hundreds of miles of barbed wire from a factory, the bricks and lumber from crushed houses and businesses, along with trees and animals. Because of the debris, the water at the top of the flood wave moved faster than the water at the bottom. Engineers estimated that the crushing force caused by that difference in speeds was as great as the power behind the water flowing over Niagara Falls. Nothing could stand in its way.

Except for the heroic efforts of many of the townspeople, many more lives would have been lost. Those who managed to escape the flood stood on the edge and hauled other people out. Some in buildings on the edge of the waters pulled others through windows to the safety of the buildings. Some people even leaped into the rushing waters to make rescues.

Every town along the flood's path was flattened. Finally, the waters were stopped at a bridge in Johnstown, where the debris piled up thirty feet high over sixty acres. Behind the debris, Johnstown had become a twenty-foot-deep lake. Then to make matters worse, the debris caught fire. Some that had escaped drowning but were pinned in the rubble were killed by the fire. Nearly one thousand people were never found.

Wreckage and debris from the Johnstown Flood

America and the world came to the rescue of the survivors. Clara Barton and her newly formed Red Cross reacted magnificently to its first major disaster. People from all over the world donated money and food to aid the needy. The millionaires who owned the lake did little except go into hiding to avoid the press.

In a remarkably short time Johnstown was rebuilt and again became a thriving iron and steel town. A coroner's investigation held the dam's owners responsible for the flood, but few people sued and no one won a suit against the millionaires. The total damages, staggering in 1889, came to seventeen million dollars. None of the survivors would ever forget the tragic day when neglect and indifference brought a rushing wall of death into unprepared Johnstown, Pennsylvania.

then became what kind of union employers would work with. They discouraged anti-capitalistic, socialistic, revolutionary unions and encouraged contact with conservative procapitalistic unions.

The Dangers of Materialism

Another obvious result of industrialism was an increase in wealth, both nationally and individually. By the year 1900 the nation counted four hundred millionaires. The buying power of the average worker had increased by fifty per cent over forty years. God's Word does not denounce wealth or money; instead, it denounces the love of money, its unwise use, and the envy and greed it can encourage. Christians are told to give God the first fruits of their labor. Sadly, in the industrial era as well as today,

Left: *The devastation of Johnstown*
Bottom: *This bedroom in the house of Cornelius Vanderbilt displays some of the extravagant luxury of the wealthy and materialistic.*

many Americans who had wealth were never satisfied. They wanted and sought more. Some of the rich competed with one another in showing off their wealth. **Materialism,** putting a higher value on money and possessions than Scripture and common sense dictate, surfaced as an American problem. It was a problem that would appear repeatedly throughout the twentieth century.

Section Review

1. List at least six major changes in America that resulted from industrial growth.
2. How did the industrial revolution affect the American family?
3. What is *social Darwinism?*
4. Why did labor unions emerge?
5. Who was the first president of the American Federation of Labor?

Summary

The late 1800s was a time of great industrial expansion for the United States. Growing industries used the nation's resources, its labor supply, railroad networks, and developing technology to produce more and more. Businesses also used forms of organization such as incorporation, trusts, and holding companies to increase capital and grow more powerful. While industrial expansion was generally good for the country, it did allow some men to take advantage of others while amassing large personal fortunes. Fear of ruthless business practices aided the growth of labor unions and eventually prompted the beginnings of government regulation of industry.

Chapter Review

Do You Remember?

■ Fill in the blanks with the appropriate word or phrase.

1. A business owned by just one person is called a _____.
2. The first transcontinental railroad was formed by the union of the _____ and the _____ in 1869.
3. Businesses need large amounts of money or _____ to finance their operations.
4. The _____ kept the Chinese from immigrating to the United States.

5. The Interstate Commerce Act was intended to regulate some of the abuses in the ____ industry.
6. Union members wanted ____ so that the union could negotiate with owners and management for them.
7. ____ is an improper concern for money and possessions.
8. Many of America's immigrants around the turn of the century landed first at ____.
9. A ____ is an advantageous business organization assembled under a charter by individual stockholders.
10. A theory of ____ was used to support the idea that the biggest and best businesses would survive while others would fail.
11. Uriah P. Stephens first led an early labor union called the ____.
12. The ____ was legislation intended to break up the unfair advantages of trusts.
13. ____ provided much of the labor for industries in the late 1800s.

Match these men with their achievements.

14. Alexander Graham Bell
15. Andrew Carnegie
16. Thomas Edison
17. Samuel Gompers
18. James J. Hill
19. John D. Rockefeller
20. Cornelius Vanderbilt

a. built the Great Northern Railroad
b. invented the incandescent light
c. formed a trust in the oil industry
d. consolidated railroads in the Northeast
e. invented the telephone
f. built a huge steel empire
g. president of the American Federation of Labor

Why Is It So?

1. Why was immigration important to the development of American industry?
2. How could consolidation help the railroads?
3. How did industries acquire the money they needed for capital?
4. Why were trusts and holding companies harmful to some?
5. Why were labor unions created?

What Do You Think?

1. Why did American industry expand so much in the late 1800s?
2. Why was it important for the United States to have transcontinental railroads?
3. Should government place controls on industries? Explain your answer.
4. Can Christians be wealthy without being materialistic? Can Christians be materialistic without being wealthy? Explain your answers.

Leaders of Industry and Invention

Andrew Carnegie: Steel

An industrial developer named Andrew Carnegie built huge steel mills in Pennsylvania. He used hard (anthracite) coal from the mines of eastern Pennsylvania and soft (bituminous) coal from other Appalachian areas to stoke huge ovens and converters.

Carnegie's parents were penniless Scottish immigrants. Carnegie himself had spent his childhood as a bobbin winder in a textile factory, earning only twelve and one-half cents a day. In America he got a job as a railroad telegraph boy. Because he acted quickly to prevent an accident and kept traffic moving in his boss's absence, he was promoted.

Carnegie saved his money and looked for ways to invest it. He believed that steel would be needed to build America and found the best ways to produce great amounts of it cheaply. A British engineer, Sir Henry Bessemer, had invented a converter that produced huge amounts of steel by blowing heated air through molten pig iron. This method was far superior to the forges used by blacksmiths, who could produce only small amounts. Carnegie got his foot in the door in the steel industry when he invested in the Keystone Bridge Company. Its steel bridges were stronger and easier to construct than wood bridges and soon replaced them.

Carnegie then started his own steel company, and new uses for the product made his business boom. Structural steel was soon used to build large buildings and even made skyscrapers possible. Barbed wire replaced wooden fences. Wire nails took the place of forged nails. In 1887 the U.S. Navy began to use steel armor plate on ships. Railroads used steel for rails and railroad cars.

Carnegie hired metallurgical engineers. They improved the quality of steel and also derived new alloys, mixtures of steel and other elements, for special uses. Making hard steel that could resist high temperatures without melting was basic to the development of dynamos for electric motors and generators, gasoline and diesel engines, and the machine tool industry.

Carnegie constantly sought ways to cut production and labor costs by mechanizing many procedures, and by holding his employees accountable for every penny spent. He formed partnerships with other men to gain capital for investments or to eliminate the risks of competing with them. Eventually all his partners became millionaires too.

Carnegie was the first captain of industry who viewed productivity and wealth as a means to achieve social goals. He did not believe that his business success resulted just from his ability to beat the competition. He believed that America's industrial supremacy was also the result of the triumph of its form of government over a monarchy. Education, churches, and libraries were some of the advantages brought by the American economic system.

Carnegie believed that along with wealth came responsibility. He was a steward, a wise caretaker, of the wealth he had gained. In an essay, *The Gospel of Wealth,* Carnegie spoke on the duties of the wealthy. Carnegie believed each man had a responsibility to provide for his own family just as the Word of God teaches in I Timothy 5:8, "But if any provide not for his own, and specially for those of his own house, he hath denied the faith, and is worse than an infidel." After that Carnegie believed each man had a duty to plunge wealth back into society. "The man who dies . . . rich dies disgraced. Surplus wealth is a sacred trust which its possessor is bound to administer in his lifetime for the good of the community." Before his death Carnegie gave away a vast fortune to libraries and charitable institutions.

James J. Hill

Because it was built without any federal land or federal funds, the most unusual railroad of the late 1800s was probably the Great Northern Railroad owned by James J. Hill. He had begun his career as a clerk for a steamboat line. In 1865 he started his own business as a salesman, and five years later he used his savings to buy a little steamship named the *Selkirk*.

Next, with the help of a state land grant, Hill bought the almost defunct St. Paul and Pacific Railroad. By January, 1879, he had connected St. Paul, Minnesota, to Winnipeg, Canada. The sale of grant lands alone brought him $100,000 a month, not to mention the money he made from shipping rich grain harvests on his line.

In 1893 his line finally reached the Pacific. When a financial panic in 1893 toppled the Northern Pacific, Hill bought it, too. In 1901 he bargained with J. P. Morgan to buy half the stock of another line, the Burlington and Quincy, that ran to Illinois. This meant that his railroads now linked the West Coast with Chicago, St. Louis, Omaha, and Denver.

Hill did not limit his trade to farm products; he diversified in mining interests, passenger service, and the lumber industry. He even created the international Great Northern Steamship Company. His ships sailed to Yokohama, Japan, and to Hong Kong.

In 1901 Edward Harriman, a New York stockbroker tried to buy Hill out. When the price of stock climbed so high that smaller investors were ruined, Hill and Harriman compromised. They united to form Northern Securities Holding Company, a monster monopoly. Because the federal government sued to dissolve it under the Sherman Anti-Trust Act, this merger or union was short-lived.

Both Harriman and Hill died rich men. Some people hated Hill, claiming he had gained his wealth unjustly at the expense of loggers, miners, and farmers. Others praised him as the man who unlocked the wealth of the Great Northwest. Without him, Hill's admirers said, the Great Northwest and the prairie states would have been wilderness for a longer time.

Frederick Weyerhaeuser: Timber Supplier for a Growing Nation

The lumber industry was tied directly to the use of a natural resource. Because most early settlers could cut enough trees from their own land to build a home, New England forests had been able to keep up with the demand for commercial users of timber for ship building and eastern cities. In the late 1800s, however, the demand for timber increased. Thousands of miles of railroad track were laid on wooden ties, and cities sprang up across the Midwest, requiring more and more lumber.

Frederick Weyerhaeuser (WIE ur HOU zur) was a young German immigrant working for day wages in a Rock Island, Illinois, sawmill. In 1860 Weyerhaeuser and his brother-in-law, Frederick Denkmann, pooled their earnings, borrowed some more money, and bought the sawmill.

Weyerhaeuser expanded the operation north to forests along the rivers of Wisconsin and soon moved his headquarters to St. Paul, Minnesota. Unlike some heads of corporations, Weyerhaeuser was always willing to share the responsibilities with a large circle of capable men. He rarely held more than a 15-20% interest in any company; yet his partners took his advice as though he owned a controlling interest because his past decisions had brought great profits. Weyerhaeuser's most innovative practice was his formation of a sales company, which served as a nation-wide wholesaler handling saw-mill products from more than twenty firms. The Weyerhaeuser Sales Company greatly improved the marketing of forest products across America and eventually became the world's largest lumber company.

When the forests of the Great Lake State had fallen to ax and saw, Weyerhaeuser sought land elsewhere. James J. Hill, the railroad baron who lived next door to him in St. Paul, sent him to tour the Pacific Northwest. Weyerhaeuser paid Hill $5.4 million dollars for 900,000 acres of timber-land. The value of the land soon quadrupled, and the company moved its headquarters to Tacoma, Washington, where it remains active today. It also set up subsidiaries (sub-companies) such as Potlatch Lumber and the Boise Cascade Corporation. The parent company also cut timber in southern states such as Louisiana and North Carolina.

The giant firms were often criticized because of their size and methods. But Weyerhaeuser was reluctant to hurt small owners. He often bought wood locally by contract. His company cut timber, milled it, and then left or sold the scarred land. While conservationists in the twentieth century have sharply rebuked these methods, their charges are not totally fair. Vast forests were available at the time, and the company acted in response to public need and to the public policy of that day. As the years went by, this practice of "cut and run" ended. Reforestation and conservation practices were employed, and research was done to find better ways to grow timber. New uses for wood by-products developed so that today much less is wasted.

Alexander Graham Bell: Pioneer in Communication

Alexander Graham Bell taught teachers of the deaf. As a result of his interest in technical devices to help the deaf, he envisioned the possibility of uniting two hearing aids, and so he invented the telephone.

The public found Bell's device fascinating. Yet when Bell sought to market it, no company showed any interest. Western Union, the telegraph company and the most logical vendor in the communications industry, ignored him. They could have bought the telephone for a mere $100,000 and made millions over the years.

Bell decided that if he were going to succeed with his invention, he would have to do it on his own. He began with a small company in New York, and soon the use of the telephone grew. Even the president of the United States, Rutherford B. Hayes, wanted, and got, a telephone for the White House. In 1876, just four years after the telephone's invention, fifty thousand American homes had phones. In the next decade 800,000 more telephones were sold. With Bell's success, many competitors tried to take over the telephone industry by claiming Bell had infringed upon their patents. Nonetheless, Bell was able to defend his invention and win the lawsuits.

Early phone systems were local ones. In 1892 the Bell Telephone Company formed the first long distance telephone network, the American Telephone and Telegraph Company. By the 1896 election campaign William McKinley was able to talk by telephone to campaign managers in thirty-eight different states. AT&T held almost total control of the communications industry until 1985 when the federal government forced it to break up into smaller units.

Thomas Alva Edison: Pioneer in Electricity

Born in Milan, Ohio, Thomas Edison loved both reading and chemistry but detested math. While selling newspapers on trains, he learned about telegraphy. He then worked as a telegrapher and tried to make improvements that would allow him more free time to read. Before he was twenty-two, he had perfected a vote recorder and an alphabetical dial telegraphic device. When he could not sell them, he set a policy he followed the rest of his life: he would not invent any item for which there was no commercial or public demand. Next he invented a stock ticker. With the money gained from the sale of the device, he set up an "invention factory." He hired fifty people to work in his lab at Menlo Park, New Jersey. His factory became the General Electric Company.

The first important product to come from Edison's lab was the carbon telephone transmitter. It improved the clarity and range of Bell's telephone. His second lab invention, the phonograph, was Edison's own favorite, and the only totally original invention credited to him. "Mary Had a Little Lamb" was the first voice recording ever made.

In 1878 Edison began experimenting to find a way to manufacture light bulbs. Edison applied the work ethic to invention, saying: "There is no substitute for hard work. Genius," he said, "is one per cent inspiration, and ninety-nine percent perspiration." After thousands of experiments, Edison tried carbonizing (burning) cotton threads. In October 1879 he made a bulb that burned forty hours. In 1882 he opened the first commercial electrical station. It sold electricity to eighty-five customers and kept four-hundred new electric lights burning.

By the time he died in 1931, he owned more than a thousand patents. Most were improvements on existing inventions or processes. But a few—the alkaline storage battery, the movie projector, and the phonograph—were innovations that led to whole new industries.

John D. Rockefeller: Trust Innovator

In the year 1859 Edwin Drake drilled America's first oil well near Titusville, Pennsylvania. At that time oil had few uses. One of its major uses was for the production of kerosene. Since kerosene was cheap and easy to make and burned more efficiently than whale oil, it had become popular for fueling lamps. Soon hundreds of small firms existed to make kerosene from rock oil or petroleum.

Later, during the Civil War, John D. Rockefeller, a bookkeeper in Cleveland, Ohio, was looking for an investment for his savings. Because he believed petroleum would have a role in America's growth, he invested in a refinery with a good profit record. He correctly guessed that the refinery business was the key to success in the oil industry. He also felt that small refineries were cutting profits and that such duplication was wasteful. In 1870, by acquiring the various refineries within his area, Rockefeller formed the Standard Oil Company. Rockefeller promised the railroads large-scale shipments in return for a reduction on his freight rates. On paper the railroad charged him the public rate, but they gave him a rebate or kickback for each barrel shipped. Rockefeller's methods, though not illegal at the time, were unfair.

Within two years Rockefeller had gained control of one-fourth of the refining industry. By 1910 Standard had gained control of ninety per cent of the nation's refineries and ninety-two per cent of the crude oil supply from the Appalachians, the nation's major oil source at the time.

20

The Last Frontier

A windmill on the Kansas horizon

The term *frontier* refers to the outer fringe of settlement. America's frontier had moved west gradually. First men moved across the Appalachians and then on to the Mississippi River. The next frontier, however, had been the far West. The discovery of gold and rich lands on the West Coast had lured numbers of settlers west. At the same time, much of the land between the Mississippi River and the Rocky Mountains, the mountains themselves, and the Great Basin were by-passed and remained unsettled until after the Civil War.

Western explorers and wagon trains crossing the plains and deserts believed that the hard soil was not fertile. The climate seemed unsuitable, too. The winters were cold, and the summers almost unbearably hot. Even worse, rainfall was scarce. Many areas received less than twenty inches annually. The area could have made up for its lack of rainfall had a good water supply been available. But the flow of most of the rivers and the underground water supply rose and fell with the amount of precipitation. A further hindrance to settlement crops could easily move across the grasslands. As the railroads crisscrossed the prairies, the vast herds of buffalo on which the nomadic Indians depended declined. Railroad crews shot buffalo for meat, to prevent the buffalo from damaging the tracks, and for the sheer sport. This activity took away the Plains Indian's source of food, shelter, and clothing, and made him a less formidable enemy.

New inventions and pioneer flexibility also aided the plains settler in his quest to conquer and adapt to the prairie environment. Although earlier writers had predicted it would take seventy-five to a hundred years to settle the remaining lands, by 1890 the frontier was closed. There were no more large tracts of land that had enough water available to make them useful for settlement. The frontier had been conquered largely by three groups of Americans who had sought its wealth and opportunity. They were the miners, the cattlemen, and the settled farmers.

A. Gold and Silver Miners

In 1848 the discovery of gold had drawn thousands to California. When the California gold fields had no more to offer, prospectors turned to other jobs or moved elsewhere to seek their fortunes. Some wandered into the mountain areas of the West that had known few explorers, and many were not disappointed by what they found. For about a generation these lands yielded new riches.

Riches in the West

There were several great strikes of gold and silver that brought miners into the West. The first was near Pike's Peak in Colorado. (Colorado was then part of the Kansas Territory.) Many prospectors raced across the

was the lack of trees on the plains. Not only would it be hard for settlers to get used to the glaring sun, but they also could not build the log cabins and wooden houses that had been their homes in the East.

As if the geography of the vast region were not enough to deter settlement, the Indians added to the risk. The land west of the 95th meridian of longitude (roughly west of the first tier of states west of the Mississippi) was occupied by the Plains Indian tribes, and the Plains Indians were the most warlike. Their lands had been invaded by eastern Woodland tribes who had been forced west by previous white settlement. The Plains Indians knew enough American history to realize that the eastern Indians had been cheated out of their land. These Plains Indians knew that white settlement meant being uprooted, and they were not about to give up the plains lands without a fight.

Despite these many discouragements to pioneers, the West would be settled. The building of the transcontinental railroad brought change to the Great Plains. With this new form of transportation, people and

Buffalo roaming in the American West

prairie with "Pike's Peak or bust!" written on their wagons. This strike made few men rich, but it brought attention to the region.

A richer strike was made in northern Nevada. There James Fenimore and Henry Comstock mined gold. At ground level they made $5.00 a day. Two feet down, their take rose to $20.00 a day. At a depth of four feet, they hit heavy blue black sand. It had gold in it, but the gold did not seem as pure because it was being affected by a blue substance. They did not know what the blue mineral was, nor did they know that they had found the northern end of a rich lode, or deposit, of precious metal. Several weeks later someone else found out that the "blue stuff" was silver, nearly pure. Over the next thirty years the **Comstock Lode** yielded more than $400 million worth of metal. (Fifty-five per cent of the wealth from the lode was from silver; forty-five per cent from gold.)

Farther north the Fraser and Columbia river valleys also yielded rich finds. Strikes in Idaho and Montana along the Bitterroot and Salmon rivers attracted thousands of miners. Gold was discovered in Helena, Montana, in 1864 and also in Butte. In the 1880s copper mines were developed in Butte as well. The city is built over a vein one mile deep.

In 1876 two soldiers with prospecting experience discovered gold in the Black Hills of South Dakota, an area that was supposed to belong to the Indians. Fortune-seekers soon invaded the area. Although the army had been sent to keep the whites out, it did not. When the government tried to buy back the land from the Sioux—land they had just given them in 1868—the Indians went on a rampage. Nevertheless, the miners got their claim, and the resulting **Homestake Mine** became the world's richest single gold mine.

Mining Camps and Boom Towns

Some miners came west alone, but for safety and for economy in buying supplies, mining guidebooks suggested four-man companies. Miners gathered into make-shift mining camps, living in tents or hastily constructed brush arbors. They staked claims quickly. To keep a claim, a miner

Mining the West

had to work it one day out of every three. If a miner did not show up after ten days, someone else could take the claim. Of course the mining claims were not really official, since the miners did not own the land. They depended on claim societies that they had organized to protect their interests.

As more people came, businesses came with them. Supply stores and saloons were usually first. Soon after, a meeting would be called to plan a town. Streets were drawn out and a town name picked. Lots were drawn for home sites. A church, school, miner's union hall, and processing mills for ore soon dotted the town's horizon. Where services were lacking, enterprising people could just about name their own fees. For example, one woman made $18,000 in one year just baking pies for the miners.

A few people made fortunes in mining. Many more made only a living. If the ore ran out or prices dropped, the mines closed down. Often miners, storekeepers, hotel owners, newsmen, and their families left when a mine closed. If everyone left, the empty buildings became weather-beaten over the years and were known as ghost towns. In addition to the mining towns, other ghost towns resulted from abandoned railroad towns, cow towns, lumber towns, and even farm towns across the West.

Silver and the Currency System

The mining of silver and gold aided the growth of the nation's economy. From before the Civil War until 1873, the government had minted both gold and silver coins. These coins were the nation's money during that time, along with greenbacks (paper money) printed during the war. When both the greenbacks and the silver coins were phased out, however, the money supply rested on its gold. The country was on the "gold standard."

Naturally, the price of silver plunged sharply once the government quit buying it for coins. Miners were disappointed by this action, and so were many other Westerners. The public began to pressure Congress for legislation that would put money backed by silver into circulation along with that backed by gold. They wanted more money (which would cause inflation) because they believed it would be easier for them to buy goods and to pay off old debts.

Finally in 1878 Congress passed the **Bland-Allison Act.** It set the price of silver at a 16:1 ratio (sixteen ounces of silver would be equal to one ounce of gold) and also required the secretary of the treasury to buy $2 to $4 million a month in silver at the market price. This silver was coined but only into token silver dollars that were still backed by gold in the treasury's vaults. Farmers, silver miners, and mine owners were not satisfied. When six new states having agricultural and mining interests came into the Union, supporters of the free coinage of silver had more leverage. They were able to force the issue, and by 1896 the Democratic party supported free silver in its party platform.

Section Review

1. List at least four reasons settlers were hesitant to explore the frontier.
2. What system of transportation encouraged the settlement of the frontier?
3. The discovery of what two metals drew thousands into the Great Plains territories?
4. Why did ghost towns emerge?
5. What did the Bland-Allison Act do?

B. The Cowboys

Cattlemen played an important role in developing the American West. Acre for acre, they were responsible for taming more of the new frontier than the miners or pioneer farmers, and they did so with a relish and a romance that have appealed to people ever since.

The era of the cattle frontier was short. Although the animals had roamed the Southwest since the Spanish explorers brought the first cattle to the New World, a large cattle industry did not boom until after the Civil War. The peak of cowboy activity came in the 1880s, and by the early 1890s most of the cowboy legend had passed into history, leaving the dress and song to be copied and idealized by twentieth-century Americans. In the twenty-five short years that the cattle trade flourished, forty thousand men drove ten million head of cattle over a network of trails, most of which led north from Texas.

The term cow*boy* was a fitting one. Photographs of the era, and there are many, and artwork by such cowboy artists as Charles M. Russell, Frederic Remington, and Olaf Seltzer show faces of young men. Booking and arrest records from cowboy towns show that most were under twenty. Young cowboys spent a few years riding the range or trail and then usually married, settling down as farmers or ranchers.

A Wealth of Cattle

Following the Civil War, Texans began to realize that the growing herds of long-horn cattle on their lands would bring large prices at market. The Easterners were hungry for beef, and they had the money to buy the cattle. Since there were no railroads reaching to Texas, the only way to get the cattle to market was to walk them there.

The Cattle Trails—Cattle could be sold at a much higher price in the East than in the West. Steers cost $5.00 when fed on the open range on free public lands. It cost about one cent per mile to drive them north. There they could be sold for between $25 and $50 a head. To take advantage of such profits, cattlemen began to move herds across the Red River in 1866.

The closest railroad at that time reached to Sedalia, Missouri. But cowboys moving north on the Sedalia Trail did not find a warm welcome. For one thing, the cowboys had trouble driving the cattle through the forests and brush of eastern Oklahoma and southern Missouri. For another, cattle ticks clung to the Texas longhorns for hundreds of miles. The insects then fell off and attached themselves to stock in Oklahoma and Missouri. Those cattle lacked the immunity of the longhorns, and many animals died from outbreaks of Texas fever. Some laws were passed to prohibit the passage of Texas herds, but some people

The Outlaws: Men Who Reaped What They Sowed

Jesse and Frank James: Both had been Confederate raiders with a rebel leader named Quantrill. After the war they took up a career of robbing banks, trains, and stagecoaches in Missouri and other nearby states. Their gang included the four Younger brothers. They claimed that the Northerners drove them to their life of crime, and they gained many sympathizers who regarded them as modern "Robin Hoods" instead of the thieves that they were. Jesse, whom his friends called Dingus, was shot in the back by a "friend" who wanted the reward. He was thirty-four. Frank surrendered, was tried, and was acquitted because of a great deal of political pressure.

Billy the Kid: At the age of seventeen he became involved in the Lincoln County, New Mexico, cattle wars. He fought for an English gentleman, John H. Tunstall, who became a father-image to the young boy. When a crooked sheriff and his posse murdered Tunstall, Billy swore to get revenge, and he did. By the time that he was eighteen, Billy was charged with twelve murders. Captured by a former friend, Pat Garrett, Billy murdered his two guards and escaped again. Garrett eventually found him again and killed him. He was only twenty-one years old.

Black Bart: He was called "the gentleman bandit." Primarily a stagecoach robber, he wore a flour sack with eyeholes as a mask, treated everyone with the best of manners, and left a poem at the scene of each crime. Bart was captured when a handkerchief he dropped at one job was traced to him, and his real name was discovered to be Charles Bolton. After his release from prison, Bolton disappeared.

The Dalton Gang: Most of their crime spree took place over an eighteen-month period. All the gangmen were in their twenties. While attempting to rob a bank at Coffeyville, Kansas, all except one were killed. The survivor, Emmett, had eighteen wounds. After spending fourteen years in prison, he married the girl who had waited for him. They moved to Los Angeles, where Emmett worked as a building contractor, a real estate man, and a movie writer. Outspoken in his condemnation of outlaws, Emmett died in 1937, a respected businessman.

Harry Tracy: Tracy inspired one of the greatest manhunts in the nation's history. Being pursued throughout the state of Oregon, he could have escaped back to the hideouts in the West but seemed to relish the hunt. He stole a boat and sailed around Puget Sound, stole a train, had lunch with farmers and their families, joined the posses looking for him, called sheriffs on the telephone to tell them he was in town, and even helped do some of the work on the farms he visited. Eventually cornered by a group of farmers, Tracy killed himself.

took matters into their own hands. They set up "shotgun quarantines" to keep the longhorns from passing through their lands.

In 1867 Joseph G. McCoy, a shrewd cattle broker from Illinois, built large corrals in Abilene (AB uh LEEN), Kansas. Using the railroad, which had just reached Abilene, he shipped cattle to the Chicago stockyards. This cut the distance of the long drives and freed the cattlemen from the dangers of armed farmers further east. It also made the **Chisholm** (CHIZ um) **Trail** the busiest trail north.

The Chisholm Trail took its name from an Indian trader, Jesse Chisholm, who used the 225-mile trail not to move cattle, but to take supplies to Indian Territory (modern Oklahoma).

Although cattle drives became common, they continued to meet difficulties. The trail ran through Indian Territory, and the Chickasaw Indians began levying a grazing tax of up to fifty cents a head on all the cattle driven through. Also farmers near the trails began putting up fences to keep the cattle out. This meant less open range and fewer water holes for moving stock. Thus, the cowboys began to swing farther west before heading north. They connected with new railroad lines at Ellsworth and Dodge City, Kansas. The Ellsworth route was a cutoff from the Chisholm Trail. The trail to Dodge City was named the Western Trail.

Two New Mexico ranchers looked for a southeasterly route that would allow them to drive their cattle to the Pecos River and then up the Pecos to the markets in Colorado. Many people thought such a trail to be impossible, primarily because of one stretch of eighty miles that had no water. Nonetheless, Charles Goodnight and Oliver Loving hired eighteen well-armed men, rounded up two thousand head of cattle, and set out for the Pecos in 1866. On the first trip they lost nearly four hundred cattle, but on their second trip they lost no cattle at all. By 1895 ten thousand head of cattle had taken the **Goodnight-Loving Trail** to western markets. The greatest danger along the route became Comanche Indians, who were on the lookout for free steak on the hoof. In fact, Loving, who had also opened the Shawnee Trail, was killed in an Indian raid on one of his drives.

The Cattle Drive—The heart of the cattle industry and the most important part of a cowboy's job was the trail drive. Getting ready for the drive took careful planning. A rancher or cattle buyer set out to gather a herd in the early spring. The ideal size

The Lawmen: The Guys in the White Hats

Tom Smith: He served as the sheriff of Abilene, Kansas, before Wild Bill Hickock. Smith was actually the man who cleaned up Abilene, and he did it with his fists more than with his guns. He was widely respected by the citizens. He was killed when trying to arrest a homesteader.

Wyatt Earp: Wherever he was sheriff, Earp was not well liked. He and a brother and some friends killed three cowboys in the famous gunfight at the O.K. Corral in Tombstone, Arizona. The townspeople considered Earp and his group murderers. They left town shortly thereafter. Earp died in 1927 at the age of seventy-one.

Bat Masterson: His first love was gambling, but he also served as a rider for the railroads. As sheriff of Tombstone, Arizona, for two years, he did an excellent job of maintaining the peace. Later he became a sportswriter in New York. Teddy Roosevelt made him a deputy U.S. marshal.

The Pinkertons: This detective agency hunted down and captured many criminals. They also established the first Rogues Gallery for identifying known outlaws. The Pinkertons also became known as strikebreakers and union infiltrators as well.

Bill Tilghman: Like Tom Smith, Tilghman used his guns only when he had to. He served as the U.S. marshal in Perry, Oklahoma, for thirty-five years. Tilghman was so well respected by even the outlaws and their gangs that one famous thief refused to let a henchman shoot Tilghman in the back because he was "too good a man." Tilghman was killed when he grabbed a gunman and asked a bystander to take the man's gun. The bystander did, and then he shot Tilghman.

for a herd was two thousand head of four-year-olds.

The **trail boss,** who was paid around $125 a month, was in charge of the men, equipment, and animals. It was his responsibility to get the herd to market safely. About eight cowboys were hired to work the herd at salaries ranging from $25 to $40 a month. Two were "point" men who rode in the lead. Two "swing" men and two "flank" men rode beside the herd and kept the stock from wandering off. Two "drag" men brought up the rear. Riding in choking dust, they had to keep any weak and tired stragglers moving along. The outfit was accompanied by a cook. He hauled the chuck wagon a mile or two ahead of the herd. Thus he could stop to have food ready for a tired crew. The cook's day could start as early as 3:00 A.M. and sometimes lasted until midnight. A **wrangler** was usually the youngest of the hands and paid the least. He took care of the horses and the riding equipment.

The drive started at daylight and went until dusk or even later—if the trail boss couldn't find good grass and water. After dinner, a cowboy's work was still not done. At night there were four two-hour watches. Pairs of riders circled the herd, riding in opposite directions, on guard for any signs of trouble. Night riding was not only hated for its loneliness but feared because of its dangers. Almost all stampedes, the most frightening experience faced by a cowboy, started at night. The snap of a twig, the bolt of a jack rabbit, a strange smell, or a streak of lightning could set off a dreaded stampede. If a stampede could not be stopped quickly, the cowboys faced several days of gathering the scattered herd. Even worse, cowboys often died if their horses stumbled and they fell in the dust to be trampled by the herd.

The Development of the Meat Packing Industry

The continued success of the open-range cattle industry was assured for a time by the development of a new industry, meat packing. Two men, **Philip Armour** and **Gustavus Swift,** led the way in making the meat packing industry successful. Their success came because they were willing to try new ideas and ways of doing things.

Philip Armour left his Massachusetts home to build sluices (long boxes for separating ore) for California forty-niners. Becoming bored on his return east, he went to Milwaukee, Wisconsin, where he became his brother's partner in a firm dealing in wholesale grains and provisions. Armour's business boomed when he contracted to sell barrels of meat to the Union armies.

A meat market in the late 1800s

Before and during the Civil War, meat was usually slaughtered locally because the only ways to preserve it for transport were by salting, drying, or pickling. Armour's meat packing operation during the war was a success, and after the war he realized that there would be a large market in the eastern cities for meat if it were shipped there in large quantities. The trail drives helped supply the cattle his business needed, and the railroads provided the transportation to the packing plants. Because the cattle were transported quickly and slaughtered almost immediately, they lost little weight during their journey and yielded large amounts of beef.

In 1875 Armour moved to Chicago and opened a packing plant. Hogs and steers moved down narrow wooden chutes to the slaughterhouse. On entrance, they were stunned by a hammer blow on the head. Slung up by the hind legs from a moving overhead belt, they moved past men who cut their throats, took out their organs, peeled off their hides and bristles, and cut up the meat.

Armour also saw the possible value of using **by-products**—bones, hide, and other parts of the animal not generally used for meat. Since his company handled many thousands of cattle and hogs a day, it would be better to turn the by-products into something profitable than to discard them. Consequently, he hired chemists to find uses for them. The fat was used to make soap; bones to make glue, buttons, and fertilizer; and hides to make shoes and gloves. It was said that the meat packers used "every part of a pig but the squeal."

Gustavus Swift believed there was a market for more fresh meat in his native Massachusetts. In 1875 he also set up a meat packing company in Chicago, and he began shipping fresh meat across the country a few years later. The meat packers knew that chilled meat, whether frozen in winter or chilled on ice in summer, stayed fresh as long as a month. With this knowledge, beef had been put on ice in a railroad car and sent to Boston in 1877. But since the meat had lain directly on the ice, it had discolored. Soon after, specially designed refrigerator cars with separate ice bins came into common use. Their ability to carry fresh meat long distances from the meat packing plants boosted the industry.

The End of the Open Range

By the 1890s the open-range cattle industry was declining. The last long drive was in 1896. Many factors combined to cause this decline. One problem was a drop in meat prices. With the efficiency of production and the amount of meat produced, meat prices went way down. Thus it became less profitable to raise livestock.

Overgrazing was also a problem. When more and more people became involved in the cattle industry, grazing grasses became shorter and more scarce. Overgrazing was a greater problem as the season wore on, particularly if there had been little rain. In the summer of 1885, especially dry ranges with short grasses left the herds in poor condition. With overgrazing, pure clear springs became stinking mudholes. Harmful weeds took the place of lush prairie grasses. Erosion turned cattle trails into ravines.

Even water could prove a danger to the cattle. Sometimes steers broke for water holes or rivers, and as they charged in on top of each other, some drowned. Some died while crossing rain-swollen rivers like the Colorado, the Brazos, the Red, the Washita (WOSH ih TAW), or the Arkansas. Deadly flash floods were frequent because the sun-baked prairie ground simply could not absorb all of the run-off from sudden thunderstorms.

Droughts and blizzards threatened the cattle as well. When water could not be found, both the cowboys and the cattle suffered terribly. Dehydration made the cattle unmanageable; some even went blind. Winter's cold could freeze the livestock to death if they were stranded in a blizzard without food or shelter.

The summer of 1884 brought severe drought; the winter that followed was the most severe of the century. A raging December blizzard laid a thick coat of ice and sleet over the thin grasses. Cattle drifted south until they reached a 170-mile-long fence that stockmen had built to end earlier feuding with farmers. There thousands of cattle starved or froze to death. More than 10,000 dead cows were found along the fence. Over fifty per cent of the stock had died that winter, and the cattle that survived faced another severe drought the following summer. The cycle of drought and blizzard was repeated again in 1886-87. The weather in those years dealt the extensive cattle operations in the West a blow from which they did not quickly recover. President Grover Cleveland, although sympathetic with the plight of the cattlemen, wisely did not offer government aid. This forced American agriculture to face its own problems and adjust to the needs of the market at that time instead of letting the government give it immediate help.

Indians and horse thieves also plagued the cowboy trails. Indians often demanded a toll of beef or horses. If the cowboys

Grover Cleveland
22ND AND 24TH PRESIDENT
(1885-1889; 1893-1897)

Born: Caldwell, New Jersey, March 18, 1837

Family: married Frances Folsom; three daughters, two sons

Occupation: lawyer

Home: Buffalo, New York

Religion: Presbyterian

Elections: 1884—defeated James G. Blaine (Republican), Benjamin F. Butler (Greenback-Labor), and John B. St. John (Prohibition party)
1892—defeated Benjamin Harrison (Republican) and James B. Weaver (Populist)

Political Party: Democrat

Vice Presidents: Thomas A. Hendricks (first term) and Adlai E. Stevenson (second term)

Interesting Facts and Accomplishments:
first Democratic president elected after the Civil War

only president to serve two terms not in succession

was a bachelor until age 49 when he became the first president to marry for the first time while in the White House

the "Baby Ruth" candy bar was named for his daughter

had surgery for cancer of the mouth while president; it was done secretly on a ship so that the public would not panic

Death: June 24, 1908

refused to pay the toll, the Indians would set off a stampede. Horse thieves and cattle rustlers hid along the trail. Stockgrowers' associations tried to rid the plains of such thieves by hanging or shooting them.

Sheep on the Range

One more problem for the cattlemen was the sheepherders. The vast vacant grasslands of the plains were as attractive to sheep owners as they were to cattlemen. In 1880 there were about 200,000 sheep in the northern mountain states and territories. By 1890 there were 1.5 million and by 1900, 15 million.

Cattlemen had reached the grasslands first. Now they eyed the "woollyback" invasion with anger. To the already overstocked ranges, sheep meant disaster. Sheep ate grass down to the roots, and they cut and trampled what little grass they left behind. Ground stripped by sheep did not have any new growth until the next spring's rain. Sheep also fouled water holes, leaving a smell that made cattle refuse to drink.

As grass ran out and tempers grew short, the more numerous cowboys resorted to bullying, intimidating, and even attacking sheepmen and their flocks. Clubbing, shooting, torching, stampeding, and rim-rocking (driving sheep over cliffs) were all effective means of destroying herds. The murder of sheepherders was common, too.

A combination of events lessened disputes: the winter of 1886-87 reduced the number of cattle that needed to be grazed; fencing began to divide range lands; some found that it was possible for sheep and cattle to share some of the same range lands.

The Candlish Movable Home on the Range

Until the late nineteenth century sheepherders slept on the ground on blankets. Home on the range was very bumpy and cold. But finally a Wyoming blacksmith came to the rescue. His name was James Candlish. In 1884 he took an old wagon and converted it into the first home on wheels. Open in the front, the wagon had a canvas flap to block the wind. In 1892 a hardware company came out with an improved model that had a stove with an oven, a window, and Dutch doors among other "conveniences." Soon most sheepherders, especially on the northern plains, were owners of their own home on wheels.

There, of course, were some die-hards who thought the manufacturers were just trying to pull the wool over their eyes. Some sheep ranchers wouldn't even hire herders who used a wagon. The most legitimate complaint was that to return to his wagon each night the sheepherder had to herd his sheep back over land already grazed.

Nevertheless, for a vast majority of the sheepherders "home, home, on the range" came with wheels in what was the forerunner of the mobile home.

Section Review

1. Where did the cowboy era begin? How long did it last?
2. How were longhorns profitable to both the North and South immediately following the Civil War?
3. List two trails that were used to herd longhorns from the South to the North.
4. List four reasons for the decline of the cattle industry.

C. The Homesteaders

Rich lands and the promise of a better lifestyle lured people steadily west. Easterners who had farmed worn-out soil left for the West. They were joined by immigrants and Civil War veterans who were looking for a place to settle down. Even a few thousand freed slaves joined these other pioneers on the plains.

Conflict with the Cattlemen

As more and more farmers went west to stake claims on western public lands (the public domain), the acreage left for open-range grazing decreased. Because these homesteaders did not appreciate having their crops overrun by marauding livestock, they put up fences. Since wood for fencing was practically nonexistent, the invention of barbed wire gave farmers the fencing material they needed.

For a time cattlemen fought the homesteader, cutting the fences and threatening the farmers. There were even some range wars. The cattlemen eventually changed their style. Rather than grazing their cattle on the public domain, they took up ranching on their own lands or land that they leased from the government or other owners.

Farmers on the Plains

The **Homestead Act** of 1862 opened western lands for free settlement. Although the 160 acres allowed to a homesteader was

hardly enough to sustain a family in these areas, no one seemed to mind. A settler was supposed to build a 12′ by 12′ house with windows, have a well, improve the land, and live on the homestead for five years. If he met these terms, the land became his. To cheat on the homesteading terms, some built 12″ by 12″ houses or had a house on wheels with a bucket of water on it rolled onto (and off) the land. Some lived on the land seasonally. This last practice was a legal option, however.

Settlers could also increase land holdings legally by outright purchase of as much as an extra quarter-section (160 acres) at $1.25 per acre. The smallest amount someone could purchase was forty acres. That would have cost the princely sum of $50.00, a large amount in those days. If a pioneer filed a timber claim and planted ten acres in trees, another quarter-section could be added to his holdings. In the first six months after the Homestead Act was passed, settlers gobbled up 224,550 acres of land in Kansas and Nebraska alone.

The railroads sold farmland too, at $2.50 an acre. They sent agents to Europe with millions of pamphlets and posters. Thus the news of cheap American lands circulated in Norway, Denmark, Germany, England, and Wales. The Nebraska and Dakota territorial legislatures also paid immigration bureaus to attract settlers.

The Morrill Land Grant Act of 1862 gave states thirty thousand acres of federal land for every representative and senator they had. Most of the states sold the land to speculators. They in turn sold it to lumber companies, mining companies, and farmers.

The Oklahoma Land Rush

You have read how the government moved the Cherokee and other eastern

A family traveling in 1886 through Loup Valley, Nebraska, to a new homestead

Indian tribes west in the 1830s. Five tribes from the Southwest, all farming tribes, also were moved to **Indian Territory** (Oklahoma). By the 1880s most of the desirable farmland in the West had been claimed. Then the white man began to look greedily at this Indian Territory.

The railroads, some federal officials, land-hungry white settlers and speculators, and even some Indians who saw the opportunity to make some money all pressured the federal government to open up Oklahoma to white settlers.

In 1885 the government bought lands in the territory. President Benjamin Harrison announced that some of these lands would be opened to settlers at noon on April 22, 1889. The U.S. Army was on hand to keep the settlers out until the given hour. More than twenty thousand pioneers were poised on the border that day. At the sound of cannons, they raced across the border to claim their land. Those who made their way into the area in this land boom were nicknamed "Boomers." (Some had "jumped the gun" illegally and made their claim ahead of time. These people were called **Sooners.**) Some 1.9 million acres of land were claimed in a few hours. In the year 1893 another part of Oklahoma, the Cherokee Strip, was opened to settlement. Oklahoma gained territorial status in 1890, and in 1907 President Theodore Roosevelt welcomed the "Sooner State" as the 46th state in the Union.

Overcoming the Obstacles to Settlement

As the farmers settled on the plains in the later 1800s, they faced some of the same obstacles that cowboys and ranchers had faced. They faced some additional problems

Benjamin Harrison
23RD PRESIDENT
(1889-1893)

Born: North Bend, Ohio, August 20, 1833

Family: married Caroline Scott and after her death, married Mary Dimmick; two children by first wife, one by second wife

Occupation: lawyer

Home: Indianapolis, Indiana

Religion: Presbyterian

Election: 1888—defeated Grover Cleveland (Democrat) and Clinton Fisk (Prohibition party)

Political Party: Republican

Vice President: Levi P. Morton

Interesting Facts and Accomplishments:

grandson of William Henry Harrison, the ninth president

graduated from Miami University of Ohio

served as a Civil War general

received fewer popular votes than Cleveland in the 1888 election but won more electoral votes

started the custom of flying the American flag from all public buildings

Death: March 13, 1901

besides. The ways that the homesteaders overcame these difficulties are a tribute to their faith in God, their perseverance, and their ingenuity.

A Lack of Some Resources—Since trees were rare on the plains, wood had to be brought from other places. This made the log cabin both expensive and impractical. Some settlers began by living in sod dugouts braced by a few purchased boards. These dreary homes were little more than ditches dug into a hillside and covered with a roof of sod (grass and soil). The **sod house,** however, was a little more pleasant, and it became the classic dwelling on the prairie.

A sod house was drier, sturdier, and more comfortable than a dugout. The sod strips used to build it were twelve to eighteen inches wide, three inches deep, and two or three feet long. The sod blocks were staggered like bricks, grass side down, to form the thick walls of the house. Soddies, as such shelters were called, were warm in winter and cool in summer. Usually a lattice of willow branches was woven and covered with clay from a nearby creek bed for the base of the roof. Then sod shingles were laid over it. In heavy rains, however, such roofs leaked water like oversoaked sponges. Debris often fell from the roof, but pioneer wives hung cheesecloth below the rafters to catch the mud and bugs. Inside walls were whitewashed with a mixture of lime and sand. Tight construction was crucial, not just to keep out the cold but also to

make snakes and field mice unwelcome. Some sod houses were real works of art; a few, combined with some lumber, were two stories high.

The lack of wood also gave the farmers a couple of other obstacles to overcome. One was scarcity of fuel for fires. Until the railroads brought coal to heat prairie homes, corncobs, hay, and even manure served as fuel. Another problem was the lack of wood for the split rail fences commonly used back east. Although prairie farmers were generally glad their lands were not rocky, they did lack stones to be used for building purposes. There was no practical material for constructing fences until barbed wire was invented.

A sodbuster had to have an adequate water supply. Some settlers set out rain barrels or cisterns to collect rain. Some homesteaded near creeks. Most found water by digging wells, but wells had to be exceptionally deep to reach water in many areas of the dry plains. Even with wells, the farmers could not pump enough water by hand to water their stock and irrigate their crop land. The invention of the **windmill,** however, put the strong breezes of the region to this use.

Even wells or rivers could not necessarily irrigate many crops. Other means of overcoming this lack of water included raising crops that required less water or using dry-farming techniques that included using a mulch to protect what little moisture there was in the ground.

Help for the Prairie Farmers—The late 1800s brought many new and helpful developments for western settlers. One was barbed wire. Without lumber and rocks, fences could not be built. And with cattle

Sod houses were common on the plains, but when wood was available, settlers sometimes built a sod-roofed house like this one.

grazing contentedly in his corn and wheat, a farmer could not hope to prosper. Plain wire fences were tried, but they failed to hold up when herds pressed on them. Some farmers started thorn hedges, but it was often years before the hedges were high enough to do any good. In 1874 an Illinois farmer, **Joseph Glidden,** designed the first practical barbed wire. He used part of a coffee grinder to cut and coil small lengths of wire and then strung the barbs on by hand. Soon a machine was invented to do the work. Within a decade 120 million pounds of wire were being sold per year.

A Connecticut mechanic, David Halladay, perfected a windmill that helped farmers get water they needed for their family and stock. His device pivoted to face the wind and used centrifugal force to adjust the pitch of its wooden vanes. This feature allowed the windmill to withstand the pressure of high prairie winds. A crankshaft transferred the mill's rotary motion to force the pump to go up and down.

Railroads helped alleviate some of the transportation problems on the vast plains. Many lines built spurs (extensions) to the scattered towns to bring in needed goods and to carry out the farmers' harvests. The lines also made trips to other cities or regions easier.

American ingenuity helped the prairie farmer, too. Heavier steel plows were designed to cut through the matted sod, and mechanical grain drills planted seeds of grain at the proper depth. The crops were harvested using a binder, an improvement on the reaper. Steam engines provided power for the larger inventions, and threshing crews often traveled through areas with this equipment for harvesting the crops of many farmers. The steam-driven tractor also appeared later in the century to aid the farmer.

Hardships of the Prairie Settler—Not only did the homesteaders have to overcome the lack of some needed resources, they also had to deal with many hazards of prairie life. One of these problems arose as more and more western lands were plowed. Especially in dry years, the wind blew tons of top soil across the dry ground. It was impossible to keep a house clean since the dust settled everywhere. Outside the dust was blinding. Sadly, in addition to the inconvenience, the erosion of precious topsoil left much land infertile. In their eagerness to cultivate more land, settlers plowed up soil that God in His wisdom had given a protective coat of grasses. The grasses had prevented erosion and helped hold the moisture in the ground.

The prairie fire was another danger for the sodbuster. What little rain there was came in spring and early summer. As the season wore on, the grasses became dry. The smallest spark from a campfire or chimney or a stroke of lightning could turn the prairie into an inferno. When the flames were fanned by winds, the settler was powerless to stop the spreading fire. Damp clothing and blankets were used to beat out small fires. Sometimes farmers used the carcasses of slaughtered livestock, dragging them over the flaming grass. Backfires were lit to slow the progress of the flames. More often the only thing to do was to go inside the dugouts or soddies and pray. The heavy sod of the house and wet sheets over openings might protect people; but it could not keep the crops from going up in smoke.

Hailstorms did as much damage as fires. Crops were flattened and little could be salvaged for harvest. Sometimes the settlers themselves were battered. Another one of nature's assaults on the prairie was the tornado. These small intense whirlwinds formed by severe thunderstorms destroyed everything in their paths. There were so many tornadoes on the plains that the region was called "tornado alley." For protection against such storms the sod-busters often dug root cellars. These cellars could be used for storing food, and they doubled as storm shelters when tornadoes threatened.

Plagues of locusts and grasshoppers were a further scourge. Swarming across the prairies in the 1870s, they devoured everything that grew. "Their fluttering wings," wrote the editor of the *Wichita City Eagle* "looked like a sweeping snowstorm in the heavens, until their dark bodies covered everything green upon the earth." Accounts say the locusts covered the ground in a wiggling layer up to six inches deep. They ate crops, grasses, leaves, tree bark, leather boots, harness straps, and even fence posts and door frames. No one knew what caused the swarms to drop from the skies or what caused them to leave, but everyone feared them. Their arrival usually meant a two-year crop loss, because the locusts laid eggs that hatched the next year.

Homesteads were often miles from a settlement. Because neighbors were few and the distances between homesteads great, loneliness was a problem. Of course, efforts were made to deal with loneliness. For example, pioneers made great efforts to go long distances to churches built in towns. Another link to the outside world was mail. After pressure by farmers, the post office began **rural free delivery** (RFD), making it cost no more to send a letter to a soddie than to send one across New York City. Mail-order catalog houses also began. The first, Montgomery Ward and Company, began in Chicago in 1872, and soon afterward, Sears Roebuck and Company started. These businesses offered settlers a wide array of products to be ordered from their catalogs. Most could be delivered to the door; some were shipped by rail to the nearest town for pickup. Farmers also formed their own social groups. The **Grange,** founded in 1867 by Oliver H. Kelley, a Minnesotan, began as a social organization. Later it became a political tool to promote the interests of farmers. It may even have encouraged the rise of the Populists, a political party that sought to help relieve farmers from some of their problems.

Section Review

1. How did the homesteaders react to the cattle drives?
2. What major territory was the last to open to homesteaders?
3. What two important resources did homesteaders often lack?
4. What inventions and developments aided prairie farmers?
5. List at least five hardships faced by plains settlers.

Oliver H. Kelley

D. The Indians

The Indians who terrorized the miners and cowboys terrorized the settlers too. Disgruntled over the loss of their lands and the destruction of the buffalo, the Indians were quick to go on the rampage.

Indian attacks and uprisings were common during the latter part of the nineteenth century. The United States Cavalry often galloped to the rescue of settlers and traders. Probably the best known Indian battle of these Indian wars was at Little Big Horn in 1876. There Colonel **George Armstrong Custer** misjudged the strength and ferocity of a group of Sioux warriors. His massacre at Little Big Horn ("Custer's Last Stand"), was led by **Crazy Horse** and Gall. **Sitting Bull,** who stayed behind the lines, was the medicine man who inspired the attack.

Indians Surrender

After years of fighting, the outnumbered Indians began to face the fact that they could no longer continue their dominance of the plains. By 1885 almost all the Indians had been forced onto **reservations,** tracts of land set aside just for them.

Chief Joseph of the Nez Perce surrendered in 1877 after being chased seventeen hundred miles and nearly reaching safety in Canada. Geronimo, a Plains Apache, gave up in 1888. That year, as final defeat for the Indian seemed apparent, the Dakota Sioux had gathered for a Ghost Dance. The ritual celebrated a time when the Indians envisioned the earth would die and be reborn. The white men would go to another world; the Indians would then get their lands back. These strange ceremonies stirred fears among whites. Army troops sent in to disarm the Indians panicked, and mowed down two hundred Sioux at the

massacre of Wounded Knee in 1890. This action proved to be the last of many Indian battles—the Indians were conquered.

Those Indians who had not resisted were made **wards** of the federal government. The government supported them with an annual payment system and placed them under federal protection. Missionaries often proved to be the Indian's best friends as he was settled on the reservations. They offered not only help for the physical needs of the Indian, but also the gospel to meet his spiritual need. Unfortunately, the greed and malice of some other whites caused many Indians to reject the aid of the missionaries.

The Dawes Act

By 1887 pro-Indian sentiment was strong enough to force Congress to do something for the Indians. The **Dawes Act** of 1887 assumed that the Indian way of life would no longer work. Hence the Indian should be Americanized and assimilated (absorbed culturally) into the mainstream of American life. Under this act tribal unions were to be dissolved, and individual Indians were to receive lands and become self-supporting.

A romanticized lithograph of Custer's Last Stand entitled General Custer's Death Struggle

Each head of a household was assigned 160 acres.

The reformers, mostly Easterners, did not understand the Indian's needs, however. First, most western Indians who were given lands had been hunters and traders, not farmers. Second, the lands the Indians had been allotted were very dry. Whites had given them to the Indians because they were undesirable for their own use. Such small plots of arid land could not sustain a family. Third, Indians were not used to the idea of private ownership of land, and so the land deeds were meaningless to them. Also, their basic social units were the tribe and extended family (several generations of a family, including grandparents, aunts, uncles, and cousins). When these two units were broken down on the reservations, the Indian way of life suffered.

Defeated militarily, economically, and psychologically, the Indians became idle and often turned to alcohol. All too eager to make money, some whites also offered to buy Indian lands. Since Indians now owned the land personally, they had the option to sell it and often did. They were not used to a money economy, however, and were easily cheated. When oil was found on Indian lands, speculators bought up even more Indian land.

Left: *The Sioux chief and medicine man, Sitting Bull*
Center: *The Apache warrior, Geronimo*
Right: *The Sioux warrior, Gall*

The Indian Today

By the late 1960s, Indian problems regained federal attention when militant Indian groups pressed for rights for Indians. Not all of the pressure has been peaceful, nor have all the motives involved been for the good of the Indians.

In 1970 the Nixon administration set up a policy of Indian self-determination. This allowed Indians to set up their own tribal system on reservations. The federal government would assist them by providing housing and vocational training as well as money for economic development. The Department of the Interior also set up a new official to coordinate these programs for the Indians: the Assistant Secretary of the Interior for Indian Affairs.

During the 1980s Indian tribes that gave up land under questionable treaties in earlier centuries sued the federal government for the value of those lands. Although not much can be done to restore lands now owned by others, the Indians have called attention to their plight.

One of the Indians' greatest needs in both centuries has been their need for the gospel. Few other Americans have faced such rapid change, change they did not seek but yet had to accept. Since few Indians had a spiritual foundation on which they could stand, they suffered greatly. Alcoholism and suicide remain major problems among Indians today.

Section Review

1. How did the Indians react to white settlers taking over their land?
2. What was probably the most famous Indian battle? Who was defeated during this battle?
3. What was the significance of the Dawes Act?
4. How has the government's attitude toward the treatment of Indians changed over the last century?

Summary

Settlement had moved across the continent to the Pacific Coast before the Civil War, but the vast areas of the Great Plains and Rocky Mountains had been passed by. The dry climate, fierce Indians, and rugged terrain had discouraged early settlement. After the war, however, settlement in these regions began. Gold and silver brought miners, especially to mountain regions of the West. The demand for beef in the East prompted cattlemen on the plains to expand their herds and drive them to the railheads where they could be shipped to market. Farmers joined the cattlemen on the plains, attempting to raise their crops in the prairie soil. Although settlement was not dense on the plains or in the mountains, the advances of the miners, cattlemen, and farmers pushed the Indians off the land and onto reservations.

Chapter Review

Do You Remember?

■ Indicate whether each of the following would be most closely associated with the miners, the cattlemen, the homesteaders, or the Indians.

1. windmills
2. Chisholm Trail
3. Comstock Lode
4. wrangler
5. Ghost Dance
6. sod house
7. Dawes Act
8. "Pike's Peak or bust!"
9. Sooners
10. stampedes

■ Who am I?

11. I am the man who invented barbed wire.
12. I am the colonel killed at the battle of Little Big Horn.
13. I am the Nez Perce chief who sought refuge in Canada.
14. I am the Sioux medicine man.
15. I am the businessman who sold meat to the Union army.

■ Which one of the terms in the following sets does not belong with the others?

16. Chisholm, Comstock, Goodnight-Loving
17. Sooners, Indian Territory, Grange
18. ghost town, sod house, windmill
19. by-products, refrigerator car, wrangler

Why Is It So?

1. Why was the Pacific Coast settled before the Great Plains and Rocky Mountains?
2. Why did towns become ghost towns?
3. Why did miners and farmers want the federal government to use silver coins?
4. Why did the cattle drives begin?
5. Why did the open range close in the late 1800s?
6. How was Oklahoma's settlement unusual?
7. Why was barbed wire important to homesteaders?

What Do You Think?

1. Why can homesteaders, rather than miners and cowboys, be given more credit for actually settling the frontier?
2. How could the Indians have been treated differently during the settlement of the West?

21

America and the World

Throughout the nineteenth century America had increased its population, built its industries, and expanded its settlement across the continent. As it had grown, the United States had extended its influence and developed its strength. By the turn of the century, much of the world would begin to recognize that America was an impressive new world power.

A. Imperialism in the Late Nineteenth Century

The Civil War and Reconstruction, the settlement of the frontier, and the development of new businesses had kept the attention of America through much of the 1800s.

The United States showed little concern for foreign affairs that did not affect its borders or its people. This attitude of minding the country's own business and staying out of world politics is known as **isolationism.**

During the late 1800s, however, the United States began to look on as other countries were building world empires. Britain, France, Germany, and a few other nations were taking control of foreign lands. This **imperialism,** the extension of one's way of life over another people, brought many of these controlling countries greater wealth and power. Soon Americans began to wonder if their own country would end its isolationism and join these imperialist powers by building its own overseas empire.

Teddy Roosevelt's home, Sagamore Hill, in Oyster Bay, New York

Reasons for Imperialism

Aside from the prestige of building a large world empire, imperialist countries had several reasons for extending their control around the world. One concerned military strength. Because taking control of foreign lands often required military force, an imperialist power could naturally be proud of its strong army. It kept a large and well-trained army ready to handle the needs of its empire and ready to use against its enemies. The military also gained important naval bases and army bases around the world in the lands it controlled. These bases increased the nation's strength as a world power.

Another major reason for imperialism was wealth. An imperialist country could regulate the trade and the development of natural resources in its colonies. The country could send its own businessmen to oversee the industries of the colony. They could hire the natives for very low wages and send the profits back to the mother country. The mother country could benefit from the products of the mines and plantations, and it could also make sure that the colony bought all its imported items from the mother country. Thus the imperialist country held every economic advantage over the colony. Sometimes the imperialist country took extreme advantage of the native people and their poverty and ignorance to keep them working for the benefit of the mother country. Such practices are called **exploitation.**

The final major reason for imperialist activity in the late 1800s was a desire to help the unlearned and poor peoples in undeveloped lands. Some people in the imperialist countries wished to teach the "uncivilized" peoples of the world how to read and write, especially in European languages. They wanted to extend the benefits of education and western art and science to the natives of their colonies so that the natives could learn to live like Europeans.

Many imperialists wished to extend not only education but also food and health care for the hungry and sick. Helping poorer peoples who need food, medicine, education, or other assistance is called **humanitarianism.** British writer Rudyard Kipling spoke of the task of aiding the needy lands of the world as the "white man's burden." This burden, or responsibility, motivated many western Europeans and Americans to take not only humanitarian aid but also Christianity to lands in Asia, Africa, and the Pacific. Thousands of missionaries were recruited, and many sincerely spread the gospel of Jesus Christ. Others, lacking a personal knowledge of Christ as Saviour themselves, spread a "social gospel" which stressed the good works of humanitarian aid rather than salvation through Jesus Christ.

America's desire to evangelize foreign fields is exemplified by some of the work of the evangelist **Dwight L. Moody.** He had a profound influence on both American and British missions through his preaching and recruiting at many universities. Mission-minded American students were invited to a summer session at Moody's schools in Northfield, Massachusetts in 1886. In one month, one hundred students pledged themselves to be foreign missionaries. By the next summer school there were twenty-one hundred young men and women. In 1888 the Student Volunteer Movement was set up with the goal of "the evangelization of the world in this generation." Although it did not attain its lofty goal, missionaries fanned

Dwight L. Moody

out across India, Africa, China, and Japan. Sadly, within forty years even this group had strayed from preaching the Bible as God's truth and preached instead the social gospel.

Arguments on American Imperialism

The United States saw the economic benefits and other advantages of empire building. By 1880 Americans were producing far more food and goods than could be sold at home. They were also looking for new supplies of raw materials, and some were wanting a stronger army and navy. As a result, Americans began to think about imperialism as an aid for their own country.

Some Americans were opposed to the nation's expanding. Since the United States was large and lacked few natural resources, it really did not need to acquire the raw materials of lands overseas as the smaller countries did. Moreover, Americans opposed imperialism because it contradicted their ideals. Americans had fought for their own liberty. Could they now take away the liberty of foreign lands? Some people were also concerned that exploitation of other peoples violates God's Word.

Other Americans favored expanding beyond the nation's shores. First, some believed that the United States would become a second-rate nation if it did not enter the race for an empire. Second, America's supply of raw materials was not inexhaustible. New sources of raw materials might be needed. Third, new markets for America's manufactured products would be needed if the market at home became saturated. Fourth, the nation needed Pacific islands so that American ships traveling west could refuel at coaling stations. Fifth, the United States needed to extend its military power and position to protect itself from other countries.

America Acquires New Territory

The United States had first practiced imperialism when it purchased Alaska from Russia in 1867. Unlike all the land acquired before that time, Alaska was not connected to the other land areas of the United States. It was a "distant land" bought for America's benefit. As it turned out, Alaska proved to be a big benefit.

A gold rush in 1897 brought a flood of miners to the area around the Yukon River. The rush also boosted the economy of the United States. Later, silver, copper, and oil were found to add to the nation's resources. Fishing became important to Alaska's economy; salmon fishing produced far more wealth for the area than gold ever did. In later years Alaska also became important for national defense. And, of course, Alaska did become the forty-ninth state when it joined the union in 1959. Yet when it was purchased in 1867, no one realized it was the beginning of American imperialism.

Another advance toward America's world empire also took place in 1867 with a far smaller acquisition than Alaska. American seamen had discovered Midway Island, located to the northwest of Hawaii, in 1859. Midway, however, remained a little-known Pacific outpost until it became the focus of a major battle for control of the Pacific Ocean in World War II.

Alaska and Midway aside, the first intentional imperial gain for the United States did not come until early in 1898, when Congress annexed the islands of Hawaii. American missionaries and businessmen had gone to the islands in the early 1800s. The large pineapple and sugar-cane plantations built by the businessmen had taken advantage of the native Hawaiian workers. The Americans had also gained influence in the Hawaiian government. In 1893, they forced Hawaii's queen, Liliuokalani (lee LEE oo oh kah LAH nee), out of power, declared a republic, and asked the United States for annexation. President Cleveland, however, refused to purchase the islands because the queen had been removed from power illegally. But in 1898 President McKinley agreed to the purchase, and Hawaii became the first in a series of imperial gains for the nation.

Section Review

1. Define *Imperialism*.
2. What were the three major reasons for imperialism?
3. What part did missions play in furthering nineteenth century imperialism?
4. List at least three reasons for opposition to American expansion in the early 1900s.
5. What American acquisition in the Pacific in 1898 started the country on its quest for an empire?

B. The Spanish-American War

Along with adding Hawaii to its territories in 1898, America also entered a war that would greatly expand its overseas empire. Although a short and relatively inexpensive war (as wars go), the **Spanish-American War** was an action of great consequence for American imperialism.

The island of Cuba, lying less than one hundred miles off the coast of Florida in the Caribbean Sea, was the source of America's quarrel with Spain. Although four centuries had passed since Cuba's discovery and the beginning of Spanish rule, this island nation had really experienced only about a dozen years of well-run, peaceful, productive existence. Spain had allowed this colony to suffer from exploitation and poor government. The United States and other nations had tried to help the Cubans and had encouraged Spain to improve the situation, but little change occurred.

Causes of the War

As Americans watched the plight of their Cuban neighbors, conditions developed that encouraged them to do something to help.

Cuban Dissatisfaction—The Cubans had long been dissatisfied with conditions in their land. Many of the people suffered from poverty and cruel treatment. Several rebellions had erupted in the land, and in 1895 revolution again came to Cuba. The revolutionaries had three goals: terrorizing Cuba, destroying its livelihood (the sugar industry), and drawing the United States into the conflict. While fighting in Cuba, the revolutionary forces were smart enough to have agents in the United States who helped to raise money for the revolution and feed the American press a steady diet of overblown incidents, all blamed on Spain.

The Yellow Press—The news that the revolutionaries wanted the Americans to hear was funneled to key newspapers. Many of these newspapers were themselves locked in deadly warfare to sell subscriptions. One way to increase sales was to subject the reading public to a steady diet of sensational stories. They manipulated news stories, trying to make each one more exciting and attention-getting than the others, a technique called **yellow journalism.** Two powerful newspapermen facing off in this struggle were **William Randolph Hearst** (HURST) owner of the *New York Journal,* and **Joseph Pulitzer** (POOL it sur) with the *New York World.* Unfortunately, some of what they reported was either inaccurate or greatly exaggerated. They knew that if they wrote about extremely poor conditions in Cuba and about Spain insulting the United States, they could stir up great interest in a growing conflict. Their reporting intentionally drove America toward war.

United States Sympathies—Humanitarian sympathies also caused Americans to want to help. Many believed that the Cubans were oppressed by Spain. They also wished that Cuba could obtain the freedoms and advantages that they enjoyed as Americans. Influenced by the press, most Americans favored helping the Cubans rid themselves of Spanish oppression.

American Investment—Another reason for United States interest in Cuba was that American businessmen had invested in Cuban sugar plantations and refineries. These investors feared that if the government stayed unstable and the terrorist acts continued, they might lose their money. The investors frantically pressured President **William McKinley** to protect their financial interests.

Joseph Pulitzer

Immediate Causes—As tensions rose concerning the Cuban situation, two important events took place that spurred the United States into action.

In February 1898 Hearst's *New York Journal* published a letter written by **Dupuy DeLôme,** the Spanish minister to the United States. The letter, to a personal friend of the minister, was never meant for publication, but it was stolen by Cuban rebels who conveniently gave it to the Hearst press. The letter described President McKinley as "weak and a bidder for the admiration of the crowd, besides being a common politician." At this time Americans held the presidency in such high esteem that they considered any criticism of the person holding the office as a national insult. The press

The Press, Public Opinion, and Comic Strips, Too

Joseph Pulitzer, a Hungarian immigrant, had refined his journalistic trade in St. Louis with his powerful paper, the *St. Louis Post-Dispatch*. In 1883 he invaded New York City and bought out the dying *New York World*. Alert reporting, sensational stunts, and pictures helped the *World* make a profit. Pulitzer was a crusader. No matter what the cause, he was able to drum up excitement and inspiration much like a bandmaster did with a band.

Editors across America studied his techniques and imitated them. His most successful imitator, William Randolph Hearst, copied him so well that he soon became his chief competitor. Hearst had been given the *San Francisco Examiner* by his father. When he later inherited his father's millions, he enlarged his base and bought the *New York Journal*. He used some of his fortune to hire writers away from Pulitzer. When news was lacking, Hearst made his own news. He turned reporters into detectives to pursue criminals and made crime columns more exciting. He hired preachers to furnish religious material that would fire editorial controversy.

In 1897 Hearst challenged Pulitzer to a duel for subscribers. The battleground became events leading to the Spanish-American War. In 1897 artist-reporter Frederic Remington was ready to leave Cuba, believing that there was nothing of importance to report. Pulitzer is said to have cabled him: "Please remain. You furnish the pictures and I'll furnish the war." Hearst entered the journalistic battleground claiming that he was just doing his patriotic duty.

Smaller newspapers copied the style of Hearst and Pulitzer; their pages were filled with the same jingoism (extreme nationalism). Some thoughtful citizens were troubled when they realized that these journalists were not just reporting public opinion, but creating and controlling it. And the issue involved, entry into a war, was deadly serious. This was not the first time the American press had created rather than reflected opinion. But it had never happened before on such a wide scale.

Once this round with Hearst was over, Pulitzer quit the fight and decided to compete on a higher level. He turned his paper into a responsible journal. Although liberal, it did maintain high standards of journalism. He tried to raise standards for future journalists by endowing a School of Journalism at Columbia University in 1912. Hearst meanwhile created a chain of newspapers and bought magazines. He had political ambitions, but he was widely distrusted, and his ambitions were frustrated.

The Hearst press did leave a lasting legacy to journalism: the funnies or Sunday comics. Trying to capture working-class families as readers, Hearst's Sunday *Journal* tried an eight-page colored Sunday supplement in 1896. Hearst hired the artist who drew Pulitzer's "Yellow Kid" drawings away from him. The Journal then published the first real comic strip. Called the "Katzenjammer Kids," it was written by a cartoonist named Rudolph Dirks. Other comics included "Mutt and Jeff" and "Krazy Kat." Editors found that the funnies were the first part of the paper most people read. The funnies became a kind of American folk art expressing what some Americans thought or felt or at least what tickled them.

William McKinley
25TH PRESIDENT
(1897-1901)

Born: Niles, Ohio, January 29, 1843
Family: married Ida Saxton; two
  daughters (both died in infancy)
Occupation: teacher, clerk, lawyer
Home: Canton, Ohio
Religion: Methodist
Elections: 1896—defeated William
  Jennings Bryan
1900—defeated William Jennings Bryan
  (Democrat) and John C. Wooley
  (Prohibition)
Political Party: Republican
Vice President: Garret Hobart (first term)
  and Theodore Roosevelt (second term)
Interesting Facts and Accomplishments:
campaigned in 1900 on the slogan "a full
  dinner pail for four years more"
last Civil War veteran to become
  president
his wife suffered epileptic seizures, and
  McKinley would shield her from view
  with a napkin or handkerchief when she
  suffered a seizure during a public
  function.
Death: was shot by Leon Czolgosz, an
  anarchist, on September 6, 1901 and
  died on September 14, 1901

demanded Spain be punished. DeLôme resigned, but the furor did not lessen.

Less than a week after the DeLôme letter, a second incident occurred. On February 15, 1898, an American warship, the **U.S.S.** *Maine,* had anchored in Havana, Cuba, for an indefinite stay. The navy called it a goodwill mission, and Spain reacted appropriately. However, on February 15th at 9:40 P.M. the *Maine* mysteriously blew up. Two officers and 250 enlisted men died in the initial blast. Of course, the conclusion the yellow press made was that Spain had done it. There were other possible explanations, but Americans wished to blame Spain. The public yelled "Remember the *Maine*!" and cried for action.

The president and Congress stalled briefly, but they issued a resolution that approved the use of force to end hostilities in Cuba and set up a stable government there. They also added the **Teller Amendment** to the resolution. It said that the United States had no intention of adding Cuba to its empire but only desired the independence of that land. This statement gave Americans confidence that further action would only be to help the Cubans and not to further American imperialism.

Some believe that McKinley yielded to public pressure. McKinley believed Spain would never grant Cuba independence on its own and that only independence would satisfy the American public. When Congress recognized Cuba's independence (even though Cuba did not have its own government at the time), Spain tried to uphold its honor by declaring war on the United States. And on April 25, 1898, the United States declared war on Spain.

Many historians today believe that United States involvement in the Spanish-

The destruction of the U.S.S. Maine

American War was not justified. However, we need to remember that we are far removed from the feelings that Americans shared in 1898. It is much easier for us to pass judgment on events and motives of the past than it is to evaluate our own actions and motives honestly. As we study history, it is important that we do not look at an event with a modern, critical eye. We must also examine it in context with the culture of that day, considering the information and attitudes we would have had if we had lived at that time.

Americans desired a better way of life for Cuba, and most honestly thought that the United States could help the Cubans achieve progress. As it turned out, however, their interest in Cuba opened the way for the expansion of American power and influence along with the problems of empire.

Course of the War

The Spanish-American War was over in one hundred days. The United States was not really ready for a full-scale war, but the Spanish government and army were weak. The United States won every battle fought in this war.

Military Preparedness—Most of the fighting men came from the state national guards. By late spring, troops had gathered at a military base in Tampa, Florida. Although the war would be fought in a sub-tropical area, many had been issued wool uniforms, and some cavalry troops lacked horses. But the invasion force sailed on June 14.

While the army fought bravely, and several regiments like the **Rough Riders** gained special fame, the navy played the most important role. President Cleveland

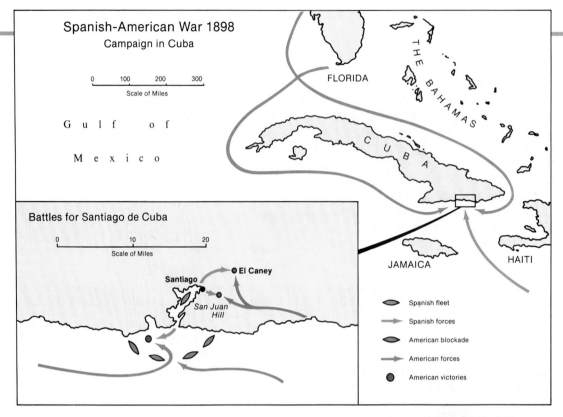

Spanish-American War 1898
Campaign in Cuba

0 100 200 300
Scale of Miles

G u l f   o f

M e x i c o

FLORIDA

THE BAHAMAS

C U B A

JAMAICA

HAITI

Battles for Santiago de Cuba

0 10 20
Scale of Miles

Santiago

El Caney

San Juan
Hill

Spanish fleet
Spanish forces
American blockade
American forces
American victories

had approved a program to build a fleet of steel ships, and the ships now came in handy. More than anything, the navy's success showed that the United States had arrived as one of the world's great powers.

Battles of the Spanish-American War— Long before war was declared, Assistant Secretary of the Navy **Theodore Roosevelt** sent secret orders to Commodore George Dewey, who was in Hong Kong with the American fleet in the Pacific. Dewey was told to prepare for an attack on the Spanish fleet in the Philippines in case war broke out with Spain. The American force arrived in Manila on April 30 and met the Spanish fleet the next morning. By noon the **battle of Manila Bay** was over. No Americans died from wounds, though one engineer died from sunstroke. Spain lost 167 men and

Theodore Roosevelt served as a colonel in the Spanish-American War and became a hero as the leader of the Rough Riders.

much of its fleet, and it was quickly defeated in the Pacific.

In the Caribbean, the American fleet was able to trap the Spanish fleet in the harbor at Santiago, then the capital of Cuba. American troops then came to storm their way to the city. The soldiers landed near Santiago and pushed the Spanish back to their defenses on San Juan Hill. Theodore Roosevelt's all-volunteer group, the "Rough Riders," was among the troops. Their famous charge up San Juan Hill helped defeat the Spanish on land while the Caribbean Spanish fleet lost every ship in a sea battle. On July 17 Santiago was officially surrendered. The American army took Puerto Rico, another Spanish possession, without resistance on July 25.

When the war was officially over in August, fewer than four hundred American soldiers had died in battle or from combat wounds. Disease, however, took a far greater toll. Over five thousand died from typhoid, malaria, yellow fever, or other diseases.

The Treaty of Paris—The Spanish sued for peace and signed a truce on August 12, 1898. Spanish and American treaty commissioners met in Paris on October 1, and by December 10, 1898, a treaty had been worked out. Spain agreed to give up its claim to Cuba and also to cede Guam and the Philippines in the Pacific and Puerto Rico in the Caribbean to the United States. In return the United States gave Spain $20 million.

However, a great debate soon ensued in the Senate. Influential anti-imperialists, including Charles Francis Adams, Andrew Carnegie, former presidents Cleveland and Harrison, and authors Mark Twain and William Dean Howells, opposed the treaty. They said the treaty violated the principles of the Monroe Doctrine. It was only when William Jennings Bryan, the leader of the Democratic party, supported the treaty and promised Filipino independence that the treaty was ratified, by two votes.

More New Territories and Responsibilities

By the terms of the peace treaty the United States, like it or not, now had an empire and all the problems that came with taking care of one.

Governing Cuba—The Teller Amendment had promised Cuba its independence. But until Cuba was ready for independence, the United States oversaw the government. In 1901 Congress passed the **Platt Amendment,** which gave Cuba strict regulations for its new independent government. In effect this legislation kept Cuba from alliances with countries other than the United States, allowed the United States to oversee Cuba's financial affairs, and allowed the United States to send forces to Cuba to keep order. This was not exactly "independence." In addition, the United States was permitted to establish and keep a navy base in Cuba. The U.S. Navy still uses the base at **Guantanamo Bay** today.

Despite its reluctance to give up control of Cuba after the war, the United States did a great deal to help the island. The tropical disease yellow fever was a scourge in the Caribbean. A Cuban doctor, Dr. Carlos Finlay, believed the disease was carried by a certain type of mosquito. An American army doctor, Dr. **Walter Reed,** proved that Finlay was right. Major **William Gorgas** (GOR gus) and a crew of army engineers then drained the swamps and low-lying areas and succeeded in getting rid of the water where the mosquitoes bred. The United States also provided food and clothing for the poor and built roads, schools, railroads, and hospitals.

Puerto Rico—The United States gave Puerto Rico much of the same aid that Cuba had received. Puerto Rico also got special economic considerations such as duty-free trade with the United States. This was of special benefit to the sugar industry. Puerto Rico was also exempted from having to contribute to the federal treasury. In 1917 under the Jones Act, Puerto Rico became a territory with the governor appointed by the president and a two-house legislative assembly. In 1952 at Puerto Rico's request it became a commonwealth, a freely associated part of the United States.

Governing the Philippines—Many Americans were skeptical about taking the Philippines, a land made up of over seven thousand Pacific islands. It would be hard for the United States to provide even the most basic government to rule the people of the entire area. Since the Filipinos were largely uneducated and had almost no experience in self-government, it would be difficult to help them set up a republican form of government. Opponents also held that annexing the Philippines violated the American ideal of liberty and might even be unconstitutional. Some even believed that the United States' presence in the Philippines might involve the United States in a needless foreign war.

Nonetheless, President McKinley believed that if left to themselves, the Philippines might be taken over by another major

New responsibilities in Cuba, Puerto Rico, the Philippines, and other lands forced the United States to commit troops to the defense and administration of those lands.

power or fall into anarchy. The land would also make a good base for trade with China, and American missionaries could go to help the Filipinos. McKinley's view won, and Congress decided to take over the islands.

The Philippines had long been fighting against Spanish rule under the leadership of **Emilio Aguinaldo.** When the United States won the war, Aguinaldo and his followers hoped that the Philippines would be given their independence. The news of the takeover by the United States angered the Filipinos, and Aguinaldo and his forces went to work again. The United States then had to fight the rebels for two and one half years to suppress the insurrection. This problem cost the United States far more time, military expense, and casualties than had the entire Spanish-American War.

The United States worked to prepare the Philippines for eventual independence. It established a public school system to train Filipinos for citizenship. Hospitals, railroads, power plants, and greatly improved communication systems were also built. The islands were ruled for a few years by American governors. In the year 1934 the islands were granted commonwealth status. World War II delayed Philippine independence, however, until July 4, 1946.

Section Review

1. What were the two immediate causes of the Spanish-American war?
2. What other causes provoked the Spanish-American war?
3. How long did the war last?
4. What were the provisions of the treaty that ended the Spanish-American War?
5. What was the significance of the Teller Amendment?
6. Why were the Philippines so difficult to govern?

C. American Foreign Policy

As American interests widened in the late 1800s, United States foreign policy began to steer away from isolationism. The government was no longer careful to stay out of disputes between foreign countries if it was to America's advantage to become involved. If American trade and power could be advanced, the United States began to get involved in world affairs, especially those in Latin America and Eastern Asia.

In Latin America

Ever since the Monroe Doctrine the United States had been protective of its American neighbors. In 1867 the United States had driven French forces out of Mexico. In 1895 it had forced Britain to allow it to settle a boundary dispute between Venezuela and British Guiana. By 1900, America was ready to take its place as leader of the Western Hemisphere.

The Panama Canal

A first priority for the United States in Latin America was to build a canal. Naval officers had pressed for the building of a canal across Central America to enable what few ships the United States had to defend both the Atlantic and Pacific coasts more easily. The Spanish-American War helped prove the point. It took two months to sail a warship from Puget Sound to the East Coast by way of the Cape Horn of South America.

The idea of a canal was not new. In 1851 the United States and England had signed a treaty to build an inter-ocean canal open to both nations. The construction of a canal, however, fell to a French company headed by Ferdinand de Lesseps (LES ups). The French chose a route across the isthmus of Panama. But when the project took much longer than expected, the company went bankrupt. The United States then stepped in to take over the project.

Although the United States had considered an alternate route across Nicaragua, it decided to pursue the Panama canal. Since Panama was legally a part of Colombia, the United States now took steps to obtain the land from her. The United States offered Colombia $10 million for the right to build the canal and an annual rental fee of $250,000. Colombia refused, holding out for $25 million.

Meanwhile, leaders in Panama wanted independence. America realized that if there were a revolt against Colombia, and Panama gained its independence, the new Panamanian government would gladly sell the United States rights for a canal. No time was wasted. Several American warships moved into positions off the coast on November 2, 1903. The next day Panamanians rioted and declared their independence from Colombia. When Colombia tried to send troops, American ships conveniently blocked the harbors. Then the rebels

A modern container ship enters the locks of the Panama Canal.

Digging the Big Ditch

Building the Panama Canal was no easy task. The United States first attacked the problem of disease in the isthmus. Colonel William Gorgas and his workers made war on the mosquitoes that spread yellow fever and malaria, and on the rats that carried the dreaded bubonic plague. By 1906 swamps had been drained and brush and grassy marshes eliminated.

An army engineer, Colonel George W. Goethals, supervised construction of the canal itself. Sixty-eight huge steam shovels hacked away. For seven years Goethals supervised 43,000 workers, 5,000 of whom were Americans. The final cost came to $400 million.

On August 5, 1914, the *Ancon* became the first ship to pass through the completed canal, saving almost seven thousand travel miles. The formal opening of the canal under President Woodrow Wilson came on July 12, 1915. Most of the credit for completing the canal was claimed by Theodore Roosevelt. "If I had followed traditional, conservative methods," he said in 1911, "the debates on it would have been going on yet; but I took the Canal Zone and let Congress debate: and while the debate goes on, the Canal does also."

overcame the Colombian opposition within the country. On November 6 President Roosevelt used his presidential power to extend diplomatic recognition to the new nation of Panama.

On November 18, 1903, the United States signed the **Hay-Bunau-Varilla Treaty** with Panama. Negotiated by Secretary of State **John Hay** and Panama's new foreign minister, Philippe Bunau-Varilla (BYOO-NOH VA-REE-YA), the terms were generous. The United States received perpetual use of a ten-mile-wide strip of land. This "canal zone" would be controlled and fortified by the United States, and the canal built on it would be open to all nations on equal terms through payment of tolls. Eleven years later, the **Panama Canal** opened.

Theodore Roosevelt and the Big Stick— Theodore Roosevelt operated his foreign policy in Latin America with the same zest he showed in his charge up San Juan Hill. He summarized his policy by saying: "I have always been fond of the West African proverb, 'Speak softly and carry a big stick, and you will go far!' " Roosevelt believed that the United States was the most important nation in the Western Hemisphere; in fact, he believed that this hemisphere was actually an American sphere of influence and that the Caribbean was an American lake. Roosevelt's foreign policy relied on America's military strength to persuade foreign nations to act properly, and this became known as the **"big stick" policy.**

In 1902, Britain, Germany, and Italy sent warships to blockade Venezuelan ports to collect unpaid loans. Venezuela asked the United States to intervene, and Great Britain asked Roosevelt to mediate. He eagerly obliged, but he saw the incident as

One of Teddy Roosevelt's hobbies was big game hunting, and this room in his home, Sagamore Hill, displays some of his trophies.

a warning that European interests in Latin America were growing. This European presence was perhaps a possible violation of the Monroe Doctrine of 1823. Hence he made a new policy to clear up any misunderstanding: the **Roosevelt Corollary** to the Monroe Doctrine. In this statement the United States asserted the right to be an "international police power" in the Western Hemisphere. Whenever a country was guilty of long-term wrongdoing, the United States reserved the right to intervene.

Because of Roosevelt's policy, the United States would send forces to Cuba, Venezuela, the Dominican Republic, Haiti, Nicaragua, Guatemala, and Mexico during the next sixty years. Although the policy kept European powers out of Latin America and made Americans happy by protecting their financial interests, some Latin Americans began to regard the United States as an unwelcome powerful neighbor, "the colossus of the North."

***Dollar Diplomacy and Moral Diplomacy*—**Roosevelt's successors modified his policy slightly. **William Howard Taft** substituted dollars for bullets, a policy known as **"dollar diplomacy."** American investments in Latin America helped those countries develop their industries and improve the lives of their peoples. But if the Latin American countries did not follow the wishes of the United States, investments could be withdrawn.

Woodrow Wilson and his secretary of state, William Jennings Bryan, turned the policy into **"moral diplomacy."** They wanted to use negotiation in international affairs. Not wanting to pressure countries into decisions, Wilson wished to talk these countries into following the example of the United States. He believed that "the force of America is the force of moral principle." Wilson tried to promote democratic principles and secure American interests overseas while maintaining peace on all fronts. Wilson's policy proved overly idealistic, and before he left office the president had been forced to send troops into the Dominican Republic, Haiti, and Mexico.

In Asia

In the late 1800s China was becoming one of the most profitable trading spots in the world. Britain, France, Germany, Russia, and Japan had divided China into **"spheres of influence."** Each of these countries controlled all the trading operations within its "sphere" or division of the country. The United States, however, had missed out in this arrangement and was now ready to seek some trading opportunities of its own.

***China and the Open Door Policy*—**Some of the foreign powers in China wanted more than control of trade—they wanted land. Some European nations as well as Japan began to seize land, literally creating their own colonies. The United States objected to such European and Asian colonization in China. Americans wanted all of China open to everyone.

In 1899 Secretary of State John Hay sent a series of circular letters to those countries involved in China. These memos formally stated an **Open Door Policy.** No nation would have its own sphere any longer: all of China would be open to all nations on equal terms. No more Chinese land was to be seized. Germany and Japan were not at all eager to follow this policy, but to go against it, they would have to risk the wrath of two major powers, America and Britain. Consequently, they agreed.

Since Chinese territories were not united and no army existed to protect them, China had no choice but to tolerate the invasion of foreign traders. Even so, some Chinese took action. They formed a secret group called the Fists of Universal Harmony. Foreigners called them the **Boxers** because one of their rituals was shadowboxing.

The Boxers decided to force all foreigners to leave China. The uprising began in rural areas and then moved to Peking (now Beijing), the capital of China. The Boxers surrounded the sections of the city where foreigners lived and terrorized them. Some foreigners were murdered. Boxers also attacked and killed many Chinese Christians. The foreigners and Chinese Christians took refuge together and tried to hold out until help could arrive.

The United States acted to protect the lives of its citizens. The first relief expedition on June 10 was forced back. By August, John Hay had played European powers against each other enough to engineer an international force of twenty thousand men. These soldiers marched from Tientsin (TIN tsin) to Peking and freed the hostages.

Some of the eleven countries involved thought they should get land. But under the Boxer Protocol, signed September 7, 1901, none of them did. Ten high Chinese officials responsible for the **Boxer Rebellion** were executed and twenty-five Chinese forts destroyed. Instead of land, China was to pay damage payments totaling $333 million over the next forty years.

The United States government put most of its share into a fund for educating Chinese students in America. Schools and colleges in China were also built using this money. In addition American churches and mission boards sent personnel and money to China. Because of such efforts, the Chinese response to the United States was friendlier than to other imperialist powers. The United States and China remained friends until the Communists took over that land in 1949.

The United States and Japan—After Commodore Matthew Perry and the United States Navy had opened Japan to trade with the outside world in 1853, Japan quickly grew to be a powerful Asian country. In less than forty years Japan transformed itself into a modern industrial nation. Japan also gained the technical know-how that allowed her to build a modern military power. She became a militaristic nation by building up a strong army and navy.

It was a short step from being a militaristic nation to being an imperialistic one. Japan had demanded a sphere of influence from China, and in 1894-95 the Japanese easily defeated the Chinese and took the land they wanted. They also joined the international force that defeated the Boxers, and in 1905 they defeated Russia in the Russo-Japanese War.

John Hay and President Roosevelt sought to use American power in Asia to maintain a **balance of power.** President Roosevelt could see that Japan would soon be one of the great powers and might be a threat to the rest of the world. He believed that the power of the United States could be used to offset Japan's and that the United States should command the respect of the world. In 1905 President Roosevelt persuaded representatives from Russia and Japan to meet him at Portsmouth, New Hampshire. There he helped negotiate a treaty that maintained a balance of power in Asia while upholding Chinese independence. For his efforts he became the first

American president to win a Nobel Prize for Peace.

In 1907 Roosevelt made a dramatic show of American military strength. He sent the entire U.S. battle fleet on a world cruise. While Congress protested the expense, the Great White Fleet, as the American ships were called, sailed on. The fleet visited the Japanese ports and so impressed the Japanese that their imperialistic designs were curbed for the time being.

Section Review

1. Why did American naval officers want the United States to build the Panama Canal?
2. What was the significance of the Hay-Bunau-Varilla Treaty?
3. Who was the army engineer who supervised the canal's construction?
4. What famous quotation summarized Theodore Roosevelt's foreign policy?
5. Who was John Hay? What part did he play in American relations with China?
6. Who were the "Boxers"?

Summary

As imperialism became a common practice among the world's nations in the late 1800s, the United States began to break away from its traditional isolationist stance. After acquiring Alaska, Hawaii, and Midway Island peacefully, it entered the Spanish-American War in 1898. Although the conflict was intended to aid Cuba, it also resulted in adding new territories to the United States. The United States also began to boldly assert its strong position in world affairs after the turn of the century. American strength brought about the building of the Panama Canal, the opening of China to more foreign trade, and the establishment of the leadership of the United States in the Western Hemisphere.

Chapter Review

Do You Remember?

■ Match these terms with their descriptions.

1. exploitation
2. humanitarianism
3. imperialism
4. isolationism
5. yellow journalism

a. helping to meet the physical needs of poor people
b. distorting the news to make it more exciting
c. taking advantage of a people's weakness
d. not getting involved in world affairs
e. taking control of foreign lands

■ Match each of the items below with the president to which it is most closely related. Answers may be used more than once.

6. "Rough Riders"
7. moral diplomacy
8. DeLôme Letter
9. dollar diplomacy
10. "big stick" policy
11. balance of power

a. William McKinley
b. Theodore Roosevelt
c. William Howard Taft
d. Woodrow Wilson

■ Fill in the blanks.

12. The sinking of the ____ helped to trigger the Spanish-American War.
13. The ____ assured Americans that action against Spain was intended to secure Cuban independence and not to build an American empire.
14. The United States allowed Cuba independence, but it kept a part of it called ____ for use as a military base.
15. ____ was a leader in the Philippines who wanted independence for his land.
16. Secretary of State ____ negotiated a treaty with Panama and helped establish the Open-Door Policy with China.
17. Britain and other countries had gained trading privileges in areas called ____ in China.
18. The ____ staged a rebellion in China because of their dislike for foreigners.

Why Is It So?

1. Why did countries build empires?
2. Why was the Spanish-American War important to American imperialism?
3. How did the United States get involved in the Spanish-American War?
4. Why was the Panama Canal needed?
5. Why did Latin Americans begin to call the United States the "colossus of the North"?
6. How did the foreign policy of Taft and Wilson differ from that of Theodore Roosevelt?
7. How did the United States win friendship with the Chinese?

What Do You Think?

1. Is humanitarianism good or bad? Explain your answer.
2. Does the news media still use yellow journalism today? Explain your answer.
3. Was the Philippines a good acquisition for the United States? Why or why not?

22

Progressivism

The last few years of the nineteenth century and the first few years of the twentieth century were exciting for America. These years contained good prospects for growth as a world power and as a prosperous nation. Cities and industries were expanding while technology was making more and more conveniences available to the American people. Yet while life in the United States had so much to offer, it also held many problems. Sins such as greed, dishonesty, and immorality afflicted the nation then as they afflict all nations. In recognition of the evils of society, many Americans began to try to right the wrongs

and cure the ills in hopes of achieving social progress. Making life in America even better through reform was the goal of these "progressives," and their movement was called **progressivism.**

A. Changing American Life

Life was changing in the United States. New living and working conditions, new opportunities, new possessions, and new attitudes resulted from the changes and also brought more changes. Americans soon found that while some of these changes were pleasant, others were full of problems.

Downtown Chicago in the early 1900s

More People

The population of the United States at the turn of the century was seventy-five million, and it was growing by over a million a year. Involved in this tremendous growth was a trend toward urbanization and the contribution of immigration.

By 1900 **urbanization** (UR bun ih ZAY shun), the movement of people to cities, had changed America. There were more cities, and the population in the cities was growing. Many young people reared in rural areas had moved to the cities seeking greater opportunities. Between 1860 and 1910 the percentage of Americans involved in agriculture decreased from sixty per cent to thirty-one per cent. By 1920 more than one-half of America's population lived in towns and cities. Urban areas, especially large cities such as New York, Philadelphia, Boston, and Chicago, became sprawling giants. Inner-city areas were often plagued by crowded tenements (apartments), poor sanitation, crime, and poverty.

America welcomed 5.2 million immigrants in the 1880s, 3.7 million in the 1890s, and in the peak decade between 1901 and 1910, 8.8 million. Almost all these immigrants faced problems in adjusting to their new home. In fact, not all of the original immigrants would become "Americanized." That plateau would be reached, however, by most of their children. Most of them learned English quickly, although the first few months of their early education was difficult. Few schools at this time offered bilingual education. Many foreign parents opposed it because they wanted their offspring to become a part of American life as quickly as possible.

The new immigrant groups contributed a great deal to the building of America.

They extracted raw materials from the land and became the work force for much of America's diverse new industries. But immigrants brought more than labor. They brought the traditions and customs of their homelands as well, including their foods, music, and literature. All these things added more diversity to America's unique culture.

More Opportunity

America's millions were able to enjoy many opportunities to improve their lives and amuse themselves.

Education—Education was becoming more widespread. Through much of the 1800s, public education had been available at taxpayer's expense only on the elementary level. In 1860 there were only three hundred secondary schools in America, and only one hundred of them did not charge tuition. But by 1900, six thousand free secondary schools existed and by 1915, twelve thousand.

Opportunities for higher education reflected the same trend. Through the Civil War era, upper-class white males were about the only people who attended colleges or universities. By 1900, however, increasing numbers of people, including blacks and women, enrolled, and those who did go to college had a wider choice of study. Many

New York City policemen inspect the cluttered basement living room of a tenement around 1900.

new curriculums designed to prepare students for more specific professions were introduced. For example, schools in agriculture and the mechanical arts multiplied, more elective courses became available, and more graduate schools offered advanced training.

Some of the colleges and universities were aided by millionaire businessmen who provided endowments (large sums of money) to finance specific programs or salaries. Some even founded schools. Tulane (1834), Cornell (1865), Drew (1866), Vanderbilt (1873), Johns Hopkins (1876), and Stanford (1885) all bear the names of such educational **philanthropists** (fih LAN thruh pists; wealthy people who donate money to charitable causes). Philadelphia's Temple University (1884) was established by Russell Conway to educate young men who had talent and the desire to succeed but who lacked the money. The University of Chicago (1890) was founded with gifts made by John D. Rockefeller.

More educational opportunities also became available for women. In the Midwest and in the West women had an easier time getting university educations than elsewhere. They were admitted to most programs and attended classes with the men. But in the

East women tended to be educated separately in women's colleges. It was unusual for women to attend state universities. Those who did needed to be strongly motivated in order to outlast the ridicule of male students.

Blacks were able to go to college too, but they almost always attended segregated schools founded just for them. The first black university, Lincoln University in Pennsylvania, opened its doors in 1854. Nashville's Fisk University and Howard University in Washington, D.C., were both founded in 1867.

The most famous black school was **Tuskegee** (tus KEE gee) **Institute** in Alabama, founded by **Booker T. Washington,** a self-educated former slave. The school's philosophy focused on hard work, self-worth, and self-reliance. An Iowa-educated botanist, Dr. **George Washington Carver,** aided the school's reputation and finances through his work. He found more than 300 new uses for the peanut and 118 uses for the sweet potato. He also explored ways to use pecans. His work was important because it helped the South become less dependent on its cotton crop.

A Rising Middle Class—Education and opportunities to work and advance in business and industry helped many Americans improve their standard of living. A significant number of people who had been penniless immigrants, poor farmers, or poverty-stricken factory workers had found a way to improve their situation. Hard work and some business sense could bring financial gain. The fact that a person was born in poverty did not condemn him to stay there.

Only a few Americans became millionaires, and some never escaped poverty, but many Americans joined the ranks of the

The kitchen from Booker T. Washington's reconstructed home in Virginia

middle class. They had enough money to enjoy a comfortable home, adequate food, and some of the newly available consumer goods.

Leisure Time Activities

In the early 1800s, factories, mines, and other employers often demanded that their laborers work six days a week, often for a total of seventy hours or more. Complaints against such long hours (and the poor conditions and wages that often accompanied such labor) began to bring great changes during the era of progressivism. By 1910 the average workweek had dropped to 54.6 hours. Such a change gave many Americans some leisure time—time they could use to improve themselves or enjoy recreation and amusements.

Interest in both spectator sports and sports participation mushroomed. Baseball, basketball, and football were all relatively new sports that had developed in the United States. All three were popular, but baseball became the favorite. The first World Series took place in 1903. After baseball, boxing was America's most popular sport of the era. Watching heavyweights fight it out attracted many crowds. Rollerskating and bicycling were new crazes of the day, and many other sports like golf and tennis were gaining attention.

Besides sports, amusement parks, concerts, theaters, and other attractions offered entertainment for Americans. There was a surge of interest in opera and classical music especially in areas where European immigrants had settled. Many symphony orchestra members and almost all the conductors were born overseas. Of course immigrants packed the concert halls to listen to the music of European composers.

Although reading books was not new, literature did take on new importance in the era. Throughout the 1800s more people who became part of the middle class could read and had money for books. Reading then became more popular. Americans were especially fond of new American themes and regional settings. The most popular writer of the day was Samuel L. Clemens, whose pen name was Mark Twain.

Magazines appealing to literary circles were common in the 1800s. But because they were expensive (thirty-five cents per issue), magazines like *Harper's* and the *Atlantic Monthly* never enjoyed wide circulation. The invention of better printing presses and better methods of making paper eventually lowered prices. Publisher Hermann Cyrus Curtis introduced *Ladies' Home Journal* for ten cents a copy and *Saturday Evening Post* for only a nickel.

Different Values

America had received a godly heritage from its early Pilgrim and Puritan fathers. Even through the 1700s and early 1800s, most of the people who had come to America were from a Protestant background. While many were not true Christians, most of these earlier Americans had

Samuel Langhorne Clemens, better known as "Mark Twain"

a respect for the Bible as the Word of God and a belief in its moral standards. The immigration of the 1800s and the changes in American society, however, greatly altered the nation's religious attitudes.

Between 1860 and 1910 almost twenty-one million immigrants entered the United States. Some German immigrants were Lutheran, some Roman Catholic, and others rationalists (those who exalted man's reason above the revelation of God's Word). Most immigrants from Ireland had been strong Roman Catholics. Later groups of Scandinavian immigrants were largely Lutheran, while Italian immigrants were usually Roman Catholics. Immigrants from eastern Europe were a mixed group including Mennonites, Russian Orthodox, Catholics, and Jews.

Almost all churches increased their memberships in these years, including the well known, "mainline" denominations such as the Methodists, Presbyterians, and Baptists. When some of the mainline groups failed to meet people's needs, however, new denominations such as the Holiness and Pentecostal groups, and other religious organizations

began. Several newly organized cults that denied Biblical truths also began during this period. For example, Mary Baker Eddy founded Christian Science with its teaching that "matter and death are mental illusions," as are sin, pain, and disease. Seventh-Day Adventism grew under the leadership of Ellen G. Harmon White. Another cult, the Jehovah's Witnesses (Watch-Tower Society) was founded in 1872 by Charles Taze Russell. These cults offered attractive ideas to religious Americans and won great followings, but they also blinded people to the truths of God's Word.

As German rationalists and other theologians cast doubts on the truth of Scripture, their ideas began to break down the standards of many religious groups in America. Some people began to accept the notion that the Bible was just a good book written by man. Men began to think they had the right to examine Scripture and to say what parts were right and what parts were in error. This "liberalism" led ministers to emphasize the social gospel because doing good to mankind was obviously right. Many quit preaching the true gospel—repentance from sin and faith in Jesus Christ who alone can give salvation—because they wished to think that man could solve his own problems. The focus of many American churches was quickly changing from God's provision for man's need in eternity to man's abilities to solve temporal needs.

Some men, called **agnostics,** even scoffed at the existence of God, saying that we cannot know whether there is a God. The most famous agnostic, Robert Ingersoll, traveled the country giving lectures. People paid to hear him mock true faith, though many attended his lectures more out of curiosity than agreement.

LOVE, PURITY & FIDELITY.

GRAND, NATIONAL, TEMPERANCE BANNER.

Dedicated to every Son & Daughter of Temperance, throughout the Union.

In 1859 in England, one of the influential works of the nineteenth century was published. Written by Charles Darwin, *Origin of Species* proposed a theory of evolution. While most Americans did not readily accept evolution at that time, the theory began to influence both science and religious thought. In 1874 Charles Hodge, a leading conservative theologian, made what was probably the most successful attack on evolution. He attacked natural selection, showing that it contradicted the existence of an all-powerful, all-knowing Creator.

While religious liberalism and other common philosophies prompted men to humanitarianism, they also hardened many

A temperance banner from the 1800s

Americans in their sin. But many Bible-believing pastors and evangelists were still preaching salvation through Christ. The existence of both liberal religion and true Christianity in American culture led to a mixture of religious goals in the progressive era. Some endeavors sincerely sought to reach souls for Christ. Others aimed at improving morals or living conditions, and some tried to do both.

Temperance Groups—The heavy use of alcohol had become a big problem in many areas of the country. Some immigrant groups were particularly heavy drinkers, and their actions were offensive to many others. Wherever alcoholism occurred, abuse of family members, increased poverty, and crime were often the result.

Many religious Americans saw the need to correct the problem and formed **temperance societies** to fight against the evils of liquor. Most of them were associated with the Anti-Saloon League (1893) or the Women's Christian Temperance Union (1874). The efforts of these societies, combined with the efforts of evangelists who preached against the sin of drunkenness, led to the prohibition movement and the passage of Amendment Eighteen in 1919. That amendment outlawed the sale and manufacture of alcoholic beverages.

Interdenominational Organizations—Laymen founded interdenominational organizations that crossed church boundary lines. The Young Men's Christian Association (YMCA), which had originated in England, came to America. The "Y," as it was called, stressed four areas of growth: physical, educational, social, and religious. Another group of British origin was the Salvation Army. It provided relief for the poor and set up rescue missions to convert

"Rescue the Perishing"

As American cities grew in the 1800s, so did their problems. Sections of large cities such as New York became slum areas, places where the poor, usually immigrants, lived close together in dirty, noisy tenements. The main "entertainment" in the slums was often found in saloons, where drinking, gambling, and other vices took much of the little money that the people had. Churches tended to move away from the slums, locating where more prosperous and "respectable" people could support them.

Some Christians did try to reach the people in the slums. They held services in rented halls, passed out tracts, and attempted to witness to the people. One man, Jerry McAuley, wanted to do more. Born in Ireland in 1837, he came to New York City at the age of thirteen. McAuley soon became a thief; at the age of nineteen he was arrested for robbery and sent to prison.

In prison McAuley was converted through the testimony of a former convict. After getting out, McAuley thought that Christians were not doing enough to help the real "down-and-outs," the drunks, prostitutes, and others who dwelt in the worst parts of the city. He decided to start a "rescue mission," a work located in the slums and designed to "rescue" people from sin. His Water Street Mission in New York is usually considered the first rescue mission in the United States.

Probably the most famous rescue mission was the Pacific Garden Mission in Chicago. This mission was started in 1877 by Colonel George Clark and his wife, Sarah Dunn. D. L. Moody helped to name it. Thousands of people were reached for Christ through the Pacific Garden Mission. In 1886 a half-drunk baseball player named Billy Sunday heard a group of mission workers singing on a street

corner. He followed them back to the Garden, where he was converted. Later, of course, he became a well-known evangelist.

Other people started rescue missions in other cities. Mel Trotter, for example, began a successful work in Grand Rapids, Michigan, and later helped found missions in other cities. Trotter loved the mission work because he had been saved in a mission. In 1897 he had stumbled into the Pacific Garden Mission. Although it was January, he was barefoot because he had sold his shoes to buy a drink. Converted, Trotter dedicated his life to reaching people like himself who had reached the bottom physically, mentally, and spiritually.

Rescue mission work varied in operation from city to city. Usually missions were open day and night to minister to anyone who came in. Services normally consisted of the singing of gospel songs, testimonies of converted sinners from the slums, and simple salvation sermons. The missions also tried to provide hot meals and a place to stay, at least for a night or two. Some more ambitious missions tried to provide work for their people. In these missions the people repaired clothing, made brooms, or did some other kind of work to help pay for their room and board.

Poor children, such as these in Washington, D.C., were also reached by gospel missions.

and rebuild the lives of those people who knew only defeat. Various other groups began rescue missions to work with such people. Probably the most famous rescue mission was Chicago's Pacific Garden Mission, founded in 1877. Other groups set up missions to work with specific immigrant groups.

Foreign Missions and Evangelistic Efforts—Americans were also concerned about taking the gospel to others. America sent out more missionary workers than any other country. The evangelistic and cultural impact of Christianity was so great at the end of the nineteenth century that some historians have called it "the Great Century" of Christianity.

Important throughout the era was the work of evangelists and revival leaders. Camp meetings were held, but tents and brush arbors were abandoned for wood-frame tabernacles. Some groups even held meetings at modern campgrounds with cabins for the visitors to stay in.

Section Review

1. What is urbanization?
2. Who founded Tuskegee Institute?
3. List at least three ways in which the American laborer used his newly acquired leisure time.
4. What was one reason for the increased diversity of religious groups from 1860-1910?
5. List at least two characteristics of religious liberalism.
6. List at least three cults that began during this time.
7. What does an agnostic believe?
8. What was the purpose of the temperance groups?

B. The Progressive Era

Besides its growing spiritual needs, America's growing and changing society was beset with many problems. Some of the problems were very big—too big for individuals to solve alone. The progressives began to look for help in solving America's problems. More and more they looked to government for the answers.

Progressive Aims

Progressives sought to abolish corruption and unfair practices in government, industry, labor, and even society. They were able to make permanent changes in the way the cities, the states, and the nation were governed, although social reforms were harder to accomplish.

A second progressive aim was to give people more say in governing. Some progressives believed that the evils of government could be cured by making government more democratic (giving the individual citizens more power over laws and government officials). Some governmental practices thought commonplace today, such as primary elections and voting by secret ballot, were started by progressives.

Third, progressives believed that the quality of life in America could be improved by government. Many thought that government should improve society, that it was to be a minister of good. Some of the progressive ideals were definitely moral in tone. Combating crime in cities, establishing prohibition, and eliminating prostitution were among such moral aims.

Uncovering Corruption

Progressives sought to correct widespread corruption through reform. There was corruption on all levels of government:

city, state, and national. In New York City, for example, "Boss" William Marcy Tweed milked the city of millions of dollars by using city funds to give himself and his friends large profits on city contracts. One example of corruption on the state level was the bribing of officials to give special favors to certain industries. In Pennsylvania, Standard Oil had been accused of doing everything to the state legislature except refine it. On the national level, the presidency of U. S. Grant had produced such scandal that the term *grantism* became a synonym for illegal dealings in public office.

The spoils system used by Andrew Jackson and other presidents who followed him had allowed much corruption in the appointment of government employees. This was curbed in the late 1800s by the implementation of several civil service reforms that made merit, or ability, the standard by which jobs were awarded instead of loyalty to the political party in power. Even the reforms in the civil service system, however, were not enough to prevent some politicians from finding ways to abuse the policies.

Corruption was also rampant in industry. The public, especially western farmers, had been victimized by corrupt and unfair

A cartoon from an 1871 issue of Harper's Weekly attacks the political corruption of Boss Tweed and his gang by asking, "Who stole the people's money?"

practices of the railroads. The railroads had been guilty of overcharging some customers while offering rebates to petroleum shippers. In states where timber was being harvested, some lumber companies stripped public lands for their own profit.

Some industrialists were not only dishonest in their business dealings but also unfair and even cruel to their workers. The workers often labored under terrible and unsafe conditions. Perhaps the worst disaster was the Triangle Shirtwaist Company fire in New York City in March 1911. Nearly one hundred and fifty people, mostly girls and women, perished because doors had been locked to keep the workers on the job until the end of the shift. Because filtering systems in southern textile plants were rare, textile workers inhaled cotton lint dust. Some then got "brown lung" disease and later died from it. Long hours at low pay were normal. Since almost all jobs had the same hours, and since employers exchanged lists of employees who caused trouble or went on strike, it did little good to try to change jobs. Women and children were also victimized by industry. Early efforts to protect women from some occupations and to forbid the employment of children under fourteen years of age failed.

Revealing Society's Ills

Living conditions were worst in crowded cities. Rents were high and housing was limited, and so the poor huddled together. Small, often one-room, apartments were common for entire families and sometimes even boarders. More than 400,000 residents of New York City lived in windowless tenements. Twenty thousand more lived in damp cellar apartments where their rooms often flooded with water.

Muckrakers: Journalists Who Exposed the Worst

If it had not been for muckraking journalists, it is possible that progressivism would have died; certainly it would have been less influential. **Muckrakers,** journalists who exposed society's ills, were given their name by Teddy Roosevelt. But the term was not original with him. It is the name of a character in John Bunyan's *Pilgrim's Progress* who was always looking down and could not look up even when offered a heavenly crown.

Muckraker journalists and authors named specific financiers, industrialists, and congressmen who undermined public interests. Muckraker Lincoln Steffens revealed city problems in articles for *McClure's.* Later they were put into a book, *The Shame of the Cities.* Steffens charged Philadelphia politicians with using the votes of "dead dogs, children, and nonexistent persons" to keep themselves in power.

Ida M. Tarbell was a Pennsylvania school teacher turned author. She had grown up near Titusville, Pennsylvania, at the height of Standard Oil's attempt to squeeze out its competitors. She later wrote a series of articles on the company's ruthless tactics. In 1903 the articles were printed in a two-volume work, *History of the Standard Oil Company.* Her book led to the court case requiring the company to break down its holdings.

John Spargo wrote of the ills of child labor and of the poverty that sent many children to school hungry each day. His work *The Bitter Cry of Children* (1906) aided the passage of child labor laws. Ray Stannard Baker attacked lynching, executing blacks without trial, in southern states. Upton Sinclair used his novel *The Jungle* to show that Chicago meat packers killed diseased cattle and used chemicals and dyes to cover up bad meat. His descriptions were effective enough to spark the final drive for the Pure Food and Drug Act.

The political and religious views of many of the muckraking writers were not sound, but their work did force some hidden problems to the attention of the American public and the government.

Epidemics were common. Diphtheria, smallpox, cholera, typhus, scarlet fever, and tuberculosis took many lives. Even "childhood" diseases such as measles, mumps, and chicken pox became dangerous under such conditions. Garbage created a terrible stench and became a breeding ground for insects, germs, and disease. Even where sanitation departments existed, they could not keep pace.

An insufficient water supply and inadequate plumbing were other urban problems. Many tenements did not have running water or indoor bathrooms. People got water from street wells. Because run-off water flowed into them, the water was impure.

Fire hydrants were opened at certain times for bathing or other uses. Where indoor plumbing existed, it was usually shared by many people and was undependable.

While housing conditions for the poor were bad, those for people confined in prisons, mental hospitals, and other institutions were even worse. Filth and cruel treatment were commonplace.

Reforms

During this era many city officials had little ability, limited knowledge, and no character. To overcome these problems, new methods of running city governments were tried. Rather than electing a mayor, some cities hired a trained expert called a city manager. Since his position did not depend on his popularity, the manager was under less pressure to bow to special interest groups. Other cities tried a commission form of government. Several commissioners were selected, each of which was put in charge of a specific area of government. This system made it much easier to detect corruption.

Two states, Oregon and Wisconsin, were leaders in progressive reforms. Oregon reformed so many parts of its government that the package of ideas they tried was called the Oregon System. One new democratic practice was the **recall** of elected officials. If citizens became unhappy with the actions of an elected official, they could get a required number of signatures on a petition and force the official either to resign or to stand for special election, even if his term of office had not yet expired.

Two other government reforms enacted in many states were the initiative and referendum. An **initiative** allowed voters to propose their own legislation. First a set number of voters' signatures had to be collected on a petition. Next the proposed law would go on a ballot allowing voters to accept or reject it. **Referendums,** on the other hand, allowed voters to pass judgment on acts already passed by their state legislatures. A similar petition and election system were used.

One other major government reform was the direct election of senators, brought about in 1913 by Amendment Seventeen. Up to that time senators had been elected by state legislatures. The progressives believed that responsibility belonged to the people. They also believed that such an approach would put elections out of the reach of corrupt manipulators in state government. However, they failed to recognize that senators elected directly by the people would be more likely to follow the immediate desires of the public rather than stand for what was right or better for the nation in the long run. Thus a practical part of America's republican government was lost.

Many attempts were made to cure some of the problems of the cities. Individuals responded to the terrible conditions in tenements by founding settlement houses. The first settlement house, Toynbee Hall, was in Whitehall, a London slum. Americans modeled theirs after it. Besides providing food, clothing, and child care, the settlement houses offered recreation and classes to slum area women. America's first settlement house, called Neighborhood Guild, was founded in 1886 in New York City. Probably the most famous was Chicago's Hull House. Jane Addams, an avowed socialist, founded the work in 1889. She was assisted by Florence Kelly who later channeled her energies into law. Her efforts led to the passage of child labor laws in several states.

Other citizens and social groups worked for improving prisons and mental institutions and for aiding people in distressed conditions. While government stayed out of most of these social programs, it did begin to press regulations on industries' abuses of employees and consumers.

Section Review

1. List three of the progressives' aims.
2. Who was William Tweed?
3. List three government reform ideas that gave more control to individual citizens.
4. What was the purpose of Toynbee Hall and Hull House?

C. Roosevelt Brings Progressivism to the White House

During the years when these issues of corruption, reform, and government regulation and aid were chief concerns for the country, Americans elected three presidents with progressive goals: Theodore Roosevelt, William Howard Taft, and Woodrow Wilson.

Theodore Roosevelt had been governor of New York when Tom Platt, the state political boss, discovered he could not control him. He then urged Republicans to nominate Roosevelt for the vice-presidency of the United States. Since the vice-presidency was thought to be a political graveyard, Platt hoped that it would shut Roosevelt up and keep him out of the public

Theodore Roosevelt
26TH PRESIDENT
(1901-1909)

Born: New York, New York, October 27, 1858

Family: married Alice Hathaway Lee, and after her death, Edith Kermit Carow; had one daughter by his first wife, one daughter and four sons by his second

Occupation: historian, rancher

Home: Sagamore Hill, Oyster Bay, New York

Religion: Dutch Reformed

Election: took office after the death of McKinley

1904—defeated Alton B. Parker

Political Party: Republican, Progressive or "Bull Moose" (1912)

Vice President: none during first term; Charles Fairbanks (second term)

Interesting Facts and Accomplishments:

educated at Harvard University and Columbia University Law School

lost his mother and his first wife on the same day in 1884; in grief went to live on his ranch in the Dakota Territory for two years

lost the sight in his left eye after blood vessels were ruptured during a boxing match

first president to travel outside the United States while president, and first to fly in an airplane

received the Nobel Peace Prize of 1906 for his efforts in ending the Russo-Japanese War

spoke four foreign languages

survived an assassination attempt in the 1912 election when the metal case for his glasses in his pocket stopped a bullet from going through to his heart

went big-game hunting in Africa and went on an exploring expedition in the jungles of Brazil

Death: January 6, 1919

eye. However, when President McKinley was assassinated, Theodore Roosevelt became president. Although Roosevelt believed it was "a dreadful thing" to gain the presidency that way, few people have enjoyed the office as much as he did.

· Roosevelt had some critics, but he gained a large popular following. He was wealthy and well educated, but his adventures as a cowboy and a soldier had given him an ability to identify with the people and endeared him to the public. A candy store owner even named a new toy, the Teddy bear, for him. A graduate of Harvard, Roosevelt spoke several languages and had written at least a dozen books before becoming president. Roosevelt was also a skilled politician with many progressive goals. Unlike many Republican leaders of the day, he wanted change and improvement for the nation's government.

Theodore Roosevelt's Square Deal

Roosevelt believed that the government should control big business and promote competition. Government should also promote better working conditions and job safety. Roosevelt's views and his efforts to put big business under the government's thumb won over other progressives.

Like other progressives, Roosevelt thought that workers should receive just and fair treatment. An example of Roosevelt's labor policy came when the United Mine Workers went on strike in 1902. They demanded a shorter workday, raises, and recognition for their union. The strike dragged on for months as management refused to negotiate, and coal shortages caused public discomfort. Instead of siding with the owners and forcing the workers back to the mines, Roosevelt warned that

he might use troops to run the coal mines. He also formed a special commission to help settle the dispute. This was the first time that the federal government had become a third party in settling a dispute between labor and management. Roosevelt claimed that he wanted to give both labor and management "a square deal." The question over whether such intervention is a proper use of federal powers remains. Nevertheless, a compromise reduced the working day for the miners to nine hours and raised pay by ten per cent.

Protecting People and Resources

Upton Sinclair's *The Jungle* had exposed corruption in the meat packing industry. In 1906 Congress passed the **Pure Food and Drug Act.** Federal inspectors gained the right to inspect all slaughterhouses and meat companies that shipped across state lines. Provisions forbade the use of harmful additives, even if they were designed to stop spoilage.

Many contemporary patent medicines, widely advertised and available over the counter or by mail, contained opium derivatives or a high percentage of alcohol. Although these medicines were often useful, they were also addictive. The Pure Food and Drug Act regulated the use of narcotics and required a list of contents on product labels. It also made it illegal to make claims about medicines that could not be verified.

Another issue very dear to Roosevelt's heart was conservation. An outdoorsman, he readily responded to demands that the government protect lands for future generations to enjoy. America's first national park, Yellowstone, had become federal property in 1872. By 1901 there were three more national parks: Sequoia (sih KWOY uh;

1890), Yosemite (yoh SEM ih tee; 1890), and Mount Rainier (ray NEER; 1891). When Roosevelt left office in 1909, he had more than doubled the number of national parks, adding Wind Cave (1901), Crater Lake (1902), Mesa Verde (MAY-suh VURD; 1906), the Petrified Forest (1906), and Platt (1906).

To protect forest lands from loggers, Congress had started a forest reserve system in 1891. While presidents Harrison, Cleveland, and McKinley had all added to the forest acreage, Theodore Roosevelt more than doubled the acreage in reserve. Theodore Roosevelt's close personal friend and a professionally trained forester, **Gifford Pinchot** (PIN SHOW), was appointed chief forester. Pinchot not only helped to preserve America's forest resources but also set up a program to conserve its grasslands.

In 1902 Congress passed the New Lands Act, which permitted the sale of federal lands in arid areas. The money gained through such a sale was to pay for irrigation projects to make arid lands usable.

Roosevelt Steps Down

Although Theodore Roosevelt could have run again in 1908, he chose instead to hand-pick his successor. This was the first time since Andrew Jackson that a president in power had enough backing to do so. Theodore Roosevelt picked William Howard Taft, who had given him loyal service.

Section Review

1. How did Roosevelt gain the presidency?
2. What was Theodore Roosevelt's attitude toward big business?
3. What was Roosevelt's reaction to the coal strike in 1902?
4. Whom did Roosevelt wish to be his successor?

D.   The Taft Administration

William Howard Taft was a lawyer who had spent most of his career in the federal court system. Although Roosevelt had named him civil governor of the Philippines and later secretary of war, Taft preferred the courts. His lifelong dream was to be chief justice of the Supreme Court. However, he set aside that dream temporarily at the urging of Roosevelt. (In 1921, nine years after Taft left the presidency, he. was appointed to the Supreme Court as chief justice by President Harding.)

Taft agreed with Roosevelt that government should control big business. However, when he won the 1908 election over Democrat William Jennings Bryan, the course he took as president was somewhat different from Roosevelt's. He followed the advice of Republican leaders more readily, and he did not publicly push progressive reforms. Although his methods and personality made him appear to be more easygoing than Roosevelt, Taft actually initiated eighty-nine antitrust suits, compared to Roosevelt's forty-three. But Taft was unable to dramatize his successes as Roosevelt had done. People saw only Taft's mistakes, and he left office a failure in the eyes of many Americans.

Taft's Term in Office

Nevertheless, Taft could claim many progressive actions. He helped to give the Interstate Commerce Commission more power to control the railroads, and he put telegraph and telephone companies under federal control. Taft backed reforms in the post office, created the Department of Labor to protect workers, and organized the Children's Bureau to end child labor. Also during Taft's administration the Sixteenth

William Howard Taft

27TH PRESIDENT
(1909-1913)

Born: Cincinnati, Ohio, September 5, 1857

Family: married Helen Herron; had one daughter, two sons

Occupation: lawyer

Home: Cincinnati, Ohio

Religion: Unitarian

Election: 1908—defeated William Jennings Bryan

Political Party: Republican

Vice President: James Sherman

Interesting Facts and Accomplishments:

only American to have headed two branches of government—executive and judicial

started the tradition of the president throwing out the first ball for the opening of baseball season

last president to keep a cow (Pauline Wayne) on the White House lawn

heaviest president, with a weight reaching 320 pounds

first president to have an official automobile

first president to be buried in Arlington National Cemetery

Death: March 8, 1930

and Seventeenth Amendments to the Constitution were ratified. The income tax amendment (sixteenth) gave government a source of revenues that would allow it to expand its activities greatly in later years. The Seventeenth Amendment required the direct election of senators.

The Republican Party Splits

Taft's political future was endangered by fighting within the Republican party. Disputes over the passage of the Payne-Aldrich Tariff in 1909 made some Republicans think Taft had sold out Roosevelt's ideas. A bitter dispute between two of Taft's cabinet members over some western forest lands was the final straw. When Taft wanted Gifford Pinchot dismissed from his cabinet, Theodore Roosevelt came home from an African safari convinced that Taft had sold out progressive Republican principles.

The Election of 1912

Theodore Roosevelt had been home less than two months when he hit the campaign trail. He said that he was out to persuade voters to elect progressive Republicans to the House and Senate. But he was really widening the rift within the Republican party and building his own support for the

Theodore Roosevelt

1912 convention. By February 1912, Theodore Roosevelt "gave in" to the urging of progressive Republicans and announced: "My hat is in the ring. I will accept the nomination for president if it is tendered' to me."

But Taft and his followers had the support of most of the Republican party leaders. They helped him win the Republican nomination on the first ballot. Theodore Roosevelt declared that Taft Republican conservatives had stolen the nomination from him. Thus the new Progressive party was launched, with Theodore Roosevelt as its candidate. When Roosevelt announced that he felt "as fit as a Bull Moose," his party became known as the **Bull Moose party.** Theodore Roosevelt's political ideals were known as "The New Nationalism" and would have involved the federal government in still more areas had he won.

The Democratic candidate was New Jersey's progressive Democratic governor, Woodrow Wilson. His campaign catchwords spoke of the "New Freedom." He wanted strict government regulation to restore business competition. Although Roosevelt and Taft together got more votes than Wilson, Wilson won because of the split Republican vote.

Section Review

1. During his career, Taft headed what other branch of government besides the executive branch?
2. What were the provisions of the Sixteenth and Seventeenth amendments?
3. Why did the Republican party split during Taft's term in office?
4. The Republican split enabled what Democrat to win the 1912 election?

E. Progressivism with a Democrat

Woodrow Wilson, son of a Presbyterian pastor, grew up in the South. His ideas reflected his background. He believed that there were two sides to every issue, "a right side and a wrong side," and he stubbornly hung on to principles, refusing to compromise. He had confidence in his judgment perhaps because he believed God had led him. He viewed men idealistically, sincerely believing that most people learned from experience and desired to do right. Politically this meant that he often underestimated his opposition, whether at home or abroad.

Wilson and Business

At first Wilson favored less government regulation of business than either Roosevelt or Taft. But rather than try to regulate large trusts, he believed that the government should break them up into smaller companies. He believed small companies would be less monopolistic and more likely to operate in the public interest.

Woodrow Wilson and his wife, Edith

Woodrow Wilson
28TH PRESIDENT
(1913-1921)

Born: Staunton, Virginia, December 28, 1856

Family: married Ellen Axson, and after her death, Edith Galt; had three daughters by his first wife

Occupation: lawyer, teacher, university president

Home: Washington, D.C.

Religion: Presbyterian

Elections: 1912—defeated William Howard Taft (Republican) and Theodore Roosevelt (Bull Moose) 1916—defeated Charles Evans Hughes

Political Party: Democrat

Vice President: Thomas Marshall

Interesting Facts and Accomplishments:
served as president of Princeton University

was the first president to have an earned Ph.D.

kept sheep on the White House lawn to crop the grass during World War I because of the manpower shortage

played golf year-round to get over his first wife's death; painted the balls black in the winter so that he could see them on the snow

suffered a stroke while in office, so his second wife managed much of his presidential affairs and is sometimes called "the nation's first lady president"

Death: February 3, 1924

To deal with big business and get around the courts, which usually decided in favor of big business, Wilson took two steps. First, he set up the Federal Trade Commission. This independent regulatory agency had the power to get data from corporations and to issue orders to stop abuses. Second, Congress passed the **Clayton Anti-Trust Act** of 1914. This act closed some loopholes of the earlier Sherman Anti-Trust Act. It defined the unfair acts for which corporations could be fined or their executives jailed. The act also exempted both labor unions and farmers' cooperatives from antitrust laws so that these groups could lawfully protest unfair practices.

The Tariff and Income Tax

One of Wilson's major accomplishments concerned the tariff. Since the Democrats had gained majorities in both the House and Senate, Wilson had the support for the reforms he had proposed in his 1912 campaign. Wilson believed that a high protective tariff encouraged monopolies and led to higher charges for consumers. Lowering the tariff would force American businesses to compete with rivals and become more efficient. The Underwood Tariff of 1913 gave the first major tariff decrease since the Civil War. The tariff rate on imports went down from forty per cent to less than thirty per cent.

Since the Sixteenth Amendment had legalized the income tax, Congress used it to make up for the loss of tariff revenue. Incomes under $4,000 were not taxed. Annual incomes between $4,000 and $20,000 were taxed one per cent. The income tax was a graduated tax: the more a person made, the higher percentage of his income he had to pay. The top bracket was six per cent on incomes over $500,000. This beginning of income taxes paved the way for higher taxes and more government spending in the future.

Another financial reform accomplished during the Wilson presidency was the establishment of the **Federal Reserve System.** It set up twelve district banks under a national Federal Reserve Board. The Federal Reserve Banks served as bankers' banks. The district reserve banks could increase or decrease the amount of money in circulation. The Board could use its power to control many banking operations throughout the country and thus try to manage the nation's economy.

The Election of 1916

As the nation approached the 1916 election, Wilson was more and more preoccupied with events in war-torn Europe. Seeking to avoid American involvement in the conflict, his campaign slogan became: "He kept us out of war."

When Teddy Roosevelt refused to run as a progressive candidate, the Bull Moose party dissolved. Progressive followers then had to decide whom to follow. Some backed Wilson because of his reforms, while others returned to the Republican fold.

The election of 1916 was a very close one. Wilson narrowly defeated Republican Charles Evans Hughes. Hughes was a former governor of New York and a Supreme Court justice. The key state in the election proved to be California. Election returns from that state were late to arrive, and Hughes went to bed believing he was the next president. The next morning he found out that Wilson had been reelected.

Wilson's Second Term

During his second term Wilson was forced to focus on foreign affairs and the eventual entry of the United States into World War I. In addition to problems in Europe, Wilson faced problems in Latin America, where he tried to implement his moral diplomacy. With all this attention on actions in other lands, progressive politics

A New York City Women's Suffrage parade in 1913

began to fall by the wayside. Two major issues that were resolved, however, were the questions of prohibition and women's suffrage. To the delight of prohibitionists, an amendment banning the manufacture and sale of alcoholic beverages passed in 1919. One year later the suffragettes won their right to vote. However, the progressive era in American history was over.

Section Review

1. What three important financial changes were made during Wilson's administration?
2. What gained most of the national government's attention during Wilson's second term?
3. What is women's suffrage, and when was it gained?

Summary

Americans generally enjoyed great prosperity at the turn of the century, but they also realized that there were many problems in their nation. Greed, poverty, alcoholism, corruption in government, and other evils troubled many people in the United States, and so Americans began to pressure government leaders to do something about these conditions. Progressive politicians campaigned for government reforms as well as regulations for industry. Although a few of the accomplishments of progressivism did prove helpful, their basic effect was to increase the government's activity and power in a search for solutions. Most people failed to realize that government could never solve the underlying problems of sin.

Chapter Review

Do You Remember?

■ Match each of the following terms with its description.

1. agnostic
2. initiative
3. muckraker
4. philanthropist
5. progressivism
6. recall
7. referendum
8. temperance society
9. urbanization

a. an effort to get rid of the evils in society
b. movement to the cities
c. one who donates money to public causes
d. one who does not believe people can know whether God really exists
e. worked to prohibit alcohol use and abuse
f. one who reported poor conditions in society
g. voters' reaction to a law already passed by their legislature
h. voters propose legislation themselves
i. voters' attempt to remove elected officials

■ Answer the following questions.
   10. What was the famous black school founded by Booker T. Washington?
   11. What scientist helped to give that school a good reputation?
   12. Name three religious cults that became popular around the turn of the century.
   13. What did progressives turn to for help in solving the problems of American society?
   14. Who were the three progressive presidents?
   15. What legislation helped to combat corruption in meat packing companies and the abuse of patent medicines?
   16. What was Roosevelt's party called in 1912?
   17. What did the Sixteenth and Seventeenth amendments do?
   18. What is the term for the group of twelve banks and their board that regulates the nation's money system?

Why Is It So?

   1. How was education in America changing by the turn of the century?
   2. Why did Americans in the early 1900s have more leisure time than those in earlier years?
   3. Why did America's religious values change in the late 1800s and early 1900s?
   4. Why did Americans think government needed to be reformed?
   5. How did muckrakers aid the progressive movement?

What Do You Think?

   1. In what ways was progressivism helpful to the country, and in what ways was it harmful?
   2. How did America's government change during the progressive era?
   3. What should have been the attitude of true Christians toward the social and religious changes of the progressive era?

23

World War I

On June 29, 1914, Americans read in their newspapers of the assassination the day before in Sarajevo (SAH RAH yeh voh), Bosnia, of Archduke Francis Ferdinand, heir to the Austro-Hungarian throne. Most Americans probably asked: "Where is Sarajevo, Bosnia?" Little did they realize how soon all their lives would be drastically affected by that political assassination in a little town on the Balkan Peninsula that few Americans had heard of. World War I would soon follow.

World War I shocked Americans. For three years—1914, 1915, and 1916—the United States looked on as "the Great War" ravaged Europe, destroying more property and life than any other war in history up to that time. Most Americans believed that the war was Europe's affair. They agreed with President Wilson that Americans needed to be neutral in word and deed. They hoped that having the Atlantic Ocean between them and the conflict would keep America out of the war. In 1916 Americans

Childe Kassam, Allies Day, May 1917, *National Gallery of Art, Washington, D.C.*©

had reelected Wilson because "he kept them out of war." But on April 6, 1917, hopes for staying at peace were dashed. The United States entered World War I.

A. The War as America Watched

The United States tried to mind its own business as the war began, but it could not help seeing the trouble that was brewing in Europe.

Reasons for War

There were several reasons for Europe's turmoil, and one was extreme nationalism. A devotion to and a pride in one's own nation is a natural and proper feeling, but some countries had been building a distorted nationalism in their people in the years before the war. Some nations, like Germany, began to believe they had the right to build up and expand their country no matter what the effect might be on others.

Imperialism and militarism were two more reasons for the growing tensions in Europe. Several countries had or wanted large empires, and some were willing to fight each other to gain control of colonies or nearby territories. Several nations had also built large armies to further imperial goals or protect possessions. Large and powerful military forces, however, were threatening to weaker neighbors and caused rivals to increase their forces as well.

One more major reason for the eruption of World War I was the alliances of European nations. In their effort to insure security against aggression, European nations formed alliances, agreements to support one another militarily. The **Triple Alliance** included Germany, Austria-Hungary, and Italy, nations united by common imperialistic goals. The **Triple Entente** (on TONT; *entente* is a French word for "agreement") included Britain, France, and Russia, na-

Troops of both the Allies and the Central Powers spent much of the war locked in uncomfortable trench warfare.

tions united by a common fear of Germany. Because these two opposing alliances involved all the major powers of Europe, once any of these powers entered a conflict, all the others were likely to be drawn in.

The Spark and Spread of War

The assassination of the Austrian archduke was the spark that ignited the conflict. Russia quickly came to the aid of Serbia, the little Balkan land that Austria-Hungary blamed for the deed. Thus Russia and Austria-Hungary were soon at war with each other, and the allies of both joined in the conflict.

On August 1, Germany declared war on Russia, and France joined with Russia against Germany and Austria-Hungary two days later. When German armies marched across the neutral country of Belgium to attack France, Britain quickly stepped into the war. A few other nations also took sides. Ahead was a long and bloody war between the **Central Powers**—Germany, Austria-Hungary, Bulgaria, and Turkey—and the **Allies**—Britain, France, Russia, Italy, and later the United States. (Italy switched to the Allied side in 1915.)

Action in the War

Since the United States was not involved in the European alliances and rivalries, it had no reason to enter the war with the other powers in the beginning. It simply watched in horror as soldiers slaughtered each other across Europe in their bitter fight.

Germany led the first major assault of the war by pressing its armies through Belgium to northern France. British troops came to France's aid before the Germans could take the land, however, and the two sides settled into trenches from the English Channel to the Rhine River. At the same time, the Russian armies began to attack Germany and Austria-Hungary from the east with little success.

The war dragged on with neither the Central Powers nor the Allies making large gains. However, both sides did introduce new weapons and equipment that made warfare more efficient and sometimes more brutal.

The British developed the tank, an armored vehicle that could fire shells while moving on caterpillar tracks. It was capable of almost continuous advance over rugged

Tanks such as this French one became important weapons in World War 1.

terrain. Soon the other powers developed their own tanks.

On April 22, 1915, at the battle of Ypres, the Germans unleashed a new deadly weapon: poison gas. Made from chlorine, the gas harmed the nose, throat, and lungs. Poison gases made whole armies temporarily helpless in the face of enemy attacks. Mustard gas, as it came to be known, soon became the most feared and common gas on the battlefield. About two per cent of those who came into contact with it died. As a result, the gas mask was developed and became standard equipment in some war areas.

Fighting also took to the air. For a while the Germans used zeppelins, large aircraft similar to blimps, to bomb Britain. But because zeppelins were slow-moving, they were soon replaced by the airplane. This new flying machine could be used for aerial reconnaissance, bombing, and "dogfighting." Dogfighting, shooting between enemy planes, became possible after machine guns were synchronized with the airplane's propellers. (Before that development in 1915, pilots could not fire their guns forward without shooting their own propellers.) Fighter pilots who shot down many planes became special heroes, called "flying aces." Manfred von Richthofen, "the Red Baron," was Germany's top ace. Britain's flying hero was Mick Mannock, and when the United States entered the war, Eddie Rickenbacker became the most famous American ace.

Trucks and automobiles aided the transportation of military goods and personnel. Rifles, cannon, grenades, mines, and other weapons were improved or invented for effective fighting. And for battling on the sea, the Germans were able to perfect the submarine. These "U-Boats" (underwater

The Wild Blue Yonder

America's air force had its beginnings in France during World War I. Actually the first American air squadron was in the French armed forces. Since the United States did not have an air corps of its own at that time, many young Americans went to Europe to fly for France. At first these adventurers could join only the French Foreign Legion. They were forbidden by French law from enlisting in the regular French forces. Soon the law changed, though, and a group of young and wealthy Americans joined the French Air Corps. (The rich became pilots simply because before the war they were the only ones who had the money to buy planes and learn to fly.)

Soon a group of these American pilots began petitioning the French government to form an all-American French squadron. Finally permission was granted, and in March 1916 the *Escadrille Americaine* (ES-kuh-DRIL uh-mehr-ih-CAN) was begun. When

boats) could remain unseen below the water while launching a surprise torpedo attack against enemy ships.

Section Review

1. List four causes that contributed to the outbreak of World War I.
2. What countries comprised the Allies?
3. What countries comprised the Central Powers?
4. Which country made the first major assault?
5. What country was the first to use poison gas?
6. How did the war extend to the skies?

President Wilson complained that the name violated America's official neutral position, the squadron changed its name to the *Lafayette Escadrille.* The young men claimed that they were repaying France for the help that the Frenchman Lafayette had given the United States during the War for Independence.

The Lafayette Escadrille began with seven pilots and a lion cub for a mascot. During the war a total of thirty-eight men served as pilots for the group, and many of them died in their cockpits. When the United States entered World War I, the Lafayette Escadrille switched over to become the first American air squadron.

B. Effects of the European War on America

Although the United States was not participating in the war, it was not totally isolated from the warring nations either. Transportation, trade, and diplomatic relationships with Europe were all affected by the war, and these matters concerned Americans.

Reasons for American Interest

Although President Wilson had stated that Americans should remain neutral, maintaining neutrality proved difficult for several reasons.

First, American sentiment favored the Allied cause. Although there were eleven million Americans who had some tie to Germany, there were substantially more who had British ties. America's background, its legal system, some of its form of government, and even its language were English. Americans also recalled that another ally, France, had come to America's aid during the War for Independence. Moreover, Americans had been upset by the German invasion of neutral Belgium.

A second factor was economic. Although American businessmen sold goods and lent money to both the Allied and Central Powers, more traded with Allied countries, especially Britain. Consequently, Americans were more sympathetic to Allied interests just to protect their investments.

Gradually the United States began aiding the Allies. Right after the outbreak of war, British and French agents had come to place orders with American firms. They contracted for shipments of grain, cotton, and other needed supplies. At first these countries had paid cash for their items and carried them back home on their own ships.

But when their cash ran low, they asked for and received loans. By early 1917 the United States had lent Britain over $1 billion and France over $300 million. The Germans protested that this violated neutrality because American-made shells and guns were killing Germans. Wilson, however, chose not to restrict these business deals. He believed that restricting them would help the Central Powers.

Another factor was Allied propaganda. Britain and France controlled the trans-Atlantic cables that brought the news to American newspapers. The Germans had to rely on the still imperfect radio to transmit messages to the United States. In addition, the Germans, with the few messages they did get through, did not project the right image to Americans. Because they emphasized hate and destruction, more anger than sympathy was aroused. The Allies easily won the Americans over just by reprinting German hate propaganda word for word. Germany's deeds were also harmful to its relationship with America. When it invaded Belgium, a violation of an earlier treaty, the German government explained away the betrayal by calling the treaty only "a scrap of paper." About five thousand Belgian civilians who had resisted the Germans were executed. British propagandists were quick to let Americans know of this and other atrocities, including a few that never happened.

Violations of America's Neutral Rights

The biggest difficulty in maintaining neutrality revolved around Britain's and Germany's violations of America's neutral rights at sea. Since Britain was a small island nation, it was almost totally dependent on overseas trade for raw materials. Over the years Britain developed the best and largest navy and merchant marine (trading) fleet. The United States had benefited greatly from trade with Britain, and it did not wish to lose that trade during the war. The United States wished to continue trade with Germany as well, but all sea trade with Europe was put in jeopardy by the naval strategies of Britain and Germany.

Early in the war Britain had put mines in the entrances to the North Sea. This was done to prevent nations from trading with Germany. However, instead of trading directly with Germany, some countries, including the United States, sent their goods to the Germans through neutral countries like the Netherlands, Denmark, or Sweden, who resold them. Such actions angered the British, and they began to stop American shipping bound for neutral nations.

The British were ready to seize anything that could be useful to Germany. American ships were stopped at sea and ordered to British ports for searches. The time wasted pushed up the cost of goods. Sometimes foodstuffs spoiled before they could be delivered. The British claimed this action was necessary because of the danger of attack by German submarines. British firms also made "blacklists" of American firms that they suspected of trading with Germany through neutral nations. These actions angered Americans because they were a violation of the rights of a neutral country.

Britain did not receive all of America's anger, however. Realizing that Britain was dependent on foreign trade, too, Germany sought to cut British imports. Rather than using just a blockade, Germany chose to use **unrestricted submarine warfare.** They fired on all ships in a designated war zone around Britain.

The S.S. Lusitania *on its last voyage*

Attacking neutral ships without giving them a warning and a chance to remove their passengers was a violation of international law. Therefore the United States protested Germany's policy as inhumane. Americans also said it violated the concept of freedom of the seas. Germans, however, argued that submarines were at a disadvantage. If they surfaced to give a warning, it was easy for even a merchant ship armed with guns to sink them.

Although the German Embassy put ads in newspapers warning Americans not to travel on British vessels, the warnings were ignored. In May 1916 a British liner, the ***Lusitania,*** was sunk without warning off the coast of Ireland. Among the 1,198 who perished were 128 Americans. President Wilson demanded that the Germans apologize and renounce this strategy. He later threatened to withdraw diplomatic recognition if another passenger ship was attacked. Germany cooperated for a while.

Growing American Fears

When the German offensives in France slowed, however, Germany decided that the only way to win the war was to cut Britain's supply lines and force her surrender. It could accomplish this by using its large fleet of U-boats. After the German announcement in February 1917 that it was going

President Wilson delivering his war message to Congress on April 2, 1917

to resume its unrestricted submarine warfare, the United States broke off diplomatic relations with Germany.

Added to the submarine tension was the discovery of a German plot. Early in March the German foreign minister, Arthur Zimmerman, sent a dispatch to Mexico. In it he said that if war broke out between Germany and the United States, Mexico would be rewarded for entering the war against the Americans. Its reward would be the return to Mexico of Texas, New Mexico, and Arizona.

British intelligence intercepted the telegram. The next day President Wilson asked Congress to arm American merchant ships, and he released the Zimmerman telegram to the public. The nation was outraged. When three more American merchant ships were sunk, the pressure increased. Finally, on April 2, 1917, a solemn president appeared before both houses of Congress asking for a declaration of war. Four days later, on April 6, 1917, the approval was given. The United States was joining the fight in Europe.

Section Review

1. List four reasons that American neutrality was difficult to maintain.
2. How did Britain violate American neutrality?
3. How did Germany violate American neutrality?
4. What was the significance of the Zimmerman telegram?

C. The United States at War

By the time the United States entered the war, the Allies were in a desperate condition. At one time, because of the success of Germany's unrestricted submarine warfare, the British were down to a three-week supply of food.

The United States responded with huge shipments of supplies to Europe. To insure safe arrival, American ships traveled in groups called *convoys*. Naval destroyers with antisubmarine guns escorted them. With such protection, shipping losses were

cut. The **convoy system** worked so well that not one of the two million American soldiers bound for Europe was lost at sea. Although American manpower gave a boost to Allied morale, the biggest contribution was in needed war materials. Food, clothing, munitions, ships, and vehicles poured into European ports. The Central Powers were unable to match this production themselves and soon fell behind. To provide these needs for the Allied cause, America faced the challenge of gearing up for war. The peacetime economy and production needed to be channeled into a great effort for victory.

Military Preparedness

Since Americans feared having a strong standing army, its military force had purposely been kept small, consisting of only 200,000 men. Allied losses had already exceeded the size of the whole American army. The United States had only four hundred heavy guns and enough ammunition for a nine-hour bombardment. It had no tanks, and it lacked an air force. Now,

Top: *American artillerymen at work during World War I*
Bottom: *American airplane and ships*

suddenly, the United States had to train men, make equipment, and build ships to carry everything to Europe.

For the first time since the Civil War, the nation resorted to a draft. Under the Selective Service Act, local draft boards under civilian leadership supplied the men. The system worked well, and there was far less opposition than there had been during the Civil War. About four million men went into the service. The recruits were trained at thirty-two training camps across the nation.

Producing for the War

As America sent its soldiers off to battle, the entire nation had to adjust to the necessities of war. As a result the government had to begin many programs and agencies that could coordinate the war effort. Everything the American forces needed had to be obtained or manufactured and transported in a hurry.

The **War Industries Board** organized the industrial production needed. Factories were transformed to produce needed war materials—uniforms, guns and ammunition, vehicles, medical supplies. The board set criteria to standardize thousands of needed items and set economic priorities for the nation.

To insure that the railroads operated efficiently to carry the extra freight and passengers, the United States Railroad Administration took control of all railroads. It organized regional units, set rates and schedules, and set shipping priorities to insure that munitions (weapons, ammunition, and other war material) reached ports even if nonessential goods had to be held up.

The Fuel Administration had the job of conserving and directing the use of the

A Little Bird Named Enza

There was a little bird,
its name was Enza.
I opened the window
and in-flu-enza.

In 1918 this was the favorite poem of America's children. But the "little bird Enza" was no laughing matter. The deadly virus struck many American soldiers either while they were still in training or after they had arrived in Europe. In four months influenza killed twenty-one million people world-wide, more people than the war killed in four years. At the height of the epidemic, the last week in October 1917, 2,700 American soldiers died in Europe; 21,000 American citizens died of the flu back home. But the flu was completely impartial: close to a quarter of a million Germans died from influenza as well.

The flu epidemic left as suddenly and mysteriously as it had come. By the middle of November 1918, it was over. Ironically, at about the same time, so was the war. Some estimate that over forty million of the world's people died in the four years of World War I, and at least half of those were victims of "the little bird Enza."

nation's fuel. It asked the people to walk more and added "gasless days" to weekly calendars. Auto owners were asked to save gasoline so that trucks could run to carry war goods. The actions of these federal agencies designed to aid the war effort coordinated the activities of the nation in a remarkable way. They could do so because the national emergency had lessened the public's resistance to government power and restrictions.

A war bond rally in Atlanta during World War I

With Allied armies facing starvation, increasing America's food production received top priority. Herbert Hoover, who had already gained fame as organizer of a massive food relief program to Belgium, headed the Food Administration. Rather than force the public to conserve food, the administration set up a voluntary program. Americans were asked to make Mondays wheatless, Tuesdays meatless, and Thursdays porkless. Americans also raised their own vegetables in "Victory Gardens" so that more food would be available for the soldiers. With these efforts huge savings were made. Moreover, the people felt they were a part of the great war effort. Just before the war began the annual average of food shipped to Europe was 7 million tons. By 1919 it had reached 18.6 million tons.

The war also brought changes in the American normal work force. Since four million men were drafted, the normal work force was depleted. Because of the urgent need, many women now worked outside their homes for the first time. Some gratefully returned home when the war ended; others stayed on the job.

Volunteer groups were formed to support the "boys" in France. Memberships in the American Red Cross multiplied as women in local chapters met to roll bandages, knit sweaters or socks, and prepare packages to be sent abroad. Men who could not serve in the military also offered their time to support volunteer efforts.

Because the war caused a labor shortage, wages shot up and more jobs were available. Even with high taxes, loan drives, and increased prices for most goods, Americans were earning more than they ever had. Of course, prices went up for what the government bought, too, raising the cost of fighting the war. To keep costs and wages under control, however, the government created the **War Labor Policies Board** to regulate laborers. While unions were allowed to organize and even showed significant gains in membership during the war years, the board stepped in to help settle disputes between labor and management. The board also set an eight-hour working day, stressed fair wages, and set standards for employing women and children.

The shortage of workers and the drop in immigration opened the doors of opportunity to black laborers. There was a movement of more than one-half million blacks to northern cities during the war. When the war ended, many blacks kept their jobs and remained in the North. This migration permanently changed the ethnic makeup of many northern cities.

Public Information

President Wilson did not want to leave anything to chance. He wanted Americans to know that their cause was just. To unite them behind the war effort, there was a Committee on Public Information. Headed by journalist George Creel, 150,000 people became involved in a giant propaganda crusade to "advertise America." Talented artists designed war recruitment posters and ads. An army of lecturers appeared at local assemblies and even at silent movies. Called "four-minute men," they gave short talks on any number of patriotic topics and moved crowds to cheers or tears.

On the other hand the attitude toward the Central Powers or even things distantly related to them became negative. All things German were hated. Even though they had been in America for years and had proved their loyalty, some German-Americans were sorely persecuted. Schools stopped teaching German, and school orchestras refused to play pieces by German composers such as Bach and Wagner. Sauerkraut became "Liberty Cabbage," hamburgers became "Liberty Burgers," and dachshunds were renamed "Liberty Pups." If you had caught the German measles, your mother would have been careful to tell the neighbors you had "patriotic spots" or "patriotic measles."

Paying for the War

The cost of the war was enormous. The United States spent about $24 billion, and the Allies borrowed $8 billion. About one-fourth of the money came from the new income and corporate taxes. The rest came from bank loans and loan drives.

Four times during the war the government went to the American people for money, raising more than $18 billion. "Liberty" and "Victory" loan drives were held in every community. Loan chairmen went door to door asking their neighbors to buy bonds. Workers also bought bonds at their places of employment. Buyers received "Liberty Buttons" for their lapels. Goals were set, and there were great celebrations when the drives went "over the top."

Even children became involved. They sold produce to earn money to finance the war, and they bought thrift stamps each week on "stamp day." A filled thrift card could be swapped for a $5 savings stamp; ten stamps on a card were proudly exchanged for a $50 bond.

Section Review

1. What did the Selective Service Act do?
2. What was the purpose of the War Industries Board?
3. List some of the changes for the laborers at home during wartime.
4. How did America finance the war?

D. The American Forces "Over There"

The chief role of the navy was to get troops and supplies safely to Europe. Congress had voted for money to enlarge the navy before war broke out. During the war it tried to build or buy more ships to carry men and supplies to the troops fighting in Europe. It was on the battlefields, particularly those in northern France, that America's soldiers were needed.

The American Expeditionary Force

The American troops who joined the European fighting force were called the **American Expeditionary Force.** Although the United States declared war in April 1917, the first American troops did not arrive in Europe until the fall of 1917. The minimum training time was three months. Often the troops were called **"doughboys"** because they were like raw dough waiting to be shaped. Most combat troops did not reach Europe until the spring of 1918 because of the period of training and other delays.

American "doughboys"

The American Expeditionary Force (AEF) was commanded by General **John Pershing.** Pershing worked under Marshal **Ferdinand Foch** (FOSH), a Frenchman who served as Supreme Allied Commander. The British and French troops were weary and discouraged from three years of war, and the arrival of the "Yanks," as they called the Americans, was a welcome relief. The Allies wanted to place American doughboys in already existing armies and use them to replace British and French losses, but Pershing disagreed. Fearing that American morale would suffer, he requested that the American troops fight as a separate force. American units were then assigned their own segments of the front to defend.

Doughboys in Action

By the time the Americans arrived, the Germans had accomplished a major goal—getting Russia out of the fight. The Germans had aided the return of **Vladimir Lenin** to Russia in 1917 after the Russians had already overthrown their czar. Weary of war, the Russians followed Lenin in the Communist Revolution. Lenin had promised peace to the Russians, and he also had promised the Germans that he would pull Russia out of the war. When he gained power, he pulled Russian troops out of the war and ended support for the Allied cause. Thus Germany had one less enemy to fight. The German armies that had been fighting the Russians could now be moved to the western front to fight France, Britain, and the United States.

The Central Powers launched an all-out offensive on the western front during the spring of 1918. The Germans hoped to reach the English Channel and also to take Paris. By June 3, 1918, they had reached the Marne River and were only about fifty miles from the French capital.

The combined American and French forces launched a counter-offensive and pushed the Germans back at a place on the Marne River called Château-Thierry (shah-TOH-tyeh-REE). Next the Americans moved up to a hunting preserve called Belleau-Wood (BEL oh) and stopped the Germans from making a run on Paris from that point. By the beginning of July, Paris had been saved and the German advance was falling apart.

Top: *General John J. Pershing (fourth from the left) and his staf.*
Bottom: *American soldiers engaged in battle against the Germa*

World War I 1918

0   50   100
Scale of Miles

American thrusts

Foch planned and carried off a massive assault at Amiens on August 8. The German general Ludendorff was to call it "the black day of the German army." Despite heavy German losses, Amiens was not the end of the war.

With more than 250,000 American soldiers arriving monthly, Allied morale climbed. Pershing got permission to apply the separate strength of the U.S. Army as a part of the larger counter-offensive. The place was St. Mihiel (SAHN mee-YEL), just south of Verdun. More than half a million

doughboys came to push back the last big German attack. An air corps of fifteen hundred planes was poised, and thirty-two hundred American guns roared in protest against the German army. In forty-eight hours the battle was over.

Two weeks later the American forces launched an offensive into the Argonne (AHR gon) Forest. Foch had assigned the American troops the worst possible spot. American forces faced a maze of barbed wire, steel, and concrete. The hills and ridges offered almost perfect terrain for a

German defensive. Historians have called this "the meat grinder offensive" because of the heavy losses.

By August 8 the British had broken through the German line. Having destroyed German resistance, the Allied troops moved swiftly across France, regaining lost lands for the Allies. The last major American activity took place in late October at Mézières, a link to the main German railway. By the end of September, however, the German commander, General Paul von Hindenburg, knew that all was lost.

At 11:00 A.M. on November 11, 1918, the slaughter stopped. Germany signed an armistice or agreement to stop fighting. This day became an American national holiday called **Armistice Day.** (After World War II and the Korean Conflict, the name was changed to Veterans' Day, honoring all veterans.)

The war had taken the lives of over eight million people and had wounded nearly twenty million. The United States had lost 115,000 of its men in its year and a half of activity in the war. Over 200,000 Americans came home wounded. Although these casualties were light in comparison to

those of the other major powers, Americans had known the heartache of war. Yet they hoped that this had been the "War to End All Wars" and the "War to Make the World Safe for Democracy." They believed they had fought for such noble goals.

Section Review

1. Who was commander of the American Expeditionary Force?
2. What were American troops who joined European fighting forces called?
3. Who was Marshal Foch?
4. When did the war officially end?

Top: *American soldiers and sailors in Paris*
Bottom: *An Allied hospital in France*

E. Peace Comes to Europe

The end of the war brought many questions for the participants. How would Germany and the other defeated countries be treated? Would the victors claim conquered territories and possessions? Could peace be maintained in Europe?

Wilson's Fourteen Points

Even before the war ended, Woodrow Wilson had proposed a set of guidelines to help rebuild European peace. His **Fourteen Points** had been announced in January 1918. Most of the points of his program centered on establishing a just peace and building a postwar world in which war would be less likely. The crucial point to Wilson was Point 14, providing for a **League of Nations.** He idealistically believed that an organization of cooperating nations could talk over problems and settle them peacefully, preventing future wars. Freedom of the seas, a ban against secret agreements, and general disarmament were some of the other key points.

President Wilson spoke of "peace without victory," urging generous terms that would preserve the German nation. He rejected territorial gains for the winners and **reparations** or payment for damages by the losers. He said that weak nations should have the right of self-determination—that is, they could choose to be independent.

The Paris Peace Conference

The Allied leaders met at the Palace of Versailles outside Paris on January 18, 1919, to shape the peace. President Wilson traveled to Europe to represent the United States at the conference himself. He believed that his presence would insure the victors' acceptance of a just and lasting peace. About two million people welcomed Wilson to

Paris, regarding him almost as the savior of Europe. His reception strengthened his resolve to push for a treaty based on his Fourteen Points.

But the representatives from the other nations were equally determined. **Georges Clemenceau** (ZHORJ KLEM-un-SOH), the French premier, knew that his country had suffered at German hands in both the Franco-Prussian War and World War I. He wanted to insure that Germany would never again be strong enough to hurt France. **David Lloyd-George** represented Britain and **Vittorio Orlando,** Italy. These men plus Wilson were sometimes called "The Big Four." The nations that had lost and Russia were not included at the peace table. Thus the treaty has sometimes been called "a victors' peace." Leaving out the losers caused them to be resentful and to reject the treaty's provisions. Germany was forced to sign the **Treaty of Versailles** anyway on June 28, 1919. The other defeated countries signed other individual treaties.

The signing of the peace treaty at Versailles

The 264-page Treaty of Versailles with Germany was very detailed. Against Wilson's wishes, it placed all the blame for the war on Germany and forced Germany to pay for its actions. Germany had to give up its overseas empire and some of its own land and resources. It had to allow foreign troops to remain on its land. Germany was also forced to pay huge reparations (damage payments) to Britain and France. While Wilson was disappointed about these and some of the other details of the treaty, he did convince the other leaders to provide for the formation of the League of Nations. Wilson believed that all the weaknesses of the peace could be worked out through further negotiations in the League.

American Responses to the Treaty

When Wilson returned to the United States, he took the treaty directly to the Senate, whose approval is required for all treaties. Although most Americans probably supported the treaty, many senators were not pleased with it. Wilson had unwisely ignored the Republican leaders in the Senate while he helped formulate the treaty, and now those senators refused to ratify it without some changes. Wilson refused their changes, and the situation became deadlocked. Time passed, and the United States never did ratify the treaty. It simply declared the war to be over. Wilson was further disappointed by the fact that the United States did not join the League of Nations.

Section Review

1. Who were the "Big Four" at the Paris Peace Conference, and what country did each represent?
2. What treaty stated the conditions for peace with Germany?
3. What key point did Wilson succeed in placing in the treaty?
4. How did the Senate respond to the treaty?

Summary

America had grown to be a powerful industrial nation by the beginning of the twentieth century. Although it attempted to remain aloof from the conflict that grew in Europe, its culture and interests made keeping a neutral position difficult. Eventually the nation abandoned neutrality and entered World War I in 1917. The United States made a gigantic effort to supply the faultering Allies with men and materials for the war effort. With this American aid the Allies defeated the Central Powers. President Wilson tried to persuade the delegates at the peace conference to follow his Fourteen Point program for establishing a lasting peace, but he found little support at the conference or in the United States.

Chapter Review

Do You Remember?

■ What significant event happened on each of the following dates?
1. June 28, 1914

2. April 6, 1917
3. November 11, 1918
4. January 18, 1919
■ Who was he?
5. Who was president of the United States during World War I?
6. Who commanded the American Expeditionary Force?
7. Who was commander of all the Allied forces?
8. Who were the "Big Four" that met at Versailles, and what country did each represent?
■ Fill in the blanks with the appropriate term.

When World War I broke out in 1914, Germany, Austria-Hungary, and the nations that sided with them were called the __(9)__, and Britain, France, and the nations that sided with them were called the __(10)__.

Germany's policy of __(11)__ greatly angered Americans. It brought about the sinking of the __(12)__ and eventually helped to prompt America to enter the war. The American soldiers who arrived in Europe were commonly called __(13)__. They helped the Allies win the war. Fighting stopped on __(14)__ Day.

Allied leaders met at Versailles to draw up a treaty. President Wilson's plan for peace consisted of __(15)__, but most of his plan was rejected, except for the formation of a __(16)__ to help settle international problems. Britain and France especially wanted Germany to pay __(17)__ for the damages caused by the war. The resulting treaty with Germany, called the __(18)__, was never signed by the United States.

Why Is It So?
1. Why did World War I begin?
2. Why did the assassination of Archduke Francis Ferdinand cause the war to erupt?
3. How did propaganda hurt the Germans before America entered the war?
4. How did the American government become more powerful during World War I?
5. Why did the Germans help Vladimir Lenin return to Russia?
6. What role did Americans play in winning the war?

What Do You Think?
1. What were the advantages of the United States remaining neutral during the early years of the war?
2. Why was poison gas a weapon feared more than any other?
3. Should America have joined the League of Nations? Why or why not?

Doing Research

The study of history often requires more than the reading of a textbook. You may choose to study a particular area in more detail, you may be asked to write a report on a certain topic, or you may want to locate a novel on a certain subject to read for enjoyment.

You will save a great deal of time if you know how and where to locate the information you need. The first type of book to check is the reference book. These will be found in the reference section of your library. The most common type of reference book is the encyclopedia. An encyclopedia will give you a general overview of your subject and also provide additional topics to read. Some encyclopedias also list other sources (a bibliography).

Other reference books which provide information are atlases, almanacs, and concordances. Some reference books are designed to help you locate additional information on your topics. *Books In Print* and *The Reader's Guide to Periodical Literature* are two valuable sources of information.

The next stop in your search for material is the card catalog in the library. Cards in the catalog are filed alphabetically according to subject, author, and title. These cards

not only provide books in your area to study but also indicate the location of the book in the library: fiction, nonfiction, or biographies.

Nonfiction books are organized according to the Dewey Decimal System in most school libraries. This method of organization houses books on related subjects in the

```
                    European War, 1914-1918

940.3         Everett, Susanne.
Ev27               World War I: an illustrated
              history / Susanne Everett ; introd.
              by John Keegan. -- Chicago : Rand
              McNally, 1980.
                   256 p. : ill. ; 32 cm.

                   "A Bison book."
                   Includes index.
                   ISBN 0-528-81539-3
```

Subject Card

same area of the library. For instance, the number 900 in the Dewey System indicates the location of books on history. Books numbered in the 970s contain material on North America. Those numbered 973 contain material about the United States. Additional numbers indicate different periods in United States history.

In addition to books, valuable information can be secured from other sources. The best type of source to examine is a *primary source*. This may be a letter or journal written by someone who witnessed the event or who lived in the specific time period. Primary sources give the researcher special insight into his area of study. For the individual involved in the reconstruction

Main Classifications of the Dewey Decimal System

000-099 General works (including reference books, collected essays, and journalism)

100-199 Philosophy (including psychology, logic, and ethics)

200-299 Religion (including church history and pagan religions)

300-399 Social sciences (including politics, economics, government, education, and customs)

400-499 Languages (including phonetics, English, and foreign languages)

500-599 Pure science (including mathematics, physics, chemistry, and biology)

600-699 Applied science (including medicine, engineering, and home economics)

700-799 Fine arts (including architecture, drawing, photography, and music)

800-899 Literature (including works about the drama, fiction, and poetry of many countries)

900-999 History (including geography, biography, and ancient and modern history)

and restoration of old buildings, blueprints, inventories, and artifacts all provide necessary knowledge to make accurate interpretation possible. For a student, primary sources can add excitement to and increase interest in the study of history.

While the primary source is the best source, it is not always accurate. Even an eyewitness account can be colored by a person's bias or may be distorted or misunderstood. Primary sources may occasionally be difficult to use because we don't always see exactly how they fit into our study. But with some time and thought, you can learn to use them.

Another good source of information is the *secondary source,* those sources that, although not primary, are based on carefully researched material. A secondary may be a map, diagram, picture, or verbal description of a period or event.

By doing your research in an organized manner, you can accomplish much more in less time than if you go about it in a haphazard way.

173

EDITION

Nazi Planes Return as Britain Digs In

By United Press

LONDON, July 15—German airplanes bombed the British Isles again today. Aerial bombs killed several persons in southern and southwestern England.

But there was mounting public approval of intensified defense preparations, including stricter food rationing, and of Prime Minister Winston Churchill's promise of a last-ditch fight until the empire can rally its full strength—possibly in 1942—against Hitler.

New successes of Royal Air Force planes in opposing the dreaded Ger-

24

The 1920s: Decade of Change

With the end of World War I, most Americans looked forward to better times. Some thought that they could return to the ideals and ways of earlier days. Instead the 1920s, sometimes called the "Roaring Twenties," became a decade of startling changes.

In prewar years progressive Americans had united to check big industry and to gain reforms. Then they had united to wage a war that would make the world safe for democracy. In the twenties diversity replaced that unity. After sacrificing for a war, many Americans now wanted a good life for themselves. They wanted all the goods big industries could supply, and they were

not as interested in righting society's wrongs. Since some of the restraints that they sought to throw off were Biblical ones, the 1920s was an era when sin was practiced more openly than in earlier periods of American history.

While many Americans were prosperous enough to enjoy "a chicken in every pot and two cars in every garage," as the Republicans promised in 1928, others struggled to put food on the table. Serious economic problems lurked below the surface prosperity of the era, and these problems led to calamity for many Americans in the 1930s.

In America the 1920s marked the transition from a predominantly rural society to a predominantly urban one.

A. Postwar Problems

America emerged from the war with some attitudes and problems that would set the stage for the decade to come. First was a desire to stay out of any other foreign conflicts that might come along.

Isolationism and Peace

President Wilson had diligently sought American approval of the Treaty of Versailles with its provision for a new League of Nations. In his battle with the Senate, he decided to travel across the country and present his views to the people. While on his tour he had a stroke that left him unable to carry on his duties for a few weeks. In the remaining months of his presidency he never regained full strength; yet he continued to plead for the United States to ratify the treaty and join the League. The Senate and many Americans, however, feared that the obligations of the League of Nations would draw America into future wars. This fear, and a general lack of concern for foreign affairs now that the war was over, made most Americans ready to isolate themselves from problems outside the United States.

When the 1920 election came, the attitude of wanting to get back to business and forget about foreign problems resulted in a strong win for the Republican candidate, **Warren G. Harding.** His campaign, stressing a "return to normalcy," was victorious over James Cox, the Democrat. Ideas of signing the treaty and joining the League were soon forgotten.

Throughout the 1920s the United States remained true to its isolationist goals in that it stayed out of most foreign affairs. Wishing to cut expenses and to avoid temptation for future war, the government sought a way to trim down its navy. Harding's secretary of state, Charles Evans Hughes, and others believed that one cause of the war had been an arms race. Hence he suggested that the five major powers limit naval shipbuilding. This was done through the **Treaty of Washington** in 1921. Britain, the United States, Japan, France, and Italy scaled down their navies. For every five British or American ships built, Japan would be allowed three, and France and Italy one and three-quarters. The treaty allowed the United States to cut its budget and delighted Republicans seeking bigger cuts in spending. Japan, however, considered the treaty unfair and turned its hurt feelings against the United States in later years. In reality the treaty had little impact because the powers got around it by building smaller ships and submarines that were not limited under the agreement.

Another attempt to keep America free from the threat of future war was the **Kellogg-Briand Peace Pact.** Coolidge's secretary of state, Frank B. Kellogg, optimistically signed a treaty with sixty-two other nations in 1928. The countries agreed to outlaw war as a means of settling international disputes. As with most peace agreements, only some nations took it seriously. Men cannot establish peace on their own, and World War II would soon prove how futile their agreement was. It would also prove that the United States could not remain isolated from the world.

Depression

Following the war came a time of economic depression for the United States. The big demand for war products had kept industries and farms busy, but when the war was over, the demand dropped. Because many of the war products were no longer needed, factories had to change over to peace-time industry. It took time to build these new businesses. American farms had sent millions of tons of food to Europe during the war, but now Europe could start feeding itself again. There was no market for the great surplus of food.

Unemployment became a problem in the cities. Soldiers returning home from the war found few jobs available. War industries were closing down, and many jobs that were available had been taken by blacks and immigrants. For a while the blacks and immigrants were resented by white Americans who were without jobs. Unfortunately, violence eventually erupted from the frustration of the unemployed. Race riots occurred in both the North and the South.

A new Ku Klux Klan arose in the South and Midwest to terrorize not only blacks but also Roman Catholics and Jews. New immigration laws were passed that set quotas (fixed numbers) of immigrants who could enter the United States. These laws were intended to stop the heavy flow of immigrants, especially those from the Roman Catholic countries of southern and eastern Europe.

Although the nation's economy picked up quickly and unemployment ceased to be a problem, the veterans continued to pressure the government until they received a bonus of a $1,000 life insurance policy. The farmers' problems continued through the 1920s as high production and low prices continued. Although representatives of the farming states moved for government aid and regulation, President Harding and his successor, **Calvin Coolidge,** believed that the federal government should not interfere by regulating the farm economy.

Fear of Communism

Although Americans had read of events in Russia leading up to and including the Communist Revolution in 1917, few really were aware of the Communist presence until it involved them directly.

Top: *Warren G. Harding*
Bottom: *A 1928 Ku Klux Klan parade in Washington, D.C.*

Americans had heard reports of massacres in Communist Russia. A fear of communism began to grow, especially when Americans learned that the Communists intended to spread their rule. Leaders of the Soviet Union, as the Russian nation now called itself and the surrounding nations it controlled, had organized the Third International. This agency for world revolution would export communism anywhere, using any method. It was already making gains in Germany and Hungary.

The Communists had two political parties working in America by 1919. One of their aims was to create a struggle between common workers and the property-owning capitalists. During this time Americans began to think of any sign of worker discontent, and strikes in particular, as part of the Communist plot. In April 1919 there was also a wave of terrorist bombings. The post office intercepted letter bombs addressed to thirty-eight prominent businessmen or government officials, including John D. Rockefeller, Justice Oliver Wendell Holmes, and both the postmaster and the attorney general. In June there were direct bombings. One bomb exploded in front of Attorney General A. Mitchell Palmer's home. In September a terrorist planted a bomb in front of the New York Stock Exchange, killing thirty-eight people.

Some have called this period the "Red Scare," for some Americans did overreact to the Communist threat. However, we should remember that the threat itself was real. Believing that Communists were involved in the attacks, Attorney General Palmer crusaded for increased government investigation and arrests in these cases. Government agents raided offices of radical organizations and arrested 250 members of the Union of Russian Workers. In December the Labor Department sent 249 aliens, some of whom were Communists, back to Russia. Eventually the scare died down, but Americans maintained a fear of communism and its infiltration into the United States for most of the decade.

The fear of the Communists added to the resentment toward immigrants, many of whom were from southern and eastern Europe, where radical political ideas were spreading. Ill feeling toward both Communists and immigrants combined in a noted court case in 1921. Two Italian anarchists, Nicola Sacco and Bartolomeo Vanzetti, were arrested and tried for murdering two shoe company employees in a payroll robbery. They were found guilty and were sentenced to death. Protests led to the reopening of the case. Some charged that the two men had been sentenced to death because they were foreigners who held unpopular political views and not because they had committed a crime. The case dragged on for six years. Sacco and Vanzetti were convicted, and in 1927 the two were executed. Many, however, tried to make the case an example of injustice in American society.

Section Review

1. What did Warren G. Harding stress in his presidential campaign?
2. What two agreements did the United States pursue in hopes of avoiding future international conflict?
3. What two groups tried to gain help from the government during the postwar depression?
4. What was the "Red Scare"?

B. A Desire for Prosperity

As America recovered from the war's effects, it developed a great desire for material prosperity. The humanitarian and reform goals of the earlier progressives were forgotten. They were replaced by desires for the possessions and the pleasures that the new decade was to offer.

Technology's Products

Inventions and improvements of industrial products greatly changed the American way of life in the 1920s. The automobile and the application of electricity to household appliances revolutionized daily life for many Americans.

The Automobile—The first successful American automobile had been built by Charles and Frank Duryea in 1894. Henry Ford had begun making Model Ts in 1903, and many other automobile producers had also plunged into the business. Although cars had become common before the war, there were still many American families without a "horseless carriage." After the war, however, factories geared up to produce cars by the thousands. Families were eager to have their own car, and the prices of all but the luxury models were affordable. Even if a family did not have enough money to pay for the car in full, they could buy it on the installment plan (paying for an item with weekly or monthly payments).

The great shift of transportation to the automobile had many direct effects on Americans. For example, the automobile allowed farmers to end some of the isolation of their lives in rural areas. When town was several hours away by horseback or horse and wagon, the farmer and his family ventured into town only a few times a year. With a car, however, the whole family could make the same trip in minutes, day or night. Now farm families could go to town often to shop or to attend social functions.

The automobile also changed the life of many city workers by making it possible for them to live away from the inner-city area where they worked. They could instead buy a house in the "suburbs" at the edge of the city and commute back and forth by car. With this practice came a by-product of the automobile, traffic jams.

Cars made travel easy for common Americans. As they began to drive everywhere, many other industries had to grow to meet the needs of these people and cars on the move. Service stations, drive-in res-

The sleek new Model A Ford began to roll off the assembly lines in the late 1920s.

taurants, and motels sprang up everywhere. Department stores, grocery stores, and other businesses built where they could be easily reached by car and where they could have large parking lots for their customers.

Other results of the popularity of the automobile were the spread of paved roads, the death of many people in automobile accidents, and even fast getaways for criminals as they fled from the scenes of their crimes. The automobile certainly made the average American's way of life more mobile.

The Airplane—Although the airplane was not a major form of transportation for most Americans in the 1920s, the airplane won admiration for its capabilities. In 1903 Orville and Wilbur Wright had made what is generally accepted as the first successful powered flight. World War I boosted aviation. Soon the government provided airmail service between major cities. Budding pilots pursued their interests by putting on air circuses at county fairs and by taking people up for short rides over towns.

The biggest air sensation came in 1927, when a twenty-five-year-old aviator from Little Falls, Minnesota, won a prize for being the first to fly solo across the Atlantic Ocean. **Charles A. Lindbergh** (LIND BURG) flew his specially designed plane, the *Spirit of St. Louis,* from New York to Paris in thirty-three and one-half hours. When Lindbergh touched down in Paris, he became an instant hero. Called "Lucky Lindy" or "the Lone Eagle," Lindbergh came home to a ticker-tape parade in New York and an invitation to the White House. Wherever he appeared over the next few years, he was mobbed by admiring fans.

Lindbergh's transatlantic flight and the record flights of other pilots did much to encourage air transportation. The first

public international passenger carrier was the Pan-American "Clipper." Regularly scheduled commercial flights soon connected all of the major American cities. They also linked America to European and South American capitals.

Electric Wonders—Second only to cars in changing American society was electricity. By 1929 generators were producing more electricity in the United States than in all the rest of the world combined. Nearly all American cities and towns had electricity by the 1920s, and some rural areas had it as well. Americans were ready not just for electric lights but also for fancy new gadgets to plug in.

Inventors added electricity to many already existing household appliances like the ice box, stove, iron, and washing machine. They also came up with hundreds more.

Charles Lindbergh and his plane, the Spirit of St. Louis

Housewives boasted of all-electric kitchens, complete with fan, water heater, toaster, electric percolator, and waffle iron.

Of course, electricity was also applied to industry where it powered large machines. When applied to the communications network, electricity further improved the quality of American life. The greatest mass communication device of the 1920s was the radio.

The basis for the invention of the radio was a sound transmitter invented by an Italian, Guglielmo Marconi (mahr COH nee), in 1895. The "wireless" could transmit messages without using the usual telegraph or telephone wires. Soon inventors began using the wireless to transmit the human voice. The resulting radio provided Americans with hours of news and entertainment. The Westinghouse Company made special home receivers and sold them in quantity during the fall of 1920. Station KDKA in Pittsburgh received its broadcasting license six days before the 1920 presidential elections. The first commercial broadcast—November 2, 1920—announced Harding's election to the presidency.

The radio soon changed the way Americans lived. News, music, entertainment, and advertising reached into more than twelve million American homes by 1930. Many Americans listened to comedian Jack Benny, singer Rudy Vallee, and Will Rogers's comic impersonations of Calvin Coolidge. Broadcasts of sports events also gained large popular followings. With Americans from different areas listening to the same programs, some regional differences soon began to fade. The radio drew Americans closer to events and people that affected their lives. They could hear the voices of the president and other leaders,

and they could hear broadcasts of events as they happened.

Business Boom

After the initial depression that followed the war, America soon took off on an amazing business boom. Some workers had saved money during the war while wages were high. Others were making money on new businesses. They were all ready to spend it on automobiles, electric appliances, clothes, entertainment, and the new pleasures of the 1920s. When Americans did not have the money, they borrowed it or bought items on credit.

The demand for new industrial goods caused industries to grow. Many manufacturers used the mass production techniques devised by Henry Ford. He placed workers along a moving conveyer belt, where each performed a certain task or added a certain part to the product. This assembly line allowed him to turn out a new car every ten seconds. Similar assembly lines turned out refrigerators, phonographs, and vacuum cleaners. Clever advertising campaigns convinced customers that they had to buy more and more of the new products.

The assembly line idea, developed by Henry Ford, boosted industrial production in the 1920s.

The Man Nobody Knows

President Coolidge's pointed remark that "the business of America is business" reflected the nation's widespread enthusiasm for business—an enthusiasm that affected even religion.

Bruce Barton, a preacher's son who had become a famous advertising executive, wrote a book, *The Man Nobody Knows,* which portrayed Jesus as a model businessman. Christ, according to Barton, was "the founder of modern business. . . . He picked up twelve men from the bottom ranks of business and forged them into an organization that conquered the world." Christ, Barton said, was a "sociable man," and "the most popular dinner guest in Jerusalem." Barton claimed that Jesus practiced "modern salesmanship," persuading by asking pointed questions, and even advertising by using parables. Barton's favorite quotation from the Bible was Christ's reply to his parents in Luke 2:49, "Wist ye not that I must be about my Father's business?"

The Man Nobody Knows enjoyed great success. In the mid-twenties it was on the best-seller list for two years. Despite its popularity, however, the book revealed the author's lack of a knowledge of true Christianity. In a book entitled *The Christ We Know,* conservative Bible teacher A. C. Gaebelein argued that Barton's sketch of Christ struck at the heart of Christianity by denying Christ's incarnation as the Son of God: "Can the conception of Christ as a businessman, as a leader, or advertiser or sociable man, give our conscience rest and bring us nigh unto God? No! Nothing but the blood of Jesus." Furthermore, Barton's book ended with Christ's death, not his resurrection. Clearly *The Man Nobody Knows* misinterpreted Christ's work, but it does show how religion and business were mixed in the 1920s. What Barton wanted to do was bring Christ down to the level of business, rather than elevate business to the standards of Christ's teachings.

Big businesses were providing new jobs. Some Americans with money left over after paying routine expenses invested in the stock market. As stockholders were paid larger dividends, more people purchased stocks, even using credit to do so. Other people invested in real estate. Property, especially in Florida, became a tempting deal as the land was presented as a future resort paradise. Thousands bought property and resold it for higher prices, although little development took place. Many people went into debt on these get-rich-quick land speculations.

Both public attitudes and government favored big business. While attitudes toward big business had been negative from 1880 to 1920, Americans now respected or almost worshiped business and businessmen. "The man who builds a factory builds a temple, and the man who works there worships there," said President Coolidge. Business had become the god of the age. Government rarely interfered with any of the growing business empires of the 1920s. And since the prosperity of business was most important, labor unions gained little while they appeared to be fighting against American business.

Section Review

1. List three changes in American life caused by the automobile.
2. Who was the American pilot hero of the 1920s? What did he accomplish?
3. How did the radio help to unify American culture?
4. How did Henry Ford bring about mass production?

C. Moral Decay

The new prosperity of the 1920s helped to foster not only excessive materialism but also a flagrant disregard for moral standards by many. The horrors of war had prompted some of the soldiers who returned to take a "live-for-today" attitude. They wanted to experience all the pleasure they could, regardless of their future. Other Americans had been affected by the new sights and sounds of the age. The changes sometimes challenged their values, especially if those values were not firmly grounded in the truths of God's unchanging Word.

In this era changes in morals and culture were more readily expressed than they had been in earlier eras. Poets and novelists freely expressed their dissatisfaction with the world, its values, its standards, and its morals. They were quick to draw attention to Christians who were hypocritical or legalistic. Such Christians indeed brought reproach on God's name. Unfortunately, those same writers and artists refused to acknowledge that there were sincere Christians. They preferred instead to reject Christianity. Nor did they offer anything to replace what they had cast aside. Men and women were left in a moral vacuum, where many did not recognize right and wrong. Thus this generation has sometimes been called "the lost generation."

In Pursuit of Pleasure

The young people of "the lost generation" sought satisfaction in many pursuits. Some were new and unusual and lasted. Others were passing fancies or "fads" that soon faded. Some were harmless; others were harmful; a few were fatal.

Alvin "Shipwreck" Kelly set a record by sitting atop a flagpole for 145 days. His food and drink were hoisted to him in a bucket. While atop the pole, Kelly met the girl who became his fiancée when she came up to interview him. Others set records in marathon dancing. Raccoon coats, crossword puzzles, and a Chinese-inspired game called mahjong (MAH-ZHONG) became popular. Silent movies were the rage through most of the decade. Movie stars became American heroes and heroines, although their lifestyles were rarely worthy of emulation. Clara Bow, Greta Garbo, Mary Pickford, Rudolf "the Sheik" Valentino, and Douglas Fairbanks soon were recognized faces throughout the nation. Comic stars Buster Keaton and Charlie Chaplin made viewers laugh.

America's young people were soon copying the dress, hair style, and mannerisms of the stars. "Bobbed hair," much shortened from earlier years, became the rage for girls. For some, such imitations were signs of rebellion. The undisciplined lifestyle gave rise to the term "flaming youth."

Sadly, many women abandoned dress and conduct codes of the past to become **"flappers."** These frolicsome girls became the symbol of the "Roaring Twenties." Always restless, the flappers delighted in shocking their elders with short skirts,

Americans often looked for pleasure in the popular forms of entertainment.

slang, new dances, heavy makeup, and drinking or smoking in public. The young people of the lost generation did not seem to care that the pleasures of sin are but for a season.

Interest in sports grew, too, whether by actual participation, attendance at events, or by listening to the radio. Women made names for themselves in sports. In 1925 Gertrude Ederle became the first woman to swim the twenty-two miles across the English Channel. Helen Wills slammed her way to glory on the tennis court.

College football drew thousands of fans. Harold "Red" Grange, the University of Illinois's "galloping ghost" won the longest ovation in the history of college football when he ran for four touchdowns within twelve minutes. Knute Rockne (NOOT ROK-nee), a Norwegian immigrant who became head football coach at Notre Dame, unleashed his players' talents to thrill radio audiences each Saturday afternoon. The "Four Horsemen of Notre Dame," as his running backs were called, dazzled their way to gridiron glories.

Boxer Jack Dempsey, who was described as having "a neck like a bull, a granite jaw, and fists like iron," cashed in the first million-dollar gate for a sporting event. Horse and auto racing drew crowds. Some people were attracted to such sports, not for their excitement, but for a wrong reason, gambling.

Famous names in sports included a baseball star George Herman "Babe" Ruth, a home run hitter for the New York Yankees. Bobby Jones won fame on the links as a golfer. Besides entering major car races, Barney Oldfield raced at county fairs. And a horse named Man O'War won twenty of the twenty-one races he entered.

The "Roaring Twenties" are memorable partly because, more than in most eras, there was a greater emphasis on the sensational. Murders and other forms of crime filled American papers. Each crime seemed more sensational than the previous one reported. Americans seemed to thrive on all the excitement they could find.

Accidents and human misfortune captured the attention of the press. A hero dog named Balto and a spelunker (spih LUNG kur; one who explores caves) named Floyd Collins were two of the big stories in 1925. Balto carried diphtheria antitoxin 655 miles across Alaska to Nome. To save lives, this lead dog covered the distance in a blinding blizzard while the temperature plunged to fifty below zero. Floyd Collins had gained fame for his explorations of Mammoth Cave in Kentucky. On another cave

Babe Ruth began his baseball career as a talented pitcher, but he became a home run hitting hero for the New York Yankees.

adventure, however, a seven-ton boulder pinned him in. A thin reporter managed to wriggle down the treacherous hole to interview him. The vivid descriptions riveted the attention of the nation on Sand Cave, Kentucky, where Collins was trapped. Floyd's voice became weaker by the day. On the eighteenth day of reporting, there was no reply from the trapped man; he was dead.

The Failure of Prohibition

Prohibition was also an important issue. In 1919 the Eighteenth Amendment had been ratified. It had established prohibition by making illegal the manufacture, sale, transportation, import, and export of intoxicating liquors as a beverage. The outlawing of liquor had come with the support of many Americans. Thousands had rallied to the temperance societies of the 1800s, and the progressives of the early 1900s had made prohibition a major issue.

By 1915 fifteen states had voted out "demon rum." By 1918 thirty-three states were in the prohibition column. Since the United States was selling all its surplus grain to the Allies for food, it was considered unpatriotic to make liquor. The prohibition amendment passed Congress and went to the states for ratification. Its widespread support at the time is evidenced by its quick approval. All the states except Rhode Island and Connecticut had ratified it in just over a year. In most states prohibition won by a large majority.

Prohibition, however, proved difficult to enforce. The Volstead Act of 1919 had made any beverage with more than 0.5% alcohol illegal. It also set up a Prohibition Bureau to enforce the law. But the bureau had a small budget and only three thousand

Detroit police discover an illegal brewery during prohibition.

agents to enforce the law. Soon the problems of prohibition appeared.

Illegal taverns called **"speakeasies"** appeared across the nation. The border with Canada, where alcohol was legal, stretched nearly three thousand miles. Officers could not effectively patrol the long border, and liquor flowed freely across it. The Atlantic seaboard also had its share of rum runners. **Bootlegging**, selling illegal liquor, became a big business and made many rich. Since it was legal to have alcohol for medicinal reasons, some people got it by doctor's prescription. Others made their own home brew in stills.

Violence often accompanied the criminals who organized bootlegging rings. "Scarface" **Al Capone**, leader of Chicago's large crime ring, made $60 million on liquor alone in 1927. He and other ruthless crooks organized liquor networks to supply those who wanted liquor and were willing to pay any price for it. They also extended their activity to crimes such as illegal gambling and prostitution. Criminal gangs controlled these activities in certain areas, and if a rival gang tried to operate in another's territory, the gangs sometimes went to "war" with one another. Innocent people were killed in their raids, and such crimes shocked the public. Although periodic crackdowns came, it proved hard to put these gangsters behind bars. Not only would the criminals refuse to testify against each other, but the gangs also threatened the lives of honest citizens called as witnesses and bought off judges and officials.

By the late 1920s it seemed apparent that prohibition was not working. More and more Americans cried out for its repeal, which finally came in 1933. Prohibition has been called the "noble experiment" because the government tried to do away with an evil in society. Liquor is certainly the source of much pain and sin, but laws cannot be expected to change the moral character of men. Only salvation through Jesus Christ can change the hearts of individuals. As long as most of society remains without Christ, it will reject restrictions on its moral actions.

Nevertheless, prohibition did bring some benefits. Less alcohol was consumed, and some people gave up drinking. There was less gambling. Alcohol-related diseases and deaths decreased, and sober workers were more efficient. When prohibition was repealed, liquor freely began to afflict Americans with its sad effects again.

Ridicule of True Christianity

Because many Americans of the 1920s wanted fortune and pleasure without moral restrictions, they attacked the authority of Scripture. They did not want to be accountable to God and the standards set forth in His Word. Instead they followed the ideas of men that gave them excuses for rejecting the truth of the Bible. The theory of evolution, popularized by Darwin, told men that God had not created them. They reasoned that if God was not their Creator, then they did not need His salvation.

They also found other ideas that they thought freed them from responsibility. The psychologist Sigmund Freud taught that man behaves the way he does because of subconscious drives. Men took his work to mean that people cannot help what they do; therefore, they should do whatever they please and not feel guilty. Even Albert Einstein, the mathematician and scientist, added to the sense of moral freedom. His theory of relativity stated that time, space, and mass were not fixed or absolute.

Although Einstein himself was not talking about moral matters, many people began to think that everything was relative. These men said that there are no absolute rights and wrongs and that everyone should do what is right in his own eyes.

Of course the Bible clearly states the standard God has set for man. Men who preached about the responsibility of man to a holy God and the truth of Scripture soon found themselves scorned by the society around them. The greatest example of the 1920s came with a trial concerning the teaching of evolution in schools.

In the 1920s Christians, angry because evolution was being taught in the public schools, pressured state legislatures to pass laws forbidding teachers to teach evolution. The Tennessee state legislature passed such a law. John Scopes, a high school biology teacher, broke the law and was brought to trial. He was convicted and fined $100.

Actually, the **Scopes Trial** had been a publicity stunt of two businessmen in Dayton, Tennessee. Eager to attract attention to their town, they asked Scopes to teach evolution with the assurance that the American Civil Liberties Union would provide legal support. The two businessmen hoped that a dramatic trial would draw attention to Dayton and thus attract industry to the town.

In the summer of 1925, the trial turned into the hoped-for gigantic "media event." Two hundred reporters converged on the small town of Dayton, and for the first time a trial was covered by radio. One of the prosecutors was William Jennings Bryan, three-time Democratic presidential nominee. Clarence Darrow, a famous trial lawyer and agnostic, defended Scopes. H. L. Mencken (MENG kun), a nationally known reporter who made fun of Christians, called the people of Dayton "gaping primates," and the event in Dayton the "Monkey Trial."

Bryan testified in the trial and was ridiculed by Darrow's questions. While Bryan was a staunch defender of the faith, he did not always handle Darrow's questions well. Bryan was not a Bible scholar or a scientist. Even though Scopes was convicted for teaching evolution, the trial had made Bible-believing Christians appear ignorant and unscientific. The Scopes trial was a disappointment to true Christians, yet they knew that their faith rested in the sure Word of God. Even in such an era of open sin and ridicule of the Bible, some men still stood firm as they preached the truth of Scripture.

Williams Jennings Bryan had been a prominent politician during the Progressive Era, but his participation in the Scopes trial brought him ridicule.

J. Gresham Machen (1881-1937)

J. Gresham Machen (MAY chun) was perhaps the most scholarly spokesman for the the faith during the 1920s. He studied at some of the best schools in the United States and Europe, and he was a professor at Princeton Seminary until its liberalism caused him to leave. During the 1920s he believed that the Presbyterian church was falling away from Scriptural truth and wrote several scholarly books defending truths such as the virgin birth, the inspiration of the Bible, the atonement, and the bodily resurrection of Christ. Machen argued that if someone held other views, he was not a Christian.

Because of liberalism in Princeton Seminary, Machen left it after teaching there several years. In 1929 he helped found Westminster Seminary in Philadelphia, where he taught until his death. He also set up a new independent mission board because of liberalism in the denominational one. Because of his stand for the truth, Machen was dismissed from the Presbyterian church, and by 1936 he and other conservatives formed the Orthodox Presbyterian Church. One of Machen's best books is *Christianity and Liberalism,* an attack on modernism.

Section Review

1. Why was the 1920s called "the lost generation"?
2. What were three fads of the 1920s?
3. What is "bootlegging"?
4. What famous trial took place as a result of the teaching of evolution? Where did it take place?

D. Political Inaction

The presidents of the 1920s reflected the attitudes and goals of the day. They promoted the unhindered growth of business and the general enjoyment of prosperity. The business and prosperity were indeed enjoyable, but some of the nation's serious problems were brushed aside at the time. Eventually the fruits of the materialism and selfishness of the era turned out to be a severe crisis for the country.

Harding's Weakness

Warren G. Harding was a likable newspaper editor from the small town of Marion, Ohio. He had come up the political ladder through Ohio politics, eventually becoming a U.S. senator. The political leaders in the state at that time were called the "Ohio Gang," and Harding did his share of favors for these friends to achieve his political success.

Harding had promised to get the country back to normal after the war, and since that was what the country wanted, he was easily elected to the presidency. It may also be noted that the 1920 election was the first time that women could vote for a president. Harding was considered to be handsome, and that quality did not hurt his popularity.

Once in office, Harding supported most of the popular programs of the day, especially big business. Unfortunately, he had allowed many of his political friends to take important offices in which they could use the government to promote their own gain. Although Harding was basically honest, his friends turned his administration into a great scandal.

Warren G. Harding
29TH PRESIDENT
(1921-1923)

Born: Blooming Grove, Ohio, November 2, 1865

Family: married Florence Kling DeWolfe

Occupation: newspaper editor and publisher

Home: Marion, Ohio

Religion: Baptist

Election: 1920—defeated James M. Cox (Democrat) and Eugene V. Debs (Socialist)

Political Party: Republican

Vice President: Calvin Coolidge

Interesting Facts and Accomplishments:
liked to play ping pong and golf
first president to ride to his inauguration in an automobile and first to use a radio
had an Airedale dog, Laddie Boy, who delivered his newspapers and is now depicted in a statue in the Smithsonian

Death: August 2, 1923

The most prominent criminal was Harding's secretary of the interior, **Albert B. Fall.** Fall persuaded Harding and the secretary of the navy to transfer control of government-owned oil reserves from the Navy Department to Fall's Interior Department. He then leased the reserves at Teapot Dome, Wyoming, and Elk Hills, California, to two oil men, who paid him back with a $400,000 "loan." When Fall's crime was uncovered, he went to prison, the first cabinet member in history to be imprisoned for misdeeds in office.

Although not involved in public scandal for financial gain, Harding was weak and at fault personally for allowing the law to be disobeyed within White House walls. Harding was obviously a poor leader who failed to take his executive responsibility seriously. Instead of providing firm direction, Harding allowed national affairs to simply drift along without guidance. By the summer of 1923 Harding knew something was wrong. He told journalist William Allen White, "I have no trouble with my enemies. I can take care of them all right. But my friends, White, they're the ones that keep me walking the floor nights."

Harding took a vacation to Alaska in 1923. Enroute back the president became seriously ill July 28 in his hotel room in California. He died August 2. The officially listed cause of death was ptomaine poisoning. Since no one else in the party of sixty-five got food poisoning, however, it is more likely that he died of a heart attack. The **Teapot Dome Scandal** was uncovered after his death.

Coolidge's Administration

Calvin Coolidge, born in Vermont, had studied law in Massachusetts and entered

Calvin Coolidge
30TH PRESIDENT
(1923-1929)

Born: Plymouth, Vermont, July 4, 1872
Family: married Grace Goodhue; two sons
Occupation: lawyer
Home: Plymouth, Vermont
Religion: Congregationalist
Election: succeeded to the presidency in 1923 upon the death of Harding
1924—defeated John W. Davis (Democrat) and Robert M. La Follette (Progressive)
Political Party: Republican
Vice President: none (first term), Charles G. Dawes (second term)
Interesting Facts and Accomplishments:
played the harmonica
was notified of Harding's death while visiting his father in Vermont, and was sworn into office by his father, a notary public, at 2:47 A.M. on August 3, 1923, by the light of a kerosene lamp
noted for his frugality and his silence—often called "Silent Cal"
while sitting beside a young woman at a dinner party, she told him she had bet that she could get at least three words out of him. Coolidge's reply was, "you lose."
Death: January 5, 1933

politics there. He had gained a reputation as a "law and order" man when as governor of Massachusetts he had taken a stand during a Boston police strike in 1919. He declared, "There is no right to strike against the public safety by anybody, anywhere, any time," and forced the police back to work. To a nation that was in fear of disorder and crime, this stand won him admiration.

Succeeding to the presidency on Harding's death, Coolidge was in charge when most of the Harding scandals were revealed. By firmly prosecuting the corrupt officials, Coolidge won enough support to win the presidential election of 1924. Then he carried on the same basic policies that Harding had supported. While business appeared to be successful during the Coolidge administration, ominous conditions were developing. Because of the unwise speculation of investors, prices were going higher and higher on the stock market. Buying on credit was so popular that millions of Americans were in serious debt. Farmers were still overproducing and receiving low prices for their produce. These and other features of the American economy would soon lead the nation into calamity.

Hoover's Inheritance

The nation was still enjoying prosperity, however, when the election of 1928 came around. The Republican candidate, **Herbert Hoover,** was swept into office by a nation satisfied with success. Hoover, a poor, orphaned farm boy, had proved his abilities by becoming a wealthy mining engineer, and then devoting his talents to public service. His Democratic opponent, Al Smith, was a Roman Catholic and was against Prohibition. The nation was not yet ready to vote a Catholic into the presidency.

Home: West Branch, Iowa
Religion: Quaker
Election: 1928—defeated Alfred Smith
  (Democrat) and Norman Thomas
  (Socialist)
Political Party: Republican
Vice President: Charles Curtis
Interesting Facts and Accomplishments:
an expert angler (fisherman)
first president born west of the
  Mississippi
never accepted a salary while president
  and personally paid for all entertaining
  functions in the White House
received honorary degrees from fifty
  American universities
his wife spoke four languages fluently
  and could read six
was writing a book at age ninety when he
  died
the "Star-Spangled Banner" became the
  national anthem while he was president
Death: October 20, 1964

Herbert Hoover

31ST PRESIDENT
(1929-1933)

Born: West Branch, Iowa, August 10,
1874
Family: married Lou Henry; two sons
Occupation: engineer, relief
  administrator during World War I

Hoover was talented, but he had inherited the impending fall of prosperity. The excesses of the twenties were about to result in disaster, and Hoover would be saddled with the responsibility for the Great Depression that was to come.

Section Review

1. Name the three Republican presidents of the 1920s.
2. What conditions of the 1920s would help bring the nation's prosperity to an end?

Summary

The "Roaring Twenties" was a time of prosperity for the nation, following the sacrifices of World War I. Businesses boomed, and Americans enjoyed the new consumer goods and amusements. The United States generally isolated itself from foreign problems and distrusted foreigners within the country, while it concerned itself with issues and events at home such as Prohibition, Lindbergh's flight, and the fads of the "flaming youth." Unfortunately, the 1920s was also a time of great decline in moral character. Americans pursued material possessions, often risking their future by buying too much on credit or speculating in stock and land. They ridiculed Christianity, rebelled against moral restraints, and turned to the pleasures of sin and selfishness. Although the decade was one of general prosperity, Americans would pay for some of their excess with the hardships of the decade to come.

Chapter Review

Do You Remember?

■ Match each of these men with the statement or description most closely related to him.

1. Al Capone
2. Calvin Coolidge
3. Albert B. Fall
4. Warren G. Harding
5. Herbert Hoover
6. Charles Lindbergh

a. America should "return to normalcy"
b. flew the *Spirit of St. Louis* to Paris
c. a Chicago gangster
d. organizer of Teapot Dome scheme
e. "the business of America is business"
f. inherited the collapse of prosperity

■ Answer the following questions about the 1920s.

7. What two international agreements did the United States sign in the 1920s?
8. What is a "Red Scare"?
9. When was the first commercial radio broadcast, and what did it announce?
10. In what fad did "Shipwreck" Kelly participate?
11. What were the shockingly fashionable young women of the 1920s called?
12. When did Prohibition begin, and when did it end?
13. What is bootlegging?
14. What famous trial convicted a teacher of teaching evolution but ridiculed Biblical Christianity?

Why Is It So?

1. Why was there a short depression following World War I?
2. Why did radicals point to the Sacco and Vanzetti case as an example of injustice?
3. How did the automobile bring changes to American life in the 1920s?
4. Why did Prohibition fail to keep all Americans from drinking?
5. How did the ideas of Charles Darwin, Sigmund Freud, and Albert Einstein affect American morals?

What Do You Think?

1. Why is the "Roaring Twenties" a good name for the 1920s?
2. How does a person make business his "god"? How could a Christian businessman avoid making business his "god"?
3. Are fads ever bad? Explain your answer.
4. With Warren G. Harding's example in mind, why must a person be careful to keep the right kind of friends?

25

Crash and Depression

American businesses appeared to be flourishing as stock prices rose higher and higher in 1929. Although prices reached a new high in September, conservative investors were beginning to grow cautious. Those who sold stocks found fewer buyers, and prices began to slide down. By October, orders to brokers to sell surpassed orders to buy. On Thursday, October 24, a record-breaking thirteen million shares changed hands. Prices slid so low that investors lost $9 billion on that "Black Thursday." Many investors, who lost all of their money, could not pay the stock brokers the additional money that the investors owed. When the investors could not pay, brokers tried desperately to sell the stock, flooding the market still more.

A panic broke out the following Tuesday, October 29, when there were orders to sell sixteen million shares on the exchange. Fortunes made over a period of years vanished in minutes. Some people became so depressed they took their lives.

An Oklahoma farmer and sons during a dust storm in 1936

This **stock market crash of 1929** signaled the beginning of the **Great Depression,** a time of hardship for many Americans.

A. The Fall of Prosperity

President Hoover had declared: "We in America today are nearer to the final triumph over poverty than ever before in the history of any land," but soon millions of Americans would join the ranks of the unemployed, the homeless, and the hungry. The "Roaring Twenties" ended with a financial collapse of the nation that would afflict Americans for the next decade.

Causes of the Crash

The great desires for wealth and pleasure in the 1920s had much to do with the crash that followed. We should note a few specific causes of the financial crisis.

Industrial Problems—Despite the overall air of prosperity in the 1920s, many common workers had already faced economic woes. Farmers were suffering from low prices. Textile workers and coal miners were hurt by layoffs as demand for their products declined. These workers could no longer buy the industrial goods that were filling the market. Eventually, many other Americans either had bought many goods or were running out of credit to buy more. With a decreased demand for goods, industrial output slowed. Laborers worked fewer hours or were laid off, cutting incomes and causing hardships. Since industries were often interdependent, when one cut back, it forced others to do the same. As consumer spending continued to drop, industrial expansion came almost to a standstill long before the crash actually took place.

Overuse of Credit—The use of credit, especially of installment buying, had grown steadily. While credit covered some of the early symptoms of economic illness, its unwise and often unrestrained use made things worse. Before long, people were having to make such high payments on the things they had bought on credit that they could not afford to buy anything new. Auto sales and construction lagged and workers were laid off; these people were then unable to meet their payments at all. Merchants, who had extended the credit loans, lost money and their businesses began to falter.

Speculation—In the late twenties newspapers carried accounts of people who had profited from get-rich-quick schemes. These speculators, often motivated by greed, bought properties at a low price, hoping to sell them quickly for a much higher price. Most had speculated in land or stock.

Land prices went up in the 1920s, especially in urban areas or near recreational settings as people moved outward to the suburbs. The biggest land boom was in Florida, where the semitropical climate attracted hoards of speculators. Miami alone boasted two thousand real estate offices in 1925. Those who had speculated early and bought good land did make big profits. But others who bought land on credit found they could not make their payments. Some people were swindled into buying undesirable lands and even swamps. In 1926 hurricanes struck, helping to put an end to the desire to invest in the area. Homes were left vacant, and few further sales were made. Bank failures in Florida climbed when loans were not repaid.

While risky land investments did not tempt many Americans, stock speculation did. Prices of corporate stock had risen steadily beginning in 1927. By September 1929 stock prices were 400 per cent higher than they had been in 1925. People of modest means were attracted to stock purchases. The ticker-tape machine allowed purchasers across America to follow price changes almost as they happened. The number of those "playing the market" grew to about 1.5 million in 1929. But most were not buying stocks to collect quarterly dividends. Rather they wanted to sell stocks for quick profits when the prices rose. Many investors paid scant attention to the earnings of the companies they had invested in, an indication of the actual value of the stock. They assumed stock prices would keep going up no matter what the industries did.

The problem was made even more complex because brokers allowed investors to **buy on the margin.** The investors or buyers paid only part of the purchase price in cash, usually ten per cent, and borrowed the rest from the broker, using the stock as collateral. The broker borrowed money from banks and corporations to cover loans made to his investors. If the value of the stock went up, there was no problem. The buyer could repay his loan with interest and gain a profit. If the stock's value went below the value of the loan, however, the buyer's margin was "called in." The speculator then had to get more cash or risk loss of the shares along with his cash investment. If the buyer could not repay his loan, the

Investors in the stock market watched stock tickers eagerly to discover how well their investments were doing.

broker could take the stock.

The system satisfied many and seemed to stimulate the economy. Stock prices climbed, and in March 1928 both the volume of shares traded and their value soared. The boom lasted through the summer of 1929, although economists were baffled because both prices and business profits were falling at the same time.

International Economic Problems—In addition to economic problems such as the lack of industrial expansion, the overuse of credit, and wild speculation on land and stock, several other problems helped to bring the downfall of prosperity. Many of these involved not only the financial operations of the United States but also those of other countries, particularly European countries.

America had lent the Allies money during World War I, and the debts and their interest amounted to over $11 billion. War-torn Europe had little cash to repay this debt. In addition, the United States had passed a high tariff on foreign goods that kept European nations from trading with America. Without profitable trade, Europe could not repay the debt. The only source of money for repayment to American creditors was the money they received from German reparations payments. Yet the Germans were also too poor to make these large payments for the war as the Treaty of Versailles had demanded. To this complex situation of international debt was added the fact that Americans began to lend Germany millions of dollars so that it could make the reparations payments. When the crash came, most of the money from these international loans was lost, and the end of American credit and prosperity threw Europe into a severe depression too.

Conditions of the Depression

Once the crash came, most Americans lost all their optimism. They saw prosperity disappear, and most had little hope that it would return very soon. Investments, money, jobs, and even homes were no longer safe.

The Run on Banks—People became increasingly afraid that the money they had deposited in banks would be lost. Some drew money out of banks to pay their brokers. Others panicked and withdrew all their money. Banks could not keep pace with the demand. In the last two weeks before Hoover left office, depositors pulled out $1 billion. Banks ran out of cash and were forced to close their doors, some permanently. Others reopened to offer depositors only a percentage of their total deposit.

Banks had unwittingly contributed to the collapse through unwise extension of credit. In September 1927 there was $1.3 billion out in loans. The same month in 1929 the total had reached $8.5 billion. When many of these loans could not be repaid, the banks ran out of money. By 1931 about five thousand banks had closed their doors. Not all were large, but some were; the failure of the Bank of the United States in New York City affected 400,000 people.

Unemployment—Millions of Americans were thrown out of work by the depression. By 1931, thirteen million Americans, one of every four workers, were unemployed. While some workers kept their jobs, they labored only a few days a week or a few hours a day. Others who kept their jobs took wage cuts.

The loss of a man's job usually meant no steady income for his family. Even so, the family needed food. The mortgage or

rent payments had to be made. Any person or business that had given credit was now beating on the door to receive payment. The situation seemed desperate to millions of Americans.

Wives and mothers helped out as best they could. They took in laundry and took cleaning jobs. If families had an empty room or children could double up, they took in renters. They planted gardens and canned vegetables to save on grocery bills. Clothing was patched; socks were darned. Children wore hand-me-downs. Sometimes unemployed husbands or older sons left home to search for work in another town.

Many families could not continue paying the installments on their loans. Because of mortgage foreclosures, some eventually lost their homes. Some moved to abandoned boxcars or hastily built shacks on the edges of towns. Since these poverty dwellings were blamed on the president and his policies, they were called "Hoovervilles."

The depression caused great despair and suffering among America's poor.

Many who needed help were aided by others. Family members helped their relatives. Friends and churches also offered help. People helped each other, trading their skills and materials.

The depression forced most Americans to lower their living standards. For many the depression destroyed their sense of independence and accomplishment. It was difficult, especially for a family's primary breadwinner, to be unemployed, unable to support his own family. Some men searched for work in vain and then waited for handouts at soup kitchens or stood in bread lines. Sometimes they gleaned fields, scavenged city dumps, or searched for food in garbage cans. It was not uncommon to see once-prosperous men selling apples on the street corner. A few men tried to escape from their troubles by jumping on freight trains to ride the rails as hobos.

The depression forced some Americans to reexamine their values. They found they could live on less. For Christians the depression offered many opportunities to trust the Lord in new ways. They continually saw God's provision for His people as He supplied their needs. They saw anew the truth of Psalm 37:25: "I have been young, and now am old; yet have I not seen the righteous forsaken, nor his seed begging bread."

Yet during this economic depression, there was no significant major religious revival. Many Americans when hard pressed turned not to God but to the government.

Further Farm Problems—Few farmers had been prosperous, even in the booming 1920s. They produced so much grain, livestock, and other farm products that prices had stayed low. Many farmers could not make payments on farmland they had bought or on the car, equipment, and other items that they had bought on credit. Without higher prices for their products, many were in danger of losing their farms.

Conditions for farmers became even worse, especially on the western edge of the Central Plains and on the Great Plains, where the **"Dust Bowl"** brought extreme poverty. This area, already semiarid, had first been overgrazed by cattle. Then with the increased demand for food during World War I, it had been plowed into farms. Since there had been enough rainfall then, farmers were able to make money. But in the 1930s droughts came, adding to the farmers' economic woes.

The unemployed often found a warm meal at charitable soup kitchens.

"I Remember the Drought "

The droughts of the 1930s created desperate conditions for farmers. One victim of the droughts recalled his family's situation:

"I know from experience what it means to have no rain. For three years in the thirties we had very, very little rain. There was no pasture for the cows on our dairy farm. My dad chopped down trees so the cows could eat leaves all summer. They would bellow when they heard Dad chopping. We had to make leaf haystacks, which the cows ate in the winter. The grass was so thin Mother used a hand rake and a gunnysack to pick up the hay. The winds blew every day, day after day. The grasshoppers were the only ones who were happy and multiplied easily. They skinned the thistles to live. We poisoned them at every turn. . . . To this day, I still conserve [water] and feel that it's almost a sin to use too much of it because you just don't know when it might be scarce again."

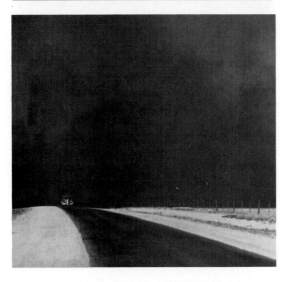

A black cloud of dust rises over the prairie in 1936.

First the crops dried up. Next the land turned to dust. Then winds whipped the rich topsoil off the dry exposed ground. By late fall of 1933, "black blizzards" blew from west to east across the country. The clouds of dust darkened skies as far away as Albany, New York. By 1934 the lands from Texas to Canada were ravaged by the dust storms. The soil drifted into banks like snow. Cars had to use their headlights in the daytime. Families put wet towels in window sills and under doors to keep out the choking dust. Livestock died of thirst. Thousands of farm families fled from their homes. Some went to areas, especially in California, where farm workers were needed to tend vegetable fields and orchards.

Hoover's Plight

President Herbert Hoover tried to deal with the onset of the depression by being optimistic. The more people panicked, the more damage was done to the economy, and so he tried to encourage Americans to believe that these trials would soon pass and business would boom again. Few people seemed to listen. Stock prices continued to fall as investors tried to sell. Runs on banks continued, and industry remained inactive. Although Hoover was not responsible for the problems that beset America, he was the president, and thus he received most of the blame for everything that was going wrong.

The Veterans Demand Aid—The veterans of World War I had been promised a life insurance bonus to be paid in 1945. Although the veterans were no worse off than most other Americans in the depression, many began to ask for the government to pay them part of the face value of their insurance policies at an earlier date.

In the spring of 1932, Walter Waters, an unemployed veteran from Oregon, journeyed east to the capital to pressure Congress to pay the "bonus." Soon men from all parts of the country joined him. About 20,000 veterans became a part of this "Bonus Army" and camped on a low-lying muddy area near the Potomac River. The men were there most of the summer. When the Senate defeated the Bonus Bill, many veterans left, but a few thousand remained. Hoover refused to meet with them, but he did ask Congress to advance them money from their insurance policies so they could get home. They were told that any who were left after July 28 would be evicted. At this point radicals in the group tried to start a riot. After two policemen were beaten to the ground, two Bonus marchers were killed. Hoover then opted to use troops, and the soldiers routed the veterans and set fire to their shacks. Although stern action was needed, Hoover received much criticism for treating the veterans harshly.

Hoover's Theory—The President was not insensitive to how the depression was affecting Americans. He believed first in "local responsibility. The best hearts and brains of every community could best serve their neighbors." He believed that creating government agencies to handle the problems would give the sufferers more red tape than relief. His position was that federal funds should be used only after all voluntary and local resources were exhausted.

When federal monies were used, Hoover believed they needed to be carefully regulated. They should not be given directly to people as a **dole,** or handout, such as welfare is today. Instead, they should be used for projects where the effects of the funds would benefit more people. If cities and states, for example, were given loans to pay for public works projects, they could hire local people who would benefit from the employment.

Hoover did not believe in government regulation of big business. He saw federal control of activities as an invitation to dictatorship, corruption, waste, and inefficiency. He defended personal freedoms against government encroachment. He greatly feared socialism. He also wanted to keep the federal budget balanced, and so he was reluctant to spend large amounts of money for aid programs.

Hoover's ideas were basically good, but he soon met opposition. Sound though his policies might have been, they required both time and the cooperation of the people to

Herbert C. Hoover by Douglas Chandor, National Portrait Gallery, Washington, D.C.©

bring the desired results. Many Americans saw only their immediate hardships and wanted relief right away. When the president's ideas brought no quick remedy, many Americans began to complain.

Hoover did try to establish programs to help the people. He set up some government work projects to employ thousands of men and supply useful work. Public buildings were constructed, and in 1931 construction was started on what became Hoover Dam on the Colorado River. The federal government also subsidized the building of thousands of miles of roads.

In January of 1932, Congress passed Hoover's bill creating the **Reconstruction Finance Corporation.** It could lend up to $2 billion to businesses, industries, and banks to undertake projects that would employ more men. Therefore, there would be less need for direct relief. Congress also approved the president's request for twelve Federal District Home Loans Banks. These banks could lend money to loan associations, banks, and insurance companies, who in turn could aid homeowners who were having trouble making mortgage payments.

Despite these actions, Hoover continued to receive criticism. The steps he took were not dramatic enough to satisfy the many Americans who were still waiting for help.

Section Review

1. What evidence was there in the late 1920s that industries were declining?
2. What is installment buying?
3. Speculators were especially involved in what two properties?
4. What were "Hoovervilles"?
5. What problems did farmers face during the depression?

B. FDR and the New Deal

While Hoover was reluctant to take dramatic action, discontent grew. Because many Americans continued to blame the problems of the depression on Hoover and the Republicans, the Democrats gained followers.

The Election of 1932

The election of 1932 was one of the most decisive in American history. The Republicans renominated Herbert Hoover. The Democrats chose New York's governor, **Franklin Delano Roosevelt,** and John Nance Garner of Texas as his running mate. Some Americans believed that the regular parties were not solving America's problems, and so they turned to radical leaders. The Socialist party nominated Norman

President Franklin Delano Roosevelt

Thomas, and the Communists ran William Foster.

Roosevelt campaigned with buoyant enthusiasm and confidence. He favored programs that were very costly, while promising to cut government spending by twenty-five per cent. He promised the voters a **"New Deal,"** and many were drawn to him because he gave hope for strong actions that might bring change.

Hoover praised "rugged individualism" and encouraged voluntary efforts by industry and labor to deal with their problems. Although he did pledge more government action than before, by the fall of 1932 millions of voters were convinced that Hoover's way would not work. Roosevelt carried forty-two of the forty-eight states to become the new president.

Putting the New Deal into Action

Franklin D. Roosevelt brought optimism to a depressed nation when he took office March 4, 1933. With confident voice he asserted: "This great nation will endure as it has endured, will revive and will prosper. . . . The only thing we have to fear is fear itself. . . . We do not distrust the future of essential democracy. The people of the United States have not failed. In their need they have registered a mandate that they want direct, vigorous action."

Roosevelt and his advisers, a **"Brain Trust"** of college professors (most of whom were from Columbia University), were ready to take that "vigorous action." The president began by proclaiming a **bank holiday,** closing banks temporarily, to stabilize banking. Next he called Congress into special session to deal with the crisis and to put his policies into effect. Then he went on the radio for the first of his many

The President's Polio

President Roosevelt may have been handicapped, but he wasn't disabled. Stricken with polio in 1921 at the age of thirty-nine, Roosevelt was permanently paralyzed from the hips down. To most people that would have signaled the end of any political aspirations. To Franklin Delano Roosevelt it was just another obstacle to push aside on his way to the highest office in the land.

It was not always easy. Roosevelt had to use metal braces just to stand. In order to minimize the effect of his handicap on the public, Roosevelt refused to be seen in his wheelchair. He had to be helped to "walk" up to the podiums to give his speeches. One time the podium had not been fastened down, and it and the president went tumbling off the platform into the orchestra pit. Returning to the reset stand, Roosevelt simply picked up his speech right where he had left off. For traveling, a railroad car with a special elevator and a special wheelchair were designed for the president.

Roosevelt's condition also gave him a special burden for the similarly handicapped. He was constantly visiting the hospitals and working with handicapped patients, children or soldiers. He had a car designed with hand controls and often he would take a particularly discouraged child for a ride and talk. Always the child returned with a positive attitude and a desire to go on. Roosevelt also invested heavily in a treatment center at Warm Springs, Georgia. The springs there had a therapeutic effect on those who used them.

Whatever one's view of Roosevelt's political philosophy, his courage and perseverance in confronting his physical handicap must be admired and applauded.

Franklin D. Roosevelt
32ND PRESIDENT
(1933-1945)

Born: Hyde Park, New York, January 30, 1882

Family: married Anna Eleanor Roosevelt (his fifth cousin); one daughter, five sons

Occupation: lawyer

Home: Hyde Park, New York

Religion: Episcopalian

Elections: 1932—defeated Herbert Hoover

1936—defeated Alfred M. Landon

1940—defeated Wendell L. Willkie

1944—defeated Thomas E. Dewey

Political Party: Democrat

Vice Presidents: John Nance Garner (first and second terms), Henry A. Wallace (third term), Harry S. Truman (fourth term)

Interesting Facts and Accomplishments:

a fifth cousin of Theodore Roosevelt

appointed the first woman cabinet member, Frances Perkins, as secretary of labor

only president elected to serve more than two terms—served a total of twelve years and thirty-nine days

was paralyzed from the hips down as a result of polio

served hot dogs to King George VI of England and his queen on their visit to his home at Hyde Park

collected stamps

Death: April 12, 1945

"fireside chats" to the nation. A good public speaker with an understanding of people, Roosevelt radiated warmth, even on the radio. He made extensive use of press conferences, seeking to make the press his allies. As allies they could sway lagging public opinion to rally support for his ideas. Soon there appeared a long line of legislation and programs that would be FDR's New Deal.

Early New Deal Legislation—Congress, realizing that the American people wanted the action that Roosevelt promised, became a "rubber stamp," approving almost anything the president proposed. In the first one hundred days, legislation for New Deal programs moved quickly.

As soon as Congress convened after Roosevelt's inauguration, it passed the Emergency Banking Act. This act suspended all banking activity, creating a bank holiday until banks could restabilize. The Treasury Department had the power to decide which banks were sound enough to reopen. Half of the banks, holding ninety per cent of all banking resources, were back in operation by March 15. Only about one bank in twenty never reopened. When the banks reopened three weeks later, confidence returned and more than $1 billion was redeposited.

In May 1933 Congress also approved Roosevelt's creation of the Federal Emergency Relief Administration (FERA). This temporary agency (later replaced by the WPA or Works Progress Administration) had $500 million in federal money to disburse. The agency provided funds for the states to use for relief needs. The money was to be channeled into work relief where possible so that the recipients would work for their pay. However, because the immediate need seemed so great, more of it went out as direct relief (doles) than as work relief.

Congress founded the Home Owners' Loan Corporation in June of 1933. This agency bought mortgages from holders and rewrote them on easier payment schedules. By 1936 one-fifth of all mortgaged nonfarm homes had mortgages under this agency. It was one of the most popular of the New Deal relief acts.

While the general public got relief through FERA and the Home Owners Loan Corporation, special efforts were made to help farmers. The Farm Credit Administration (FCA) refinanced mortgages for farmers who would have lost their lands. The government also hoped to restore the farmers' purchasing power through the **Agriculture Adjustment Act** (AAA). To raise farm prices, farmers were asked to cut production. Rather than sell their products at a loss, the farmers were told to destroy crops. In 1933 they were asked to plow under between one-quarter and one-half of their crop. Milk was poured into ditches; grain was burned; cattle, sheep, and hogs were killed. Cotton and wool were stored in warehouses and held off the market until greater need would raise the prices.

Ironically, while this was being done, many Americans were hungry or in need of clothing. Yet the action seemed to offer hope to the farmers because they were being paid to cooperate with the plan. The act allowed the government to pay farmers for not producing crops. The government also bought surplus crops that it planned to store and sell when prices were higher. Farm income did go up about fifty per cent over the next two years.

Despite the AAA's immediate benefits for the farmers, it was soon attacked. When the policies forced farm prices up, consumers had to pay more for their goods. Moreover, the subsidies for not producing were given to landowners. In the South, where sharecropping was used, the landowners were not the ones who actually farmed the land. The sharecropper who had labored on the land did not receive any benefits. In fact, he often lost money because he had to cut his production. Meanwhile the landlord received all the monetary gain.

In 1936 the Supreme Court nullified the AAA, but a dangerous precedent had already been set. Many farmers became dependent upon government subsidies. Farmers would soon regain those subsidies and agricultural regulation, and they would protect them. Such policies require tremendous government expense while they artificially control the industry. Other New Deal programs would similarly hamper other industries from adjusting to the market demands.

The **National Recovery Administration** (NRA) was designed to help businesses recover from the effects of the depression. The logic behind the act was to eliminate "wasteful competition" among firms. Codes were written and given to businesses. Each company was assigned a share of the national market and given annual production quotas. The codes also set maximum hours to be worked and minimum wages. An additional provision required a company to recognize a union if the majority of the employees wished to form one. Each firm or business that complied with the NRA codes was allowed to display the NRA's Blue Eagle seal. Rather than clutching arrows in its talons as on the Great Seal, this eagle clutched lightning bolts and a gearwheel. The NRA was soon criticized as a violation of the free enterprise system. Big businesses seemed to be favored over smaller ones, and the consumer was caught in the middle when prices went up. The Supreme Court declared the NRA unconstitutional in 1935.

Another law established the **Civilian Conservation Corps.** This act gave unemployed young men jobs and at the same time conserved natural resources. In the seven years of its existence, the CCC employed two and a half million young men.

In May 1933 Congress also established permanent New Deal agencies with long-range as well as immediate goals. The **Tennessee Valley Authority** (TVA) involved seven southeastern states. The agency provided for public power projects on the

Tennessee River. The thirty multi-purpose dams produced and sold electric power, controlled floods, eased erosion, manufactured fertilizer, and created recreation areas. Because it involved the federal government in areas where it had never been involved before and put the government in the position of competing with private companies, the act was controversial.

Further Action—Americans were generally pleased that the new president was taking firm actions to deal with the depression. When one measure did not work, Roosevelt quickly tried another one. The actions, however, were not bringing a real economic recovery to the nation, and millions were still in need. Roosevelt continued to experiment with new programs that he

A cartoon depicts the cooperation between labor and management under the NRA.

hoped would solve some of the problems. In 1935 he launched the Works Progress Administration (WPA). This agency put more people to work on construction projects. WPA workers built hospitals, schools, parks, playgrounds, and airports.

Eventually the WPA was extended to other areas, including the arts. Actors, actresses, and directors were employed to put on programs. Authors were hired under the Federal Writers' Project to write historical and geographical guides for the forty-eight states. Artists were hired under a Federal Art Project. They painted murals in public buildings such as post offices. The National Youth Administration (NYA) helped young people. High school and college students were hired for part-time jobs that enabled them to stay in school. Together the WPA and NYA provided jobs for almost five million Americans.

Even though Roosevelt took many daring actions, some New Deal critics believed that the president was not doing enough to relieve the poverty of many Americans. Some suggested radical plans to distribute wealth and won many supporters. One such critic was Dr. Elmer Townsend, a retired California medical doctor who designed a plan to help the elderly. His plan required the government to pay each person over sixty a $200-a-month pension. The money for the pensions would come from a national sales tax. To receive pensions, retirees would have to agree to spend every cent each month. He thought such spending would pump up the economy.

Another radical plan was proposed by Huey Long, a masterful politician from Louisiana. He suggested taxing large incomes heavily to provide a minimum income for the poor. Another popular

The Cees Get Passing Grades

They planted over two billion trees and spent 6.5 million manhours fighting forest fires. They built over 420,000 dams, fixed up old parks and built new ones, and built or improved miles of trails and access roads. They made thirty dollars a week, twenty-five of which was sent home to help support their families. "They" were the *Cees,* the young men who worked for the Civilian Conservation Corps.

There were over two and one half million jobless youths hired by the Civilian Conservation Corps. The CCC was the most popular New Deal program; even the Republicans praised it. They were the first relief agency to go into action. Some have called them "The Tree Army," and others, "The Soil Soldiers." The program lasted from 1933 until World War II called most of the young men into the armed forces.

The camps for the Cees were directed by army officers. Extracurricular activities were usually oriented toward sports, particularly boxing. Rising time was 5:45 A.M. and taps was at 10:00 P.M. The food had the flavor of Army meals with lots of potatoes and bologna. For most of the men, the times spent in the Cees were rewarding, and for some it was character building. Hard outdoor work kept

speaker with a plan was Father Charles Coughlin, a Detroit priest who had a nationwide radio broadcast. He suggested government-stimulated inflation, government takeover of certain industries, and a guaranteed living wage for laborers. He also wanted to overhaul the currency system and abolish the Federal Reserve System for

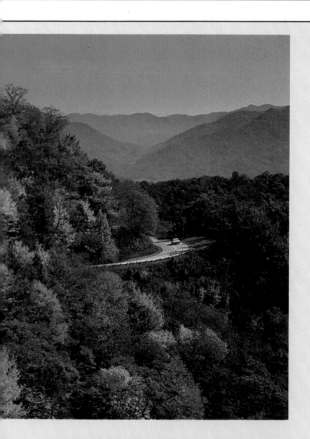

them busy. The conservation emphasis gave meaning to their efforts. The money sent home to help their families gave them a purpose. It's easy to see why the Civilian Conservation Corps received the most praise of any of Roosevelt's programs.

regulating the nation's banks. Most of the ideas of these critics were even more socialistic than Roosevelt's programs, and they would have led the government deeper into debt. They also would have discouraged people from working for their money.

Roosevelt countered these ideas with a government-sponsored insurance plan. It

The Blue Ridge Parkway and the Appalachian Trail were projects that benefited from the labors of the CCC.

offered smaller monthly pensions by giving federal aid to the states for the elderly as well as funds for unemployment insurance, aid to dependent children, and public health programs. The old age insurance, commonly called **Social Security** today, was only a part of the program. The program was to be financed by a federal tax on wages (one per cent in 1935) paid by both employer and employee.

Roosevelt supported the National Labor Relations Act of 1935, also called the Wagner Act. With it he tried to salvage some of the benefits labor had been offered under the now-outlawed NRA. This act encouraged the growth of labor unions. The largest labor union, the American Federation of Labor, now faced competition from another union, the Congress of Industrial Organizations. Formed in 1935, this union boasted a membership of 3.7 million within two years. Other regulations intended to help workers came with the Fair Labor Standards Act in 1938. It established the nation's first legal minimum wage and maximum hours for workers producing goods that crossed state lines. The wage was twenty-five cents per hour, and the workweek was to be forty-four hours. The act also forbade children under sixteen from working in most industries.

Section Review

1. Who were the presidential candidates in 1932?
2. List at least two of the New Deal's agencies and state the purpose of each.
3. What provisions were made for the nation's farmers?
4. What provisions were made for the aged?

C. Opposition to the New Deal

Although Roosevelt had gained office with a large popular vote, there were many who opposed him. Liberals and leftists opposed him because they did not think that his New Deal policies had gone far enough. They believed that the New Deal needed to be more socialistic, providing for government ownership of certain industries or providing people with income at government's expense.

Conservatives also voiced their opposition. Under Roosevelt's New Deal, the government had gained control in areas previously left to private interests. Conservatives distrusted such governmental control and feared the extension of government's power into more areas. The New Deal was giving the federal government wide powers over industry and commerce, areas that were not government's rightful sphere. Roosevelt's agencies were replacing the free enterprises of capitalism with the government regulations of socialism. Federal powers gained during the crisis of the Depression would never be curbed in the decades to come. The Supreme Court decisions in 1935 and 1936 outlawing several New Deal measures and agencies fueled the conservative opposition and reflected its thinking.

The Election of 1936

The New Deal president faced a political test in the 1936 election. A group called the American Liberty League unsuccessfully sought to block the president's renomination. The Democrats, however, chose Roosevelt on the first ballot. The party platform praised the New Deal and promised similar additional reforms.

During his first term Roosevelt had been working to change the Democratic party's image. Until 1935 he had urged business, agriculture, bankers, and workers to settle conflicts among themselves. But in 1935 he began using the government's power to alter the balance between employees and employers, and between the rich and the middle class or poor. He tried to identify the Democratic party with the underprivileged. Reforming liberals, blacks, urban immigrants, and workers tended to join the Democratic party from this time on.

Although Roosevelt had refused to support both civil rights regulations and an anti-lynching law in 1936, he still got black support. The depression hit blacks hard, and they were particularly grateful for the New Deal's financial relief. Many blacks believed that the Roosevelt's programs had saved them from starvation. The public works projects offered blacks employment at equal wages with whites (although they were not allowed to work with whites). Such policies landed FDR seventy-five per cent of the black vote in 1936.

Black children on a North Carolina farm in 1938

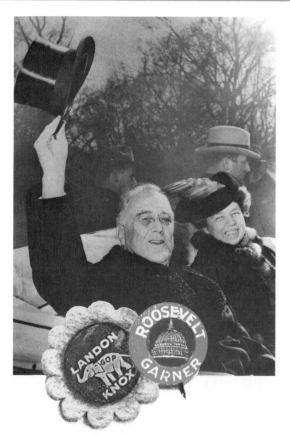

The Republicans had lost heavily in the congressional elections in 1932 and 1934. Because they lacked a leader and a program to attract voters, a 1936 win looked impossible as well. The Republicans ran Alfred M. Landon, who had been a progressive governor in Kansas. Using the phrase "America is in Peril," the Republicans criticized the New Deal for its overthrow of traditional ways and for betraying its promises to the people.

Although Landon campaigned hard, he carried only two states, Maine and Vermont. Roosevelt beat him by more than eleven million votes. The Congress elected in 1936 was also heavily Democratic.

Top: *President Roosevelt and his wife, Eleanor*
Bottom: *Republican and Democratic campaign buttons from 1936*

Declining Popularity of the New Deal

Roosevelt's strong win and congressional support encouraged him to challenge the make-up of the Supreme Court. Because it had outlawed several New Deal measures, FDR became more and more critical of the court's conservative nature.

In February 1937 he presented a plan to "pack" the Supreme Court with new justices. He hoped that adding to the number of justices would protect his New Deal measures. Roosevelt requested that the number of justices be increased from nine to as many as fifteen. Each time a justice reached seventy and did not retire, FDR wanted to appoint a new justice. This court-packing plan would have allowed him to add justices who would support his programs.

For the first time, Congress defeated a Roosevelt request. They saw his action as a serious threat to the balance of power among the branches of government. Increasing the court's size in this way would have limited the independence of the judicial branch by giving the president more power to control it.

The New Deal had reached high tide in 1936. In 1937 it ebbed. Suddenly there was a **recession,** a slump in business that was supposed to be less serious than a full depression. The decline between September 1937 and June 1938 was one of the worst in American economic history. The stock market dipped and industrial production declined. In early 1937 federal spending had dropped off. This spending cut reduced personal incomes and in turn cut the purchasing power that had been artificially sustaining industry's production.

Roosevelt had accepted the use of government spending to get the economy started up, even if it meant going into debt. But when the government reduced its spending after four years, the pumped-up economy did not stand on its own. It was becoming evident that the New Deal measures had only helped to cover the problems; they had not brought the United States recovery.

Consequences of the New Deal

The New Deal had improved conditions from their 1932 depressed state in some respects. Business profits and farm prices were up; unemployment was down. Annual per capita income had gone up from $678 in 1933 to $925 in 1939. Electricity had been extended to many rural areas, and other public works had improved buildings and parks and encouraged conservation. These benefits, however, had come at a tremendous price for the country—the growth of federal power and federal spending.

Perhaps the one positive thing that the New Deal had accomplished was the restoration of people's faith and confidence in America. Roosevelt, despite the dangers and failures of many of his programs, had offered hope and action for people who were in a panic. People trusted him to do something about their problems.

In 1939, however, after six years of Roosevelt programs, the United States had not really recovered from the depression. Prices for farm products were still low. Overall manufacturing production and corporate profits lagged far behind 1929 levels. Nine million Americans were still unemployed.

Roosevelt's money policies and excessive spending had a great effect in the following years. He had taken the United States off the gold standard in 1933. Paper money and coins were no longer convertible into gold coins. Although this action did little to aid the economy at the time, it gave the government much power over national currency for the future. And because of its high spending, the New Deal had left the country with a record debt. The national debt in 1933 was $2.6 billion. In 1939 it was $6.5 billion. Unfortunately, in future years the precedents of high government spending and unbalanced budgets continued. The public just did not want the government to cut back on what they were used to having.

In the long run the New Deal had brought other changes. The government, especially the executive branch, had greatly increased its power. Under Roosevelt both the size and scope of the federal government had been greatly increased. Unfortunately, once the government assumes the responsibility for something, it rarely gives up control. And when the people give up their personal rights and responsibilities to government, they rarely get them back.

The government had also intervened in, perhaps even managed, the economy. The economy was no longer solely based on private enterprise. Although private businesses remained the mainspring of economic activity, government had assumed a major role. The government had taken responsibility for individual and national economic welfare. It had provided special help to farmers and industrial workers. It left Americans with the idea that when there was a crisis in future years, the government would help them then, too. Some people now believed that they were entitled to public help if they became victims of any circumstances over which they had no real control.

The depression was a time of great trials for many Americans and for the nation as a whole. Those who lived through it often learned many lessons about the uncertainty of money and positions in this world. Too few, however, learned to fully trust in God in the midst of their hardships. It was easier to ask the government for aid. We who are Christians must realize that men and governments may fail. The only one worthy of our trust in any crisis is our Saviour, Jesus Christ. He who feeds the birds of the air and clothes the lilies of the field is certainly able to take care of His own children. "But seek ye first the kingdom of God, and his righteousness; and all these things shall be added unto you" (Matt. 6:33).

Section Review

1. What groups of voters did the Democratic party begin to attract in 1936?
2. What Republican candidate ran against Franklin Roosevelt in the 1936 election?
3. Describe Franklin Roosevelt's court-packing scheme.
4. List at least three consequences of the New Deal.

Summary

The stock market crash in 1929 signaled the end of a generally prosperous and carefree time for the nation. It also signaled the beginning of a severe economic depression that would last throughout the 1930s. Failing banks and closing businesses plagued the country after the crash, and millions of Americans began to experience the hardships of unemployment, the loss of their homes or farms, and even hunger. In their distress, many looked to the government to give them aid. When President Hoover's reactions did not bring them quick relief, they turned to Franklin Roosevelt for swift action. He offered one New Deal program after another in an attempt to bring recovery. The programs increased government power and federal debt, but they ultimately failed to solve the underlying problems of the depression. The American people survived the trying times of the 1930s, but in the process they learned to depend on government aid and regulation to protect them from crisis.

A family on their way to Oregon during the depression

Chapter Review

Do You Remember?

■ Define each of the following terms.
1. Dust Bowl
2. buying stock on the margin
3. dole
4. bank holiday
5. recession

■ Match each of the following terms with its description.

6. Great Depression	a. Roosevelt's group of advisors
7. Reconstruction Finance Corporation	b. Hoover's aid program
	c. "old age insurance"
8. New Deal	d. the 1930s
9. Brain Trust	e. Roosevelt's attempt to bring
10. Social Security	the nation relief and recovery

■ The New Deal contained many programs and pieces of legislation that were commonly known by their initials. For that reason they were sometimes called an "alphabet soup." What were the full names of the programs listed below, and what did each one do?
11. AAA
12. NRA
13. CCC
14. TVA

Why Is It So?

1. How was America's economy declining before the stock market crash?
2. How did buying on the margin make stock speculation especially risky?
3. Why did Americans criticize Hoover's policies?
4. How did FDR get public support for his New Deal?
5. Why did conservatives oppose the New Deal?
6. Why did Roosevelt wish to "pack" the Supreme Court? Why did he fail?
7. What example did the New Deal era leave for future administrations?

What Do You Think?

1. Why are government doles dangerous?
2. Is the Social Security program, established during the New Deal, a benefit to the nation? Explain your answer.
3. How did the depression change Americans?

26

World War II

American marines raising the flag on Iwo Jima in 1945

On Sunday morning, the seventh of December in 1941, the Japanese bombed Pearl Harbor in Hawaii. The attack on the American naval base resulted in the sinking or disabling of nineteen American ships, the destruction of nearly two hundred planes, the death of over two thousand men, and the wounding of two thousand more. The treacherous surprise attack prompted President Franklin D. Roosevelt to address Congress the next day with these words:

Yesterday, December 7, 1941—a date which will live in infamy—the United States of America was suddenly and deliberately attacked by naval and air forces of the Empire of Japan.

Roosevelt then asked the Congress to declare war, and immediately America was thrown into a conflict not only with Japan but also with Germany and Italy. The United States had joined the worldwide conflict known as World War II.

A. Trouble Brewing

Although Americans fighting in World War I had idealistically believed that they were "fighting a war to end all wars," in less than twenty-five years Americans were back on the battlefields. The conditions that led to another, even wider, conflict were many; the troubles had begun almost before the guns of World War I had cooled.

Leaders of War

Not everyone was pleased with the outcome of World War I. The peace settlements had satisfied only a few of the participants. Most countries had not gotten all they wanted from victory or had lost more than they wanted to lose from defeat. Some of this dissatisfaction aided the rise of three strong imperialist countries in the 1930s.

Hitler Builds His Third Reich—The German nation was most upset by the Treaty of Versailles. That settlement had placed all the blame for the war on Germany and had stripped the country of some of its land, its colonial possessions, its strong army, and its self-respect. The treaty had also forced a large debt upon Germany to be paid to the Allies as reparations. Humiliated by these terms of defeat, Germany struggled through the 1920s. In the midst of the downcast German people, however, there arose a man who gave Germany a hope for future greatness.

Adolf Hitler gained Germany's attention in 1924 with the publication of his book *Mein Kampf* ("My Struggle"). In it he preached the injustice of the Treaty of Versailles, blamed the Jews for Germany's problems, and declared the superiority of the German race. Hitler also organized the National Socialist German Workers party, or **Nazi party,** around his leadership. He denounced communism (which the Germans greatly feared at that time), and he proposed a strong, organized Germany that would become a powerful leader of the world.

Although many Germans did not accept Hitler at first, they found Nazism to be full of excitement and pageantry, and almost no one wanted to be left out. Calling Hitler the *Fuehrer* (leader), many joined in his support, believing that they were building a Third Reich (German empire) that would last for a thousand years. They believed that Hitler would restore Germany to its rightful place in the world. They believed the promises Hitler made in his speeches with more enthusiasm than many Christians today carry the gospel to the lost. A few people continued to mistrust him, but their influence was not strong enough to reverse his power.

As depression increased German despair in the early 1930s, Hitler and his Nazi party swept into power. He became the German chancellor in 1933 and was given the powers of a dictator. He soon began to violate the Treaty of Versailles by sending troops into the Rhineland area near France and by organizing German men and boys into groups for military training. Hitler also set German scientists to work developing new weapons and materials that could be used in war. His power and ambition would soon threaten world peace.

Mussolini Moves to Conquer—Italy was also disappointed after World War I. It had switched to the Allied side during the war, but it had not received the extra territories it wanted when the war ended. Suffering from economic and political problems after the war, Italy allowed **Benito Mussolini** to seize power in 1922. Mussolini, called *Il Duce* (DOO chay; the leader), was the leader of a party that favored nationalism and opposed communism. Like Hitler, he had organized military groups across Italy. As dictator, Mussolini built efficient railroads and major highways, provided houses and lands for sixty thousand peasants, and made other improvements in Italy. Although he denied freedom to the people, he promised to give Italy back the pride of a bygone era by establishing a "Second Roman Empire." Such promises initially caused his followers to rank him with Julius Caesar.

Mussolini's first attempt to expand his empire began in 1935, when Italian soldiers crossed the Mediterranean to attack the African land of Ethiopia. Ethiopian tribesmen faced Italy's machine guns and bombers with spears and rifles. Although Europe and the United States looked on in horror, no one went to Ethiopia's aid.

Mussolini found an ally in Hitler. Both men had formed **fascist** (FASH ist) **governments,** strong dictatorships that stressed nationalism and power. They formed an alliance called the Rome-Berlin Axis. Later, Japan joined this alliance, becoming the third of the **Axis powers.**

Benito Mussolini, the fascist dictator of Italy

Changes in Japan—Japan's industrial and military power had been growing since the turn of the century. A group of military leaders had gained control of Japan, and they intended to increase Japanese power in China and in other areas of Eastern Asia and the Pacific. These leaders were convinced that Japan had deserved greater recognition as a world power after World War I. They convinced the Japanese people that the United States was a threat to further growth of the Japanese Empire and that Japan should establish control of the trade and resources of Eastern Asia.

After World War I the League of Nations had assigned Japan the responsibility of governing some Pacific islands formerly held by Germany. Fortifying these islands enabled Japan to invade China and take over the northern region called Manchuria in 1931. The United States believed that Japan's conquest of Manchuria was wrong, but the United States' request to the League of Nations to take action against Japan was ineffective, and Japan stayed in Manchuria. Since no American possessions in the Pacific were yet threatened, the United States did nothing except to slightly strengthen the defenses of the Philippines.

Roosevelt and Foreign Policy

The United States was aware that the growing powers of Hitler, Mussolini, and the Japanese military leaders were threatening the delicate balance of world peace. Even so, the isolationist attitude that had ruled in the 1920s also prevailed in the 1930s. Most Americans were more concerned that the nation take care of the problems of its own economic depression than that it get involved in foreign affairs. They hoped that the limits set for navies and the peace pacts that the major nations had signed in the 1920s would be enough to discourage future war. Americans did want the League of Nations to take appropriate actions against the threatening powers. Yet the League was very weak and never able to act as an effective restraint against villainous nations.

President Roosevelt was among those who wanted the United States to take a major role in foreign affairs. But without popular support little was done about the trouble that was brewing in Europe and Eastern Asia. A significant step, however, was accomplished in the United States' relationships to the countries of Latin America. President Hoover had initiated a **"Good Neighbor Policy"** in dealings with these lands, and Roosevelt continued this policy. Instead of marching into Latin American countries with a "big stick" when troubles arose, as had been done since the presidency of Theodore Roosevelt, the United States began to let these countries handle their own affairs. The Good Neighbor Policy did much to improve relations with these countries, which had grown tired and suspicious of U.S. intervention in their lands.

Section Review

1. What event brought America into World War II?
2. What two European leaders built strong military dictatorships after World War I?
3. What part of China had Japan conquered?
4. What was the general attitude of Americans toward foreign affairs in the 1930s?
5. What new policy was the United States following in its dealings with Latin America?

B.   World War II Begins

In the late 1930s the world watched as Hitler began his conquest of European territory. His actions soon made France and Britain realize that something had to be done about this fascist leader.

German Expansion

Because other nations had not really protested Hitler's disregard of the Treaty of Versailles, Hitler chanced violating it again by uniting Austria (a German-speaking land) with Germany in 1938. In four weeks Austria came under Hitler's control. Foreign powers still did not protest too strongly against him, and so he next demanded an area in Czechoslovakia, the Sudetenland. He claimed that the 3.5 million Germans who lived there "deserved to be a part of the Fatherland." However, he had secretly instructed his military to invade Czechoslovakia if he did not gain it peacefully by October 1, 1938. Hitler promised that this would be "the last territorial claim I have to make in Europe."

A Nazi rally in Nuremburg in 1935

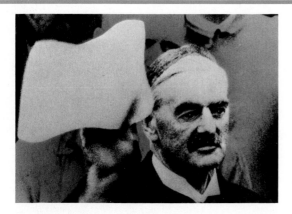

Great Britain's prime minister, Neville Chamberlain, and Hitler reached an agreement during a meeting in Munich, Germany. Chamberlain thought that if Europe would "appease" Hitler by giving in to his demand, peace would be saved. Many Europeans were relieved that war had been avoided, but they soon found that giving in to evil usually causes it to resurface in an uglier form. Chamberlain returned to Britain and announced that there would be "peace in our time." **Winston Churchill,** who would soon take Chamberlain's place as prime minister, violently disagreed, saying: "You chose dishonor and you will have war!"

Hitler took the Sudetenland peacefully, but the **appeasement** did not work. Only about six months later, Hitler forcefully took over all of Czechoslovakia. Europe began to realize that Hitler intended to keep increasing his power and his empire. No European nation was safe.

By the spring of 1939, Hitler wanted Poland. This time both Britain and France warned that such action would lead to war. Hitler ignored them, saying: "Our enemies are little worms. I saw them at Munich." But Hitler was worried that the Soviet Union would also protest his actions. He realized it would be unwise to fight too

Neville Chamberlain, prime minister of Britain, returning home after the Munich conference

much of Europe at one time. Therefore, in August he signed a nonaggression pact with **Joseph Stalin,** the dictator of the Soviet Union. They agreed not to attack each other as they both expanded their territory. Although Hitler had said that he hated the Communist Soviet Union, he would wait until later to attack that enemy. The stage was now set for the beginning of World War II.

War Envelops Europe

On September 1, 1939, Hitler unleashed his mechanized war machine on Poland. Hundreds of bombers soared over Poland while armored tanks, called *panzers,* and thousands of soldiers moved in to take control. The Soviet Union also attacked Poland from the east. Within hours Poland had lost almost all hope for avoiding conquest. A few Poles continued to resist for several weeks, but the fall of Poland was complete before the month ended. The world had seen a new type of warfare— "lightning war" or **blitzkrieg.** Nine more European countries soon would fall under Nazi control as the Germans advanced.

Britain and France, the **Allies,** knowing that Hitler had to be stopped, declared war on Germany on September 3, 1939. They rushed to prepare their armies, but little fighting took place for eight months. Then on April 9, Hitler's forces took control of Denmark and Norway. A few weeks later, on May 10, 1940, Hitler staged another blitzkrieg, sending his forces into Belgium, the Netherlands, and Luxembourg. The Belgians and the Dutch, unable to fight against his strong armies, soon became conquered states. Next, by-passing France's heavy fortifications, the Germans moved on to conquer the French.

Chapter 26

Britain sent soldiers and equipment to help France, but the Allied army of 338,000 men was forced to retreat to northeastern France near the port of Dunkirk. The Germans rushed to cut off an escape across the English Channel. Having trapped the Allied army at Dunkirk, the Germans waited for their air force to finish the task. Bad weather, however, prevented German planes from bombing the fleeing forces. Meanwhile, the British and French brought every available boat to Dunkirk. Fishing boats, steamers, yachts, and even lifeboats were used to evacuate the Allied army. Fishermen, dockworkers, merchants, and farmers all helped ferry the army across the Channel to safety. The evacuation of an army, however, was hardly enough to save France. On June 14, 1940, German troops entered Paris. France had fallen to the Nazis.

While Hitler was conquering the French, Mussolini announced that Italy was joining Germany in the fight against the Allies. Mussolini had already taken control of Albania before the war began, and he intended to gain more land from an Axis conquest of Europe.

Britain Stands Alone

With the fall of France, Britain stood alone to face Hitler and Mussolini. Most believed that the Germans would cross the English Channel to invade and conquer the British Isles, but Hitler chose another way to try to defeat Great Britain. He ordered devastating bombing raids on English cities, including the capital, London. These bombing attacks became known as "the battle of Britain," and they began in July 1940 and lasted for one year.

The Germans hoped to drive Britain's Royal Air Force (RAF) from the skies and to force a surrender by inflicting heavy damage on civilians. The RAF courageously tried to protect Britain from the bombings. Because of a shortage of pilots, RAF pilots made as many as five flights a day to defend their homeland. Their efforts prevented the fall of Britain. The new prime minister, Winston Churchill said of the RAF, "Never in the field of human conflict was so much owed by so many to so few." Had the attacks continued, the outcome might have been different. But because of the British determination to stop Hitler, he had to seek another approach to victory over Britain.

Left: *Allied troops evacuate Dunkirk in 1940*
Right: *Smoke rises above London during the battle of Britain*

Hitler Turns Against the Soviet Union

Although mired in a stalemate in Great Britain, Hitler was winning elsewhere. German armies had control of Hungary and Rumania by the spring of 1941. Turkey had signed a treaty of neutrality. In early summer Hitler swept into southeastern Europe. Bulgaria, Yugoslavia, and Greece were soon Axis victims.

Hitler then made a decision that would have tremendous consequences—a decision to attack the Soviet Union. Hitler believed that the British were holding out in the hope that the Soviets would change sides and come to the aid of the Allies. While the Germans were still fighting the Allies in Western Europe, Hitler's generals tried to warn him that opening up another front, or battleground, in the East would be unwise. Expanding the war into the Soviet Union late in the summer could be dangerous, but Hitler did not listen. He wanted to crush the Soviet Union and to take its resources for German use. On June 22, 1941, the blitzkrieg against the Soviet Union began. Hitler thought he could take control of the land in just eight weeks.

At first the Russian people accepted Hitler's armies as a relief from the terrors of Stalin's Communist rule. However, they soon learned that the Nazis were not friendly. Germans ravaged Soviet towns and tortured the Russians they met. The Russians began to use a "scorched earth" policy. Instead of leaving crops and livestock for Hitler to use to feed his men, the Russians, as they retreated, burned their crops and killed their animals. Thus the supplies the German army had hoped to capture were gone. With every mile conquered, the supply lines back to Germany became longer.

Axis-Controlled Area—1941

Scale of Miles: 0 100 300 500

- Axis & Axis-controlled
- Allies & Allied-controlled
- Neutral nations

In mid-October German troops were only forty miles from Moscow, and they had killed over two million Russians. Even though the autumn days grew shorter and temperatures grew colder, Hitler refused to stop and wait until spring for further action. He did not want to give Stalin more time to ready his defenses. The Germans marched on with only their summer uniforms and light-weight oil for their vehicles. Ironically, Hitler had not learned from history. A century before, Napoleon had found that the Russian winter was far more dangerous than Russian troops. On December 6, as the freezing Soviet winter closed in, the Soviet troops attacked Hitler's cold and weary forces, and they actually broke through the German lines. The Soviet army and the Russian winter had kept Hitler from defeating the Soviet Union.

American Sympathies and Fears

Americans looked at European affairs with increased alarm. The European dictators had made it clear that they were opposed to any form of republican government. Some Americans feared that if Britain fell, Germany might try to wage war on the United States. Most Americans generally opposed Hitler and wanted the Allies to win. Yet since Congress had passed a series of neutrality acts in the 1930s, Americans were limited in what they could do to help the Allies.

In 1939 Congress had allowed the Allied powers to buy war materials from American companies if the Allies paid cash and carried the supplies on their own ships. Congress also passed a Selective Service Act in 1940. Once again young men aged twenty-one to thirty-five were required to register for possible military service. Some 375,000 men were drafted and started training to be ready for attack. But since the armistice in 1918, America had not been concerned with building a strong armed force; so the new soldiers had to train on old or substitute equipment until new pieces were available.

Many Americans still feared war and wanted to avoid it at all costs. The America First Committee, with such prominent members as Charles Lindbergh, and other organizations pleaded for American neutrality. Roosevelt ran for a third term as president in 1940, and he won. Because of the fear of war, however, Roosevelt had to promise that he would keep American boys out of a foreign war, a war that did not directly involve the United States.

As the battle of Britain was threatening to crush the Allies in the summer of 1941, President Roosevelt decided that Britain desperately needed more help. He sought a way for the Allies to obtain vital war equipment from the United States more easily. Congress complied by approving the **Lend-Lease Act.** This act permitted the president to send needed equipment to any nation in which the receipt of such equip-

Left: *Adolf Hitler salutes Nazi soldiers in a parade in Munich*
Right: *A political cartoon of the 1930s warns that the policy of isolationism in the face of the Nazi threat was placing the United States in danger.*

ment might be vital to American defense. Rather than paying with money, the countries could pay with property, services, or equipment for American use. In this way the United States received land for seven air bases in exchange for war supplies sent to Britain.

Americans also began to realize that the European Axis powers (Germany and Italy) might not be their only enemies. Japan had joined the Axis powers, and it was pursuing interests in Asia. Japanese forces had already entered Southeast Asia; Australia, New Zealand, or the Philippines might be Japan's next target. Most Americans did not know that Japan also intended to take control of a vast area in the Pacific. The Japanese were strengthening their position in Asia in preparation for their attack on American possessions in the area.

President Roosevelt decided to forbid almost all trade with Japan. The strain between the two nations increased as Japan continued to expand its power in defiance of American interests. In November 1941 Japanese diplomats arrived in Washington for talks. At the same time, however, Japanese aircraft carriers were sailing across the Pacific to take up positions within bombing distance of Hawaii.

Section Review

1. Hitler's invasion of what country actually triggered World War II?
2. Which of the major Allied countries did Hitler capture within a year?
3. With what major power did Hitler make a nonaggression treaty that he later broke?
4. What did the America First Committee want?
5. What was the Lend-Lease Act?

C. America Enters the War

The attack on the naval base at **Pearl Harbor** on December 7, 1941, put an end to American neutrality. When the United States declared war on Japan after the attack, Japan's allies, Germany and Italy, also declared war on the United States. The war now directly involved America in a fight against all the Axis powers.

The attack on Pearl Harbor was a great blow to the United States Navy. The damage was severe, but heavier losses were avoided because the American carrier fleet was at sea that Sunday morning. Nonetheless, the United States had much to do to prepare itself for the long fight ahead.

Manpower for War

Following Pearl Harbor, patriotic volunteers deluged army and navy recruiting centers. Eventually about sixteen million Americans, one in eleven, wore military uniforms. Those Americans who sincerely believed that war was wrong registered as **conscientious objectors** and served in the medical corps or in nonmilitary roles.

Destruction during the bombing of Pearl Harbor

Women also became involved in the war effort in military or civilian jobs. Some served in the Women's Air Corps (WACS); others joined the Women's Naval Reserve or the WAVES (Women Accepted for Voluntary Emergency Service). The WAFS (Women's Auxiliary Ferrying Squadron) helped to fly aircraft from the factories to air force bases. Although women were not assigned to combat roles, they did serve overseas, especially in tasks that freed men to fight.

More women also became a part of the job force, taking the places of men who were drafted. Posters picturing "Rosie the Riveter" were used to recruit women to join workforces everywhere. Some joined the Red Cross and others worked with the USO (United Service Organizations), entertaining troops and providing other services.

As some jobs previously closed to them opened up, black Americans joined the work force in larger numbers than ever before. Blacks also enlisted in all-black units in the armed forces.

Beginning February 1, 1943, Japanese-Americans could enlist, too. They trained as an all-Nisei (American-born Japanese) force. Because of their Japanese association, however, most were sent to fight in Europe. Some Japanese-Americans did do intelligence work in the Pacific, cracking the secret Japanese telegraph codes.

Materials for War

The United States entered the war without materials and preparation for the conflict, but Americans rose to meet the challenge. Factories were soon retooled to produce war goods, such as jeeps and tanks, rather than cars. Through teamwork and sacrifice, production doubled in less than four years. By 1945 more than 300,000 planes, 100,000 tanks and self-propelled guns, 2.5 million military trucks, 1.1 million rifles and carbines, 400,000 artillery weapons, and 50 billion rounds of ammunition had become a part of the American arsenal.

Shipbuilders set to work to increase the United States' naval fleet. Ships dubbed "Liberty Ships" were christened as quickly as every three and a half working days. Liberty Ships were employed to carry war materials to far-flung fronts. Aircraft carriers, destroyers, submarines, and other vessels also were built with amazing speed.

To meet the ever-increasing need for war goods, Americans at home had to sacrifice during the war. After 1942, automobiles were no longer made for private sale. Gasoline and oil as well as meat, butter, sugar, coffee, most canned or frozen goods, and shoes were **rationed** (restricted in use) because of shortages. Americans received books of ration stamps. They could buy a rationed item only if they had an unused stamp for it. When scarce products were available in stores, there were often long lines to buy them. Nothing was thrown

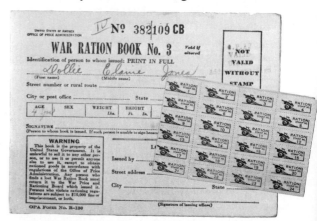

The government used ration stamps, issued to Americans in ration books, to limit purchases of goods that were in short supply during the war.

away. Drives to collect tin cans, waste paper, aluminum, and scrap iron became common.

As they had in World War I, most Americans patriotically added to their food supply with "victory gardens." These vegetable gardens popped up everywhere, in backyards, along edges of parking lots, in zoos and parks, and in window boxes. By 1943 they supplied Americans with a third of all their vegetables. These efforts insured that there would be more food available for the boys fighting in the war. Americans also bought war bonds to help pay for the war effort.

The supply lines used to carry goods to the armed forces stretched around the globe. In addition to supplying its own men, the United States supplied much of the Allied forces. President Roosevelt called the United States "the arsenal of democracy."

Mapping the War

As commander-in-chief of all American armed forces, the president mapped the war strategy with the help of the leading military officers and advisors. Roosevelt also met with Britain's Prime Minister Winston Churchill. Their first meeting was held secretly aboard an American destroyer off the coast of Newfoundland in August 1941, before the United States had joined in the war on the Allied side. Later the Arcadia talks, held near Washington, D.C., made public the Allied leaders' "Hitler first" policy. This policy made Nazi Germany the first target. The United States agreed that the Germans were the biggest threat to the Allies. Once Hitler was defeated, Japan could not stand long.

Other meetings among Allied leaders allowed them to discuss their military strategy and to plan for dealing with the prob-

lems that would be faced after the war was over. At Casablanca (CAS uh BLANG kuh) in Morocco in January 1943, the Allies decided to invade Europe through Sicily and Italy. After Hitler had turned against the Soviet Union, that country had joined the Allies. Therefore, at the next meeting in Teheran (TEH uh RAN) in Iran, Soviet dictator Joseph Stalin joined the meetings. Stalin pressed for the Allies to invade northern Europe to take pressure off his troops. With the fall of France and the end of the battle of Britain, most of the fighting was taking place in the east between the Germans and the Soviets. Stalin was promised a second European front to take the pressure off the eastern front in return for his promise that the Soviet Union would help defeat Japan once Hitler was defeated.

Section Review

1. About how many Americans served in the armed forces during World War II?
2. How did women serve in this war?
3. What had to be done with America's factory production?
4. List three ways that Americans sacrificed to help the war effort.

The "Big Three": Stalin, Roosevelt, and Churchill at Teheran

D. American Efforts in Europe

Although the United States did not totally neglect events in the Pacific, it sent its major forces into the European portion of the conflict first.

Attacking North Africa

Prior to Germany's invasion of Russia, Italy had launched a major campaign in North Africa. The British, however, defeated the Italians and threatened to drive the Italians out of Africa altogether. In order to prop up his faltering ally, Hitler sent German troops, called the "Afrika Korps," to Africa under the command of the brilliant General Erwin Rommel (ROM ul). By clever maneuvering and swift movement, Rommel succeeded in driving back the British. He even threatened to drive into Egypt and capture the Suez Canal. The battle lines in North Africa shifted back and forth for hundreds of miles in 1941 and 1942 as first Rommel, and then the British, were victorious.

By the middle of the year 1942, however, American troops began to arrive. Under the

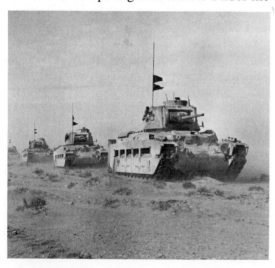

Tanks in the African campaign

skilled command of General **Dwight D. Eisenhower,** the Americans landed in western North Africa and began to push east toward Libya. The British in the meantime began to drive west from Egypt. With this "Operation Torch," as the African campaign was called, the Allies crushed the Axis forces between them. Rommel and some of his men escaped to Europe, but 240,000 Axis troops surrendered to the Allies in Tunisia in May of 1943.

The Allies Attack Italy

Although Hitler had lost in North Africa, he now fought to keep "Fortress Europe" or the lands that the Reich held in Europe. The Allies under American General George Patton launched "Operation Husky" to free Italy by invading Sicily, the island off the tip of Italy. American troops under General Mark Clark and British troops under General Bernard Montgomery then crossed to Italy. Working their way up the Italian coast, the Americans captured Naples in October 1943. But the push to take Rome was slowed by the Germans during a murderous four-month assault through Italy's snow-clad mountains.

As they had done in World War I, the Italians decided to switch sides. They overthrew Mussolini, surrendered to the Allies, and declared war on Germany. Although the American forces freed Rome on June 5, 1944, fighting continued with German forces in Italy for another year. The Allies decided to focus their assault elsewhere in Europe. Leaving behind the fewest possible troops to hold the German army where it was in Italy, General Eisenhower worked in Britain to prepare for a bigger invasion. American generals Omar Bradley and George Patton and British general Bernard

European Theater, 1943-44

Montgomery assisted Eisenhower in the planning.

The Allies began preparations for a great invasion of Germany through France, "Operation Overlord." They assembled men and equipment in southern England while they sent planes on bombing attacks in Germany. The RAF planes conducted night raids over German cities, systematically destroying two and a half cities per month. The American air force bombed by day, focusing on industrial and military sites.

Invasion at Normandy

At dawn on June 6, 1944, the largest invasion force in history moved into position in the English Channel. Twenty miles away, across the Channel, lay the German-held northwest region of France, called Normandy. Allied leaders had considered tide schedules and weather reports when they picked June 6 as **"D-Day,"** the day for the operation to begin. General Eisenhower led the Allied forces in the Normandy invasion. He announced by radio: "The tide has turned. The free men of the world are marching together to victory." The D-Day invasion was the turning point of the European war.

While the Allied air forces sought to provide air protection, American soldiers landed on Normandy beaches code-named Utah and Omaha, and the British landed on other nearby beaches. German defenses were strong and the Allied landing was challenged. Losses were heavy, but a beachhead was secured. The Allies then pushed inland yard by yard and mile by mile across some of the same ground fought over in World War I.

On August 25, after a grueling, three-month battle, the Allies liberated Paris. German resistance collapsed rapidly after Paris fell, and by October, just two months

Supplies and troops pour into France during the Normandy invasion. Balloons overhead protect against air attacks on the landing.

later, the Allies had advanced all the way to the Rhine River. But in mid-December the German retreat stopped. Hitler launched an immense counterattack into Belgium in an attempt to recapture the strategic port of Antwerp and divide the Allied forces. Although the Germans did not succeed in taking the port, they did succeed in pushing the Allied lines sixty miles westward at one point. This "bulge" in the lines allowed the Germans to surround an American division in the Belgian town of Bastogne. Other Allied forces rushed to the trapped forces in the resulting **battle of the Bulge.** After a month of battle, the German attack began to slow. The Allies moved in to free those in Bastogne and started pushing the Germans back toward Germany again. Hitler's forces were faltering.

German Defeat

As the Americans and other Allies fought northward from Italy and east from the Rhine, the Soviets were fighting their way west toward Berlin. Although the American forces probably could have won the race and arrived at Berlin first, they elected not to, concentrating instead on capturing Nazi forces and liberating concentration camps.

An additional factor that kept them from Berlin was the **Yalta Meeting** of FDR, Churchill, and Stalin in February 1945. There Soviet "special interests" in Eastern Europe were recognized in return for Stalin's promises of entry into the Pacific war and of holding postwar elections in any countries the Soviets liberated. The Soviet promises proved worthless, but nonetheless, Roosevelt thought these agreements necessary, and Churchill was forced to go along. Yalta would prove to be the last meeting of these two leaders with Stalin. Within a few months Roosevelt was dead, and Britain elected a new prime minister to replace Churchill.

Berlin fell on May 2, 1945, after Hitler had committed suicide two days earlier. On May 7, 1945, the Germans surrendered at a schoolhouse near Rheims (REEMZ). An elated America paused briefly to celebrate "V-E Day" ("Victory in Europe") on May 8. All efforts could be centered on forcing the Japanese to surrender in the Pacific.

Section Review

1. Where was the first major battleground for American soldiers against the Germans in World War II?
2. What country was liberated from Axis rule under "Operation Husky"?
3. What action did the RAF and the U.S. Air Force take against Germany so that the Allies could invade it?
4. Where and when did the largest invasion in history take place? What was this day called?
5. When did Germany finally surrender?

Berlin shortly after the end of the war

E. The War in the Pacific

While the war in Europe was being won, events in the Pacific did not come to a standstill. America put men, ships, and planes into the Japanese conflict as it was able, but the early results were discouraging.

The Japanese Advance

The same day that Japan attacked Pearl Harbor, it also struck at other major targets in the Pacific, including the Philippines. At that time the Philippines still belonged to the United States, and they served as an important American base in the Pacific. On Christmas Eve, 1941, the Japanese made their second large-scale landing on the Philippines. By January they held Manila. The American-Filipino troops, under General **Douglas MacArthur,** held only the Philippine peninsula of Bataan (BAH tahn) and the small, nearby island of Corregidor (kuh REHG ih DOR). But when it was realized that it would be impossible for American forces to keep the Philippines, MacArthur was ordered to leave. The United States did not want to risk the capture of a valuable general; so MacArthur escaped to safety in Australia. As he left, he promised the Filipinos, "I shall return."

With supply lines cut off, the American troops remaining in the Philippines ran low on supplies. They suffered from disease and starvation. Even in their weakened condition, they battled to defend Bataan, but it was not enough. On April 8, 1942, most troops on the Bataan peninsula had to surrender to the Japanese. The captured Allied troops were forced to march in tropical heat, without food or water, for sixty-five miles to a prison camp. Thirteen thousand of the American forces in the Philippines had escaped to Corregidor. By early May the

World War II in the Pacific

Japanese were shelling the island constantly. Finally the remaining men surrendered. The Japanese controlled all of the Philippines.

Meanwhile the Japanese had also captured most of Southeast Asia and many of the islands in the Pacific. In June the Japanese turned northward and even snatched two of the Aleutian Islands just off the tip of southern Alaska. To America's dismay, the Japanese seemed to control the entire region of eastern Asia and the western Pacific.

American shipyards and munitions factories were gradually making progress. They were soon able to launch and equip new aircraft carriers within fifteen months from the time their construction began. Soon, battleships, aircraft carriers, and escort vessels sailed westward to help push back the Japanese.

The Rising Sun Begins to Set

In the spring and summer of 1942, Americans saw a ray of hope in the Pacific war. On April 8, 1942, the aircraft carrier *Hornet* secretly sailed within seven hundred miles of the Japanese mainland. Sixteen B-25 bombers under the command of Jimmy Doolittle shocked the Japanese by dropping bombs on Tokyo and other Japanese cities. This successful operation was a tremendous boost to the morale of the Americans.

After the bombings, Japan changed its war strategy. The Japanese split their force of aircraft carriers. Two were sent to harass Allied naval supply lines near Australia. The other four giant carriers moved into the middle of the Pacific, acting as magnets to draw the United States into battle there. Because the Japanese lacked the productive power to fight a long war, they gambled everything on a quick victory.

The Japanese aircraft carriers heading for Australia used the Coral Sea as an approach lane. In May of 1942 they met an American naval force led by two aircraft carriers, the *Yorktown* and the *Lexington*. The resulting three-day **battle of the Coral Sea** was unusual because it was the first sea battle in which all of the fighting was done by airplanes. The Japanese force turned back, and one of its carriers was sunk. The *Lexington* suffered such extensive damage that it had to be destroyed, but the battle successfully stopped Japanese advances toward Australia.

The other Japanese aircraft carriers had headed toward Midway Island, an American island west of Hawaii. The Japanese hoped to attack the island base and then lure American carriers into a battle. But by this time American naval intelligence had cracked the Japanese radio code and had advance warning. Planes from American carriers bombed the Japanese ships in advance, preventing the attack on Midway. The Americans sank three Japanese carriers in a few minutes, and the fourth went down the next day. The cost to America was also high. The Americans lost one aircraft carrier, and most of the planes and their pilots had been shot down. However, the huge Japanese sea offensive was stopped and the Japanese navy had suffered a defeat.

The Americans then planned a strategy to capture the Japanese-held islands in the Pacific. Starting with the southern islands,

Bottom: *The sinking of the U.S.S.* Yorktown *in the battle of Midway*
Right: *American planes soaring toward a defeat of Japan*

they would work their way northward until they reached islands within bombing distance of Japan. General MacArthur would head one operation that would push northward from New Guinea to the Philippines. Admiral **Chester Nimitz** (NIM itz) would "island-hop" across the mid-Pacific, taking certain key islands in three chains: the Gilberts, the Marshalls, and the Marianas. Then both forces would converge on the Japanese mainland.

MacArthur Moves Northward

The Japanese, meanwhile, had almost finished an airfield on **Guadalcanal** (GWOD ul kuh NAL) in the Solomon Islands near New Guinea. From there they could bomb Allied convoys at will. Consequently, MacArthur began his offensive there in 1943, but it took six months to drive the Japanese out. The Japanese fought tena-

General MacArthur (front right) returning to the Philippines

ciously, and American casualties were heavy. Finally, the marines dynamited the island's caves to force out the last Japanese defenders.

The American attack on New Guinea became bogged down and was saved only when General MacArthur airlifted fifteen thousand troops there. By October 1944 MacArthur's forces were ready to retake the Philippines, landing first at Leyte (LAY tee). Many liberty-loving Filipino fighters who had hidden in the mountains and jungles now undertook guerrilla warfare to help the Americans free the Philippines. MacArthur said: "I have returned. By the grace of Almighty God, our forces stand again on Philippine soil, soil consecrated by the blood of our two peoples." By March 1945 the forces had moved northward and had freed the Philippine capital of Manila on the island of Luzon.

Nimitz Moves West

The first target of Admiral Nimitz's Pacific operation was Tarawa, the largest atoll (a ring-like island of coral) in the Gilbert Islands. After bombing the island for a whole week and pounding it for hours with heavy gunfire, the Americans did not expect much resistance. They soon discovered how well the Japanese held out. While American losses soared, the Japanese held on until only seventeen of more than forty-five hundred defenders remained alive.

The Americans learned lessons for future attacks. The Japanese did not surrender easily. Two months of bombing before landing troops became normal. Thousands of tons of explosives would be hurled shoreward by battleships at Japanese targets from this point on.

After launching such attacks in the Marshall Islands, the Nimitz forces recaptured Guam in the Marianas. Next the sea east of the Philippines was retaken from the Japanese. The fleet then angled northward to take **Iwo Jima** (EE-woh JEE-muh). This small island, only seven hundred miles from Tokyo, had been a station from which the Japanese could intercept American bombers headed for Japan. If the United States could capture it, Iwo Jima could serve as an emergency landing place and refueling stop for American bombers. It could also provide a takeoff point for shorter-range fighter planes. But Iwo Jima proved to be the costliest chunk of rock and black sand captured by the U.S. Marine Corps in their 168 year history. Over five thousand marines died during its capture in early 1945.

As war with the Japanese intensified, the Allied seamen began to fear a new type of Japanese attack: the **kamikazes** (KAH mih KAH zeez). Kamikazes were suicide attack planes. Their pilots deliberately hurled these planes at an enemy target. Such attacks were a product of the Japanese teaching that the highest gift one could give the emperor was one's life. Furthermore,

Japan had lost both its first-rate pilots and its best planes. In kamikaze warfare out-of-date planes could be loaded with explosives and flown by inexperienced pilots who had only to dive into a ship. The results were devastating. Kamikazes sank 30 ships, damaged 368 more, and killed 11,000 sailors. In spite of the kamikaze attacks, the American forces pushed on toward Japan.

Taking **Okinawa** (OH kih NOW wah) was the last obstacle to reaching the Japanese mainland. The assault on Okinawa began in April 1945 and was completed in June. The Japanese fought hard; over 110,000 died, leaving 11,000 to surrender. But now Americans were just 325 miles from mainland Japan and able to attack both Japan's industrial and population centers. In one ten-day bombing blitz American planes turned thirty-two square miles of factories into wastelands. Fire bombing of residential areas was especially destructive because the Japanese homes were built close together and were constructed of highly inflammable materials.

Section Review

1. What American general was forced to evacuate while attempting to hold the Philippines?
2. What two American military leaders took command of much of the action against Japan?
3. An airfield on which of the Solomon Islands took the Americans six months to capture?
4. What were kamikazes? Why did the Japanese use them despite the tragic waste of human life?
5. What was the last American conquest before attacking the Japanese mainland?

Sailors attempt to control the blaze after a kamikaze plane crashes into the U.S.S. Enterprise.

F. The End of the War

American forces were closing in on all sides, and Japan was suffering heavily from bombing raids. The American military had learned, however, how hard the Japanese would fight. Many feared that it would take hundreds of thousands of American lives to invade and conquer Japan.

The Beginning of the Atomic Era

In 1933, when Hitler had gained power and had taken action against the German Jews, a professor of physics named Albert Einstein had taken refuge in the United States. Aware of the Nazis' efforts to develop a uranium bomb, Einstein wrote the president in July 1939 to advise him of the possibilities and dangers of such a weapon. Leaders in the United States decided to set up a secret program to make such a bomb before the Germans could.

A group of brilliant scientists joined this **"Manhattan Project."** In Los Alamos, New Mexico, the Manhattan Project engineers assembled the materials for the bomb. At dawn on July 16, 1945, the first device was successfully tested in New Mexico.

On April 12, 1945, Franklin Roosevelt, by then in his fourth term as president, died from the effects of a stroke. The day after he stepped into the presidency, **Harry S. Truman** was told of the Manhattan Project. He decided that it would be better to end the war quickly with the new weapon than to spend countless thousands of lives in an invasion of Japan. Although in later years people debated Truman's approval of dropping the bomb, Truman wrote in his *Memoirs:* "Let there be no mistake about it. I regarded the bomb as a military weapon and never had any doubt that it should be used."

On July 26, when President Truman met at Potsdam in Germany for a conference with the major powers, he issued the **Potsdam Declaration.** It demanded that Japan surrender unconditionally or face total destruction.

Although the original military leaders in Japan's war effort were no longer in power, the new premier refused to surrender. Eleven days later, on August 6, 1945, at 8:15 A.M., an American bomber dropped a single uranium bomb on **Hiroshima** (HIR uh SHE muh). Although it was only a little more than two feet in diameter and ten feet long, the bomb's explosive power was equal to twenty thousand tons of dynamite. The blast killed eighty thousand Japanese civilians, and an equal number suffered radiation burns.

After another warning to surrender was ignored, the United States dropped a single plutonium bomb, called "Fat Boy," on **Nagasaki** (NAH guh SAH kee) on August 9. This bomb flattened the city and killed about forty thousand people.

Peace

The next day Japan sued for peace. On August 15, 1945, the Japanese people heard the voice of their emperor Hirohito. In a taped radio broadcast, the emperor told his subjects that the war was over. Americans

A "mushroom" cloud rises above Nagasaki, Japan, following the atomic explosion in 1945.

Harry S. Truman
33RD PRESIDENT
(1945-1953)

Born: Lamar, Missouri, May 8, 1884
Family: married Bess Wallace; one
daughter
Occupation: clerk, haberdasher, farmer,
soldier
Home: Independence, Missouri
Religion: Baptist
Election: succeeded to the presidency
upon the death of Franklin Roosevelt
1948—defeated Thomas E. Dewey
(Republican), Strom Thurmond (States'
Rights), and Henry Wallace
(Progressive)
Political Party: Democrat
Vice President: none (first term), Alben
Barkley (second term)
Interesting Facts and Accomplishments:
lived in the Blair House (across the street
from the White House) during most of
his administration because the White
House was under renovation
an accomplished pianist who played for a
White House gathering when Kennedy
was president
was the only twentieth century president
who did not attend college
Death: December 26, 1972

at home ran into the streets, temporarily leaving their jobs, and hugged one another from sheer joy.

Although a few Japanese groups in distant spots continued to fight, the war was really over. On August 21 General MacArthur was in Tokyo. As he watched the same flag that had flown over the U.S. Capitol on December 7, 1941, go up over the reestablished American embassy, he said, "Let it wave in full glory as a symbol of hope for the oppressed and as a harbinger of victory."

On September 2, 1945, MacArthur accepted two of the emperor's representatives on board the battleship *Missouri* anchored in Tokyo Bay. There they signed the formal treaty of surrender.

World War II was the costliest war in history. It is estimated that over fifteen million soldiers and twenty million civilians died in the war. The United States lost nearly three hundred thousand of its military personnel, and many more were wounded. On top of its human effort and loss, the nation spent about $300 billion on the war.

Americans returned to peacetime with great relief that the price had been paid and the war had been won. It then remained for them to take their place in the postwar world.

Section Review

1. What was the Manhattan Project?
2. Who became president before the war ended?
3. On what two cities were the atomic bombs dropped?
4. Where, when, and by whom was the Japanese surrender accepted?
5. How many American servicemen died in the war?

Summary

The fascist governments that arose in Germany and Italy began to threaten Europe in the late 1930s, while Japan's militaristic government wanted more control in Asia and the Pacific. The desires of these nations led them to band together as the Axis powers and brought Britain and France into war against them in 1939. Hitler's German armies soon took control of most of Europe, including France. For over a year, Britain stood alone against the Axis powers. The United States aided the Allied cause by supplying materials, but it was unwilling to join in the war until Japan bombed the American naval base at Pearl Harbor in December 1941.

With that attack, the United States entered the war and began to build its military strength to defeat its enemies. With Britain, the United States concentrated first on defeating Hitler and Mussolini in Europe. Campaigns were launched in North Africa, Italy, and France, and the Allied advances finally brought victory in Europe on May 8, 1945.

In the east the Japanese had taken control of much of Southeast Asia and the Pacific Islands. They had even taken control of America's Philippine Islands. But American forces began to battle back, winning control of island after island until they reached islands within bombing distance of Japan. Rather than risk a large scale invasion, two atomic bombs were dropped on Japan. This action forced the Japanese to surrender and ended World War II in August 1945. The United States emerged from the war as leader of the free world and as a nation with many postwar problems.

Chapter Review

Do You Remember?

■ What word or words best describe each of the following things?
1. governments (or leaders) of strong, controlled dictatorships that stress nationalism and power
2. giving in to someone's demands in an attempt to settle a disagreement peacefully
3. a swift attack of bombers, tanks, and troops—a "lighting war"
4. young men who were sincerely opposed to war and were thus allowed to serve in noncombat roles instead of regular military service
5. Japanese planes flown on suicide missions to destroy American ships

■ Match each of the following men with his country.
  6. Franklin Roosevelt   a. Britain
  7. Benito Mussolini   b. Germany
  8. Joseph Stalin   c. Italy
  9. Adolf Hitler   d. Soviet Union
  10. Harry Truman   e. United States
  11. Winston Churchill

■ Match the appropriate letter on the timeline that corresponds with the date of each of these events. Also indicate why each one of these events was significant.
  12. V-E Day
  13. attack on Pearl Harbor
  14. Hitler invades Poland
  15. bomb dropped on Hiroshima
  16. D-Day

Why Is It So?
  1. Why were Germany, Italy, and Japan displeased with the outcome of World War I?
  2. Why did Hitler sign a pact with Stalin in 1939?
  3. Why was the United States not well prepared for war in 1941?
  4. Why was the United States called "the arsenal of democracy"?
  5. Why did the United States agree to help the Allies defeat Hitler first?
  6. Why did the Americans wish to gain control of Iwo Jima and Okinawa?

What Do You Think?
  1. Should the United States have been better prepared for World War II? Should it be constantly prepared for war? Explain your answers.
  2. How does a man like Hitler gain such popularity and power? Could such a man rise to power in the United States? Explain your answer.
  3. Why did the United States drop the atomic bomb on Japan? Was it a good decision? Explain your answer.

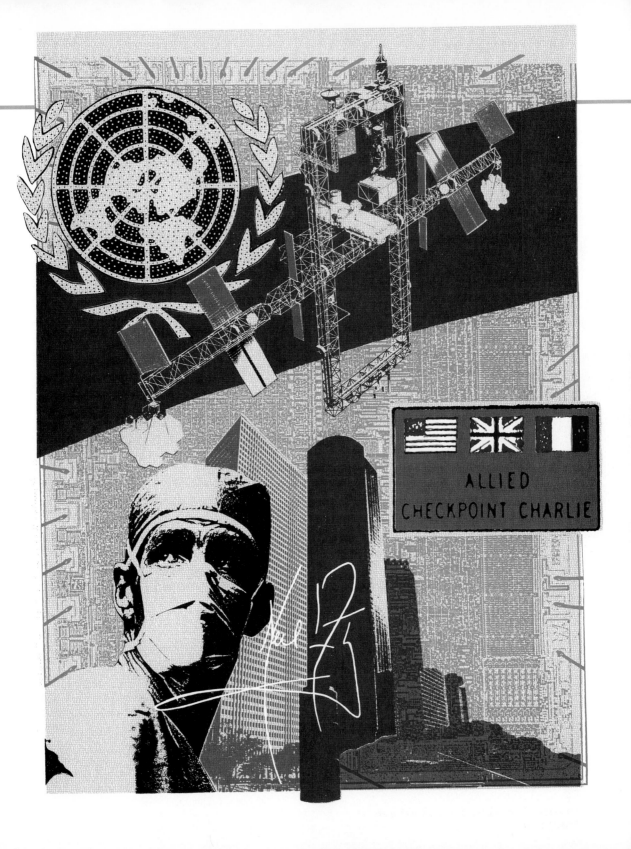

27

Recovery, Cold War, and Coexistence

President Truman shakes hands with General Eisenhower.

At 7:00 P.M. (EST) on August 14, 1945, President Harry Truman announced to the nation that Japan had finally accepted the terms of surrender. Church bells rang. Whistles blew. Troop ships halfway across the Pacific turned around and headed home. World War II was over! Four years of conflict on the battlefields, on the seas, and in the air had come to a halt. The United States was at peace.

The war was over, but the United States faced new challenges that would prove to be almost as trying as the war had been. The world after the war was not the same as the one that had existed before. New problems, new threats, and new fears emerged in the postwar era. But the country would also have new opportunities and new technological improvements that would bring a new prosperity.

A. Home from the War

The end of the war brought nine million men in uniform home to civilian life. It brought the retooling of industries to produce peacetime goods instead of guns and tanks. It opened the way for new inventions, new styles, and new fads to change America's way of life.

Changing Times

Many Americans feared that a depression would follow World War II as it had World War I or that the nation would return to the hardships of the Great Depression. Instead of another depression, however, Americans found plenty of jobs, and they kept businesses booming with their desire for more and more material goods. They wanted new comforts and labor-saving devices such as dishwashers, automatic washers, electric dryers, power lawn mowers, and boats. The easy availability of credit encouraged such purchasing.

Since some consumer goods had been either rationed or totally unavailable during the war, people were now ready to buy what they could not buy before. In 1944 factories had produced 100,000 planes and only 70,000 passenger cars. In 1949 only 6,000 planes were produced, but 3.7 million passenger cars rolled off assembly lines. The major problem was that so many goods were in demand, factories could not produce enough to satisfy the public. Prices on many goods skyrocketed until the demand was met. But as more factories got in gear to produce needed items, inflation settled down, and the economy became stable.

Another aid to Americans after the war was the **GI Bill.** Fearful that soldiers returning from war would be unemployed, as many were after World War I, Congress passed a bill that helped the veterans move right into civilian life. Veterans were granted benefits in many areas, including help in finding jobs and money for education and for home purchases.

While the young men were away at war, many young couples had postponed marriage. With the war over, many newlyweds began to start families, and the resulting

"baby boom" created tremendous new demands, which changed over the years as the children grew. A demand for housing was followed by a demand for baby goods such as diapers, baby food, and strollers. When these children started school, there were acute shortages of classrooms and teachers.

With housing shortages in the early postwar years and the high cost of land in the cities, more Americans became willing to move to the suburbs. Contractors built homes cheaply and quickly, using the techniques of mass production. Bulldozers graded the lots, and work crews came to lay water, gas, sewer, and electrical lines. They were followed by carpenters, who built row after row of identical houses. Roofers, plumbers, electricians, and painters applied their skills as well. Rolling fields turned into suburbs in a few weeks or months.

Most (about ninety-five per cent) of those who moved to homes in the suburbs were younger whites. Cities were left to be occupied by the poor (mostly the elderly and racial minorities). Since cities could not collect heavy taxes from the poor, they had to function with less money. Thus cities started to decay and sought government aid for urban renewal projects.

To live in the suburbs, Americans needed more cars. Two-car families became common as the breadwinner needed a car to drive to work and the family wanted to use another. With more cars came more automotive-related industries like service stations and car washes. To cut the travel distance to stores, shopping centers were started. Cities spread out so much that some described the situation as "urban sprawl."

Naturally, the traffic increased, and commuter traffic jams became more common. These problems and the desire to be able to move troops and equipment in case of war prompted the government to promote more and better highways. In 1956 a **Federal Aid Highway Act** was passed. This allowed construction of 41,000 miles of interstate highways at a cost of $28 million over thirteen years. Increased use of

auto, truck, and air transportation cut back the use of railroads.

With cars, highways, and the availability of new jobs, Americans were willing to move from their hometowns and to relocate. They moved to sections of the country that offered new jobs. The West, especially California, offered the biggest attraction. The South and the Southwest also grew. This was the beginning of the **"sunbelt migrations,"** movements toward the areas of the country with warmer climates.

The war had produced changes in technology. Scientists had worked hard during the war to find new materials and inventions that would improve the war effort and

Beginning in the 1950s, the interstate highway system changed the landscape of America.

President Truman delivering a radio address

supply substitutes for materials that were in low supply. Now that the war was over, some war inventions and materials had peacetime applications. New medicines and vaccines had been developed for diseases. Synthetic fibers, plastics, and other new materials became useful for industries. New hybrid crops, insecticides, machinery, fertilizer, and better irrigation techniques allowed American farmers to grow more crops than ever before. These changes in American agriculture have sometimes been called the **"green revolution."**

Changes in technology also affected the use of leisure time. Although television had been made workable as early as 1927, it was not perfected until after World War II. In 1946 there were seven thousand televisions. By 1950 there were four million TV sets. By 1960 there were 74 million sets. Television had many effects on Americans.

One was the lessening of regional differences as people from the North, South, East, and West all watched the same TV programs.

Crazes were also common in the postwar decade. More than thirty million Americans purchased hula hoops, large plastic rings that could be twirled for exercise. A Walt Disney television series based on the life of a frontier hero, Davy Crockett, led to a whole series of products. Children carried Davy Crockett lunch boxes and wore "coonskin" caps and buckskin jackets while singing about the "King of the Wild Frontier."

The Fair Deal

Although the depression of the 1930s had ended, many people still wanted the government aid that Franklin Roosevelt's New Deal had given them. Americans wondered if the new president, Harry Truman, would continue support of similar programs. Their answer came in September 1945. The president called Congress into special session to detail a twenty-one-point domestic program that he called a **"Fair Deal."** The policies were similar to those of the New Deal but included the GI Bill, provided better treatment of black Americans, increased aid to science and public education, and subsidized medical insurance. Not all of Truman's ideas were accepted by Congress, but they helped give the American people some assurance that government would continue to come to their aid.

One of the issues that did not go Truman's way was the control of labor unions. During the days of high inflation after the war, laborers wanted higher wages without price increases. Some of the unions resorted to major strikes to get their way. Auto, steel, coal, and railroad workers went on strike for higher wages. With the growing number of strikes, some Americans thought that unions had gained too much power. Truman had difficulty controlling the labor unrest himself, but he did not like the way the Republican Congress dealt with it either.

Congress passed the **Taft-Hartley Act** of 1947 over the veto of Truman. The act limited the powers of unions by giving employees more freedom to work against unions. The bill outlawed the closed shop, a practice that forced businesses to hire only union members. It permitted states to pass laws prohibiting union shops that required workers to join the union within a certain date of their hiring. In addition, unions had to give a sixty-day notice before changing or ending work contracts. During that time they could not strike. Moreover, if a proposed strike threatened the nation's health or safety, an eighty-day **injunction,** a court

order forbidding the strike, could be issued. During that time the strikers and the management were required to settle the dispute through negotiations.

In the years following the war, **civil rights** (rights guaranteed by the Constitution to every American citizen) for America's blacks became an increasingly important issue. Although Congress rejected Truman's civil rights legislation, the president did try to lessen discrimination against blacks through the influence of his position.

Both the North and the South practiced segregation. Although not required by law in the North, segregation existed in fact. Blacks generally lived in their own neighborhoods and went to black neighborhood schools and businesses. In the South **Jim Crow laws** segregated blacks from whites in schools, theaters, restaurants, and on buses.

Changes came slowly. In 1946 President Truman appointed the President's Committee on Civil Rights. In 1948, by executive order, the president banned segregation in the armed forces. In World War II President Roosevelt had issued an executive order saying that the federal government would not contract its business to any firms that discriminated against minorities. President Truman continued the policy and also formed a committee to investigate instances of alleged discrimination.

These actions during the Truman administration advanced the civil rights movement. Other changes were made to help integrate blacks in other areas. In 1947 Jackie Robinson became the first black to play major league baseball when he joined the Brooklyn Dodgers. Higher education also began to open to blacks as the University of Oklahoma began to admit blacks to graduate school in 1948.

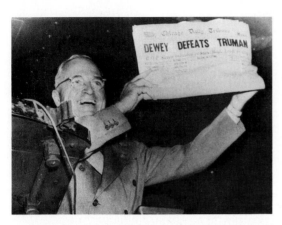

Truman's idea of giving a Fair Deal to the American people helped him win the presidential election of 1948. He had not been especially popular in his first few years as president. Political pollsters said his Republican opponent, Thomas E. Dewey, was a sure winner, and newspapers printed on election night declared the same. But when the ballots were counted, both the pollsters and the papers were wrong. Truman had waged an exhausting campaign, traveling across America making speeches from the end of a railroad car. The public apparently admired his fighting spirit. "I met the people face to face," he explained, "and . . . they voted for me."

Section Review

1. What happened to America's economy after the war?
2. What were some of the benefits of the GI Bill?
3. To what areas (local and regional) did many Americans move in the postwar years?
4. What was Truman's overall program called?
5. What act was passed to limit excessive power of labor unions?

Truman could smile because the headlines were wrong.

B.   Postwar Problems

The United States emerged from World War II as the most powerful nation in the world, but it now had one strong rival— the Soviet Union. These two nations had fought as allies in the war, but the differences of these two postwar world powers would create great tensions. As Europe and Eastern Asia lay in ruin after the havoc of war, they needed help for rebuilding from the superpowers. The problem was that American ideas on how they should be rebuilt often conflicted with the demands of the Soviet Union.

Postwar Germany

Because Germany's government under Hitler had been defeated, the Germans were left without a government at the war's end. To fill this power vacuum, the Allies divided Germany into four sectors or sections. The three sectors of what is now West Germany were occupied by American, British, and French troops. Modern East Germany was the Soviet-occupied sector. The Soviet Union quickly showed that it would have its way in East Germany by making sure that its economy and politics were Communist-controlled. Tensions developed in Germany that would soon result in major problems between the United States and the Soviet Union.

Another concern for the Allies was what to do with Germany's former Nazi leaders. As Allied troops liberated the German-occupied areas of Europe, they discovered concentration camps. Terrible atrocities had taken place in these camps, especially against Jews. The Allies decided to try the Nazi leaders publicly as war criminals. The trials began in 1945 in Nuremberg, Germany, and further unraveled the grim story of

Hitler's Germany. In October 1946 the international court at the **Nuremberg trials** condemned twelve Nazi leaders to death for "crimes against peace" and "crimes against humanity." The trials of lesser Nazi officials continued over many more months, though more quietly.

Dealing With Japan

Japan had been destroyed by the war. Her cities and harbors lay in ruin. Her merchant fleet had been sunk. The United States avoided trouble with the Soviet Union over the rebuilding of Japan by taking sole responsibility for helping that country. Truman appointed General Douglas MacArthur to head a military government in postwar Japan that could supervise its recovery.

The United States helped the Japanese write a new constitution. The Japanese elected a legislative body and gave rights to all citizens. Women got the right to vote. As in Germany, war criminals went to trial. In an effort to help rebuild the lives of the Japanese and to instill spiritual values, General MacArthur encouraged missionaries to come to Japan. Thus the door to Japan again opened to the gospel.

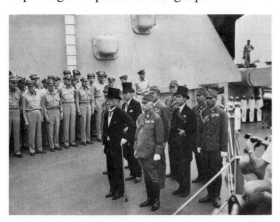

Japanese officials signing the surrender aboard the U.S.S. Missouri *in 1945*

The UNRRA (United Nations Relief and Recovery Administration) sent aid to the Japanese from 1945 to 1948. The United States was the chief donor to this organization, which provided food, clothing, and medicine to meet immediate needs. Japan rebuilt quickly, soon becoming a thriving industrial nation. In 1951 the United States ended its military occupation of Japan. The United States had helped Japan to rebuild, gaining her as a powerful ally for the free world.

The United States Aids Europe

Europeans, who had seen World War II fought on their own lands, had suffered more than Americans. Millions of their soldiers and civilians had been killed. Millions of the survivors were homeless, wandering from place to place seeking shelter and food. To many of these "displaced persons" life seemed hopeless. There was no one to hire them. The war-time governments of the defeated countries no longer existed, and the winners were so deeply in debt from their own war efforts that they could do little to help. Bombing and fighting had destroyed most industries. Railroads and roads were in ruin. Because they had been bombed or burned, farmlands did not produce, and near-famine conditions existed in Europe.

The United States went to work aiding Europe. First it furnished aid through the UNRRA. Immediate needs were met through shipment of tons of food, clothing, and medicine. Because Communists could and did make easy inroads among the discontented and downtrodden, the United States demonstrated a special concern for such people in an effort to keep them from ignorantly accepting Communist influence.

On June 5, 1947, Secretary of State **George Marshall** proposed a vast new aid program for Europe. He asked Congress for huge sums of money to rebuild the European countries ravaged by war. The **Marshall Plan** offered aid even to Eastern European countries already subjected to Soviet control. But the Soviet Union rejected the offer. It would not allow its satellites (Soviet-dominated countries) to take advantage of the offer.

Although the Marshall Plan cost a great deal (more than $17 billion), it did aid European recovery. The Western European countries who received American help rebuilt quickly and soon surpassed their prewar production.

The Formation of the United Nations

Throughout World War II the Allies had held eleven conferences to plot strategy and

deal with problems. The idea of a postwar peace-keeping organization to replace the League of Nations was voiced at the meeting in Teheran late in 1943. Because of increased tensions among the Allies, especially between free countries and the Soviet Union, the topic was raised again at Yalta in February 1945. The Big Three—the United States, Britain, and the Soviet Union—called for a meeting of nations at San Francisco to write a charter for another world peace-keeping organization.

On April 25, 1945, just thirteen days after the death of President Roosevelt, President Truman welcomed delegates from fifty nations to San Francisco. During the two months of discussion, the delegates had many arguments. Some threatened to leave the meetings because the Soviet demands were too selfish. Finally enough concessions

Secretary of State George C. Marshall

were made to forge a charter for the new **United Nations** organization.

A permanent world headquarters for the United Nations was established in 1947 when John D. Rockefeller, Jr., provided $8.5 million to construct a building. The city of New York gave land; the United States provided a generous loan of $65 million. The new headquarters opened in 1952.

The Organizational Structure of the United Nations—The three most important parts of the U.N. are the **General Assembly,** the **Security Council,** and the **Secretariat.** The General Assembly was to be somewhat like a legislature. Every member nation was to send a representative. By 1986 it consisted of the delegates of 159 countries. The General Assembly really has little power, however, since the nations are not forced to abide by its decisions.

The Security Council had five permanent member nations and six (now ten) nonpermanent members. The latter are elected by the General Assembly for two-year terms and are usually drawn from the smaller countries. The Security Council is the strongest part of the U.N. because it has the power to enforce U.N. policy with military action. But because any one of the five permanent members (the United States, Britain, France, China, and the Soviet Union) can exercise veto power to stop a decision, the council's power is often curtailed. It has acted successfully only in minor disputes or when the Big Five decided to use force. The Soviet Union has vetoed more than a hundred decisions of the council—more than all the other members combined. Moreover, since the seat of Free China has now been given to Communist China, the chance of a veto by a Communist power is doubled.

The final major body of the U.N. is the Secretariat. The Secretariat is a type of executive branch, composed of U.N. agencies and administrators that handle the daily affairs of the organization. It is headed by a secretary-general elected by the General Assembly.

Weighing the Successes of the United Nations—From a Christian viewpoint it is admirable to settle disputes peacefully, as the United Nations intends. Knowing the possible consequences of today's weapons, few people want war. Yet no matter how strong and exemplary the desires for peace may be, the sinful nature of man works against them.

Although some people and nations believe that it is important to do right and keep one's word, others are mainly concerned with what will benefit them most. Sinful man will often do what he can to get ahead, even if he must disregard the rights of others to do so. Because they are led by sinful men, countries are often guilty of unjust actions. Communist countries in particular tend to honor an agreement only when it benefits them. Appealing to a higher level, that of honoring God, is fruitless because God means nothing to them. Thus, agreements made in the United Nations have little chance for success.

Moreover, the record of the U.N. shows its ineffectiveness. It has neither brought peace nor ended war. Since its founding, at least seventy-five wars have erupted in the world, and more than one-third of the world's population has come under Communist domination. The member nations of the United Nations fall into three major categories—free world nations, Communist nations, and the **third world.** (The third world includes the many poor nations of

Africa, Asia, and Latin America.) Because the third-world nations are generally poor and politically unstable, Communist influences have often swayed these countries to accept Communist ideas and side with the Soviet Union in disputes at the United Nations. This Communist influence creates problems for the United States in its dealings with these third-world countries. In addition, the existence of the U.N. in New York has allowed many foreign countries to spy in the United States legally, a practice contrary to the best interests of Americans.

Although the words of Isaiah 2:4—"They shall beat their swords into plowshares, and their spears into pruning hooks: nation shall not lift up sword against nation, neither shall they learn war any more"—appear in the U.N. headquarters, in God's Word the verses refer to Christ's coming kingdom. Only after Christ's return to earth will there be true peace. The United Nations cannot stop that turmoil; only God can. Yet Christians are not to be troubled over these things. The Christian's refuge is not in the organizations of man, but in the arms of the almighty God.

Section Review

1. How was Germany divided after the war?
2. Why were the Nuremberg trials necessary?
3. Who was in charge of military occupation in postwar Japan? What were some of the changes that resulted?
4. What plan was developed for giving aid to Europe after the war?
5. What are the three major bodies of the United Nations? Which body is the strongest?

C. Cold War Crises

Because the threat of Hitler and Nazism was great, the United States and the Soviet Union became allies in World War II. When the war was over, however, the United States soon learned that the Soviets were out to gain all they could in the postwar disarray. In the years after the war there developed what was called the **Cold War.** The United States and the Soviet Union did not go into a direct military conflict with each other, but they found themselves in many disputes that sprang from the tensions between them. Fear of a third world war erupting between the two countries was often present.

At Yalta Stalin had pledged to hold free elections in Poland and in other areas where the Soviets took control. But he had no intention of allowing any nation that the Soviets occupied to choose its own form of government. By organizing Communist parties in the countries of Eastern Europe even before World War II, the Soviets had laid the groundwork for Communist takeover. As Soviet troops moved in to occupy Eastern Europe at the war's end, they placed Communists in government positions. In this way they took over the governments of Bulgaria, Yugoslavia, Albania, Rumania, Poland, Hungary, and later Czechoslovakia. To insure that these countries remained in the Communist camp, Red Army units remained in each nation, keeping pro-Soviet leaders in control despite opposition from the people.

On March 5, 1946, Britain's World War II leader, Winston Churchill, came to Fulton, Missouri, to speak at Westminster College. Churchill graphically described the problem in Eastern Europe: "From Stettin in the Baltic to Trieste in the Adriatic, an iron curtain has descended across the Continent." From then on countries who came under Communist control were said to be "behind the Iron Curtain." Churchill believed that the West would have to take firm action to halt future Communist expansion.

The Truman Doctrine: Containing Communism

The Soviets soon proved Churchill's point by showing that they were not content to control only Eastern Europe. Their next goal was to claim the oil-rich Middle East.

Allied troops had occupied Iran during World War II to keep open its vital oil supply. When the war ended, American and British troops withdrew, but Soviet troops remained. Soviet-inspired rioting took place, and Iranian troops who sought to restore order were kept from doing so. When Iran, with American backing, complained to the U.N., the Soviet troops left.

Meanwhile, Communist-led guerrillas in Greece were gaining ground in their efforts to take control. Turkey also seemed to be on the brink of tumbling into the Soviet camp. President Truman finally saw that it was essential for the United States to "contain" communism, that is, to stop the Soviets from overtaking more governments. To carry out the **containment** policy, the president asked Congress to approve $400 million for military aid to support the pro-Western governments in Greece and Turkey. The idea of using military aid to support pro-Western, anti-Communist governments soon got the name **Truman Doctrine.**

Confrontation in Germany

When Germany was divided among the Allies after the war, the country's old capital of Berlin was in the middle of Soviet-controlled East Germany. Because Berlin was such an important city, the Allies agreed to divide its control among themselves. It had four zones, one each for France, Britain, the United States, and the Soviet Union. Supplies were shipped to the French, British, and American zones of Berlin from the West by truck or train across Soviet-held lands.

When the United States, Britain, and France decided to combine their sectors of Germany, the Soviet Union responded by denying all road, rail, and river access across East Germany to Berlin, beginning June 24, 1948. This violation of the Yalta agreement left two million residents of West Berlin without food and other supplies. The Soviet Union thought that its blockade would force the Allies out of Berlin. Stalin also believed that his action would undermine the confidence of the European Allies in the United States.

President Truman responded quickly to the Soviet threat. He announced that the United States would use a massive airlift to West Berlin. For the next 321 days, more than 250,000 flights carried supplies into West Berlin. More than 2.5 million tons of supplies were airlifted to the blockaded city. The Soviets did not attack the planes, as some had predicted. When the Soviets realized that the United States was prepared to keep the **Berlin airlift** going indefinitely, it lifted its blockade in May 1949.

Since the Soviet Union had taken such a strong grip on East Germany, attempts for unification of Germany seemed futile. In September 1949, the United States, Britain, and France allowed the sectors of Germany they held to become an independent nation. The new Federal Republic of Germany (West Germany) was formed, with Bonn as its capital.

Alliances and Aid

Because of the Soviet threat to the parts of Europe that remained free, President Truman believed that these nations needed more than financial aid. He asked Congress for military support and the formation of a joint alliance, with the United States as a member. The alliance, called the **North Atlantic Treaty Organization** (NATO), united the Western European nations of Britain, France, Italy, Portugal, the Netherlands, Denmark, Norway, Belgium, and Luxemburg, as well as the North Atlantic countries of Canada, Iceland, and the United States. In 1952 Greece and Turkey joined, and in 1959, West Germany. These nations agreed to provide money, troops, and military equipment for mutual protection. General Dwight D. Eisenhower became the first supreme commander of NATO forces. America's membership in NATO meant a change in its long-standing policy of isolationism. It was the first peace-time alliance that the United States had ever joined for the possible defense of other nations.

The Soviets, responding to the Berlin airlift and the formation of NATO, gathered representatives of their Eastern European satellites in Warsaw, Poland. The Soviets then organized their own military alliance, called the **Warsaw Pact.** The Warsaw Pact nations included Poland, Albania, East Germany, Bulgaria, Rumania, Czechoslovakia, and the Soviet Union.

The China Question

Just as postwar Europe was undergoing change, so was the Far East. China became a special problem. China was the most populous nation in the world. The Communists, led by **Mao Tse-Tung,** were poised to gain control of the country after World War II.

China had suffered from fighting warlords and domineering foreign countries in the decades before the war. Generalissimo **Chiang Kai-shek,** had emerged as leader of the strong "Nationalist" group in China. The United States had made trade agreements with Chiang and had aided the Chinese against Japan in World War II. Chiang's efforts to defeat the Japanese in China and to control China, however, were being sabotaged from within his own party by corruption and internal conflicts. Some American troops were sent to aid Chiang, but they were pulled out in 1947.

Almost immediately China was again engulfed in war. This conflict was between the Communists, led by Mao, and the Nationalists, led by Chiang. Mao's forces were highly motivated. The Communists had promised to give land to the poor. By 1949 the Communists had gained control

Mao Tse-Tung, Communist leader of China

of the mainland. They forced Chiang to flee with his army to the coastal island of Taiwan, where he set up Nationalist China (also called the Republic of China or Free China). Mainland China became the Communist "People's Republic of China."

The presence of communism in China posed a new threat. China and the Soviet Union signed the Sino-Soviet Pact in February 1950, confirming American suspicions that the Communists might try to work together against the free world. President Truman, and several presidents who followed him, steadfastly supported Chiang and his government on Taiwan, at least in theory. Some Americans preferred, however, to recognize the Communist People's Republic, which controlled the mainland, as the one legitimate government of China. Americans knew that the Chinese Communists were persecuting Christians, squelching free ideas, and killing or imprisoning those who opposed Chairman Mao. Even so, in 1971 the United States reversed its policy and recognized Communist China instead of Free China.

Korea and the Korean Conflict

China was not the only Communist target in Eastern Asia. The Soviet Union had begun to take a grip on part of Korea before World War II ended. As the United States was defeating Japan, the Soviet Union was pouring troops into Korea. The Yalta agreement allowed the Soviets to occupy Korea north of the 38th parallel. The Soviets again promised that at the proper time, free elections would be held. Of course, the Communists established their style of government in North Korea in the meantime. South Korea held its own elections, and the Republic of Korea was formed with Seoul as capital. Korea, like

Germany, was thus divided—part Communist, part free.

Talks were held in hopes of unifying Korea, but they broke down. Then North Korea invaded South Korea on June 25, 1950. The U.N. Security Council quickly called an emergency session to deal with the crisis. It demanded North Korea's

The Korean War, 1950-53

immediate withdrawal. When the troops were still there two days later, the Council suggested that the U.N. aid South Korea. (The Security Council was able to approve this because the Soviet Union was boycotting sessions at that time.)

That same day President Truman committed American planes and ships to support the South Koreans. On June 30 American troops were ordered to Korea. Within a week the U.N. voted to send a peacekeeping force to Korea to seek an end to the conflict. Since four-fifths of its men were American, President Truman was allowed to pick its commander. He chose General Douglas MacArthur, the most experienced American Pacific officer.

Truman hoped the troops could drive Communist troops out of South Korea. But a shortage of needed equipment and American unreadiness produced a shabby start for the **Korean War.** North Korean troops, well equipped by the Soviets, continued to push their way south. By the end of August, U.N. forces held only the southeastern corner of Korea near Pusan. MacArthur then surprised the North Koreans by going behind their lines and attacking from Inchon. All the ground lost was regained in two weeks.

When the troops reached the 38th parallel a decision was needed. Truman and the U.N. approved MacArthur's order to cross into North Korea. The U.N. hoped that MacArthur's northward push would lead to reunifying Korea. On October 26, 1950, MacArthur's advance guard reached the Yalu River, the dividing line between North Korea and China. China reacted by sending more than two hundred thousand "volunteers" across the Yalu River into North Korea to stop the U.N. forces.

Fierce fighting broke out, and U.N. troops were pushed back past the 38th parallel down into South Korea. MacArthur now believed that winning a land war in Korea required the bombing of Chinese bases and supply lines in China. MacArthur declared, "There is no substitute for victory."

President Truman and his advisors, however, thought differently. They were now content simply to restore the boundary to the 38th parallel. Although MacArthur pushed for all-out war and total victory, Truman decided on a limited war with very specific aims. He did not want to risk the

MacArthur as leader of the U.N. forces in Korea

use of nuclear weapons in Korea. He was also afraid that the Soviet Union might fight back somewhere in Europe or Asia if the United States pushed for control of North Korea. When MacArthur publicly denounced the president's policy of limited war, Truman removed him from his command.

In July 1951 talks for a cease-fire started, but both the talks and the fighting dragged on. Following his election in 1952, President Dwight D. Eisenhower traveled to Korea to revive the stalled talks. A cease-fire was signed on July 27, 1953, restoring the 38th parallel as the boundary. There was to be a demilitarized (nonfortified) zone between Communist North Korea and free South Korea.

Section Review

1. What do we commonly call the line separating the Eastern European countries under Communist control from the free Western countries? What British statesman coined the phrase?
2. What term was given the practice of using the military to support prowestern governments and to prevent the spread of communism?
3. How did the United States keep West Berlin from falling into Communist hands?
4. What military alliance was formed to halt the threat of aggression in Europe?
5. Who was the leader of Free China? Who led the Communist takeover of China?
6. Which China does the United States now recognize?
7. What were the dates of the beginning and end of the Korean Conflict?

D. The Eisenhower Era

Both the Republicans and Democrats would have been happy to have World War II hero Dwight D. Eisenhower as their candidate in 1952. He ran on the Republican ticket against Adlai E. Stevenson, governor of Illinois. The public decided that they "liked Ike" (as he was called), because his grandfatherly image made many Americans feel comfortable. Eisenhower won handily.

Southeast Asia

Problems with Communist expansion continued during the Eisenhower era. The Southeast Asian area of Indochina (Vietnam, Cambodia, and Laos) became a target for Communist control. The area had been a French colony, but after World War II French control in the land was deteriorating. **Ho Chi Minh,** a Communist leader, tried to gain independence for Vietnam. His forces defeated the French at Dien Bien Phu in May 1954. The United States did not intervene with troops at this time, because it did not want to risk another land war in Asia.

The conflict was referred to an international conference in Geneva, Switzerland, for settlement. As in Germany and Korea, it was decided to have two Vietnams. North Vietnam under Ho Chi Minh would be Communist. South Vietnam would be non-Communist and would receive American support. But North Vietnam was not content. Using guerrilla tactics it attacked, seeking to gain control of South Vietnam. Before long the United States discovered that the North Vietnamese were receiving Chinese and Soviet military aid.

Activities in Korea and Indochina not only had made the United States tense but

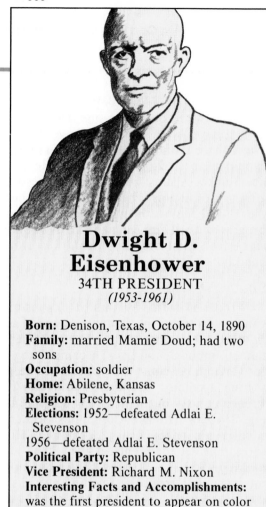

Dwight D. Eisenhower

34TH PRESIDENT
(1953-1961)

Born: Denison, Texas, October 14, 1890
Family: married Mamie Doud; had two sons
Occupation: soldier
Home: Abilene, Kansas
Religion: Presbyterian
Elections: 1952—defeated Adlai E. Stevenson
1956—defeated Adlai E. Stevenson
Political Party: Republican
Vice President: Richard M. Nixon
Interesting Facts and Accomplishments:
was the first president to appear on color television
only president who was a licensed pilot
liked to paint for relaxation, but he could not draw, and so someone else sketched the picture and then he painted it
only five-star general to become president
retired to a home overlooking the battlefield at Gettysburg, Pennsylvania
Death: March 28, 1969

also had alarmed other free countries in Southeast Asia and the southern Pacific. Therefore, in 1954 eight countries formed an alliance to contain the spread of communism there. The **Southeast Asia Treaty Organization** (SEATO) united the United States, Britain, France, Australia, New Zealand, Thailand, Pakistan, and the Philippines. The United States agreed to aid any of these nations threatened by an aggressor. By the end of 1955, America was sending military advisors to South Vietnam to train Vietnamese forces. The United States also pledged to aid Taiwan if it was attacked by mainland China.

Soviet-American Relations

The United States had become the leading nation of the free world. America could no longer remain isolated from international affairs as it had in earlier times. Because the interests of the United States were affected by conditions abroad, it had to get involved in international problems. America's greatest international problems lay in the Cold War tensions with the Soviets. The affairs between the United States and the Soviet Union were always gaining world attention.

In July 1955 Britain, France, the Soviet Union, and the United States met in Geneva, Switzerland, to attempt to put to rest some of the Cold War tensions. About the only thing that was agreed on was that they would not resort to war to resolve differences. President Eisenhower suggested that the United States and the Soviet Union submit to air inspections of each other's military installations to see whether there were missiles present. The Soviets, however, rejected the idea.

The Soviet Union was struggling to project a new image. Stalin had died in 1953, and **Nikita Khrushchev** (KROOSH chef), his successor, claimed to be critical of the former leader's terror tactics. One time he declared that the Soviets wanted to be friends and promote peace with the United

States; yet Soviet intentions had not really changed. At another time Khrushchev threatened, "We will bury you."

The United States and the Soviet Union settled into a policy of **"peaceful coexistence."** The two countries agreed to try to settle the many tension-filled situations between them without hostility. They also tried to arrange events that would promote good will between the two countries. Khrushchev even visited America in 1959, the first Soviet leader to do so. Unfortunately, the attitude of peaceful coexistence committed the United States to settling each issue with the Soviets peacefully even if Soviet wrongs were not stopped or punished.

European Developments

Further examples of Soviet Communist oppression came in Eastern Europe. People in the Soviet satellite countries were unhappy under Communist rule. In October 1956, freedom fighters in Hungary bravely led a revolt. They pleaded for help from the West on short-wave radio broadcasts, but help never came. For four days the people of Hungary had hope. Their revolt forced Soviet troops to leave their capital of Budapest. But then the Soviet army rolled back down the streets in tanks and crushed the freedom fighters. The freedom fighters were brave, but with only homemade grenades and their bare hands, they could not stop the tanks.

The Soviet invasion of Hungary was brought before the U.N. That body voted to condemn the Soviets. When the Soviets ignored the U.N. decision, the U.N. took no real action. Because the nations feared that aid to Hungary might start a third world war, the Soviets ruthlessly crushed the freedom movement with no hindrance from the free world.

Cuba

Latin America soon became another source of Cold War tensions. Communism was winning support in the region because so many of the people were poor and uneducated. Many believed the Communist promises. The growth of Communist activity in Latin America alarmed Americans since it brought the Soviet threat closer to home.

The most disturbing Communist gain for the Americans was that of Cuba. In 1959 Americans heard that Fulgencio Batista, a long time dictator of Cuba, had been overthrown by a revolutionary leader, **Fidel Castro.** Although the State Department was aware of Castro's Communist leanings from the outset, the American people were not. Thus Americans idealistically believed that conditions might get better in Cuba if Castro took control.

Instead, conditions got worse. Castro, a cruel dictator, jailed thousands of his political enemies. He seized the property of Americans and American business investments in Cuba and declared himself a Communist. Cuban refugees attempted to escape Castro's regime by fleeing to Florida any way they could. Some flew; more floated on rickety boats. Soon Soviet aid was on its way to Cuba. The Caribbean was no longer an American lake. Ninety miles off Florida lay a Communist threat to American freedom.

Activities at Home

The United States was involved in some important activities at home during the Eisenhower era. Two of the most pleasant accomplishments were the completion of the **St. Lawrence Seaway** and the addition of two new states.

In 1954 the United States and Canada had undertaken a joint project called the St. Lawrence Seaway. The two countries cooperated to deepen the St. Lawrence River and build canals and locks where necessary. The completed seaway allowed ocean-going vessels to sail from the Atlantic Ocean through the seaway to the Great Lakes. The project helped the economies of both nations and turned cities along the Great Lakes into major inland seaports. The moving water through the seaway was also used to provide electrical power.

In 1959 Congress admitted two territories to the Union. Alaska and Hawaii became the forty-ninth and fiftieth states. Alaska and Hawaii differ from the other states because they are noncontiguous, or unattached territories away from the other forty-eight states. The states are also unique because of their populations. About one-fifth of Alaskan citizens are Indian (Eskimo, Aleut, or other tribes). One-half of Hawaii's citizens descend from Japanese, Chinese, Filipino, or Korean immigrants. The additions of Alaska and Hawaii gave the United States an even wider cultural heritage.

Section Review

1. Who was elected president in 1952?
2. What alliance was started to thwart communism in Southeast Asia?
3. What Soviet satellite country revolted against communism in 1956? Why did these freedom fighters fail?
4. What Latin American country turned Communist in 1959? Who became its leader?

Summary

The United States emerged from World War II as the prosperous leader of the free world. Americans eagerly returned to peacetime activities, but international problems continued to concern the nation. Because of Communist actions after the war, great tensions arose between the United States and the Soviet Union. The two nations avoided a direct shooting conflict, but a "Cold War" continued between the two throughout the 1950s. The ideals and demands of the United States and the Communists clashed in Germany, Korea, and many other areas of the world. The new United Nations organization did little to stop regional conflicts and did not control the spread of communism. All the while, the United States continually provided protection for the free world and increased its aid to faltering free nations. The United States found its new role as world leader to be both expensive and entangling.

Chapter Review

Do You Remember?

▪ Answer each of the following questions.
1. What legislation initiated the interstate highway system?
2. What did President Truman call his domestic program?

3. What postwar legislation curbed some of the powers of labor unions?
4. Where were the Nazi leaders tried for their deeds in World War II?
5. Who was given command of the military occupation of Japan?
6. Who devised a plan for helping the war-torn countries of Europe?
7. What are the three important divisions of the United Nations?
8. Who succeeded Truman as president?
9. What two states entered the union in 1959?

■ Explain the meaning of each of the following terms.

10. baby boom
11. green revolution
12. civil rights
13. third world
14. Cold War
15. containment
16. peaceful coexistence

■ Match each of the following men with their country.

17. Fidel Castro	a. Communist China
18. Chiang Kai-shek	b. Free China
19. Ho Chi Minh	c. Cuba
20. Nikita Khrushchev	d. Soviet Union
21. Mao Tse-tung	e. Vietnam

Why Is It So?

1. How did the GI Bill help soldiers returning from the war?
2. How did Germany become divided into two nations after World War II?
3. Why did Churchill say that an "iron curtain" had fallen across Europe?
4. How was the Truman Doctrine supposed to support the policy of containment?
5. Why was the Berlin airlift necessary?
6. How did Korea become a divided nation after World War II?
7. Why was the Communist presence in Cuba disturbing to Americans?

What Do You Think?

1. How did Jim Crow laws violate the civil rights of blacks?
2. Why is the United Nations unable to maintain world peace?
3. How was the Korean War different from previous wars in which America fought?
4. What would have happened if the United States had taken an isolationist position after World War II?

28

The Sixties

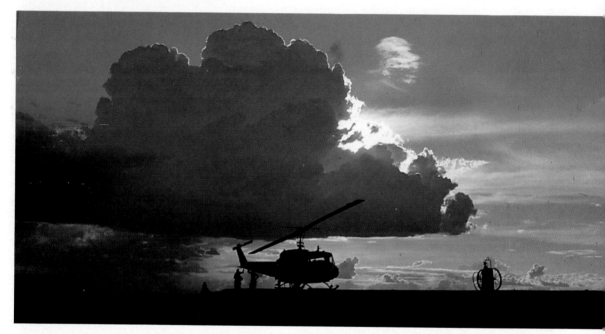

The 1960s was a turbulent decade in American history. Riots, assassinations, war, and general discontent are vivid memories of that time period. Photographs show protesters seeking civil rights for blacks, peace in Vietnam, or the breakdown of moral restraints. Cold War tensions occasionally flared. Inflation caused prices to soar. Even with these problems and challenges, the sixties was also a decade of accomplishment for the United States. Science and medicine made great advances. Civil rights issues gained attention. Some improvements were made in international relations. The prosperity of most Americans

An American helicopter lands at a South Vietnamese base during the Vietnam War.

continued. Both turmoil and triumphs were characteristic of this colorful decade in American history.

A. Kennedy and the New Frontier

The Sixties began with the rise of a young senator to the presidency and the hope of conquering the nation's "New Frontier," the challenges that lay ahead.

The Election of 1960

The Republicans chose Eisenhower's vice president, **Richard Nixon,** as their candidate in 1960. The Democrats chose Massachusetts Senator **John F. Kennedy.**

Kennedy's running mate was Texan **Lyndon B. Johnson,** the well-known Senate majority leader. With this ticket the party hoped to win the votes of both northern and southern Democrats. Kennedy was young, only 43, and he was a Roman Catholic. In a major change from earlier campaigns, Nixon and Kennedy engaged in a series of four television debates. Kennedy entered the debates as an underdog, but he was able to use his youthful appearance and charm to good effect. In contrast, Nixon seemed to lack energy and appeal. The election was a close one. Out of 68.3 million votes cast, Kennedy won by only 120,000. This was less than one vote per precinct (local voting place). The election highlighted the importance of individual votes even in a large country.

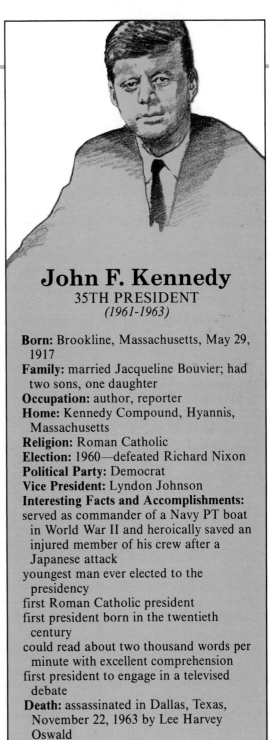

John F. Kennedy
35TH PRESIDENT
(1961-1963)

Born: Brookline, Massachusetts, May 29, 1917

Family: married Jacqueline Bouvier; had two sons, one daughter

Occupation: author, reporter

Home: Kennedy Compound, Hyannis, Massachusetts

Religion: Roman Catholic

Election: 1960—defeated Richard Nixon

Political Party: Democrat

Vice President: Lyndon Johnson

Interesting Facts and Accomplishments:
served as commander of a Navy PT boat in World War II and heroically saved an injured member of his crew after a Japanese attack

youngest man ever elected to the presidency

first Roman Catholic president

first president born in the twentieth century

could read about two thousand words per minute with excellent comprehension

first president to engage in a televised debate

Death: assassinated in Dallas, Texas, November 22, 1963 by Lee Harvey Oswald

John F. Kennedy makes his inaugural speech with President Eisenhower and Mrs. Kennedy looking on.

Kennedy's Plans

Kennedy's campaign had promised a new program, the **"New Frontier."** Kennedy pressed for measures similar to those of the New Deal—economic aid to depressed areas, medical insurance for the aged (called Medicare), federal aid for college students, and an ambitious space program. Although Kennedy supported civil rights, he offered no new legislation but did insist on active enforcement of existing laws and court decisions. Kennedy's inaugural speech encouraged foreign adversaries to join the United States in a quest for lasting peace. He challenged Americans to "ask not what your country can do for you; ask what you can do for your country."

Since Kennedy's victory was a narrow one, and since southern Democrats often voted with House and Senate Republicans, Kennedy's "New Frontier" met opposition in Congress. Although Congress agreed to a few of Kennedy's goals—such as raising the minimum wage to one dollar per hour, passing the Trade Expansion Act, and making improvements in the Social Security system—it rejected Medicare, federal aid to education, and a bill to create a department of urban affairs.

Kennedy's Foreign Program and Problems

President Kennedy had several ideas for helping other countries that were in need. As he was implementing these plans, he met some serious Cold War problems.

One popular idea that Kennedy introduced was a volunteer program called the **Peace Corps.** American teachers, technicians, engineers, and businessmen offered to serve for two years to help improve conditions in Third World countries. Schooling, health, and conservation programs were thus provided for more than sixty foreign countries. This humanitarian program was especially popular among idealistic young Americans who wanted to make the world a better place.

Much of the work of the Peace Corps was good, but it met only a few of the temporal needs of the people the Corps intended to help. Its work provided no permanent solutions for the world's needs. Christians should realize that although helping the poor and needy is good, people have a spiritual need that only the Lord Jesus can satisfy.

Realizing that communism could spread from Cuba, where Communist soldiers were being trained, Kennedy announced an **Alliance for Progress.** Under this plan almost $12 billion went to Latin American nations to provide housing, schools, and health clinics or hospitals in the 1960s. It was hoped that relieving poverty would ease some of the unrest that allowed communism to spread. Unfortunately, money cannot improve people's minds and hearts. The large expenses of the program served mainly to encourage corruption instead of benefiting the poor.

Problems with Cuba—Under Communist dictator Fidel Castro, Cuba's problems were growing worse. Castro had seized all American property in Cuba and refused to pay for any of it. President Eisenhower, in reaction, had cut Cuban sugar imports and later had broken off relations completely. The Cuban economic troubles that resulted from Castro's policies caused great hardships for the people. As life under Castro's regime worsened, many Cubans fled their native land and sought refuge in the United

States. The Central Intelligence Agency (CIA) devised a plan to train fifteen hundred exiled anti-Castro Cubans to overthrow Castro. Kennedy allowed the plan to proceed. The CIA believed that when the Cubans heard about the invasion, they would rally to the cause and help free Cuba.

Unfortunately, nothing went as planned. On April 17, 1961, the force landed at the **Bay of Pigs,** but Castro's forces repelled the invasion because Kennedy withheld promised air support. More than four hundred died, and the rest of the force was captured. Castro was able to use the unsuccessful invasion to embarrass the United States and make other Latin Americans think that America was trying to interfere in Latin American affairs.

America's problems with Cuba were far from finished. On October 14, 1962, American military patrol planes flying over Cuba confirmed American suspicions that the Soviet Union was shipping missiles to Cuba, missiles that could destroy American cities. President Kennedy told the American people of the missiles, and he demanded that the Soviets remove them. Meanwhile the United States put Cuba under a blockade. The U.S. Navy waited off the coast of Cuba ready, to stop and search Soviet ships en route to Cuba. The nation's forces were on full military alert. On October 28 Khrushchev wrote Kennedy that the Soviet Union would remove the missiles on the condition that the United States not invade Cuba. The **Cuban Missile Crisis** was over, and Americans were relieved that the threat of war with the Soviet Union had subsided. Kennedy's secretary of state, Dean Rusk, summarized what happened: "We're eyeball to eyeball, and I think the other fellow just blinked."

More Trouble in Berlin—The Cuban Missile Crisis was not the only confrontation that the United States had with the Soviets during the Kennedy Administration. Because of the Communist control in East Germany, thousands of East Germans—mostly professional people—were escaping from behind the iron curtain by going into the free city of West Berlin. As a result, in 1961 the Soviet dictator, Khrushchev, ordered the construction of a concrete wall topped by tangles of barbed wire around West Berlin. Armed guards stood waiting to shoot any who would try to cross the **Berlin Wall** to gain freedom in West Berlin.

President Kennedy sent more troops to West Berlin, and in 1963 he traveled to Berlin. He made a nighttime visit to the Berlin Wall, where thousands of Berliners lit candles to show their support of freedom. Kennedy tried to tell the people there that he was concerned with their situation by saying, *"Ich bin ein Berliner."* ("I am a Berliner.") Nevertheless, the existence of the wall was a blow to the free world.

President Kennedy looking over the Berlin Wall

A Slight Thaw in the Cold War—In 1963 relations with the Soviet Union seemed better. A "hot line," a direct telephone line between the White House and the Kremlin in Moscow, the Soviet capital, was installed. The same year at Geneva, Switzerland, the United States, Britain, and the Soviet Union signed a Limited Test Ban Treaty. They agreed that there would be no above-ground testing of nuclear weapons. Each nation was to tell the others of any underground tests and was to police itself. But France and China, who also had nuclear weapons, refused to sign the treaty.

Section Review

1. Who were the presidential candidates in the 1960 election?
2. What was the name Kennedy gave to the program for his administration?
3. What was the purpose of the Peace Corps?
4. What two situations in Cuba created problems for the United States?
5. What did the Soviets build to stop escapes from their Communist-controlled area of Germany?

An East German Communist soldier

B. The End of Camelot

The Kennedy administration ended abruptly in late 1963. On November 22, President Kennedy went to Dallas, Texas, to speak. While traveling down a street in Dallas in an open car, the President was shot and killed by Lee Harvey Oswald. Kennedy was only 46.

The Kennedy Mystique

When Kennedy came to office, the musical *Camelot* was popular on Broadway. The play retold the story of King Arthur and his Round Table, recounting how Arthur dreamt of creating a new England where truth, justice, and equality would reign. Since many of Kennedy's hopes for America sounded just as noble and idealistic, some began to refer to his administration as "Camelot." After Kennedy's assassination he became even more of a hero, and the high ideals of Camelot seemed even more glorious. Even people who disagreed with Kennedy personally remembered the things they liked about him—his youth, his idealism, and his vitality. Kennedy and his Camelot seemed to represent hope and optimism for America's future. Before Kennedy's death his "New Frontier" program was hardly moving at all. After his assassination, Congress passed many of Kennedy's programs as memorials to the late president.

Despite the admiration Americans developed for their slain president, they soon came to face some major problems that had been growing during the Kennedy years. The tensions of civil rights issues and the question of American involvement in Vietnam had already come to the attention of the Kennedy administration. Soon these two concerns would fill America's headlines.

The Great Society

Lyndon Johnson took his oath of office on the president's plane, Air Force One, after Kennedy's death. Since Johnson had been on Capitol Hill for thirty-two years, serving in both the House and the Senate, he knew the political system and how to work it. A powerful and persuasive man, he was able to get bills passed. Johnson's legislative program was called **"The Great Society."** This program was supposed to make American society great again.

The Great Society program declared a "War on Poverty." It created a Job Corps, similar to the CCC of the 1930s. Another Great Society program offered aid to distressed areas of the eleven states in Appalachia. A food stamp program made better nutrition possible for some. A Head Start Program gave underprivileged children educational help before they started

Lyndon B. Johnson
36TH PRESIDENT
(1963-1969)

Born: Stonewall, Texas, August 27, 1908
Family: married Claudia "Lady Bird" Taylor; had two daughters
Occupation: teacher, rancher
Home: LBJ Ranch, Johnson City, Texas
Religion: Disciples of Christ
Election: succeeded to the presidency upon the death of Kennedy
1964—defeated Barry Goldwater
Political Party: Democrat
Vice President: none (first term); Hubert Humphrey (second term)
Interesting Facts and Accomplishments:
was the second tallest president at 6′ 3″
his entire family had "LBJ" initials (Lyndon Baines, Lady Bird, Lynda Bird, and Luci Baines)
first president to have his oath of office administered by a woman (Judge Sarah Hughes)
Death: January 22, 1973

Lyndon Johnson takes the oath of office shortly after Kennedy's death.

regular school classes. Johnson also persuaded Congress to pass new legislation for labeling and packaging foods, drugs, cosmetics, and household supplies.

Another program—and one in which the first lady, Lady Bird Johnson, played an active role—was the beautification of America. More than $3.7 billion was spent to clean up the country's lakes and rivers. An antipollution crusade spent $186 million to insure purer air. **Ecology,** the study of man's relationship to his environment, became the new issue of the era.

In 1965 the Great Society program pushed through a bill providing for Medicare and Medicaid. Two months of low-cost hospital care and allowances for other medical costs were among its provisions. Two new departments of government—Housing and Urban Development, and Transportation—were also formed. Many of these Great Society programs were actually the fulfillment of Kennedy's New Frontier. All of these programs were expensive, costing more than the government brought in. The resulting deficit spending put the nation in debt and encouraged inflation, a problem that plagued America in the future. The Great Society programs also made Americans more dependent on government programs and gave the federal government more power over people's lives.

Section Review

1. In what city was Kennedy assassinated?
2. Why was the Kennedy administration called "Camelot"?
3. Who became president when Kennedy died?
4. Why did many of Kennedy's programs proceed after his death?

C. Civil Rights in the Sixties

Civil rights had been in controversy even at the Constitutional Convention. Although many rights were ensured in the Constitution, some of them were still being denied to Americans, especially to racial minorities. Because of the emphasis of these problems in the 1960s, *civil rights* now often refers to racial matters.

Blacks particularly had been struggling for years to gain the same rights and privileges as others. The struggle for both legal and actual equality had been a long, hard one. In the 1950s and 1960s, unprecedented changes finally came.

The Role of the Courts in Civil Rights

For many years the National Association for the Advancement of Colored People (NAACP) had been working quietly through the court system to remedy inequality. In a series of earlier cases, they won the right for black graduate students to be educated in white universities. They were able to do this because there were no black schools on the graduate level that offered blacks equal training. Thus these changes were made without overruling an 1896 Supreme Court case, which had allowed blacks to be separated as long as facilities were theoretically equal.

Eventually a court case challenged the idea of "separate but equal." In 1954 in **Brown v. Board of Education,** the Supreme Court ruled that segregation of children in public schools based solely on race violated the equal treatment that all citizens were guaranteed under the Fourteenth Amendment. The decision overturned the earlier case. The *Brown* case applied to school districts in seventeen states plus the District of Columbia. School districts were told to integrate "with all deliberate speed." However, some districts did not start to integrate until 1969, some fifteen years later.

Neither presidents Eisenhower nor Kennedy put particular pressure on the states to integrate. They hoped the states would follow the court's instructions on their own. When challenged by the government of Arkansas, however, Eisenhower put the state National Guard under his control to insure the safe enrollment of black students at Little Rock's Central High School in 1957.

Although Kennedy personally believed that more legislation should be passed to insure equality, he realized that the legislation would not go through. He did, however, take a strong stand to enforce existing laws and to act on the *Brown* case. In less than three years, the Justice Department took action to integrate 183 schools. In September 1962 and June 1963, Kennedy sent federal marshals to the Universities of Mississippi and Alabama to insure that black students could enroll. The Justice Department also defended freedom riders—blacks and whites who rode interstate buses from place to place in the South, seeking to integrate the buses and waiting rooms. Often they were arrested; some were pulled off the buses and beaten while the buses were burned by angry whites.

The Kennedy administration also passed the **Twenty-third Amendment.** It gave the residents of the District of Columbia the right to vote in national elections. Since the district's population was heavily black, this was regarded as a step forward in civil rights.

Blacks Stage Civil Rights Protests

In 1955 Rosa Parks, a black seamstress in Montgomery, Alabama, rode a city bus

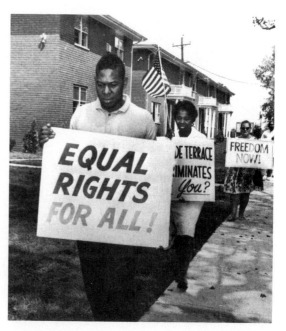

home from work. Tradition and the law had divided the bus into two sections: one in back for blacks, the other in front for whites. Mrs. Parks sat in one of the few empty seats on the bus, at the rear of the white section. A white person asked her to give it up. When she refused, she was arrested. To show support for her action, other blacks started a bus boycott. They refused to ride city buses for almost a year. Then the city's segregated bus law was declared unconstitutional.

Blacks began to try other forms of protest. Sit-ins at white lunch counters and freedom marches or rides soon followed. The biggest single demonstration took place in August 1963. Organized by **Martin Luther King, Jr.,** its purpose was to rally support for proposed civil rights legislation. About 250,000 blacks and whites converged on Washington, D.C., where they heard King deliver an address in which he repeated

A demonstration against segregation

the phrase "I have a dream." King spoke of an ideal America where liberty and equality would be a reality for all—both black and white.

Black Leaders in the Sixties

Martin Luther King, Jr. was the most famous black leader of the sixties, and today he has a federal holiday named for him. King was a Baptist minister and the founder and leader of the Southern Christian Leadership Conference. Instead of preaching the gospel, however, he spoke of liberating the poor and underprivileged peoples from their misery through social action. He used his pulpit and his influence in black churches to inspire blacks to work for their civil rights and to test federal laws. An inspiring speaker, he encouraged blacks to use passive (nonviolent) resistance or civil disobedience to oppose laws they believed

The 1963 civil rights march on Washington, D.C.

to be unjust. Such techniques, however, sometimes resulted in violence.

In April of 1968 King went to Memphis, Tennessee, to take part in a demonstration. While there, he was murdered. As with President Kennedy before him, King's death helped to make him a hero in the eyes of many Americans.

Although no other black leader gained the popularity of Martin Luther King, several did establish significant movements in the sixties. Stokely Carmichael became the darling of young blacks by advocating "black power." No one was sure what the term meant, but its slogan—"violence is as American as cherry pie"—frightened some whites and angered conservative blacks, who could see that it would ruin a good cause. As a result of the actions of the extremists and the riots that occurred, the civil rights movement became a highly emotional and frustrating challenge for America.

Civil Rights Legislation

Following Kennedy's assassination, Congress rallied to pass some important pieces of civil rights legislation. The **Civil Rights Act of 1964** forbade segregation and discrimination based on race in schools and public places, including public accommodations (such as motels). Any private companies that discriminated would not receive government business contracts. Institutions that discriminated in employment would not be eligible for public funds.

The **Twenty-fourth Amendment,** ratified in 1964, forbade states from levying poll taxes. Southern states had required their voters to pay these poll taxes before they could vote. These taxes kept both poor blacks and poor whites from voting.

The **Voting Rights Acts of 1965** ended long-standing injustices in voting in federal elections. Although the Fifteenth Amendment (1870) kept the states from denying any one race the right to vote, southern states had gotten around the law in a variety of ways. Many required literacy tests. Often these not only tested reading knowledge but also required understanding of obscure, difficult portions of state constitutions. Blacks who sought to register had also been harassed. The new act gave the national government the power to register blacks in states where the registered black vote was significantly lower than census population. Federal officials also had the power to check any complaints of discrimination.

In the eyes of many blacks, however, the changes had come too slowly. A few black radicals could not be satisfied by peaceful legislation. Bitter because of past injustice, they encouraged violence, and riots began to break out. Parts of Detroit, Newark, and Los Angeles were burned, and people were killed in some of the riots. The looting and destruction shocked Americans who saw it on their TV screens. This racial violence in the late sixties signaled the end of a decade of improved civil rights and made future improvements more difficult to obtain.

Section Review

1. What major court case affected civil rights? How?
2. Who was the most prominent black civil rights leader?
3. What two amendments to the Constitution were gains for the civil rights movement? Why?
4. Name two other pieces of legislation that improved civil rights, and explain how they did so.

Civil rights leader Martin Luther King, Jr., (front left) and Robert Kennedy (next to King) in an appearance with President Johnson (front right)

Chapter 28

D. The Vietnam War

The biggest single issue in foreign affairs in the 1960s was the **Vietnam War.** Lyndon Johnson inherited the conflict that had been brewing in Southeast Asia for nearly a decade (pp. 559-60). During his administration, Vietnam became a raging issue as American involvement increased.

Beginning American Involvement

Although the Eisenhower administration had pledged that South Vietnam would not be allowed to fall to Communists and had supplied financial aid, the Kennedy administration was the first to send large numbers of Americans. By December 1962, 11,200 United States troops were in Vietnam. Most served in advisory roles, training the Vietnamese to fight their own war.

Kennedy had refused to send a large number of ground troops (rather than advisors) to South Vietnam, but President Johnson thought Vietnam deserved American help. He was concerned that Southeast Asia not be conquered by the Communists as China had been in 1949. "I am not going to be the president who saw Southeast Asia go the way China went," he said.

In August 1964 three North Vietnamese patrol boats supposedly attacked an American destroyer in international waters off the coast of Vietnam in the Gulf of Tonkin.

South Vietnamese soldiers

The president reported this incident to Congress and requested power to act. The resulting **Gulf of Tonkin Resolution** said that the United States was now ready "to take all necessary steps, including the use of armed forces" against the North Vietnamese. The resolution was not a declaration of war, but it gave the president broad powers to increase American involvement in Vietnam. The United States wanted to prevent Communist North Vietnam from moving south past the 17th parallel into South Vietnam and from taking control of that free area.

The American involvement in Vietnam quickly became a debated issue in the United States. Congressmen and leaders who favored increased American presence in Vietnam, or an escalation of the war, were called **hawks.** Others wanted to de-escalate the war, or lessen American involvement. Those who wanted the United States to pull out completely were called **doves.** Despite the debate, American involvement increased rapidly. When President Johnson was elected in November 1964, there were 28,000 American troops in Vietnam. In May 1965 more than half a million Americans were in Vietnam.

A Sticky Situation

From the beginning the United States committed itself to protecting the free government of South Vietnam from Communist assaults. The United States effort might have had a better chance of success had Vietnamese politics been free of corruption and had the South Vietnamese people consistently backed their own government, but this was not so. During the war the United States not only had to fight the Communist assaults from the North but also had to struggle to keep the South Vietnamese united under an anti-Communist government. Furthermore many South Vietnamese, known as **Vietcong,** favored the Communists and carried out guerilla warfare against both the Americans and the South Vietnamese troops.

The United States entered the conflict at a disadvantage. Since Congress had never officially declared war, technically it was engaged in only a police action. The United States feared that if it declared war, many more countries would be involved, causing perhaps even a world war. Yet frustration resulted because thousands of Americans were dying in Vietnam for a cause that politicians were still debating. As the war dragged on, it seemed that the United States was not fighting to win anything. There seemed to be no glorious cause to rally public support for the conflict.

Furthermore, although the United States had the most modern and sophisticated weapons, this advantage could not be easily used in Vietnam. In World War II the United States had defeated Germany by bombing its industrial cities. North Vietnamese had no large industrial plants but rather relied on thousands of little shops scattered across the land to produce war materiel. The vegetation and terrain also made bombing difficult. The United States conducted bombing raids on the **Ho Chi Minh Trail,** the route that the Vietcong forces used to move their men and goods, but it was hard to identify specific targets. Even when specific targets were identified, success was not guaranteed. One bridge on the trail was destroyed at least twenty times. But since it was built of logs, the North Vietnamese could rebuild it in only a few days. Moreover, the North Vietnamese received military supplies from both China and the Soviet Union.

In addition, United States servicemen could not identify the enemy. Obviously, the North Vietnamese and Vietcong looked just like the loyal South Vietnamese. While those in the cities south of the 17th parallel usually gave the Americans support, in rural areas no one knew whom to trust. The Vietcong even employed children to lob hand grenades at American soldiers. Many soldiers were killed by children; yet when children were killed in the war, the American public was appalled.

Finally, the lack of unity at home undermined the war effort. As war continued, political activists who strongly opposed the war gained increased public attention. Communist agitation helped the antiwar movement get its start among liberal college professors and students. Their "New Left" grew as civil rights workers looking for a new cause and other disenchanted Americans joined their ranks. Because college students were subject to the draft and some did not want to fight, they joined the protests. A few defiant ones burned their draft cards and the American flag. Some

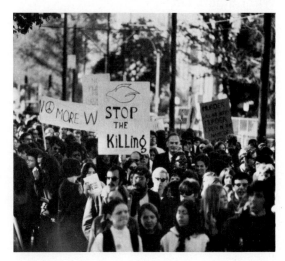

Antiwar demonstrations were common in the late 1960s.

The Vietnam War

0   100   200   300

Scale of Miles

young men fled to Sweden or Canada, both of which harbored the draft dodgers. In October 1965 more than ninety cities had antiwar demonstrations. A left-wing organization, the Students for Democratic Society, was in the forefront. In April 1967 antiwar marches in New York and San Francisco attracted up to 300,000 people.

War Lingers On

By clever use of Communist manpower, of Soviet and Chinese supply lines, and of guerrilla warfare, the North Vietnamese, led by Ho Chi Minh, made headway. They believed that if the war were prolonged, they could win. Americans would become so disenchanted with the war that they would pull out.

To counter Communist successes and hinder Soviet and Chinese aid, the United States organized bombing raids on the northern port of Haiphong and the capital city, Hanoi. Each time the bombing raids were stepped up, the North Vietnamese hinted that they might go to the peace table if the bombings halted. The president then slowed the bombings, only to find that the Communists used the lulls to their advantage, quickly moving in troops and supplies by sea or along the Ho Chi Minh Trail.

Despite the frustrations of the conflict, the fighting in Vietnam continued and became more effective in 1966. The president and his leading general, William Westmoreland, were more optimistic in 1967. The air war was expanded, and additional American soldiers were sent into the battle. Some believed the fight would be over in two to three years.

Over the Christmas holidays of 1967 and through the lunar or Chinese New Year (the Tet), the United States called another cease-fire. As usual, the Communists used the lull to their advantage. This time, however, they moved huge quantities of supplies and troops into South Vietnam. Large numbers of young strangers walked or rode into South Vietnam's cities. Many more funerals were held than usual, but the coffins towed through the crowded streets by a hidden enemy contained weapons, not corpses.

With their troops and weapons in position, the Communists were ready to attack. On January 30, 1968, the North Vietnamese and the Vietcong unleashed their largest offensive yet. Shortly after midnight, when all the Tet celebrators were asleep, the attack began. They assaulted key points in the capital of Saigon and a hundred other cities. From one end of the country to the other, police stations, military bases, government buildings, radio and power stations, and foreign embassies fell under North Vietnamese attack. More than sixty thousand additional Vietcong troops appeared. They took the old imperial city of Hue (HWAY) and assaulted Saigon, the capital city.

The **Tet Offensive** was a blow to the American effort in Vietnam, but within weeks American forces had regained what was captured and had begun to take the offensive themselves. Nonetheless, television, radio, magazines, and newspapers in the United States continually reported the incident as a miserable defeat. Such publicity, along with a continual report of the growing casualty list in Vietnam, began to make more and more Americans sympathetic with the doves. The nightly scenes of blood and death on the evening news made Americans anxious to get out of Vietnam.

The Election of 1968

Before Christmas of 1967, most Americans thought that the incumbent, Lyndon Johnson, would be the 1968 Democratic candidate. But after the Tet Offensive, there were second thoughts. Democratic politicians, some of whom already opposed Johnson on the war, now pushed the issue further. In November 1967, a Minnesota antiwar senator, Eugene McCarthy, voiced his intention to run for president. With the help of hundreds of college students, his campaign gained momentum. In the New

C-130 cargo and troop transport planes unload equipment in South Vietnam.

Hampshire primary in March 1968, he showed a strong following.

McCarthy's popularity led New York's Senator **Robert Kennedy** (the brother of the late president) to believe that an antiwar candidate might have more of a chance to win than he had originally believed. Moreover, Kennedy could count on the popularity of his name, as well as the support of minorities and labor. Five days after the presidential primary in New Hampshire, he threw his hat into the ring.

A political poll in late March 1968 revealed that only thirty-six per cent of the country supported Johnson. Johnson could see that he might not win the nomination. On March 31 he surprised the country with a double announcement. He said that he had ordered a reduction in the bombings in North Vietnam. Then he said, "I should not permit the presidency to become involved in the partisan divisions that are developing in this political year. . . . Accordingly, . . . I will not accept the nomination of my party for another term as your president." Vice President **Hubert Humphrey** then declared his candidacy.

The Democratic front-runner, especially after his victory in the California primary, was Robert Kennedy. But after meeting with his California campaign workers the night of the election, Kennedy was assassinated in a Los Angeles hotel. This was a blow from which the Democrats could not recover before the election. Their party convention in Chicago chose Humphrey as its candidate. The convention, however, was surrounded by a wave of antiwar riots and demonstrations.

The Republicans revived the hopes of Richard Nixon and put him on their ticket with **Spiro T. Agnew** of Maryland. A third

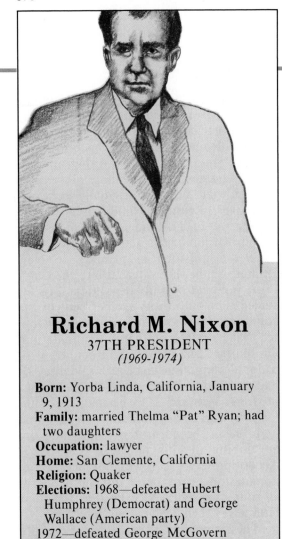

Richard M. Nixon
37TH PRESIDENT
(1969-1974)

Born: Yorba Linda, California, January 9, 1913

Family: married Thelma "Pat" Ryan; had two daughters

Occupation: lawyer

Home: San Clemente, California

Religion: Quaker

Elections: 1968—defeated Hubert Humphrey (Democrat) and George Wallace (American party)
1972—defeated George McGovern

Political Party: Republican

Vice Presidents: Spiro T. Agnew (resigned); Gerald R. Ford

Interesting Facts and Accomplishments:
was named for Richard the Lionhearted, king of England
had served as Eisenhower's vice president
first president to visit all fifty states while in office
visited both the Soviet Union and Communist China while president
his youngest daughter married President Eisenhower's grandson
only president to resign (Aug. 9, 1974)

party, the American party, ran George C. Wallace, an Alabama governor noted for his opposition to integration. His party shopped for votes from those who were tired of high taxes, liberal court decisions, and federal interference in the lives of citizens. The election was close between Nixon and Humphrey, but Nixon was elected.

From Johnson to Nixon

President Johnson's Council of Economic Advisors had told him that he could not fight a war, continue the Great Society programs, and limit inflation without a tax increase. Since he was already unpopular, the president had no desire to become more so by raising taxes. To avoid the problem, he lied. When congressmen talked to him about a tax increase and discussed the cost of the war, Johnson gave them false figures.

The national debt in 1966 was $9.8 billion, and the war was costing about $100 million a day. The White House, however, reported a much lower cost. Within a year the debt reached $23 billion. Johnson's deceit encouraged runaway inflation and added to a staggering debt. The American public never sacrificed at home the way they had in other wars. Americans continued to buy all the material goods they wanted while the government spent money not only for the war but also for growing domestic programs, such as taking care of the poor. The increased dependence on government aid for the poor put more people on welfare and gave them the idea that people did not have to work to end poverty; the government would end it for them. As a result, people unwisely began to expect that the government would do more and more for them.

Nixon inherited an unfinished war in Vietnam and a "no-win" war policy, as well as a huge national debt and an inflated economy that was nearly out of control.

Since the escalation of the Vietnam War had led to the end of Johnson's career, one of Nixon's priorities was ending American involvement in that conflict. Nixon intended to pull the large numbers of American ground troops out of Vietnam while continuing the more effective air attacks. He did not want it to look as if the United States had been defeated in Vietnam, however, and so he was concerned that the American withdrawal be carried out with dignity. The White House courted public support for its Vietnam policy by calling radical antiwar protesters "defeatists."

In the fall of 1969 Nixon announced his plan for the **Vietnamization** of the war. This meant that the responsibility for the fighting would gradually be returned to the South Vietnamese. The United States would continue to support the South Vietnamese with supplies, air attacks, and other assistance. As Vietnamization was carried out, more American troops came home. When Nixon took office, 543,400 Americans were in Vietnam. An accelerated American pullout left 157,000 by December 1971, and only 24,000 by the end of 1972.

Section Review

1. What action of Congress gave President Johnson the authority to increase American involvement in Vietnam?
2. What were the South Vietnamese Communists called?
3. By what route did the Communists send troops and supplies into South Vietnam?
4. Who won the election of 1968?
5. What was "Vietnamization"?

Summary

The decade of the 1960s was a trying time for the United States. Divided opinions on major issues such as civil rights and the Vietnam War created tensions that affected all Americans. Reports of violence on television and in other media stirred fears, anger, and unrest. The Great Society increased government agencies and welfare programs in attempts to regulate and improve American life. The national debt increased dramatically; yet most Americans continued to seek wealth and benefit for themselves while ignoring their own responsibilities.

Chapter Review

Do You Remember?

■ Indicate whether each of the following items is most closely associated with (A) John Kennedy, (B) Lyndon Johnson, or (C) Richard Nixon.

1. Camelot
2. The Great Society
3. Vietnamization of the war
4. Gulf of Tonkin Resolution
5. the New Frontier
6. Cuban Missile Crisis

■ Match each of the following items with its description.
   7. Alliance for Progress
   8. *Brown* v. *Board of Education*
   9. ecology
   10. Gulf of Tonkin Resolution
   11. Twenty-third Amendment
   12. Twenty-fourth Amendment

   a. gave residents of the District of Columbia the right to vote
   b. allowed the president to increase activity in the Vietnam War
   c. dealt with man's relationship to his environment
   d. forbade states from levying poll taxes
   e. promised help to Latin Americans
   f. overturned the policy of "separate but equal"

■ Answer these questions about the 1960s.
   13. What Kennedy program sent American volunteers to needy parts of the world?
   14. A plan to recapture Cuba from the Communists failed when an unsuccessful invasion force landed where?
   15. What black preacher led much of the civil rights activity of the 1960s?
   16. Name three men involved in the race for the Democratic presidential nomination in 1968. Which one won the nomination?
   17. Who was Nixon's vice president?
   18. What word describes Nixon's plan for handling the Vietnam War?

Why Is It So?

1. Why was the 1960 presidential election different from past elections?
2. Why was the Berlin Wall an embarrassment for Kennedy and the free world?
3. How did blacks benefit from the civil rights legislation of the 1960s?
4. How did the civil rights movement turn violent?
5. Why was it difficult for American soldiers to fight in Vietnam?
6. How was the Tet Offensive both a victory and a defeat for the United States?

What Do You Think?

1. Should Kennedy have been tougher with Cuba and the Soviet Union? Explain your answer.
2. Was the civil rights movement of the 1960s necessary? Why or why not? Is a continued civil rights movement necessary today? Why or why not?
3. Why do you suppose the assassination of leaders often enhances their reputations?

29

Beginning a Third Century

President Nixon visiting the Great Wall of China in 1972

On July 4, 1976, Americans united to celebrate their **Bicentennial,** the two hundredth anniversary of the signing of the Declaration of Independence. Fireworks, special events, and celebrations throughout the country marked the entry of the United States into its third century. The Bicentennial reminded Americans to recount successes and to be thankful for their freedoms. Ten years later the country saw the one hundredth birthday of the Statue of Liberty. The special tribute to that monument reminded Americans that America has been a land of liberty and opportunity for those who have come to its shores. Then, in 1987,

the United States marked one more special anniversary—the bicentennial of the Constitution. For two hundred years this country's unique system of government has withstood trials and adapted to meet the needs of modern generations. Even in the nation's recent history, Americans have had reason to remember that their political heritage should be protected and preserved.

A. Leaders

During this time Americans had leaders who were very different from one another. Each tried to address the issues of the time with his own style.

Richard Nixon

Richard Nixon took office at the end of the turbulent sixties. Although antiwar protests continued for a while, much of the unrest among Americans seemed to be disappearing. The United States had sent astronauts to the moon. Foreign relations seemed to be improving, and there was hope for even greater accomplishments and an end to the war in Vietnam. Americans approached the new decade with hopes for an end to the turmoil they had experienced in the sixties. President Nixon was taking firm control of national affairs, and his leadership gave the country a new confidence.

Nixon's Approach—Nixon had received much of his support from a group of people he called "the silent majority"—decent, law-abiding, tax-paying Americans. Although President Johnson's interest had been in domestic affairs, Nixon's emphasis was on foreign affairs. He dealt with the problem of Vietnam, and he gained friendlier relations with Communist China and the Soviet

Union. Nixon brought in a new era of **détente,** an easing or relaxation of tensions, with the Soviet Union. In foreign affairs Nixon relied heavily on Dr. **Henry Kissinger,** a Harvard professor who became his special advisor. In 1973 Kissinger became Nixon's secretary of state.

Many Americans objected to these developments, arguing that because Communist governments could not be trusted, "better" relations with them were actually more dangerous. Because some called Nixon a conservative, however, he was able to quiet such fears where a more liberal president would have been viewed with more suspicion.

Nixon won the election of 1972, easily defeating a liberal Democrat, Senator George McGovern of South Dakota. Pleased with an economy that appeared stable, efforts at détente, and what they viewed as favorable developments in Vietnam, the people felt confident under Nixon's leadership.

Nixon's Vice President—Nixon's running mate, Vice President Spiro T. Agnew, was charged with accepting bribes from construction companies while he had been governor of Maryland. He was also charged with income tax evasion, to which he pleaded no contest (similar to pleading guilty). Facing a possible prison sentence, Agnew resigned the vice-presidency on October 10, 1973. He was the first vice president to resign since 1833 and the first vice president ever to resign because of a criminal charge.

For the first time since its ratification in 1967, the Twenty-fifth Amendment was used to pick a new vice president. Following the guidelines in the amendment, Nixon selected a vice president, and both houses of Congress confirmed his choice. The new

President Richard Nixon

vice president was **Gerald R. Ford,** a Michigan congressman. He took the oath of office on December 6, 1973.

Nixon's Downfall: Watergate—During the election of 1972, the Democratic party's National Campaign Headquarters had been burglarized. The headquarters was in a building called the Watergate complex in Washington, D.C., and its name, **"Watergate,"** soon became a household word. The police caught five men who were accused of planting electronic listening devices in the Democratic offices. One of the men arrested was a member of President Nixon's reelection committee.

The Watergate Cover-up Uncovered— The trial of the Watergate burglars and two other Nixon officials began in January 1973. One defendant claimed that the witnesses had committed perjury (lied in court). He also said that the defendants had been told to plead guilty by someone higher in the administration, giving the impression that the White House was covering up the burglary.

In May 1973 the U.S. Senate began its own independent investigation of the matter. The Senate committee found that the White House had tape recordings of all the president's office conversations. By listening to the tapes, the committee would be able to determine whether the president had instigated Watergate or whether he had known of it and was covering it up. But when the courts ordered Nixon to turn over the tapes, the president refused. He argued that he had executive privilege and that turning them over to the court or a committee would endanger national security.

Nixon's Resignation—The American public began to respond. They wrote angry letters to Congress asking for Nixon's impeachment. The House Judiciary Committee then began hearings on fifteen listed charges. The president responded by agreeing to turn over the tapes to a new special prosecutor. However, some of the tapes were missing, and on one tape, an eighteen-and-a-half minute section had been erased. Nixon claimed it was a secretary's error. When a court order asked for more tapes, the president refused to comply. However, he did supply a tape transcript. The transcript showed that the president had known about the efforts to cover up Watergate.

Watergate dragged on. By the end of July, the House Judiciary Committee had voted to impeach the president for obstructing justice, misusing his presidential powers, and refusing to comply with their requests for evidence. When the committee showed its determination to examine additional charges, the president's lawyers persuaded him to release more transcripts. These showed that the president not only had known of the burglary but also had acted to stop an FBI investigation of it. Rather than face an impeachment trial before the Senate that would probably have removed

President Nixon in the Oval Office with some of his staff who were involved in the Watergate affair

him from office, President Nixon resigned, the only president ever to do so.

The Watergate conspiracy troubled the public not only because of the corruption it uncovered but also because it revealed the power held by a president. Actually the power of the executive branch and the power of the president had been increasing steadily since the time of Franklin Roosevelt. Congress acted to prevent another Watergate. It forbade the president from refusing to release budget funds set aside by Congress in order to stop a congressional program or action. It strengthened the Freedom of Information Act, allowing the public more access to government decisions and acts. A Federal Campaign Reform Act in 1974 allowed taxpayers to designate money for candidates for federal offices and also placed a limit on the amount of money private individuals could give one candidate. This last action was an attempt to avoid corruption in future presidential campaigns.

The Watergate conspiracy was exposed and dealt with rather than pushed under a rug. Although the exposure was an embarrassment to the nation, it did show that the presidency was not all-powerful and above the law. The Constitution's system of checks and balances still worked.

Gerald Ford

Vice President Gerald R. Ford took the oath of office when Nixon resigned on August 9, 1974. Ford's position was unique: the public had not elected him as either vice president or president, but they seemed pleased to find a man who promised "openness and candor" and who said he was only an ordinary man who would try his best. Ford promised regular news conferences so that the public would be informed of his

Gerald R. Ford
38TH PRESIDENT
(1974-1977)

Born: Omaha, Nebraska, July 14, 1913
Family: married Elizabeth "Betty" Bloomer; had three sons, one daughter
Occupation: lawyer
Home: Grand Rapids, Michigan
Religion: Episcopalian
Election: none; appointed as vice president and succeeded to the presidency upon the resignation of Nixon
Political Party: Republican
Vice President: Nelson Rockefeller (appointed)
Interesting Facts and Accomplishments:
only president not elected to national office (was appointed vice president and approved by Congress)
was born Leslie Lynch King, Jr., but was adopted by his stepfather after his mother remarried; his name was changed to Gerald R. Ford, Jr., and he did not know he was adopted until he was sixteen years old
often made his own breakfast while in the White House
two assassination attempts were made on his life during his presidency—both by women
was left-handed

actions. He saw the need to restore the public's confidence in the presidential office. He chose a former New York governor and Republican politician, Nelson Rockefeller, as his vice president. He kept Henry Kissinger, Nixon's secretary of state, on his cabinet and said that he would pursue a foreign policy like Nixon's.

One month into office Ford ignited his first spark of controversy by pardoning Richard Nixon for any crimes he might have committed while in office. Ford said that trying the former president would only subject the country to added agony. Many Americans, however, were displeased. They reasoned that if those under Nixon had been tried and sentenced, he should be too.

Jimmy Carter

Ford had the chance to run for office himself in 1976. But since he had not been in office long, he had not made many of his own policies. Moreover, the Republican party was still recovering from the scars of Watergate.

The Democratic party nominated **Jimmy Carter,** a former governor of Georgia. Because he had taken a strong stand on civil rights in Georgia, he won black voters. He also won a following among laborers. Carter stressed his honesty and his lack of ties to politics in Washington. It was a lackluster election that Carter won by only a narrow margin.

Since Carter had worked with nuclear submarines in the U.S. Navy, he had a good understanding of science and technology. However, he did not have a solid grasp of foreign affairs. He wanted to bring new faces to Washington and use the same simple, down-home style he had used to run his father's peanut warehouse in Georgia. Although that style made Americans feel

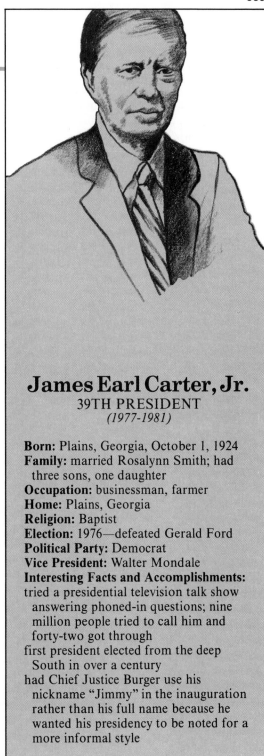

James Earl Carter, Jr.
39TH PRESIDENT
(1977-1981)

Born: Plains, Georgia, October 1, 1924
Family: married Rosalynn Smith; had three sons, one daughter
Occupation: businessman, farmer
Home: Plains, Georgia
Religion: Baptist
Election: 1976—defeated Gerald Ford
Political Party: Democrat
Vice President: Walter Mondale
Interesting Facts and Accomplishments:
tried a presidential television talk show answering phoned-in questions; nine million people tried to call him and forty-two got through
first president elected from the deep South in over a century
had Chief Justice Burger use his nickname "Jimmy" in the inauguration rather than his full name because he wanted his presidency to be noted for a more informal style

closer to him, Washington politicians neither appreciated nor cooperated with it. Carter did not take the right steps to build support for his programs. He tended to be bogged down in details, and few people, even in his own party, really knew if the president had any long-term goals that he wanted to reach while he was in office.

In his inaugural address Carter declared that human rights would be central in his foreign policy decisions. "Because we are free, we can never be indifferent to the fact of freedom elsewhere," he said. "Thus people everywhere should have freedom to make political choices, exercise their ideas free of intimidation or persecution, and to own property." Although such ideas sound wonderful, they are hard to bring into reality in areas of the world where the United States has no control and little influence.

Ronald Reagan

Carter's Republican opponent in the election of 1980 was California's former governor **Ronald Reagan.** Reagan's speeches were direct, sincere, and stirring. His policies were conservative, and many Americans accepted them. He pushed for strengthening the national defense, for cutting the size of the federal bureaucracy, and for getting big government "off the backs of the people."

Reagan carried all but six states and the District of Columbia in the election. The Republicans even won a small majority in the Senate. Although Democrats still held a majority in the House, a group of somewhat conservative Democrats sometimes voted with the Republicans. This meant that, in his early years as president, Reagan was able to get his programs passed by Congress, especially laws dealing with the economy and with military spending.

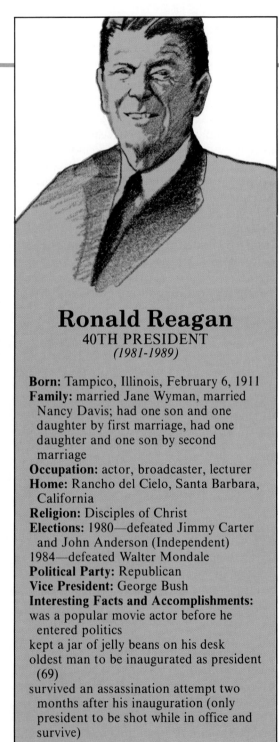

Ronald Reagan
40TH PRESIDENT
(1981-1989)

Born: Tampico, Illinois, February 6, 1911
Family: married Jane Wyman, married Nancy Davis; had one son and one daughter by first marriage, had one daughter and one son by second marriage
Occupation: actor, broadcaster, lecturer
Home: Rancho del Cielo, Santa Barbara, California
Religion: Disciples of Christ
Elections: 1980—defeated Jimmy Carter and John Anderson (Independent) 1984—defeated Walter Mondale
Political Party: Republican
Vice President: George Bush
Interesting Facts and Accomplishments:
was a popular movie actor before he entered politics
kept a jar of jelly beans on his desk
oldest man to be inaugurated as president (69)
survived an assassination attempt two months after his inauguration (only president to be shot while in office and survive)

The Democrats were optimistic about the election of 1984. Former Vice President Walter Mondale eventually won the nomination and surprised many by choosing a woman as his running mate—Geraldine Ferraro Zaccaro, a congresswoman from New York. The Democrats attacked the high deficit, the arms build-up, and decreased spending on social programs.

Ronald Reagan easily won the Republican nomination. He led in the polls the entire campaign. Americans trusted the president, and he carried every state but Mondale's home state of Minnesota. It was one of the biggest landslides of the twentieth century.

After Watergate the American government had had two weak presidents. In addition, the failures in both domestic and foreign policy during the Ford and Carter years had given the whole nation a sense of weakness and an inability to deal with problems. Ronald Reagan offered to restore American strength and pride, and the people were once again willing for their leader to take charge of affairs.

Section Review

1. Who was Nixon's first vice president? What was unusual about the manner in which he left office?
2. What evidence showed that Nixon knew about the Watergate burglary and tried to cover it up?
3. How was the president's power curbed by legislation after Watergate?
4. What was unique about Ford's rise to the presidency?
5. What issue did Carter say would be central in his foreign policy decisions?
6. Why did Reagan have some success with Congress in his first term?

B. Domestic Issues

The Economy

When he came to office, Richard Nixon inherited both a war debt and inflation. He tried to curb inflation by curtailing government spending and by increasing taxes. With less money in circulation, people would not be able to buy as much. But economic recessions often result from such action, and such was the case for Nixon.

Nixon—To make the recession less painful to the average American—and to help his own chances of reelection—Nixon raised government spending, an action that increased the national debt. But Nixon did not give up on curbing inflation. In August 1971 he ordered wage and price controls. All wages, prices, and fees were frozen at August levels for ninety days. When the ninety days were up, the Cost of Living Council was organized. Under its guidelines some increases were allowed. Nixon's wage and price controls, like those used in other administrations, did not deal with the causes of inflation—excessive government spending and national debt. They only temporarily controlled some of the symptoms of the nation's economic problems.

The Twenty-sixth Amendment
Because eighteen-year-olds were eligible to be drafted for military duty but were not able to vote, many Americans began to support the idea that the voting age should be lowered. While Nixon was president, the **Twenty-sixth Amendment** was passed in 1971 to lower the voting age from twenty-one to eighteen.

Ford—When Gerald Ford succeeded Nixon, the wage and price controls had artificially slowed inflation to about three per cent annually. But with the end of these controls in 1973, inflation doubled. In 1974 it almost doubled again to 12.2 per cent.

Rather than have the government regulate the economy, Ford pushed for a voluntary anti-inflation crusade. Called WIN (*W*hip *I*nflation *N*ow), the plan encouraged consumers to boycott overpriced goods and asked workers not to seek wage increases. But since most people believed they were the victims rather than the causes of inflation and wanted more money rather than less, they ignored WIN. The economic recession grew even worse as the Federal Reserve System, which influences interest rates in the country, raised interest rates. This action added to the increased inflation. Sales slackened, and unemployment reached more than nine per cent.

President Ford then requested a tax cut, and Congress approved it. Although the cut provided more money for buying things, it also brought more inflation by increasing the government's budget deficit. The president then cut the budget and government spending. He also vetoed both spending bills the Democratic Congress passed, but inflation continued to spiral upward.

Carter—Under Jimmy Carter the economic troubles mushroomed. Because of inflation people feared prices would go still higher. To get what they wanted before prices went up, consumers purchased items using borrowed money. With this borrowed money in circulation, inflation increased and prices continued to rise. Workers then demanded higher wages. At the same time, interest rates reached some of the highest levels in years. The annual inflation rates were "double-digit"—over ten per cent. Because people could not afford home mort-

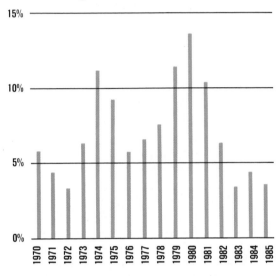

Consumer Price Index Increases Show High Inflation of the 1970s

gages, the building trade floundered. Other businesses suffered also, and unemployment rose.

Like Ford, Carter tried to curb inflation by cutting federal spending and revising the tax system. He asked people to accept voluntary wage and price controls but had little success. His tax bill was supposed to cut taxes for lower-income groups by closing loopholes open to the rich. By the time Congress finished with the bill, it had reduced some taxes for the wealthy, but it had raised Social Security taxes.

Reagan—In his campaign Ronald Reagan had promised to cut inflation and to stimulate the nation's economy. He hoped to do this by going back to a classical, free-enterprise, capitalist system. Calling it **"supply-side economics,"** Reagan hoped to decrease or remove government regulation of industry and to cut both corporate and individual taxes. Ideally, less regulation and lower taxes would encourage both businesses and people to invest more and to spend more. Thus more goods would be needed, and more unemployed could go back to work.

In 1981 Congress cut inheritance and gift taxes, corporate taxes, and income taxes. To help balance the budget, the president hoped to cut the size of the government bureaucracy and reduce increases in federal spending in almost every area except the military. Some of these reductions were in social services such as housing, aid to cities, aid to families with dependent children, loans to college students, and food stamps. About two hundred programs were trimmed, and the resulting savings was about $35 billion.

Because there was little real support for cutting federal spending, supply-side economics did not work as well as planned. The budget did not balance; in fact, the national debt reached its highest total in history. Three things hurt Reagan's plan: the already existing debt amassed by previous administrations, the nation's current spending habits, and his own underestimation of the effect of the tax cuts. Government receipts did not increase, forcing the national debt higher as the government still had to pay its obligations. Some critics of the president's economic programs referred to the policies as "Reaganomics."

Despite the growing national debt, businesses flourished during most of the Reagan administration. However, a growing trade imbalance became an additional threat to the economy. Americans were buying more foreign goods than foreigners were buying American goods. Eventually, worries over the future of the economy led to a stock market crash in 1987. The crash was not as severe as the one in 1929, but it did cause some Americans to realize that they could not count on prosperity to continue. Debts would have to be repaid—whether they were personal debts or national debts.

Energy

Arab Oil Embargo—Because Arab nations resented American support of Israel, they ordered an embargo (complete ban) on American oil shipments in October 1973. Since the United States imported one-quarter of its oil from Middle Eastern countries, the **oil embargo** soon affected Americans. There were long lines at gasoline stations. Prices of gasoline, fuel oil, and products made from petroleum, such as plastics, rose dramatically.

President Nixon asked Americans to conserve energy. The speed limit was lowered to 55 mph. Congress passed the Alaskan Pipeline Act to build a pipeline across Alaska and Canada, thus developing a new source of domestic oil. The oil crisis was eased somewhat when the Arab nations lifted their embargo in March 1974. But the oil embargo did make the nation conscious of the need to develop alternate sources of energy.

Although OPEC (the Organization of Petroleum Exporting Countries) halted its embargo, it steadily raised crude oil prices. Americans were forced to pay up to two dollars a gallon for gasoline, about four times what they had paid before the embargo. Middle Eastern countries that were anti-American, such as Libya and Iran, pushed for even higher crude oil prices to afflict America further. More moderate OPEC members, such as Saudi Arabia, tried to convince them that their tactics might bankrupt industrialized western countries. Countries with sagging economies would not be good customers for oil. The split among the OPEC countries opened up oil trade and thus helped to ease the **energy crisis.**

But with increased fuel costs, Americans made changes during the crisis. Smaller cars that got more miles per gallon became popular. Car pools or "ride-sharing" became more common in urban areas. Many Americans spent vacations close to home as the cost of travel climbed.

Energy Independence—From 1973 to 1977, the cost of imported oil for the nation skyrocketed from $8 billion to $40 billion a year. President Carter believed that the solution was for the United States to be independent in energy resources. He devised a program that he believed would bring that independence. First, he wanted nationwide conservation. Next, he proposed **deregulation,** an end to price controls on gas and oil. If foreign prices went high enough, American companies would be encouraged to search for new oil sources and to develop new energy sources. This competition might bring solutions to the nation's energy needs. Deregulation came, and fuel prices jumped higher. Although it might have been desirable in the long run, deregulation had an immediate negative effect on the average citizen's pocketbook.

Nuclear Power and Three Mile Island— Although President Carter realized that there were serious problems in disposing of nuclear waste, he believed that increasing the use of nuclear power might help solve the energy crisis. Nuclear accidents worried some Americans, but the risks seemed minimal compared to the overall gain.

On March 28, 1979, an accident occurred at the **Three Mile Island** nuclear power plant near Harrisburg, Pennsylvania. The nuclear reactor's cooling system failed. Before the reactor could be shut down, radioactive steam was released, contaminating the water in a backup stream. Although the backup system worked and the immediate crisis passed, many Americans feared that nuclear power was unsafe. The Three Mile Island accident prompted antinuclear protests and hampered the building of more nuclear power plants. Despite these problems, the cost of energy stabilized during Reagan's administration.

The Supreme Court

Nixon's Court Appointments—President Nixon had the opportunity to appoint four justices to the Supreme Court, including a new chief justice. The Warren Court, the court of the 1950s and 1960s, had grown unpopular with many Americans who thought it had overprotected criminals and tied the hands of the police. In state after state there were stories of cases where criminals had been freed on legal technicalities. When Chief Justice Earl Warren retired in 1969, Nixon replaced him with **Warren Burger.** He filled later vacancies by nominating Harry Blackmun, Lewis F.

Chief Justice Warren Burger administering the oath to Sandra Day O'Connor, the first woman to sit on the Supreme Court

Powell, and William H. Rehnquist. Although the Burger Court did not reverse the trends and landmark decisions of the Warren Court, it did limit the scope of some. The court also cut the number of cases it heard dealing with civil liberties.

Roe* v. *Wade—Unfortunately the conservatives on the court did not have enough power to prevent a liberal decision on abortion. In ***Roe* v. *Wade*** (1973), the court decided that a woman had the right to abort her unborn child within the first three months of pregnancy. Since then about 1.5 million abortions have been performed each year. This legalized murder destroys nearly one-third of all American babies each year.

Reagan's Court Appointments—President Reagan's first appointment to the Supreme Court was the first woman on the court, **Sandra Day O'Connor.** Afterwards the president named Justice **William H. Rehnquist,** a conservative justice already on the court, as the new chief justice when Warren Burger stepped down. With these and other court appointments, such as Antonin

Scalia and Anthony Kennedy, President Reagan hoped to shape the Supreme Court into a more conservative force.

Supreme Court justices are highly influential. Because most are in the court far longer than the term of a president, they can influence policies for long periods. The justices need God's guidance and wisdom as they make decisions that influence future generations. Although we do not have the opportunity to influence justices as directly as we do the president and congressmen, they need our prayers just the same.

Section Review
1. What are the causes of inflation?
2. What two names were given to Reagan's economic policies?
3. How did Arab countries react to American support for Israel in the Middle East?
4. How did Carter deal with the energy crisis?
5. Whom did Nixon appoint as chief justice?

The Supreme Court Building in Washington, D.C.

C. Foreign Affairs

Vietnam

Vietnamization—Nixon's plan in Vietnam—"Vietnamization" of the war—was to pull American troops out of Vietnam by the thousands. But the success of Vietnamization depended on continued American support for the South Vietnamese and the ability to force North Vietnam to honor negotiated settlements. While the Americans pulled out of Vietnam, the North Vietnamese and Vietcong multiplied their forces and gathered supplies from Communist China and the Soviet Union. These Communist soldiers were not only moving into Vietnam but were also lurking in safe hideouts across the border in Laos and Cambodia.

In April of 1970 President Nixon announced a temporary expansion of the war into Cambodia. The Communists had supply bases there that needed to be destroyed, and they were withdrawing to Cambodia between attacks on Americans in Vietnam. Nixon ordered the Cambodian bases bombed. In 1971 the United States also became involved in Laos. American planes provided air cover for invading South Vietnamese troops seeking to destroy the Ho Chi Minh Trail.

American response to these actions, especially the move into Cambodia, was strong. More demonstrations erupted on college campuses, sometimes with the help of leftist agitation. At Kent State University in Ohio, students disobeyed the instructions of the Ohio National Guard to disperse. When the soldiers felt threatened, they panicked and fired into the crowd. Four students died. A similar riot at Jackson State University in Mississippi led to two more deaths. In a regular war, dissent and riots such as these would have been punishable, perhaps even defined as treason. In an undeclared war, where there was no defined enemy, Americans tolerated such acts, and some even cheered them on.

Paris Peace Talks—Meanwhile Nixon sought to get the North Vietnamese to the peace table. It took six weeks to get the two sides into the same room in Paris. At the same time, Kissinger was holding secret talks with Le Duc Tho, secretary of the North Vietnamese Communist party. But as usual the Communists used the lull to ready a new offensive. When Le Duc Tho became angry and left for Hanoi, the United States responded with air strikes and heavy bombing of Hanoi and Haiphong, North Vietnamese cities. In addition, it mined Haiphong's harbor. The pressure was heavy enough that when Le Duc Tho came back to the peace talks on January 24, 1973, he was willing to sign a cease-fire agreement.

The Fall of Vietnam and Cambodia—While in Congress, Ford had voted with the hawks on Vietnam-related issues. Thus when North Vietnam violated the 1973 cease-fire and attacked Saigon in 1975, Ford asked Congress to increase aid to South Vietnam, but Congress refused. Because Congress blocked any further attempts to aid South Vietnam and force North Vietnam to remain faithful to the peace agreements, the cause was lost. The last American troops left Saigon in the spring of 1975. Within two weeks of the American departure, Saigon fell to the North Vietnamese. In April 1975 the South Vietnamese surrendered. In the years following, reports of Communist massacres and inhumanity regularly found their way out of Southeast Asia.

The statue at the Vietnam War Memorial in Washington, D.C.

President Ford offered **amnesty,** or a group pardon, to those who had illegally dodged the draft during the Vietnam conflict. The president issued the amnesty to heal the dissension left from the war. But to Americans who had complied with the law and to those who had lost a family member in the war, the action was a stinging insult. The number of people who took advantage of the amnesty offer was smaller than expected. Some draft dodgers snubbed the offer because they believed accepting it was an admission that their actions had been wrong.

The Cost of Vietnam—The cost of the Vietnam War was high: more than 50,000 Americans were killed; 200,000 more were wounded; and about $140 billion was spent. But the war cost Americans more than casualties and money. Vietnam War veterans came back to a disillusioned, frustrated country. A few were welcomed as heroes; most were ignored. Many returned maimed by injuries. Because they had risked their lives as patriots, veterans were angered when draft dodgers were granted amnesty

and allowed to return. Americans remembering past victories had a hard time comprehending the purpose of wasting lives in no-win wars such as Korea and Vietnam. It was not until 1982 that a national memorial for the Vietnam dead was dedicated.

As a result of the length and cost of this undeclared war, Congress acted in 1973 to limit the president's power to fight such a war in the future. The **War Powers Act** upheld the president's authority to go to war under certain defined circumstances, but it also required that all action be ended in thirty days unless Congress authorized action beyond that.

The Vietnam War showed that there had been many miscalculations in determining national policies. American military capabilities were overestimated; the enemy's were underestimated. Second, basic economic principles were ignored. Unwise domestic spending in addition to the war cost led to massive inflation, deficit spending, and a huge national debt. Third, the corrupt nature of the Vietnamese governments hurt American policy at home and in Vietnam. While Americans were trying to save South Vietnam, some Vietnamese began to hate Americans for what they perceived as their interference. Reports of such attitudes were exaggerated and fed to Americans as propaganda to increase questions about U.S. involvement in Vietnam. Fourth, because the war was undeclared, there were few restrictions placed on the press. Thus the press was allowed to give Americans its view of the war in such a way that it created the public opinions that restricted and shaped military policy. Such circumstances tied the hands of the military and kept them from carrying out actions in the best interest of the nation.

The war left several questions unanswered, questions such as to what extent the press should be allowed to influence the actions of the military and how much power the president should have to wage war. It gave Americans a fear of entangling themselves in other foreign conflicts that might end without victory. The war also left its veterans with many adjustments to make as they returned to the United States. Nearly six hundred American soldiers that had been taken as prisoners of war in Vietnam were released in 1973, but over two thousand soldiers that were listed as missing in action (MIA) are still unaccounted for.

Relations with the Soviet Union

SALT I—In May 1972 President Nixon made a trip to the Soviet Union. He met with Soviet leaders in Moscow to discuss a **Strategic Arms Limitations Treaty** (SALT). Both nations agreed to restrict the types and number of nuclear warheads and missiles. They also made trade agreements and an agreement to cooperate on scientific and space projects. Opponents of these agreements observed that since the Soviet Union had not developed a reputation for honoring treaties, they were worth little more than the paper on which they were written. However, they did have considerable political value at home.

SALT II—Carter continued negotiations for another Strategic Arms Limitations Treaty with the Soviets. However, in 1977 he submitted a new set of proposals for strategic arms limitations. One aim was to get equality in missile systems. This slowed the talks, and it was March 1979 before a treaty called SALT II was signed. Carter then submitted the treaty for Senate approval. Both the Senate and the press

Communist China

China had been closed to the West since the Communist Chinese takeover in 1949. In July 1971 Kissinger made a secret trip to China. There he made arrangements for a presidential visit in February of 1972. Accompanied by American magazine and TV reporters, Nixon toured the Great Wall, attended banquets, and met with Chinese leader Chairman Mao Tse-tung. This opening of diplomatic relations with the People's Republic of China, however, hurt Taiwan. When the United States recognized Red China, the U.N. admitted it into that organization and expelled Taiwan. The United States ended its diplomatic relationship with Taiwan on March 1, 1979, but it has maintained some cultural and commercial ties and continues to trade with the island nation.

reacted negatively. Opposition grew stronger when the Soviet Union invaded the nation of Afghanistan, and the president withdrew the treaty.

Afghanistan—The Soviet invasion of Afghanistan in 1979 angered Americans. Claiming they had been invited into Afghanistan, the Soviets executed the Afghan president soon after their paratroopers landed. Their plans to set up a puppet regime were hindered by Afghans who took to the hills and initiated guerrilla warfare. Although Carter had earlier been against secret operations, he now let the Central Intelligence Agency (CIA) channel aid to Afghan freedom forces. Carter's punishment for the Soviets was weak, however: he announced that the United States would not take part in the 1980 Olympic Games, to be held in Moscow. The Soviet invasion of Afghanistan led to the end of détente, at least for the time being.

Reagan's Approach—Between the Soviets and the Americans there seemed to be frost—if not ice—in the air even before Reagan took office. The Soviets had invaded Afghanistan, and Soviet-equipped Cuban troops were in Angola, Africa. Moreover, the Soviets were installing long-range missiles in their satellite countries in Eastern Europe.

President Reagan wanted to negotiate a new treaty to replace the unapproved SALT II. However, he sought to improve the national defense so that when the United States negotiated, it would do so from a stronger position. He pushed for the development of a new bomber, called the B-1, and asked for further research on nuclear and chemical weapons. While the Soviets stalled on arms limitation talks in 1982, Reagan placed more American missiles in Western European nations.

Relations with the Soviet Union seemed strained as arguments continued over the Soviet presence in Afghanistan. Tensions increased when the Soviets shot down a Korean airliner with 61 Americans, including a U.S. congressman, aboard in 1983. Also the Soviets backed the Polish government's crackdown on a labor movement for greater freedom in Poland. While Americans complained about these and other acts of Soviet repression, the Soviet Union tried to make President Reagan seem like a villain for promoting an American Strategic Defense Initiative (SDI). This antimissile system in space came to be called the "Star Wars" program.

Reagan's tough stand against the Soviet Union made many of America's NATO allies in Western Europe nervous, but Reagan soon began to negotiate with a new Soviet leader, **Mikhail Gorbachev,** who gained power in 1985. Within two years plans were being made for a reduction in the land-based nuclear weapons in Europe. Such negotiation renewed hopes for peace between the United States and the Soviet Union, but it changed none of the differences between the two governments. Gorbachev used his personal charm to influence American opinion, and many Americans began to believe that long-term peace between the U.S. and the Soviet Union—what Reagan had called an "evil empire"—might be achievable.

The Middle East

Relations Between Israel and Egypt—In October 1973 Egyptian and Syrian troops suddenly attacked Israel. Because they launched their attack on Yom Kippur (the Day of Atonement), a Jewish high holy day, the war was called the **Yom Kippur War.** In the first week of the war, the Israelis, who had been caught by surprise, lost. But in the second week they recovered lost ground and took the offensive. Since Egypt and Syria had been friendly to the Soviet Union while the United States had supported Israel, Americans feared that the Soviet Union might aid the Arabs (Egypt and Syria). The Arab states, though losing, refused to negotiate directly with Israel.

As a result, Secretary of State Henry Kissinger became the go-between. He helped negotiate an Israeli-Egyptian cease-fire in May 1974. Using **shuttle diplomacy** that took him from the United States to Damascus, Syria; to Cairo, Egypt; on to Tel Aviv, Israel; and back home again, he negotiated. Anwar Sadat, Egypt's president, became more friendly to the United States and surprised everyone by sending an ambassador to Israel.

Following the visit of Anwar Sadat to Israel and Kissinger's shuttle diplomacy,

Carter invited Sadat and Israel's Menachem Begin to Camp David, a presidential retreat in Maryland. A historic accord, or agreement, was reached, with Carter acting as mediator. In September 1978 Sadat and Begin signed a treaty ending thirty years of fighting between Israel and Egypt. Israel agreed to leave the Sinai peninsula; Egypt agreed to let Israeli ships use the Suez Canal. Carter claimed the **Camp David Accords** as a foreign relations triumph.

The Iranian Hostage Crisis—On November 4, 1979, America faced a new crisis. In the Middle Eastern country of Iran, sixty-six American embassy officials were taken hostage by a group of radical Iranian students who soon revealed their connections to Iran's new Muslim ruler, the **Ayatollah Khomeini.**

The **Iranian hostage crisis** caught most Americans by surprise, but it probably

shouldn't have. The United States had aided the former ruler of Iran, the shah. However, the shah had made many enemies in Iran. During a civil war the shah fled the country, and Khomeini emerged as ruler. To mask deep economic problems and widespread unemployment, Khomeini stirred up hatred toward the shah and the United States, which had supported him. In October 1979 President Carter allowed the shah, who was ill with cancer, to be admitted into the United States for medical treatment. Although presidential advisors told Carter the Iranians would retaliate, he made his decision on humanitarian grounds. The retaliation was seizure of the hostages.

The American people were incensed that Khomeini and his country had paralyzed the United States in such a way. Carter froze Iran's American assets (did not allow Iranians to withdraw their investments in the United States). Then he cut off the importation of Iranian oil.

Carter made one attempt to rescue the hostages by force, but in the effort one helicopter collided with a transport plane, killing eight Americans. The failure of the rescue attempt only added to the American feelings of frustration and humiliation.

By September 1980 Iran and its neighbor Iraq were at war, and the shah had died of cancer. Khomeini said he would release the hostages if America freed Iranian assets, promised never to interfere in Iranian affairs, and returned the shah's wealth that he had sent out of the country. Since the United States had no access to the shah's wealth, it could not meet the conditions. And furthermore, most Americans thought the country should not submit to Iranian demands.

President Jimmy Carter

Just before Reagan's inauguration Iran announced the release of the hostages. On January 21, 1981, after 444 days in captivity, the American hostages boarded a plane in Teheran, Iran, beginning a journey to freedom. Americans rejoiced with an outpouring of patriotism upon the return of the hostages. They were relieved that the crisis was over.

Middle-Eastern Terrorism—Early in Reagan's first term civil war and foreign intervention in Lebanon led the U.N. to send in peace-keeping troops. American marines were stationed in Lebanon as a part of this force. But on October 23, 1983, a truck loaded with heavy explosives ran a series of barricades and slammed into the marine headquarters on the outskirts of Beirut. The suicide attack killed over two hundred marines.

Tensions in the Middle East also led to a series of terrorist attacks in Europe and the Mediterranean. Many of these attacks were aimed at Americans, and the United States grew weary of these surprise bombings and shootings. When it was learned that Libya and its leader, **Muammar Qaddafi,** were behind some of the terrorism, and when Qaddafi further threatened the United States, Reagan responded with a surprise bombing raid. The American attack on

Soldiers in Beirut, Lebanon, a major center of Middle Eastern discord and terrorism in the 1980s

Libya on March 31, 1986, was brief, but it helped quiet the terrorist rampage.

Iran-Iraq War—Another major problem was a war between Iran and Iraq. Fighting in the Persian Gulf threatened the sea transportation of the neighboring oil-exporting countries. These countries also feared that Iran might push the war beyond Iraq and into their lands. Because the petroleum supplies of these lands were in danger, and because that petroleum was very important to western industrial nations and their economies, the United States began to send a large naval force into the Persian Gulf to protect the neutral oil tankers. Americans grew uneasy, thinking that this involvement might lead the United States into war.

Latin America

The Panama Canal Treaty—Early in the 1970s Secretary of State Henry Kissinger had been working on an agreement dealing with the future of the Panama Canal. The United States had a ninety-nine-year lease beginning in 1903, but Panamanian nationalists demanded that the canal be put under their control immediately. Carter resumed negotiations and in 1978 signed a new **Panama Canal Treaty.** Control of the Canal Zone was transferred to Panama in 1979, and all control of the canal would be exchanged in the year 2000. The United States, however, retained the right to intervene with military force if the canal's neutrality were ever threatened.

The Senate approved the treaty after hot debate. Those who supported the treaty believed that the United States had no right to the Canal Zone. Many Americans, however, believed that the United States had given up something of value much too easily.

They also believed that under Panamanian rule, the canal might fall into Communist hands.

Growth of Communist Influence— Since Fidel Castro's rise to power in Cuba in 1959, the United States had been especially concerned about limiting the spread of communism throughout Latin America. Conditions in Latin American countries—such as high birth rates, poverty, ownership of land primarily by the rich, and dictatorships—made it easy to convince the people to support revolution.

President Reagan became increasingly concerned about Grenada, a small island country in the Caribbean. Grenada had been ruled by an anti-American government since the 1970s. In 1983 Grenada was permitting Cuba to build a major airport runway on the island. Such a runway could be used to spread supplies for Communist revolutions in the Caribbean area. To this threat was added a political upheaval and the murder of the president of Grenada.

Neighboring islands feared for their safety, and civil war in Grenada threatened the lives of about seven hundred young Americans enrolled in medical school there. Several Caribbean nations asked the United States to intervene. In a surprise attack American paratroopers and forces from five Caribbean nations restored peace to Grenada. The United States finished the airstrip and oversaw a free election in December 1984. American troops were in Grenada only a matter of weeks. The Grenada incident helped Castro and other Communists see that not all of Latin America would tolerate Communist expansion.

Another revolution had taken place in Nicaragua before Reagan took office. The Communist **Sandinistas** had used Cuban

advisors to set up a Communist government. The CIA had channeled aid to the anti-Sandinista rebels, called **Contras** (short for the Spanish word for *counter-revolutionary*). President Reagan feared that Communist-backed revolution would spread to Nicaragua's neighbors: Guatemala, Costa Rica, Honduras, and El Salvador. Reagan's particular concern was El Salvador. He believed that it was the next target; and if it fell, all Central America and even Mexico might fall under Communist domination. At first Congress went along with Reagan's plans to give aid to the Contras and to El Salvador. Eventually, however, the unstable conditions in those lands led to a fear that America might be pulled into another conflict like Vietnam. Support for Reagan's plans dwindled.

Another incident relating to Contra support came to light in 1987. Some of the

President Reagan addressing Congress with Vice President Bush and the Speaker of the House looking on

administration's personnel organized a sale of weapons to Iran in exchange for Iran's help in freeing some of the American hostages in Lebanon. The president apparently approved this deal, contrary to his official stand of not bargaining with terrorists. The situation grew worse when it was learned that money from the sale of the weapons was sent to aid the Contras in Nicaragua. Congress had cut all government aid to the Contras during the time the transaction had been made, and so many charged that sending money to the Contras was a violation of the law. Reagan claimed he knew nothing of this diversion of funds. Many Americans believed him, but opponents made much of his apparent lack of control over his subordinates. This Iran-Contra scandal hampered Reagan's effectiveness in the final years of his presidency.

Section Review

1. When did the United States pull all of its troops out of Vietnam? What was the result?
2. What two Communist countries did Nixon visit?
3. What was Carter's major triumph in foreign affairs?
4. What situation caused a great crisis in the last year of the Carter administration?
5. What two major treaties did Carter support? Were they approved by the Senate?
6. Who were the Contras? Why was President Reagan concerned for them?

Summary

The United States entered its third century carrying a heavy load of difficulties. The Watergate scandal had left the presidency weak. Growing national debt and inflation threatened the economy. The Communists were making advances in Southeast Asia and Latin America, and Middle Eastern terrorism added to the problems abroad; yet Americans celebrated their Bicentennial as leaders of the free world. The nation continued to meet the challenges of the times, not always successfully, but with assurance that the republic would continue to work if the people fulfilled their responsibilities.

Chapter Review

Do You Remember?

◼ Answer these questions.
1. What two bicentennial celebrations did America have during the 1970s and 1980s?
2. What treaty did Nixon make with the Soviets?
3. What court case legalized abortion in America?

4. What two scandals occurred during President Nixon's second term?
5. What two especially controversial actions did President Ford take?
6. What was President Carter's greatest foreign relations triumph?
7. What two groups were fighting against each other in Nicaragua in the 1980s?
8. Who was the first woman appointed as a Supreme Court justice?

■ Match these men with their descriptions.

9. Warren Burger	a. Iranian Muslim ruler
10. Mikhail Gorbachev	b. Libyan leader
11. Ayatollah Khomeini	c. Soviet leader
12. Henry Kissinger	d. chief justice appointed by Reagan
13. Muammar Qaddafi	e. chief justice appointed by Nixon
14. William Rehnquist	f. prominent American diplomat

■ Indicate whether each of the following items is most closely associated with (A) President Nixon, (B) President Ford, (C) President Carter, or (D) President Reagan.
15. Panama Canal Treaty
16. Watergate
17. Supply-Side Economics
18. amnesty for draft evaders
19. Grenada invasion
20. détente
21. Iranian hostage crisis

Why Is It So?

1. Why did the Arab nations place an embargo on American oil shipments in 1973?
2. Why was the American public upset by the revelations of Watergate?
3. Why did Vietnamization fail?
4. What was unique about the way Ford became president?
5. Why did Ford's WIN crusade fail?
6. How was Carter's foreign policy unsuccessful?
7. Why were Americans embarrassed by the Iranian hostage crisis?

What Do You Think?

1. Was détente with the Soviet Union good for the United States? Explain your answer.
2. Should America have become involved in Vietnam? Explain your answer.
3. Why do America's presidents receive much criticism?

30

Continued Change, Continued Challenge

"Man Lands on the Moon," "Heart Transplant Saves Life," "Robots Do the Work of Men on Assembly Line," "Computer Solves Mathematical Questions," "Solar Heat Saves Electricity"—headlines such as these have become commonplace in the United States over the past few decades. Technological advances have provided Americans with many achievements, conveniences, entertainments, and medical improvements and safeguards. Although Americans enjoy these remarkable achievements, such advances cannot provide an escape from common troubles such as poverty, crime, and discontent. Modern America has many blessings, but it also faces many difficulties. As the United States presses further into its third century, it will have to continue to deal with both the triumphs and the trials of modern life.

A. Scientific Advances

Almost every day Americans learn of discoveries in science and medicine that may benefit man. Computers, lasers, robots, and new chemicals that can help man in his work or contribute to his health are constantly being developed and improved. Today small hand-held calculators powered by light can perform far greater tasks than the old bulky

A solar energy plant in California's Mojave Desert uses technology that may help America produce more electricity in the future.

adding machines of the 1950s and 1960s. Patients who would have faced death or permanent handicap only a few years ago can now hope that plastic joints, pacemakers, transplanted organs, and many other medical wonders and new medicines may help to restore their health. New cars are generally more aerodynamic and fuel efficient and offer more new features every year. New electronic equipment continually seems to make older televisions, stereos, videotape recorders, and other goods seem obsolete. These are just some of the ways that technology is changing the manner in which Americans live. The United States, probably more than any nation on earth, offers these advances to many of its people.

Space Travel

Perhaps some of the greatest technological achievements the United States has made have come with the pursuit of its space program. America's space program began as a desperate race—a race against the Soviets, who were first to launch a satellite and then were also first to put a man into space. The Soviets put their first satellite, *Sputnik,* into orbit on October 4, 1957. This action concerned Americans because they realized that the United States had not yet achieved this capability. Immediately the United States set to work to catch up with the Soviet Union and to surpass it in

New technology makes cars more sophisticated and aerodynamic each year.

Lasers

Science fiction authors of the 1930s and 1940s wrote stories with characters using ray guns. Such guns shot beams of light instead of bullets. In 1957 an American scientist, Gordon Gould, invented a device that came close to doing what the writers had described. A LASER (Light Amplification by Stimulated Emission of Radiation) creates intense light with narrow ranges of wavelength. Interestingly enough, lasers have been developed and adapted through the years for many purposes, one of which is to provide toy "ray guns" for children (and for many adolescents and adults as well).

Laser lights are so precise that they can be used for medical purposes to burn away diseased tissue without touching surrounding normal tissue. High heat from lasers can also cauterize, or seal off, incisions, preventing a great deal of bleeding.

Another use of lasers may be for military purposes. Although not yet fully developed, lasers can strike down planes or missiles, and they could be used against an enemy in other ways. Lasers also have applications in the realm of entertainment and communication. Stereo and videodisc equipment use lasers. Lasers can create unusual visual effects in films or for programs. Lasers are also being combined with computers. Grocery stores use lasers linked to computers to read product bar code lines on items. The computer "reads" the price of goods that are purchased and also updates the store's inventory.

space technology. Congress established the **National Aeronautics and Space Administration** (NASA) to operate the new space program and also put aside money to promote science and math education in American schools and colleges. Congress hoped that better education in these fields would provide many future scientists who could help to improve the U.S. space program.

President Kennedy had expressed his hope that America would place a man on the moon before the 1960s were over. NASA pursued that goal, beginning its manned space flights in 1961. The Mercury, Gemini, and Apollo programs proceeded through the 1960s, providing more needed knowledge for space exploration. Finally, in July 1969, two American astronauts walked on the moon and returned safely to earth. Five more Apollo missions also carried men to the moon and back. Following the lunar exploration, the United States began to concentrate its efforts on the unmanned exploration of other planets and the study and use of space activities. The space shuttle program has provided reusable spacecraft for some of this space research activity.

Energy

The oil embargo and energy crisis of the 1970s made the United States become aware of the depletion of its nonrenewable energy resources. These nonrenewable resources (mainly the fossil fuels such as coal and oil) are in a limited supply. Continued heavy use of petroleum, natural gas, and coal may exhaust most of the world's supplies within the next century. This prospect, along with rising prices for the remaining fuel supplies, has made Americans realize that other sources of energy must be found.

A Space Shuttle launch in the early 1980s

The Space Race

American Activity		Soviet Activity
	1988	V. Titov & M. Manarov—Record 366 days in space
	1987	
Voyager 2—First probe to pass near Uranus Jan. 28 Space shuttle *Challenger* explodes	1986	*Mir*—First permanently inhabited space station *Vega* 1—Probe past Halley's Comet △
	1985	
	1984	*Salyut* 7—Space flight lasting 237 days
S. Ride—First American woman in space	1983	
	1982	
STS 1—First reusable manned space shuttle	1981	
	1980	
Voyager 1—First close probe of Jupiter and its moons *Pioneer* 2—First probe to pass near Saturn	1979	
	1978	
	1977	
Viking 1—First successful Mars landing (unmanned)	1976	
July 15 *Apollo/Soyez*—First international cooperative space flight*	1975	*Venera* 9—First photos from the surface of Venus
Mariner 10—First probe to pass near Mercury	1974	
May 14 *Skylab* 1—First American space station	1973	
Dec. *Apollo* 17—Last manned moon mission March 2 *Pioneer* 10—Probe passes near Jupiter	1972	
	1971	June—Three cosmonauts perish on reentry April 19 *Salyut*—Orbiting laboratory launched
	1970	Sept. *Luna* 16—First unmanned spacecraft to land on moon and return safely
July 20 *Apollo* 11—First men to walk on moon N. Armstrong, E. Aldrin	1969	
Dec. 21 *Apollo* 8—First manned lunar orbital flight	1968	Sept. 15 *Zond* 5—First unmanned round trip to moon
Jan. 27 Three astronauts die in fire in *Apollo* tests	1967	Oct. 18 *Venera* 4—Returns data on Venus atmosphere April 23 Soviet cosmonaut killed in reentry
Aug. 10 *Lunar Orbiter* 1—First American lunar orbit	1966	March 31 *Luna* 10—First probe to achieve lunar orbit Jan. 31 *Luna* 9—First soft landing probe on moon
Dec. 15 *Gemini* 6 & 7—First space rendezvous July 14 *Mariner* 4—Probe passes near Mars June 3 E. White of *Gemini* 4—First American space walk	1965	
July 28 *Ranger* 7—Moon's surface photographed	1964	Oct. 12 *Voskhod* 1—First three-man space flight
	1963	June 16 V. Tereshkova—First woman in space
Dec. 14 *Mariner* 2—Probe passes near Venus Feb. 20 *Friendship* 7—First American in orbit (J. Glenn)	1962	
May 5 *Freedom* 7—First American in space (A. Shepard)	1961	April 12 Y. Gagarin, *Vostok* 1—First manned orbit
Aug. 12 *Echo* 1—First communications satellite Aug. 10 *Discoverer* 13—First satellite recovered from space	1960	
Aug. 7 *Explorer* 6—First TV images of earth from space	1959	Sept. 12 *Luna* 2—First probe to the moon Jan. *Luna* 1—First probe to pass close to the moon
Jan. 31 *Explorer* 1—First American satellite	1958	
	1957	Nov. 3 Dog "Laika" in *Sputnik* 2—First animal in space Oct. 4 *Sputnik* 1—First earth satellite

Note: The U.S. & USSR conducted many more space missions than those included in this chart.

△ Japanese and European space agencies send probes *Suisei*, *Sakigake*, and *Giotto* past Halley's Comet

Apollo 8's Christmas Message

Americans have intently watched the major missions of the space program. They have thrilled over the great accomplishments and have wept over the tragedies. The Apollo 8 mission in 1968 was one of the exciting triumphs. The crew of Apollo 8—Frank Borman, James A. Lovell, Jr., and William A. Anders—became the first men to orbit the moon. Not only Americans but people around the world watched televised pictures of these astronauts on their journey to the moon. On December 24, after three days of flight, Apollo 8 went into lunar orbit and remained there, over 200,000 miles from earth, for about twenty hours.

On that Christmas Eve, before leaving their lunar orbit, the three astronauts expressed their wonder at the sight of the moon, the earth, and the vastness of space. The three gave a most memorable message from space for the world to hear.

"For all the people back on earth, the crew of Apollo 8 has a message that we would like to send to you." In turn, the three began to read the story of creation from Genesis 1. "In the beginning God created the heaven and the earth. . . ." People around the world listened as the astronauts quoted the Scripture passage on this special broadcast from space.

"And from the crew of Apollo 8, we pause with good night, good luck, a Merry Christmas, and God bless all of you—all of you on the good earth."

The American astronauts who read that passage recognized that the worlds they saw were the work of a divine Creator. Man's greatest accomplishments in space or on earth can never compare with God's wondrous work of creation.

Nuclear power has offered one alternative. Although nuclear fuels can provide tremendous amounts of power, they have several drawbacks. Accidents in nuclear power plants can be very dangerous. The hazardous waste material left when the fuel is used must be disposed of, and this waste remains dangerously radioactive for many years. Furthermore, the fuel itself is not renewable, and thus may later be in short supply. Therefore nuclear power does not seem to provide a complete solution for America's fuel needs.

Renewable energy sources may hold the best promise for fueling America's future. Solar power, water power, and wind are now being used to meet many energy needs. Solar energy heats a growing number of American homes and buildings, and experiments are increasing the number of ways that the sun's energy can be used. Water-power has found its most important use in producing electricity. Rivers and reservoirs usually supply the energy for generating hydroelectricity, but research may also bring about the use of the power of tides, waves, and other water movements. Windmills, once commonly used on American plains for

A solar energy conversion system

pumping water, are now returning in modern forms to generate electricity. Further research with these and other possible renewable energy sources may provide answers to tomorrow's energy needs. Converting garbage to energy may even become a practical option.

Environmental Problems

America's fast-paced lifestyle has brought many technological advances in recent years, but it has also brought some problems. One of the most notable has been the growing problem of pollution. Cars, factories, mills, power plants, and other fuel-burning sources discharge over 250 million tons of pollution into the air every year. Over 15 million cars and trucks in the Los Angeles area help to give that region frequent smog problems. Other cities suffer from similar air pollution that is not only unsightly but also dangerous for health. Congress passed the Clean Air Act in 1970 to help control some of the worst offenders. Air pollution standards for smokestacks and cars have helped some, but air pollution continues to be a problem for Americans in urban areas. Part of the problem, however, spills out of the air even far away from the source of the pollution. **Acid rain** has become a menace as acids form from some pollutants in the air and then fall in rain and snow to harm plants and animals.

Water pollution has also increased as agricultural chemicals are washed into rivers and lakes, and as sewage is dumped into these waters by cities and factories. The Water Pollution Control Act of 1972 was intended to cut down the waste dumped into America's waters, but much extra effort is needed to keep America's waters safe for man, fish, and other creatures.

In addition to air and water pollution, the United States has had to deal with the

problem of disposing solid waste. Americans dispose of about 250 million tons of garbage every year. Old cars, refrigerators, newspapers, bottles, and cans along with multitudes of other items are discarded. Most of this trash ends up in sanitary landfills, dumps where the garbage is promptly covered with dirt. Although better than open dumps where rats, insects, and odors can accumulate, landfills also spread over large areas of land. They may leak harmful liquids into the ground water beneath the landfill. Some garbage can be burned (causing air pollution), and some can be recycled. But the remaining huge amounts of waste pose a definite problem for the future.

Air pollution threatens health.

In the 1960s and 1970s many people became concerned not only with the problems of pollution but also with the way man was crowding out wilderness areas and endangering wildlife. The ecology movement focused attention on the need for man to protect his environment. Some Americans became so worried that pollution or development would kill or endanger certain plants or animals that they took extreme and sometimes violent measures to try to protect them. They used protests to block the way of machinery, court cases to block construction of dams, and other tactics to stop any project they targeted as harmful. In the process they sometimes hindered projects that would benefit many Americans so that they could save a few plants or animals.

It is true that Christians should be good stewards of the resources God has provided on earth, and so we should try to control pollution and protect wildlife. However, we must be careful to use Biblical methods and common sense. Some who fight for ecology matters believe that improving the environment will solve man's greatest problems. A few are even pantheists who almost worship nature as a god. However, we should recognize that God created nature for man, and not man for nature. (See Gen. 1:28-30.) Man should use nature for his good with as little waste of resources and damage to the environment as possible.

Section Review

1. Who put the first satellite into space? What was it called?
2. What American agency operates the space program?
3. When did man first land on the moon?
4. What are renewable energy resources?
5. What is acid rain?

B. Human Need

Events and trends in the past few decades have shown America to be a strong and wealthy country, but also a needy country. Although Americans have not suffered from famine, plague, the destruction of war, and other great calamities experienced in other parts of the world, the people of the United States have many needs of their own.

Poverty

Christ said in Mark 14:7, "For ye have the poor with you always, and whensoever ye will ye may do them good: but me ye have not always." We can look throughout history and see that there has always been some poverty. When we see it in America in contrast to the wealth and comfort of many, however, it appears especially sad. President Johnson declared a "War on Poverty" in the 1960s, and other presidents and government leaders have tried to promote programs that would give additional aid to the poor. Some of this government aid has helped a few who were in need, but it cannot wipe out poverty.

Churches and charity groups once took responsibility for helping the poor and needy, but now most of this function has been assumed by government. This situation has two regrettable features. It becomes easier for those who want aid for whatever reason to cry to the government for help. Also, it relieves Americans of the responsibility and blessing of helping those who are truly in need. The Bible often commands that Christians should help the poor, but it is easy to overlook that duty when the government is distributing welfare checks. (See Matt. 25:34-46.)

Statistics on those who are poor and lack the ability to help themselves are difficult to obtain, but they are still very few in comparison to the comfort of most Americans. Far worse than their problems of poverty, however, is a problem that is much more prevalent in America—spiritual poverty. Even those who lack money to buy food, shelter, or clothing can obtain the most precious possession, salvation through the Lord Jesus Christ. Millions of Americans, both rich and poor alike, need the Saviour. We who are Christians should be ever mindful of the needs of those around us. We should try to help those who suffer from poverty if we can, and we should be ever ready to tell others of how they may find eternal life.

Rights Movements

In recent decades Americans have become more vocal in expressing their discontent with the society around them. A few of these people, such as some within the civil rights movement, were legitimately concerned over mistreatment or unfair discrimination. Other groups were simply rebelling against rules or restrictions they did not like.

As we studied the 1960s, we noted some of the actions and accomplishments of the civil rights movement. Although the movement died down somewhat in the 1970s, some groups continued to push for more rights for blacks. To these were added many other groups that began to rise up and to pressure the government to give them what they thought were their rights as citizens. Among these groups were American Indians, Hispanic Americans, the handicapped, and women.

Indian Rights—The Indians sought repayment for the government's mishandling of old treaties. They also wanted aid for the many Indians who suffered from poor education, unemployment, alcoholism, and other problems. One protest became violent when a group of Indians seized a government trading post at Wounded Knee, South Dakota, in 1973. The violence was regrettable, but it drew attention to some of the legitimate problems of the Indians. The federal government soon began to improve its Indian policies.

Hispanic Grievances—Most of America's immigrants in the past few decades have come from the Spanish-speaking lands of Latin America. Mexicans, Puerto Ricans, Dominicans, and others have given many areas of the South and West as well as some northern urban areas a large Hispanic population. Many of these Hispanics have become American citizens, while others have come on temporary visas or have entered the United States as illegal aliens.

Escaping poverty in their homelands, many of these Hispanics have taken low-paying jobs as factory workers or as agricultural workers. These jobs in America are much better than those in their homelands, but the Hispanics have often faced difficulties because of their low incomes and lack of education. Hispanics began to protest, seeking aid. In the 1970s they did see the passage of two new laws. One provided education for Hispanic children in Spanish while they were learning English. The other required ballots in Hispanic areas of the country to be printed in both English and Spanish so that those citizens who had not yet mastered the language could still vote. These laws seemed to benefit the Hispanics, but they also made it difficult for them to adjust to American culture.

Aid for the Handicapped—The return of many disabled veterans from Vietnam prompted a new concern for the handicapped. People on crutches or in wheelchairs could not get around in many public buildings, were hampered by high curbs on city streets, and had other difficulties getting from place to place. Printed materials were not always available in braille for the blind, and no signs were printed to warn the deaf of possible danger for them.

Much legislation has been passed to provide ramps, wide doors, special parking spaces, and other needs for the physically handicapped as they use public facilities. Materials and protection for the blind and the deaf have also increased, and educational opportunities have been expanded for all the handicapped. In addition, measures were taken to make sure that handicapped people are not discriminated against by employers.

Women's Rights—Another rights movement that gained far more publicity was that promoting rights for women. While some who joined the women's movement thought they were fighting merely for equal pay for equal work with men and opportunities to work in jobs previously dominated by men, the movement actually sought far more. It unwisely sought to tear down the distinctions of womanhood. Women's groups, particularly the radical National Organization for Women (NOW), tried to push the addition of the **Equal Rights Amendment (ERA)** to the Constitution.

> **Section 1.** Equality of rights under the law shall not be denied or abridged by the United States or by any state on account of sex.
> **Section 2.** The Congress shall have the power to enforce by appropriate legislation the provisions of this article.
> **Section 3.** This amendment shall take effect two years after the date of ratification.

This amendment seemed harmless, but it would have given the government virtually unlimited power to interfere in women's lives, taking away every privilege that laws had given them. Moreover, many feminists were seeking to erase the God-given differences between men and women as well as their different responsibilities. Some even went so far as to attack marriage, support abortion, and advocate other immoral and un-Biblical practices. The ERA did not pass, even though it was given extended time for ratification.

Women have stepped into many new occupations because of the push of the women's movement. America now has women business leaders, politicians, and workers in many jobs traditionally held by men. The movement also resulted in women astronauts and a woman justice on the Supreme Court. Even so, the women's rights movement has not died out. It continues to press for the acceptance of its more radical ideas.

Rights and Wrongs—Many other groups have joined these in seeking just or unjust aid. Older Americans have sought help for special needs of the elderly, who may be easily abused by others. Along with such good causes appear despicable movements such as that for "gay rights" for homosexuals. These immoral Americans not only try to excuse their sin as simply another choice of lifestyle but also try to demand special recognition and privilege. Such a situation serves to illustrate man's sinful condition and his great need for the Saviour.

Are "rights activists" right or wrong? Depending on the issue, they may be either, or even both. Many of these rights movements have addressed real problems in our society and have helped to decrease those problems. As Christians, we should be especially concerned whenever citizens are not treated with justice and truth (Isa. 1:16-17; Jer. 22:3).

Many rights activists, however, have failed to recognize two Biblical principles. First, the Bible places the blame for our problems not on our institutions or on "the system," but on us (Jer. 17:9). If something is wrong, we should not depend on the government or anyone else to fix it. History bears out the fact that the best way to accomplish something is to do it yourself.

A second Biblical principle that applies to the rights movements is that man's problems spring from his heart. We can pass thousands of laws forcing races to act a certain way toward each other, for example, but we cannot erase racism with laws. The government cannot change man's heart, and the solution to many of these problems is not in legislation, but in the changing power of the gospel. The only true solution for these problems is found when people accept Jesus Christ as their Saviour and show Christian love to their neighbors.

Finally, rights activists have often failed to realize that in a republic, *they* are the government. Every new responsibility they force upon government becomes new restrictions and new expenses they place upon themselves. Each American must be concerned not just with what he wants, but with what is best for the nation as a whole. The American republic has been formed to protect the rights and freedoms of individuals. The Constitution, with its Bill of Rights and other amendments, has insured these privileges for Americans and provided legal and organized methods of maintaining them. By asking for further restrictions, agencies, and aid, Americans often unwit-

tingly increase the size and expense of their government while they decrease their own rights and freedoms.

Changes in Thinking and Morals

Whereas the 1960s had been characterized by individual involvement and commitment to political and social issues, the 1970s gradually brought changes in thinking. Rather than getting involved, individuals became more apathetic to most social causes. They were concerned about their private lives and own desires, not about social issues. Some have called the 1970s the "Me decade" because so many people seemed to be seeking to satisfy only themselves. Self-centered attitudes continued in the 1980s. Many Americans coveted material possessions—designer label clothes, fancy cars, electronic equipment—and they admired successful businessmen and businesswomen.

Although the United States has never been a sinless nation, conditions of the 1960s and 1970s saw much open defiance of God's standards. Indications of a breakdown in national morality included everything from the elimination of dress codes in most schools to the legalization of abortion. Some Americans pursuing their own selfish whims wanted to throw off almost all restrictions on their behavior. They wanted the freedom to sin openly. For example, some believed that it was all right for a couple to live together without being married. They tried to use the privilege of "free speech" to advocate the open use of vulgar or obscene language. Many young people and adults used illegal drugs.

In the late sixties and early seventies young people followed the styles set by the "hippies." These rebellious youth delighted in rejecting all standards and creating their own "counterculture," a culture deliberately different from and opposed to the established way of life. Hair styles, clothing, vocabularies, and other features of the hippies reflected their rebellion against "old-fashioned" standards. Although the hippie trend died out by the late 1970s, hard rock music, drugs, and open immorality continued to plague America.

Recent decades have also seen the further breakdown of strong family unity. Because of the high cost of living, more mothers worked. Watching television at home and an increased number of activities outside the home meant that families often spent less time together. Lack of communication among family members was frequently cited as a problem. The divorce rate continued to climb as couples broke their marriage vows—sometimes for minor reasons. In the eyes of many in the world, marriages were not to fulfill God's divine purpose, but only for short-range self-fulfillment. Single-parent homes multiplied as divorces and the number of unwed mothers increased.

One of Satan's strongest attacks on America and on the church comes from his attacks on the family unit. Good marriages and strong families require commitment, work, effort, and a willingness to please God and others. Most people since the 1970s have been far more interested in "doing their own thing" and in serving their own selfish interests than in putting someone else's interest before their own. And, sadly, that trend is reflected across the nation in the many families, even Christian ones.

Crime and Unrest

With the breakdown of other standards, it was only natural that crimes such as murder and robbery would increase. Illegal drugs prompted some of the crime as pushers competed for buyers, and as the drug users stole to get money to buy their next dose of drugs. The crime rates in many urban areas shot up, encouraging more and more people to move to the safer suburbs.

Protests against the Vietnam War continued into the 1970s, and much of the rioting of the antiwar movement occurred on college campuses. Although student protests quieted when the United States pulled its troops out of Vietnam, other causes occasionally raised interest around the country. Ecology matters, protests by different rights groups, and antinuclear protests were common in the 1970s.

In the 1980s the antinuclear protests continued, attacking not only nuclear power plants but also any nuclear weapon buildup. Civil rights activists became interested in the political conditions in South Africa, where blacks were denied the same rights as whites. Protests began in America to encourage the United States government and American businesses to act against the white government of South Africa. Several rights groups also continued their political action. These and other crusades, though rarely violent like those in the sixties, continued to show the unrest and discontent that cannot really be satisfied in a society where God is commonly rejected.

Section Review

1. List at least five rights movements common in America since the 1960s.
2. From where have most of America's recent immigrants come?
3. What was the Equal Rights Amendment?

C. One Hope for the Future

In comparison to the turmoil of the sixties and early seventies, life in America has seemed more settled in recent years. Nonetheless, Americans still have great problems. The teen-age suicide rate is high, and so is the consumption of alcohol. Experimentation with and increased addiction to hard drugs show that many Americans are still looking for ways to escape their problems. Few of the spiritual needs of the nation have been met, despite a general popularity of religion and even more national awareness of the term *born again*. Being religious, however, does not serve as a substitute for true salvation. It remains the task of Bible-preaching churches and truly born-again Christians to tell their fellow Americans that peace is to be found through accepting Christ as their personal Saviour.

Dramatic changes have taken place in American life in the past decade. America faces many troublesome problems. There will always be challenges; there will always be needs. But because God has blessed America with abundant resources, there is hope that America can remain a great nation. Young people who trust in God and pray to Him can help meet those challenges.

Summary

The last few decades of America's history have contained triumphs in many fields such as medical science, space technology, and electronic engineering. Americans have enjoyed the products of these and other advances while they have faced adjustments to the changing society around them. Changing values have led to a general acceptance of low moral standards. And as many Americans have sought to abandon their responsibilities in the home, church, neighborhood, and government, their demands for greater government action to meet social needs have increased. Unrest and discontent are common among Americans who lack salvation through the Lord Jesus Christ. Those without the Saviour lack the peace and hope that can help them meet the challenges of America's future.

Chapter Review

Do You Remember?

■ Fill in the blank with the appropriate word or phrase.
1. The Soviets called their first satellite _____.
2. _____ operates America's space program.
3. Solar power, water power, and wind are examples of _____.
4. Pollutants in the air sometimes form _____, which may fall to earth to harm plants and animals.
5. Since the 1960s, many groups of Americans have been petitioning the government to protect their _____.
6. The _____ was a proposed amendment that was pleasing to radical feminist groups.
7. Because of rampant selfishness, the 1970s have been called the "_____ decade."
8. Young people called _____ created their own counterculture in the late 1960s and early 1970s.

Why Is It So?

1. Why did the American government become especially concerned with math and science education in the late 1950s?
2. Why must America search for new ways to produce energy?
3. How have some environmental concerns been exaggerated?
4. Why was the Equal Rights Amendment dangerous?
5. Why has increased government activity on the behalf of Americans sometimes become an increased burden for them?

What Do You Think?

1. Should the United States continue its space program? Why or why not?
2. Why is poverty a continual problem? What is the Christian's responsibility toward the poor?
3. How far should the government go to protect the rights of its citizens?
4. What will America be like in the future?

Epilogue

A Christian historian, introducing his history of the Reformation, said, "These volumes . . . lay down in the chief and foremost place this simple . . . principle: *God in History.*" He desired to give proper place to God's direction and guidance of history. You have finished reading about the history of the United States. You have read about many different people, places, and events. Each of these people, places, and events are but small components of the overall history of the United States. Furthermore, the history of America is but one component of the history of mankind. Not only should you realize that all the pieces of history are parts of one whole, but you should also realize that God directs all of history according to His good and wise purpose. As a Christian, you too should "lay down" that "simple principle": God is always at work guiding and shaping history.

Appendix

The States of the Union

Order of Admission into Union	State	Year of Admission	Postal Abbrev.	Capital City	Nickname	Area in Sq. Miles
1	Delaware	1787	DE	Dover	Diamond State, First State	2,044
2	Pennsylvania	1787	PA	Harrisburg	Keystone State	45,308
3	New Jersey	1787	NJ	Trenton	Garden State	7,787
4	Georgia	1788	GA	Atlanta	Empire State of the South	58,910
5	Connecticut	1788	CT	Hartford	Constitution State	5,018
6	Massachusetts	1788	MA	Boston	Bay State, Old Colony	8,284
7	Maryland	1788	MD	Annapolis	Old Line State, Free State	10,460
8	South Carolina	1788	SC	Columbia	Palmetto State	31,113
9	New Hampshire	1788	NH	Concord	Granite State	9,279
10	Virginia	1788	VA	Richmond	Old Dominion State	40,767
11	New York	1788	NY	Albany	Empire State	49,108
12	North Carolina	1789	NC	Raleigh	Tar Heel State	52,669
13	Rhode Island	1790	RI	Providence	Little Rhody	1,212
14	Vermont	1791	VT	Montpelier	Green Mountain State	9,614
15	Kentucky	1792	KY	Frankfort	Bluegrass State	40,409
16	Tennessee	1796	TN	Nashville	Volunteer State	42,144
17	Ohio	1803	OH	Columbus	Buckeye State	41,330
18	Louisiana	1812	LA	Baton Rouge	Pelican State	47,752
19	Indiana	1816	IN	Indianapolis	Hoosier State	36,185
20	Mississippi	1817	MS	Jackson	Magnolia State	47,689
21	Illinois	1818	IL	Springfield	Land of Lincoln, Prairie State	56,345
22	Alabama	1819	AL	Montgomery	Heart of Dixie, Cotton State	51,705
23	Maine	1820	ME	Augusta	Pine Tree State	33,265
24	Missouri	1821	MO	Jefferson City	"Show Me" State	69,697
25	Arkansas	1836	AR	Little Rock	Land of Opportunity	53,187
26	Michigan	1837	MI	Lansing	Wolverine State	58,527
27	Florida	1845	FL	Tallahassee	Sunshine State	58,664
28	Texas	1845	TX	Austin	Lone Star State	266,807
29	Iowa	1846	IA	Des Moines	Hawkeye State	56,275
30	Wisconsin	1848	WI	Madison	Badger State	56,153
31	California	1850	CA	Sacramento	Golden State	158,706
32	Minnesota	1858	MN	St. Paul	North Star State, Gopher State	84,402
33	Oregon	1859	OR	Salem	Beaver State	97,073
34	Kansas	1861	KS	Topeka	Sunflower State	82,277
35	West Virginia	1863	WV	Charleston	Mountain State	24,231
36	Nevada	1864	NV	Carson City	Sagebrush State, Silver State	110,561
37	Nebraska	1867	NE	Lincoln	Beef State, Cornhusker State	77,355
38	Colorado	1876	CO	Denver	Centennial State	104,091
39	North Dakota	1889	ND	Bismarck	Sioux State, Flickertail State	70,702
40	South Dakota	1889	SD	Pierre	Coyote State, Sunshine State	77,116
41	Montana	1889	MT	Helena	Treasure State	147,046
42	Washington	1889	WA	Olympia	Evergreen State	68,139
43	Idaho	1890	ID	Boise	Gem State	83,564
44	Wyoming	1890	WY	Cheyenne	Equality State	97,809
45	Utah	1896	UT	Salt Lake City	Beehive State	84,899
46	Oklahoma	1907	OK	Oklahoma City	Sooner State	69,956
47	New Mexico	1912	NM	Santa Fe	Land of Enchantment	121,593
48	Arizona	1912	AZ	Phoenix	Grand Canyon State	114,000
49	Alaska	1959	AK	Juneau	The Last Frontier	591,004
50	Hawaii	1959	HI	Honolulu	Aloha State	6,471
	District of Columbia	1791	DC	Washington		70

The Presidents of the United States

Presidents	Term	Political Party	Home State	Vice-President
George Washington	1789-1797	None	Virginia	John Adams
John Adams	1797-1801	Federalist	Massachusetts	Thomas Jefferson
Thomas Jefferson	1801-1809	Republican	Virginia	Aaron Burr
				George Clinton
James Madison	1809-1817	Republican	Virginia	George Clinton
				Elbridge Gerry
James Monroe	1817-1825	Republican	Virginia	Daniel D. Tompkins
John Quincy Adams	1825-1829	Republican	Massachusetts	John C. Calhoun
Andrew Jackson	1829-1837	Democrat	Tennessee	John C. Calhoun
				Martin Van Buren
Martin Van Buren	1837-1841	Democrat	New York	Richard M. Johnson
William H. Harrison	1841	Whig	Ohio	John Tyler
John Tyler	1841-1845	Whig	Virginia	
James K. Polk	1845-1849	Democrat	Tennessee	George M. Dallas
Zachary Taylor	1849-1850	Whig	Louisiana	Millard Fillmore
Millard Fillmore	1850-1853	Whig	New York	
Franklin Pierce	1853-1857	Democrat	New Hampshire	William R. King
James Buchanan	1857-1861	Democrat	Pennsylvania	John C. Breckinridge
Abraham Lincoln	1861-1865	Republican	Illinois	Hannibal Hamlin
				Andrew Johnson
Andrew Johnson	1865-1869	Republican	Tennessee	
Ulysses S. Grant	1869-1877	Republican	Illinois	Schuyler Colfax
				Henry Wilson
Rutherford B. Hayes	1877-1881	Republican	Ohio	William A. Wheeler
James A. Garfield	1881	Republican	Ohio	Chester A. Arthur
Chester A. Arthur	1881-1885	Republican	New York	
Grover Cleveland	1885-1889	Democrat	New York	Thomas A. Hendricks
Benjamin Harrison	1889-1893	Republican	Indiana	Levi P. Morton
Grover Cleveland	1893-1897	Democrat	New York	Adlai E. Stevenson
William McKinley	1897-1901	Republican	Ohio	Garret A. Hobart
				Theodore Roosevelt
Theodore Roosevelt	1901-1909	Republican	New York	Charles W. Fairbanks
William H. Taft	1909-1913	Republican	Ohio	James S. Sherman
Woodrow Wilson	1913-1921	Democrat	New Jersey	Thomas R. Marshall
Warren G. Harding	1921-1923	Republican	Ohio	Calvin Coolidge
Calvin Coolidge	1923-1929	Republican	Massachusetts	Charles G. Dawes
Herbert Hoover	1929-1933	Republican	California	Charles Curtis
Franklin D. Roosevelt	1933-1945	Democrat	New York	John Garner
				John Garner
				Henry A. Wallace
				Harry S. Truman
Harry S. Truman	1945-1953	Democrat	Missouri	Alben W. Barkley
Dwight D. Eisenhower	1953-1961	Republican	Pennsylvania	Richard M. Nixon
John F. Kennedy	1961-1963	Democrat	Massachusetts	Lyndon B. Johnson
Lyndon B. Johnson	1963-1969	Democrat	Texas	Hubert H. Humphrey
Richard M. Nixon	1969-1974	Republican	California	Spiro T. Agnew
				Gerald R. Ford
Gerald R. Ford	1974-1977	Republican	Michigan	Nelson A. Rockefeller
Jimmy Carter	1977-1981	Democrat	Georgia	Walter F. Mondale
Ronald Reagan	1981-	Republican	California	George Bush

Index

Photo Credits